THE
AMERICAN AUTOMOBILE
A CENTENARY
1893 – 1993

This edition first published in the United States in 1992 by
SMITHMARK Publishers Inc.,
16 East 32nd Street, New York, NY 10016.

First published in the United Kingdom in 1992 by
PRION, an imprint of Multimedia Books Limited,
32/34 Gordon House Road, London NW5 1LP

Editors Anne Cope, Nicholas Bevan
Copy editing Raymond Kaye
Picture research Mirco De Cet
Design concept Patricia Houden
Design Kelly j Maskall
Production Hugh Allan

ISBN 0-8317-0286-9

SMITHMARK books are available for bulk purchase for
sales promotion and premium use. For details write or call
the manager of special sales, SMITHMARK Publishers Inc.,
16 East 32nd Street, New York, NY 10016; (212) 532-6600.

Printed in Italy

THE
AMERICAN AUTOMOBILE
A CENTENARY
1893 – 1993

Nick Georgano
with photographs by
Nicky Wright

SMITHMARK

TABLE OF CONTENTS

TABLE OF CONTENTS

1929 PACKARD CUSTOM 645 DIETRICH
OWNER: DUKE DAVENPORT (PHOTO NICKY WRIGHT)

O f all twentieth-century artifacts none is more quintessentially American than the automobile. Germany may have been the birthplace of the automobile and France its cradle, but it was in America that the car first became a part of the lives of ordinary people, and an important contributor to the economy. Although overtaken in recent years by Japan, for eight decades the United States led the world in auto manufacture, passing France in 1906 with an output of 33,200 passenger cars. Automobiles of American manufacture or design have been sold in every country of the world, even in those with opposing political ideologies. The Soviet tractor, car, and truck industry could not have come into existence without the help of Ford; even the architect of the vast Gorki plant was a Ford man, Albert Kahn. The first Chinese trucks of the 1930s used American-made components, while the Jeep Cherokee-based Beijing BJ was China's second largest production car in 1990. The auto industries of Australia, South Africa, and most Latin American countries were founded on American designs. Mass-production was brought to Europe by Ford and, later, General Motors. In 1919 two-fifths of all the motor vehicles on British roads were Fords, made in the company's Manchester plant.

What is more, almost all the associated aspects of an auto-centered world which we now take for granted originated in the United States — electric traffic lights, parking meters, multilane highways, multistory car parks, and motels, as well as some almost exclusively American ideas such as drive-in movies, restaurants, and banks. It is a cliché to say that the automobile revolutionized the way of life of millions of Americans, but today we often forget just how drastic that revolution was. Take vacations, for instance. Up to the third decade of this century, most working-class families in cities and farming communities never dreamed of taking a vacation. Ownership of an automobile, which became widespread between 1920 and 1930, enabled them to takes short trips away from home, even if only for a weekend. The lure of the big outdoors took Americans by storm; cooking and washing far from modern conveniences became a welcome challenge, while a bed was often no more than a plank propped between two running boards. Hardship was, if anything, an attraction: "We cheerfully endure wet, cold, mosquitoes, blackflies and sleepless nights just to touch naked reality once more," said one of Henry Ford's traveling companions.

It has been estimated that the inhabitants of North America collectively spend 62,000 years a week in their cars. It has also been said that 20 percent of Americans are conceived in automobiles. A few are also born in them, and alas many die in them. Some individualists even choose to be buried in them. And greater mobility has improved the breed — inbreeding in country districts ended once cars became widespread. "The farmer's boy found that he could court the lady of his choice even if she lived fifty miles away. He could select his mate from the whole wide world" (*Middletown: a Study in Contemporary American Culture*, 1929).

The part played by the auto industry in the American economy is no less striking. More than 2.5 million U.S. citizens earn their living from manufacturing, selling, or repairing motor vehicles, or ministering to them with gasoline and other fuels. Thousands of others are involved in the building and maintenance of the country's highways. In fact the economic health of the nation is closely tied to the success or failure of the industry centered on Detroit. A close watch is kept on the Goodyear display on the road from the airport into Detroit which registers each time a car is completed. In a good year it clicks down every second of every working day.

To squeeze 100 years of history, some 4,000 makes of automobile, and an output of about 1.757 billion units into 288 pages has inevitably meant compression and summary, but I have tried to achieve a balance between the technical, social, and personal factors that have created the American automobile in all its variety. All the significant models have been included, as well as many that were interesting.

Detailed credits are given elsewhere, but I would like to pay tribute to the magnificent photography of my friend Nicky Wright, without whom this book would never have existed.

Nick Georgano, 1992

1900 MOBILE STEAMER ▼
OWNERS: MARK AND TOOTSIE ACCOMAZZO (PHOTO NICKY WRIGHT)

CHAPTER ONE

PRECURSORS AND PIONEERS

1805 – 1900

"It ran no faster than an old man could walk . . . but it did run."

Charles Duryea, 1893

I T WAS REPORTED IN 1803 that there were no more than six steam engines in America, while Britain boasted several hundred — the Industrial Revolution came late. The United States was still largely a country of farmers and merchants; manufactured goods were imported or made in small home-based workshops, and for long-distance travel rivers were much more suitable than roads. It was not an encouraging climate for inventing motor vehicles of any kind, yet Nathan Read of Warren, Massachusetts, produced drawings for a steam carriage as early as 1790, and actually gained an audience with George Washington to expound his ideas. Fifteen years later a self-propelled vehicle actually ran on the streets of Philadelphia.

Oliver Evans (1755–1819) was probably America's leading engineer in the eighteenth century, author of the definitive work on milling technology, *The Young Millwright and Miller's Guide*, still the standard work in the 1860s. James Watt's interest in steam was sparked by a tea kettle, Evans' by a heated gun barrel with water in it. If one end of the gun barrel was sealed with tightly packed wadding and the other end heated in a fire, after a while the wadding blew out as loudly as if

the barrel had been filled with gunpowder. Surely, the young Evans thought, here was a power that could be harnessed usefully. Although he later built stationary engines to grind plaster of paris and saw marble, his first thoughts were of steam-powered wagons and boats. In 1805 he realized his ambitions in a rather unusual way.

The Philadelphia Board of Health, impressed by several Evans engines working in the city, commissioned him to build a steam-powered dredger to remove silt from the docks on the Delaware River. For this Evans designed a new engine which used steam supplied at a pressure of 120 pounds per square inch in a cylinder of 5 inches bore and 19 inches stroke. This was mounted in flat-bottomed barge 30 feet long and 12 feet wide driven by a paddle wheel at the stern; the mud was to be brought up by a chain of buckets. The machine was built in Evans' yard at Market and Ninth Street, about half a mile from the Delaware and 1½ miles from the River Schuylkill where it was eventually launched. The fact that it went the long way round to reach water and that Evans christened it Orukter Amphibolos (Amphibious Digger) indicate that he intended it to travel on land, at least temporarily. Perhaps, since nobody had commissioned a road vehicle

from him, he saw this as the only way to achieve an ambition that had absorbed him for more than 30 years. He hoped that Orukter would demonstrate that the self-propelled carriage was a practical proposition.

For the journey from workshop to river Evans fitted a simple rope drive from the end of the crankshaft to the rear axle; the paddle wheel was not to be installed until Orukter entered the water. The wheels broke under the weight of the vehicle after a few yards, but the workmen volunteered to make a new set of wheels and axles in their own time. The machine left the works successfully on July 13, 1805, the first time a vehicle had moved under its own power on the streets of an American city.

Evans could not resist taking his creation to Centre Square (now the site of City Hall) where stood two enormous atmospheric beam engines, installed by the Englishman Benjamin Latrobe for pumping water. Like Watt, Latrobe was scornful of high-pressure steam and had made no secret of his contempt for Evans' theories, so it must have been sweet revenge for Evans to parade his comparatively small machine under his detractor's nose. And parade he did, for Orukter attracted so much attention from the crowd that it circled Centre Square for three days. Spectators who had the money were asked to contribute 25 cents, but the less affluent were not turned away (at the time, a workman's daily wage was around 90 cents). Half the receipts went to Evans and half to the workmen who had given their evenings free of charge.

After three days on display, Orukter clanked and rattled its way down Market Street to the Schuylkill, where it settled into the water. The rope drive to the wheels was disconnected, and when the tide had floated the barge from its undercarriage the paddle wheel was installed and Orukter began its maiden voyage, down the Schuylkill, up the Delaware to Dunks Ferry, New Jersey, and back to Philadelphia, a distance of nearly 45 miles. It could not begin its work until the dredging equipment had been fitted, and this caused endless problems. Three years later Orukter had still not done a day's work. The Board of Health tried to blame Evans, but he retaliated and eventually received in full his payment of $5,000, although the Board never had a satisfactory dredger. After all the excitement in Centre Square, it is a sad anticlimax to record Orukter's obituary in the minutes of the Board of Health for June 9, 1809: "The Committee appointed to superintend the sale of the Mud Machine reported that they had received twenty seven dollars for Pig Iron sold to James Ash June, and four dollars ten cents for bricks sold to Mr. Hamilton, both articles taken out of said Mud Machine."

Evans continued to make high-pressure stationary engines, selling licenses to other manufacturers. Although he never made another moving vehicle, he did not abandon his dreams. In 1812 he wrote: "The time will come when people will travel in stages moved by steam engines, from one city to another, almost as fast as birds fly.... A carriage will set out from Washington in the morning, the passengers will breakfast in Baltimore, dine in Philadelphia and sup in New York the same day." And so they did, eventually, but not until a century later.

▶ WISCONSIN'S FIRST STEAM CAR WAS "THE SPARK" OF 1871, DESIGNED BY A PROFESSOR OF PHYSICS, H.S. CARHART, AT THE SUGGESTION OF HIS BROTHER DR. J.W. CARHART. THE BOILER WAS MADE BY THE BUTTON FIRE ENGINE WORKS OF WATERFORD, NEW YORK; MUCH OF THE REST OF THE ENGINEERING WAS THE WORK OF RACINE'S J. I. CASE COMPANY. IT RAN SUCCESSFULLY, ALTHOUGH WITH MUCH NOISE, AND INSPIRED THE STATE OF WISCONSIN TO OFFER A $10,000 PRIZE SEVEN YEARS LATER.

STATE HISTORICAL SOCIETY OF WISCONSIN

▼ THE TWO COMPETITORS GREEN BAY AND OSHKOSH IN THE 1878 200-MILE RACE. THE GREEN BAY WAS THE FASTER BUT RAN INTO A CULVERT, GIVING THE PRIZE TO THE OSHKOSH WHICH AVERAGED 6mph. THIS DRAWING WAS MADE MANY YEARS AFTER THE EVENT AND MAY NOT BE AN ACCURATE REPRESENTATION OF THE VEHICLES.

STATE HISTORICAL SOCIETY OF WISCONSIN

THE STEAM PASSENGER CAR

On both sides of the Atlantic early experimenters were concerned with the utility of the road vehicle. The ancestor of them all, Nicolas Cugnot's *fardier* of 1770, was a gun tractor, Orukter was a dredger, and nearly all the British vehicles of the 1820s and 1830s were buses or stage coaches. In 1826 Thomas Blanchard of Springfield, Massachusetts, built an eight-seater steam carriage, and 14 years later the first self-propelled fire engine, by Hodge, ran on the streets of New York. Passenger cars for pleasure rather than commerce did not begin to appear until the next decade. The honor of being the first American to offer vehicles for sale belongs to New Yorker John Kenrick Fisher, who formed the American Steam Carriage Company. In 1853 the company advertised steamers with a promised speed of 15mph on good gravel roads at the then very high price of $2,000. Sadly, it seems, nobody bought.

Four years after Fisher's advertisements another New Yorker, Richard Dudgeon, built a steam passenger car, but this was destroyed by fire. He built a second machine in 1866 and this has survived to the present day. It looks like a small locomotive, with a bench seat on either side of the boiler. The engine consists of two single cylinders, each driving a rear wheel; these, like those at the front, are of solid red cedar wood, with iron tires.

▲ THE SECOND STEAM CAR BUILT BY RANSOM OLDS, THIS DATES FROM 1890. IT HAD A FLASH BOILER, LIQUID FUEL, AND AN OUTPUT OF 4hp. IT WAS SOLD TO A CLIENT IN INDIA, BUT HE NEVER TOOK DELIVERY AS IT WAS LOST AT SEA.
OLDSMOBILE HISTORY CENTER

Steering is by a centrally-pivoted front axle, which seems to have been a bugbear of the Dudgeon down the ages. No one but its builder could master it and even he once ran into a barber shop at Oyster Bay. When the Dudgeon was tried out in the 1950s, historian Phil Dumka reported that it seemed to need 50 turns from lock to lock, "slower than an oil tanker," and that driver Joe Knowles "...wore himself out correcting for the drift, then correcting for the correction." This was in a journey of less than 1 mile.

Dudgeon used his car for some time in New York City, for business journeys and for taking his family to church, but eventually the noise and smoke so scared the horses that the police ordered him off the city streets. He also got on the wrong side of Tammany Hall politicians, who retaliated in the way they thought would hurt Dudgeon most. He then took his car to his country home at Locust Valley, Long Island, where he continued his experiments. Presumably country horses were no more pleased with his machine than city ones, but at least there were fewer of them.

From the 1860s onward steam cars multiplied across the United States, although few achieved more than fleeting local fame. Despite their dedication, their inventors seldom received any financial reward and were frequently the despair of their families. Sometimes they despaired themselves. John Gore of Brattleboro, Vermont, weary of complaints from the neighbors and the restriction of having to have a boy walk in front of his car ringing a bell, one day inadvertently ran his machine into a ditch, climbed out, and said that as far as he was concerned the thing could stay there. He walked home and the engine was later removed for a local bakery.

Most of these pioneer cars were light steam buggies, although some were heavier wagons, such as that built in Quincy, Massachusetts, in 1861 by Louis Badger. Intended for hauling granite, it also carried the West Quincy Brass Band on occasion, although most local people thought it was no match for a good team of oxen. The most extraordinary invention was the Steam Man, patented in 1870 by Zadoc P. Dederick and Isaac Grass of Newark, New Jersey. This was a life-size figure of a man, complete with top hat, with a boiler inside his jacket and a two-cylinder engine behind his back which worked his legs by a very complex system of cranks. The ingenious inventors even gave their man two speeds forward and two in reverse. He would only function when attached to a cart or carriage. One might be forgiven for doubting that he ever functioned at all, but the famous gasoline car pioneer Charles E. Duryea said in later years that he definitely saw the Steam Man in action.

The most persistent builder of steam cars in America was Sylvester Hayward Roper of Roxbury, Massachusetts. His first vehicle was announced in *Scientific American* in 1863, but may well have been completed earlier. The front portion was a two-passenger horse buggy, behind which was a vertical boiler producing a pressure of up to 60 pounds per square inch (half that of Evans' boiler of nearly 60 years before) and a 2hp engine. Roper later sold the machine to a fairground promoter, the self-styled Professor W.W. Austen, who exhibited it under his own name at numerous fairs in New England and other East Coast states from 1865 to at least 1870, possibly later. With a claimed top speed of 30mph, it was a great draw at circuses, and was frequently matched against the fastest horse the neighborhood could offer. Roper subsequently built about ten other vehicles, including two steam motorcycles. The first of these, made in 1869, was a crude-looking velocipede with iron tires, but in 1894 he produced a very neat-looking machine with a tiny water tube boiler and a marine-type two-cylinder engine of 2 x 4 inches fitted into the frame of a standard Columbia bicycle, driving the rear wheel directly from the connecting rods. When turning at only 200rpm, this engine gave a theoretical top speed of 60mph. Whether the machine ever attained this is not known, but Roper was traveling pretty fast when he crashed his machine at Boston's Charles River Track and was instantly killed. This was in 1896, when he was aged over 60. Ironically, Austen had met his death at the same track two years earlier when he collided with another steamer, almost certainly the first two-car accident in American history.

Most of the early steamers originated from New England, but there were exceptions. Wisconsin's first self-propelled vehicle, built in 1871, was the idea of Racine resident Dr. J.W. Carhart, with design by his brother H.S. Carhart, a professor of physics at Northwestern University and Michigan State University. Construction was mainly by the J. I. Case Company, still famous for their agricultural equipment, and automobile builders from 1911 to 1927. Named "The Spark," the Carhart machine had a large vertical boiler behind the buggy-like seat and was very noisy. The doctor recalled in later years that no racing car of 1914 could exceed the decibels emitted by "The Spark," and that "...we usually had the street entirely to ourselves, for when they had seen it the citizens were unanimous in predicting that The Spark would blow up."

In 1878 the State of Wisconsin offered a prize of $10,000 for "a cheap and practical substitute for the use of horses and other animals on the highway and farm." The contestants had to complete a 200-mile journey, and although seven entered only two showed up at the start line in Green Bay. One was called, appropriately, the Green Bay, although built in the nearby community of Wequiock, and the other was the Oshkosh from the city of that name. Both were heavy vehicles, the Green Bay turning the scales at 14,255 pounds, about a third heavier than the Oshkosh. Both pulled trailers carrying fuel and water. The Green Bay was the faster, but its driver/builder E. P. Cowles ran it into a culvert and had to stop for repairs, so, in true hare and tortoise fashion, the Oshkosh plodded on to win at an average spread of just over 6mph. The State tried to deny the Oshkosh builders the prize on the grounds that a speed of 6mph did not make the machine practical, but after some argument its builders were awarded half the money.

Other pioneer steamers included those of Elijah Ware of Bayonne, New Jersey, who built several between 1861 and 1867, one of which he sold to a Canadian Roman Catholic priest living on Prince Edward Island. Priced at $300, this was almost certainly the first American-built vehicle to be exported. George Alexander Long of Northfield, Massachusetts, and Lucius Copeland of Phoenix, Arizona, and later Camden, New Jersey, both made steam-powered tricycles based on Columbia bicycles between 1880 and 1890, while mass-production pioneer Ransom Eli Olds made two steamers, with three and four wheels, in 1887 and 1890 respectively. The Philion steamer from Akron, Ohio, had an interesting background; Achille Philion was a French-born circus artist who married an Akron girl, Belle Melvin, and built his small four-wheeled car to publicize the circus in the parades that announced its arrival in town. Begun in 1887, it was not completed until 1892. By 1904 Philion was operating a movie theater and many years later his car featured in such movies as *The Magnificent Ambersons* and *Excuse My Dust*.

THE FIRST DURYEA CAR, AS MODIFIED IN JANUARY 1894. SOON AFTERWARD FRANK DURYEA BEGAN WORK ON HIS SECOND CAR, AND THE PIONEER WAS PUT INTO STORAGE UNTIL 1920, WHEN IT WAS RESCUED BY INGLIS M. UPPERCU AND PRESENTED TO THE UNITED STATES NATIONAL MUSEUM.

MOTOR VEHICLE MANUFACTURERS' ASSOCIATION

THE ARRIVAL OF GASOLINE AND ELECTRIC POWER

The claim to the title of America's First Gasoline Car has been disputed many times, but the first to give rise to a car manufactured for sale was undoubtedly that of the brothers Frank and Charles Duryea.

The Duryea brothers were born in Illinois, Charles in 1861 and Frank in 1869, but were living in Springfield, Massachusetts, when they began work on their first car. In later years there was a lot of undignified controversy between the brothers and their families about who was really responsible for the car's design. It seems that the original idea was Charles', that the initial construction work was perhaps shared between the brothers, but that after Charles' departure to Peoria, Illinois, in September 1892 development work was solely that of Frank. Charles was perhaps disillusioned with the slow progress on the car, which would not run at all after nearly a year's work, and anyway he had a successful bicycle business in Peoria to look after. Frank continued, alone, with financial assistance from Erwin F. Markham; the car was running by February 1893 and in September was ready for road trials.

The body and frame of this first Duryea were those of a horse-drawn buggy purchased secondhand for $70, and the engine was a horizontal single-cylinder unit of 1,302cc which developed a theoretical 4hp. Features included low-tension ignition and a spray carburetor. Transmission was by friction drive. The car's first recorded run on public roads took place on September 21, 1893. Frank recorded in a letter to Charles: "...have tried it finally and thoroughly, and have quit trying until some changes are made." Presumably it did not run very well, and the next known trial did not take place until November 10, when the *Springfield Morning Union* recorded that the car ran up and down two streets, then "stopped short, refusing to move. Investigation revealed that the bearing had been worn smooth by the friction, and a little water sprinkled upon it put it in working condition again." Incidentally, although the news item referred to a "vehicle operated by gasoline," the headline read "An Electric Carriage Tried in Springfield." This was not untypical of the confusion spread by journalists of the day, who had

▲ ELWOOD P. HAYNES IN HIS FIRST CAR, COMPLETED IN 1894 (ALTHOUGH HE LATER CLAIMED IT WAS MADE A YEAR EARLIER).
MOTOR VEHICLE MANUFACTURERS' ASSOCIATION

▼ ANOTHER VIEW OF THE FIRST HAYNES, WITH ITS MAKER AT THE TILLER, NEXT TO A LARGE TOURING MODEL OF 1908.
MOTOR VEHICLE MANUFACTURERS' ASSOCIATION

little idea of even the basic workings of the automobile. Many years later Charles Duryea said of one of these early trials: "It ran no faster than an old man could walk, but it did run."

Further changes were made during the winter of 1893/4, but the following year Frank was working on a new design with spur gear drive to the rear axle. He sent drawings to Charles, who applied for a patent which was granted on June 11, 1895. Unfortunately Charles made no mention of his brother on the application, which bears the title C.E. Duryea, Road Vehicle. This poor treatment of his brother was continued when he described Frank merely as the "operator" of the car which won the *Chicago Times-Herald* race in November 1895. He circulated a photograph of himself at the wheel of the car in Springfield the previous summer, but at the time it was taken Charles had not yet learned to drive. His part in the great race was limited to a ride in a sleigh.

Self-publicists often fare better than dedicated engineers, but in the long run Frank earned more from the automobile than Charles did. Together they set up the Duryea Motor Wagon Company in Springfield, but built no more than 13 cars between 1895 and 1898, then went their separate ways. Charles then organized several companies which made cars of his own highly eccentric design; from 1902 to 1906 these had three-cylinder engines mounted at the rear behind the seat, and tiller steering, although by this time most other auto makers had gone over to wheel steering. Among the advantages Charles claimed for the tiller was that it only occupied one hand, so that the other could hold a passenger's waist, a good five-cent cigar, or, in inclement weather, an umbrella. He later made a solid-tired high-wheel buggy called the Buggyaut, and cyclecars with three or four wheels called the Gem. That was until 1916, after which he wrote technical books and articles until his death in September 1938. While it would not be true to say that he died a pauper, he was certainly not a rich man. Frank, on the other hand, designed a car which was taken up by the Stevens Arms & Tool Company as the Stevens-Duryea. The car grew increasingly large and expensive, and in 1915 the company was sold to Westinghouse, Frank's share of the proceeds being $0.5 million dollars, which enabled him to live comfortably for the rest

◄ A HAYNES-APPERSON TOURING OF c.1900. THESE CARS HAD HORIZONTAL TWO-CYLINDER ENGINES OF 190-CUBIC-INCHES DISPLACEMENT MOUNTED UNDER THE REAR SEAT, AND COST $1,500 IN FOUR-PASSENGER FORM. THEY WERE KNOWN SIMPLY AS HAYNES FROM 1905 ONWARD.
MOTOR VEHICLE MANUFACTURERS' ASSOCIATION

of his long life. He died in February 1967, seven months before his 98th birthday.

The Duryeas were not the only engineers who tinkered with road vehicles. In Anderson, Indiana, John William Lambert built a three-wheeled car in 1891, but it was destroyed in a fire before manufacture could begin. Two years later Elwood P. Haynes (1857–1925), field superintendent of the Indiana Natural Gas & Oil Company, purchased a single-cylinder two-stroke Sintz marine engine with the intention of using it in a road vehicle. He approached the Riverside Machine Works in Kokomo, Indiana, which was run by the Apperson brothers, Elmer and Edgar, asking them to build the car for him. This they did, and on July 4, 1894, the car was ready for testing. The makers were so afraid of ridicule that they had it towed by horses out of town for testing. The car had a spur gear transmission with three forward speeds but no reverse, a foot-operated throttle, and tiller steering. A few similar cars were turned out over the next four years, although Haynes kept his job with the gas and oil company, and the Appersons continued with general engineering work. In 1898 they formed the Haynes-Apperson Automobile Company and began turning out cars at the rate of one every two or three weeks. By this time Haynes had decided that he wanted to be a pioneer, so he not only discounted the part the Appersons had

played in his first car, but predated it by a year, claiming it was made in 1893, when it was only an idea in his head. The Lambert car was also a problem to him, having been made in the same state, so he visited William Lambert and asked him not to object if he called his vehicle "America's First Car." Lambert agreed, and although he subsequently made cars under his own name, he never referred to his three-wheeler of 1891. Haynes does not seem to have worried about the Duryea brothers, probably figuring that they were too busy arguing with each other to notice his claim.

There were other pioneers, some of whom pre-dated the Duryeas, such as Gottfried Schloemer and Frank Toepfer who built a car in Milwaukee in 1892. Like Haynes, they used a Sintz engine, and the car was tested, but they never made another. Even earlier was William Morrison of Des Moines, Iowa, who built a seven-passenger electric car in 1890. The electric buggy, as he called it, took part in a parade in September 1890, attracting nationwide publicity through magazines such as *Scientific American*. This prompted more than 16,000 inquiries, and it took Morrison and his partner Louis Schmidt all their time just to open the mail. They soon gave up reading the letters, simply opening them for the sake of the postage stamps enclosed, which filled two bushel baskets.

Morrison had no intention of becoming a car manufacturer, although he may have built a few more vehicles to test his batteries. He sold his buggy to Harold Sturges, who entered it in the 1895 *Chicago Times-Herald* race. As late as 1907 Morrison declared: "I wouldn't give ten cents for an automobile for my own use."

In Philadelphia Henry Morris and Pedro Salom also made electric cars which they called Electrobats. At first, each car carried its own name, in the manner of railroad locomotives or ships, Crawford Wagon, Fish Wagon, Skeleton Wagon, and so on, but they soon ran out of names and for 1896 their vehicles were simply called Electrobats. They had front drive, and many were used as taxicabs in Philadelphia and New York.

CHICAGO TIMES-HERALD RACE

In the early 1890s America's various automobile pioneers were working largely in ignorance of each other and well out of the gaze of the general public, but in 1895 most of the inventors just mentioned, plus many others, were brought together through America's first automobile contest. This was the idea of H.H. Kohlsaat, publisher of the *Chicago Times-Herald* newspaper, who had been inspired by the French contests from Paris to Rouen and to Bordeaux in 1894 and 1895 respectively. He thought that a similar event in America would act as a catalyst to arouse interest in the horseless carriage, and also bring useful publicity to his newspaper.

The event was announced on July 9, 1895, with the entry list closing on September 13. The race was to take place on November 2. A total of 89 entries was received, but 30 pleaded that they could not be ready in time, so the contest was postponed to Thanksgiving Day, November 28. Even then only 11 announced that they would actually start, and of these five failed to make it to the start line for various reasons. The actual starters were a Duryea, an Electrobat, the five-year-old Morrison electric entered by Harold Sturges, and three cars based more or less on the German Benz. Late November was far from an ideal time to hold a contest in Chicago, and the cars were hampered by slushy snow for most of the 54-mile journey from Jackson Park to Evanston and back. Only two

cars completed the course, the Duryea in first place, followed by a Mueller-Benz. Large crowds turned out to see the start, but their enthusiasm did not last for 11 hours of a chilly November day. As Gerald Rose, the British chronicler of early auto racing, wrote: "The Duryea...passed through the dark and snowy streets almost unobserved."

The prize money was $5,000, of which $2,000 went to the Duryeas, $1,500 to the H. Mueller Company, and $500 each to Macy's department store for its Benz and to Sturges, even though their cars did not complete the course. The rest of the money went to other entrants, even those who did not reach the start line, for various technical points, while Morris and Salom were awarded a gold medal for their Electrobat, for its "safety, ease of control, absence of noise, vibration, heat or odor, cleanliness and general excellence of design and workmanship."

The *Times-Herald* event may not have been a brilliant success, but it did attract a great deal of public attention to the new vehicles. It was certainly more useful to the cause than the next contest, the race organized in May 1896 by the

New York magazine *Cosmopolitan*, between the city and Irvington. Of the six starters, only the Duryea completed the course, its time of 7 hours 13 minutes over 60 miles being a great improvement over the 10 hours 23 minutes for the 54 miles of the Times-Herald race. The failure of its competitors, which included three other Duryeas, a Carlos Booth, and an Armstrong electric, prompted the following rhyme:

Six horseless carriages entered for a drive,
Wheel came off one, and then there were five,

Five horseless carriages, racing as before,
Chain slipped on one, and then there were four;

Four horseless carriages, speeding merrily,
Bicycle ran into one, and then there were three;

Three horseless carriages came to a hill,
Hill stayed right where it was, so the drivers had to get off and push, and that was why the time between City Hall and Irvington for the prize of 3,000 dols., offered by a magazine, was not what it

might have been if there had not been any hill there.

The poem appeared in *The Wheel*, a leading bicycle magazine, which explains the disparaging sentiments about automobiles. In fact the cyclists who set out to follow the cars reached Irvington ahead of them.

The Duryea distinguished itself later in the year when it was the first car to arrive at the conclusion of the famous London to Brighton run held in England in November. There were no more important races held in America for a number of years.

AN INDUSTRY GETS GOING

The year 1896 was of great significance in the history of the American automobile, not least because it was then that the French word "automobile" first came into common use in American publications. Before that, "horseless carriage" was the most common term, although motocycle was also used, and America's first trade journal, published by H.H. Kohlsaat, was entitled *The Motocycle (Automobile) Maker & Dealer*. A better-known and longer-lived journal, *The Horseless Age*, appeared a month later, in November 1895, and was published until May 1918.

The year 1896 was also the first in which more than one car was made from the same design; the Duryeas turned out 13 examples of what must be called America's first production car, and the first known purchaser was George H. Morill Jr. of Norwood, Massachusetts. It is not known if any other car makers actually sold cars in 1896, but several noteworthy experimenters built their first vehicles. The first to be made in the motor capital, Detroit, was the work of Charles Brady King (1868–1957), who had made his engine in 1894, and hoped to have a car ready for the *Times-Herald* race. The engine was unusual in having four cylinders,

▶ THE DURYEA FACTORY AT SPRINGFIELD, FROM WHICH 13 CARS EMERGED DURING 1896, MAKING IT THE FIRST MOTOR VEHICLE MANUFACTURING PLANT IN THE UNITED STATES.
MOTOR VEHICLE MANUFACTURERS' ASSOCIATION

when most of his rivals had not ventured beyond one, or at most two. Unable to compete in the Chicago contest, King contented himself with riding as an official umpire on the Mueller-Benz (and driving it for the final hour), but in March 1896 his car was ready and made its first trials on the city's streets. Following in hot pursuit on a bicycle was a young electrical engineer named Henry Ford.

Charles King, in fact, played an important part in the building of the first Ford car, for he obtained some of its components, such as the chain for transmitting power to the rear wheels. Ford, like all the other builders of his day, had no ready-made components to work with. The cylinders for his engine came from a length of scrap pipe from a

▲ ONE OF THE FIRST AUTOMOBILE ADVERTISEMENTS IN AMERICA, PROMOTING THE 1897 DURYEA. FROM THE PRINTING OF THE DATE IT LOOKS AS IF THIS AD ORIGINALLY APPEARED THE PREVIOUS YEAR, AND WAS MADE TO LAST A FURTHER SEASON BY CHANGING THE 6 TO A 7. THE DAIMLER MOTOR COMPANY, U.S. BRANCH OF THE GERMAN FIRM THAT LATER MADE THE MERCEDES, WAS PRESUMABLY THE DURYEA AGENT FOR THE NEW YORK AREA.
MOTOR VEHICLE MANUFACTURERS' ASSOCIATION

steam engine, cut in half and bored out to the required diameter; the flywheel came from an old lathe; the wheels and seat came from bicycles; and the "horn" was a domestic doorbell screwed to the front. Because of its cycle ancestry, Ford's first car was lighter than those of most of his contemporaries, weighing just over 500 pounds compared with 1,300 for King's, and 700 for the Duryeas'. It had a top speed of 20mph, compared with 5mph for the King. Ford had his car ready on June 4, 1896, but in his enthusiasm to get it finished had failed to consider how it was to get out of his tiny workshop. Finding the door too narrow, he demolished the frame with a pickax, and after removing some bricks was able to manhandle his little machine into Bagley Avenue. It ran around

Detroit for a while (at 2:00 A.M.) and only broke down once, outside the Cadillac Hotel on Washington Boulevard.

Soon Ford felt able to venture outside the city limits, to visit the family farm at Dearborn. Here he ran into the greatest threat to all auto pioneers, the atrocious state of country roads. His particular problem was that the roads were deeply rutted, and as the track of his car was smaller than that of ordinary wagons he was forced to drive with one side of the car in the ruts and the other several inches higher, with the car sharply tilted. This was hardly helpful to the primitive mechanism, let alone the comfort of the driver, his wife, or their three-year-old son Edsel. It has always seemed most unfair that the pioneer cars, which needed

good roads more than any of their successors, had to cope with the worst possible conditions.

By the end of 1896 Ford had sold his first car, or Quadricycle as he called it, for $200, and used the proceeds to help build his second. For this he was also financed by Detroit's Mayor William C. Maybury, and the resulting machine, which was ready by the end of 1897, was a much more sophisticated vehicle than the Quadricycle. The chain drive was now to the center of the rear axle rather than to the offside, and there was proper buggy-type seating (although the modified Quadricycle had this as well). There were stylish mudguards over front and rear wheels, and two headlights. With backing from Maybury and other wealthy Detroiters, the Detroit Automobile Company was organized in July 1899, but although a few more prototypes emerged, no production cars were ever made by the company. Many problems were encountered with inexperienced workmen and inferior quality of components, while one of the partners told a reporter, with delightful candor: "You would be surprised at the amount of detail about an automobile." There was also Ford's grasshopper mind, forever seeking new solutions and jumping to a new model before the one in hand had been perfected. The Detroit Automobile Company was wound up in January 1901, and it was to be another two years before Ford cars were offered in the marketplace.

Meanwhile, in Cleveland, Ohio, a Scottish-born bicycle maker called Alexander Winton (1860–1932) had been enthused by reports of the *Times-Herald* race, even though he did not witness it. He decided that cars should combat the falling sales of two-wheelers, and by October 1896 he announced his first automobile in *The Horseless Age*. It was curious looking, with a short, stubby appearance and a single-cylinder engine mounted between the front and rear seats. The latter faced backwards, an arrangement known in France as the dos-à-dos (back-to-back). The steering tiller also incorporated the speed control, and ahead of it was a dashboard which housed the gas tank. Warning was given by a pedal-operated bell. Weight was over 1,000 pounds, which must have hampered performance, for Winton decided that his next car would be lighter and capable of 30mph.

The actual speed of the second Winton is not

▼ HENRY FORD'S FIRST CAR OF 1896, IN A RECONSTRUCTION OF HIS WORKSHOP AT THE HENRY FORD MUSEUM. WHEN THE CAR WAS COMPLETED, IN JUNE 1896, FORD HAD TO DEMOLISH THE DOORFRAME TO GET IT OUT.

FORD MOTOR COMPANY

known, but from its appearance it does not seem much lighter. It was longer and wider, accommodating three people abreast on both seats, which were still arranged back-to-back. The Winton Motor Carriage Company was incorporated in March 1897, and four cars were completed that year. Winton's chief engineer Leo Melanowski invited Henry Ford for an interview, but Winton was not impressed by the young man from Detroit and did not hire him. By 1898 the company was in production with a single-cylinder two-passenger motor buggy, and the first sale was recorded in March. The purchaser was not a local man, but a 70-year-old Pennsylvania mining engineer who had seen an advertisement for the Winton carriage. He traveled by train to Cleveland and, on being satisfied with his inspection of the car, handed over $1,000 cash. Before the end of the year 22 buggies had been sold, together with eight delivery wagons. One of the buyers was James Ward Packard, whose purchase had far-reaching consequences.

In 1899 more than 100 cars were delivered, which made Alexander Winton by far the largest maker of gasoline vehicles in the United States. The earliest known auto dealership was opened in 1898 by H.W. Koller of Reading, Pennsylvania, to sell Wintons. In fact, after the Duryea brothers ended production at Springfield in 1898 and went their separate ways, there were very few gasoline cars made anywhere until the turn of the century. With steam and electric cars, though, it was a different story.

THE AMERICAN AUTOMOBILE: A CENTENARY 1893–1993

▲ TWO FOLDING FRONT-SEAT STANLEY STEAMERS, SECOND AND FOURTH IN THE LINE-UP, AT THE AQUIDNECK TRACK, NEWPORT, RHODE ISLAND. THE CAR IN THE FOREGROUND IS A TWO-CYLINDER AUTOCAR.
MOTOR VEHICLE MANUFACTURERS' ASSOCIATION

1899 WINTON PHAETON ◀
THE CLEVELAND-BASED WINTON MOTOR CARRIAGE COMPANY WAS THE FIRST TO MAKE GASOLINE AUTOMOBILES IN ANY QUANTITY IN THE UNITED STATES, AND IN 1899 DELIVERED MORE THAN 100 TWO-PASSENGER PHAETONS SIMILAR TO THIS ONE. THEY HAD HORIZONTAL SINGLE-CYLINDER ENGINES, TWO-SPEED TRANSMISSIONS, AND LAMINATED WOOD FRAMES. THE PRICE WAS $1,000, WHICH ROSE TO $1,200 BY 1901.
OWNER: NATIONAL AUTOMOBILE MUSEUM, RENO, NEVADA
(PHOTO NICKY WRIGHT)

N EW ENGLAND STEAMERS

The steam car played a much larger part in the United States than it ever did in Europe, and nearly all the successful makes came from New England. They were totally different from vehicles such as the Oshkosh and Green Bay, which weighed up to 14,000 pounds and used coal fuel (the turn-of-the-century steamers weighed 600–1,000 pounds and were kerosene-fueled). One of the first was built by George Eli Whitney (1862–1963; — no, this isn't a misprint, he really did live to 101), grand nephew of the Eli Whitney who invented the cotton gin. He completed his first car in October 1896, and in the spring of the following year set up the Whitney Motor Wagon Company in Boston. Like so many of the pioneers, Whitney was a tinkerer rather than a dedicated manufacturer; he had built seven cars by the summer of 1898, but they were all different, most with vertical engines, although at least one was horizontal. His designs were subsequently made by Frank F. Stanley of Newton, Massachusetts (no

relation to the better known Stanley twins who were just starting up steam car manufacture in nearby Watertown).

The Stanleys, Francis E. and Freelan O., were identical twins born in 1849. They ran a photographic equipment business, first in Lewiston, Maine, and then at Watertown, although they lived in Newton where Frank F. Stanley was making his steam cars. This has caused much confusion ever since, even though Frank F. Stanley's cars were sold under the name McKay. While in Lewiston, they saw a steamer made by Edwin Field, which inspired them to build one of their own. This was in 1888, and it seems that it was a complete failure. Eight years later they saw George Whitney's steam car in Boston and this inspired them to try again.

The light steamer they built was typical of the breed, with a vertical two-cylinder engine and single chain drive. It was completed in 1897, and

▲ AN 1899 STANLEY STEAM CAR. A SIMILAR MODEL TO THIS WAS THE FIRST CAR TO CLIMB MOUNT WASHINGTON, A FEAT ACHIEVED BY MR. AND MRS. F. O. STANLEY ON AUGUST 31, 1899.
MOTOR VEHICLE MANUFACTURERS' ASSOCIATION

▲ 1900 MOBILE STEAMER

THE MOBILE, LIKE THE LOCOMOBILE, WAS DEVELOPED FROM THE ORIGINAL STANLEY DESIGN. A VERTICAL TWO-
CYLINDER ENGINE DROVE THE REAR AXLE BY SINGLE CHAIN, AND THE FIRE-TUBE BOILER WORKED AT A PRESSURE OF 180
POUNDS/SQUARE INCH. THE WATER TANK HELD 22.5 GALLONS, YET HAD TO BE REFILLED EVERY 20 MILES OR SO. FOR
THE MOBILE, MADE IN A FACTORY AT TARRYTOWN, NEW YORK, AND DESIGNED BY THE CELEBRATED ARCHITECT
STANFORD WHITE, 1900 WAS THE FIRST YEAR. THIS DOS-À-DOS COST $1,100, BUT THE FRINGED SURREY TOP WAS EXTRA.
OWNERS: MARK AND TOOTSIE ACCOMAZZO (PHOTO NICKY WRIGHT)

by the spring of 1898 they had completed two more, one of which was sold for $600. Later in the year they took one to Boston's Charles River Park, where it won the hill-climbing contest. This involved ascending an 80-foot incline; a Whitney was defeated at 76 feet 8 inches, but the Stanley sailed to the top with little apparent effort. This feat amazed the crowd and resulted in orders for 200 of the little cars within two weeks. It was no easy matter for men whose expertise lay in photographic plates to start making cars in such numbers. Nevertheless, they set about obtaining components for an initial run of 100. In early 1899, before these orders were completed, they were visited by John Brisben Walker (1847–1931), the publisher of *Cosmopolitan* magazine which had sponsored the calamitous New York to Irvington race three years before. He offered to buy the twins out, but they were reluctant to sell because they felt they were overcoming the headaches involved

in quantity production. They decided to ask a ridiculously high price — $250,000 — but to their surprise Walker accepted. Since their investment in the business had been around $20,000, they were not unnaturally delighted, and the sale went through.

To help him raise the purchase price (equivalent to more than $5 million today) Walker secured the backing of asphalt millionaire Amzi Lorenzo Barber (1843–1909). They formed a new company called the Locomobile Company of America in June 1899, and began to make cars of Stanley type in the Watertown factory. Before long the partners quarreled, and Walker left to make a similar design which he called the Mobile at Tarrytown, N.Y. Barber continued with the Locomobile at Watertown, but in 1900 he bought a much larger factory at Bridgeport, Connecticut. This enabled production to rise from 400 in 1899 to 1,500 in 1901 and 2,750 in 1902, when Locomobile

was the largest automobile producer in the country. Mobile was a much smaller operation, and when production ceased at the end of 1903 not more than 600 had been made. Coincidentally, Locomobile also ended steamer production in 1903, going on thenceforth to make gasoline cars, but their total was more than 5,000.

As one would expect, the design of the Stanley/Locomobile/Mobile was very similar. It consisted of a fire-tube boiler working at 180 pounds of pressure per square inch which fed a vertical two-cylinder engine mounted in the center of the tubular frame. Behind the boiler was a 22.5-gallon water tank which occupied the full width of the car, yet only gave a range of about 20 miles before a refill was necessary. Drive was by a single chain from the crankshaft to the center of the rear axle. One of the advantages of the steam engine was that it delivered full power at any speed, so a gearbox was unnecessary. Bodies were mostly

◄ THE LOCOMOBILE WAS MADE TO A STANLEY DESIGN, AND WAS THEREFORE VERY SIMILAR TO THE MOBILE IN SPECIFICATION — AND IN ITS THIRST. BY CONTRAST THE LAST STEAM CARS FROM DOBLE WOULD RUN 1,500 MILES ON A 24-GALLON TANKFUL. ALTHOUGH NOT VERY STRONG, THE LITTLE LOCOMOBILES WERE GOOD VALUE AT $600 IN 1898, AND BY MAY 1902 MORE THAN 4,000 HAD BEEN SOLD. AMONG OVERSEAS CUSTOMERS WAS THE BRITISH WRITER RUDYARD KIPLING.

OWNER: NATIONAL AUTOMOBILE MUSEUM, RENO, NEVADA
(PHOTO NICKY WRIGHT)

proportion of steamers from New England must have been around 80 percent. The one prominent make from outside the area was the White from Cleveland, Ohio. This was the product of a sewing machine manufacturer, and although the first model of 1900 looked not unlike a Stanley or Locomobile, it was more sophisticated, with a flash boiler which generated steam much more quickly. A condenser to recycle exhaust steam was added in 1902, and the following year the White took on the appearance of a gasoline car, with its condenser mounted up front and resembling a radiator.

THE SILENT AND ODORLESS ELECTRIC

In many ways battery electric power was the best way to drive an automobile at the turn of the century. It had none of the noise, vibration, or smell of the gasoline car, nor did it need a gearbox whose operation was one of the major challenges to the driver. Admittedly the steamer was also free of gear shifting, but it took up to 45 minutes to start it on a cold morning. No wonder that in 1899 and 1900 electrics outsold all other types of car; the Columbia was the production leader of all U.S. makes.

The history of the Columbia was a complex one, and was tied in with the ambitions of Colonel Albert Augustus Pope (1843–1909), whose aim was to dominate the vehicle industry as Billy Durant was to try to do later. A Civil War veteran, he began bicycle manufacture in 1877, and by 1899 had formed the American Bicycle Company, a trust controlling some 45 manufacturers. He had experimented with a gas-powered tricycle in 1894, but, finding it unsatisfactory, he decided that the future lay with electric vehicles. Unlike Olds and Ford, Pope was a businessman rather than an engineer and had his vehicles built for him by employees. His first electric came in 1896 and by October of that year he began production of a series of light two-seater runabouts which he sold under the name Columbia, also used for his bicycles. For his chief engineer he hired Hiram Percy Maxim, son of the inventor of the machine gun, and in 1898 Maxim came up with a whole range of designs from the runabout to a heavy enclosed brougham. Electric power was selected "for convenience in charging from the ordinary

simple open two-passenger buggy types, although four-passenger versions were offered, and Mobile made a wide range of more expensive types up to a nine-passenger enclosed limousine at $3,000. A two-passenger Locomobile runabout sold for only $750.

The success of the Locomobile led to many imitators, most of whom followed the same basic design. Most manufacturers assembled their cars from bought-out components, which explains the general uniformity. Variations, which on the whole did not sell well, included the shaft-driven Century from Syracuse, N.Y., and the Cotta from Lanark, Illinois, which featured chain drive to all four wheels and four-wheel steering. Variations in

engine design included the V-twin Crouch from New Brighton, Pennsylvania, the three-cylinder shaft-driven Eclipse from Boston, and four cylinders in the Henrietta from New York and the Hood Electronic Safety Steam Vehicle from Danvers, Massachusetts. The latter had magnetic inlet valves operated by three batteries guaranteed for six months. The company itself lasted barely twelve months.

Of the 100 or so makes of American steam car, most of which flourished between 1898 and 1905, 40 were originated in the states of Massachusetts, New Hampshire, New York, and Maine, but as these included nearly all the successful makes, the

worked for Morris & Salom) and Woods in Chicago, but at the turn of the century they were insignificant compared with Columbia.

For obvious reasons, the popularity of electric vehicles was limited to cities, and in the early days many were hired from cab companies rather than bought outright. Wealthy New Yorkers such as Frank Gould and Cornelius Vanderbilt had a cab constantly on call, for which they paid $180 per month. Doctors were also keen users of electric cabs, and one found an ingenious use for his. Wanting to X-ray a broken arm at the patient's home, he was unable to do so because the house was not supplied with electricity. He simply linked up his machine with the battery in his cab and quickly located the fracture.

type of electric light station circuits common to all towns of any size." The range of a middle-sized four-seater surrey was 35 miles between charges, at a speed of 12mph.

Meanwhile two other manufacturers were getting into the electric car act. The Electric Vehicle Company of Elizabethport, New Jersey, headed by Isaac L. Rice, acquired the Electrobat rights from Morris & Salom, and expanded manufacture of the front-drive taxicabs, and New York electrical engineer A.L. Riker began to make a range of vehicles from a two-passenger runabout to heavy trucks. In 1899 financier William Collins Whitney bought out the Electric Vehicle Company with the idea of making 2,000 taxicabs for use in America's major cities. He merged his activities

with Pope's, the idea being that Electric Vehicle would make the cabs and Pope's Columbia Automobile Company the passenger cars, both gasoline and electric. In 1901 the Columbia name was dropped for the company, although cars and cabs continued to be called Columbias. Riker had been working on a gasoline car, but Pope was not interested in this, so Riker offered it to Locomobile, it became the basis of the first gas car from that company and soon ousted the steamers. In 1900 output of electric passenger cars totaled about 1,500, double the number of Locomobile steamers, and to this figure should be added a quantity of cabs and trucks. There were a few other electric car makers, such as Baker in Cleveland (whose founder Walter Baker had

1913 RAMBLER TOURING ▼

OWNER: DAN OBERLE (PHOTO NICKY WRIGHT)

THE ROAD TO MASS PRODUCTION

1900 – 1920

"The way to make automobiles is to make one automobile like another,
to make them all alike, to make them come through the factory all alike,
just as one pin is like another pin when it comes from the pin factory."

Henry Ford, 1903

1903 AUTOCAR TONNEAU ▲▼

THE AUTOCAR COMPANY GREW OUT OF A PITTSBURGH, PENNSYLVANIA, FIRM THAT MADE TRICYCLES AND
QUADRICYCLES. IN 1901, FOUNDER LEWIS CLARK SET UP AN AUTOMOBILE FACTORY AT ARDMORE, PENNSYLVANIA,
AND BY 1903 WAS MAKING THE 10hp TWO-CYLINDER CAR SEEN HERE.
THE ONLY BODY STYLE WAS THIS REAR-ENTRANCE TONNEAU, SOON TO GIVE WAY TO THE SIDE-ENTRANCE TONNEAU,
OR TOURING CAR, ONCE WHEELBASES WERE LONG ENOUGH. THE GILLED TUBE RADIATOR MOUNTED BELOW THE HOOD
WAS TYPICAL OF THE PERIOD.

OWNER: AUBURN-CORD-DUESENBERG MUSEUM (PHOTO NICKY WRIGHT)

N JULY 1899 *McCLURE'S Magazine* published an article extolling the progress that the automobile had made in America over the preceding twelve months. A hundred electric cabs were plying New York, with 200 more on order, a motor ambulance was in operation in Chicago, at least two cities were using self-propelled fire engines, and the Santa Fe railroad had ordered a number of horseless coaches for an Arizona mountain route.

These and other examples were undoubtedly true, but nonetheless even at the turn of the century the impact of the automobile was very small. In 1900 production of passenger automobiles was 4,192, and the total number registered was about 8,000. Manufacture was confined largely to the East Coast, with a few exceptions such as White and Winton in Cleveland, Ohio. Outside the big cities many Americans had never seen a self-propelled vehicle, and the horse and mule reigned supreme. In 1900 it was estimated that the horse population of America numbered some 30 million. There would not be that number of motor vehicles until 1937. To displace the horse from the loyalty of rural Americans was not easy, for the animal was a companion, almost a member of the family, and only the very poorest citizens were without one. The maintenance of horses was easily understood, they reproduced themselves, and they could find their way home if their owner were too tired or intoxicated to do so. Rural communities tended to side with the horse against the automobile, requiring drivers to pull into the side of the road or at least stop and switch off their engine at the approach of a horse.

In order to calm the horse's fears one motorist,

Uriah Smith of Battle Creek, Michigan, made a sculpted, life-size horse's head which he mounted on the dashboard of his car. "It will have all the appearance of a horse and carriage," he wrote to *The Horseless Age* in 1899, "and hence raise no fears in any skittish animal, for the live horse would be thinking of another horse, and before he could discover his error and see that he had been fooled, the strange carriage would be passed, and then it would be too late to grow frantic and fractious." Smith recommended that the horse's head be made hollow, so that it could be used as a gasoline tank.

Less considerate motorists than Mr. Smith aroused great anger among farmers, who sometimes spread tacks and broken glass on the roads or ran strands of rope, or barbed wire across them, especially effective at twilight. Automobiles were frequently stoned, and not only by children, while horse whips were used on occasion. To be fair, these incidents were as often as not provoked by the drivers, who killed chickens and dogs with little thought for their owners. An investigator in Iowa counted on one journey (unfortunately we do not know how long it was) 225 dead animals, representing 29 wild and domestic species.

Against this background, the spread of the automobile across America in the first two decades of this century was a remarkable phenomenon. It began in the cities, not only because paved streets were kinder to primitive and low-powered vehicles, but also because the horse was less favored there. In the 1890s New York and Brooklyn had a horse population of some 175,000, and the accumulations of dung posed a serious health problem. Overworked and underfed horses often died in harness and were left by the curbside for several days to add to the pollution.

FIRST STEPS TOWARD MASS PRODUCTION

No industry springs into life without antecedents. The auto industry in America could not have grown in the way that it did without the existence of two established, large-scale businesses, bicycles and carriages. They not only provided the technology on which many early autos were based, but also trained men who subsequently made their name with cars. Colonel Pope's car empire was built on bicycle money, and other well-known names who began their working life with cycles included Alexander Winton, the Duryeas, Thomas B. Jeffery, George N. Pierce, and Erwin R. Thomas. William S. Knudsen, head of General Motors from 1937 to 1940, was a bicycle mechanic, while John N. Willys was a bicycle salesmen.

The best-known name from the carriage and wagon world belonged to the Studebaker brothers, whose business was founded in 1852. By the 1890s it was the largest vehicle builder in the world, with annual sales of over $2 million. Overland, later taken over by Willys, originated as a branch of an Indianapolis buggy maker, while Billy Durant and J. Dallas Dort, both famous for their cars in the 1920s, were partners in a successful carriage business from 1885 to the turn of the century. Other companies that grew from carriage and buggy making included Gardner and Moon.

There were, of course, other apprenticeships that led to auto making. Henry Ford and James Packard were electrical engineers, David Buick was in the plumbing business, International Harvester was well-known in the agricultural equipment field, while the first man to make cars in serious quantities was Ransom Olds, whose father ran a machine shop in Lansing, Michigan. Olds was also a graduate of Lansing Business University, so had the valuable combination of commercial acumen and mechanical skills.

Ransom Eli Olds (1864–1950) was born in Geneva, Ohio, the son of a locksmith of English extraction, Pliny F. Olds. After a spell of farming near Cleveland, the family moved in 1880 to Lansing where Pliny became more ambitious, announcing his new company as practical machinists, manufacturers of steam yachts, steam engines, brass and iron castings. Ransom joined the firm in 1883 and soon bought out his brother's share, becoming a fully fledged partner when he was 21, in 1885. Two years later he built his first vehicle and, given the nature of the family business, it is not surprising that it was a steamer. A three-wheeler with tiller-steered front wheel and seating for two passengers, it does not seem to have been a great success. It was followed by a four-wheeler which was sold to India, some say to a circus, others to a maharajah. The destination really doesn't really matter as the vehicle was lost in

shipwreck. Olds cannot have had much confidence in it, for he said that as a result of the shipwreck "the reputation of the company was saved."

During the 1890s Olds experimented with electric cars before deciding that internal combustion was the motive power of the future. Pliny had retired in 1894, and his son reorganized the firm as the Olds Gas Engine Works. While the money was being brought in from stationary gasoline engines, Ransom Olds tinkered with automobiles. His first was running toward the end of 1896, and in August 1897 he set up a separate company, the Olds Motor Vehicle Company Capitalization was $50,000, with support from Lansing businessmen, but two years later, during which time he had built only five or six cars, Olds set up a new company in Detroit, since he thought that Lansing's population of 2,000 was too small to support a new industry such as he had in mind. In May 1899 the Olds Motor Works came into existence, with nominal capitalization of $350,000, nearly all the money being provided by Samuel L. Smith, a copper and lumber millionaire who had already invested heavily in the Olds Gas Engine

▲ PART OF THE EXTENSIVE OLDSMOBILE WORKS IN 1904, WITH ENGINES AND FRAMES ALREADY ASSEMBLED. ENGINES CAME FROM LELAND & FAULCONER AT THIS TIME.

OLDSMOBILE HISTORY CENTER, MIRCO DE CET COLLECTION

▲ ONE OF MANY STUNTS PERFORMED TO SHOW THE VERSATILITY OF THE CURVED DASH WAS CLIMBING THE STEPS OF THE MICHIGAN STATE CAPITOL.

OLDSMOBILE HISTORY CENTER, MIRCO DE CET COLLECTION

◄ ANOTHER PART OF THE OLDS PLANT AT LANSING, MICHIGAN, SHOWING CURVED DASH MODELS ALMOST COMPLETED. THIS PHOTO WAS TAKEN IN 1905, WHEN OLDS PRODUCED 6,500 VEHICLES, MORE THAN ANY OTHER AUTO MAKER IN THE WORLD.

OLDSMOBILE HISTORY CENTER, MIRCO DE CET COLLECTION

Works which was kept entirely separate, just in case the auto business foundered. Olds' stake in the new company was limited to $400.

By the beginning of 1901 the new company had built no more than a dozen cars, and sold even fewer. Little information about them has survived, but they were probably not unlike the 1896/97 models, with 5hp single-cylinder engines slung below the high-built four-passenger carriage-like body, and final drive by double belts. However, a completely new model was in the planning stage when a disastrous fire struck the Detroit plant on March 9, 1901. There were several prototypes in the factory, but there was time to save only one, a light two-passenger runabout. It has been said that because this was the only car saved, Olds had no choice but to concentrate on it, and thus mere chance gave rise to America's first mass-produced automobile, the Curved Dash Olds. It is a good story, but research suggests that the company had decided on that model anyway, and that plans and patterns did survive the fire.

Whatever the story behind it, the Curved Dash Olds was an attractive little car, 98 inches long and weighing 700 pounds. It was powered by a 4½hp single-cylinder engine of 95.5 cubic inches displacement, mounted horizontally under the seat, with a two-speed planetary transmission and final drive by single chain. The front part of the body curved upwards to form the dash, hence the name, while the springs ran from front to rear and formed the side members of the frame. Olds set a price of $650, which remained unchanged through the car's seven-year life. This was a very reasonable figure when compared with competing models, of which there were not many. A Winton cost $1,500, and although it was larger it was still a single-cylinder two-passenger car. Even a Locomobile runabout cost $750, and it was not so simple to operate as the Olds. From the first year, Olds offered extras which included a rear-facing dos-à-dos seat for $25, mudguards for $10 a set, and a folding top which cost $50 in leather and $25 in rubber.

Because of the fire, Olds had to contract out many of his car's components, which gave a boost to several Detroit firms later to become famous in the auto industry. The engines were made for him by Leland & Faulconer (Henry Leland later built the first Cadillac), transmissions by the Dodge

brothers, and radiators by the Briscoe brothers. By the end of 1901, Olds had sold 425 of his little runabouts; production jumped to 2,500 in 1902, 4,000 in 1903, 5,508 in 1904, and 6,500 in 1905. The last two years' figures included some larger cars, but the bulk of production was still devoted to the Curved Dash Runabout. Although the rebuilt Detroit factory was continued, Olds moved back to Lansing and operated a larger factory there as well.

This level of production put Olds well in the lead of American auto manufacturers. Once Locomobile gave up its light steamers it was no longer in the race, and indeed Olds overtook Locomobile before this, topping the charts in 1903. Oldsmobile was undisputed leader in 1904 and 1905 as well, but in 1906 sales fell drastically as the

1902 OLDSMOBILE CURVED DASH RUNABOUT ▼
THE CURVED DASH WAS AMERICA'S FIRST QUANTITY-BUILT CAR: MORE THAN 18,000 WERE MADE IN THE SEVEN YEARS 1901 TO 1907. THIS 1902 MODEL HAS WIRE WHEELS, ALTHOUGH WOOD-SPOKED ARTILLERY WHEELS WERE MORE COMMON BY THIS DATE. IN 1905 THE GUS EDWARDS POPULAR SONG, "IN MY MERRY OLDSMOBILE," GAVE THE COMPANY MUCH USEFUL PUBLICITY. THE CURVED DASH WAS MADE UNDER LICENSE IN SEVERAL FOREIGN COUNTRIES, INCLUDING CANADA (AS THE LEROY) AND GERMANY (AS THE POLYMOBIL).
OWNER: CRAWFORD COLLECTION OF THE WESTERN HISTORICAL SOCIETY (PHOTO NICKY WRIGHT)

▲ LINE-UP OF OLDSMOBILES OUTSIDE THEIR MINNEAPOLIS DEALERS, A.F. CHASE & COMPANY. LEFT TO RIGHT:
10hp TONNEAU, CURVED DASH DELIVERY WAGON, 10hp TONNEAU, CURVED DASH RUNABOUT, TONNEAU
OF UNKNOWN MAKE. THE OLDS TONNEAU WAS INTRODUCED IN 1904. THE LARGE STATIONARY ENGINE
IN THE SHOWROOM WINDOW IS ALSO PROBABLY OF OLDS MAKE.
OLDSMOBILE HISTORY CENTER,
MIRCO DE CET COLLECTION

1910 REO ▶
THE REO MOTOR CAR COMPANY
WAS FORMED WHEN RANSOM OLDS
PARTED FROM HIS COLLEAGUES
IN THE OLDS MOTOR WORKS. BY 1910,
WHEN THIS FIVE-PASSENGER TOURING
WAS MADE, REO WAS THE EIGHTH
LARGEST U.S. AUTO MANUFACTURER,
WITH 6,588 CARS DELIVERED.
OWNER: BOB BENNETT (PHOTO NICKY WRIGHT)

Curved Dash was dropped in favor of more costly cars. This was against Ransom Olds' wishes, but he had left the company at the end of 1904. He was outvoted by the Smith family, who of course owned nearly all the company stock. It is interesting to speculate what might have happened if he had remained in charge. Perhaps Ford would never have become the leading U.S. manufacturer? Instead, Olds found other backers to set him up in a new business which he called Reo Motor Car Company, making a car called the Reo. Similar in general conception to the Curved Dash, but with a small hood at the front, it cost $680 and consistently outsold Oldsmobiles for several years. It was made in Lansing, not far from the Oldsmobile's home. (Although the company name remained Olds Motor Works up to 1943, the cars were known as Oldsmobiles from the early days of the Curved Dash.)

Ransom Olds continued with his new company until 1936, although he went into semi-retirement in the mid-1920s, concentrating on rural subsistence living. He founded a combined agricultural/industrial colony in Florida called Oldsmar, which still exists today. He was also a pioneer in the manufacture of powered lawn mowers, an interest that continued until his death at the age of 86 in 1950.

THE IMPACT OF HENRY FORD

The make which displaced Oldsmobile in 1906 and was to remain at the top of the production league until 1927 was Ford. Credit is always given to the Model T as being the first mass-produced car, and certainly output did not reach massive proportions until the T era, but Ford was making substantial numbers of cars several years before the T's debut in 1908.

We last saw Henry Ford struggling with the Detroit Automobile Company, which was dissolved in January 1901 after hardly any cars had been built. He then turned to racing, with the express aim of beating the Frenchman Henri Fournier, who was achieving great speeds with his 60hp Mors and who was to set a flying mile record of 69.5mph in November 1901. Ford built a massive two-cylinder car with 540-cubic-inch displacement (surely the largest two-cylinder auto engine ever made

THE MASSIVE ENGINE OF FORD'S 999 RACING CAR, EACH CYLINDER OF WHICH DISPLACED 288.83 CUBIC INCHES — THE SAME AS A FORD V8 OF THE 1960s. THE FOUR CYLINDERS WERE CAST IN ONE BLOCK — UNUSUAL FOR THE PERIOD — BUT THE VALVES WERE UNCOVERED, AND THE HUGE CRANKSHAFT WAS ALSO UNPROTECTED FROM THE MUD AND DIRT OF THE ROAD.

FORD MOTOR COMPANY

anywhere in the world) in which he beat Alexander Winton over a 25-mile course at Grosse Pointe track in October 1901. He never competed directly against Fournier, although he had plans to go into partnership with the Frenchman in making cars, but in 1904 he took the flying mile record at 91.37mph in a massive four-cylinder car with 1,155.3-cubic-inch displacement, called 999 after the famous New York Central express train. This and a similar car called Arrow had been built in 1902 with financial backing from racing cyclist Tom Cooper. At first, neither Ford nor Cooper drove the monster cars; this they entrusted to another racing cyclist called Barney Oldfield, who had never driven a car of any sort when he first climbed into the seat of 999. He covered 1 mile in 1 minute 1.2 seconds, reducing the time to under 1 minute (59.6 seconds) in June 1903 and going on to a career as one of America's best-known racing drivers. Ford and Cooper parted company in October 1902, and Clara Ford for one was not sorry. "He thinks too much of low down women to suit me," she said.

If Clara was unhappy with Henry's partner, his backers were unhappy with Henry, for they saw no chance of making money from his racing involvement. The Henry Ford Company had been founded in November 1901 with backing from

William Murphy, who had been among the supporters of the Detroit Automobile Company in 1899, but Murphy refused to allow the building of racing cars in company time. Ford said that he was not ready for production yet, so Murphy brought in Henry Leland as a production consultant. Ford was furious and left in March 1902, with $900 compensation and a promise from Murphy that he would not use the Ford name in connection with any car. Murphy was true to his word. The Leland-designed car which he put into production in 1903 was called the Cadillac.

Ford had quarreled with two partners in little over six months and had still earned no money from making or selling cars. Many observers might have forecast that he would fizzle out like countless contemporary tinkerers, warranting no more than a few lines in specialist encyclopedias. However, in 1902 he found a new supporter. In his days with the Edison Illuminating Company, one of his jobs had been to buy coal, and the best merchant to go to was Alexander Young

Malcomson, whose products were marketed as "Hotter Than Sunshine." The two men remained friends, and when Malcomson became bitten by the auto bug he bought a Winton. Hearing that young Ford had beaten Winton, he thought a Ford car might be just what he wanted, and in August 1902 he agreed to provide funds for the manufacture of automobiles. Knowing Ford's doubtful reputation, he kept his involvement quiet at first, but in November agreed to the formation of the Ford & Malcomson Company This became the Ford Motor Company on June 16, 1903, and so it

HENRY FORD (LEFT) ON HIS 999 RACER DURING AN EXHIBITION RUN AT THE GROSSE POINTE HORSE-RACING TRACK IN 1903. ALONGSIDE HIM IS HARRY HARKNESS ON A SIMPLEX. BY THIS DATE FORD HAD ALREADY GIVEN UP RACING, HAVING DECLARED "ONCE IS ENOUGH" AFTER BEATING ALEXANDER WINTON AT GROSSE POINTE IN 1901.

FORD ARCHIVES, MIRCO DE CET COLLECTION

has remained ever since that day.

The car that Ford put into production as the Model A was similar to the one he had been working on for William Murphy. In appearance it was close to the first Cadillac, the main difference being in the engine, which in the Ford was a horizontally-opposed twin, while Leland's design for the Cadillac was a single-cylinder. Transmission was by two-speed planetary gear and single chain, as on the Curved Dash Olds, Cadillac, and most other American cars of that time. The body had a

single seat for two passengers, but a rear-entrance tonneau giving two additional seats was available for an extra $100 over the basic price of $750. This was more than the Olds, but in the Ford all four passengers faced the same way. Top speed was around 25mph.

The first Ford factory, on Mack Avenue, Detroit, was little more than an assembly plant for the various bought-in components — chassis and engines from the Dodge brothers, bodies from the C.R. Wilson Carriage Company, tires from the Hartford Rubber Company, and wheels from the Prudden Company of Lansing. Profit margin was estimated at $200 on the two-seaters, but only $150 on the four-seaters.

The first sale of a Model A, to Dr. E. Pfennig, a Chicago dentist, took place on July 15, 1903, and by October of 1904 a total of 1,708 cars had been delivered. Toward the end of 1904 a new factory, on Piquette Avenue, came into use, and by April 1905 Ford was making an average of 25 cars a day, with 300 employees. The huge factory sign said "Home of the Celebrated Ford Automobile." By now the Model A had been superseded by the Models B

and C. The C was similar to the A, although different in appearance because the sloping dash had been replaced by a short hood which looked as if it concealed an engine, though in fact it contained a fuel tank and the engine still lived under the front seat. The B was a different matter altogether, a larger and more expensive car with a front-mounted four-cylinder engine of 318 cubic inches and 24hp, with a side-entrance touring body and shaft drive. It cost $2,000 compared with the C's $800, and marked a change in direction which Malcomson favored but Ford did not.

Malcomson reasoned that a higher profit could be made on an expensive car than on a cheap one. Ford clung to the belief that there was a vast market for cars among poorer people, if only the cars could be made cheap enough, and the only answer to this was to make them in larger numbers. The Model B was made only for the 1904 and 1905 seasons and production figures are not known,

although they must have been pretty small. The Malcomson theory had one more airing in the Model K which was even larger, a massive 40hp six of 405 cubic inches on a 114- or 120-inch wheelbase and priced at $2,800. It never sold well, and by 1907 Ford was having to force the car onto dealers by telling them that they must take one Model K for every ten of the popular Model Ns, and by insisting that new dealers took at least one K before they were accepted at all. When even this failed to move the cars, prices were reduced to $1,800 at the end of 1907. Only 584 of the Model Ks were made.

The Model N was a direct ancestor of the T in that it was a four-cylinder car, yet modestly priced at $500 for a two-seater. Its success took Ford from fourth place in the production league in 1905 with 1,599 deliveries, to first place, with 8,729, in 1906. Henry Ford was also changing his manufacturing process. Up to this time "manufacture" was really assembly with components being bought in. Ford was particularly niggled by having to buy from the Dodge brothers because they were profiting from his success twice over, from sales of their components and from the sizable investments they had in the Ford company. In November 1905, therefore, Ford set up the Ford Manufacturing Company to organize the production of engines and transmissions. In fact this work could have been done under the name of the Ford Motor Company but the main purpose of setting up a new company was to exclude Alexander Malcomson. Ford thought that Malcomson's fondness for large cars would lead the company into disaster.

Malcomson was allocated no shares in Ford Manufacturing and responded angrily by setting up a new firm, the Aerocar Company, to make a large air-cooled car priced at $2,800, the same as the Model K Ford. He also retained his holdings in the Ford Motor Company but Henry claimed this was improper as Malcomson would be using his profits from Ford to build up a rival concern. In November 1906, with legal backing, Malcomson was ousted from the Ford Motor Company, although his associate James Couzens remained with Ford. Another important figure close to Ford was Childe Harold Wills, a highly skilled young draftsman who became chief engineer and played a

large part in the development of the Model T.

Once Malcomson was out of the way, Ford quickly reabsorbed Ford Manufacturing into the Ford Motor Company, but he persevered with its aims. If he was to make all the components previously contracted out, he would need greatly increased manufacturing space, so in April 1907 he began work on a new factory at Highland Park six times the size of the one at Piquette Avenue. It was not completed until January 1910, and is still a Ford property today, although used largely for storing machinery rather than manufacturing. Piquette Avenue was sold to Studebaker in 1911.

1911 FORD MODEL T TOURING ▲
THE MODEL T WAS CONSIDERABLY REDESIGNED FOR 1911, WITH NEW FENDERS, WHEELS, AXLES, AND MODIFICATIONS TO THE ENGINE. ITEMS THAT HAD BEEN OPTIONS, SUCH AS HEADLIGHTS AND HORN, BECAME STANDARD EQUIPMENT; INDEED FORD SAID THAT THE COMPANY'S WARRANTY WOULD BECOME VOID IF OTHER ACCESSORIES WERE ADDED, ALTHOUGH IT IS NOT KNOWN IF THIS RULE WAS EVER ENFORCED. CERTAINLY, IN LATER YEARS A VAST INDUSTRY SUPPLYING MODEL T ACCESSORIES GREW UP.

OWNER: GEORGE SANDERS (PHOTO NICKY WRIGHT)

THE MODEL T

The low-priced four-cylinder Model N was joined in 1907 by the Model R, which was essentially the same car, but with additional trimming such as full-length running boards in place of steps, and more brass fittings. These took the price up to $750, and to bridge the gap between the N and the R, Ford brought out the $700 Model S for 1908; with a four-passenger body this also cost $750. These three models kept Ford at the head of the production league, with 14,887 in 1907 and 10,202 in 1908. Ford's nearest rival was Buick, with figures of 4,641 and 8,820 respectively.

During the winter of 1906/07 Henry Ford had a section of the top floor at Piquette Avenue, as yet unused, partitioned off, with a door large enough to get a car through (he hadn't forgotten wielding his pickax in 1896) and a good lock. Here he and a small team which included Wills, a Danish-born woodworker, Charles Sorensen, and a Hungarian-born engineer, Joseph Galamb, worked on the design of the new car which would emerge in the Fall of 1908 as the Model T. In some ways the Model T was evolutionary, using ideas already proved in the Models N, R, and S, in other ways revolutionary, particularly in the ease of servicing the engine. The Model N's engine had four separately cast cylinders and a fixed head; in the T the cylinders were cast in one block and the head was detachable. The crankshaft was made of vanadium steel, which Henry had come across when examining a French racing car in 1905. Much stronger than regular steel, it was made for him by a small steel company in Canton, Ohio, and although the crankshaft looked frail it would withstand twice the actual load given by the engine. The transmission was an improved version of the two forward speed planetary unit used in previous Fords. Ignition was by low-tension magneto incorporated in the flywheel, and another innovation was the left-mounted steering wheel. Although Americans always drove on the right, the majority of cars, including the previous Fords, had right-hand drive. The enormous numbers of Model Ts which soon came onto the roads influenced other makers to follow Ford's lead in this matter. Within ten years only a few high-priced cars such as Pierce-Arrow and Stutz still had steering wheels on the right.

When it was launched in October 1908 the Model T was offered in five body styles, two-passenger coupe and runabout, five-passenger touring, and seven-passenger town car or landaulet. Prices ran from $825 for the runabout to $1,000 for the town car. As one would expect, the open models sold the best, 7,728 tourings and 2,351 runabouts in the first model year. Rarest was the sentry-box-like coupe, of which only 47 were delivered. Most components were Ford-made, apart from tires, which Ford bought from his friend Harvey Firestone, and bodies, which came from a number of suppliers, notably Kelsey and O.J. Beaudette.

Production started slowly, but by the summer of 1909 was running at 100 cars per day. 1909 saw 17,771 cars delivered, and within four years Ford factories were turning out more than ten times this number. The moving assembly line, the key to mass production, was installed at Highland Park in 1913, in which year production rose to 202,667. The following year saw another jump, to 308,162, while

▲ FORD MODEL T STRIPPED TO THE BARE ESSENTIALS. THIS IS THE CAR IN WHICH BERT SCOTT AND JIMMY SMITH WON THE 1909 NEW YORK–SEATTLE RACE, BEATING A $4,500 ACME, A $5,000 SHAWMUT, AND AN IMPORTED ITALA THAT PROBABLY COST MORE STILL. THEIR TIME WAS 22 DAYS AND 55 MINUTES.
FORD MOTOR COMPANY

1909 FORD MODEL T ◄
THE FIRST FULL YEAR OF PRODUCTION FOR THE MODEL T WAS 1909, AND 17,771 WERE DELIVERED IN THE 12 MONTHS. THREE COLORS WERE OFFERED: RED ON THE TOURINGS, GRAY ON THE RUNABOUTS, AND GREEN ON THE TOWN CARS AND LANDAULETS. VARIOUS COLORS WERE AVAILABLE UP TO 1914, AFTER WHICH MODEL Ts WERE SUPPLIED ONLY IN BLACK, ALTHOUGH COLOR WAS TO RETURN IN 1926. THE TWO ACETYLENE GAS HEADLIGHTS ON THIS CAR WERE EXTRAS, AS STANDARD LIGHTING IN 1909 DID NOT EXTEND BEYOND TWO SIDELIGHTS AND ONE TAILLIGHT. THE TOP WAS AN EXTRA AS WELL.
OWNER: CRAWFORD COLLECTION OF THE WESTERN HISTORICAL SOCIETY (PHOTO NICKY WRIGHT)

the figures for 1915 and 1916 were 501,462 and 734,811 respectively.

Henry Ford is sometimes credited with inventing the moving assembly line, but this is not so. Interchangeable parts were used in the assembly of rifles well before the Civil War, and a little later, in the watch and clock industry. Henry, who had planned to mass-produce a watch at one time, is said to have gained his inspiration from the Chicago meat-packing industry, where hog carcasses were brought on overhead trolleys past each worker who would take his cut. Ford's achievement was to adapt the process to the vastly more complicated process of making automobiles.

As production grew the unit price came down, so that by 1915 the touring was down to $440, little

more than half the 1908 figure, for a much better equipped car. It must be admitted that the original Model T was a pretty basic vehicle. Standard equipment consisted of three oil lamps only, two side and one tail. Headlights, windshield, top, horn, bumpers, and speedometer were all extras. By 1915 these were all included in the price, except for bumpers, which were seldom seen on Model Ts. A debit from 1914 onward was that the cars were only available in black. This was because japan black enamel was the only paint that would dry quickly enough to keep up with the assembly line. From 1926 a choice of colors was again provided, thanks to fast-drying Duco lacquer.

The Model T was not the only mass-produced car of its day, but it has passed into folklore as the car that put America on wheels. Certainly no other car aroused such affection, as well as exasperation, among owners. It was the first car owned by most Americans in the first two decades of this century, and even after it went out of production in 1927 it

was bought by many as a "starter car" because of the wide availability and low price of used Ts. Henry Ford came of farming stock and he was particularly pleased that farmers took to the T in such a big way. It was the first car to wean them away from the horse and buggy. "You know," wrote a Georgia farmer's wife to Henry in 1918, "your car lifted us out of the mud. It brought joy into our lives. We loved every rattle of its bones...."

After a slight dip in production during World War I, the Model T surged ahead in the 1920s, topping the million mark each year from 1922 to 1926, and reaching a peak of 1,817,891 in 1923. This was more than four times the number of cars made by Ford's nearest rival, Chevrolet. Prices were down too, with the cheapest two-passenger runabout of 1924 costing a mere $260. Because the car was still pretty basic, an enormous trade in accessories grew up. In the early 1920s the Sears Roebuck catalog offered as many as 5,000 different items for the Model T, fancy lamps, horns, disk wheels, and almost anything that could be bolted or screwed to the car. Some firms offered complete body kits to transform the T's homely appearance, others provided overhead valve conversions to boost its performance. The planetary transmission, widely used and familiar in 1908, was obsolete on every car but the T in the 1920s, and some firms offered conventional three-speed sliding transmissions. The Mayfair Manufacturing Company of Boston bought up used T sedans, tested and replaced parts where necessary, and fitted a sliding transmission and their own style of radiator, selling the result for $485, $175 less than a new 1925 T sedan. Not many people were impressed with this offer, and fewer than ten Mayfairs were sold.

THE SELDEN PATENT

In September 1909, just as the Model T was approaching its first birthday, Judge Charles Merrill Hough of the Circuit Court of Southern New York upheld a patent claim against Ford by the Association of Licensed Automobile Manufacturers (ALAM). This awarded millions of dollars to ALAM in unpaid royalties on every Ford car made since 1903, the year in which the ALAM was set up.

The ALAM arose from the activities of a patent attorney from Rochester, N.Y., called George Baldwin Selden (1846–1932). He had filed a patent in 1879 for an internal combustion motor vehicle, and had gradually updated it as he saw the design of such vehicles changing. His definitive patent was filed in November 1895, and four years later he signed the patent over (for a fee) to a group of Wall Street men headed by William C. Whitney, who acquired the Electric Vehicle Company and allied himself with Colonel Pope. They bought Selden's 1895 patent for $10,000. One may wonder why a maker of electric cars should obtain a patent for gasoline cars, but so long as they held the patent they could enforce it against anyone they liked. Since no one was certain at this point what type of motive power would prove the most popular, they were hedging their bets. Alexander Winton was the first manufacturer to be brought into line, in 1900, and in 1903 the representatives of five other companies, Knox, Locomobile, Oldsmobile, Packard, and Pierce-Arrow formed the ALAM

which agreed the validity of the Selden patent and promised to pay a royalty of 1¼ percent on the price of every car sold. This royalty was to be split, 20 percent to Selden, 40 percent to the Electric Vehicle Company and 40 percent to the ALAM to cover any litigation which might arise.

Up to this time Selden had not made a single car, but in 1903 he had two made to the design he had worked out in 1877, two years before he took out his first patent. They were crude-looking machines, with the two-cycle engines mounted over, and driving, the front axle, which steered on the center pivot system. Henry Cave of Hartford, Connecticut, who built one of them, said that it did not run very well. The other car was made by Selden and his sons, who painted the date 1877 on the side. Surviving photos have led some people to think that the car really was made in 1877, and numerous mugs, beer mats, and other such items have been made illustrating the "1877 Selden."

Membership of the ALAM was not open to everyone, only to those considered to be bona fide manufacturers. In 1903 Henry Ford made inquiries about membership and was told by F. L. Smith, treasurer of Oldsmobile, that he would not be accepted as his company was "a mere assemblage plant." Smith should have known better than to cross swords with as feisty an individual as Ford, or his associates. James Couzens is reported to have said: "Selden can take his patent and go to hell with it." The Ford company resolutely refused to pay any royalties and offered to protect any dealers or users of its cars against prosecution. The battle was on.

In 1907 Selden tried to demonstrate one of his cars to Judge Hough; it required an air compressor to start it and ran no more than 5 yards before spluttering to a standstill, but the judge did not consider that its failure was relevant to the case. In 1909 he rendered his verdict, and so overawed were the auto manufacturers that 30 more joined the ALAM in a matter of weeks. Durant, whose Buick, Cadillac and Oldsmobile companies were longstanding ALAM members, decided to pay up.

Ford was not without supporters, who had formed the American Motor Car Manufacturers' Association. They included Marmon, Reo, Maxwell-Briscoe, Mitchell, and the truck maker Mack, but most of these fell in line with the ALAM

▲ GEORGE B. SELDEN AT THE WHEEL OF THE CRUDE FRONT-DRIVE CAR HE BUILT IN 1903 TO JUSTIFY HIS PATENT. NEITHER IT NOR ITS FELLOW RAN AT ALL WELL, BUT HE USED THEIR EXISTENCE TO EXTRACT MILLIONS OF DOLLARS IN ROYALTIES, UNTIL HE WAS CHALLENGED AT LAW BY HENRY FORD, WHO WAS FINALLY SUCCESSFUL IN 1911.

MOTOR VEHICLE MANUFACTURERS' ASSOCIATION

after the 1909 decision. However, Ford appealed, and on January 9, 1911, Judge Hough's decision was dismissed on the grounds that the Selden patent applied only to two-cycle engines of the Brayton type and those of Ford and nearly all other auto manufacturers used the four-cycle Otto system.

Through his fight against the ALAM Ford became a folk hero, the lone fighter against the large organization, which was ironic as his own company went on to become one of the biggest industrial organizations in the world. But he was for a long time seen as a friend of the common man, and epitomized the distrust felt by the Middle Western country dweller for East Coast big business. He was not a joiner, and never became a member of the National Automobile Chamber of Commerce (NACC), so that up to the end of the 1920s the NACC Handbook, which listed and illustrated a wide variety of cars from companies great and small, never carried a mention of Ford, the greatest of them all.

▲ ONE OF THE MANY FIRMS THAT BILLY DURANT INCORPORATED INTO GENERAL MOTORS WAS THE RELIANCE MOTOR TRUCK COMPANY OF DETROIT. FROM 1912 RELIANCE MODELS SUCH AS THIS CHAIN-DRIVE CAB-OVER TRUCK BORE THE NAME GENERAL MOTORS TRUCK, STARTING A LINE OF GMC TRUCKS THAT LASTED UNTIL THE 1980s AND MERGER WITH THE WHITE RANGE. THIS TRUCK IS CARRYING A LOAD OF TIRES, WHICH WERE FITTED TO NONDETACHABLE RIMS. YOU CHANGED A TIRE IN THOSE DAYS, NOT A WHEEL.

MOTOR VEHICLE MANUFACTURERS' ASSOCIATION

► THE TWO MEN WITHOUT WHOM GENERAL MOTORS WOULD NEVER HAVE COME INTO EXISTENCE: LEFT, THE DEDICATED BUT UNWORLDLY ENGINEER DAVID DUNBAR BUICK (1855–1929); RIGHT, THE DYNAMIC BUT SOMETIMES UNWISE ENTREPRENEUR WILLIAM CRAPO DURANT (1860–1947). BOTH MEN ENDED THEIR LIVES IN HUMBLE JOBS, BUICK AS A RECEPTIONIST, DURANT RUNNING A HAMBURGER JOINT.

MOTOR VEHICLE MANUFACTURERS' ASSOCIATION

B ILLY DURANT AND THE FORMATION OF GENERAL MOTORS

Although Ford certainly dominated American production until the late 1920s, his lead was soon followed by other ambitious men. The most prominent of these was William Crapo Durant (1860–1947), born in Boston but raised in Flint, Michigan. Often described as self-made, Billy Durant did not come from poor stock, for his grandfather William H. Crapo had made a fortune in whaling on the East Coast, then moved west to Michigan where he operated a successful lumber mill. Young Billy worked in the mill until he was 21, then set out on his own in the carriage business, which was a major activity in Flint. He patented a two-wheeled cart, which he sold for $12.50, and in 1885 went into partnership with Josiah Dallas Dort (1861–1925). By the turn of the century they had built up a thriving carriage business; at their peak they made 50,000 carriages a year. Among their employees was future auto maker Charles Nash.

Durant noticed a locally built car with an advanced valve-in-head engine made by Scottish-born David Dunbar Buick (1855–1929). Buick had entered the plumbing business and in the 1890s perfected a technique for applying enamel to cast-iron bathtubs. Today his name is associated only with cars and his major contribution to modern domestic living is forgotten. His plumbing business, Buick and Sherwood, brought him a considerable fortune, but he chose to turn his energies to a new obsession, the automobile. Founded in 1902, the Buick Manufacturing Company made only six cars in 1903 and no more than 37 in 1904 when Billy Durant stepped in, bought a controlling interest, and raised capitalization to $1.5 million.

Durant reorganized production with assembly in a disused Durant-Dort carriage factory at Jackson, Michigan, and manufacture of engines at the Buick factory at Flint and bodies by the Flint Wagon Works. Production jumped to 750 cars in 1905, and to 1,400 in 1906. Manufacture was gradually concentrated in Flint, the Jackson plant being wound down and finally closed in 1912. The 1907 output from Buick was 4,641 cars, which put the make second among U.S. manufacturers, outdone only by Ford.

As Buick prospered under Durant's leadership,

there seemed to be less room in the organization for its founder. David Buick was a tinkerer rather than a mass-production man, and he was constantly making suggestions to the engineers, who were mostly Durant men. These met with little sympathy because they would have interrupted the drive toward large-scale manufacture. Buick was also keen on selling his engines to other car makers. Durant was not happy with this either, so in 1908 Buick left the company, with $100,000 as a personal gift from Durant.

1911 OVERLAND MODEL 55 TOURING ▲
THE WILLYS-OVERLAND COMPANY WAS AMERICA'S THIRD LARGEST AUTO MAKER IN 1911, BEATEN ONLY BY FORD AND BUICK. THIS MODEL 55 WAS PART OF THE 40hp RANGE THAT INCLUDED FIVE STYLES ON A 118-INCH WHEELBASE, FROM THE 55 AT $1,300 TO THE 52 LIMOUSINE AT MORE THAN DOUBLE THE PRICE, $2,750.
OWNER: GEORGE SANDERS (PHOTO NICKY WRIGHT)

The rest of David Buick's story is a sad one. Nothing he touched seemed to go right, from oil and land speculation to the manufacture of carburetors and automobiles. Others made fortunes from oil in the years before World War I, but Buick lost most of what he took out of the Buick Motor Company. Back in Michigan, he tried carburetors with his son Tom, followed by manufacture of a car in Walden, New York. For this he used his other family name, Dunbar, launching the David Dunbar Buick Corporation with a supposed capitalization of $5 million. Nowhere near this figure was ever raised, and only one car was ever made, a roadster powered by a six-cylinder Continental engine. Buick invested the little money he had left in real estate in Florida, but lost this too. In 1927 he took a job as an instructor at the Detroit School of Trades, but he was 72 years old and so frail that he was soon transferred to the reception desk. Outside in the streets countless Buick cars rolled by, but their original creator toiled away unnoticed. David Buick could never afford to retire, and died in 1929.

By then Billy Durant had made and lost two fortunes. He also had a car bearing his own name, but far more important was his organization of General Motors. He had originally hoped to include Maxwell-Briscoe, Ford, and Reo in his empire, but his plan never materialized because of the lack of enthusiasm from Henry Ford, among other reasons. So he used the Buick Company as a base to found General Motors in September 1908, although the only make in it was Buick. On December 28 Oldsmobile was brought into the group, followed by Oakland in May 1909, and

1913 RAMBLER TOURING ▲▼

FOR THE RAMBLER NAME 1913 WAS THE LAST YEAR, FOR 1914 MODELS WERE CALLED JEFFERY FOR THE FAMILY WHO MADE THEM. THIS 42hp FOUR-CYLINDER TOURING WAS CALLED THE CROSS COUNTRY, ALTHOUGH IT WAS HARDLY IN THE JEEP/BRONCO CLASS. PERHAPS THE FACT THAT NED JORDAN WAS GENERAL MANAGER HAD SOMETHING TO DO WITH IT, FOR OTHER RAMBLER MODELS BORE EXOTIC NAMES LIKE VALKYRIE, KNICKERBOCKER, AND COUNTRY CLUB. RAMBLERS WERE UNUSUAL IN 1913 IN HAVING RIGHT-HAND DRIVE. HOWEVER, WHEN THE NAME WAS CHANGED SO WAS THE STEERING WHEEL POSITION. IN 1918 THE JEFFERY BECAME THE NASH.

OWNER: DAN OBERLE (PHOTO NICKY WRIGHT)

1908 BRUSH MODEL B RUNABOUT ▶

THE BRUSH MOTOR CAR COMPANY OF DETROIT WAS ONE OF THE FIRMS MERGED BY BENJAMIN BRISCOE INTO HIS UNITED STATES MOTOR CORPORATION, WHICH HE SAW AS A RIVAL TO GENERAL MOTORS. THE BRUSH WAS THE CHEAPEST CAR IN THE GROUP; THE 6hp SINGLE-CYLINDER RUNABOUT SOLD FOR ONLY $500. IT WAS UNUSUAL IN HAVING SUSPENSION BY COIL SPRINGS ALL ROUND — THE FRONT PAIR ARE CLEARLY VISIBLE HERE. DESIGNER ALANSON P. BRUSH HAD HELPED WITH THE FIRST SINGLE-CYLINDER CADILLAC.

OWNER: NATIONAL AUTOMOBILE MUSEUM, RENO, NAVADA

(PHOTO NICKY WRIGHT)

Cadillac in July. Oakland was eventually replaced by its companion make, Pontiac, so four of the five makes that constitute today's General Motors Corporation were already in the group a year after it was founded. Over the next few years numerous other short-lived companies also became part of General Motors, including Carter, Elmore, Ewing, Marquette, Rainier, Rapid, Reliance, and Welch. Rapid and Reliance were truck makers, and in 1912 evolved into GMC trucks, still being made today. Most of these companies were acquired by issuing General Motors stock, although Cadillac had to be bought for $4.4 million in cash.

The early days of General Motors were by no means easy. Durant wasted a lot of money buying up companies because their patents "might come in useful one day" if design changed. Thus he paid $140,000 for Cartercar because of its friction transmission, and $600,000 for Elmore to secure its two-cycle engine. Neither prospered, and Cartercar was sold in 1915 for only $50,000. Elmore had to be written off completely. Worse still, Durant paid $7 million for the Heany Lamp Company which held a patent on an incandescent light that turned out to be fraudulent, so the whole $7 million went down the drain.

Of the car-making companies, only Cadillac was really profitable by 1910; Buick had been mortgaged to the hilt to provide the purchase price for Cadillac, Oldsmobile sales had declined sharply after the end of the Curved Dash, and Oakland was an untried newcomer. General Motors had to turn to the banks for support, and one of their conditions was that Durant should step down from the presidency of Buick and the vice-presidency of GM. He remained on the board of directors, and a few years later, with the success of Chevrolet, was back in charge.

E XPANSION BY OTHER FIRMS
While Durant was expanding Buick and Ford was embarking on mass production, other makers were contributing cars in the same market. Chief among them were John North Willys, the Studebaker brothers, Thomas Jeffery, and Jonathan D. Maxwell with his partner Benjamin Briscoe.

John North Willys (1873–1935) differed from most contemporary auto men in that he was a dealer before he became a manufacturer. Like many others, he began with bicycles, selling and repairing them in his home town of Canandaigua, New York. He later bought a larger business in Elmira, and at the turn of the century began selling Pierce, Rambler, and Overland automobiles. The Overland was a small car made by the Standard Wheel Company of Indianapolis, one of the largest wheel makers in the country. Willys had seen the car on a visit to Indianapolis in 1905 and had ordered as many as could be made of the 1906 models, a 9hp two-cylinder runabout and a 16hp four-cylinder touring. Overland made 47 cars and Willys took all of them, following this with an order for 500 of the 1907 models.

When no cars arrived and letters went unanswered, an anxious Willys set out for Indianapolis, where he found the Overland company in disarray. No cars were being made, there were parts for only three, and the workforce was rapidly vanishing; those who remained only did so because they had not been paid for several weeks. Willys had $10,000 invested in his order and was determined to see some cars produced, so he borrowed the money to pay off the company's debts and asked his hotel to make no payments until they had enough cash to meet his check to settle the payroll. As the factory premises were inadequate for the production of 500 cars, Willys acquired an enormous circus tent and began making cars there until a new factory could be built.

Thus Willys became, in his own words,

▼ ALTHOUGH NOT IN THE TOP FIVE, COMPANIES SUCH AS HUDSON, HUPMOBILE, AND RAMBLER MADE A SIZABLE CONTRIBUTION TO AMERICA'S AUTOMOBILE OUTPUT IN THE YEARS BEFORE WORLD WAR I. HUDSON BEGAN IN 1909, AND THIS 1911 MODEL 20 FOUR-CYLINDER ROADSTER WAS SIMILAR TO THE FIRM'S INITIAL MODEL.
MOTOR VEHICLE MANUFACTURERS' ASSOCIATION

"manufacturer, president, treasurer, general manager — everything from Lord High Executioner down" of the Overland Company. Output from the circus tent was 465 cars in 1908, all 20/22hp tourings or runabouts with two-speed planetary transmissions. In 1909 he moved to Toledo, Ohio, and changed the company name to Willys-Overland; 4,860 cars were made that year, including models with conventional three-speed transmission as an alternative to the planetary (at $100 extra), and a 45hp six at $2,250 which was called a Willys rather than an Overland. This move upmarket was not continued, and for 1910 all cars were Overlands and none cost more than $1,850. Most were in the $1,000–$1,450 range, and production shot up to 15,598. Willys was now the third largest manufacturer after Ford and Buick. In 1912 the company moved into second place, with 28,572 deliveries, the lowest-priced model being a two-passenger roadster at $850. Willys was to remain in second place until 1918.

In 1913 Willys made an enforced trip to Europe, enforced by his doctor who threatened him with the alternative of a sanatorium if he kept on working so hard. While traveling he met another American, the engineer Charles Yale Knight, who had patented the sleeve-valve engine and had already sold it to European car makers such as Daimler in Britain, Panhard in France, Minerva in Belgium, and Mercedes in Germany. Willys bought up a company which was already making a sleeve-valve car, the Edwards Motor Car Company of New York City, moved production to Elyria, Ohio, and renamed it the Willys-Knight. By the 1920s Willys was making more sleeve-valve engines than all other car makers combined, and continued to produce them up to 1933.

Studebaker was a famous name in American motordom for six decades, yet for some time Studebakers were built by other firms. A history dating back to the middle of the nineteenth century made Studebaker the oldest vehicle-making company in America, its first wagons having been built at South Bend, Indiana, in 1852. The company prospered greatly during the Civil War, and one of the brothers, John Mohler Studebaker, made a separate fortune building wheelbarrows for California gold miners. The first Studebaker automobiles were electrics, made in

1902; they were joined by gasoline cars in 1903. The latter were made for Studebaker by the General Automobile Company of Cleveland and later by the Garford Company of Elyria, Ohio (whose factory was bought by Willys in 1913 for the Willys-Knight).

Garford's production enabled Studebaker to sell 8,142 cars in 1908 (nearly all badged as Studebakers), but they were expensive at $3,750–$4,500, and Studebaker needed a cheaper product in order to compete with Ford and Buick. The answer was the EMF 30, a conventional $1,250 touring put on the market in 1908 by the Everitt-Metzger-Flanders Company of Detroit. The men behind it had plenty of the right experience; Barney Everitt had made a fortune as a body builder, William E. Metzger was a successful salesman who had contributed much to the early success of Cadillac, and Walter E. Flanders had been Henry Ford's production manager. Studebaker contracted to take half of EMF's 1909 production, estimated to be 12,000 cars. The actual figure was 8,132, including 172 made the previous year, but output jumped to 15,598 in 1910 and reached a peak of 28,032 in 1912. Despite good sales, EMF 30s were not without problems, particularly with the rear-axle-mounted gearbox. The initials inevitably gave rise to rude nicknames, such as "Every Morning Fixit" and "Every Mechanical Failure."

In 1909 Everitt and Metzger left the company, and Walter Flanders bought the factory of the defunct Deluxe Company, helped by Studebaker money, to make a smaller car than the EMF, giving it his own name. The Flanders 20 runabout sold for $700 in 1911, only $20 above the price of an equivalent Model T. Walter Flanders remained a Studebaker associate until March 1912, devoting an increasing amount of company time to his own projects, which included an electric car and a four-cylinder motorcycle. This led to a parting of the ways, and for the 1913 season both Flanders and EMF were renamed, the former becoming the Studebaker 25 and the latter the Studebaker 35. The two Detroit factories were kept, as was an EMF plant in Walkerville, Ontario; this began an association with Canada that was to last until after production ceased in the United States, although the last Canadian-made Studebakers were

produced in Hamilton rather than Walkerville.

There is no space to mention all the other companies that contributed to the rise of mass production, but Maxwell is a name to remember, if only because it led to the Chrysler empire, the last of the large groups to emerge. The Maxwell-Briscoe Motor Company was built on the familiar combination of one man's technical skills combined with another man's money. Jonathan D. Maxwell (1864–1928) had been with the Apperson brothers when they built their first car for Elwood Haynes, and later worked for Olds before designing a single-cylinder car for the Northern Manufacturing Company of Detroit. His partner at Northern was Charles King, who had helped Henry Ford to build his first prototype, but he and Maxwell did not get on, so the latter found a new partner in Benjamin Briscoe (1869–1945), a successful maker of sheet metal goods who had got into the auto business by

making radiators for Olds and a number of other manufacturers. He had briefly backed David Buick, but left before Durant arrived on the scene.

Briscoe was impressed with Maxwell's ability and in 1904 set up Maxwell-Briscoe, renting the Tarrytown, N.Y., plant which John Brisben Walker had used for making Mobile steamers. Although Briscoe raised the money, more than two-thirds of it came from the financial house of J.P. Morgan in New York. The first Maxwell-Briscoe was a two-passenger runabout with a horizontally opposed two-cylinder engine of square dimensions (4 x 4 inches). Only ten cars were made in 1904, but two years later this had burgeoned to nearly 2,200; putting Maxwell into fifth place. Third place arrived in 1909 with 9,460 deliveries; Maxwell-Briscoe generally managed to remain in the top six up to 1920.

In 1906 Briscoe, feeling insecure in a rented factory, started to construct a large new plant at

New Castle, Indiana, which was not completed until 1909. He also bought premises at Pawtucket, Rhode Island, and Auburn, N.Y., all of which contributed to the output of about 20,000 Maxwells in 1910. Their super-salesman Cadwallader Washburn Kelsey (1880–1970) promoted them by making short films showing the cars in police chases, driving up the steps of churches and other public buildings, and showing them in nickelodeons. He also supported long-distance trials such as the Glidden Tours, which Maxwell won outright in 1911 and 1912. It was a Maxwell that Alice Huyler Ramsey and her three lady companions drove across the continent in 1909, earning more press coverage than all Kelsey's other activities combined.

Unfortunately, in 1910 Briscoe, using his company as the base, organized a rival to General Motors which he called the United States Motor Corporation, for which he acquired the car-producing companies of Brush, Columbia, Courier, and Stoddard-Dayton, among others. The new group was unwieldy from the start, with seven marque names, 52 models, and 18 factories, and soon found itself in a similar position to British Leyland Motor Corporation in the early 1970s. However, Briscoe had no government to bail him out, and the group collapsed in 1912. He later made cars under his own name, while Maxwell, having the soundest of the United States Motor Corporation's companies, saw control pass to Walter Flanders, one of the partners in Everitt-Mitzger-Flanders. Maxwell left, but he must have derived some satisfaction from knowing that Flanders retained the Maxwell name, as a good selling point. The four-cylinder Maxwells were now being made at New Castle and in the former Stoddard-Dayton plant at Dayton, Ohio, while the six-cylinder 50-6 model was made in the Flanders plant in Detroit. The six was soon dropped, and Maxwell concentrated on a low-price 25hp four selling for $750. Sales jumped to 75,000 by 1917, but dropped after World War I when the company was combined with Chalmers, the maker of a more expensive six-cylinder car. Maxwell-Chalmers came under the control of Walter P. Chrysler in November 1921, and for 1926 the Maxwell four was renamed the Chrysler 58, having the same engine with Chrysler styling. The same basic car, with important improvements such as four-wheel hydraulic brakes, was renamed Plymouth for the 1929 season.

Another empire that rose and fell was that of Colonel Albert Pope. In addition to the Columbia electrics described earlier, he bought up another electric car maker, Waverley of Indianapolis, and built four makes of gasoline car, the Pope-Hartford, Pope-Robinson, Pope-Toledo, and Pope-Tribune. The latter, located at Hagerstown, Maryland, in a plant managed by the Colonel's son Harold, was a low-priced single-cylinder runabout initially, although prices rose with the introduction of four-cylinder cars to a peak of $2,750 in 1908, the Pope-Tribune's last year. Other marques in the empire were costlier, in particular the massive Pope-Toledo, which reached a peak of $6,000 for a 50hp limousine in 1907. The unwieldy Pope group was already in difficulties when the Colonel died in August 1909: Pope-Hartford went into receivership, Pope-Waverley was sold and the product renamed Waverley, Pope-Toledo closed, and Pope-Tribune had already gone. The Hartford business continued until 1914 under the Colonel's brother George, when it, too, closed down.

CHEVROLET AND DODGE

By 1920 the major U.S. makes were the same as they are today; Ford had the biggest market share, followed by Dodge, Chevrolet, and Buick. The rise of two new names represented almost the last successful intrusion of fresh blood into the established Detroit hierarchy: Chrysler was the first intruder in the 1920s, building on the base of Maxwell-Chalmers and later acquiring Dodge, and Kaiser-Frazer came to prominence after World War II, but the latter, "the last onslaught on Detroit," failed after ten years.

In their early years Chevrolet and Dodge built much the same sort of cars, but their histories were different. Louis Chevrolet was new to the auto industry when he planned his first car in 1910, although he was already well known as a racing driver, while the Dodge brothers had been prominent suppliers to the industry since the turn of the century, first to Olds and then to Ford. Indeed as far as components were concerned, the early Fords had more Dodge than Ford in them, being largely assembled machines.

The Chevrolet brothers, Gaston, Arthur, and Louis, were Swiss-born but lived in France before emigrating to Canada and thence to the United States around 1900. Louis was the mechanically minded one, having invented a pump for extracting wine from barrels when the family lived in the Beaune region of France, and later worked for the New York De Dion Bouton importer and the fellow Swiss vehicle maker, William Walter. From 1908 he raced cars for Buick, which brought him to the attention of Billy Durant. In 1910 Durant was out of a job, having been eased out of General Motors, and on the lookout for a new opportunity. It is not certain whether Chevrolet had begun work on a car design before Durant approached him, or whether the idea was Billy's from the start. Anyway, Chevrolet was soon planning a car, and as he had little engineering training he sought the assistance of Etienne Planche, a Frenchman he had met at the Walter company who had designed a car for Walter which eventually evolved into the Mercer.

Although Chevrolet and Planche had promised a "French-type light car," the vehicle they came up with was more typically American and by no means light. Launched late in 1911, the Chevrolet Classic Six had a T-head six-cylinder engine whose displacement of 299 cubic inches was larger than that of any other Chevrolet until 1958. Its wheelbase was 120 inches, as long as any Chevrolet ever made, and Durant could not juggle the price below $2,250. The Classic Six was clearly not the car to rebuild his career with, so he also brought out a smaller four called the Little, not for its size but for William H. Little, his former production manager at Buick. This sold for $690, closer to Durant's ideal, but it did not sell very well, perhaps because the name was unappealing, but also because it was not very well made. Durant himself remarked that it would be "driven to its death in less than 25,000 miles."

Between early 1912 and its discontinuance in May 1913, the Little sold about 3,500 units, including a six at $1,250, less than the Chevrolet Classic Six, which managed nearly 9,000 sales between the summer of 1912 and the end of the 1914 season. It was then replaced by a smaller L-head six, but much more important was the new Chevrolet four, the Series H. This was somewhat larger than the Little, with a 104-inch wheelbase against 90 inches for the earlier car, and an overhead valve engine. It did not please Louis Chevrolet who, for all his European ancestry, favored a larger, American-style car.

There was also the matter of his smoking habits. Durant had suggested that cigars were more appropriate than cheap cigarettes now that Chevrolet was a motor industry executive, and he particularly objected to the way Louis constantly had a cigarette hanging on his lower lip. This was too much for Louis; he is reported to have exploded: "I sold you my car and I sold you my name, but I'm not going to sell myself to you." This was the final flashpoint reflecting deep

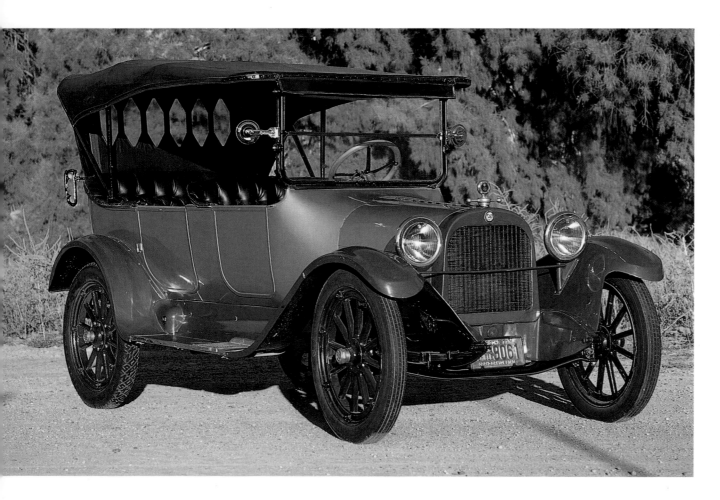

1918 DODGE TOURING ◄ ►

DODGES OF THIS PERIOD COULD BE IDENTIFIED BY THE SIX VERTICAL WINDOWS IN THE REAR OF THE TOP, ALSO SEEN ON TWO-PASSENGER ROADSTERS. THE RUGGED FOUR-CYLINDER DODGE WAS A LEADING STAFF CAR FOR THE U.S. ARMY. THE TYPE WAS USED BY GENERAL JOHN PERSHING IN THE MEXICAN CAMPAIGNS OF 1916 AGAINST PANCHO VILLA; THE FIRST MECHANIZED CAVALRY CHARGE WAS LED BY AN UNKNOWN YOUNG OFFICER, LT. GEORGE S. PATTON, IN A DODGE. THE SAME CAR WAS THEN USED BY PERSHING DURING WORLD WAR I IN EUROPE, WHERE HE WAS CHAUFFEURED BY CAPT. EDDIE RICKENBACKER, LATER TO MAKE HIS OWN CARS.

OWNER: DICK TRAVERS (PHOTOS NICKY WRIGHT)

disagreement, and Chevrolet left the company in 1914. He later built successful racing cars under the name Frontenac, which won the Indianapolis 500 in 1920 and 1921. He never made the money he could have done with Durant, and died in obscurity in 1941. He always said that he was prouder of his Indy winners than of all the millions of cars that bore his name, which is understandable, as he had nothing to do with their design. His partner Etienne Planche joined Durant's erstwhile partner J. Dallas Dort, for whom he designed a four-cylinder car not unlike the Chevrolet, although it was never so successful.

The Series H was continued for the 1915 season, priced at a modest $750 for a roadster. There was also a de luxe model called the Amesbury Special, with more attractive lines, one-piece windshield with wiper, and rumble seat with its own windshield. The Amesbury Special was mostly delivered in white and cost $985 or, with optional Houk wire wheels, $1,110. The other models were

a two-passenger roadster called the Royal Mail and a five-passenger touring called the Baby Grand. The Series H engine, designed by Arthur Mason and made by the Durant-owned Mason Motor Company, was a 170.9-cubic-inch four whose dimensions remained unchanged until fours were discontinued in 1928. This was the basis for the car with which Durant planned to meet Henry Ford head on, the 490. Announced in December 1914 but not put into production until the summer of 1915, the 490 was named for the price of a Model T touring, and this was to be the Chevrolet's price too. Six weeks after the 490 went on sale, Henry reduced the T to $440 and Durant was soon forced to up the price of his car to $550, although this included electric lighting and starting. He managed to have it both ways by claiming that the basic price was still $490, but adding in the brochure: "We strongly recommend the purchase of the Model 490 with electric lighting and starting equipment, as no car is complete today without it. If you buy a car

without electric lights and starter you will make a mistake." This was a dig at Ford, which still had to be hand-cranked, and whose side- and tail-lights were lit by kerosene.

To build the 490 in the numbers planned, Durant had to find more factory space, so he began by buying up the former Maxwell plant at Tarrytown, N.Y. (still a GM plant today), and followed this by obtaining manufacturing space from his former carriage-building friend Russell Gardner at St. Louis and Norman de Vaux in Oakland, California. He wanted a Canadian plant as well and talked the McLaughlins, who were already making Buicks for him in their carriage works at Oshawa, Ontario, into giving up carriages in favor of Chevrolets.

The 490 took Chevrolet into the big league very rapidly; in 1915, only 13,292 cars were made, but in the following year production shot up to 62,898, putting the company into sixth place. By 1919 this had become second place, with 123,371 cars sold. From 1922, Chevrolet was in second place behind Ford, a position it held until it overtook Ford in 1927. With the profits accruing from Chevrolet, Durant was able to buy back into General Motors. And aided by explosives makers E. I. duPont he regained control of the company he had started and lost on the seventh anniversary of its founding, September 16, 1915. The Chevrolet Motors Company now owned the General Motors Company, which in 1918 assumed its present title of the General Motors Corporation.

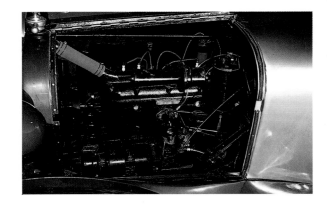

Durant's triumph was not to last long, however, for he overextended the corporation's finances in 1919, as he had done earlier, by rash purchases, notably of the Samson Tractor Company of Stockton, California. This purchase was clear evidence of Durant's ambition to challenge Henry Ford all along the line. He had a successful car in the Chevrolet 490, but the Samson was a failure. Durant bought the rights to the Samson Sieve Grip tractor and put it into production in a large plant at Janesville, Wisconsin, but the $1,750 tractor was no competition for the $750 Fordson. It was hastily replaced by the Model M, which sold for $650 and was better equipped than the Fordson. This might have been the basis for a successful business, but Durant spoiled it all by buying up the rights to the Dandy motor cultivator, which he sold under the name Iron Horse. This was a curious machine with steering by reins rather than wheel, and belt-and-pulley transmission with independent clutch control for the pair of wheels on each side of the tractor. Even at $450 it did not sell, and the small profits made on the Model M were eaten up by the losses on the Iron Horse. Durant's judgment was once again called into question by his partners, particularly Walter Chrysler, who resigned over the tractor affair, and GM's vice-president, Alfred P. Sloan. Durant's personal finances were shaky, due to stock market losses in the 1920 slump, and a convenient solution to both problems was for Durant to sell his 2.5 million GM shares to pay off his debts. His place as president of General Motors was taken by Pierre S. duPont, but Billy was by no means finished. He was soon back with fresh supporters in Durant Motors Inc. but that story belongs to the next chapter.

THE DODGE STORY

They were born four years apart, but they looked as alike as twins and were seldom separated. The Dodge brothers, John and Horace, grew up in a little wooden cottage in a poor district of Niles, Michigan, and left school early to help their father and uncle run a small machine shop. It made little money, and John earned extra by driving a cow to pasture twice a day for 50 cents a week.

Both brothers were gifted mechanically, Horace probably more than John, and after various spells of employment in Detroit and across the border in Windsor, Ontario, they set up in business on their own account in 1901. The Dodge Brothers Machine Shop on Beaubien Street, Detroit, turned its hand to any machining jobs, but soon most of its business was being done with the Olds Motor Works. At first Dodge Brothers supplied engines, then transmissions. In 1903 the company began to deliver 8hp two-cylinder engines to Henry Ford, and was soon making engines, transmissions, and axles for him. The contract was worth $5,000 a month, with the brothers also receiving 50 Ford shares each; this alone was sufficient to make them millionaires ten years later. The company continued to supply Ford for some time, making the engines of the Models B and K. Even after Ford built his Highland Park plant he continued to obtain some supplies from the company. This state of affairs lasted until the summer of 1914, but by then the Dodge brothers were ready to launch a car of their own.

In many ways the Dodge Four was a grown-up version of Ford's Model T. Its engine was larger, at 212.3 cubic inches, and gave 35bhp to the Ford's 20bhp, and the transmission was a three-speed sliding one, although with a distinctive gearshift pattern, the reverse of the normal. The 12-volt electrical system was unusual in a low-priced car, but the most radical feature was the all-steel welded body developed in Philadelphia by Edward Budd. The Dodge brothers did not understand wood, and a steel body seemed the logical way to go. Being a little apprehensive about the all-welded construction that was Budd's pride, "they added rivets here and there, just in case," recalled employee Ralph Vail.

Announced in November 1914, the Dodge Four touring cost $785 and was an immediate sensation,

thanks to the well-established reputation of the brothers. No new make could have had a better start. Some 22,000 firms applied for dealerships before the car was even launched. Production in the last six weeks of 1914 was 249 cars, but by the end of 1915 45,000 had been made, putting Dodge in third place behind Ford and Willys-Overland. By 1920 Dodge was second, the highest position it ever reached, with 141,000 sales. Design did not change greatly during the company's first six years: however, a two-passenger roadster was added in 1915 and a center-door sedan for 1916. More significant was the company's first all-steel four-door sedan, new in 1919.

For the Dodge family 1920 was a sad year. While on a visit to New York for the Auto Show in January, Horace contracted pneumonia and very nearly died. Although the doctors offered little hope, John encouraged him to keep fighting and just as Horace rallied, John himself also caught pneumonia and died on January 14. The brothers had always been very close and Horace never got over John's death. He struggled through the year, and went to Florida for his usual winter vacation, where he died on December 10, officially of cirrhosis of the liver, but many people said of a broken heart. He was a great music lover and supporter of the Detroit Symphony Orchestra, which turned out *in toto* for his funeral and later gave a concert in his honor. Both brothers died very wealthy, leaving more than $20 million apiece. Inheritance taxes of $900,000 were the highest ever paid in Michigan history. Their widows remarried and lived a long time; John's widow Matilda died in 1967, aged 83, and Horace's widow Anna lived three years longer, dying at the age of 103. Thanks to their inheritances, careful investments, and wealthy second husbands, Matilda and Anna were among the richest women in the world.

1913 CADILLAC 30 TOURING ▼

OWNER: AALHOLM MUSEUM, DENMARK (PHOTO AALHOLM MUSEUM)

CHAPTER THREE

LUXURY AND UNORTHODOXY

1900 – 1920

"Price is secondary. We build always the highest
attainable quality, and the price is fixed
by the production cost."

Packard advertisement, 1915

▲ GENERAL VIEW OF THE 1915 NEW YORK SHOW; THE WINTON, BUICK, HAYNES, AND FRANKLIN STANDS ARE VISIBLE. COMPARED WITH TODAY'S SHOWS ONLY A LITTLE SPACE WAS ALLOTTED TO EACH MAKE, BUT THEN THERE WERE MANY, MANY MORE AUTO BUILDERS TO FIT IN!

MOTOR VEHICLE MANUFACTURERS' ASSOCIATION

WHILE THE LIKES OF FORD and Durant were putting America on wheels, another group of engineers set about catering to the wishes of the rich. They did not make their mark straightaway, and often started with modestly priced small cars, while the limited market for expensive machines was mostly filled by foreign imports. In the first few years of the century the wealthy American who wanted the best in private transportation bought a French-built Panhard or C.G.V., or a German-made Mercedes, but from 1905 onward he had a growing choice of home-built luxury cars. By coincidence, three of the best began with P. The Packard, Peerless, and Pierce-Arrow have become known as the "three Ps" of American motordom.

THE THREE Ps AND THEIR RIVALS
In 1898 an Ohio electrical engineer named James Ward Packard (1863–1928) bought the twelfth Winton car to be made. Like many early motorists he was not entirely satisfied with his purchase and took it back for adjustments, with some suggestions about how it could be improved. The irascible Alexander Winton, who by then had made more than 20 cars, was not pleased to be told his job by a man who had made none. No one knows exactly what the two men said to each other, but the story that has gone down in history is derived from the account by journalist Hugh Dolnar, written in 1901. He wrote: "Mr. Winton...replied...to the effect that the Winton

1910 HAYNES TOURING ◄▲
ELWOOD HAYNES PARTED COMPANY WITH THE APPERSON BROTHERS IN 1902 AND SET UP A RIVAL FACTORY IN THE
SAME TOWN, KOKOMO, INDIANA. IN 1910, WHEN THIS MODEL 20 FOUR-CYLINDER TOURING WAS MADE, HAYNES
PRODUCTS WERE CONVENTIONAL CARS BUILT IN TOURING AND ROADSTER FORMS. HAYNES WAS LATER TO MAKE
A PIONEER V12. PRODUCTION ENDED IN 1925.
OWNER: TOM BARRETT (PHOTO NICKY WRIGHT)

wagon as it stood was the ripened and perfected product of many years of lofty thought, aided by mechanical skill of the highest grade, and could not be improved in any detail, and that if Mr. Packard wanted any of his own cats and dogs worked into a wagon, he had better build it himself, as he, Winton, would not stultify himself by any departure whatever from his own incontestably superior productions."

It is said that, following this outburst, Packard promptly went off and built himself a car. He had been thinking about automobiles since 1893, and before the Winton he had bought a De Dion Bouton tricycle. However, he did set to work on his own car in 1899, aided by his brother William Doud Packard and two former Winton men, George L. Weiss and William A. Hatcher. The first Packard left the workshops of the New York & Ohio Company in November 1899, and by the end of the year it had been followed by four more. They were quite typical of their time, relatively light two-passenger buggies with single-cylinder engines, two-speed planetary transmission, chain drive, and tiller steering. They did have one advanced feature, though: an H-pattern gearshift.

Only one of the 1899 Packards, called the Model A, was sold, the others being retained for experimental purposes. The Model B of 1900 was generally similar, but it had an automatic spark advance and a foot throttle. There was also a dual warning system, a normal hand-operated bulb horn

and a pedal-operated chime. Production was 49 cars, of which two were bought by William D. Rockefeller at the New York Auto Show in November 1900. These were the first of many Packards bought by the Rockefeller family. In 1901 Packard built 81 model Cs, whose chief improvement over previous designs was a steering wheel which replaced the tiller. Whereas the Model B could carry four passengers with a dos-à-dos seat, the Model C was offered with four forward-facing seats in addition to the dos-à-dos. All body styles were priced at a uniform $1,500.

The Model C was shown at the 1901 New York Show, and seen by a railroad and banking magnate from Detroit, Henry Bourne Joy (1864–1936). He and a friend were admiring a Packard outside the show when a fire engine went by. The Packard's owner gave the crank handle one turn, starting the motor immediately, and set off in hot pursuit of the fire engine. Joy was so impressed that he contacted the Packards and decided to invest in the business. This enabled them to expand and move from Ohio to Detroit in 1903. Without the intervention of Henry Joy, the Packard might never have become the world-renowned make that it did, for William Packard did not favor a move to multicylinders. "More than one cylinder in a Packard would be like two tails on a cat — you just don't need it." However, Joy thought otherwise and therefore hired a French engineer, Charles Schmidt, to design a four-cylinder for 1903.

Schmidt's first design was the Model K, a large 24hp car with four-speed sliding transmission and shaft drive. Expensive to manufacture, it had to be priced at an enormous $7,300, but still lost money for the company. Only 34 were made, and the K was hastily replaced by the smaller Model L. This was still a four-cylinder shaft-drive car, but with a three-speed transmission, and the price was a more reasonable $3,000. The longer wheelbase Model N came in 1905 and was the first Packard to be offered with closed bodywork, a brougham or limousine at $4,100 and $4,600 respectively. Packard was now set to become one of America's leading quality automobiles.

Peerless and Pierce-Arrow had quite similar backgrounds. Both were making bicycles in the 1890s, following such diverse productions as clothes wringers (Peerless) and bird cages (Pierce, hence the nickname "Fierce Sparrow"). Peerless was made in Cleveland and Pierce in Buffalo, and both entered the car world with small buggies powered by single-cylinder De Dion Bouton engines. What is more, both companies called their little cars Motorettes.

Larger machines soon followed, twin cylinders from Peerless in 1902 and Pierce in 1903, and by 1904 they had joined Packard in making four-cylinder cars. Pierce's was named the Great Arrow (the marque name Pierce-Arrow was not adopted until 1909); it was quite like a Mercedes in appearance, and had a 24/28hp T-head engine and shaft drive. The price for a touring was $4,000, and for 1905 there were three closed models on a longer wheelbase at $5,000. Peerless manufactured three four-cylinder cars in 1904, from $4,000 to $6,000,

beating both Packard and Pierce by having closed models that year.

The similarity of year-by-year changes is hardly surprising, for every manufacturer followed his rivals closely, workers moved from one factory to another, and there was undoubtedly a degree of industrial espionage. Each year wheelbases grew longer and bodies more elaborate, with electrically lit interiors, flower vases, and even hand washbasins. Packard had its own body-building department, as did most other American companies, in contrast to European luxury car makers such as Rolls-Royce, who supplied only chassis for specialist coachbuilders to work on. However, coachbuilders flourished in America as well, and being specialists were often in advance of the auto makers in their ideas. Most of the coachbuilders in the pre-1920 era were horse carriage makers, and some of the best known were Brewster of Long Island City, whose history dated back to 1810, Cunningham of Rochester, New York, who began making complete cars in 1908, Judkins of Merrimac, Massachusetts, and Quinby of Newark, New Jersey.

The next major mechanical development to hit the auto industry was the six-cylinder engine. This had appeared in Europe on the Dutch Spyker of 1902 (which also offered four-wheel drive), and on the better-known British Napier of 1904, and the first in the United States appeared on the 1906 Franklin Type H 30hp. The six was promoted as giving a smoother-running engine, there being more explosions per revolution, an argument later used to justify eights, twelves, and sixteens. The overlapping power impulses gave better low-speed torque, which reduced the need for gear shifting. This was undoubtedly true, but on the debit side six-cylinder crankshafts were generally lighter in build and their greater length made them subject to torsional stresses that led to fractures and total destruction of the engine. The solution was to mount an extra flywheel at the front of the crankshaft; this was proposed by the English engineer Frederick Lanchester and marketed in the United States as the Warner Crankshaft Damper. The Franklin adopted it in late 1905.

Following the Franklin's lead, numerous other American companies launched sixes; Ford with the Model K and Stevens-Duryea in 1906, Chadwick, Pierce-Arrow, and Stearns in 1907, Lozier, Oldsmobile, Peerless Thomas, and Winton in 1908. Packard ignored the trend longer than most and did not make a six until the 1912 season.

Some of these early sixes were monstrous cars. The Stearns 45/90hp had a displacement of 795 cubic inches and an engine so long that the rear pair of cylinders projected into the driving compartment. Prices ranged from $6,250 for a touring roadster to $7,500 for a limousine. The Oldsmobile Limited, made from 1910 to 1912, was one of the most impressive American cars

1911 ALCO FOUR-PASSENGER SPEEDSTER ◄ ►
THE AMERICAN LOCOMOTIVE COMPANY WAS ONE OF THE COUNTRY'S LARGEST BUILDERS OF STEAM LOCOMOTIVES, WITH EIGHT PLANTS IN THE EASTERN STATES. IN 1905 AUTOMOBILE MANUFACTURE BEGAN IN THE PROVIDENCE, RHODE ISLAND, PLANT, USING THE FRENCH BERLIET AS A MODEL. UP TO 1909 THE CARS WERE KNOWN AS AMERICAN BERLIETS, THEN ALCOS. THEY WERE HIGH-QUALITY, HIGH-PRICED VEHICLES WITH HUGE ENGINES: 453 CUBIC INCHES IN THIS 40hp FOUR, AND 579 CUBIC INCHES IN THE 60hp SIX. ALCO BOASTED THAT IT TOOK A YEAR AND SEVEN MONTHS TO BUILD A SINGLE CAR.
OWNER: DUKE DAVENPORT (PHOTO NICKY WRIGHT)

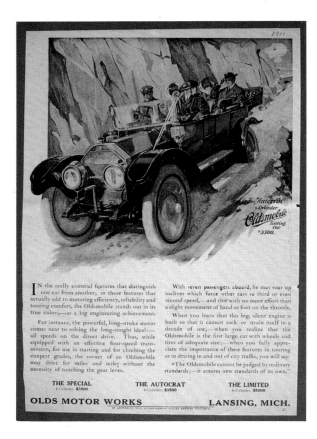

ever built, with 42-inch wheels and an engine displacement of 706 cubic inches. Passengers needed two steps to climb into the Limited, which looked deceptively low because of its enormous wheels (other Oldsmobiles had 36- or 38-inch wheels, while the Model T's were only 30 inches). The Limited was made for three seasons, 1910–1912, prices starting at $4,600 for a 1910 runabout and rising to $6,300 for a 1912 limousine. Total production was only 825, but Oldsmobile was at a low ebb anyway, output of all models being only 4,175 for the three years.

▲ A 1911 ADVERTISEMENT FOR THE ENORMOUS AND POWERFUL OLDSMOBILE LIMITED. THE CLAIM THAT IT COULD SOAR UP INCLINES IN HIGH GEAR WITH SEVEN PASSENGERS ABOARD WAS NO EXAGGERATION.

MIRCO DE CET COLLECTION

At the same time that Oldsmobile was making the Limited, over in Buffalo Pierce-Arrow had introduced the mighty 66, which vied with the Peerless for the largest engine of any production American car. With a displacement of 824 cubic inches, it exceeded even the famed Bugatti Royale (778 cubic inches), while the short-lived Fageol of 1917/18, often claimed as America's largest car, had the same displacement as the 66, although it was more expensive. The 66 was the largest of three Pierce-Arrow sixes, all of which had pair-cast T-head engines. Pierce-Arrows were among the

1903 PIERCE MOTORETTE ▶

PIERCE AND RIVAL PEERLESS BOTH BEGAN WITH SMALL CARS POWERED BY FRENCH-BUILT DE DION BOUTON ENGINES. AFTER STARTING WITH A 2¾hp UNIT, PIERCE WENT UP TO 3½hp IN 1902, AND TO 5hp AND 6hp IN 1903 WHEN THIS MOTORETTE WAS BUILT. BY THEN GEORGE PIERCE WAS MAKING HIS OWN ENGINES WITH SEVERAL IMPROVEMENTS OVER THE FRENCH DESIGN. THIS IS THE FOLDING FRONT SEAT MODEL SIMILAR TO THE ONE IN WHICH GEORGE'S SON, PERCY PIERCE, WON HIS CLASS IN THE NEW YORK–PITTSBURGH ENDURANCE TEST IN OCTOBER 1903.

OWNER: GEORGE SANDERS (PHOTO NICKY WRIGHT)

highest-quality American cars, and were much favored by conservative East Coast buyers who wanted the best without ostentation. The 66 was introduced in 1910, although it did not reach its full size of 824 cubic inches until 1912, while the longest wheelbase of 147½ inches did not arrive until 1913. The car was made up to 1918, production reaching a total of a very respectable 1,071 units.

Features of the big Pierce-Arrows included compressed air starters and a power air pump driven from the transmission, for pumping up tires. Prices ran from around $4,000 for the "small" Model UU to over $7,000 for a Model 66 vestibule suburban, which was a limousine with raised rear doors to allow ladies with fancy hats to enter without too much bending. Custom-built models were even more costly; Pierce-Arrow president George Birge had a special touring landau on the 66-QQ chassis, with running boards enlarged to contain storage compartments, a sliding drawer under the rear seat, and a fold-out washbasin supplied with running water from a pressurized tank under the body. This car cost $8,250, and two others were subsequently made, one of them for the cereal magnate Charles W. Post.

Locomobile also made big and expensive sixes, starting in 1911 with the 522-cubic-inch Model 48.

The engine was a T-head, like the Pierce-Arrow's, and Locomobile persisted with this layout up to the end of production in 1929, when it had long been abandoned by all other manufacturers in favor of the L-head. Indeed the 48 itself was still made in 1929, but with power upped from 48 to 103bhp and modern features such as balloon tires and four-wheel brakes. Late in 1914 Locomobile set up a custom body department headed by Frank de Causse, who later worked for Franklin. This turned out some very handsome and advanced coachwork, and Locomobiles were found in the garages of many famous names such as William Carnegie, Lawrence Copley Thaw, and Willie K. Vanderbilt. In 1916 de Causse designed a dual cowl phaeton for Rodman Wanamaker, the first of its kind, subsequently cataloged as the Sportif. Fittings and metal work for Locomobile bodies were designed by Tiffany and interiors were planned by the well-known actress and interior decorator Elsie de Wolf. In 1918 General John "Black Jack" Pershing had two 48s built for his use in France, with sloping Vee windshield, narrow body to reduce wind resistance, and dual rear tires. Ordinary 48s were also used by the U.S. Army in France, but it was found that at top speed (80mph) the vertical windshield had a tendency to crack, hence Pershing's request for a Vee-shaped one.

V8s AND V12s

By 1914 the six-cylinder engine was commonplace on medium-priced cars such as Buick, Chalmers, and Studebaker. But for still greater smoothness eight cylinders were needed, and in order not to have too long a crankshaft a Vee layout was preferable to an in-line one (in-line eights became very popular and fashionable in the 1920s when crankshaft strengths were greater).

The first V8 engine had been made in 1903 by the Frenchman Clément Ader, but it was little more than four V-twins coupled together. In America Buffum had offered a V8 touring in 1906 and Hewitt had one in 1907, but few if any were sold. Another French make, De Dion Bouton, was the first to commercialize the V8 engine, from 1910 onward, but the honor for the first successful large-

1913 CADILLAC ROADSTER ◄ ▲
THE 1913 CADILLACS CONTINUED THE DELCO INTEGRATED ELECTRIC LIGHTING AND STARTING SYSTEM INTRODUCED IN 1912, AND ALSO HAD LARGER ENGINES WITH POWER UPPED FROM 40bhp TO 50bhp, AND WHEELBASES WERE EXTENDED BY 4 INCHES TO 120 INCHES. APPEARANCE WAS IMPROVED WHEN A CURVED COWL REPLACED THE STRAIGHT DASH. THE SLOGAN "STANDARD OF THE WORLD" WAS USED FOR THE FIRST TIME IN 1913.
OWNER: NATIONAL AUTOMOBILE MUSEUM, RENO, NEVADA
(PHOTO NICKY WRIGHT)

1915 CADILLAC V8 TOURING ▲
THE WORLD'S FIRST SUCCESSFUL QUANTITY-BUILT V8,
THE CADILLAC TYPE 51 WAS LAUNCHED IN SEPTEMBER
1914 IN NINE BODY STYLES, OF WHICH THE FIVE- AND
SEVEN-PASSENGER TOURING CARS WERE THE LOWEST
PRICED AT $1,975. BEFORE THE CADILLAC, THE FEW V8s
MADE HAD BEEN VERY EXPENSIVE AND OF DOUBTFUL
RELIABILITY. CADILLAC'S ENGINEER D. McCALL WHITE
GAVE THE WORLD A DEPENDABLE, SMOOTH, AND
POWERFUL UNIT THAT WAS COPIED BY MANY OTHER
FIRMS, AND BECAME THE STANDARD LAYOUT FOR
AMERICAN ENGINES AFTER WORLD WAR II.
OWNER: CRAWFORD COLLECTION OF THE WESTERN HISTORICAL SOCIETY
(PHOTO NICKY WRIGHT)

scale production V8 goes to Cadillac.

In 1914 Cadillac did not hold the prestige position among American automobiles that it enjoyed in later years. Rather Cadillacs were well-respected four-cylinder cars in the upper-middle price bracket, selling for $1,975 to $3,250, around half the asking price for the larger Pierce-Arrows and Locomobiles. In 1912 Cadillac had set a lead with the introduction of a combined electric lighting and starting set. This was largely the work of Charles F. Kettering of the Dayton Engineering Laboratories Company (later Delco), but the V8 engine was designed by Cadillac's own D. McCall White, a Scottish-born engineer whose previous appointments had been with Daimler and Napier in England.

The two banks of cylinders were mounted at 90° to each other and had a displacement of 314 cubic inches. They were in cast-iron blocks of four on an aluminum crankcase. Maximum output was 70bhp at 2,400rpm, but in 1916 this went up to 77bhp at 2,600rpm, and in the 1920s the V8 was advertised as giving 80+bhp. This was a great improvement over the 40bhp given by the larger 365.8-cubic-inch four-cylinder engine. As on the four, the V8 engine drove through a three-speed transmission, but the driver was now on the left, with a central gear lever, although right-hand drives could still be had as an option. The V8's wheelbase was 2 inches longer than its predecessor's, but the car's appearance was virtually the same — the same body styles were offered at almost the same prices. This made the V8 remarkable value. The four was dropped for 1915, not to be reintroduced for another 67 years.

The Cadillac V8 was announced in September 1914 and seems to have taken the industry by surprise. Rivals were quick to criticize it, and to counter such criticism Cadillac's advertising agency came up with one of the most famous advertising slogans in history, "The Penalty of Leadership." Cadillac sold 13,002 cars in the 1915 model year, and 18,004 for 1916. Imitations came initially not from the big manufacturers who made their own engines, but from proprietary engine builders such as Ferro, Herschell-Spillman, Massnick-Phipps, Northway, and Perkins, who began to offer V8s that enabled many smaller car makers to get in on the act. For 1916 Detroiter and Remington offered V8s (by Perkins and Massnick-Phipps respectively), and by 1918 at least 20 American car makers were listing V8s, from the $1,050 Homer-Laughlin to the 566-cubic-inch nine-passenger RiChard listed at $8,000. Cadillac's engines were made by the GM-owned Northway company, which also supplied V8s to Oldsmobile from 1915 and, perhaps surprisingly, sold them to companies outside the GM fold, such as Cole of Indianapolis and Jackson of Jackson, Michigan. The discreet luxury car maker Cunningham of Rochester, N.Y., used its own 442-cubic-inch V8 from 1917, while the equally discreet Daniels, which carried its name nowhere on the car, only the letter D on the hubcaps, used a Herschell-Spillman V8 from 1915 to 1919, then made its own.

The V8 was followed with remarkable speed by the V12. In May 1915 Packard announced the Twin Six, which had been under development for nearly two years, designed by Jesse Vincent, who had come from Hudson three years earlier. The two banks of six cylinders were mounted at a narrower angle than in the V8 Cadillac, at 60°. Displacement was 424.1 cubic inches and output 88bhp at 2,600rpm. The Twin Six engine weighed 400 pounds less than the previous Packard six, yet torque was 100 percent better, and 50 percent better than it would have been had he used a V8, said Vincent.

The Packard Six was continued to September 1915 to allow Twin Six production to build up, but thereafter the new model took over and was the sole Packard until the 1921 season. For such a sophisticated car it was remarkably cheap. In 1916 the lowest-priced model was the touring on the shorter of two wheelbases, which sold for $2,750, while the most expensive was a long-wheelbase imperial limousine at $4,650. In its first season the Twin Six sold 3,606 units, slightly fewer than for all models the previous year, but the 1917 season saw nearly 9,000 sold, and 9,586 in 1918/19. By the end of Twin Six production in 1923, sales reached over

30,900. Twin Sixes were very popular in Latin America, where Packard agencies were set up for the first time in Buenos Aires and Rio de Janeiro.

As with Cadillac's V8, so Packard's Twin Six encouraged imitators. National of Indianapolis launched its Highway Twelve just after Packard. In 1916 the proprietary engine maker Weidely brought out a 390-cubic-inch V12 which enabled several small firms to offer the prestige of a twelve, something they could never have done if they had had to make their own engines. The HAL from Cleveland, Pathfinder from Indianapolis, and Singer from Mount Vernon, New York, were all twelves. However, none of them had much success, and by 1921 Packard was almost the only purveyor of twelve-cylinder automobiles.

▲ THE NATIONAL WAS A RESPECTED MAKE THAT FLOURISHED IN INDIANAPOLIS FROM 1900 TO 1924. THIS IS A 1913 SERIES V FOUR-CYLINDER TOURING, WHICH SOLD FOR $3,000. FOR 1915 NATIONAL WENT OVER TO SIXES, AND THEN THE FOLLOWING YEAR INTRODUCED ITS V12 HIGHWAY TWELVE.

MOTOR VEHICLE MANUFACTURERS' ASSOCIATION

ONE OF THE GREATEST GIFTS OF THE AUTOMOBILE TO
THE AMERICAN PEOPLE WAS THE FREEDOM OF THE
COUNTRYSIDE, ESPECIALLY ENJOYABLE IN THE DAYS
BEFORE THERE WERE TOO MANY TOURISTS. PICNICS
WERE POPULAR, AS THESE PHOTOS SHOW.

▲ THE CAR HERE IS A 1911 ABBOTT-DETROIT.

▶ A c.1914 PICTURE WHERE, NOT SURPRISINGLY,
MOST OF THE CARS ARE FORD MODEL Ts.

MOTOR VEHICLE MANUFACTURERS' ASSOCIATION

◀ TIRE CHANGING WAS PROBABLY THE EARLY
MOTORIST'S GREATEST PROBLEM. BURSTS
OCCURRED FREQUENTLY BECAUSE OF
INFERIOR RUBBER AND ALSO THE VARIETY
OF OBJECTS LITTERING THE ROADS,
SUCH AS STONES AND HORSESHOE NAILS.
TIRES HAD TO BE LEVERED OFF THE RIMS,
AS DETACHABLE RIMS DID NOT COME IN
UNTIL AROUND 1910, AND DETACHABLE
WHEELS EVEN LATER.
MOTOR VEHICLE MANUFACTURERS' ASSOCIATION

▲ "G & J TIRE DOES NOT BURST" SAID THE 1910
ADVERTISEMENT, BUT THIS INNER TUBE HAD BALLOONED
TO AN ALARMING SIZE.
MOTOR VEHICLE MANUFACTURERS' ASSOCIATION

◀ ▼ BEFORE THE DAYS OF DRIVE-IN
FORECOURTS, GASOLINE WAS
SUPPLIED TO CARS STANDING AT THE
CURBSIDE BY OVERHEAD PIPE.
MORE CONVENTIONAL DELIVERY OF
GASOLINE, NEW YORK, c.1920.
MOTOR VEHICLE MANUFACTURERS' ASSOCIATION

1909 SEARS HIGH-WHEEL BUGGY ◄▲

THE SEARS ROEBUCK CATALOG WAS SECOND ONLY TO
THE BIBLE IN MANY AMERICAN HOMES, AND FROM 1908
TO 1912 YOU COULD ORDER AN AUTOMOBILE FROM IT.
THE SEARS HIGHWHEELER (CATALOG NUMBER 21R333)
WAS TYPICAL OF ITS KIND, WITH 10hp HORIZONTAL
TWIN ENGINE, FRICTION TRANSMISSION, AND DOUBLE
CHAIN DRIVE. UP TO THE END OF 1909 THE BUGGIES
WERE MADE FOR SEARS BY COLONEL WILLIAM H.
McCURDY AT EVANSVILLE, INDIANA, BUT AFTER THAT
SEARS OPENED ITS OWN PLANT IN CHICAGO. ABOUT
3,500 SEARS WERE MADE BETWEEN 1908 AND 1912.

OWNER: CRAWFORD COLLECTION OF THE WESTERN HISTORICAL SOCIETY
(PHOTO NICKY WRIGHT)

HIGHWHEELERS, CYCLECARS AND ODDITIES

By about 1905 automobile design had settled down
to a general pattern of front-mounted vertical
water-cooled engines, driving through planetary or
sliding gear transmission to a bevel gear rear axle.
There were, of course, exceptions, such as the air-
cooled Franklin and cars defined as highwheelers
and cyclecars, and a few machines that were
downright weird.

The highwheeler, as historian Beverly Rae
Kimes has observed, may or
may not have been a practical
answer to a crying need, but it
was definitely as American as
the Fourth of July. It was born
just after the turn of the
century in response to the
appalling state of country roads. As a correspondent
from Montana wrote in *The Horseless Age*: "All roads
have ruts at each side varying from two to fifteen
inches deep. To run a car with a nine inch
clearance over these roads in daylight is
exasperating, and it is practically impossible to run
after dark."

Horse-drawn buggies with 44-inch wheels could
cope with these conditions, so the highwheeler in
its simplest form was a motorized buggy. The first
of the breed by several years was the Chicago-built
Holsman, which appeared in 1903. It was a two-
passenger buggy with a two-cylinder horizontally
opposed engine which drove the rear wheels by
⅞-inch manila rope. This did not fare well in wet
weather, and Holsman soon substituted a chain
braided over with manila and steel wire, later using
a plain chain like many of his rivals. The 42-inch
wheels had solid tires and initially the brakes
operated directly on the tires. The brakes were
hand-operated, Henry Holsman being of the
opinion that the foot could not be relied upon to
act instantly in an emergency.

In many ways the Holsman and its rivals looked
at least ten years behind the times with their
spidery wheels, lack of fenders, and piano box
bodies perched on full elliptic springs. Many of the
companies making them were in the buggy trade,
and it showed in their appearance. The Holsman
company had increased its factory space sixfold by
1906, and was working night shifts to keep up with
demand. This spurred others to get in on the
lucrative field, and in the next few years nearly 100
makers offered highwheelers. Chicago was the
center of production; apart from the Holsman, it
was home to the International Harvester Company,
makers of the I.H.C., and to the Sears, offered from
1908 to 1912 in Sears Roebuck's famous catalog. A
Sears owner probably spoke for many when he
wrote to the company: "It beats a horse bad as it
don't eat when I ain't working it, and it stands
without hitching, and best of all it don't get scared
at automobiles."

St. Louis had a number of
well-known makes such as the
A:B.C. and Success, while
Auburn, Indiana, was home to
the Kiblinger, McIntyre, and
Zimmerman, and Cincinnati to
the Schacht. Most highwheelers came from the
Midwest, although exceptions included the Kearns
from Beavertown, Pennsylvania, and the White
Star from Atlanta, Georgia. North of the border the
Tudhope Carriage Company of Orillia, Ontario,
made a highwheeler using the McIntyre engine.
Highwheelers appealed particularly to farmers, but

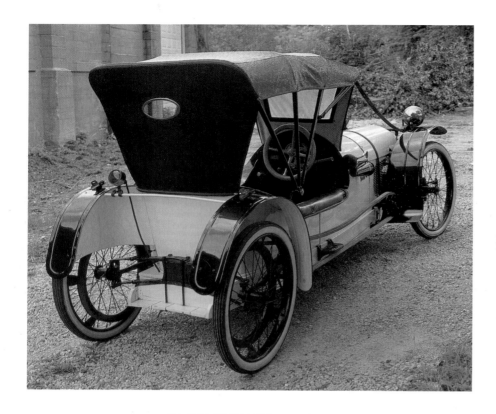

1913 IMP CYCLECAR ◄

THE IMP, BUILT AT AUBURN, INDIANA, LOOKED A TYPICAL CYCLECAR, BUT IT HAD A NUMBER OF UNUSUAL FEATURES. THESE INCLUDED WHEELS MOUNTED ON THE ENDS OF TRANSVERSE SPRINGS, WHICH DID AWAY WITH AXLES, AND STARTING FROM THE DRIVER'S SEAT. THIS WAS EFFECTED BY INSERTING A CRANK IN THE CENTER OF THE STEERING COLUMN, WHICH CONNECTED WITH A RATCHET ON THE CRANKSHAFT. THE AIR-COOLED V-TWIN ENGINE GAVE 15bhp, AND DROVE VIA FRICTION TRANSMISSION AND LONG BELTS TO THE REAR WHEELS.

OWNER: AUBURN-CORD-DUESENBERG MUSEUM (PHOTO NICKY WRIGHT)

1908 ZIMMERMAN HIGH-WHEEL BUGGY ◄▼

THE ZIMMERMAN MANUFACTURING COMPANY OF AUBURN, INDIANA, WAS ONE OF MANY HORSE BUGGY-BUILDING FIRMS THAT TURNED TO MOTOR POWER. THIS EXAMPLE FROM THE FIRST YEAR OF PRODUCTION HAD A 14hp TWO-CYLINDER AIR-COOLED ENGINE AND CHAIN DRIVE. NOTE THE DOUBLE-LEAVED TRANSVERSE FRONT SPRING. THE COMPANY LATER OFFERED STANDARD FOUR-CYLINDER CARS, WHICH WERE BUILT FOR ZIMMERMAN BY THE AUBURN AUTOMOBILE COMPANY. THESE WERE MADE UP TO 1914; THE LAST ZIMMERMAN WAS A SIX, BUILT FROM 1913 TO 1915.

OWNER: AUBURN-CORD-DUESENBERG MUSEUM (PHOTO NICKY WRIGHT)

were not exclusively country vehicles. In 1907 there were nearly 100 Holsmans operating in Chicago, and of these 75 percent were owned by physicians.

After about six years highwheelers fell victim to progress. They were very slow, 25mph being a good top speed, and offered little in the way of weather protection, although Holsman did make a closed model called the coupelette. Cheaper than most cars initially, they were soon undercut by the Model T, which was also pretty good at coping with bad roads. Better sometimes, for the highwheeler's narrow solid tires would break through the frozen crust to the mud below while wider pneumatic tires stayed on top. By 1913 practically all the highwheelers had gone. I.H.C. and Schacht turned to trucks, McIntyre to cyclecars, and most of the others gave up altogether.

If the highwheeler was uniquely American, the next craze to hit the industry was an import from Europe: the cyclecar. This was a light two-passenger auto using many motorcycle components in its specification, which emerged in France in 1910 and spawned a large number of makes there and in Britain over the next ten years. The fashion did not hit America until 1913, but when it did, it hit hard.

Between the summer of 1913 and the end of 1915 at least 215 ambitious individuals or companies tried to build cyclecars, although probably not more than 30 ever got as far as serious production. They were widespread geographically, from Laconia, New Hampshire (Laconia), to Seattle, Washington (Tilikum), while Detroit had at least nine by November 1913.

As in Europe, none of the big car makers turned to the cyclecar. A lone Ford cyclecar, resembling a scaled-down Model T, did show up in front of Detroit's Pontchartrain Hotel, but this was Henry's ruse to deter a possible threat to the T. He reasoned that if the smaller makers thought that Ford was going to enter the cyclecar market they would give up.

In January 1914 the American Cyclecar Manufacturers' Association was founded, defining the cyclecar as a four-wheeled vehicle with an engine displacement of not more than 71 cubic inches. A consequence of this was that cyclecars were almost all two-passenger cars, although

1904 ORIENT BUCKBOARD ▲

BILLED AS "THE CHEAPEST AUTOMOBILE IN THE WORLD — EVERYBODY SHOULD HAVE ONE," THE ORIENT BUCKBOARD WAS BUILT BY THE WALTHAM MANUFACTURING COMPANY OF WALTHAM, MASSACHUSETTS, AND COST ONLY $375 IN 1903. RIDING ON AN 80-INCH WHEELBASE, IT HAD A 4hp SINGLE-CYLINDER ENGINE AND NO SPRINGS, AS THE FLEXING OF THE WOODEN SLATS THAT FORMED THE CHASSIS WAS CONSIDERED SUFFICIENT SUSPENSION. EVIDENTLY CUSTOMERS THOUGHT OTHERWISE, FOR THIS 1904 MODEL HAS FULLY ELLIPTIC SPRINGS AT THE FRONT. BUCKBOARDS WERE BUILT THROUGH THE 1907 SEASON.

OWNER: CRAWFORD COLLECTION OF THE WESTERN HISTORICAL SOCIETY (PHOTO NICKY WRIGHT)

designers differed as to whether the passengers should sit side by side, staggered, or in line one behind the other. If the latter, should the driver be in front or behind? The driver-behind solution was favored by the makers of the Automobilette, Davis, Greyhound, and one or two others, and was practical so long as the passenger in front was not fatter or taller than the driver.

Cyclecar engines were mostly V-twins, with their crankshafts mounted transversely so that they could drive a belt transmission to a pulley on the back wheel. The engines were usually under a hood, but the Detroit-built Cricket carried its engine beside the driver on the running board.

This had the advantage of needing a shorter belt, but against this the weight distribution must have been distinctly odd, while the driver had to scramble over a hot engine or enter from the passenger side. Throttles were usually hand-controlled, as on a motorcycle.

One of the cyclecar's advantages was its size, in particular the tread, which seldom exceeded 36 inches. This meant that it could be driven through the garden gate, up the path, and garaged beneath the porch. For those who did not have porches, a simple garage could be fashioned from rough lumber by almost anyone, and did not need to be more than 4½ feet high, 3½ feet wide, and 9 feet

1912 INTERNATIONAL HARVESTER ▲
INTERNATIONAL MADE HIGH-WHEEL PASSENGER CARS FROM 1907 TO 1911, AND TRUCKS UP TO 1916.
THIS 1912 MOTOR TRUCK HAD A HORIZONTALLY OPPOSED TWO-CYLINDER ENGINE GIVING 18-20hp, AND
COULD BE FITTED WITH "SUNDAY-GO-TO-MEETIN'" SEATS IN THE LOAD-CARRYING SPACE.
OWNER: CRAWFORD COLLECTION OF THE WESTERN HISTORICAL SOCIETY (PHOTO NICKY WRIGHT)

keeping out driving rain. And by 1915 even their low price had ceased to be an advantage, for Henry Ford had lowered the price of a Model T two-passenger roadster to $440. The cyclecar makers couldn't afford to reduce their prices. It cost only an extra $40 to buy a full-sized car with a four-cylinder engine, shaft transmission, and proper weather protection, and all the benefits of an established reputation and nationwide servicing facilities.

The demise of the cyclecar was as rapid as its birth; by the end of 1915 the breed was just about extinct, as were the magazines that had promoted it. The spidery belt-drive tandem-seated models went first, while cars like the Trumbull, which had a four-cylinder engine and sliding gear transmission, lasted into 1915. The Trumbull might have survived longer if its founder Isaac Trumbull, together with 20 cars, had not gone to the bottom of the Atlantic when the liner *Lusitania* was sunk by a German torpedo in May 1915.

Given their flimsy construction, it is not surprising that the survival rate of cyclecars was very low, much lower than that of larger cars made in the same era. Nothing is left of most of the 200-odd makes beyond a few photographs.

Apart from highwheelers and cyclecars, there were other automobiles which differed from the norm. Strange though these may seem today, one must remember that in the early days there was no

long. Another advantage, initially, was its price, which ran from just under $300 for the simplest machines and seldom exceeded $400. In 1913 the cheapest Model T was $525.

There was boundless optimism among cyclecar manufacturers and dealers. Charles Coey of Chicago, who had begun manufacture of his Coey Bear as a sideline to his full-size Flyers, said: "We believe that the 1,125,000 horse-drawn buggies that were sold in 1913 will all be supplanted by two-passenger light cars." The nation's first female cyclecar dealer, 21-year-old Anna Sheeley of Passaic, New Jersey, expected to sell 500 cyclecars in southern New Jersey alone in 1914, and added "...there is no limit apparently to the number of cars I can sell."

At least three magazines sprang up in 1913 to cater for the new craze, *Cyclecar Age* (New York), *The American Cyclecar* (Chicago), and *Cyclecar and Motorette*. However in 1914 *Cyclecar Age* changed its name to *Light Car Age*, and *The American Cyclecar* to *Carette*, reflecting a growing disillusion with the cyclecar concept. The little cars were just too flimsy in their design, and when this was coupled with sometimes bad workmanship and harsh usage, they did not offer what the American motorist expected. Transmissions were a particular weakness, for the long belts slipped, stretched, and sometimes broke, and friction drives became increasingly useless in wet weather, so that the slightest hill brought the vehicle to a standstill. Tops were either nonexistent or hopeless at

tradition of car design, nothing except a certain degree of common sense, to keep their makers on the straight and narrow.

Take motive power, for example. Gasoline, steam, and electricity sufficed for most car makers, but a few were lured by compressed air stored in large cylinders at pressures up to 3,000 pounds per square inch and admitted to the working cylinders through a pressure regulating gauge giving a constant 100 pounds per square inch. The expanded air drove pistons in the same way as hot air in a steam engine. The idea was first proposed by MacKenzie and MacArthur of New Haven, Connecticut, in 1895, although it is not certain if they ever built a running vehicle. In 1896 a six-seater carriage called the Pneumatic, built by the American Wheelock Engine Company of Worcester, Massachusetts, definitely took to the road, reaching 15mph at the low engine speed of 350rpm. In the Pneumatic, the expansion of air was aided by hot water stored in a separate tank, presumably very well lagged so that it kept hot for a reasonable length of time. Limited range was the main drawback of the compressed air engine, whose proposers tended to be visionaries who imagined a vast network of storage facilities with their attendant compressing plants. Six companies proposed or built compressed-air cars between 1895 and 1900, all in the states of New York, Connecticut, or Massachusetts, but none went into production.

A variation on compressed air was liquid air, whose evaporation produced the compressing force for the engine. This seems to have been even less practical than compressed air, and the much touted Liquid Air Power & Automobile Company of New York and Boston was a stock promotion fraud which may never have built a car at all. More modest was the Tripler Liquid Air Company, also of New York City, which built at least one car that still exists today. The company claimed that the liquid air could be stored safely for up to ten days, but the car's prospects were doomed by the scandal surrounding the other company. Both ventures had collapsed by 1901.

Kerosene-powered cars were not unknown in the early days, but none came stranger than the Brooklyn-built Tuck of 1904. In this the oil was admitted to the cylinder without being vaporized, and there was no explosion. One wonders how any motive power was developed, but the maker claimed that high torque was developed at low speed, so there was no need for gears. There was no reverse either; when the driver wanted to back up he just reversed the direction of the engine, although to do so he had to stop the motor and pull a lever which "shifted the cams in such a manner that the direction of rotation was changed." An easily impressed reporter said that the Tuck was "full of very novel ideas, of which much is expected," but it not surprising that no more was heard of it.

Another kerosene-driven car from a later era was the Ingram Hatch, made in a former steam laundry on Staten Island in 1917. It was exceptional for what it lacked rather than otherwise. It was advertised as having "no clutch, no radiator, no magneto, no gearshift, no water system, no central controlled shaft, no carburetor, no water jackets, no timers, no selective transmission, no need for gasoline." What did it have, one wonders? It had an air-cooled four-cylinder engine with friction transmission from which twin shafts took power to each half of the rear axle. So the boasted "no central shaft" was replaced by two shafts, more complication rather than less! The most unusual feature of the Ingram Hatch was its wheel design, which consisted of heart-shaped springs in place of spokes, with compressed-air cushions between them to reduce road shock. With all this there was no need for pneumatic tires, so these were made of leather and steel in sections that could be replaced if they became worn, rather than changing whole tires. Alas, no one seemed to take Joseph Ingram or William Hatch very seriously, and only one car was made.

Most designers were content with three or four wheels, but cars were made with five, six, or eight. The best-known five-wheeler was the Smith Flyer, also sold under the names Briggs & Stratton and Auto Red Bug. First marketed in 1917, it was a very simple buckboard with four cycle-type wheels at each corner and six wooden slats for a frame. There were no springs, as the slats were thought to be sufficiently flexible to provide a reasonably comfortable ride. Power came from a 2½hp single-cylinder engine mounted on a wheel which was let down onto the road behind the buckboard. The engine was started first, and care had to taken with the throttle; too little and the engine stalled, too much and you burned all the tread off the tire! Still, the buckboard was quite popular, and several hundred were sold at around $200 each. From 1924

▲ THE EXTRAORDINARY DIAMOND-WHEEL-PATTERN SERPENTINA CAR, BUILT BY CLAUDIUS MEZZACASA IN NEW YORK CITY IN 1915. BESIDES THE U.S. AUTOCYCLE, CARS WITH THIS LAYOUT WERE MADE BY SUNBEAM MABLEY IN ENGLAND — ABOUT 150 OF THEM BETWEEN 1901 AND 1903. A LATER AMERICAN PROTOTYPE WAS GORDON HANSEN'S GORDON DIAMOND OF 1947.
SCIENTIFIC AMERICAN

to 1930 they were made by a firm in New Jersey that offered electrically-powered models as well; these used a 12-volt battery and motor employed in Dodge cars, which drove directly to the rear axle, so there was no need for the fifth wheel.

Another, more obscure, five-wheeler was the Chicago-built Glover of 1902, which had a traction drum in the middle of the frame, with face plates of soft steel between two disks. Chain-driven from a four-cylinder engine, the drum was spring-loaded to keep contact with the ground and was said to enable the car to pull two heavy coal wagons, one with its brakes locked. Glover also built a steam-powered version in which the drum could be filled with hot water from the boiler to melt snow in winter!

The six- and eight-wheelers were built by Milton O. Reeves of Columbus, Indiana, who took his inspiration from a Pullman railroad coach, believing that more wheels equaled greater comfort. His Octo-Auto of 1911 was converted from an Overland touring, with two pairs of wheels at each end. Wheelbase was 180 inches and overall length 248 inches. The first rear axle was powered, and steering was on all eight wheels, the front pair of axles turning in the normal direction, the rear pair in the opposite direction, as in today's Honda Prelude and Mazda 626. Reeves quoted a price of $3,200 for his Octo-Auto, but received no orders, and in 1912 decided to think a little smaller. He made two Sexto-Autos, the first the Octo-Auto with only one front axle, the second based on a Stutz. For this he asked $5,000, doubtless because of the greater price of the base car (a standard Overland 40 touring cost $1,300, a Stutz $2,250).

You would think that there would be little disagreement over where to place the wheels on a four-wheeled car, but at least two designers arranged them in a diamond pattern, one each at front and back and one on each side. In 1907 Thomas Vandergrift's Autocycle emerged from its Philadelphia workshop. Powered by an air-cooled 6hp twin driving the rear wheel by belt, it had two normal-sized wheels front and back, and two smaller ones on either side, almost like the stabilizers on a child's bike. With a very small turning circle (three of the four wheels steered), a 45mph top speed, and a $400 price tag, the Autocycle seemed an attractive proposition, but production lasted only one year.

1905 STANLEY ROADSTER ▲▶
BY 1905 STANLEY HAD ADOPTED THE
CHARACTERISTIC ROUNDED HOOD,
UNDER WHICH LURKED THE BOILER.
THE HORIZONTAL TWO-CYLINDER ENGINE
WAS LOCATED AHEAD OF THE REAR AXLE,
WHICH IT DROVE DIRECTLY WITHOUT ANY
NEED FOR VARIABLE GEARS.
OWNER: CRAWFORD COLLECTION OF THE WESTERN
HISTORICAL SOCIETY (PHOTO NICKY WRIGHT)

On similar lines was the Serpentina roadster made in New York City in 1915 by Claudius Mezzacasa. This was more streamlined than the Autocycle, almost torpedo-shaped, and the wheels were of equal size, those at the front and rear steering in opposite directions, whereas on the Autocycle the front and center pair steered, the rear wheel being fixed. *Scientific American* reported: "A traffic policeman at Columbus Circle did not trust his eyes when the car showed up for the first time. The driver swung the steering wheel round just as the car reached the policeman, and it performed a pirouette of the most amazing swiftness. Before the surprised policeman could

open his mouth, it had darted off in a right-handed direction — after having described an arc of 450 degrees." Sadly, no more were made than of the Autocycle, possibly only Mezzacasa's prototype.

S TEAM AND ELECTRICITY

Although they were to become marginal by the 1920s, steam- and electric-powered cars were a significant part of the automotive scene in the first two decades of the century. Particularly in the northeastern United States steam was dominant at the turn of the century; more than 50 percent of all cars registered in the state of New York in 1902 were steam-powered. But Locomobile's changeover to gasoline at the end of the 1903 season marked a sharp downturn, and during the next two years many smaller makes followed suit or went out of business altogether. Only two significant makes carried on, Stanley and White.

The Stanley had been redesigned in 1902 to avoid infringing the patents which the brothers had

granted to A. L. Barber of Locomobile and J. B. Walker of Mobile. The engine was now horizontal and geared directly to the rear axle, a layout which Stanley maintained until the last one left the factory in 1927. In 1905 the frontal boiler was covered under a rounded hood. This became the marque's characteristic feature until 1915, when a Vee-shaped dummy radiator was substituted. It acted as a condenser to reduce the exhaust steam to water for re-use, a feature seen on many steamers ten years earlier, but the cautious Stanley twins were never in a hurry to adopt other people's ideas. They retained wooden frames until 1915, long after most other American car makers, with the exception of Franklin, had gone over to steel.

For their price, Stanleys gave excellent performance, something appreciated by the Boston police department as early as 1903 when it bought several of the folding front seat models. The

1902 WHITE STANHOPE ▲

ALTHOUGH THE WHITE LOOKED SIMILAR TO THE STANLEY AT THIS TIME, IT WAS A MORE ADVANCED DESIGN, WITH SEMIFLASH BOILER. THIS MUST BE AN EARLY 1902 MODEL, FOR THAT YEAR BROUGHT THE INTRODUCTION OF THE FRONT-MOUNTED CONDENSER, WHICH LOOKED LIKE A RADIATOR AND RECYCLED THE EXHAUST STEAM. IN 1903 WHITES LOST THEIR BUGGY LOOK, FOR THEY NOW HAD HOODS LIKE A GASOLINE CAR.

OWNER: CRAWFORD COLLECTION OF THE WESTERN HISTORICAL SOCIETY
(PHOTO NICKY WRIGHT)

1913 BAKER ELECTRIC VICTORIA ▲▶

BY 1913 THE TYPICAL ELECTRIC CAR WAS A CLOSED COUPE, BUT BAKER STILL OFFERED THIS OPEN TWO-PASSENGER VICTORIA. IT IS UNMISTAKABLY AN ELECTRIC, BUT SOME BAKERS HAD LONG HOODS GIVING THEM THE APPEARANCE OF GASOLINE CARS. TOP SPEED WAS NOT MORE THAN 25mph, ALTHOUGH IN 1902 WALTER BAKER COVERED A MILE IN 47 SECONDS (EQUAL TO 76.6mph) IN HIS STREAMLINED ELECTRIC TORPEDO. SADLY, HE CRASHED INTO THE CROWD AT THE END OF THE RUN, KILLING TWO SPECTATORS.

OWNER: CRAWFORD COLLECTION OF THE WESTERN HISTORICAL SOCIETY
(PHOTO NICKY WRIGHT)

Newton fire department bought them as well. In 1906 the company brought out a range of roadsters, in 10, 20, and 30hp sizes, the latter capable of 68mph yet costing only $1,800. The 10hp roadster was priced at only $850. The 20hp, selling for $1,350, went by the charming name of Gentleman's Speedy Roadster. Some Stanleys were faster still. F. E. Stanley was once driving an experimental model on a straight road near Boston when he was stopped by a policeman who, although he was a friend, said he would have to book him because he was going so fast. When the case came up in court, the officer said the car was doing nearly 60mph, to which Stanley pleaded "not guilty." When the judge asked how this could be in face of the evidence, Stanley replied: "I plead not guilty to going 60mph. When I passed the officer my speedometer showed I was going 87mph." He was fined $5 and all the Boston papers carried the story.

In 1906 a streamlined Stanley racecar called the Beetle took the unofficial Land Speed Record at 127.66mph at Daytona Beach in Florida. This was the company's peak period, although production was no higher than 700 cars per year. As time passed the Stanley Steamer grew heavier, more complicated, and more expensive in an attempt to keep up with gasoline cars. A particular blow was the arrival of Cadillac's self-starter in 1914, for this was a system both easy and quick. The Stanley took up to 45 minutes to start on a cold morning, but before 1914 it could at least boast that this involved no muscular cranking. Stanley never took to the flash boiler, which gave quicker starting, but did introduce electric lighting in 1913.

By the end of World War I prices ranged from $3,425 to $5,100, above those of Cadillac, and sales dwindled year by year.

The White is not as well remembered as the Stanley, although more Whites were made in the years 1900–1910, after which the company went over to gasoline. Whites were more sophisticated than Stanleys, with condensers from 1902 and flash boilers, or steam generators as the company preferred to call them, from 1903. By 1905 Whites had a water feed controlled by the driver, and a clutch which allowed the engine to run and operate the pumps while the car was stationary. Previously, when the car was not moving, the pumps had to be operated by hand. Although more expensive than Stanleys, Whites sold better, reaching 1,534 deliveries in 1906 and totaling 9,122 over their ten-year lifetime, compared with 5,122 Stanleys sold in the same period. Whites were the first official White House cars, President William Howard Taft using one from 1909. His predecessor Theodore Roosevelt had been the first U.S. president to drive a car, also a White steamer, in Puerto Rico in 1906. In 1910 White made 1,208 steamers and 1,200 gasoline cars, and that was that for the steamers. Gas cars were made up to 1918, after which White concentrated on trucks, still making them today, under Volvo ownership. Steam had a final flowering in the California-built Doble, but that belongs to the next chapter.

The electric car was proportionally more important than the steamer, and was a familar feature of city life, particularly between about 1906 and 1916. Columbia led the field in the early days, and was then joined by Baker and Rauch & Lang from Cleveland (merged in 1915) and Detroit, which became the best-known makers of electric cars, with 1,500 sales in 1910 and a peak of 4,669 in 1914. There were also about 20 other electrics of some importance, such as Argo, Borland, Chicago (which sold a car to the Pope in 1915), Fritchle, Milburn, Ohio, and Woods. The electric car's appeal was

▲ 1904 POPE-WAVERLEY ELECTRIC RUNABOUT WITH TWO FASHIONABLY DRESSED LADIES, TYPICAL USERS OF SUCH CARS. WITHIN A FEW YEARS, MOST ELECTRICS WERE CLOSED COUPES, NICKNAMED "MOBILE CHINA CLOSETS."
MOTOR VEHICLE MANUFACTURERS' ASSOCIATION

to women, who appreciated its silence and ease of driving, and who found hand-cranking undignified at best and often physically impossible. Most electrics were closed broughams, sometimes nicknamed "mobile china closets" because of their tall, angular lines and generous areas of glass all round. With her electric brougham, the American matron could go shopping and pay social calls independent of husband or chauffeur, fully protected from the weather. What she could not do was to travel more than about 50 miles a day, or venture beyond the city's paved roads, but then on the whole she didn't want to.

The importance of the electric car is shown in a photograph taken outside the Detroit Athletic Club in about 1914, when the members threw open the club for their wives' inspection. There are about 35 cars visible in the photo, and all but three are electrics. This preponderance did not last for long. By 1920 the electric was definitely on the wane. The advent of the self-starter had something

1911 RAUCH & LANG ELECTRIC COUPE ▲
RAUCH & LANG WERE AMONG THE BETTER-KNOWN MAKERS OF ELECTRIC CARS, AND BEGAN AS CARRIAGE BUILDERS
IN CLEVELAND IN 1884. ELECTRIC POWER WAS ADDED IN 1905, AND BY 1911 THE COMPANY WAS MAKING SIX DIFFERENT
DESIGNS ON 77- OR 85-INCH WHEELBASES. THIS COUPE, ALMOST AS TALL AS IT IS LONG, WAS TYPICAL OF ELECTRICS
AT THIS TIME. IN 1915 RAUCH & LANG MERGED WITH BAKER, ANOTHER CLEVELAND ELECTRIC VEHICLE MAKER.
OWNERS: MARK AND TOOTSIE ACCOMAZZO (PHOTO NICKY WRIGHT)

to do with it, but also the public's expectations had risen. In 1914 a top speed of 20mph and a limited range seemed acceptable, but not so six years later, when improved roads made out-of-town journeys more possible. The electric car always had a "lady image," but by the 1920s this had become an "old lady image." Younger women went for a Dodge or Chevrolet coupe, or, if sufficiently sporting, for a Jordan Playboy. In 1921, out of 9 million passenger cars registered in the United States, only 18,184 were electric. There were more Auburns or Peerlesses, not particularly well-known makes, than all the electrics put together. Ten years later the number of electrics was so insignificant that it did not feature in statistics.

THE FRONTIERS OPEN UP

Ever since the 1895 *Chicago Times-Herald* race, autombile enthusiasts had been pushing back the frontiers imposed on their vehicles. By the turn of the century town-to-town endurance runs of several hundred miles were becoming common. In 1901, the 380-mile New York to Buffalo run involved some 50 cars, and soon roadside touring signs were being set up on popular routes such as New York to Boston or Philadelphia. Also in 1901, 21-year-old Roy Chapin achieved fame when he drove a Curved Dash Olds from Detroit to New York for the Auto Show, taking 7½ days for the trip. On his arrival he was so muddy that the doorman of the Waldorf Astoria where Ransom Olds was staying turned him away. Chapin later became president of Hudson. However, the real challenge was the crossing of the continent, coast to coast, and although there were several attempts, no one succeeded until the summer of 1903.

Horatio Nelson Jackson was a 31-year-old Vermont doctor who accepted a $50 wager that he could not drive across the continent. He bought a Winton, and with a hired driver, Sewell Crocker, and camping equipment, picks, and shovels, set off from San Francisco on May 23. He also took a rifle and pistols, just in case of hostilities, and a fishing rod to help with food along the way. In Wyoming the pair rescued a bulldog from a fight and, given the name Bud, he became part of the crew for the

▼ "REFUELING STOP" FOR A DETROIT ELECTRIC COUPE. THE 40-CELL BATTERIES WERE HOUSED UNDER THE HOOD AND AT THE REAR. IN A COMPANY-SPONSORED TEST A DETROIT ELECTRIC RAN 211 MILES ON A SINGLE CHARGE, ALTHOUGH 80 MILES WAS THE GENERALLY ADVERTISED FIGURE.
U.S. LIBRARY OF CONGRESS

▲ ELECTRIC CARS WERE GENERALLY USED IN CITIES, BUT THIS DETROIT WENT ON A PROMOTIONAL TRIP FROM SEATTLE TO MOUNT RAINIER AROUND 1915.
U.S. LIBRARY OF CONGRESS

▲ THE LITTLE CURVED DASH OLDSMOBILE IN WHICH L. L. WHITMAN (LEFT) AND EUGENE HAMMOND CROSSED
THE CONTINENT, PAUSING IN DETROIT, WHICH THEY REACHED IN 60 DAYS FROM SAN FRANCISCO. ALTHOUGH THEY
TOOK LONGER TO REACH NEW YORK THAN THE JACKSON/CROCKER OR FETCH/KRARUP TEAMS, THEIR CAR WAS
CHEAPER AND SMALLER, WITH ONLY ONE CYLINDER.
OLDSMOBILE HISTORY CENTER

▶ A PAUSE FOR WHEEL
ADJUSTMENTS DURING THE
NEW YORK TO ST. LOUIS TOUR
IN JULY 1904. THE CAR IS
AN OLDSMOBILE LIGHT TONNEAU,
THE FIRST OLDS TO HAVE
A STEERING WHEEL IN PLACE
OF A TILLER.
MOTOR VEHICLE MANUFACTURERS'
ASSOCIATION

rest of that pioneering car journey.

Jackson's worst enemies were not hostile animals or humans, but punctures and mud. The car constantly bogged down in Idaho, and in Wyoming Jackson and Crocker frequently resorted to block and tackle to get out of sand dunes and river beds. Reactions to their passing varied from intense curiosity to sheer terror. One young man who heard of their arrival in his state rode 70 miles across the prairie just to look at an automobile. "I have seen lots of pictures of them," he said, "but this is the first real live one I ever saw."

Jackson and Crocker reached New York after 64 days, and were promptly followed by others. Indeed, before they had even arrived, Tom Fetch and Marius Krarup set out from San Francisco in a single-cylinder Packard, making the journey in 61 days. Krarup was editor of *The Automobile*, which ensured plenty of publicity. The next to cross were L.L. Whitman and Eugene Hammond, who drove a little Curved Dash, again from San Francisco to New York, in 73 days. Two years later, two Curved Dash models called Old Scout (the Whitman–Hammond car) and Old Steady took part in an East–West jaunt, from New York to Portland, Oregon, making the 3,890-mile trek in only 44 days.

All these journeys were accomplished by men, but in 1909 22-year-old Alice Huyler Ramsey decided that women ought to be able to do just as well. She used a four-cylinder Maxwell Model DA touring her husband had bought her when her horse bolted (after being frightened by a car). She had less than a year's driving experience when she set out with three female companions, none of whom could drive, from New York on June 9. The trip to San Francisco took 53 days, of which 13 were needed to traverse Iowa, in whose notorious gumbo (black heavy clay) horses had been known to drown. Gumbo could add 250-300 pounds of extra weight on each wheel. In Wyoming and Utah they found that heavy rains had washed out some roads to a depth of 12 feet. Often the roads were no more than wagon or horse trails, and some ran across private ranches where the travelers had to open and close gates as they went.

The appalling state of American country roads was highlighted by journeys such as that of Alice Huyler Ramsey, and gradually improvements were made. The first rural mile of concrete pavement in

the United States was laid in Wayne County, Michigan, in July 1909, and a Federal Road Act was passed in July 1916 authorizing the establishment of a nationwide system of interstate highways. Even before that conditions had become easier. In 1916 Amanda Preuss was unimpressed with the current women's record of 43 days held by movie star Anita King. "Gracious," she said "I can beat that and never half try." Driving an Oldsmobile V8 roadster, she went from San Francisco to New York in 11 days, 5 hours 45 minutes. This was little more than a fifth of Alice Ramsey's time, and although her car was undoubtedly faster, most of the credit must have been due to better roads. The outright record in 1916 was 7½ days, set by Erwin "Cannonball" Baker in a Cadillac V8.

The earliest long-distance American motorist,

who gave his name to a series of tours still commemorated today, was Charles Jasper Glidden (1857–1927), a Bostonian telephone magnate who at one time controlled one sixth of the Bell Telephone Company. Retiring a wealthy man at age 43, he looked for something to do with the rest of his life, and decided to travel the world by automobile. He began in 1901 with a British Napier, and over the next eight years covered 46,528 miles in 39 countries. Where roads were unsuitable, he fixed flanged wheels to his Napier and drove on the railroad tracks, scheduled as a regular train and carrying flags and a whistle.

In 1904 Glidden promoted a reliability run from New York to St. Louis, and the next year organized the first Glidden Tour. Covering 870 miles from New York to Bretton Woods, New Hampshire, and back, 34 cars made the journey, their drivers including such luminaries as Ransom Olds in a Reo, Percy Pierce in a Pierce Great Arrow, and Walter White in one of his steamers. On the whole they were well received, although a Manchester, New Hampshire, newspaper disapproved of their speed: "Concord to here, 18 miles, in forty minutes. Have they any right to do such a thing?"

One who clearly thought they had no such right was a judge from Worcester, Massachusetts, who said: "If these people want to race, let them go elsewhere. If they want to come to Massachusetts, they must behave themselves and obey the law." Despite the fact that it was not a race, he fined six drivers $15 each.

The Glidden Tours were held annually through 1913, reaching a maximum length of 2,636 miles in 1909. They were revived after World War II to cater for the growing number of antique car enthusiasts who wanted to give their cars some good exercise.

There were countless other automobile tours and record attempts, but mention must be made of the New York to Paris Race of 1908, jointly sponsored by *The New York Times* and *Le Matin*. Six cars set off from Times Square on February 12, crossing the American continent to San Francisco, where they were shipped to Alaska and then again to Japan and to the Russian port of Vladivostok. After that, it was land all the way to Paris, the total journey being 13,341 miles. The winner was George Schuster driving a Buffalo-built Thomas Flyer, who took 169 days. The next finisher, a German Protos, reached Paris 16 days later. All the contestants agreed that the winter roads of upstate New York were worse than anything Siberia or Eastern Europe could offer. In some Western states they took to the railroad tracks, but not as Glidden did with flanged wheels; they just bumped along over the sleepers because even this was better than an almost nonexistent road. As a result of Schuster's victory, sales of Thomas cars jumped by 27 percent and Schuster (who died in 1972, aged 99) became a national celebrity. His car still survives as one of the most valuable exhibits in Harrah's Collection at Reno.

 THE ITALIAN-BUILT ZÜST CAR IN CHICAGO DURING THE 1908 NEW YORK–PARIS RACE. THE DRIVER IS POET/JOURNALIST ANTONIO SCARFOGLIO. THE CARS LEFT NEW YORK'S TIMES SQUARE ON FEBRUARY 12, AND THE WINNING THOMAS FLYER DID NOT REACH PARIS UNTIL JULY 30.
MOTOR VEHICLE MANUFACTURERS' ASSOCIATION

◀▶THREE PHOTOS SHOWING THE TERRIBLE ROAD CONDITIONS ENCOUNTERED ALL OVER THE UNITED STATES IN THE EARLY YEARS OF THE 20TH CENTURY. ROADS LIKE THESE WERE AN ADDITIONAL BURDEN TO DRIVERS WHOSE CARS FREQUENTLY BOILED OR SUFFERED BROKEN TRANSMISSIONS. NOT THAT TODAY'S MODELS WOULD DO ANY BETTER IN THESE CONDITIONS — APART, THAT IS, FROM FOUR-WHEEL-DRIVE CHEVROLET BLAZERS OR FORD BRONCOS.
MOTOR VEHICLE MANUFACTURERS' ASSOCIATION

1930 FORD MODEL A COUPE DE LUXE ▼
OWNER: JIM RANSOM (PHOTO NICKY WRIGHT)

CHAPTER FOUR

THE GREAT BOOM ON WHEELS

1920 – 1929

"You can't ride to town in a bathtub."
Indiana farmer's wife, 1925

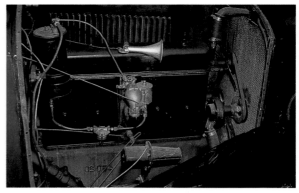

THE 1 MILLION MARK IN U.S. passenger car production was passed for the first time in 1916, slightly exceeded in 1917, then after a dip caused by the war reached nearly 2 million (1,905,560) in 1920. The market seemed to be expanding without limit, and in 1929 even these figures were dwarfed by a record 4,455,178 sales. Over the same nine years, registrations of cars rose from 8,132,000 to 23,121,000. No decade since has seen such an increase, nor is it likely ever to be repeated. In the 1920s and 1930s car ownership passed from being the pleasure of a minority, albeit a substantial minority, to one of the majority of Americans. By 1930 there was one car for every 1.3 households, compared with one for 44 households 20 years before.

This phenomenal growth was partly due to higher living standards, but also to the high value that Americans put on car ownership. They were prepared to make sacrifices on other purchases such as clothing. In 1923 *The Chicago Evening Post* reported that retailers blamed the automobile for the slump in the clothing trade. "We'd rather do without clothes than give up the car," one mother of nine children said, while another remarked, "We don't have no fancy clothes when we have the car to pay for." A survey made in Muncie, Indiana, in 1925 revealed that 21 out of 26 car-owning homes surveyed had no bathtubs with running water. When a farmer's wife was asked why they chose a car in preference to indoor plumbing, she replied: "You can't ride to town in a bathtub."

JOCKEYING FOR POSITION

The manufacturers catering to this booming demand were mostly the same as in the previous decade: Ford well ahead, followed by Chevrolet, Willys-Overland, Dodge, and Buick. The numbers were swelled for a while by Billy Durant's Durant and Star, and by Hudson's low-priced Essex, which arrived in 1919. There were also numerous smaller manufacturers, although few in the low-priced field.

Ford dominated the field in the first half of the 1920s, selling more than four times as many cars as its nearest rival, Chevrolet, between 1922 and 1926. Sales came so easily that Ford did not bother to advertise nationally between 1917 and 1923, although local dealers still did so. Prices reached an all-time low in 1923, when a two-passenger runabout cost $260 and a five-passenger touring cost $290. The closest that Chevrolet could get to these prices was $490 and $495 respectively.

By 1926, although Ford was still outselling Chevrolet, the gap was closing, and the Model T

1930 FORD MODEL A COUPE DE LUXE ▼

"FROM COUNTRY COUSIN TO COUNTRY CLUB" — THE
MODEL A TOOK FORD FROM FARMER'S FRIEND INTO
THE WORLD OF STYLE. MOVIE STARS AND POLITICIANS
FAVORED IT IN A WAY THEY NEVER DID THE T,
ALTHOUGH MECHANICALLY IT WAS NOT A VERY
REMARKABLE CAR. THE 1930 MODELS HAD LARGER
TIRES ON SMALLER SHEELS, RESULTING IN A DISTINCTLY
LOWER LOOK. AT $550 THIS DE LUXE COUPE COST
$50 MORE THAN THE STANDARD VERSION.

OWNER: JIM RANSOM (PHOTO NICKY WRIGHT)

was selling largely on its low price. With rising prosperity and expectations, this was not enough. Wire wheels and balloon tires became available in 1925 and a range of colors in 1926, thanks to quick-drying Duco lacquer, but still the T was ripe for replacement. This was clear to everyone but Henry Ford, who in his homespun way thought that getting from one place to another was all that should be expected of a car. He blamed falling sales on indolent dealers and alienated them so much that a number changed franchises in favor of General Motors. His son's

1931 FORD MODEL A CONVERTIBLE SEDAN ▶

THIS BODY STYLE WAS NEW TO THE MODEL A
RANGE FOR 1931, AND ONLY 4,864 WERE MADE.
IT WAS ONE OF THE RAREST OF ALL MODEL A
STYLES, ONLY BEATEN BY THE TAXICAB (4,850) AND
THE TOWN CAR (1,065). AT $640 IT WAS THE MOST
EXPENSIVE OF THE 1931 MODELS.

OWNER: GILMORE CAR MUSEUM, KALAMAZOO, MICHIGAN

(PHOTO NICKY WRIGHT)

brother-in-law and vice-president Ernest Kanzler was strongly in favor of a six-cylinder car to replace the T, but Ford distrusted sixes after the failure of the Model K. He considered an X-8 engine, but it was too radical and too heavy, so, after the departure of Kanzler in August 1926, work went ahead on the design of a conventional four-cylinder car.

The last Model T officially left the Highland Park factory on May 27, 1927, although production actually continued through June. Engine manufacture lasted much longer; you could still buy a new Model T engine in August 1941. Today, old models are seldom discontinued until their replacements are well into production, but this was not Henry's way. The T's successor, the Model A, was not launched until December 1927, and in the meantime 60,000 men were thrown out of work in Detroit alone, across the nation 23 assembly plants were shut down, and dealers had to survive by selling spare parts.

It is a tribute to the public's faith in the Ford name that so many people held back from buying a new car until they saw what the Model A would be like, and also that so many dealers remained loyal for the six months when they had no new cars to sell. The A was launched in Detroit, New York,

and other cities on December 2, 1927, to greater acclaim than any other new car. In New York crowds began gathering at three in the morning outside the Broadway showroom, and in Cleveland mounted police had to be called out to control the crowds. Dallas newspapers described it as the greatest event there since the signing of the Armistice. In less than a week 25 million people had looked at the A, and by Christmas nearly half a million firm orders had been taken, even though there were virtually no cars available for a test drive. So scarce were the new cars that they were driven around the country, stopping for no more than a few hours' display in each city before speeding on to the next.

The car that aroused everyone's excitement was not really very remarkable. It had a four-cylinder L-head engine of slightly larger displacement than the T, with 200.5 against 176.7 cubic inches, but output was doubled from 20 to 40bhp. Weights were 20–25 percent up on the equivalent T models, but the extra power gave a 65mph top speed, better than many more costly cars. Henry

▲ EVEN AT THE BEGINNING OF THE 1920s THE AUTOMOBILE DOMINATED THE STREETS OF LARGE CITIES. THIS NEW YORK PHOTO WAS TAKEN ON 42nd STREET WITH BRYANT PARK ON THE RIGHT. CLOSED CARS PREDOMINATE, ALTHOUGH THEY WERE IN THE MINORITY IN THE NATION AS A WHOLE. THE FEW HORSE-DRAWN VEHICLES ARE ALL TRUCKS; THE HORSE SURVIVED IN COMMERCIAL TRANSPORTATION AFTER IT HAD DISAPPEARED FROM PRIVATE USE.

MOTOR VEHICLE MANUFACTURERS' ASSOCIATION

▼ FORD BEGAN NATIONAL ADVERTISING AGAIN IN 1923; THIS ADVERTISEMENT FOR THE MODEL T TUDOR SEDAN DATES FROM 1926. BY THIS TIME COLORS WERE AGAIN AVAILABLE: HIGHLAND, MOLESKIN AND DRAKE GREEN; ROYAL MAROON OR FAWN; GRAY ON THE CLOSED MODELS. BY 1927 BLACK, SO LONG THE SOLE COLOR FOR THE MODEL T, WAS ONLY AVAILABLE TO SPECIAL ORDER ON THE PICKUP.

MIRCO DE CET COLLECTION

THE FIRST TRAFFIC CONTROL LIGHT IN AMERICA — AND PROBABLY IN THE WORLD — APPEARED IN CLEVELAND, OHIO, ON AUGUST 5, 1914. THE FIRST TRAFFIC LIGHT WITH RED, AMBER, AND GREEN CAME INTO USE IN NEW YORK IN 1918.

TWO EARLY EXAMPLES OF MECHANICAL TRAFFIC CONTROL ARE SHOWN HERE.

▲ A FAIRLY COMPLEX SYSTEM IS SEEN HERE; IT HAS THE COP IN AN ELEVATED POSITION AND GIVES INSTRUCTIONS TO PEDESTRIANS. IT DATES FROM THE EARLY 1920s.

▶ DETROIT'S FIRST ELECTRIC STOP LIGHT, INSTALLED IN 1914.

MOTOR VEHICLE MANUFACTURERS' ASSOCIATION

did not favor a conventional sliding gear transmission, largely because he did not want to be thought imitative, but the wishes of his son Edsel and others prevailed, and the A had a three-speed system modeled on that of the luxury Lincoln which Ford was making. Also inherited from Lincoln were the hydraulic shock absorbers, while safety glass in the windshield was a first in a low-priced car. The transverse leaf suspension was unchanged from the T; indeed no Ford had conventional lateral springs until 1948.

In styling the A bore some resemblance to the Lincoln, although its short wheelbase prevented it from being really elegant. Body options were similar to those on the T, with the addition of a taxicab and panel delivery van. Prices were higher,

1924 CHEVROLET ▲▼

SUPERIOR SERIES F WAS THE DESIGNATION FOR 1924 CHEVROLETS, WHICH WERE MADE
IN SIX BODY STYLES ON A SINGLE 103-INCH WHEELBASE. BETTER EQUIPPED THAN
THE RIVAL FORD MODEL T, THE CHEVROLET INCLUDED AN ELECTRIC STARTER AS STANDARD EQUIPMENT,
ALSO AN AMMETER AND ELECTRIC HORN. CLOSED MODELS HAD A WINDSHIELD WIPER.

OWNER: DICK TRAVERS (PHOTO NICKY WRIGHT)

1,310,147 As, and later years, hit by the Depression, recorded fewer Model A station wagons (a total of 11,317 in four seasons). Still, the station wagon did better than the town car, which notched up only 1,065 sales over the same period, and was the ancestor of countless station wagons in years to come made not only by Ford, but by most other U.S. manufacturers.

Ford biographer Robert Lacey couldn't have put it better when he wrote that with the unveiling of the A, the Ford swung overnight from country cousin to country club. Gone were the countless jokes about the Lizzie. Its scarcity alone gave the A considerable cachet in its early years. Few celebrities had been willing to be photographed alongside a Model T, but Douglas Fairbanks gave Mary Pickford a Model A coupe for Christmas, and both were happy to appear with the car. Other Hollywood figures who bought As included Cecil B. de Mille, Lon Chaney, Wallace Beery, and Louis B. Mayer. In Washington, Senator James Couzens requested that he receive the first A to be delivered in the capital. President-to-be Franklin D. Roosevelt recorded his pride on operating a Model A, and across the ocean Prince Nicholas of Rumania took delivery of the first A in his country.

The Model A was phased out over the winter of 1931/32. Henry Ford announced the indefinite shutdown of production in August 1931, and there were no 1932 models, but in fact the last A was not delivered until April 1932. Total production was 3,837,503, of which about 900,000 are thought to survive today. On the surface, the A would seem to have been a success, but the balance sheets showed a different story. It was not the fault of the car, but the disastrous and unnecessary halt in

from $460 for the four-passenger touring, now called a phaeton, to $600 for the taxi. For 1929 the range was extended from 9 to 18 models, including bodies by Briggs and Murphy as well as Ford, and two new styles, a station wagon at $650 and a town car at $1,200. The latter was something of a folly, and few were made, although after the Depression there was a short-lived vogue for expensive town car bodies on Ford chassis. The station wagon was another matter, however; this style had been offered on the T, often rebodying chassis which had lasted longer than the original bodies, but the 1929 Model A was the first to be a listed style. It took some time to find a niche in the market; 1929 calendar year sales were 4,954 out of a total of

production in 1927 which led to a loss of $30 million over the year. The halt was unnecessary because the A was made at Ford's vast new River Rouge plant, whereas the T had been made at Highland Park, so an overlap would have been perfectly feasible. The 1928 year saw losses up to $250 million. The assembly line was moving so slowly that Ford was losing more than $300 per car. In the same period General Motors and Chrysler were making record profits, largely due to management being delegated rather than concentrated in the hands of one strong-willed 65-year-old. Because of the changeover, Ford inevitably lost the lead to Chevrolet in 1927, and was 254,000 units behind in 1928 too. Although the company regained first position in 1929 and 1930, thereafter it came second to Chevrolet in almost every year to the present.

Chevrolet began the 1920s badly, in the wake of Billy Durant's sudden departure from GM. While Ford doubled its sales in 1921 to nearly 1 million, Chevrolet's halved to just under 62,000. Alfred P. Sloan (1875–1966) was executive vice-president of GM after the end of the Durant regime, becoming president in 1923. He realized that Chevrolet could never compete head-on with Ford, but his strategy was to take a slice off the top of the Ford market and cater to those who wanted to trade up to something a bit more stylish and better equipped than a Model T. Had Ford sales not been so good, one could say that it was a weakness of Henry Ford that his customers had nothing to move up to. This gap was not plugged until the arrival of the Edsel-inspired Mercury for 1939. Sloan, of course, had a whole range of cars carefully priced for a particular market; above Chevrolet came Oakland, then Oldsmobile, Buick, and finally Cadillac.

The cheap Chevrolet in 1922 was still the 490, priced from $510 for a two-passenger roadster to $875 for a four-door sedan. Comparable Ford prices were $269 to $725. For 1923 the 490 was renamed the Superior, with some improvements. There was also a short-lived air-cooled model called the Copper-Cooled Chevrolet. This had a 135-cubic-inch engine with square dimensions (3½ x 3½ inches) cooled by the copper fins that gave it its name. It looked much like the Superior, sharing the same wheelbase and most of the same body styles, although the Copper-Cooled range had an

additional coach. The engine was supposed to be simpler and cheaper to make than the Superior's, but this was not reflected in the price, which was $200 more. The main problem was pre-ignition, which got worse with higher temperatures, and a fan that did not give even cooling over the whole engine. The engine was in fact a complete failure; of the 739 cars made, 239 were scrapped before leaving the factory, 300 were assigned to dealers, and only about 100 went to the public. Chevrolet recalled them all in the summer of 1923, although one Bostonian refused to give his back, and this survives today, together with one other bought by Henry Ford to see if there was anything worth copying. There wasn't.

The Superior Series K of 1925 had many improvements, including a stronger crankshaft, enclosed and automatically lubricated rocker arms, dry plate disk clutch in place of cone, stiffer chassis frame, and, most important, a new banjo-type rear axle which eliminated the "Chevrolet hum" that was something of a joke about the previous models. Chevrolet was the first low-priced car to adopt the new Duco fast-drying paint. Unlike the Ford, still available in any color so long as it was black, Chevrolet cars did not include that hue in their color schemes at all.

The Chevrolet fours were continued through the 1928 season with little change apart from being named Capitols for 1927 and Nationals for 1928, when they gained four-wheel brakes and an extra 4

inches of wheelbase. Former Ford executive William S. Knudsen headed Chevrolet during these years of revival. Apart from the improvements in the Chevrolet and the obsolescence of the Model T, one of GM's most valuable weapons was a low-interest flexible instalment plan. Henry Ford refused to sell on credit, claiming that it damaged the traditional thrift on which he believed America had been built. In fact, Henry's principles, wise though they may seem in retrospect, were increasingly out of step with the business practices of the 1920s. Although he may never have heard of "built-in obsolescence," Alfred Sloan believed it was important for new models to create a certain amount of dissatisfaction with the old ones. To Ford it seemed ridiculous that a 1923 model should be rejected because it did not look like a 1924. "We want the man who buys one of our products never to have to buy another," he said. This was not a little naive when he was turning out 1.8 million cars per year, many of which must have been replacements for older Fords.

Chevrolet obviously outsold Ford in 1927, the figures being 1,749,998 to 356,188, and triumphed in 1928 too, when the Model A was up and running. To counter the A, Chevrolet launched a brand-new six-cylinder engine to go into the 1928 107-inch chassis. It had overhead valves like the previous fours, and the 195-cubic-inch displacement gave 46bhp at 2,400rpm. The pistons were of cast iron, giving rise to the nickname "Cast Iron Wonder;" an

1928 CHEVROLET ADVERTISEMENT ◄ THE 1928 CHEVROLETS WERE LARGER CARS, WITH AN ADDITIONAL FOUR INCHES IN THE WHEELBASE. THEY WERE KNOWN AS THE NATIONAL AB MODELS, AND THEIR MOST IMPORTANT INNOVATION, HIGHLIGHTED IN THIS ADVERTISEMENT, WAS FOUR-WHEEL BRAKES. CHEVROLET HAD NINE U.S. PLANTS IN 1928, AND ONE IN CANADA, WHICH MADE A TOTAL OF 1,193,212 CARS.

MIRCO DE CET COLLECTION

1926 CHEVROLET SUPERIOR SERIES V LANDAU COUPE ▲
CHEVROLETS FOR 1926 WERE LITTLE CHANGED FROM THE PREVIOUS YEAR,
BUT COULD BE DISTINGUISHED BY THE TIE BAR BETWEEN THE HEADLIGHTS.
THE BUMPERS WERE AN EXTRA, AS WAS A SPARE TIRE. THE DISK WHEELS SEEN
HERE WERE STANDARD, WOOD SPOKES BEING AN OPTIONAL EXTRA.

OWNERS: DAN AND CAROL HANSEN (PHOTO NICKY WRIGHT)

alternative name was "Stove Bolt Six," from the slotted head bolts similar to those used to hold the pipes on domestic stoves.

The company's advertising slogan for the car was "A Six for the price of a Four," which was somewhat optimistic. It all depended on what four you were looking at. Both the previous Chevrolet and the Ford Model A were somewhat cheaper model for model, but the newly introduced Plymouth Four was between $20 and $100 more expensive. The 1928 Chevrolet Four had been the National series, so the 1929 Six was the International, possibly in reference to its styling, which owed something to Harley Earl's La Salle, which in turn took its inspiration from the French Hispano-Suiza. The 1930 models were called Universal, the 1931s Independence, and the 1932s Confederate, after which the name Master was adopted, lasting until 1942.

The 1931 Independence series had subtly improved styling and an extra 2 inches of wheelbase, making them the best-looking Chevrolets yet, and definitely more expensive-looking than the Model A. Yet expensive they were not; the roadster was $475, less than the fours had ever been, and even the luxurious-looking five-passenger Landau Phaeton was only $650. Prices were lower still in 1932, very close to Ford's, but that was the year in which Ford brought out its V8 engine, giving a considerable performance advantage over Chevrolet. However, it was not enough to give Ford the lead again, and Chevrolet topped a very depressed market, with 306,716 sales to Ford's 232,125. The Depression bottomed out in 1932: sales throughout the industry were less than 25 percent of what they had been in 1929.

From 1928 there was a third challenger in the low-priced field, Walter Chrysler's Plymouth. Its ancestry could be traced back to the Maxwell Four, which was restyled and reissued as the Chrysler 58 in 1926. Two years later, with styling updated to parallel that of the six-cylinder Chryslers, the design was launched under the name Plymouth. This was the name of a popular twine used by farmers. As they were an important market for any low-priced car, Walter Chrysler chose this name, although Chrysler's PR department also made much of the connection with Plymouth Rock and the Pilgrim Fathers. The name was said to "typify

the endurance and strength, the rugged honesty and enterprise, the determination of achievement and the freedom from old limitations of that Pilgrim Band who were the first American colonists." Dealers were dressed up as Pilgrim Fathers, while the car was touted as America's lowest-priced full-size car, implying that the Ford and Chevrolet were mere compacts.

The Plymouth did have several advantages over its rivals, including four-wheel hydraulic brakes, full-pressure engine lubrication, and alloy pistons. Prices were not all that much higher, at $655–$745, and sales to the end of the first model year (February 4, 1929) were an encouraging 66,097.

To meet demand, a new factory was put up on Lynch Road, Detroit, over the winter of 1928/29. Assembly workers were making cars while the building went up around them. Heating was provided by a steam locomotive parked on a spur track nearby, and four crews of building workers were involved, two working outward from the middle and one from each end toward the middle. Completion took only three months. In 1931 Plymouth built 106,259 cars, displacing Buick from third place, a position it retained until the mid-1950s. An important factor in Plymouth's rapid rise was the dealer network, which Walter Chrysler had quickly expanded when he acquired Dodge in 1928. His existing network selling his more expensive Chryslers would not have been adequate for a popularly priced car like the Plymouth. And since mid-1928 he had another marque in his empire, the low-/medium-priced six-cylinder De Soto.

Plymouth went over to a six for 1933, but the original Model PC was unpopular. It looked no larger than the four which it succeeded. Interestingly, Ford did not suffer the same market resistance with its V8, which was externally identical with the four-cylinder Model B, yet easily outsold the four. After Plymouth had given its six an extra 5 inches of wheelbase and a good dollop of restyling, sales improved. The 190-cubic-inch L-head engine was enlarged over the years, but in its basic form it was still available in a Plymouth in 1959, and lasted into the 1960s in Dodge trucks.

Another newcomer, from the beginning of the 1920s, and one that made a significant contribution to growing production figures, was the Essex. This was Hudson's attempt to enter the low-price field to counter the dominance of the large manufacturers (Ford, General Motors, Dodge), which Hudson's secretary-treasurer Roscoe B. Jackson deplored. A separate company, Essex Motors, was set up, and a former Studebaker factory in Detroit was leased for a production start in February 1918. But the growing needs of war production put paid to this and only 92 Essexes were built in the whole year; 1919 was a different story, though, with 21,879 delivered, more than the 18,175 output from the parent Hudson company.

The Essex is said to have been named for the English county and because the name hinted at six cylinders, but in fact it was an F-head four (inlet valves in the cylinder head, exhaust valves at the side). Displacement was 180 cubic inches and output 55bhp, which gave the car sparkling

1925 HUDSON SUPER SIX BROUGHAM ▲▶
HUDSON WAS A LEADING BUILDER OF CLOSED CARS IN THE 1920s, AND THE TWO-DOOR, FOUR-WINDOW COACH WAS A POPULAR STYLE FIRST SEEN IN 1922. STYLING WAS CHANGED IN MIDSEASON 1925, WITH PILLARS BECOMING THINNER AND A CURVE TO THE LOWER EDGE OF THE WINDSHIELD — AS ON THIS FOUR-DOOR BROUGHAM, A NEW STYLE FOR 1925. THE BODY WAS BUILT FOR HUDSON BY BIDDLE & SMART. IT SOLD FOR $1,595, REDUCED TO $1,450 IN OCTOBER.
OWNER: CHRISTOPHER G. FOSTER (PHOTO NICK GEORGANO)

performance. From the start the makers entered various record-breaking attempts, such as a world long-distance endurance record of 3,037 miles in 50 hours at the Cincinnati Speedway. Also in 1919 a stock touring car covered 1,061 miles of snowy Iowa roads in 24 hours. And in 1920 four Essex tourings crossed the continent, two from East to West and two in the opposite direction. The first to arrive in New York took only 4 days, 14 hours 43 minutes.

Body styles of the 1919 Essex were a two-passenger roadster at $1,595, a five-passenger touring at $1,395, and a five-passenger sedan at $2,250. For 1922 Essex caused a sensation by offering a two-door coach sedan, nicknamed "a crackerbox on a raft," at $1,495. By the beginning of the year this had been reduced to $1,345, and a few months later to $1,245, only $200 more than the open touring car. The coach sedan was not a beauty; it used the same two-door, five-passenger body designed for the longer-wheelbase Hudson and this did not transfer very well to the 17-inches-

shorter Essex. Nevertheless its significance was not lost on rivals. Alfred Sloan wrote later that the introduction of the Essex coach was "an event which was to profoundly influence the fortunes of Pontiac, Chevrolet, and the Model T."

By the end of the 1924 season, closed models were accounting for 90 percent of Hudson-Essex production. A year later, when the coach had been redesigned with better proportions, its price of $765 was the same as the open touring and for 1926, $100 less than the open car. A new four-door sedan was the same price as the touring. Rivals such as Chevrolet and Ford were still asking up to $200 more for their closed models, and Essex was in the forefront of the trend which led to nearly 90 percent of cars sold in America in 1929 being closed models. Ten years earlier, little more than 10 percent had been closed.

Essex replaced the F-head four by a smaller L-head six in 1925, which made for smoother running but less performance. No longer would Essexes set

coast-to-coast records or storm up Pikes Peak (as they did again in the 1930s), but the public liked the sixes, and in 1928 bought 229,887 Essexes, a record for the make.

Essex and Hudson closed bodies, important though they were in terms of production, were conventional in construction, with pressed steel panels over a wooden frame. Dodge, on the other hand, brought out the world's first all-steel four-door sedan in 1919, with bodywork by the Budd Manufacturing Company of Philadelphia. Luxuriously equipped with velvet mohair upholstery and wire wheels, it cost $1,900, but by 1927 Dodge had the price down to $895, which was maintained even after the car went over to six cylinders in 1928.

Ford built its first all-steel sedan body in 1923. General Motors was slower to abandon traditional methods, not giving up on the composite body until 1937, despite the much vaunted Turret Top on the 1935 LaSalle, which was simply a one-piece steel roof over a composite frame.

Two other companies that competed in the low-price field in the 1920s were Willys-Overland and Durant. John North Willys entered the postwar era riding high, in second place behind Ford in 1918. However, 1919 saw a disastrous strike which might never have happened had Willys been on the spot at Toledo, but he was away in New York where he had made his home to suit his other interests, which included the National Committee on War Camp Recreation. It seems that the labor unions chose the Willys plant as a test case for their demands on the closed shop, increased pay, and a shorter working week. The plant was big, but not as big as those of the giants of Detroit, and it would have been a foolhardy union leader who challenged Henry Ford. Willys' deputy, Clarence Earl, refused to meet any of the unions' demands or even to negotiate, and when the work force walked out in the spring of 1919 he called in non-union labor. Riots ensued, and an auxiliary police force was called in, with the result that two workers were shot dead and 70 others injured. Toledo's mayor said that the city was powerless to protect the factory, and the State Governor placed the area under martial law. Earl closed the factory, and it did not resume full production until just before Christmas. In the circumstances, it is surprising that the company managed to make as many cars as

it did — 80,853 for the year — but finances were badly damaged. Willys owed $18 million to the banks and $14 million to suppliers.

The Chase National Bank's condition for extending its loan to Willys was that a manager should be brought in, and the man chosen was Walter Chrysler. His price for reorganizing Willys was a free hand to do as he wished and a salary of $1 million a year, a record at the time. One of his first acts was to halve Willys' salary of $150,000, which possibly led Willys to sell his $200,000 Pasadena home to Chrysler in April 1921. Chrysler stayed at Willys-Overland for two years and when he left the company was in much better shape. As well as his record salary, Chrysler took away with him the designs of a new six-cylinder car which was to have been built in Willys' New Jersey plant. He was so confident that he took a full-page advertisement in the January 1921 Show Number of *MoTor* announcing that his new Chrysler Six would be available for delivery in July. However, the plant closed before production could begin, and was acquired by Durant. The deal included Chrysler's prototype, so what would have been a Chrysler Six emerged as the Flint. Chrysler then went to work on a modified version which appeared three years later.

The mainstay of production at Toledo was the Overland Four, intended as competition for the

Model T. But the problems of 1919 meant that the price could not be brought below $945, which was not much competition at all. However, the price came steadily down over the next five years and in 1924 was only $495 for a touring or roadster. Sales soared from 48,016 in 1921 to 215,000 in 1925. In the fall of 1926 came the Overland Four's successor, the Whippet, often listed as a marque in its own right. John Willys was a frequent traveler in Europe and hankered after building a European-type small car. On one of his trips he acquired several French and British examples, and set his chief engineer A. J. Baker to test and disassemble them. He found them underpowered and too narrow for American rural roads, but some of their features found their way into the Whippet, particularly the small-bore/long-stroke cylinder dimensions which suited taxation in some foreign markets such as Britain. The radiator styling was reminiscent of the Fiat 501, and overall lines were a great improvement on the Overland Four. Other improvements included pressure lubrication, pump cooling instead of thermo-syphon, and four-wheel brakes.

With a displacement of only 134 cubic inches, the Whippet had the smallest engine of any American car, yet its 30bhp gave it good performance. The advertised top speed was 55mph, but the car was a good deal faster than that. Unfortunately its nippy ways tempted owners to

1925 STEARNS-KNIGHT MODEL 6-C TOURING ◄▼
THE CLEVELAND-BASED F .B. STEARNS COMPANY WAS THE FIRST IN AMERICA TO TAKE UP THE KNIGHT SLEEVE-VALVE ENGINE, AND USED THIS DESIGN EXCLUSIVELY FROM 1911 TO THE END IN 1929. FOUR- AND SIX-CYLINDER CARS WERE MADE IN 1925, WHEN THIS TOURING SOLD FOR $1,875. IN DECEMBER THAT YEAR JOHN NORTH WILLYS BOUGHT STEARNS, MAKING IT THE MOST EXPENSIVE OF HIS SLEEVE-VALVE RANGE.
OWNER; WOLFGANG H. GAWOR
(PHOTO NICK GEORGANO)

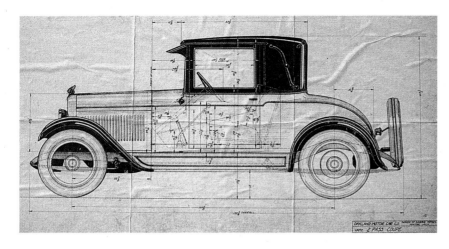

1926 PONTIAC TWO-PASSENGER COUPE ▲▼►

THE PONTIAC WAS CREATED BY GM PRESIDENT ALFRED P. SLOAN UNDER HIS POLICY
"A CAR FOR EVERY PURSE," AND WAS INTENDED TO FILL THE GAP BETWEEN THE
$525 CHEVROLET ROADSTER AND THE $890 OLDSMOBILE. BUILT BY GM'S OAKLAND
DIVISION, THE PONTIAC USED MANY CHEVROLET CHASSIS COMPONENTS, BUT HAD
A NEW SHORT-STROKE SIX-CYLINDER ENGINE. THIS WAS DESIGNED BY HENRY M.
CRANE, WHO HAD MADE THE LUXURY CRANE-SIMPLEX TEN YEARS BEFORE. IN OVERALL CHARGE OF PONTIAC
ENGINEERING WAS BENJAMIN ANIBAL. THE CAR WAS NAMED FOR ITS HOME CITY OF PONTIAC, MICHIGAN, WHICH IN
TURN TOOK ITS NAME FROM AN INDIAN CHIEF, HENCE THE PROMINENCE OF THE CHIEF'S HEAD IN PONTIAC MASCOTS.
THIS COUPE IS THE VERY FIRST PONTIAC BUILT, COMPLETED ON DECEMBER 28, 1925. LIKE THE TWO-DOOR COACH,
WHICH WAS THE ONLY OTHER STYLE FOR 1926, IT WAS PRICED AT $825.

PONTIAC DIVISION, GENERAL MOTORS

abuse it, and the long-stroke engine was not happy with sustained high speeds. The Ford Model A was slower, but it could be driven flat out all day, which the Whippet most definitely could not. At $625 for a two-door coach sedan, it undercut all its competitors apart from Ford, and in 1928 a cabriolet was down to $545, just $5 less than the equivalent Model A.

For 1927 the Whippet Four was joined by a six on a slightly longer wheelbase. In 1928 the Whippets took fourth place in the industry, with 197,910 sales, and they were fourth again in 1929. They were discontinued after 1931, with a total of 545,890 having been made. The four-cylinder engine was continued in the small Willys of the 1930s, and after extensive reworking by Barney Roos, which raised power from 30 to 61bhp, it went into the World War II Jeep.

In January 1921, less than a month after being ousted from General Motors for the second time, Billy Durant formed Durant Motors Inc. with funds of $7 million contributed by 67 individuals who had faith in the man who had built up and twice headed GM. Having supervised the making of countless cars bearing other people's names, Durant at last had one of his own, the Durant Four Model A. It was a conventional car with a 35bhp overhead valve engine made by Continental, and had a 109-inch wheelbase with three body styles — touring, coupe, and sedan — priced from $890 to $1,365. His General Motors experience led him to favor a simultaneous attack on the market in several price brackets, so in 1922 he brought out a smaller, Ford-challenging car called the Star, as well as a six-cylinder Ansted-powered Durant selling for about double the price of the four. He also acquired the prestigious Locomobile to challenge the very top-price cars.

The Star was the most important Durant Motors car in terms of sales, finding about 130,000 buyers in 1923. It was a conventional and simple car, with a 130.4-cubic-engine by Continental, giving a modest 33bhp, and a three-speed transmission separate from the engine, a feature common to all Durant's cars but very unusual at that time in America. The basic price of $348 for a five-passenger touring did not include a self-starter or demountable rims; these became available on the 1923 models, when the price had gone up to $443. A significant model for 1923 was an open-sided station wagon, the first to be offered complete by an American manufacturer. The Star's main plant was at Elizabeth, New Jersey, but it was also made at Lansing, Michigan, Oakland, California, and Toronto in Canada.

The Star was made up to the end of the 1928 season, being offered in six-cylinder form in 1926 and 1927, and more than 1 million were made. In the mid-1920s Durant's companies were taking practically all of Continental's engine output. He then launched two new makes, the Flint and the Princeton. The Flint was designed by the triumvirate responsible for the first Chrysler —

Carl Breer, Owen Skelton, Fred Zeder — and there were many similarities between the two. It had originally been planned as a Willys, but when Willys vacated the Elizabeth, New Jersey, plant, the prototype left behind was revamped as the Flint. Meanwhile the three engineers had left with Walter Chrysler to work on a further improved version which became the Chrysler 70 in 1924. The Flint was a medium-sized six-cylinder car selling in the $1,195–$2,085 bracket, remarkable for its four-wheel hydraulic brakes, also a leading feature of the first Chrysler. A rival to the six-cylinder Buick,

the Flint sold about 24,000 units in five seasons, 1923–1927.

To fill the gap between the Flint and the Locomobile, which sold for upward of $7,600, Durant created a new marque, the Princeton, which he regarded as his Cadillac. Announced in 1923, it was powered by a six-cylinder Ansted engine, had wheelbases of 128 or 132 inches, and was to come in six body styles at prices from $2,485 to $3,675. Several prototypes were made in Durant's Muncie, Indiana, plant, and then it was announced that production would begin in the Locomobile plant at Bridgeport, Connecticut, in 1924. However, the idea got lost somewhere between Muncie and Bridgeport, and the Princeton never went on the market.

The Durant lasted longer than any of the Billy's other makes, but it, too, died in the wake of the Depression, by which time the Flint factory had been sold to General Motors and the Long Island City factory to Ford. In fact Durant had closed more than half his factories before the stock market crash, but even so the company was dealt a deadly blow. Durant put $90 million of his own money into Durant Motors, only to see it all evaporate with the drastic decline in sales for every make of car; 1930 sales were 20,900, and in 1931 only 7,270 Durants found buyers. There were 1932 models, but they were only revamped 1931s and hardly any were sold. The Canadian factory, which sold cars under the name Frontenac, lasted a year longer.

In 1936 Billy Durant filed for personal bankruptcy; his debts were $914,000 and his assets only the clothes he stood up in, which he valued at $250. In his last years he ran a bowling alley and a restaurant. One unpleasant-sounding car dealer used to take customers and salesmen there so that he could show off by ordering a hamburger from the man who founded General Motors. In 1942 a stroke rendered Durant an invalid. His wife Catherine had to sell her jewelry piece by piece, and they were virtually penniless when the 85-year-old Durant died in July 1947. Unlike David Buick or Louis Chevrolet, who also died in poverty, he didn't even have a flourishing make of car to be remembered by.

1924 CHRYSLER MODEL B PHAETON ▼

ENGINEERED BY CARL BREER, OWEN SKELTON, AND FRED ZEDER, THE FIRST CHRYSLER WAS AN UP-TO-DATE CAR WITH SIX-CYLINDER HIGH-COMPRESSION ENGINE (4.7:1 WHEN THE INDUSTRY NORM WAS 4.0:1), ALUMINUM PISTONS, AND VIBRATION DAMPER. ITS 68bhp GAVE IT A TOP SPEED OF 70mph, ONLY 5mph SLOWER THAN THE PACKARD EIGHT. SUCH SPEEDS WERE CURBED BY HYDRAULIC BRAKES ON ALL FOUR WHEELS. THE CHRYSLER 70 WAS INTRODUCED IN JANUARY 1924 IN NINE BODY STYLES, FROM A FOUR-DOOR TOURING AT $1,335 TO A TOWN CAR AT $3,735. THIS PHAETON WAS A BETTER-EQUIPPED VERSION OF THE TOURING, AND COST $1,395.

OWNER: NATIONAL AUTOMOBILE MUSEUM. RENO, NEVADA (PHOTO NICKY WRIGHT)

SURVIVAL OF THE FITTEST

In 1922 nearly 200 domestic makes of car were competing for the attention of the American motorist, as well as a number of imports, mostly in the luxury field. In 1929 the figure was down to 47, and a decade later to 22. The process continued after World War II, although the number of makes has been swelled from time to time by small sports cars and latterly by kit cars and neo-classics. Statistically, however, the numbers of the latter have been unimportant. Significant marques or makes were down to 16 in 1960 and 13 in 1992, although to the latter one must add the U.S. plants of the Japanese Honda, Mazda, Nissan, and Toyota companies.

The 1920s saw by far the greatest mortality, for which there were several reasons. Chief among them was the need for greater capital investment to keep up with technical trends, and this was simply unavailable to smaller firms. Added to this was the reduced unit cost which resulted from mass production, itself only made possible by heavy investment in machinery. One mistaken design could be fatal, as for example, the "drunken Mitchell."

Mitchell Motors Company was a well-respected firm in Racine, Wisconsin, dating from 1903 as car builders, although as wagon makers Mitchell went back to 1834. In the first decade of the century Mitchell was making around 6,000 cars per year, raising this to 10,000 in the years 1917 to 1919. For 1920 Mitchells were restyled by sloping the radiator backward, presumably to give some idea of streamlining. Unfortunately the windshield remained uncompromisingly vertical, and the contrast between the two made the radiator seem to be leaning at a drunken angle, hence the uncomplimentary nickname. Mitchell did some hasty redesigning for the 1921 season, but the damage had been done; lost customers could not be regained by a conventional though not particularly good-looking car, and sales dropped to about 3,500 in 1921 and 1922.

As well as financing the redesign, Mitchell spent a lot of money on publicity stunts, such as a 1-million-mile test put up by 109 cars, but it was all to no avail. Only 100 cars were made in the first few months of 1923 and in May Mitchell filed for bankruptcy, with assets of $3.7 million and debts of

$3.9 million. Among the assets were finished and unfinished automobiles, and raw materials, worth $1.6 million, and the factory. This was sold to Nash and used for the manufacture of the Ajax. Thus passed from the industry a name, wrote *Automobile Topics*, "that was once familiar to everyone, and a concern that in the early days was a real factor in the business." As a well as Mitchell, another 49 makes closed their doors in 1923, including some that had hardly started, such as the Ace, Detroit Steamer, Rotary, and Strattan, and more or less well-known names like Biddle, Chalmers and Dorris. In 1924 a further 36 makes disappeared, including the long-established Crow-Elkhart, Paterson, Premier, and Winton.

Technical progress spelled the downfall of a number of the smaller firms. Most could cope with self-starters and electric lighting, because these were bought from outside suppliers and did not necessitate a redesign of the car. Both were practically universal by 1920. Front-wheel brakes were another matter; their first appearance on an

American car was on the high-priced Duesenberg straight-8 of 1920, and in 1923/4 there was a surge in their popularity, so that no self-respecting manufacturer in anything but the lowest price bracket could afford to be without them. But they were not cheap, for tires, steering, front axles, springs, and shock absorbers all had to be redesigned. Among those whose end was hastened by the incorporation of four-wheel brakes were Premier from Indianapolis and the two formerly joined Kokomo makes, Apperson and Haynes. All three were out of business by 1926, as were other respected makes with production of several thousand cars a year, such as Cole, Dort, King, and Stephens.

Some manufacturers who were prominent in other fields decided to abandon the automobile market when the going got too tough. One was the J.I. Case Company, which had been famous for agricultural equipment since 1842 and which introduced a medium-sized car in 1910. Sales began to fall after 1923, for the Continental-powered Case

1920 ROAMER ROADSTER ◄ ▲
THE ROAMER WAS A GOOD-LOOKING ASSEMBLED CAR FROM KALAMAZOO, MICHIGAN, WHICH SOLD QUITE WELL IN THE EARLY 1920s, THEN GRADUALLY DECLINED UNTIL ITS DEMISE IN 1929. MOST ROAMERS HAD SIX-CYLINDER CONTINENTAL ENGINES, BUT COULD BE HAD WITH THE MORE POWERFUL 80bhp ROCHESTER-DUESENBERG FOUR. THIS MODEL D-4-75 ROADSTER COST $4,375, WHICH WAS $1,000 MORE THAN THE SAME CAR WITH THE 54bhp CONTINENTAL SIX. ROAMER WAS ROCHESTER'S BEST CUSTOMER, TAKING BETWEEN 800 AND 1,000 ENGINES FROM THE FALL OF 1917 TO 1925, POSSIBLY A YEAR OR TWO LATER. THE ROAMER RADIATOR WAS AN UNASHAMED COPY OF THE ROLLS-ROYCE, BUT NEITHER THE BRITISH FIRM NOR ITS SPRINGFIELD, MASSACHUSETTS, BRANCH TOOK ANY ACTION.

OWNER: GILMORE CAR MUSEUM, KALAMAZOO, MICHIGAN (PHOTO NICKY WRIGHT)

six was not sufficiently different from many rivals and was more expensive than the Buick. It was becoming a drag on the balance sheet and Case could only have reduced the price by increasing production at the expense of its traditional products such as tractors, so after 1927 the Case car was no more.

Another factor which killed off some of the smaller firms was the improved distribution of the larger ones. The South's most prominent make was the Anderson from Rock Hill, South Carolina, made from 1916 to 1925 with the slogan "A Little Higher in Price, BUT Made in Dixie," which appealed to local pride. It was a pretty good car, although like many it used a number of bought out components, particularly its Continental engine. Anderson did sell outside its own territory, but most customers were fairly local. Once makes like Buick and Oldsmobile set up dealerships in Rock Hill and many other Southern towns the competition became too great, and Anderson closed down. The few other Southern makes, such as Hanson from Atlanta, Georgia, and the Climber from Little Rock, Arkansas, never tried to sell north of the Mason-Dixon line.

Improved communications meant that cars could be delivered from the manufacturing centers to all parts of the country, usually by railroad, although if the distances were not too great they could be driven. Haulaway trucks came into use from the early 1930s. In areas really remote from Detroit, such as the West Coast, assembly plants were set up by Ford, General Motors, and Durant. This was another blow to local manufacturers. Over the years automobiles have been built in all 49 mainland states, but many had disappeared before 1920. Probably the peak at any one time was reached in 1909, when 290 different makes were being built in 145 cities in 24 states. By 1923, 23 states were still home to 164 auto makes (excluding assembly plants), but by 1929 the figure was down to 9 states and 47 makes.

ROADSTERS AND SPEEDSTERS

Another factor which led to reduced variety among American cars was a growing conformity, a reluctance to step out of line and appear eccentric. After 1929 this was coupled with a reluctance to flaunt one's wealth, even if one still had it. A victim of these trends was the speedster, a type of car which had its origins before World War I.

The first speedsters, otherwise called roadsters, runabouts, or raceabouts, were made on stock chassis using unmodified engines with light two- or three-passenger bodies. It was a simple matter for a dealer to put a light body on a stock touring chassis and enter it in local hill climbs and races to boost sales. If the car was successful, the makers would be told and, if it made economic sense, a roadster would find its way into the next year's catalog. Although Maxwell was not thought of as a sporting make, a few 22hp roadsters were built by branch dealers to compete in 1909 events; as they did well, a two-passenger Sportsman roadster was listed for 1910. Finished in pearl gray, it had a large exterior gas tank and spare tires behind, while the seats were tilted to give a rakish look. Sportsman models won their class at two important hill climbs in 1910: Giant's Despair at Wilkes Barre, Pennsylvania, and Sunset at Ossining, New York.

Numerous other makers listed sporting models in the years 1910–1914, including Apperson, Kissel, Marion, National, Overland, Peerless, and Thomas. Better known than any of these were the Mercer Raceabout and Stutz Bearcat. The Mercer Type 35 appeared in 1910, with a Beaver T-head four of 299 cubic inches. Initial models were a touring, toy tonneau, and speedster, the last a not particularly sporting car. The immortal Raceabout came for the 1911 model year and was the idea of Washington A. Roebling II, son of Mercer's founder C.G. Roebling. It was engineered by Finlay Robertson Porter, who later made his own cars under the names F.R.P. and Porter. The engine was not large, but thanks to high gearing and low weight a top speed of 75mph was possible. The body was classically simple; two bucket seats with a bolster gas tank behind them, and behind that a small tool box and two spare tires. There were neither doors or windshield, the latter being replaced by a circular monocle attached to the steering column. It cannot have been much use as weather protection, but drivers normally wore goggles anyway.

Compared with its rivals, the Mercer Raceabout had a rather delicate appearance, which was complemented by fine handling. "The Mercer is the Steinway of the automobile world," ran a 1914 advertisement. "It is possible to thread a needle while traveling 60mph." Its great rival, the Stutz Bearcat, was an altogether more rugged and heavier vehicle, although its 390-cubic-inch engine gave about the same power, 60bhp. Harry C. Stutz entered the first car he built in the 1911 Indianapolis 500, finishing eleventh out of 40 starters. From this he coined the slogan "The Car that Made Good in a Day," which might seem a bit of hype, but the Stutz did have the smallest engine in the race, and had it not been hampered by many tire changes would undoubtedly have finished higher.

Several weeks after the race, Stutz formed the Ideal Car Company to make replicas of the race car. These were characterized by a three-speed transmission in the rear axle. Touring, coupe, and roadster models were offered, and the most sporting was called the Bearcat. The name may have been chosen in response to Marion's Bobcat, a similar type of roadster. The Stutz Bearcat sold for $2,000, some $500 less than the Mercer, and even with the optional six-cylinder engine the price was only $2,125. The roadster with doors was continued, but it was the stark, doorless Bearcat that grabbed all the attention and triggered off

intense rivalry with Mercer owners. "There's no car worser than a Mercer," they chorused, which brought forth the response "You have to be nuts to drive a Stutz." There really wasn't much to choose between the cars, which achieved countless amateur successes in hill climbs and races, although the Mercer was more fragile. Some social snobbery may have been involved; the Mercer was an East Coast make from Trenton, New Jersey, backed by blue-blooded families like the Roeblings, while Harry Stutz was a Middle Western farm boy turned mechanic.

The T-head Mercer Raceabout did not last long. In 1912 Washington Roebling II lost his life in the *Titanic* disaster, and Finlay Robertson Porter left Mercer two years later. His place was taken by Erik Delling, who designed a new line called the 22–70. This had an L-head four engine. A roadster was still in the range, but it had a proper windshield, bench seat, and enclosed coachwork with doors. Although quite popular, these "softer" Mercer raceabouts lacked the charisma of the original. For 1923 they acquired a six-cylinder valve-in-head engine by Rochester, but production ended in 1925, when Mercer went out of business. The Stutz Bearcat was also made into the early 1920s, and then the name was revived in 1932 for a very small series of short-wheelbase versions of

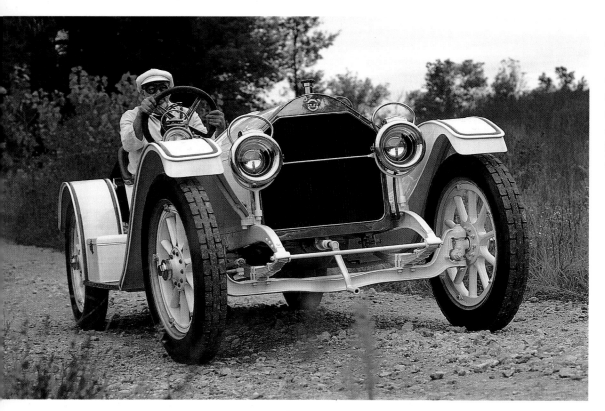

1912 STUTZ BEARCAT ◄▼

THE FAMOUS BEARCAT SPEEDSTER WAS PART OF THE STUTZ RANGE FROM THE FIRM'S FIRST PRODUCTION YEAR, AND WAS AVAILABLE WITH FOUR- AND SIX-CYLINDER ENGINES. THEY WERE NO MORE EXPENSIVE THAN TOURING STUTZES. IN 1912 STUTZ ENTERED 30 RACES AND WON 25 OF THEM. BEARCATS WERE HEAVY TO HANDLE. HOWEVER, THE STORY THAT HARRY STUTZ MADE THE CLUTCH SPRINGS SO STIFF THAT A WOMAN COULD NOT OPERATE THEM IS PROBABLY APOCRYPHAL.

OWNER: AUBURN-CORD-DUESENBERG MUSEUM (PHOTO NICKY WRIGHT)

the DV-32 Dual Valve straight-8.

Stutz and Mercer had a number of rivals in the 1920s, for there was quite a fashion for speedsters, from makes such as Biddle, Jordan, Kissel, Marmon, and Paige, as well as the lesser-known Argonne, Noma, Richelieu, and ReVere. The Biddle was an assembled car, but a high-quality one of handsome appearance thanks to its Mercedes-type pointed radiator and high-grade coachwork. Among a variety of listed bodies was a rakish roadster styled by a young Maryland girl, Miriam Warren Hubbard. Tired of Mercers and Stutzes which, she said, were always going wrong, she took Biddle up on its offer to build a car for anyone, and designed a roadster with Vee-shaped headlight glass to match the radiator, separate fenders and running boards, and no top.

Miriam's roadster was subsequently repeated for several clients. Biddles were offered with either Buda or Rochester-Duesenberg engines, the former giving 48bhp, the latter up to 100bhp in race tune. One would imagine that the roadsters would have had the more powerful engine, but one cannot be sure. Like other roadsters, Biddles were not performance automobiles; their function was to look

1920 MERCER SERIES 5 ▼►

THE MERCER 35J RACEABOUT GAVE WAY TO ERIK DELLING'S 22-70 DESIGN IN 1915. THIS SERIES 5 OF 1920 WAS A DESCENDANT, WITH DOORS AND A WINDSHIELD IN PLACE OF THE 35's MONOCLE. IT WAS 17 INCHES SHORTER THAN THE TOURING MERCERS, ON A 115-INCH WHEELBASE, AND COST $4,200.

OWNER: CRAWFORD COLLECTION OF THE WESTERN HISTORICAL SOCIETY

(PHOTO NICKY WRIGHT)

stylish and sporty, to complement their owners whose sports might be golf, polo, or deepsea fishing.

The Biddle was expensive, up to $3,750 for an Ormond two-passenger roadster in 1921, but more modestly priced and better known roadsters were made by Jordan and Kissel. Ned Jordan has become more famous for his advertisements than his cars, with the immortal "Somewhere West of Laramie," "A Golden Girl from Somewhere," "A Million Miles from Dull Care," and "I Think She Came from a Land of Fire." All these featured the Jordan Playboy, a typical roadster with a rumble seat, powered by a six-cylinder Continental engine, which was launched in 1919, three years after the first Jordan appeared. Claimed top speed was 65mph, although the British magazine *The Autocar* could not get more than 50.7mph (they must have had an off-tune model). Its price was $2,550.

The Playboy (named from J.M. Synge's *Playboy of the Western World*) was not a particularly distinguished car, and was only one of a wide range of Jordan styles, yet it is the model with which the make is always associated, even more so than Bearcat is with Stutz. Advertising must have made a big difference: "Some day in June, when happy hours abound, a wonderful girl and a wonderful boy will leave their friends in a shower of rice, and start to roam....Give them a Jordan Playboy, the blue sky overhead and the green turf flying by, and a thousand miles of open road." Only Ned Jordan wrote copy like that.

Jordan got the Playboy's price down to $1,750 in 1924, and the following year the name went onto an eight-cylinder roadster, also Continental-powered. By now it was less sporty-looking, no different from many other two-passenger open cars with rumble seats.

Kissel's speedster was called the Gold Bug and

was developed from a line of custom bodies on Kissel chassis designed and sold by New York distributor Conover T. Silver (who also built bodies on Apperson and Willys chassis). Launched in 1919, the Gold Bug had a doorless two-passenger body with an auxiliary seat which could be pulled out, with its accompanying foot rest, like a drawer from the side of the body. One would have been pretty daring to occupy this seat at any speed, but this was all part of the speedster's devil-may-care image. Historian Keith Marvin thinks that these seats were soon curtailed legally because of the horrific possibilities of a side-swipe accident. The 1922 Paige Daytona 6–66 roadster also featured such a seat, and had a 66bhp Continental six engine

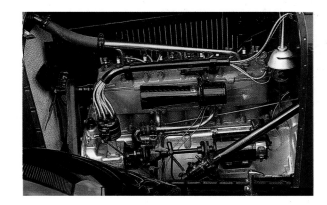

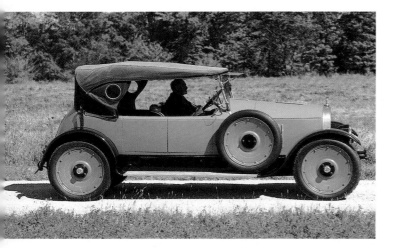

giving an 80mph top speed. For 1923 the Paige was better equipped, with two side-mounted spare wheels, front and rear bumpers, a power-operated windshield wiper, and an eight-day clock, cigar lighter, and rear-view mirror. All this for only $2,400, or $1,000 less than in 1922. The price was probably too low, for the Daytona was withdrawn after only 56 had been made in two seasons.

After the middle of the 1920s speedsters had mostly disappeared or become tamer, but the end of the decade saw a final flowering of the breed. The most striking was the Auburn, product of an Indiana firm which had been on the point of extinction in 1924 when Errett Lobban Cord joined the company. A whiz kid several decades before the phrase was coined, Cord had, by his own confession, made and lost three fortunes before he was 21. He had been a highly successful salesman for Moon cars in Chicago when he came to Auburn as general manager. He added some nickel plating and gave new paint jobs to the countless unsold Auburns he found there, and before the end of the year most of them had found customers.

In 1925 he hired a new designer, J.M. Crawford, ordered a consignment of Lycoming straight-8 engines, and launched a new line of Auburns as the 8–53 and 8–88. With stylish bodies and two-tone color schemes, the new Auburns sold very well. Cord sent his cars record-breaking, and in 1928 launched an A1 Leamy-designed speedster with Vee-windshield, pointed tail body, and an engine that gave 115bhp thanks to alloy pistons and connecting rods, larger valves, and a high-lift camshaft. All Auburns that year had hydraulic

brakes. A V12 joined the Auburn range for 1932. There was also a speedster which sold for the low price of $1,145 (the cheapest V-12 was the coupe at $975, the only twelve-cylinder car to sell for under $1,000). The Depression was not the best time to market exotic cars like the Auburn speedsters, and sales dropped alarmingly after 1931. Auburn ceased to make cars after 1936, but not before creating a final speedster, the low-slung supercharged 851 of 1935 styled by Gordon Buehrig. The Schwitzer-Cummins supercharger boosted the output of the

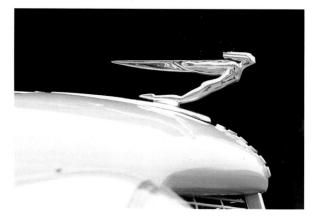

1936 AUBURN 654 SEDAN AND 852 PHAETON ▲▶▼

TWO LATE MODEL AUBURNS, A SIX-CYLINDER SEDAN AND EIGHT-CYLINDER PHAETON. LIKE THE V12S, BOTH
WERE AVAILABLE WITH STANDARD TRANSMISSION OR WITH CUSTOM DUAL RATIO REAR AXLE. THE EIGHTS
COULD BE HAD IN SUPER CHARGED FORM, LIKE THIS PHAETON. THESE MODELS WERE USED BY THE INDIANA
STATE POLICE, EARNING GOOD PUBLICITY FOR A LOCAL MAKE. HOWEVER, 1936 WAS AUBURN'S LAST YEAR,
WITH ONLY 1,848 CARS OF ALL TYPES DELIVERED.

OWNER: AUBURN-CORD-DUESENBERG MUSEUM (PHOTO NICKY WRIGHT)

274-cubic-inch Lycoming straight-8 from 115 to 150bhp, and all cars sold bore a plaque to certify that they had exceeded 100mph. About 500 were sold, at $2,245. Auburn lost money on each one, but they were intended as bait to lure customers into the showrooms to buy the regular six- and eight-cylinder sedans. Sales rose by 20 percent between 1934 and 1935, but this was not enough to save the Auburn, which went down with the other marques of Cord's empire, the Cord and the Duesenberg.

There were other short-lived speedsters at the end of the 1920s, including the straight-8 twin-camshaft Stutz Black Hawk, the Packard Model 734 with 384-cubic-inch engine, also a straight-8, and the duPont Model G. This was the speedster version of a wide range of duPonts, all powered by Continental straight-8 engines, and was very expensive at $5,335.

HIGH NOON OF THE LUXURY CAR

The 1920s were the peak years for cars at the top of the price scale, and for the fortunate few with upward of $5,000 to spend on an automobile, there was a wide choice. The more conservative East Coast rich tended to favor traditional makes such as Locomobile, Pierce-Arrow, Cunningham, and Rolls-Royce (made in Springfield, Massachusetts, from 1921), while the more flamboyant oil-rich and Hollywood families chose exotica like the Daniels, McFarlan, and the Doble Steamer, and at the end of the decade the Model J Duesenberg. Imported luxury cars were also seen in growing numbers, from Minerva, Hispano-Suiza, Isotta-Fraschini, Mercedes-Benz, and Renault. This era was also the great heyday of the American custom coachbuilder.

Many of the buyers of luxury cars, whether they were Wall Street bankers or Boston dowagers, were more interested in comfort and exclusiveness than in the latest technical innovations, which accounts for the conservatism of some of their cars. Locomobile, in particular, continued the monster T-head Model 48 through 1929 with little change to the specification, apart from a gradual updating of body styling. In December 1923 front-wheel brakes were announced as an option, at an extra cost of $350 on new cars and at $450 on cars which the owner returned to the factory. This was perhaps not exorbitant when compared with an overall price of up to $13,000, but for the same money the owner's cook could buy a Model T and have enough change for a year's gasoline.

In 1923 production of the Model 48 was only two chassis per day, and by 1929 probably not more than one per week. Prices were $9,600–$12,500 in this its last year. Locomobile was bought by Billy Durant in 1922, and four years later he brought out another luxury model, as well as cheaper sixes and eights. The new luxury car was called the Model 90 and had an

L-head monobloc six engine only a little smaller than the 525-cubic-inch 48. Wheelbase was 4 inches shorter at 138 inches, and prices were considerably lower, at $5,500–$7,500.

Pierce-Arrow entered the 1920s with designs similar to the Locomobile, big, slow-turning T-head sixes of 414 and 524 cubic inches, called the 38 and 48 respectively. They were among the last American cars to go over to left-hand drive with centrally mounted gearshift and parking brake. This move was resisted by P-A's chief engineer David Fergusson, who had tried a left-hand drive conversion back in 1911, when most other manufacturers were making the change. It has been said that Pierce-Arrow preferred right-hand drive as the chauffeur could leap onto the sidewalk and open the door for the passengers. However, this was probably a useful side effect of conservatism rather than the cause of it. In 1911 Fergusson's impressions of the left-hand drive car were not

favorable, and the change was not made until 1921, the year that Fergusson retired from Pierce-Arrow.

Other top grade manufacturers who stuck to six cylinders included Stevens-Duryea, Winton, and Rolls-Royce. The first made old-fashioned designs with pair-cast cylinders at prices up to $10,000. These sold to the same clientele as the

Locomobile, although in smaller numbers. Winton continued their sixes up to 1924. Rolls-Royce had been represented in the United States since 1906. A prominent early customer was Mrs. John Jacob Astor, so much the leader of New York society that if she grew tired of a performance at the Metropolitan Opera and left during the intermission everyone else left too and the cast sang to an empty house. She was not so slavishly followed in the matter of automobiles, however, and Rolls-Royce's New York dealer failed to meet his promise to order 50 cars in 1908. Little more was heard of Rolls-Royce in America until after World War I.

In 1919 Rolls-Royce's director Claude Johnson decided that the United States was potentially the firm's best market (he was worried about socialist legislation in Britain), but that import duties would make the price too high. Manufacture in the United States was the answer, so a factory was acquired at

1933 AUBURN 8-105 ▲ ▶
BOAT-TAIL SPEEDSTER
THE BOAT-TAIL SPEEDSTER WAS
THE MOST STRIKING STYLE
IN THE AUBURN LINE, FROM ITS
INTRODUCTION IN 1928
TO THE FINAL 852 OF 1936.
IN 1933 THE DESIGN WAS
AVAILABLE ON BOTH EIGHT-
AND TWELVE-CYLINDER
MODELS, WHICH COULD BE
HAD WITH THE COLUMBIA
DUAL RATIO AXLE.
THIS 8-105 COST $1,345.
OWNER: DUKE DAVENPORT
(PHOTO NICKY WRIGHT)

Springfield, Massachusetts, which began to turn out Silver Ghosts at first identical to the British ones. Like them, they were supplied in chassis form only, although Rolls-Royce-designed bodies were made for them by prestigious coachbuilders, including Merrimac of Merrimac, Massachusetts, Biddle & Smart of Amesbury, Massachusetts, and Willoughby of Utica, New York.

In 1923 Rolls-Royce of America set up its own bodywork department at Springfield and no longer farmed the work out, although there were always special requests for custom bodies. Even the regular coachwork made the Springfield Silver Ghost more expensive than any other American-built car. In November 1924 prices ranged from $12,930 for a Pall Mall five-passenger touring to $15,880 for a Mayfair full cabriolet. Custom work by such firms as Brewster, Brunn, Derham, or Locke could cost several thousand dollars more, while the ultimate was probably reached by the town car built by Waterhouse for Harry Orndorff of Providence, Rhode Island.

The Phantom I delivered to Mr. Orndorff in 1926 was only the fifth of this model to be made at Springfield. After five years of use, its owner returned it to the works asking for the chassis to be lengthened from 146½ to 160 inches to accommodate the body he had in mind. This was built by Waterhouse, a lesser-known coachbuilder formed to make bodies for duPont. The floor was decorated with oriental rugs, and the seats were duplicates of the owner's favorite armchairs, with winter and summer covers. Like many cars of the period, the Phantom had two spare wheels mounted on the running board; the one on the right-hand side contained not a wheel but a two-octave chime which Mr. Orndorff could operate by a keyboard located ahead of the front passenger seat. The total cost of this Phantom was in excess of $30,000. Unfortunately the additional weight on one side caused springing problems, and the car had to be returned to Springfield several times before an ideal ride was obtained.

The 1925 season prices quoted above were a considerable increase on those of the previous year, mainly because Rolls-Royce went over to left-hand drive that year, necessitating a redesign not only of the axle and steering controls but also of the exhaust manifold. A number of right-hand drive

1929 ROLLS-ROYCE PHANTOM 1 ASCOT PHAETON ▲
THE ASCOT WAS ONE OF SEVERAL BODY STYLES MADE FOR ROLLS-ROYCE OF AMERICA BY BREWSTER. THEY ALL TENDED TO HAVE VERY ENGLISH NAMES SUCH AS ASCOT, DERBY, PICCADILLY, PALL MALL, AND NEWMARKET, ALTHOUGH A FRENCH TOUCH WAS GIVEN BY THE TROUVILLE TOWN CAR. PRICES WERE VERY HIGH; THE ASCOT COST $17,250, AND A HIBBERD & DARRIN CONVERTIBLE SEDAN SET THE CUSTOMER BACK $19,665. A TOTAL OF 25 ASCOTS WERE MADE, ALL ON THE 144¾-INCH WHEELBASE.
OWNER: GILMORE CAR MUSEUM, KALAMAZOO, MICHIGAN (PHOTO NICKY WRIGHT)

cars were traded in for the new models and proved difficult to resell, since the less well-off who might have bought a used Rolls-Royce were unlikely to have chauffeurs and were therefore less happy with right-hand drive. Rolls-Royce Inc. was able to move some of the remaining right-hand drive stock by selling them in Argentina and Uruguay, both of which still favored driving on the left.

Prices went up again when the Phantom I was introduced late in 1926. Although not a very different car apart from the larger engine with overhead valves, expensive retooling was needed, so Phantom prices ran from $17,840 for a Derby four-passenger touring to $19,965 for a Trouville

town car. Sales dropped from the 325–365 per year which the Silver Ghost had enjoyed between 1923 and 1926 to 275 in 1928 and 251 in 1929. The Phantom II introduced in 1929 would have cost even more in retooling, at which point Rolls-Royce of America gave up its manufacturing rights. The Phantom I was assembled for six more years, from parts on hand, and 116 Phantom II chassis were imported from England. They were equipped with left-hand steering and most carried bodies by Brewster, which had become a Rolls-Royce subsidiary in 1926.

Customers for the American Rolls-Royce ranged right across the social spectrum and the continent,

from prominent East Coast families such as the Carnegies, Guggenheims, Rockefellers, and Vanderbilts to many Hollywood personalities, including Jackie Coogan, Pola Negri, Gloria Swanson, Tom Mix, Al Jolson, Clara Bow, Zeppo Marx, and Daryl Zanuck. The celebrated New York hostess Mrs. E.T. Stotesbury had several. It was at her Pennsylvania mansion, Whitemarsh Hall, that

Henry Ford murmured to his wife in the entrance hall: "It's instructive to see how the rich live."

Ex-president Woodrow Wilson had a Silver Ghost Oxford seven-passenger touring in 1923, although the official White House cars remained Pierce-Arrows into the 1930s. Among foreign rulers, owners of American Rolls-Royces included General Morales of Cuba (1926 Oxford touring) and

Poland's Marshal Pitsudski, who had a 1931 Phantom II with a 28-gallon gas tank and two horns, "very loud" and "loudest possible."

Other lesser known luxury cars which vied with the aforementioned included the McFarlan, Phianna, and Porter. The McFarlan from Connersville, Indiana, had the largest engine in any production American car of the 1920s. This was a

AUBURN'S V12 WAS CONSIDERABLY LOWER IN PRICE
THAN ANY OTHER TWELVE-CYLINDERED CAR, AND
THE COMPANY MANAGED TO GET ONE MODEL,
THE 1932 STANDARD COUPE, BELOW THE $1,000 MARK
AT $975. THIS TWO-DOOR SEDAN WAS KNOWN
AS THE BROUGHAM. THE "A" IN THE DESIGNATION
INDICATES THE HIGHER-PRICED CUSTOM RANGE,
WHICH INCLUDED THE DUAL-RATIO REAR AXLE
GIVING SIX FORWARD SPEEDS.

OWNERS: GARY AND SHARON VICK (PHOTO NICKY WRIGHT)

572-cubic-inch T-head six made under license from Teetor-Hartley, who had designed it for use in Maxim fire engines. In fact, the Maxim company of Middleboro, Massachusetts, acted as New England distributors for McFarlan automobiles. The engine was called the TV for Twin Valve (four valves per cylinder), a design that became common for high-performance engines in the 1980s. It developed 120bhp, a record for American engines in 1920.

The TV was a massive car standing more than 6 feet high in sedan form, and on a wheelbase of 140 inches. Up to 1925 Disteel disk wheels were usually featured, although wood-spoked or wire were available and were more common in the later 1920s. In 1921, 11 body styles were available, from a two-passenger roadster at $6,300 to the Knickerbocker cabriolet at $9,000. This spectacular vehicle was a town car with an open front for the chauffeur and a folding roof at the rear. For 1923 it became even more distinctive, with small fenders hugging the front wheels, no running board, but a smaller step plate for the driver and a slightly larger one for the rear-seat passengers. Carriage-type side lamps were mounted just ahead of the rear doors, and there were dummy landau irons behind the windows. Since they were dummies the car was no longer properly a cabriolet and for 1924 it was renamed the town car. The well-known antique car collector Cameron Peck offered one for sale in 1949, describing it as "like nothing so much as a Moorish castle on wheels" and "the largest possible motor car in the worst possible taste." He was asking only $500, including delivery to railroad, but this was not so much a reflection of his opinions of the car as of the generally low prices of old cars at that time.

McFarlan made its own bodies, and few of the

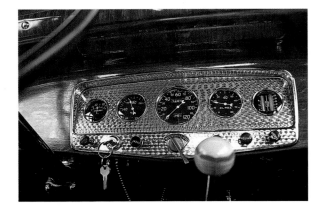

custom firms built on the TV chassis. The 1922 New York Salon did reveal a Brooks-Ostruk town car priced at $11,650, but the most remarkable body of all was exhibited by McFarlan at the 1923 Chicago Show. This had a Knickerbocker cabriolet body, but the radiator shell (one of the largest in the business), hubs, rims, door handles, and other exterior metal work, even the bumpers and canisters for the Gruss air springs, were all gold-plated. It was apparently built as a speculative venture, not specially ordered, and carried a price tag of $25,000. Unsold for six months, it was eventually bought by a lady from an oil-rich

Oklahoma family, although whether she paid the full price is not known. Other well-known McFarlan owners included heavyweight boxing champion Jack Dempsey and bandleader Paul Whiteman, who toured England in his TV and found it was too large for many small roads. Movie star Dorothy Dalton was photographed in a McFarlan, but whether she owned it or just posed for the picture we do not know. McFarlan built a smaller single-valve six from 1924 and a Lycoming-powered straight-8 from 1926, but these were cheaper and less glamorous than the mighty TV. All production ended in 1928.

The Phianna and Porter were unusual among expensive cars in having four-cylinder engines. The former began life in Newark, New Jersey, in 1917, descended from the S.G.V. and named for the daughters of one of the promoters, Phyllis and Anna. Few were made under the original ownership, but in 1919 the car was relaunched by a young enthusiast, Miles Harold Carpenter, who set up a new factory at Long Island City. He retained the four-cylinder engine with an interesting modification in the form of a laminated walnut and ash fan, the work of airplane propeller designer Fred Charavey. The wheelbase was lengthened by

1932 WILLYS-OVERLAND 6-90 ROADSTER ▲
WILLYS BUILT FOUR SERIES IN 1932, ON TWO WHEELBASES. TWO USED POPPET-VALVE ENGINES IN SIX- AND EIGHT-CYLINDER MODELS, AND TWO HAD SIX-CYLINDER KNIGHT SLEEVE-VALVE ENGINES. THIS IS A 6-90 POPPET-VALVE SIX ROADSTER WHICH SOLD FOR A MODEST $515. THERE WAS NO KNIGHT-ENGINED ROADSTER, BUT IN STYLES WHERE BOTH ENGINES WERE USED, SUCH AS SEDANS AND COUPES, THE SLEEVE-VALVE MODELS COST OVER $300 MORE. OF 26,710 CARS SOLD BY WILLYS IN 1932, ONLY 3,265 WERE WILLYS-KNIGHTS.

OWNER; GEORGE SANDERS (PHOTO NICKY WRIGHT)

10 inches to 125 inches, and custom-built coachwork was available at prices from $6,000 for a standard brougham to $11,500 for a limousine. These prices were way up in Locomobile country, and most buyers expected at least six cylinders for this kind of money.

Few Phiannas were made, probably not more than 300, although customers included R.B. Horne, president of Canadian Pacific, the president of Brazil, and Bainbridge Colby, secretary of state in President Wilson's government. When four meat tycoons, Messrs. Armour, Benjamin, Curahy, and

Swift, were discussing cars, it turned out that all of them were Phianna owners. Carpenter remembered delivering one Phianna to a splendid mansion at Irvington-on-the-Hudson where a party was in progress, and being surprised to find that the customer and all her guests were blacks. In a gathering of some 80 people, he was the only white man present. He was happy to do business with a black client, in contrast to the members of the Imported Car Association, who had an unwritten agreement that they would not sell their cars to black people.

The Porter had some similarities with the Phianna in that it was also a high-priced four-cylinder luxury car that had evolved out of a previous make, in this case the F.R.P. But if Miles Carpenter was an unknown, not so the Porter's designer, Finlay Robertson Porter, the man responsible for the famous Mercer Type 35. The Porter had a large four-cylinder engine made by the American & British Mfg Corporation of Bridgeport, Connecticut, which developed 120–125bhp, possibly putting it ahead of the McFarlan. The finest custom bodies by such firms as Brewster, Demarest, and Fleetwood were mounted on a whopping 142-inch wheelbase, and prices were in excess of $10,000. Only 36 were sold, between 1919 and 1922.

While the traditional luxury car makers stuck to six cylinders, there was a considerable vogue for eights, not only the V8s that had been popular since Cadillac launched the fashion in 1914, but also for in-line or straight-8s. Of the V8 adherents, Cadillac remained faithful throughout the 1920s, and indeed up to the present day, supplementing them with V12s and V16s in the 1930s. Peerless adopted a V8 for 1916 and through 1928, going over to a straight-8 and a cheaper six for its last few years. Other firms favoring the V8 included the luxury car makers Cunningham and Daniels, who made their own, the mid-priced Apperson and King, which also featured home-built engines, and Cole, which bought from Northway. Most of these firms went out of business by the middle of the decade, although Cunningham carried on in a small way, eventually concentrating on hearses, which had been a mainstay of production for the company from the beginning. Cunningham's final fling was a Ford V8-powered town car in the mid-1930s.

An important newcomer to the luxury car market was the Lincoln, made initially by Henry M. Leland and his son Wilfred, who walked out of Cadillac in 1917 after harsh words with Billy Durant. With America's entry into World War I threatening, the first products of the new Lincoln Motor Company were Liberty airplane engines, of which 6,500 were made. Once the war was over they had to find some way of keeping their large plant and 6,000 payroll occupied. With their background, it was hardly surprising that they turned again to automobiles.

Announced in September 1920, the Lincoln V8 was not unlike the Cadillac, except that the angle between the cylinder banks was 60° rather than the more usual 90°. This gave an uneven firing sequence alternating between 60° and 120° of crankshaft revolution. Leland's aim was to damp out the harmonic vibration periods which troubled earlier V8 engines. Both engines had side valves in an L-head. Displacement and output were 358 cubic inches and 81bhp, compared with the Cadillac's 314 cubic inches and 60bhp. This gave a good performance, a top speed of 80mph with a touring body. Prices ran from $4,300 to $6,600 for standard bodies built by the American Body Company of Buffalo, or the Anderson Electric Car Company, which had made Detroit Electric cars until the latter were hived off to a subsidiary. Custom bodies by Brunn or Judkins were considerably more expensive. Cadillac prices ran from $3,740 to $5,690 at this time.

The name of Leland carried so much weight that $6.5 million of stock was subscribed in one day and over 1,000 orders were received before the first Lincoln rolled from the plant. Unfortunately a number of these were canceled when buyers saw the cars; the engineering and performance were acceptable, but the body styling seemed uninspired, even old-fashioned. Today Lincolns do not seem too bad when compared with other 1920 cars, but the public had been led to expect something exceptional from a new make with the Leland reputation. Added to this, there was a recession at the end of 1920, which resulted in a disappointing first year for Lincoln, with 3,407 cars sold to the end of 1921 instead of an anticipated total of 6,000.

A heavy tax bill forced Lincoln into receivership in November 1921 and in February 1922 the company was put up for sale. The only bid came from Henry Ford, with an offer of $8 million, which was accepted. Clara Ford was a friend of Wilfred Leland's wife, and she said, in one of her very few public statements: "If Detroit will stand by and see the Lelands and their men who put money into that concern lose everything they've got and not lift a hand to help them, there's something wrong with our public spirit." Edsel Ford added his bit: "It would be a shame, a blot on the good name of the whole community, if Detroit

1937 LASALLE SEDAN ▲ ◄
ALTHOUGH NOT VERY DIFFERENT IN APPEARANCE FROM THE 1936 CARS, THE 1937 LASALLES WERE NOW MORE LIKE JUNIOR CADILLACS THAN THEY HAD BEEN, WITH THE SAME 322-CUBIC-INCH V8 THAT WAS USED IN CADILLAC'S SERIES 60. BOTH CARS NOW HAD A HYPOID REAR AXLE. THERE WERE FIVE BODY STYLES, INCLUDING FOR THE FIRST TIME A CONVERTIBLE SEDAN. THIS FOUR-DOOR SEDAN COST $1,145. FOR LASALLE 1937 WAS THE BEST YEAR, WITH 32,005 CARS DELIVERED.
OWNER: WALLY HERMAN (PHOTO NICKY WRIGHT)

than spectacular during the 1920s. The aluminum pistons introduced under the Ford regime boosted power to 90bhp, and the 1923 cars were better-looking thanks to the option of wire wheels and a longer wheelbase of 136 inches. This was standardized from 1924 and remained unchanged until 1931, when it went up to 145 inches. Apart from wealthy customers at home and abroad, Lincolns were favored by the members of the Detroit Police Flying Squad, who chose them after testing 11 other makes. They needed fast cars in the 1920s to apprehend the rum runners who brought their merchandise from Canada to supply the countless bootleggers and speakeasies of the Prohibition era. Police Lincolns were equipped with front-wheel brakes from 1924, although regular customers didn't get these until the 1927 season. Other features available on police vehicles included bullet-resistant glass and gun racks in the rear compartment.

Lincoln production rose satisfactorily. In 1922 5,767 cars were delivered, 255 of them Leland-built, the rest built by Ford. By 1926 the figure was 8,858, the highest until the introduction of the lower-priced Zephyr in the 1930s. These figures were small compared with those achieved by Cadillac, which sold 27,340 cars in 1926, but were ahead of the really expensive Locomobile and Pierce-Arrow.

Cadillac had a good decade, with one model of V8 until 1927, when it was joined by the smaller companion make, LaSalle. Named for the French explorer René Robert Cavalier de la Salle, who claimed Louisiana for his king, Louis XIV, in 1682,

let the Leland company go to ruin."

Henry's community spirit was not so evident. He had been approached by the Lelands in June 1921, when he could have helped with a loan, but this would not have given him full control. By waiting until Leland was forced into receivership he got a potentially valuable company at a bargain price. After a few months, during which Henry Leland celebrated his 79th birthday, the Lelands were so discouraged by the interference of Ford men that they offered to buy back their company for what Ford had paid, plus interest. "Mr. Leland," Ford replied, "I wouldn't sell the Lincoln plant for five hundred million dollars."

Ford promised to spend at least two hours a day with Henry Leland, sorting out any problems that might arise, but he never saw the Lelands again. In June 1922 an emissary from Ford requested the departure of Wilfred Leland, and not unnaturally his father resigned the same day. Lincoln Motor

Company was now wholly Henry Ford's, although styling and promotion became the special responsibility of Edsel.

Few changes were evident at first, and indeed most 1922 Lincolns carried the word "Lincoln, Leland built" on their radiators. The 151 dealers whom the Lelands had commissioned were soon replaced by Ford dealers, which extended Lincoln sales to such countries as Cuba, China, and Japan. Edsel engaged Herman Brunn of the famous Buffalo coachbuilding company to design a new range of bodies and these were adopted on a semi-custom basis on late 1922 and 1923 Lincolns, although the styles with fewer trimmings were made by the American Body Company. A wide range of open and closed styles by Judkins was also available. Prices ran from $3,800 for a standard seven-passenger touring to $7,200 for a Brunn town car version.

Development of the Lincoln was gradual rather

the make was intended to fill a gap between the highest-priced Buick ($1,995) and the lowest-priced Cadillac ($2,995). Successful competitors in this field included the Packard Single Six and Chrysler Imperial. The 303-cubic-inch LaSalle engine was more efficient than the Cadillac's, with a smaller stroke/bore ratio, 1.58:1 compared with 1.64:1. The right cylinder bank was 1⅜ inch forward of the left, making it possible to fit the rods side by side on the crankpins. Output was a respectable 75bhp, only 5bhp less than from the 314.5-cubic-inch Cadillac. The LaSalle cylinder layout was adopted in Cadillac engines from 1928 onward.

Probably the most striking aspect of the new LaSalle was its appearance. It was the first car to be styled by Harley Earl, who had worked for the Don Lee coachbuilding company in Los Angeles. Indeed it was the car that led to the setting up of an Art & Colour Section (later redesignated Styling) at GM. Earl modeled his car on the French Hispano-Suiza, at that time the ultimate in chic and luxury, but a very small seller in the United States thanks to prices in the $10,750–$19,500 region. The French car's influence was particularly strong in the radiator shape, winged radiator emblem, and the badge tie-bar between the headlights. Dual color schemes were offered on all 11 body types, eight of them on a 125-inch wheelbase, 7 inches shorter than the shortest Cadillac, and three on a 134-inch chassis. Prices ran from $2,495 for a short-wheelbase phaeton to $2,920 for a long-wheelbase seven-passenger Imperial Sedan. For 1928 a line of custom bodies by Fleetwood took the highest prices up to $4,900. At the same time, Cadillac was offering 50 different variations of body and chassis, with 500 color combinations. In the years 1927 and 1928, LaSalle accounted for more than half of the Cadillac Division's registrations, 26,807 out of 47,136.

LaSalle V8s were built until the end of the 1933 season, after which they were replaced by an Oldsmobile straight-8. From 1931, they were the same engines as in the Cadillac, yet they were at least $500 lower in price. An important technical development common to both makes was the synchromesh transmission, new for 1929. This was a world first for General Motors, although at the time few people realized that within ten years synchromesh transmission would be almost

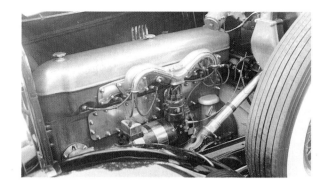

universal and double-declutching would become as obsolete as hand-cranking. There was no synchromesh on first gear, though.

The V12 layout, so popular in the first decade of the century, survived only in Packard's Twin Six, and then only to 1923, until there was a revival around 1930. The only exception was the gloriously extravagant Heine-Velox, the work of German-born piano maker Gustav Otto Heine (1868–1959). He had built a few cars in San Francisco until his plant was destroyed in the 1906 earthquake, then returned to pianos until 1921, when he announced a massive car on a 148-inch wheelbase, powered by a 389.5-cubic-inch Weidely V12 engine. The car bristled with unusual features, including hydraulic brakes on all four wheels, thought to be a first for the U.S. industry, with a five-gallon reserve tank for the hydraulic system, which could be adjusted

to refill either the front or rear brakes, or both at once. The windows pivoted instead of sliding, and the body was fastened to the side of the frame rather than the top, giving greater rigidity and a lower center of gravity. All bodywork was carried out by the Heine-Velox Engineering Company in its San Francisco workshops. The headlights were mounted on top of the fenders, rather in the manner of the Pierce-Arrow.

Heine announced prices from $17,000 to $25,000 for his car, but he never sold any. Five were built, a sporting victoria, three sedans, and an unfinished limousine. At least one purchaser, a Hollywood actor, had his check returned to him with a message from Heine scribbled across it: "We do not accept charity." One or two cars he gave away, the others he kept. At the time of his death in 1959 two remained, a sedan and the unfinished limousine, and they are still in storage in California.

A popular layout which appeared for the first time in the 1920s was the straight-8 or eight in line. The design was pioneered by the Italian Isotta-Fraschini company in 1919, and their cars were particularly popular in the United States, where about 450 were sold between 1920 and 1932. Who made America's first straight-8 has been a subject of dispute for some time. The claim has been argued between the two Duesenberg brothers of Indianapolis and Cloyd Y. Kenworthy of

Mishawaka, Indiana. Both announced their cars at the end of 1920, but the Duesenbergs had theirs on show at the New York Automobile Salon in mid-November, while the Kenworthy was not announced until December. By the acid test of subsequent success in the market place, the Duesenbergs won hands down, for few, if any, of the $5,550 Kenworthy Line-O-Eights were sold, while the Duesenberg Model A was made into 1926, to be followed by one of the most glamorous cars America has ever seen.

The Duesenberg brothers, Fred and Augie, made their name with racing cars, first under the Mason name from 1912 to 1913 and then under their own name. The Model A touring on which they worked during 1920 was their first road-going car, and employed a 260-cubic-inch straight-8 engine with a single overhead camshaft. It also had hydraulic brakes on all four wheels, a feature shared coincidentally with the Kenworthy and with the V12 Heine-Velox. Beautifully built, the Model A was far from cheap, prices running from $6,500 for a five-passenger touring to $8,800 for a town car. The first cars did not reach customers until 1922, and about 600 were made up to 1926 when Errett Lobban Cord bought the company.

Cord, who had already revitalized Auburn, saw the Duesenberg as a step into the top ranks of American motordom, but the Model A was not the car to take that step. He therefore gave the Duesenbergs a free hand to develop a car that could hold its head up among the finest that America or the rest of the world could make. While an interim design similar to the A and called the Model X was listed for 1927 (only about a dozen

were made), Fred worked on the new car. This was launched at the New York Salon on December 1, 1928. Called the Model J, it had a straight-8 engine of 420-cubic-inch displacement, with not one overhead camshaft but two, a layout hitherto only seen on racing cars and a few low-production European sports cars. Output was claimed to be 265bhp at 4,250rpm, and while this has been disputed and was almost certainly the gross figure without taking into account losses through the transmission, it was still more than double that of any other contemporary car. The massive French-built V12 Hispano-Suiza, which appeared two years later and had a 575-cubic-inch engine, gave only 220bhp, while the next most powerful American car was the Cadillac V16, which gave 175bhp when it was introduced in 1930.

The Model J was inevitably very expensive, but this was probably a bonus to Cord rather than a disappointment. He was aiming unashamedly at the ostentatious rich, the "if you've got it, flaunt it" crowd, of which there were many in pre-Depression America. Chassis price was $8,500, to which the buyer had to add anything from $2,500 to $8,000 for the body. Bodies varied from those offered by Duesenberg under the name La Grande, although they were built by other firms, to custom designs from America's finest coachbuilders. In fact few bare chassis left the factory, and most of these went to Europe. The

usual pattern was for the customer to choose a body from the wide range of designs on show in the Duesenberg styling department, which worked in close cooperation with the coachbuilders. Head of styling from 1929 to 1931 was Gordon Buehrig, later to design the Model 810 Cord. He preferred to supervise what would be appearing on a Duesenberg chassis rather than give the coachbuilder a free hand to do as he or the customer liked. Thus many Duesenberg bodies seem similar, although few were absolutely identical.

The most popular coachbuilding firm, who bodied probably 150 of the 470 Model Js, was Murphy of Pasadena, best known for its convertible sedans and Beverly sedans. Others whose work was regularly seen on Model J chassis included Brunn, Derham, Holbrook, Judkins, Locke, Rollston, Weymann, and Willoughby. Bohman & Schwartz built some original bodies, but were best-known for updating bodies in mid-1930s style, seldom improving on the original, but this is what customers wanted. One of the most unusual Bohman & Schwartz bodies was built on a chassis specially lengthened from an already long 153½ inches to 178 inches. Known as the Throne Car for its raised rear seats, it was built for the popular 1930s evangelist, Father Divine, and is said to have cost $25,000.

Duesenberg owners were not all so flamboyant

1929 PACKARD CUSTOM 645 PHAETON BY DIETRICH ▶

PACKARD BUILT ONLY STRAIGHT-8s IN 1929, AND THE 640 AND 645 SERIES WERE THE TOP OF A WIDE RANGE. THEY HAD A 384.5-CUBIC-INCH ENGINE AND CAME IN TWO WHEELBASES, 140 INCHES (640) AND 145 (645). THE INDIVIDUAL CUSTOM LINE INCLUDED THREE BODY STYLES ON THE 640 AND THIRTEEN ON THE 645, FROM DIETRICH, LEBARON, AND ROLLSTON. THIS DIETRICH PHAETON COST $4,585.

OWNER: DUKE DAVENPORT (PHOTO NICKY WRIGHT)

THE SJ WAS THE SUPERCHARGED VERSION OF THE
FAMOUS MODEL J. ALTHOUGH NOT VISIBLE HERE,
THE CHARACTERISTIC FEATURES OF THE MODEL
WERE THE FOUR-BRANCH FLEX-COVERED EXTERNAL
EXHAUST PIPES ON THE RIGHT-HAND SIDE
OF THE ENGINE. CONSIDERABLE REDESIGNING OF THE
ENGINE WAS NECESSARY, INCLUDING RELOCATION
OF THE WATER PUMP AND OIL FILTER, AND AN INTAKE
MANIFOLD EXTENSION ACROSS THE TOP OF THE HEAD.
NOT MORE THAN 35 SJs WERE MADE, BUT THE
EXTERNAL MANIFOLD PIPES BECAME A POPULAR
ACCESSORY FOR NONSUPERCHARGED CARS,
AND ARE STILL BEING ADDED BY RESTORERS TODAY.

OWNER: MR. GOODWIN (PHOTO NICKY WRIGHT)

as Father Divine, but most were very different from the conservative owners of Locomobiles and Pierce-Arrows. Relatively few Duesenbergs were sold on the East Coast, although one went to New York's mayor Jimmy Walker. Hollywood was particularly fertile ground for Duesenberg dealers: buyers included Marion Davies, Mae West, Greta Garbo, Gary Cooper, and Clark Gable, also newspaper tycoon William Randolph Hearst. Cooper and Gable had the only two short-chassis SSJ two-passenger sports cars made. Another Duesenberg owner was Cliff Durant, son of Billy, who had a 1931 Murphy boat-tail roadster which he sold to oil magnate J. Paul Getty in 1932. Getty kept it for eight years, then traded it in for a new Mercury! The car was later owned by novelist John O'Hara. Foreign owners of Duesenbergs included the Kings of Italy and Spain, Queen Marie of Yugoslovia, Prince Nicholas of Rumania, and the Holkar of Indore. Most of these cars had European bodies, such as the sedan by Franay of Paris for Queen Marie, and the Holkar's two-passenger roadster (on a long wheelbase) by Gurney Nutting of London.

In July 1932, about three weeks after an auto accident from which he was thought to be recovering well, Fred Duesenberg died of pneumonia. His last design was a centrifugal supercharger which boosted output to a claimed 320bhp. This had already gone onto some cars, which bore the designation SJ. The first was

delivered in May 1932, the last in October 1935. Mostly built on the shorter of the two standard wheelbases (142½ inches), the SJ chassis cost $8,000 in 1934 and $10,000 in 1935. An SJ convertible coupe reached 129mph at Indianapolis. Only about 36 SJs were made out of a total generally thought to be 470 Model Js, although some were converted to supercharged form after they left the factory. The last Duesenberg chassis was made in 1937, although the last car to be completed was not delivered to its owner, a German artist called Rudolph Bauer, until early in 1940. Bauer planned to have his car bodied in Germany by Erdmann & Rossi, then thought

better of it, deciding to make his home in the United States and not in the Third Reich. The commission was given to Rollson, as Rollston became in 1939, who built a fully convertible town car with wheel-hugging fenders and a sloping chromed grille quite unlike that of a regular Duesenberg.

The next important straight-8 after Duesenberg came from Packard, who replaced its Twin Six in June 1923 by the Single Eight. This had a 357.9-cubic-inch engine with nine main bearing crankshaft, side valves in an L-head and aluminum crankcase. It developed 84bhp, which rose to 160bhp by 1940, with a slightly smaller engine of

and light body, speeds of over 100mph. Four bodies were cataloged in the 734 series, a two-passenger runabout, four-passenger phaeton, victoria, and sedan. Only 113 were made, and the model was not repeated for 1931.

The fashion for straight-8s spread rapidly in the late 1920s, as medium-priced cars like Chandler and Marmon adopted them, and smaller manufacturers like Jordan, Kissel, and Roamer got in on the act thanks to straight-8 engines available from proprietary firms Continental and Lycoming. In 1929, 18 U.S. manufacturers were making straight-8s, and the following decade saw even more from famous firms such as Dodge and Hudson (1930), Buick and Chrysler (1931), Oldsmobile (1932), and Pontiac (1933). The last named were the lowest-priced straight-8s ever made, costing $585–$695.

THE LAST PUFF OF STEAM

One of America's finest and rarest luxury cars, the Doble, had only four cylinders, and these were steam-powered. Abner Doble (1895–1961) built his first steamer while still in high school, and while studying at the Massachusetts Institute of Technology he naturally visited the Stanley plant. The conservative attitudes of the Stanley twins left him quite unimpressed, and in 1914, with the help of his brothers and a family fortune founded on mining tools, he built his first car of which records survive. It had a condenser which consumed all exhaust steam, and a two-cylinder double-acting engine.

Doble built five of these Model As at Waltham, Massachusetts, then moved to Detroit where a few

all cast-iron contruction. Like the Duesenberg, it had four-wheel brakes, although these were not hydraulically operated until 1937.

The Packard Eight (the title Single Eight was dropped after the first year) came on two wheelbases, 136 and 143 inches, and was known as the 136 and 143 in its first year, 236 and 243 in its second year, and so on up to the 1931 season, which was the eighth series. After that, wheelbases no longer figured in the model name, although Packard Eights were known by Series rather than year right up to the 26th Series of 1953. Prices were

a little lower than those of the Twin Six, and production was much higher, more than 11,000 in 1924 and 43,000 in 1928. These were remarkable figures for a car in the Packard's price bracket, giving Packard a lead over Cadillac-LaSalle sales in most years through the late 1920s and early 1930s. When Packard brought out a low-priced Eight in 1935 the lead became still greater.

The rarest and most valued by collectors of Packard Eights were the Series 734 Speedsters of 1930. These had a modified De Luxe Eight engine giving up to 145bhp and, with a 3.3:1 rear axle ratio more were made under the name Doble-Detroit, but it was not until 1924 that he made his masterpiece, the Model E, for which a new factory at Emeryville, California, was built. No expense was spared in incorporating the latest technology and the finest components. The Model E had a four-cylinder engine delivering 125bhp, a very efficient condenser which gave a range of 1,500 miles on one 24-gallon tankful of water (Stanleys still had to take on fresh water every 150–250 miles), and a flash boiler which gave a working head of steam in just over 1 minute. In one test, a Doble was left in the street where the temperature was just on freezing; operating pressure was reached in 23 seconds after switching on, and 41 seconds later the car moved off with a load of four passengers. The Model E's acceleration was quite remarkable, 0–40mph in 8 seconds, while a stripped chassis went to 75mph in 10 seconds.

The Doble Model E rode on a 142-inch wheelbase and was offered with a choice of eight body styles, all of which were built by Murphy of Pasadena. Prices ran from $8,000 to $11,200, which put the Doble up against Locomobile and Rolls-Royce, or expensive imports such as Hispano-Suiza and Isotta-Fraschini. It could outperform all these and the only gasoline car Abner Doble feared was the Lincoln; even then a Doble on full throttle could get away from one.

Abner Doble's customer list was a distinguished one, including Joseph Schenk, Norma Talmadge, Howard Hughes, and the Maharajah of Bharatpur, who had a shooting brake body built by Hooper of London and used his car for tiger hunting. One California couple, the H.W. Hostetters, had two Dobles, a seven-passenger touring for him and a town car for her. Unfortunately, although distinguished, the list was also very small, for not enough wealthy people

appreciated the Doble's refinement and performance. The Doble company was also badly hit by fraudulent stock manipulations of which Abner Doble, busy in his workshops, was unaware until it was too late. Not more than a dozen Model Es were made, and even fewer of the improved Model F.

Apart from the Doble, steam was practically dead by the end of the 1920s. More steam cars were made in Canada than in the States, for the Brooks company of Stratford, Ontario, built about 180 steam sedans, many of which saw service as taxicabs in Stratford and Toronto. Stanley struggled

on with occasional improvements, rising prices, and declining sales until 1927. There was a short flurry of activity in 1922/23, with several new makes such as American, Bryan, Crossland, Delling, Detroit, Gearless, and MacDonald, but only prototypes were built, and most of MacDonald's business was in converting gasoline cars to steam, not that there were many customers who wanted such a service.

GOLDEN AGE OF THE COACHBUILDER

The 1920s saw the finest flowering of the coachbuilder's craft, with many innovative designs that later found their way onto mass-production cars, and at least 20 firms of the highest quality plying their craft. There were basically three groups of quality coachbuilders: those who had started their work in the nineteenth century with horse-drawn vehicles, of which the best-known were Brewster, Derham, Healey, Judkins, and Quinby; those who began in the early years of the twentieth century, staffed by craftsman from the first group (Brunn, Holbrook, Locke, Willoughby); and companies set up later specifically to make automobile bodies (Bohman & Schwartz, Fleetwood, LeBaron, Murphy, Rollston).

Brewster of Long Island City was the oldest established American coachbuilder, founded in 1810 and known throughout the nineteenth century as "Carriage Builders to American Gentlemen," but Quinby dated to 1834, Judkins to 1857, Biddle & Smart to 1870, and Derham to

1884. Most of these firms began to make automobile bodies in the period 1900–1910, although Brewster's first body was made for an 1896 Barrett & Perret electric car. At first the coachbuilders worked on any chassis that was submitted to them, but in some cases they later became associated with a particular make, Brewster with Rolls-Royce, Biddle & Smart with Hudson, Fleetwood with Cadillac, or Murphy with Duesenberg, and so on. Brewster was bought by Rolls-Royce in 1926 and Fleetwood by General Motors in 1925, although this did not prevent them from working on other chassis for a while.

The coachbuilding era is often thought of as a time when rich individuals went to a firm with their own ideas, which the craftsmen would put into reality. There were certainly some examples of this, but more often than not the customer did not know what he or she really wanted, so coachbuilders had pattern books from which a design could be chosen, with an almost limitless range of detailed accessories. Sometimes designs were initiated by dealers; in 1916 the New York

Packard dealer asked the major custom body builders of the Northeast to submit designs, 24 of which were incorporated in a custom body sales catalog. Those by Derham were a six-passenger limousine and a landaulet brougham, the latter with silver-plated accessories and pleated broadcloth upholstery priced at $5,800. Packard became one of Derham's best customers, although the two were not officially linked, and Derham work was also seen on Cadillac, Chrysler, Duesenberg, Franklin, Lincoln, Minerva, Rolls-Royce, and Stutz, among other chassis.

Not all coachbuilders' designs were home-grown. Locomobile had its own styling studios from 1914 commissioning bodies from Demarest and others, while Duesenberg's styling chief Gordon Buehrig penned such classics as the four-passenger Tourster made by Derham and Murphy's Beverly sport sedan. The latter was strictly a four-passenger car, with a narrow rear compartment that seated two people separated by an armchair division which could be removed when "more intimate seating arrangements were desired."

1929 DUESENBERG MODEL J DUAL-COWL PHAETON ▲▼
THE DUAL-COWL PHAETON WAS ONE OF THE MOST POPULAR BODY STYLES ON THE DUESENBERG MODEL J,
AND WAS MADE BY DERHAM, LEBARON, MURPHY, AND UNION BODY (LA GRANDE), AMONG OTHERS.
THIS MURPHY BODY WAS DESIGNED BY MAURICE SCHWARTZ WHO FORMED BOHMAN & SCHWARTZ
WITH FELLOW MURPHY EMPLOYEE CHRISTIAN BOHMAN. ALTHOUGH TO A SIMILAR BASIC DESIGN,
INDIVIDUAL MURPHY PHAETONS DIFFERED IN MANY DETAILS: SOME, FOR EXAMPLE, HAD NO EXTERNAL DOOR
HANDLES. THEY WERE MADE ON BOTH SHORT- AND LONG-WHEELBASE CHASSIS.

OWNER: GILMORE CAR MUSEUM, KALAMAZOO, MICHIGAN (PHOTO NICKY WRIGHT)

Other features included a lighted instrument panel for rear-seat passengers, a built-in radio, and a bar.

Even genuine custom bodies built for particular owners often had as much input from the coachbuilder as from the customer. One of the most striking was the enormous touring car built for comedian Roscoe "Fatty" Arbuckle by the Don Lee Studios of Los Angeles in 1919. For his chassis he chose a car already obsolete, the Pierce-Arrow 66 on its longest wheelbase of 147½ inches. Don Lee's chief stylist was Harley Earl, who later became head of General Motors' Art & Colour section, and this was the third custom car he had designed for Fatty Arbuckle. The Pierce-Arrow identity was completely disguised under a body that flowed in a straight horizontal line from radiator to windshield, while the dipped belt line from behind the windshield to the rear made the car seem lower than it was. Gone were the Pierce-Arrow frog headlights, replaced by huge drum-shaped lights, while the radiator was restyled to incorporate a badge featuring the actor's initials. Only the A pierced by an arrow atop the radiator cap gave a clue to the make of car. The estimated cost of this body was $28,000, with the chassis adding another $6,000. It was Arbuckle's last custom job from Don Lee Studios, for in 1921 he was implicated in the death of an obscure film starlet and tried for murder. Although acquitted (at a cost of $785,000), he never sought publicity again.

The Don Lee Studios, or Don Lee Coach & Body Works as the company was also called, came into being when Cadillac distributor Don Lee took over the Earl Automobile Works, started by Harley Earl's father. The firm was an interesting one in that it grew up alongside the Hollywood movie business and flourished largely through orders from the movie world. Earl's first customized Cadillacs appeared around 1917, but before that the works had built carriages to be used in films, from Roman chariots to Napoleonic coaches. One of Harley's first designs was a four-passenger sport touring on a Marmon 34 chassis, built at a cost of $7,000 for a New York banker. *The Los Angeles Times* made much of the fact that a New Yorker should go to the extra expense of ordering a body from California, when he had the cream of America's coachbuilders almost on his doorstep.

Another early Harley Earl creation was a dual-cowl phaeton on a Pierce-Arrow built in 1919 for oil millionaire E.L. Doheny. The car was a gift to his wife, and along with the car went a chauffeur. Shortly afterward car, chauffeur, and Mrs. Doheny vanished from the family home, so perhaps Mr. Doheny would have been better off with a Model T that he drove himself.

In 1919 and 1920 the Don Lee Studios built about 300 custom bodies, mostly on Cadillac chassis, but some on Packard, Locomobile, and Crane-Simplex chassis as well. These were generally flamboyant, in keeping with their owners, which included movie stars Mary Miles Minter, Anne May, Tom Mix and Blanche Sweet, Mary Pickford's brother Jack, and movie directors Cecil B. de Mille and Henry Lehrman. Bodies tended to feature step plates instead of running boards, and innovative three-piece windshields.

As the years passed, the Don Lee Studios turned to longer runs rather than individual bodies, and it was an order for 100 Cadillac chassis in 1925 that brought Harley Earl to the attention of GM's boss Alfred Sloan. Earl was hired to design the LaSalle, and in June 1927 he left Los Angeles to head the newly formed Art & Colour Section. Don

Lee Studios closed down shortly afterward.

Another West Coast coachbuilder was the Walter M. Murphy Company of Pasadena, which began in 1921 with stylish phaetons on Lincoln chassis, at a time when standard Lincolns were homely and old-fashioned. One Murphy phaeton was bought by Douglas Fairbanks. Like Don Lee, Murphy soon had many customers from the movie colony as well as among industrial chiefs and older Californian land-owning families. An early Murphy roadster had a curved glass windshield, something very difficult and expensive to fabricate at that time (Don Lee thought this too expensive and settled for three-piece windshields). Murphy built nearly all the bodies on the Doble Series E steam car chassis, and also worked on Packard, Mercedes-Benz, Minerva, and later on Duesenberg and Cord chassis. Much of Murphy's work was by in-house designers George McQuerry Jr., Franklin Hershey, and Frank Spring, although, as we have seen, the company was also willing to work to the designs of outsider Gordon Buehrig. Murphy built more bodies on Duesenberg chassis than on any other, but by no means all were Buehrig's designs. Also built were some beautiful Hershey-styled dual-cowl phaetons and town cars on the front-drive Cord L-29 chassis, although the bulk of L-29s carried standard bodywork built for Cord by his associate company, the Union City Body Company.

Like many coachbuilders, Murphy was badly hit by the Depression, and closed its doors in 1932 after building the sedan body for the prototype Peerless V16. Two Murphy employees, Christian Bohman and Maurice Schwartz, managed to bid on work on two cars which were still in the workshops, one of them for Gary Cooper. Moving some machinery to new premises, they started a custom body plant which continued until after World War II. Most of their work was in updating earlier coachwork, particularly on Duesenbergs, and converting cars for invalid use. However, they made a few original designs, including Father Divine's Throne Car and a streamlined town car for Ethel V. Mars of the Mars candy bar family on a 1936 Duesenberg J. They also built the body for Rust Heinz's extraordinary Phantom Corsair coupe on a Cord 810 chassis, which he might have put into production at $12,500 had he not died in an auto accident in 1939. Bohman and Schwartz parted in 1947, but both continued to work independently. Maurice Schwartz lived long enough to end his days (in 1961) working on classic car restoration, especially for Harrah's Automobile Collection.

Generally, coachbuilders left hoods and grilles alone, for these were features that gave distinction

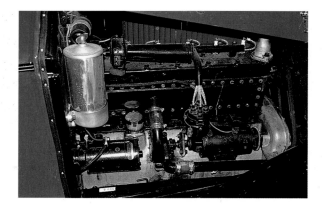

to the whole vehicle when they identified such quality marques as Rolls-Royce, Packard, Lincoln, and so on. However, there were exceptions, such as Arbuckle's Pierce-Arrow, a Packard dressed up to look like a Rolls-Royce by Don Lee in 1924, and a series of disguised Cadillacs marketed by Inglis M. Uppercu of New York in the mid-1920s. These were made for Uppercu by a little-known New England coachbuilder, Hollander & Morrill of Amesbury, Massachusetts. In the 1930s Bohman & Schwartz updated the classic vertical Duesenberg radiator with various styles of sloping grille for customers who wanted to be in fashion, in one case even using a stock 1936 Buick grille.

An appropriate setting for the exhibition of custom-bodied cars was provided by the Automobile Salon, first held in New York's Hotel Commodore in 1921. This was a very different affair from the National Automobile Show at the Field Artillery Armory, which was open to anyone who could afford the entrance charge and showed run-of-the-mill cars like Chevrolet and Maxwell. The Salon was only open to selected car manufacturers, importers, and coachbuilders, admission was by invitation only, and formal dress was expected of visitors. High-pressure salesmanship was severely frowned upon, although of course the purpose of the Salon was to sell cars. Among coachbuilders who were regular attenders were Brewster, Brunn, Derham, Judkins, Holbrook LeBaron, Locke, Rollston, and Willoughby, with Murphy exhibiting at the West Coast equivalents at the Biltmore, Los Angeles, and Palace, San Francisco. Salons were also held in Chicago at the

Drake Hotel. Some firms built cars especially for the shows, without being sure of orders. One of the more extreme examples was the English Coaching Brougham which Judkins showed on a Lincoln chassis at the Commodore in 1927. Styled after the eighteenth-century Concord coaches, it featured carriage lamps, rooftop luggage rails, and a wicker trunk. It didn't sell at the Salon, but after touring the other shows it was bought by movie actress Ethel Jackson.

The Depression spelled the end of the exclusive salons whose deliberately elitist image did not sit well with bread lines, soup kitchens, and the New Deal. The last New York Salon was held at the Park Lane Hotel in 1933, and by then the numbers of coachbuilders had been drastically reduced. Holbrook, LeBaron, Locke, Murphy, Willoughby, and many others had gone, Brewster was about to turn to quality bodies on Ford V8 chassis, and by the outbreak of World War II most of the others were out of business.

1927 PIERCE-ARROW SERIES 80 ◀▲
THE SERIES 80 WAS A SMALLER AND LOWER-PRICED PIERCE-ARROW INTRODUCED FOR 1924. BETTER SUITED TO THE OWNER-DRIVER THAN PREVIOUS PIERCES, IT HAD A 289-CUBIC-INCH L-HEAD ENGINE DEVELOPING 70bhp. IN 1927 IT WAS OFFERED IN 13 BODY STYLES, AT PRICES FROM $2,895 FOR THIS ROADSTER TO $4,045 FOR A SEVEN-PASSENGER ENCLOSED LIMOUSINE. THESE PRICES WERE WELL BELOW THOSE FOR THE LARGER MODEL 36, WHICH COULD COST AS MUCH AS $7,500.

OWNER: GEORGE SANDERS   (PHOTO NICKY WRIGHT)

1927 FRANKLIN 11-B SEDAN ◄▼

IN 1925 FRANKLINS WERE COMPLETELY RESTYLED, AND ALTHOUGH STILL AIR-COOLED, LOOKED MUCH MORE LIKE CONVENTIONAL AUTOMOBILES. THE BODY STYLIST WAS J. FRANK DE CAUSSE (1879–1928), WHO HAD FORMERLY WORKED FOR LOCOMOBILE. THIS 1927 EXAMPLE WAS KNOWN AS THE SEMICOLLAPSIBLE CUSTOM SPORT SEDAN; OTHER COACHBUILDERS MIGHT HAVE CALLED IT A LANDAULET ON ACCOUNT OF THE FOLDING REAR PORTION OF THE TOP. ITS PRICE WAS $3,150.

OWNER: DAVID BODWELL (PHOTO NICKY WRIGHT)

DEPRESSION AND RECOVERY

1929 – 1942

"Buy an automobile, and help restore prosperity."
President Herbert Hoover, 1932

1934 PONTIAC EIGHT SEDAN ▶▼

PONTIAC BROKE NEW GROUND IN LAUNCHING THIS STRAIGHT-8 FOR 1933. GIVING 77bhp FROM 223.4 CUBIC INCHES, THIS POWER UNIT WAS SMOOTH, QUIET, AND ECONOMICAL, AND WAS LESS EXPENSIVE TO MAKE THAN THE V8s USED IN THE 1932 PONTIACS. STYLING WAS NEW AND UP-TO-THE-MINUTE AS WELL; CHIEF DESIGNER FRANKLIN QUICK HERSHEY ADAPTED CHEVROLET MASTER BODY STAMPINGS TO A STRETCHED CHEVY FRAME, AND ADDED GRAHAM-LIKE SKIRTED FENDERS. FOR 1934 WHEELBASES WENT UP BY 2¼ INCHES AND POWER TO 84bhp, BUT THERE WERE NO MAJOR CHANGES. AT $805 THIS TOURING SEDAN WITH TRUNK WAS THE MOST EXPENSIVE 1934 PONTIAC.

OWNER: DICK GINTHER

(PHOTO NICKY WRIGHT)

ISTORY SELDOM FALLS into such neat categories as the turn of the decade.at the end of 1929. The year saw a boom in American business generally, and the auto industry registered a record 4,455,178 passenger cars, not to be equaled for another 20 years. The crash which wiped billions of dollars off the value of shares came toward the end of the year and had little immediate effect on production. But 1930 was another story, with sales down to 2,787,456. The depth of the Depression was reached in 1932, with only 1,103,557 sales, the worst figure since the war year of 1918. After that matters slowly improved, with 1,560,599 in 1933. By 1937 sales had recovered to a healthy 3,929,203. There was a short recession in 1938, with motor vehicle production down 48.2 percent on the previous year,

probably caused by fears of war in Europe. This sent jitters through the stock market, and with memories of 1929 very fresh, people preferred to save their money rather than spend it on automobiles. However, the industry soon bounced back. The last year of peace, 1941, saw the second best year's production since 1929, with 3,779,682 passenger cars made and total vehicle production reaching 4,840,502. Several milestones were celebrated in 1941: the 4 millionth Plymouth, 5 millionth Dodge, and 29 millionth Ford.

The auto industry was undecided how to face the Depression. Income was reduced, so there was not the money to spend on new models, yet there was a desperate need to pry out of the public the few remaining dollars it had, if the factories were to keep open at all. There were widespread lay-offs, with Ford almost halving its payroll between 1929 and 1932, from 101,069 to 56,277. For a while Henry Ford tried to keep his work force occupied with non-automotive jobs such as moving and reconstructing the historic buildings at Greenfield Village, and building America's first airport hotel, the Dearborn Inn. He also raised wages to $7.00 a day minimum in 1931 to increase spending power, "spending one's way out of the Depression," as President Franklin Roosevelt was to urge a few years later. However, even Ford couldn't keep this up in the face of declining income; the daily wage was quietly reduced to $6.00 at the end of 1931, and a year later it was only $4.00.

Of the Big Three mass producers, Chevrolet already had a new model in the Six introduced in 1929, Plymouth carried on with its existing models, although it brought out the considerably modified PA for 1932, with "Floating Power" engine mounting and "Free Wheel" drive, and Ford had a brand new engine in the V8 of 1932.

Henry Ford had planned his V8 in 1929, possibly earlier. Certainly in that year he made his ideas public, telling his engineering assistant Fred Thomas: "We're going from a four to an eight because Chevrolet is going to a six." A lot of Ford's ideas came from a determination to be different, from espousing the V8 to avoiding items like hydraulic brakes and longitudinal springs just because they were the norm with other manufacturers. The V8 was launched in March 1932, having a 221-cubic-inch displacement L-head engine, with cylinders set at 90°, giving 65bhp. This was the best specific output of 16 cars in the low and medium price range, and soon earned the Ford V8 an excellent reputation for performance. The roadster, in particular, was a favorite with young enthusiasts, and in later years became the foundation stone of the hot rod movement.

The V8 was built alongside the four-cylinder Model B, a developed version of the A. Externally there was no difference between the two, apart from the V8 emblem on the tie-bar between the headlights, and the hubcaps, which were lettered Ford on the B rather than V8. Body styles were identical, and the price difference was only $50 right across the range. Most people thought it was $50 well spent. The Model B managed to attract 261,055 buyers in the three seasons 1932 to 1934 out of a total of 1,186,175 Ford sales. After 1934 the

1936 FORD V8 COUPE ▲▼

FOR THE FORD V8, 1936 WAS THE FIFTH SEASON AND THAT YEAR'S CARS WERE KNOWN AS MODEL 68s. THEY WERE SLIGHTLY RESTYLED COMPARED WITH THE 1935 MODEL 48s, WITH NEW GRILLES, AND THEIR WHEELS WERE OF PRESSED STEEL RATHER THAN WIRE. THERE WERE TWO SERIES, STANDARD AND DE LUXE, THE LATTER BEING IDENTIFIED BY CHROME TRIM AROUND THE GRILLE AS ON THIS FIVE-WINDOW COUPE. IT WAS PRICED AT $555, WHICH WAS $45 MORE THAN THE STANDARD COUPE.

OWNER: CURLY PHILLIPS (PHOTO NICKY WRIGHT)

1932 CHEVROLET ROADSTER ▲▶
THE SIX-CYLINDER CHEVROLET WAS IN ITS FOURTH YEAR IN 1932, AND MODELS WERE KNOWN AS THE CONFEDERATE
SERIES BA. FOURTEEN BODY STYLES WERE OFFERED, THE SAME NUMBER AS FORD. THIS ROADSTER WAS THE LOWEST
PRICED AT $445. THE YEAR MARKED THE BOTTOM OF THE DEPRESSION, AND CHEVROLET SOLD ONLY 306,716 CARS, BUT
STILL BEAT FORD BY MORE THAN 74,000.
OWNER: HUBERT FRIEND (PHOTO NICKY WRIGHT)

four-cylinder engine was no longer available in passenger cars, although it was continued in light trucks and some foreign Fords until World War II.

The first V8 engines were less than perfect, particularly in their terrible thirst for oil due to leaking piston rings. However, this was put right on later examples, and the 221-cubic-inch V8 enjoyed a long career, powering Ford automobiles up to 1946 when it was enlarged to 239 cubic inches, giving it another eight years of life. Overhead valves were featured from 1954. The flathead V8

was also used in trucks (both sides had them in World War II, since the German Ford factory made V8 engines as well as the British and American), gun carriers, boats, and airplanes.

The Ford V8 was the first low-priced eight-cylinder engine, and it was a long time before the competition caught up. Chevrolet and Plymouth did not offer one until 1955, and in the 1930s the next lowest priced eight was the $585 Pontiac straight-8. V8 engines were, in fact, rare in the 1930s, being offered only by Oakland up to 1931, Cunningham in very small numbers to 1936, Cadillac and LaSalle, and Cord in the 810/812 made in relatively small numbers from 1936 through 1937. Straight-8s, on the other hand, were offered by 28 U.S. car makers, including well-known firms such as Buick, Chrysler, Nash, Oldsmobile, Packard, Pontiac, and Studebaker, who made this layout through most or all of the decade.

Despite having a performance and image advantage over its rivals, Ford struggled to match Chevrolet in sales, and in fact only beat its rival once, in 1935 with 942,439 units sold to Chevrolet's

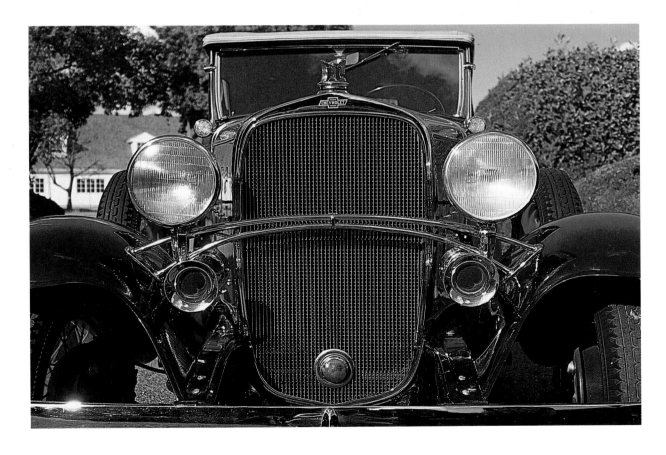

793,437. Indeed from 1936 Ford was third behind GM and Chrysler in overall sales, but at that time GM had six makes and Chrysler four, to Ford's two. These hardly spanned the market, with Ford at one end and Lincoln at the other, and it was to remedy this that Mercury was introduced as a new make for 1939.

Ford made some improvements during the 1930s. Styling was fully up to date and arguably the best of the low-priced three. Hydraulic brakes finally arrived on 1939 models, and a steering column gear change was introduced for 1940. However, springing remained the transverse leaves inherited from the Model T ("We use transverse springs for the same reason we use round wheels," said Henry, "because we have found nothing better for the purpose"). The Ford V8 certainly outperformed Chevrolet and Plymouth, but this was perhaps more appreciated overseas. British motor journals published road tests with acceleration times and maximum speeds, something their U.S. equivalents did not do at that time. Europeans were impressed by Ford victories in the 1936 and 1938 Monte Carlo Rallies, but these meant little to the average buyer in Topeka, Kansas. Ford's performance was appreciated by high school and college kids, but they seldom bought new. Others who enthused over the 85+mph top speed were Bonnie Parker and Clyde Barrow, whose bullet-

1933 BUICK SERIES 90 TOURING SEDAN ◄▲
THE SERIES 90 WAS THE LARGEST BUICK OF THE 1930s, AND INDEED ONE OF THE LARGEST OF ANY AMERICAN CARS, WITH A 138-INCH WHEELBASE AND A WEIGHT OF UP TO 4,780 POUNDS. WITH JUMP SEATS, THIS SEDAN ACCOMMODATED SEVEN PASSENGERS FOR A COST OF $1,955. THERE WAS ALSO A LIMOUSINE AT $2,055. ONLY 890 WERE BUILT FOR DOMESTIC SALES, AND 12 FOR EXPORT.

OWNER: BOB DEBOW (PHOTO NICKY WRIGHT)

ridden car started first time after the fatal shoot-out in the pine hills of north Louisiana; and John Dillinger, branded Public Enemy Number One in 1934, who wrote to Henry Ford saying: "Hello Old Pal, you have a wonderful car. It's a treat to drive one." Franklin Roosevelt drove a Ford V8, and so did Charles Lindbergh and many movie stars, but the public still bought more Chevrolets.

There were other reasons for Ford's slippage in the sales charts. Henry had little time for advertising, remembering the days when the Model T sold itself and there was no national advertising at all. Ford did advertise in the 1930s,

but Henry would not sanction a large budget. "Don't exaggerate, the truth is big enough," he said, and "There are some things we refuse to do to sell a car." His political attitudes did not help either. His strong anti-union position and the employment of strong-arm man Harry Bennett and his thugs to deal with union organizers must have alienated some liberal-minded buyers. More serious was his anti-Semitism, which surfaced in his journal *The Detroit Independent* during World War I. Although the articles were discontinued in 1921 and *The Independent* closed down in 1927, the animosity lasted a long time. Ford's erstwhile friend Rabbi Leo Franklin returned the Model T that Henry gave him, and Jewish sales lost to other makes were not easily won back.

Chevrolet and Plymouth had a number of advantages over Ford in design. In place of Ford's transverse leaf springs Chevrolet had, from 1934, independent front suspension by Dubonnet coils, the much-touted "Knee Action," and, for those who distrusted this newfangled engineering, conventional longitudinal semi-elliptics could be had up to 1940, old-fashioned but still better than Ford's suspension — except over plowed fields. Plymouth tried independent front suspension briefly in 1934, then dropped it until 1939, but both Ford's rivals had hydraulic brakes, Plymouth from 1931 and Chevrolet from 1936. This was a distinct safety argument, and customers tended to ask what was the point of Ford's faster cars if they couldn't stop as well as their slower rivals. Not that they were much slower; a 1937 Chevrolet Master Six sedan was tested (by a British magazine) at 78mph, against 87mph for a Ford V8. Hydraulic brakes finally came to Ford for 1939.

MIDDLE-PRICED CARS AND THE DECLINE OF THE INDEPENDENTS

Above the low-priced three a variety of automobiles was on offer in the 1930s, from independent manufacturers as well as Detroit's big guns, GM and Chrysler. Ford was weak in that it lacked anything between the top V8 at $750 and the cheapest Lincoln V12 at $4,200, although the introduction of the Lincoln Zephyr at $1,275–$1,320 went some way to plugging the gap, and market coverage was further extended with the arrival of the Mercury for 1939.

Many people have questioned why the Mercury did not appear before it did, but it was Edsel Ford's idea and he had a hard time persuading his father to allow him that much independence. He had contributed a lot to the styling side, particularly of Lincolns, but the Mercury was a marketing venture, although it looked pretty good as well. Introduced on October 8, 1938, a month before the 1939 model Fords, the Mercury bore a close family resemblance to them, although it was 4 inches longer in wheelbase and proportionately wider and heavier. Its engine was a Ford V8 enlarged to 239.4

cubic inches and 95bhp, and a good power-to-weight ratio gave a top speed of 93mph. Although it bridged the gap between the Ford and the Lincoln Zephyr, the Mercury was much closer to a Ford, being $165 more than the Ford as a four-door sedan and $430 less than the Zephyr.

The Mercury was aimed at the section of the market occupied by the Dodge De Luxe, Pontiac De Luxe Eight, and Studebaker Commander, and with first season sales of 70,835 was clearly a success. By 1941 Ford was able to claim: "It's made 150,000 owners change cars." Sales before the production line shut down in January 1942 totaled about 275,000. Mercurys were also built in foreign countries such as Brazil, where production continued throughout the war years, and Rumania, where production ceased in 1940.

General Motors' offerings were carefully graded, with an increasing interchangeability of engines and bodies toward the end of the decade. Above Chevrolet came Pontiac, which introduced a six in 1935 to complement its straight-8. The 80bhp six was priced from $615–$745 in the Standard series and from $675–$795 in the De Luxe series, overlapping Chevrolet's $465–$675, and at the other end the Pontiac straight-8 at $730–$860.

Pontiac sixes and eights were continued up to 1942, as were Oldsmobiles, although the latter were in a higher price bracket ($800–$970 in 1935). For the extra money, Oldsmobile owners got technical advances before other GM customers, including steel-spoke wheels in 1933, hydraulic brakes in 1934, a semi-automatic transmission in 1938, and fully automatic HydraMatic in 1940. Buick made

1938 OLDSMOBILE L-38 CONVERTIBLE ▲
OLDSMOBILE OFFERED SIX- AND EIGHT-CYLINDER ENGINES IN 1938, ON TWO WHEELBASES, WITH SLIGHTLY DIFFERENT GRILLES TO DISTINGUISH THE F-38 SIXES FROM THE L-38 EIGHTS. THIS L-38 CONVERTIBLE WAS A RARE MODEL, WITH ONLY 407 DELIVERED, OF WHICH 30 WENT FOR EXPORT. IT WAS THE COSTLIEST OLDS OF THE YEAR, AT $1,163. A RADIO ADDED $53 FOR A STANDARD UNIT, $66.50 FOR A DE LUXE.

(PHOTO NICKY WRIGHT)

only eights from 1931 onward, but in several sizes
and qualities of trim. Four different engines were
used in 1935, from 233 cubic inches and 93bhp in
the Series 40 to 345 cubic inches and 116bhp in the
Series 90. The Series 40 had a short-stroke engine
introduced in 1934; combined with bodies of
Chevrolet size and Buick styling, it gave excellent
performance. Priced from $855–$925, the Series 40
helped Buick to almost double its production in
1934 to 78,757; by 1939 the company was in fourth
position overall, with 321,219 sales. The Series 90,
or Limited as it was called from 1936, was a really
large car on a 140-inch wheelbase, priced at up to
$2,453 for a seven-passenger limousine in 1937/38.

Despite their upper middle class image ("The
Doctor's Friend" they were often called), Buicks
shot to royal fame in 1936 when England's King
Edward VIII ordered two Canadian-built Limited
limousines. One of them conveyed his bride-to-be
Mrs. Simpson on her "escape" to France later in

the year. After he became Duke of Windsor, he
ordered two more Buicks, in 1938 and 1939. His
brother, the Duke of Kent, also liked Buicks.

From the mid-1930s onward there was a
definite General Motors style of body, hardly
surprising as all bodies were made by Fisher. One
couldn't fail to identify a GM sedan from the rear,
though it might not be so easy to say if it were a
Buick, Oldsmobile, or Pontiac. The A-body four-
door sedan and coupe were used in 1940 by
Chevrolet and the lower-priced Pontiacs and
Oldsmobiles, while the 1939 B-body sedan was
seen on the 1940 Buick Century, Oldsmobile 60,
and Pontiac De Luxe. A new and more modern
style for 1940 was the C-body, inspired by the 1938
Cadillac 60 Special. A low and sleek-looking four-
door, four-window sedan, the C-body was available
on the Buick Series 50 Super and Series 70
Roadmaster, Cadillac Series 62, LaSalle Special,
Oldsmobile 90, and Pontiac Torpedo Eight. There

were also C-bodied coupes and convertibles in all five marques. 1941 saw a continuation of the C Series and also a new B Series with fastback sedans and coupes on Buick, Cadillac, Oldsmobile, and Pontiac chassis.

Chrysler Corporation had two marques between its low-priced Plymouth and Chrysler itself, which offered models between the upper-middle and upper price brackets. These were De Soto and Dodge. De Soto had been created in 1928, the same year as Plymouth, to catch the Pontiac market. Actually the cheaper Dodges were hardly more expensive, but Walter Chrysler had planned the De Soto before he bought Dodge. Indeed there is a theory that he announced the De Soto in order to alarm the bankers of Dillon Read, who owned

Dodge, into thinking that they could not compete and had better sell to Chrysler, which is what they did, in fact.

Whatever the rationale behind De Soto, Chrysler was stuck with it, and in fact the make sold very well to start with, although from the Depression onward sales never matched those of Dodge. Both makes were offered with straight-8 engines from 1930 through 1932, and the Dodge Eight was continued for 1933. De Soto was unfortunately saddled with an Airflow model (companion to Chrysler's larger car with similar styling) from 1934 through 1936. In De Soto guise it sold even more poorly than the Chrysler, only 25,737 in three seasons, against Chrysler's 31,850 in four seasons. The conventionally styled De Sotos

from 1936 onward sold better, but they were now in a higher price bracket than Dodge, and this was reflected in sales of less than a third of Dodge's. By 1939 De Sotos and Dodges were very similar in appearance, although the former had a slightly larger engine, 228.1 cubic inches and 93bhp compared with 217.8 cubic inches and 87bhp. The De Soto was 2 inches longer in wheelbase and around $100 more expensive than equivalent models. As well as standard models, both De Soto and Dodge (and Chrysler) included in their 1939 range a limited production Custom Club Coupe by the Hayes Body Company. As well as having different lines from the regular coupes, the car featured a radio, heater, overdrive, and de luxe wheel covers. It cost $1,055 in the Dodge range and $1,145 in the De Soto, and sold in very small numbers, 363 Dodges and 264 De Sotos. The Chrysler version, available with an eight-cylinder engine as well as the six, sold 497 units.

The 1930s saw Detroit's Big Three extend their grip on automobile sales. At the beginning of the decade they were in a strong position, with 75 percent of the market, leaving the remaining 25 percent to be contested by 27 makes, several of which disappeared within a year or two. By 1939 the Big Three accounted for 90 percent of sales, and only five makes of any importance remained to squabble over the rest of the market.

Setting aside the midget and luxury car makers, the independents of the 1930s fell into three categories. The largest, numerically, consisted of makers which failed within a year or two; then came those which staggered through to the middle or end of the decade, such as Auburn, Reo, Graham, and Hupmobile; then came those which survived into the postwar era, like Hudson, Nash, Packard, Studebaker, and Willys.

The Depression is often blamed for the decimation among car makers, but most casualties of the 1930s were doomed anyway. They included medium-sized companies like Chandler, Elcar, Jordan, and Kissel, which kept afloat with sales of anything from 10,000 to 20,000 units a year in the 1920s, but unit costs were high because so many components were bought in from outside suppliers. Who wanted a 1931 Jordan Eight coupe at $2,495 when he could have a Buick of the same size and quality, with better servicing facilities, for $1,765? Durant was much larger than Jordan and Kissel, but even before the Depression he was in trouble, and a planned new empire, to include Chandler, Gardner, Hupmobile, Jordan, Moon, and Peerless, came to nothing.

Makes that might have survived had there been no depression included Graham and Hupmobile.

1936 HUPMOBILE D 618 SEDAN ▼▶
THE FAILING HUPMOBILE COMPANY INTRODUCED AERODYNAMIC STYLING BY RAYMOND LOEWY ON THE 1934 MODELS, AND THIS RARE 1936 SEDAN IS A DIRECT DESCENDANT, WITH A LITTLE ADDED CHROME TO THE GRILLE. IT HAS A 101bhp SIX-CYLINDER ENGINE, BUT THE HUPP COMPANY ALSO OFFERED A 120bhp EIGHT FOR 1936. ONLY 1,556 OF ANY HUPMOBILES WERE MADE IN 1936, AND THERE WERE NO 1937 MODELS. THE FACTORY REOPENED FOR 1938 TO MAKE A NEW LINE OF SIXES AND EIGHTS WITH THE SAME ENGINES AS BEFORE, BUT EVEN FEWER WERE BUILT.

OWNER: AUBURN-CORD-DUESENBERG MUSEUM

(PHOTO NICKY WRIGHT)

The former started in 1928 as Graham-Paige, founded by the three Graham brothers who had made trucks for Dodge and who took over the Paige-Detroit Motor Car Company. Sales in the first year were 73,195, a record for a new make, and in 1929 the company had 2,270 distributors worldwide. Production that year topped 77,000, a figure never reached subsequently. The Depression forced sales down to 12,967 in 1932, the year in which Graham introduced the Blue Streak series, the first production cars to be fitted with full-skirted fenders. Bodies were styled by Amos Northup of Murray; with sloping radiator grilles, they were a

year in advance of other U.S. makes, yet sales were only 10,967. By 1935 the Graham brothers had lost their styling lead — they did not have the capital for major redesigns — and for 1936 they shared Hayes-built bodies with Reo, another make on the way out.

The Grahams had made sixes and eights, but only the former from 1936 onward. Their only distinction was the supercharger offered from 1934. The 1938 models had completely fresh styling, with a forward-sloping grille which gave rise to the nickname "Sharknose," although the makers called it "Spirit of Motion." Other features were square headlights faired into the fenders, skirts over the rear wheels, and concealed door hinges. It was said that the public either loved or intensely disliked the car. Unfortunately there seemed to be more of the latter, or perhaps too few were ready to pay out money for a new car, for 1938 saw a marked dip in car sales nationwide. The Sharknose sold only 4,139 in 1938 and 3,876 in 1939, when Joe Graham put in $560,000 from his personal fortune to keep the company afloat.

The Sharknose was still offered in 1940, but only about 1,000 found buyers. Graham was now trying a new solution to the company's problems. A joint venture was set up with another ailing firm, Hupmobile, to combine the body dies from the Cord 810 with the six-cylinder Continental engine used in the Sharknose. In contrast to the Cord, the engine drove the rear wheels. The Graham version was called the Hollywood and the Hupmobile the Skylark, and both were built in the Graham factory. Only 859 Hollywoods and 319 Skylarks were made, and by September 1940 it was all over. Some Hollywoods and Skylarks were sold as 1941 models,

and a few were assembled as late as 1946, after the factory officially belonged to Kaiser-Frazer.

Hupmobile was one of the more substantial independents, with sales of 65,862 cars and profits of more than $8.75 million in 1928. The company's history in the 1930s was much more checkered, with poorly accepted aerodynamic sedans in 1934, abortive plans for a merger with Willys, and closure of the factory between December 1935 and July 1937. Much of Hupmobile's trouble was due to Archie M. Andrews, an entrepreneur who had been involved in the front-drive Ruxton car of 1929/30, manufacture of which contributed to the downfall of both Kissel and Moon. For 1938 Hupmobile introduced a conventional four-door sedan with six-

or eight-cylinder engines, but there was only one body style, whereas rivals were offering at least four. The company made 3,483 of the 1938/39 sedans, of which only 397 had eight-cylinder engines, then joined with Graham in the Skylark/Hollywood venture.

Of the more successful independents, Hudson and Studebaker had much wider market coverage than Graham or Hupmobile, with sub-marques to reach a lower price bracket. Hudson's was the Essex, which gave way to the Terraplane, while Studebaker's was the Erskine, made from 1927 through 1930. Not a great success, the Erskine was about the size of the Model A Ford, yet sold for over $500 more. Granted, it was a higher-quality product, but Studebaker was not the first or the last company to learn that the quality small car does not appeal to American buyers. It tried again in 1932 with the Rockne, named for famed Notre Dame University football coach Knute Rockne, who had been hired by Studebaker as head of sales promotion, but died in an air crash in the spring of 1931. The Rockne came in two sizes of six-cylinder engine, giving 66 or 72bhp, and two wheelbases, 110 and 114 inches. Prices were lower than the Erskine, at $585–$795, but the car faced stiff competition from the new Ford V8, lower in price and with two extra cylinders. Total Rockne production was 23,201 in two seasons.

At the end of the decade Studebaker brought out another small car, the Champion, but this was priced low as well, around $50 less than a De Luxe Chevrolet. Price and excellent fuel economy of 20–22mpg earned the Champion many friends, and it accounted for well over half of all Studebaker's sales in the years 1939 through 1941.

Hudson's Terraplane was appreciably cheaper than its big sister, even in eight-cylinder form, but it was also a hot performer, for it followed the formula of a powerful engine in a light, short chassis. In its first season, 1932, the Terraplane was a model of Essex, with a more powerful engine of 70bhp in a 106-inch wheelbase. At $425 the roadster was $35 cheaper than the Ford V8, yet its performance was by no means inferior. For 1933 the Essex part of the name was dropped, and Hudson put its 94bhp straight-8 engine into a 113-inch Terraplane frame as an additional model to the six. Terraplanes soon acquired the nickname "Hill Busters" on account of their prowess on hill climbs all over the country. They took many records at Pikes Peak and also set speed and endurance records at Daytona Beach. The Terraplane Eight engine was used by Englishman Reid Railton for his first Railton sports cars of 1933, although he subsequently turned to the slightly larger Hudson Eight.

The Terraplane lost something of its performance image in 1934 when the eight was no

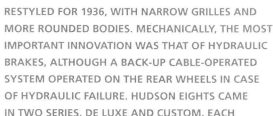

1936 HUDSON DE LUXE EIGHT SEDAN ◄
ALL HUDSONS AND TERRAPLANES WERE COMPLETELY RESTYLED FOR 1936, WITH NARROW GRILLES AND MORE ROUNDED BODIES. MECHANICALLY, THE MOST IMPORTANT INNOVATION WAS THAT OF HYDRAULIC BRAKES, ALTHOUGH A BACK-UP CABLE-OPERATED SYSTEM OPERATED ON THE REAR WHEELS IN CASE OF HYDRAULIC FAILURE. HUDSON EIGHTS CAME IN TWO SERIES, DE LUXE AND CUSTOM, EACH WITH TWO WHEELBASES OF 120 OR 127 INCHES. DIFFERENCES IN TRIM ACCOUNTED FOR AROUND $90–$100 VARIATION IN PRICE. THIS DE LUXE EIGHT SEDAN COST $855.
OWNER: NATIONAL AUTOMOBILE MUSEUM, RENO, NEVADA
(PHOTO NICKY WRIGHT)

LUXURY CARS IN A DEPRESSION ERA

It is ironical that some of the finest American cars of any age were made during the depths of the Depression. They had, of course, been planned several years before 1929, and it is a sobering thought that if the Depression had struck, say, in 1927, we might never have had such glorious machines as the Cadillac V12 and V16, Lincoln or Packard V12s, or the Marmon 16.

Cadillac was first in the field with a V16 engine, developed by a team led by Ernest W. Seaholm, who had been with Cadillac since 1913 and had therefore been in on the birth of the V8. Most of the detail work on the V16 was by former Marmon engineer Owen Nacker, who worked full-time on the project for four years. The cylinder banks were angled at a narrow 45° and had overhead valves with hydraulic valve silencers. Displacement was 452 cubic inches and output 165bhp, which made it America's second most powerful car, after the Model J Duesenberg.

The Cadillac V16, or Model 452 as it was named for its displacement, was launched at the New York Automobile Show in January 1930, although only one car was ready. This was an Imperial Landaulette by Fleetwood, of which only four were ever made. Its price does not seem

to have been recorded, but is likely to have been at least as much as the $7,350 asked for a four-door Imperial Cabriolet, also by Fleetwood. As production got underway during 1930, a vast choice of 54 semi-custom bodies was offered, all by Fleetwood, a GM-owned coachbuilder who built only on Cadillacs from 1933. Prices ran from $5,350 for a two-passenger roadster with two-passenger rumble seat to $9,700 for a five/seven-passenger four-door Town Brougham. Among the 452 range was a limited production series called the Madam X models, after a popular stage play. These had a number of styling features, including a flat windshield sloped at 18°, with very thin pillars. The 452 was also supplied in chassis form for full custom bodies, which were made by Murphy and Waterhouse in the United States, Saoutchik in France, and Pininfarina in Italy.

The V16 Cadillac sold well in its first year, with more than 2,800 finding customers; 1931 was much less encouraging, with only 364 sales, and fewer than 300 in 1932. This was partly due to the deepening Depression, but also to inroads made by rival twelve-cylinder cars from Lincoln, Packard, and Pierce-Arrow, as well as Cadillac's own V12. Introduced for 1931, this was essentially a V16 with four fewer cylinders and a displacement of 368 cubic inches. It was in no way inferior in smoothness, and with 135bhp its performance was almost as good. With prices between $800 and $2,200 lower, no wonder the V12 took sales from the larger car. It would have done

longer made, becoming a lower-priced model of Hudson, with the same body styles and the 116-inch wheelbase of the shortest Hudson. The marque was dropped for the 1938 season, becoming a model of Hudson, and for 1939 the name disappeared altogether. Hudson's small model for 1938 was the 112, named for its wheelbase. It was made in 16 different models, eight bodies in Standard and De Luxe forms, and used an 83bhp six-cylinder engine of 173-cubic-inch displacement. Styling was similar to the larger Hudsons, but the hood opened from the rear. The 112 gained useful publicity when a convertible was chosen as the Pace Car for the Indianapolis 500 Mile race. This was the only year in which a Hudson received this honor. The 112 was made for a further season, with different styling from the larger Hudsons, but for 1940 it gave way to the Series 40 Six with an extra inch on the wheelbase and the same grille as other Hudsons.

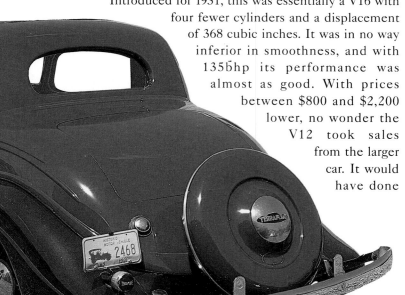

1934 TERRAPLANE KU DE LUXE SIX COUPE ▲▶
HUDSON'S TERRAPLANE WAS MADE ONLY AS A SIX IN 1934, SO WAS LESS OF A PERFORMER THAN IN PREVIOUS YEARS. STYLING WAS NEW, AND CLOSELY FOLLOWED THAT OF HUDSON. THE 116-INCH WHEELBASE WAS SHARED WITH THE SMALLEST HUDSON. THIS TWO-PASSENGER COUPE COST $600.
OWNER: IRA GAMBLE (PHOTO NICKY WRIGHT)

1931 CADILLAC V16 FLEETWOOD IMPERIAL SEDAN AND ALL-WEATHER PHAETON ◄▼
TWO MAGNIFICENT EXAMPLES OF FLEETWOOD COACHWORK ON THE SERIES 452-A CHASSIS. FLEETWOOD BECAME A DIVISION OF GENERAL MOTORS IN 1929, AND BUILT ONLY ON CADILLAC CHASSIS FROM 1933. THE LIMOUSINE IS ONE OF A LIMITED SERIES CALLED THE MADAM X MODELS, AFTER A CONTEMPORARY PLAY. THEY WERE CHARACTERIZED BY VERY THIN PILLARS TO THE WINDSHIELD, WHICH SLOPED AT 18°. THE ALL-WEATHER PHAETON SHOWN IS BELIEVED TO HAVE BEEN BOUGHT BY CHARLES F. KETTERING FOR HIS FRIEND P. PRIOR OF DAYTON, OHIO. WHEN PHOTOGRAPHED IN 1990, IT HAD ONLY DONE 22,083 MILES.

OWNERS: ELLIOTT AND KATHERINE KLEIN (PHOTO NICKY WRIGHT)

so even without the onset of the Depression.

In 1933 Cadillac and LaSalle were freshly styled, with Vee radiator grilles and skirted fenders. But it was a rock bottom year for sales, with only 6,655 from all four lines, LaSalle and Cadillac V8s, Cadillac V12s and V16s. At the beginning of the year Cadillac announced that only 400 V16s would

be made, but in fact the year's total did not exceed 126. Even fewer were made in later years, 60 in 1934, 50 in 1935, and 52 in 1936. Of the latter, 49 were complete cars from a greatly reduced Fleetwood range, and three were chassis supplied to outside coachbuilders; 49 were delivered in 1937. From 1938 through 1940 a new V16 with a short-

stroke, side-valve engine was built. This was slightly smaller, at 431 cubic inches, but power was equal to the old V16 at 185bhp. The new engine looked very different, though, for the cylinders were splayed out at a shallow 135°, giving almost the appearance of a horizontally opposed unit.

The new V16, known as the Series 90, took the industry by surprise when it was launched in the fall of 1937. With sales of the previous model so low, people wondered how GM hoped to sell any more in a market where other multicylinder cars like Lincoln and Packard's V12 were floundering. Pierce-Arrow was on the verge of going out of business. The Series 90, which looked like a larger V8 and was offered with twelve Fleetwood body styles, sold 315 units in the 1938 model year, but only 138 in 1939 and 61 in 1940. With such a limited run, it was not worth updating the styling, with the result that the 1940 Series 90 looked distinctly old-fashioned next to the sleek V8s. A few chassis were supplied to outside coachbuilders, including Derham, and two gigantic convertible sedans were built by Fleetwood on a 165-inch wheelbase for the White House. They were used by secret service staff rather than by President Roosevelt, who rode in Lincolns, and survived into the Truman era when they were repowered with V8 engines.

The only other production V16 was the pet project of Colonel Howard C. Marmon (1876–1943). Although work started on the design

1937 CADILLAC SERIES 37-85 V12 FORMAL SEDAN ▲▶
THE V12 AND V6 CADILLACS ENDED THEIR RUN IN 1937, ALTHOUGH A NEW SIXTEEN
WITH FLATTER ENGINE WAS TO APPEAR FOR 1938. SIX FLEETWOOD STYLES WERE OFFERED
ON THE V12 CHASSIS: SEDANS, CONVERTIBLE SEDANS, LIMOUSINES, AND TOWN CARS.
THIS FORMAL SEDAN, STYLE 7509F, SOLD FOR $4,195. THE LARGE TRUNK AT THE REAR
IS AN OPTIONAL EXTRA.

OWNER: DUKE DAVENPORT (PHOTO NICKY WRIGHT)

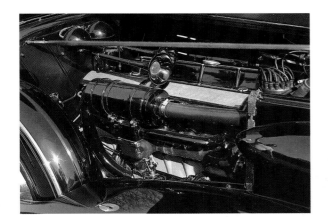

in 1926, it was not revealed to the public until November 1930, eleven months after Cadillac's V16. Known as the 16 or Sixteen, never as a V16, the Marmon was similar to the Cadillac in being an overhead valve unit with cylinders at 45°, but was larger at 490.87 cubic inches and 200bhp. The block, crankcase, intake manifold, oil pan, cylinder heads, and flywheel housing were all in light alloy, making for an exceptionally light engine and a power/weight ratio of 4.65 pounds per horsepower. The 6:1 compression ratio was the highest in the U.S. industry at that time.

Bodywork on the Marmon Sixteen was designed by Walter Dorwin Teague and built for Marmon by LeBaron. Each of the eight styles was attractive to look at, complemented by the sloping Vee radiator grille which gave a lower look than Cadillac's, but they were built to a price and did not have the quality of some other LeBaron work. Many people think that the Sixteen was priced too low, for the 1931 models were $5,200–$5,470, less than a V16 Cadillac, and by 1933 the price of a Marmon Sixteen sedan or coupe was down to $4,825. This price cutting was a desperate measure to help flagging sales, and Marmon cannot have made any profit at this figure. Only 390 Sixteens were sold in three

1936 CADILLAC SERIES 90 V16 LIMOUSINE ◀▼
THE YEAR 1936 WAS ALMOST THE LAST FOR THE FIRST GENERATION V16 CADILLAC, AND ONLY 52 WERE MADE. HALF OF THEM WERE LIMOUSINES, THE BALANCE BEING MADE UP OF CONVERTIBLE SEDANS, AND VARIOUS CUSTOM TOWN CARS, MOSTLY BY FLEETWOOD OR BRUNN. THE SAME 452-CUBIC-INCH ENGINE WAS USED AS IN THE FIRST V16s OF 1930, BUT THE WHEELBASE WAS NOW A WHOPPING 154 INCHES. THIS FLEETWOOD LIMOUSINE COST $7,750.

OWNER: TOM BARRATT (PHOTO NICKY WRIGHT)

seasons, and manufacture ceased altogether at the end of 1933. Marmon undoubtedly suffered badly from being a year later on the market than Cadillac, for while 1930 may not have the best of years to launch a new luxury car, 1931 was worse. Cadillac sold only 790 V16s in the same three-year period, out of total V16 sales of 4,403.

One other sixteen-cylinder car was planned in the early 1930s, but never reached the market place. This was the Peerless, of which just one prototype was built, with a 464-cubic-inch 170bhp engine and aluminum sedan body by Murphy on a 145-inch wheelbase. The car was enthusiastically promoted by James Bohannon, who came to Peerless from Marmon in 1929, but there is no hard evidence that he brought more than the general

idea with him. The same applies to Owen Nacker and the V16 Cadillac, for he was more of a consultant than a regular Marmon employee.

The V12 layout was offered by five manufacturers during the 1930s, Auburn, Franklin, Lincoln, Packard, and Pierce-Arrow, in addition to Cadillac already mentioned. The Auburn was the lowest-priced V12 ever made. At prices from $975 to $1,275 in 1932, it was not in the same price range as other V12s at all. It was also the only V12 of that era to have an engine bought from outside, although "outside" was perhaps not strictly accurate as engine maker Lycoming was part of the Cord empire, as was Auburn. The 390-cubic-inch engine gave 160bhp, which propelled the handsome two-passenger roadsters at over 100mph,

1932 FRANKLIN SEDAN ▲▼

THE FRANKLIN COMPANY WAS NEAR THE END OF THE ROAD IN 1932, BUT BROUGHT OUT A NEW MODEL,
THE AIRMAN LINE. THESE CARS USED THE SAME SIX-CYLINDER AIR-COOLED ENGINE AS THEIR PREDECESSORS,
BUT HAD NEW BODIES IN NINE STYLES. THIS FOUR-DOOR SEDAN COST $2,345. FRANKLIN BUILT ONLY 1,577 CARS
IN 1932, AND WENT OUT OF BUSINESS TWO YEARS LATER.

OWNERS: MARK AND TOOTSIE ACCOMAZZO (PHOTO NICKY WRIGHT)

and the five-passenger sedans and phaetons at 90+mph. There were effectively six forward speeds, thanks to the Columbia Two-speed Axle with which all Auburns were offered. The Auburn V12 was on the market for three seasons, 1932/34, but did not sell particularly well, probably not more than 2,000 or 3,000 out of total Auburn sales of 17,276 during those years.

Even rarer was the Franklin V12, whose engine was slightly larger than the Auburn's at 414 cubic inches, but gave 10 fewer bhp and was, like all Franklin units, air-cooled. It was launched for the 1933 season, but had been under development since 1927 and had undergone radical changes when the design was quite advanced. As conceived by

Herbert Franklin and his engineers Glen Shoemaker, Ed Marks, and Carl Doman, it was to have had the new V12 engine in an extended Franklin frame, with bodies by Dietrich in traditional Franklin styling. In 1929 Herbert Franklin borrowed $5 million from a bank, the first time he had done so. When the Depression struck, the bank put in one of its men, Edwin McEwan, to supervise all Franklin operations. Although four prototypes of the car as conceived by Franklin and his engineers had already been built, and two of them had been exhibited at the New York Automobile Show, McEwan ordered a complete redesign in the interests of cost cutting. The engine was about the only thing that was not altered, for the frame was made much heavier (the traditional light and flexible Franklin frame was undoubtedly expensive to make), the full elliptic springs were replaced by semi-elliptics, and the wheelbase was extended from 137 to 144 inches. This made the whole car heavier by about 1,200 pounds. The handsome Dietrich bodies were replaced by LeBaron-designed two-door club brougham and four-door sedan bodies, which Franklin expert Thomas Hubbard thinks may have been designed for Lincoln and rejected by Edsel or Henry Ford.

Despite McEwan's cost cutting, the Franklin V12 was priced from $3,885 to $4,185, too much for the depressed state of the market. For 1934, prices were reduced by $1,000 across the range, but this did not help. Only 200 V12s were made, and Franklin went out of business by the end of 1934. The four prototypes were sold off to private customers, an unusual step, for companies generally destroy prototypes, considering them inferior to production models. However, as Franklin clearly thought the prototypes were superior, perhaps it is not so surprising. None of them is known to have survived, but Thomas Hubbard has built a "Franklin that never was but should have been" by installing a V12 engine in a 1932 chassis clothed with a particularly lovely four-passenger phaeton body styled after a Merrimac design.

Lincoln, Packard, and Pierce-Arrow all launched their V12s for the 1932 season. The engines were all massive L-head units, displacements being 447.9 cubic inches for the Lincoln KB, 445.5 for the Packard Twin Six, and 398 or 429 for the Pierce-Arrow. Quoted output was

150bhp for the Lincoln and Pierce-Arrow, and 160bhp for the Packard. These were all large cars, with wheelbases between 142 and 147 inches and weighing up to 6,000 pounds. Like Cadillac, they were available with standard bodies and semi-custom styles, and also as bare chassis for individual custom work. Among the favored coachbuilders for Lincoln were Brunn, Dietrich, Judkins, and Murphy, and for Packard, Dietrich and LeBaron. Pierce-Arrow mostly made its own coachwork, although individual custom designs by Brunn, LeBaron, Rollston, and others were seen.

In price the twelves were fairly similar, starting at $3,450 for the lowest-priced smaller Pierce-Arrow and $3,895 for the Packard standard touring. Lincolns were more expensive, with nothing under $4,300. Upper prices depended on coachwork, but even the semi-customs ran to nearly $8,000. In 1933 Pierce-Arrow announced a very special model, the streamlined Silver Arrow fastback sedan. Priced at $10,000, it was the most expensive American-built car that year, with the exception of the Duesenberg. Only five were made, of which four survive. In 1934 a much less radical fastback two-door coupe was made, also called Silver Arrow. It was available on the eight-cylinder chassis as well as the twelve, and cost only $3,295, but by then all prices had been sharply reduced.

In happier times all three cars might have sold to their makers' satisfaction, but 1932 was the bottom of the Depression, and only 1,623 Lincoln V12s, 549 Packards, and 447 Pierce-Arrows found buyers that year. Prices were dropped accordingly for 1933, a Lincoln sedan costing $3,200, a Packard $3,860, and a Pierce $2,975. All three had smaller and lower-priced lines to back them up, Lincoln the KA 381.7-cubic-inch V12, Packard two lines of straight-8, and Pierce one straight-8. However, all of these were still costly cars, conceived in the expansive pre-Depression years. What was needed was a model in the upper-middle bracket to sell in numbers hitherto unknown to these luxury car builders. By 1936 Lincoln and Packard came up with such cars; Pierce-Arrow lacked the resources and perhaps the will to do so, and went under in 1938.

The luxury Lincoln and Packard twelves were continued up to 1939, but in diminishing numbers. Only 446 Packard Twelves were made in their last model year, and 139 Lincolns in the calendar year 1939. The cars which took over from them were very different in design and appearance, yet both were logical for the firms that made them. They were the conservative-looking Packard 120 and the advanced, streamlined Lincoln Zephyr V12.

Packard's 120 was introduced in January 1935, selling at $980 for a two-passenger business coupe. Other models were into four figures but only just, with the top price five-passenger club sedan costing $1,085. The 120s, which had a 120-inch wheelbase, were just over half the price of any Packard made

1936 PACKARD V12 MODEL 1407 DIETRICH CONVERTIBLE VICTORIA ►

PACKARD RETURNED TO THE 12-CYLINDER FIELD FOR 1932. FOR THIS SEASON THE CARS WERE KNOWN BY THE TRADITIONAL NAME, TWIN SIX, BUT THEREAFTER THEY WERE SIMPLY CALLED THE PACKARD TWELVE. BY 1936 OUTPUT WAS 175bhp FROM 473.3 CUBIC INCHES. THE 1936 MODEL CARS WERE THE 14th SERIES, AND 07 INDICATES THE MIDDLE OF THE THREE WHEELBASES AVAILABLE, AT 139.25 INCHES. DIETRICH WAS ONE OF THE FAVORITE BUILDERS OF SEMICUSTOM COACHWORK FOR PACKARD. THE FIRM WAS THE CUSTOM BODY SUBSIDIARY OF THE MURRAY CORPORATION; STYLING WAS BY RAYMOND DIETRICH WHO HAD BEEN LURED AWAY FROM LEBARON.

OWNER: GILMORE CAR MUSEUM, KALAMAZOO, MICHIGAN

(PHOTO NICKY WRIGHT)

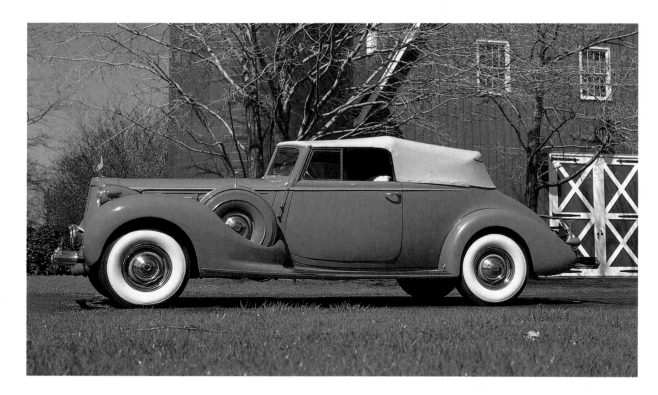

1932 PIERCE-ARROW MODEL 53 V12 LIMOUSINE ▼

PIERCE-ARROW BUILT TWO SIZES OF V12 IN 1932; THIS IS THE SMALLER TYPE 53 WITH 140bhp FROM A CAPACITY OF 429 CUBIC INCHES. THE PIERCE COMPANY HAD ITS OWN BODY SHOP, AND A LARGE PROPORTION OF THE CARS WERE DELIVERED COMPLETE. ALL-STEEL BODIES HAD REPLACED HAND-BUILT WOOD-AND-ALUMINUM ONES IN 1929.

OWNER: ED OBERHAUS (PHOTO NICKY WRIGHT)

up to then, but still a quality product, with a straight-8 engine designed by ex-Pontiac engineer G.T. Christopher. This displaced 256 cubic inches and gave 110bhp. In 1936 power went up to 120bhp, a double reason for the name. The 120 also incorporated two innovations that would not be seen on larger Packards for a few years, independent front suspension and hydraulic brakes.

In its first season the 120 sold 24,995 units, out of total Packard production of 31,889, and in the succeeding years the lower-priced Packard accounted for an increasing proportion of the firm's output. The 1937 season saw a six-cylinder companion to the 120, with basically the same engine minus two cylinders on a 115-inch wheelbase. The interior was less expensive, but very similar in appearance. Designated the 115, it sold from $795 for a business coupe to $1,295 for a station wagon, Packard's first example of this body style.

The 1937 Packard sales breakdown was 30,050 115s, 50,100 120s, 5,793 Senior Eights, and 1,300 Twelves. However, these expensive cars occupied 50 percent of the work force for only 8.8 percent of cars built. Profit margins, if any, must have been much tighter than on lower-priced models. This, combined with the continuing poor market for luxury cars, led Packard management to

manner of the Czech Tatra, but not even a prototype was made in this form. The design attracted the attention of Edsel Ford, and the first two prototypes were tested with Ford V8 engines before any definite plans were made to build the car as a Lincoln. An advanced feature that got carried over into the production models was the integral body/chassis construction.

Before the Zephyr went into production, the front end was restyled by Ford's Bob Gregorie to give it a strong resemblance to a 1937 Ford, then a year away. Tjaarda's proposed all-independent suspension gave way to Ford's traditional transverse leaves, and the engine, although a V12, was much closer to Ford than Lincoln, having many interchangeable parts with the V8 as well as the same stroke. Its displacement was 267.3 cubic inches and it developed 110bhp.

The Zephyr was priced to compete directly with Cadillac's LaSalle, and was about $200 more

1935 LINCOLN K V12 SEVEN-PASSENGER TOURING ▼
THE BIG V12 LINCOLNS WERE RESTYLED FOR 1935, WITH BULLET-SHAPED HEADLIGHTS, CLOSE-MESH GRILLES, AND LONGER HOODS WITH THERMOSTATICALLY CONTROLLED HORIZONTAL SHUTTERS. ONLY 1,400 WERE MADE, BUT EVEN SO THEY EXCEEDED THE COMBINED PRODUCTION OF RIVAL V12 MAKERS, CADILLAC, PACKARD, AND PIERCE-ARROW. THIS CAR IS REPUTED TO HAVE BEEN USED BY PRESIDENT ROOSEVELT; HE CERTAINLY USED SIMILAR CARS. LINCOLNS HAVE LONG BEEN FAVORITE WHITE HOUSE TRANSPORTATION.

OWNER: TOM BARRATT (PHOTO NICKY WRIGHT)

discontinue the big 384-cubic-inch Senior Eight after 1936, although the smaller 320-cubic-inch model was continued, giving way to the 356-cubic-inch Super Eight 160 and 180 for the 1940 season. These were closer to the 120 in appearance, especially the short-wheelbase models, and in price. The lowest-priced 160 cost $1,524 and the top price 120 cost $1,573. The big seller was now the six, designated the 110, which notched up 62,300 units compared with 28,138 of the 120s and only 7,562 Senior Packards.

The last prewar Packards were the Clippers, introduced in mid-1941 in the 120 series only, although for 1942 they were available with the six-cylinder and Super Eight 160 engines as well. Until the Clipper, Packard styling was behind other American makes, but it drew ahead, with wide, low, fastback bodies, fenders faired into the front doors, and rear wheel covers. Many rivals were not so modern-looking until their 1949 models.

Lincoln's answer to the Packard 120 was about as different as could be imagined. Named Zephyr after the streamlined train, Burlington Zephyr, which captured the nation's imagination in 1934, it had a highly streamlined body designed by John Tjaarda of the Briggs Body Corporation. Tjaarda planned his body for a rear-located engine, in the

1940 PACKARD DARRIN CONVERTIBLE VICTORIA ◄

PROMOTED AS THE "GLAMOUR CAR OF THE YEAR," THIS SPORTY-LOOKING OPEN FOUR-SEATER WAS STYLED BY HOWARD "DUTCH" DARRIN, AND BUILT IN LIMITED NUMBERS AS PART OF THE CUSTOM SUPER EIGHT SERIES. DARRIN ALSO DESIGNED A SPORTS SEDAN AND CONVERTIBLE SEDAN, BUT THE VICTORIAS ATTRACTED THE MOST ATTENTION. BODIES WERE BUILT IN A SPECIAL PLANT AT CONNERSVILLE, INDIANA, FOR 1940, THEN IN PACKARD'S DETROIT BODY PLANT FOR 1941 AND 1942. THE 1940 DARRIN VICTORIA COST $4,570: MORE THAN TWICE THE PRICE OF A REGULAR SEDAN.

OWNER: DUKE DAVENPORT (PHOTO NICKY WRIGHT)

1934 PACKARD CONVERTIBLE COUPE ▼▶

THE 1934 PACKARDS WERE THE 11th SERIES, AND WERE LAUNCHED ON AUGUST 21, 1933. THERE WERE NO DRAMATIC IMPROVEMENTS OVER THE 10th SERIES, BUT MANY DETAIL CHANGES WERE INCLUDED, SUCH AS AN OIL TEMPERATURE REGULATOR, AND FACTORY-INSTALLED RADIO WHICH NECESSITATED A LARGER, HEAVY-DUTY GENERATOR. THIS CONVERTIBLE COUPE IS A SERIES 1100 EIGHT ON THE 129½-INCH WHEELBASE, AND SOLD FOR $2,580. THE "FLYING LADY" RADIATOR ORNAMENT WAS A $10.00 EXTRA; THE TRADITIONAL PACKARD CORMORANT COST $20.00.

OWNER: AUBURN-CORD-DUESENBERG MUSEUM (PHOTO NICKY WRIGHT)

expensive than the Packard 120. A two-door sedan cost $1,275 and a four-door $1,320. Buyers got a lot of car for their money. Apart from the prestige of twelve cylinders, the body was roomier than the competition, top speed was 90mph, and 0–50mph acceleration took only 10 seconds. Fuel consumption was not at all bad, at 19mpg. The Zephyr sold very well, 14,994 in its first season, 1935/36, which was ten times the figure for the senior Lincolns, and far more than any previously achieved by Lincoln. For the 1937 season a two-door coupe was added to the range, and production rose to 29,997. A further extension of the range came in 1938 with a four-door convertible, while small grilles on either side of the prow set a new styling fashion.

After the demise of the big K Series Lincoln, the small V12 became the sole Lincoln model; displacement was raised to 292 cubic inches (120bhp) for 1940 and to 306 cubic inches (130bhp) for 1942. The car became a lot heavier (the 1942 models weighed 580 pounds more than the original 1936 Zephyr) and more expensive, 1942 prices running from $1,748 for a two-door coupe to $2,274 for a convertible. But the model that attracted most attention, although not so many sales, was the Continental, launched for the 1940 season.

Although always overshadowed by his father,

1939 PACKARD 1700 SIX AND 1703 SUPER EIGHT SEDANS ◀▲
PACKARD OFFERED A WIDE RANGE FOR 1939, FROM THE 100bhp SIX
TO THE 175bhp TWELVE, NOW IN ITS LAST YEAR. THE 1700 SERIES SIX
WAS THE MARQUE'S BEST-SELLER, WITH 24,350 DELIVERED IN SIX BODY STYLES.
THIS SEDAN WAS THE MOST POPULAR OF THESE AND SOLD FOR ONLY $995.
THE 1703 WAS OTHERWISE KNOWN AS THE SUPER EIGHT, AND WAS ALSO
MADE IN SIX MODELS, PRICED FROM $1,650 FOR A CLUB COUPE TO $2,294
FOR A LIMOUSINE ON A LONGER WHEELBASE. PRODUCTION FOR THE
1939 MODEL YEAR WAS 3,962 CARS.

OWNERS: 1700 JOHN BALL; 1703 ROSS ARMIJO (PHOTOS NICKY WRIGHT)

THE ZEPHYR WAS IN ITS FIFTH SEASON IN 1940 WHEN
IT RECEIVED A RESTYLED BODY AND MORE POWERFUL
ENGINE. THE FOUR-DOOR CONVERTIBLE SEDAN WAS NO
LONGER LISTED, BUT THERE WERE SIX STANDARD BODIES
OFFERED. THIS SEDAN WAS BY FAR THE MOST POPULAR
OF THEM WITH 15,764 MADE, OUT OF A TOTAL OF 21,642
ZEPHYRS. IN ADDITION, FOUR MODELS EACH OF
LIMOUSINE AND TOWN CAR WERE MADE, TOGETHER
WITH 404 CONTINENTAL COUPES.

LINCOLN MERCURY DIVISION, FORD MOTOR COMPANY

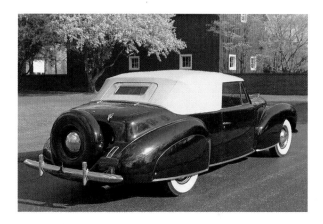

Edsel Ford was the driving force behind several cars of the 1930s, the Lincoln Zephyr, the Mercury, and the Lincoln Continental. But whereas the first two were quantity-produced cars, the Continental was a pet project of Edsel's, originally a special model for his personal use. It was styled by his friend and colleague Bob Gregorie, using a 1939 Zephyr as the starting point and retaining its front end, hood, and fenders, although the latter were lengthened by 12 inches. At the rear Gregorie gave a squared-off chunkier trunk with, at Edsel's request, an externally mounted spare wheel. While the car was under construction, Edsel paid daily visits to the studio, although he was on vacation in Florida when it was completed. The car was delivered to him there in March 1939, and the reaction of his friends was so enthusiastic that about 200 of them placed orders before it was established that there would even be a production Continental.

For the 1940 season the Continental four-passenger convertible, known as the cabriolet to emphasize its continental connections, was added to the Lincoln range. The production model did not differ greatly from Edsel's personal car, except that the rear end was somewhat bulkier. The hood was 3 inches lower and 7 inches longer than the standard Lincoln Zephyr. The cabriolet was introduced with the other Zephyrs in October 1939, and was joined in the spring of 1940 by a two-door coupe. Only 404 Continentals were made in the 1940 model year, 350 cabriolets and 54 coupes. These were minute figures when compared with the total of 22,046 Lincolns made that year.

The Continental sold on its styling and image, for its performance was no better than that of the regular Lincoln Zephyr. There were hardly any modifications to the V12 engine, and the cabriolet weighed about the same as the Zephyr convertible. Suspension was by the good old Ford transverse leaf system, which dated back to the Model T. Continental buyers paid a hefty premium for their stylish cars, $2,840 for the 1940 cabriolet, while the Zephyr convertible cost a mere $1,770.

The 1941 Lincolns were offered in three series, the Zephyrs in five body styles, the two Continentals, and two Lincoln Customs. These had wheelbases lengthened by 13 inches, and were made only as a seven-passenger sedan or limousine. Very small changes were made to the Continentals, of which the obvious identifying features were push-button doors in place of handles. In 1941 the coupe outsold the cabriolet by 850 to 400. The 1942 Lincolns carried heavier and less attractive grilles; few were made because of the war, only 6,547 altogether, of which 336 were Continentals and 113 Customs.

1940 LINCOLN CONTINENTAL CONVERTIBLE ◄▲

DERIVED FROM A PROTOTYPE BUILT FOR EDSEL FORD
IN 1939, THE CONTINENTAL COMBINED ZEPHYR
MECHANICAL COMPONENTS WITH AN INSPIRED BODY
DESIGN THAT EARNED THE MODEL CLASSIC STATUS
IN LATER YEARS. ENGINE CHANGES WERE CONFINED
TO A SIDE-MOUNTED AIR CLEANER (BECAUSE OF THE
LOWER HOOD) AND POLISHED ALUMINUM HEADS AND
MANIFOLDS. AT $2,840 THE 1940 CABRIOLET ILLUSTRATED
COST 60% MORE THAN A ZEPHYR CONVERTIBLE, AND
ONLY 350 WERE SOLD. THE 1941 CONTINENTALS HAD
PUSH-BUTTON DOOR HANDLES.

OWNER: GILMORE CAR MUSEUM, KALAMAZOO, MICHIGAN

(PHOTO NICKY WRIGHT)

TWILIGHT OF THE COACHBUILDER

From a high point in 1930 the prewar decade saw a sad decline in the number of coachbuilders, mirrored by a similar trend in other countries. The prestigious New York Salons, which were for coachbuilders as much as chassis makers, ended in 1933, by which time many of top names such as Holbrook, Locke, Murphy, and Waterhouse, had gone out of business. The survivors tended to be linked with chassis makers building small series of bodies, such as Brunn, Judkins, and Willoughby with Lincoln, LeBaron with Chrysler, and LeBaron and Darrin with Packard.

Two coachbuilders built small series on Ford V8 chassis, marketing the cars under their own names. These were Brewster and Cunningham. The Brewsters were the more distinctive, with their heart-shaped grilles and cutaway fenders, while Cunningham used standard Ford grilles and fenders. Brewsters were made under the direction of John S. Inskip, whose philosophy was that the chassis could be replaced from time to time, while the owner retained his craftsman-built Brewster body. How many people actually did this is not known, but there were doubtless some engine transplants. The first Brewster of 1934 was a town car priced at $3,500, but the following year additional body styles were offered, a four-passenger convertible, a limousine, and a "coupelet," which was no more than a two-passenger convertible with rumble seat. All carried the same price tag of $3,500, which made the limousine and town car better value, as there was much more craftsmanship in their bodies, particularly in their interiors. About 120 Brewsters were made in three seasons, 1934/36. At least one body was transferred to a 1940 Buick 90 Limited chassis and used for many years by Mr. J. Whitney of the New York Stock Exchange.

Between 100 and 150 Cunninghams were made, and only in the years 1935 and 1936. Costing less than the Brewster, at $2,600 for a town car, the Cunningham was an elegant-looking vehicle whose formal coachwork blended quite well with the Ford V8 front end, hood, and fenders. Cunningham discontinued its large cars, powered by an own-make V8 engine, in 1933, and its coachwork department concentrated on Ford-powered cars plus a few ambulances and hearses on Packard chassis. Car making ceased in 1936, although the company remained in business in other fields.

The number of true custom bodies shrank drastically as the 1930s progressed. Among them were the antique-looking town car with vertical body lines and artillery wheels built by Derham on a 1938 Packard Super Eight chassis. More typical

1940 CHRYSLER NEWPORT DUAL-COWL PHAETON ◄▲

ONE OF TWO DESIGNS OF SHOW CAR BUILT FOR CHRYSLER BY LEBARON, THE NEWPORT HAD AN ALUMINUM BODY WITH DUAL COCKPITS AND SEPARATE WINDSHIELDS, PUSH-BUTTON DOORS, AND CONCEALED HEADLIGHTS. A NEWPORT WAS THE OFFICIAL PACEMAKER FOR THE 1941 INDIANAPOLIS 500 MILE RACE, THE FIRST TIME A NONPRODUCTION CAR HAD BEEN CHOSEN FOR THIS ROLE. THIS PARTICULAR CAR WAS BOUGHT BY MILLIONAIRE PLAYBOY HENRY J. TOPPING, WHO SUBSTITUTED A CADILLAC ENGINE AND TRANSMISSION. HE ALSO PERSONALIZED THE CAR BY HAVING HIS NAME CAST IN THE HUBCAPS AND VALVE COVERS, AND ADDING HIS INITIALS TO THE GRILLE. HE WAS MARRIED TO FILM STAR LANA TURNER, HENCE THE LANA LICENSE PLATES.

OWNER: NATIONAL AUTOMOBILE MUSEUM, RENO, NAVADA

(PHOTO NICKY WRIGHT)

THE CHRYSLER THUNDERBOLT
(ADDITIONAL PICTURES SHOWN UNDER THE THUNDERBOLT PICTURE)

Here is the Thunderbolt, reproduced in four colors, exactly as it will appear on your Chrysler Calendars. The Car of the Future has an irresistible appeal that makes it an outstanding calendar illustration—commanding attention all year long.

1940 CHRYSLER THUNDERBOLT
CONVERTIBLE ◄▼
NAMED FOR GEORGE EYSTON'S LAND SPEED
RECORD CAR OF 1937, THE THUNDERBOLT WAS
THE MORE STREAMLINED OF CHRYSLER'S
TWO CONCEPT CARS. STYLED IN TEN DAYS
BY ALEX TREMULIS, IT HAD A FULL-WIDTH
BODY WITH SEATING FOR THREE ABREAST,
CONCEALED HEADLIGHTS, AND A RETRACTABLE
HARDTOP THAT WAS NOT TO SEE PRODUCTION
UNTIL THE FORD SKYLINER OF 1957. ALTHOUGH
MADE FOR CHRYSLER BY LEBARON,
THE NEWPORT AND THUNDERBOLT WERE NOT
DESIGNED BY THE COACHBUILDERS.
TREMULIS AND NEWPORT STYLIST RALPH ROBERTS
BOTH WORKED FOR BRIGGS AT THE TIME.
CHRYSLER CORPORATION, MIRCO DE CET COLLECTION

was the customizing of production bodies, adding closed rear panels for greater formality, removing the front part of the top to make a town car, or opening the rear to give a landaulette style. This was done by LeBaron on Chrysler Imperials from 1936 through 1938 and by Derham on Cadillac, Chrysler, and Packard up to 1942. More individual designs from LeBaron were the Newport parade phaeton and Thunderbolt convertible on Chrysler chassis in 1940. These anticipated the show cars of the postwar years in that they were built for the Chrysler Corporation to display around the nation. The Newports were striking enough, with their dual cockpits and windshields for both cockpits, but the Thunderbolts were the more advanced of the two designs. With all-enveloping aluminum bodies with wheels skirted front and rear, they still looked modern in 1960. Six were made of each design; four Newports and two Thunderbolts are known to exist today.

Favorite coachbuilders on the K Series Lincoln chassis were Brunn, Judkins, LeBaron, and Willoughby. Most were semi-custom designs. The Brunn brougham had a town car front and the Judkins berline was really a six-window sedan, but these were made in very small numbers, just 13 broughams and 11 berlines. The breakdown of 1938 Model K chassis figures tells an interesting story: 227 complete cars were made with Lincoln bodywork, 199 chassis were sent to the four coachbuilders just mentioned for cataloged semi-custom work, and 7 went for full custom work. Some of the last-named went to professional bodybuilders (ambulances and hearses). In 1939 only 97 standard bodies were made, 34 semi-customs and seven full customs, although the coachbuilders for the latter have not been traced. In addition, there was one extra-long 160-inch wheelbase chassis bodied by Brunn as a parade car for President Roosevelt. Known as the Sunshine Special, it was fitted with an updated grille in 1942 and accompanied the President to the famous conferences at Casablanca, Teheran, and Yalta. It also went with President Truman to the 1945 Potsdam Conference.

The demise of the Lincoln K at the end of the 1939 season spelled the end for Judkins and Willoughby, who built no more custom bodies. Brunn tried to keep going with a series of semi-custom landaulettes and town cars on the Buick Limited chassis, but Cadillac saw these as a threat to Fleetwood custom bodies and convinced GM to veto their manufacture. Four styles were proposed on 1941 chassis, and at least one of each was built. Brunn closed its doors at the end of 1941.

Packard provided chassis for some striking coachwork by Darrin, LeBaron, and Rollston. All were semicustoms cataloged from 1939 through 1942. The best known was the Darrin convertible victoria, a sporty-looking two-door four-passenger convertible with cutaway doors available on the Super Eight 180 chassis for $4,570 in 1940, and $4,595 in 1941 and 1942. Darrin also did a five-passenger sport sedan with lower lines than the regular sedans at $6,300, and Rollston an all-weather town car at $4,574. These semi-customs were expensive when compared with the regular 180 five-passenger sedan at $2,243.

The only coachbuilder to survive the war and continue with its traditional work was Derham, which built the prototype of Gordon Buehrig's futuristic Tasco coupe on a Mercury chassis in 1948, and customized a number of Cadillacs and Chryslers into the mid-1950s. Among customers for the modified Cadillac 75 were Pope Pius XII and the Sultan of Kuwait. Derham continued to produce sales catalogs up to 1957, but its last important piece of work was a convertible on the 1956 Lincoln Continental Mark II, which was delivered to Mrs. William Clay Ford. Like Bohman & Schwartz, Derham got into classic car restoration toward the end of its life. The author visited the premises in 1970, and among the interesting cars receiving attention were a 1941 Lincoln Continental, the Tasco coupe, and the only example of the French-built Pedroso twin-cam straight-8 of the 1920s. When Enos Derham died in 1974, the Derham Body Company closed down, ending 164 years of distinguished American coachbuilding.

LITTLE CARS THAT COULDN'T

After the Ford Model A had been laid to rest, and setting aside such ephemerals as the Littlemac from Muscatine, Iowa, of which no more than 12 were made, only three cars with less than six cylinders were offered by American makers in the 1930s. These were the American Austin/Bantam, Crosley, and Willys Four. The last was not a true baby car, having a 134.2-cubic-inch 48bhp engine derived from that used in the Whippet. Known as the 77 from 1933 through 1936 it was restyled for 1937 in the contemporary rounded fashion, and received hydraulic brakes for 1939, when power was raised to 62bhp and the old name of Overland was revived, just for one year. The car sold mainly on its economy and price, being just $200 cheaper than the cheapest Chevrolet in 1939. Willys was near the bottom of the production league, but nevertheless sold 76,803 cars in 1937, and between 25,000 and nearly 29,000 in the years 1939–41. The engine achieved its greatest fame in the Jeeps made by Willys and Ford during World War II.

The American Austin was an attempt to give the nation a taste of European-style motoring three decades before there was really any demand for it. The Austin Seven was small even by British standards, and was regarded with amused affection in its own country, although it sold very well, about 300,000 between 1923 and 1939. The same 45-

cubic-inch four-cylinder engine and 75-inch wheelbase were used for the American version, but the bodies were something else. Styled by Alexis de Saknoffsky and built by Hayes, they had dual color schemes, disk wheels, and on the roadster a curved color panel which cheekily aped that of the Model J Duesenberg. The cars looked larger than their actual length of 122 inches. The original 1930 models were priced from $445 for a roadster to $550 for a de luxe coupe. Unfortunately Ford

Model A prices that year started at $435, and buyers got a lot more than they did from American Austins. Admittedly fuel consumption was lower at 40mpg, but gasoline costs were not a significant factor at that time. The Austin factory was located at Butler, Pennsylvania, in the plant of the Standard Steel Car Company, maker of the Standard V8 car from 1916 through 1923.

The American Austin had plenty of novelty value, but failed to make a hit with the average

Main Street buyer. Showbusiness folk like Buster Keaton, Marion Davies, Laurel and Hardy, and Al Jolson bought them, and so did Ernest Hemingway. A fleet of Austins appeared in the Will Rogers movie *A Connecticut Yankee in King Arthur's Court*, and Austins became a stock-in-trade of radio skits and vaudeville acts. "Tell me, do you get into that car, or do you put it on?", was a favorite joke. More Austins went to California than to any other state, but overall sales for 1930 were only 8,858, a bitter disappointment to the promoters, who had spoken of 100,000 or more. 1931 was even worse, with only 1,279 cars sold and more than 1,500 unfinished cars in the factory, with no buyers in prospect.

The American Austin story might have ended there, but for super-salesman Roy Evans who had handled 80 percent of sales. He took the unfinished cars, had them completed outside the factory, and sold them in Florida for $295 each. He then assumed control of the company and built 4,726 units in 1933, including pick ups and delivery vans. The latter were very popular as mobile billboards, their small size and cute appearance attracting more attention than larger vans. Prices were as low as $275 for a business coupe, and bodies were now made in Butler instead of by Hayes at Grand Rapids, Michigan. Only 1,057 vehicles were delivered in 1934 and after that there was a three-year gap before Evans reorganized as the American Bantam Car Company.

The new car was called American Bantam, or simply Bantam (*never* Austin Bantam), and featured fresh styling by de Saknoffsky, who, aware of the precarious finances, gave his services for $300, which represented simply his expenses. The cars featured Vee grilles, and rear wheel covers on the open models, which included a convertible (for 1940) as well as a roadster, and for 1939 a station wagon. Under the hood the engine was modified by race car wizard Harry A. Miller; shortage of money prevented him from doing all he wanted, but a redesigned manifold was sufficient to avoid paying the $10 per car royalty to the Austin Motor Company Ltd. Later, displacement went up to 50 cubic inches and power to 22bhp.

Despite glamorous names like Riviera and Hollywood, the Bantams did not sell very well, about 2,000 in 1938, 1,225 in 1939, and 800 in 1940. Production ended in June 1940, although a 1941 catalog was issued. By then the company was concentrating on the four-wheel-drive army vehicle that would be immortalized as the Jeep.

America's other small car was the Crosley, made in Cincinnati by Powel Crosley (1886–1961), who was 53 years old when he launched the third automobile of his career. His previous efforts were the Marathon Six of 1909 and the DeCross cyclecar of 1913, but his fame and fortune came from making radios and refrigerators. In 1922 he was said

to have been the largest radio manufacturer in the world, while his Shelvadoor refrigerator was the first to have shelves in the doors. In 1934 he became president and owner of the Cincinnati Redlegs baseball team.

Crosley's third attempt at automobile manufacture, and the only one that achieved any success, was planned as early as 1934, but the first car did not appear until April 1939, when it was launched at the Indianapolis Motor Speedway. Smaller than the Bantam, at 120 inches overall, it seated four passengers in the convertible sedan form and sold for $350. Compared with the Bantam, it seemed rather crude, with a two-cylinder air-cooled engine made by the Waukesha Motor Company and derived from an orchard-spraying unit. Seats were simple tube frames covered in stretched fabric, and the windshield wiper was hand-operated. By 1942 an automatic wiper was offered. Top speed was 50mph, although the makers advised 40mph as a more suitable limit for touring. Although 2 inches shorter than the Bantam, the Crosley was roomier, doubtless to suit the 6-foot 4-inch frame of its creator. Another large man, Erwin "Cannonball" Baker, drove a Crosley from Cincinnati to Los Angeles to New York to

Chicago in the summer of 1940, averaging 50.4mpg for 6,517.3 miles. His costs for both gasoline and oil from Cincinnati to Los Angeles were only $9.41.

Crosleys were sold through department stores and other outlets handling Powel's radios and refrigerators. Sales in the first year were quite encouraging, at 2,017 between June and December, but serious problems with breaking driveshafts reduced 1940 sales to 422 units. After redesign by Paul Klotsch, the 1941 models sold 2,289 and the 1942 models 1,029. A $450 station wagon joined the range in 1940, while panel deliveries and pickups were also made. Crosley was to achieve greater fame after World War II with small four-cylinder cars.

1939 CROSLEY CONVERTIBLE SEDAN ◀ ▲ ▶
THE LITTLE CROSLEY WAS LAUNCHED ON APRIL 29, 1939, ONE DAY AFTER POWEL CROSLEY'S CINCINNATI REDLEGS ROUTED THE CHICAGO CUBS IN THE FIRST OF SEVERAL WINS. MORE OF A LATTER-DAY CYCLECAR THAN A FORERUNNER OF THE SUBCOMPACTS, THE CROSLEY'S FLAT-TWIN ENGINE GAVE 15BHP FROM 38.87 CUBIC INCHES, AND COULD PROPEL THE LITTLE CAR AT UP TO 50MPH. BRAKES WERE CABLE OPERATED, AND THERE WERE NO UNIVERSAL JOINTS IN THE DRIVESHAFT. ANY NECESSARY DEFLECTIONS WERE SUPPOSED TO BE HANDLED BY FLEXING OF THE RUBBER-MOUNTED ENGINE.
OWNER: AUBURN-CORD-DUESENBERG MUSEUM (PHOTO NICKY WRIGHT)

1934 CHRYSLER AIRFLOW COUPE ▲
1935 CHRYSLER AIRFLOW C-1 SEDAN ▶
AFTER THE POOR RECEPTION OF THE 1934 AIRFLOWS, CHRYSLER'S STYLIST OLIVER CLARK REDESIGNED
THE FRONT END TO GIVE IT A PRONOUNCED PROW IN PLACE OF 1934's WATERFALL GRILLE. YOU COULD
EVEN BUY A NEW HOOD TO UPDATE YOUR 1934 AIRFLOW. RESTYLING DID NOT HELP SALES, HOWEVER,
WHICH WERE LOWER THAN IN 1934.

OWNERS: STEVE AND EVELYN BENN (PHOTO NICKY WRIGHT)

THE DECADE OF STYLING AND CONVENIENCE

Although the 1930s saw the introduction of several important mechanical features, such as GM's "Knee Action" independent front suspension and "Turret Top" steel bodies, the main impact of the decade was in styling and convenience features for driver and passengers.

No decade has brought more changes in styling than the 1930s. At the beginning cars were not so different in appearance from those of the 1920s: radiators, windshields, and rear ends were vertical, headlights separate, fenders unskirted. Wheels mostly had wire or pressed steel "artillery" spokes. By 1940 the radiator had disappeared behind a stylish grille, windshields were sloping two-piece units, and sedan backs were sloping and rounded. Fenders acquired skirts around 1932–34, and by 1942 were beginning to be faired into the doors on Buicks and Packard Clippers, anticipating the straight-through lines of postwar cars. Wheels had steel disks with large hubcaps, not too different from those of today.

For their general progress in styling, three cars stood out, the Lincoln Zephyr already described, the Chrysler Airflow, and the Cord 810. The Chrysler was the most significant, since it combined advanced engineering with an ambitious market coverage, and showed auto makers that being ahead of the times could be as dangerous as lagging behind. Chief designer Carl Breer said that he was inspired to study aerodynamics as early as 1927, when cars were just "big boxes with little boxes up front." He noted that aircraft followed the shape of birds in their lines, and asked pioneer aviator Orville Wright to set up a small wind tunnel in which streamlined shapes could be tested. This was followed by a larger tunnel at Chrysler's Highland Park research center. Several prototypes were made, some runners, others merely wooden mock-ups. One had a rear-mounted straight-8 engine but was hopelessly tail heavy, and others had three-abreast seating with central steering, a design which Chrysler never put in production, although the French Panhard company did so a few years later.

The first running Airflow prototype, the Trifon Special, took to the road in December 1932, and the Airflow was shown to the public in January 1934. Its revolutionary appearance was matched by

its engineering, for underneath the waterfall grille, recessed headlights, and rounded sedan back was unitary construction of chassis and body, with a light, cage-like steel girder network carrying the body panels. Unlike most contemporary American cars, no wood whatsoever was used in the construction. Seating for six passengers was within the wheelbase, which necessitated mounting the engine further forward than was usual, about one third of the block being ahead of the front axle, and tilting it rearward at 5°. Access to the trunk was by lifting the rear seat backs, an innovation for the time. Transmission included Borg-Warner's automatic overdrive, the first use of this on an American car. At speeds above 40mph, when the driver lifted his foot from the gas pedal, overdrive was automatically engaged; below 25mph, it dropped back to underdrive.

The engines were the least innovative aspects of the Airflow, being standard Chrysler eights, the 299-cubic-inch in the CU, 323.5-cubic-inch in the

Imperial CV and CX, and 384.8-cubic-inch in the Imperial CW. This last one was the largest and heaviest car ever built by Chrysler, riding on a 146-inch wheelbase and weighing in at up to 5,900 pounds. Only 67 were built, prices being up to $5,145 for the Custom Limousine. By contrast, the cheapest Chrysler Airflow cost only $1,345, and there was an even lower-priced Airflow in the De Soto line, with a 241.5-cubic-inch six-cylinder engine, at $995. The most popular body style was a six-window sedan, but there was also a four-window town sedan and a two-door coupe. The Airflow was never offered in convertible or roadster form.

Although the Airflow was announced at the New York Automobile Show in January 1934, cars did not reach customers until April, which gave rivals, especially General Motors, ample time to spread disparaging rumors. As Carl Breer put it: "We had a lot of fallacies to combat, and no cars to combat them with." When the cars did get into customers' hands, complaints poured in, mostly

arising from faulty building. One owner suffered the engine breaking loose from the frame at 80mph. Probably the first 3,000 Airflows suffered from construction problems, and by the time these had been rectified the damage had been done to the car's reputation. Chrysler kept two conventional cars in the 1934 range, the six-cylinder CA and CB, and these easily outsold the Airflows; of 36,929 Chryslers that year, only 11,292 were Airflows. De Soto had no conventional line for 1934 and sold 13,940 Airflows.

It has been suggested that if Chrysler had had no conventional cars to siphon off sales, the streamlined Airflows might have done better, but it is equally possible that customers would have bought other makes instead. At least the conventional Chryslers kept the company in profit during the Airflow years, while the Airflow car never earned a cent for its makers. For 1935 Walter Chrysler hired Ray Dietrich to style a new line of conventional cars. Called Airstreams, these were

1937 CORD 812 BEVERLY SEDAN ◄
"IT DIDN'T LOOK LIKE AN AUTOMOBILE. SOMEHOW
IT LOOKED LIKE A BEAUTIFUL THING THAT HAD BEEN
BORN AND JUST GREW UP ON THE HIGHWAY."
THIS WAS DESIGNER GORDON BUEHRIG'S FAVORITE
COMPLIMENT ON HIS CORD, AND A VERY APT ONE.
IT WAS CERTAINLY ONE OF THE MOST INSTANTLY
RECOGNIZABLE CARS, THEN AND NOW. LIKE THE
CONTEMPORARY AUBURNS, CORD SEDANS WERE
USED BY THE INDIANA STATE POLICE.

OWNER: LEE MUZILLO (PHOTO NICKY WRIGHT)

available in six- and eight-cylinder forms, thus eating into the Airflow's market, although the most expensive Airstream undercut the cheapest Airflow by $10. The Airflow was also restyled, giving it a prow which made the front seem less radical. In retrospect, this may have been unwise, since it spoiled the pure waterfall grille which was one of the Airflow's attractions. It certainly did not help sales, which were only 7,751 out of a Chrysler total of 38,533. The front end underwent further modifications in 1936 and 1937, but to no avail; sales were 6,276 and 4,600 respectively, and the Airflow was quietly dropped in August 1937.

The Cord 810 rivaled the Airflow in innovative styling, and has been described as perhaps the most instantly recognizable of all American cars. After the demise of the front-driven straight-8 Cord L-29 in 1932, Errett Lobban Cord's name was absent from cars, although he was still making Auburns and Duesenbergs. Gordon Buehrig was retained as stylist for the group, dividing his time between the marques as Cord decided. In 1934 Cord planned to make a cheaper Duesenberg and asked Buehrig to produce a design. It was radically different from anything seen before, with a "coffin nose" hood and

horizontal louvers, headlights that disappeared into the fenders, no running boards, and a fastback sedan body. It was intended to have rear-wheel drive, and the prototype was built on an Auburn chassis.

Before the mock-up was completed Buehrig was moved to Auburn, where he designed the 851 speedster. When he returned to the Duesenberg project a year later, he found that it was to have front drive and to be called a Cord. He revised his drawings somewhat, with a lower four-window sedan in place of the original six-window design, but otherwise the appearance of the 1935 Cord was

1929 CORD L-29 SEDAN ◄▲
THE FIRST CAR TO BEAR THE NAME OF ERRETT LOBBAN CORD WAS THE L-29, NAMED FOR THE YEAR
OF ITS INTRODUCTION. ITS MOST STRIKING FEATURE WAS DRIVE TO THE FRONT WHEELS, WHICH HAD
BEEN SEEN ONLY ON A FEW EXPERIMENTAL ROAD CARS AND ON INDIANAPOLIS RACERS. INDEED,
RACE CAR ENGINEERS HARRY MILLER AND CORNELIUS VAN RANST WERE CONSULTANTS TO THE L-29
PROJECT. IT WAS POWERED BY A 125bhp STRAIGHT-8 LYCOMING ENGINE, AND WAS PRICED
FROM $3,095 to $3,295; BUT THESE PRICES WERE LOWERED FOR 1930. PRODUCTION CEASED
ON DECEMBER 31, 1931, WITH JUST OVER 5,000 CARS MADE.

OWNER: AUBURN-CORD-DUESENBERG MUSEUM (PHOTO NICKY WRIGHT)

very similar to that of the 1934 baby Duesenberg. The Cord was powered by a 288.6-cubic-inch 125bhp V-8 Lycoming engine designed to Cord's specification, Lycoming being part of his empire. It drove the front wheels through a four-speed transmission, with steering column gear selector and shifting by depression of the clutch.

Called the Model 810, the new Cord was launched at the New York and Los Angeles Shows in November 1935. The rules of the Automobile Manufacturers' Association insisted on at least 100 cars being completed before the shows opened, and the Cord company had a struggle to build these in time. In fact, they were not runners, for the transmissions could not be completed. Their appearance scored a big hit with the public, and they were voted best-looking cars at the New York Show. The Packard 120 was voted second, while the other streamlined cars of the era, Lincoln Zephyr and Chrysler Airflow, were sixth and ninth

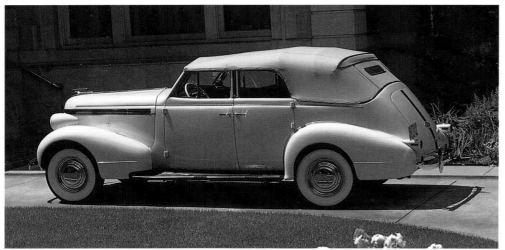

◄▲► TWO EXAMPLES OF THE RELATIVELY RARE FOUR-DOOR OPEN CARS THAT HAD THEIR LAST FLING IN THE 1930s. THE STYLE WAS OFFERED IN 1937 AND 1938 ONLY, IN BOTH THE SIX- AND EIGHT-CYLINDER PONTIAC LINES. THIS IS A 1937 DE LUXE EIGHT, WHICH AT $1,235 WAS THE MOST EXPENSIVE PONTIAC THAT YEAR. FEW WERE MADE, AND ONLY FIVE ARE KNOWN TO SURVIVE, THREE SIXES AND TWO EIGHTS. BUICK'S VERSION WAS KNOWN AS THE PHAETON, AND WAS AVAILABLE IN THE SPECIAL, CENTURY, AND ROADMASTER LINES. THIS IS A 1939 CENTURY MODEL 61-C, OF WHICH ONLY 249 WERE BUILT FOR DOMESTIC SALES, AND 20 FOR EXPORT.

PONTIAC OWNER: DICK CHOLER; BUICK OWNER: BOB DEBOW

(PHOTOS NICKY WRIGHT)

respectively. People were less enthusiastic about their prices, only 0.9 percent believing that the Cords offered best value for money, which is understandable, for they were priced from $1,995 for a Westchester sedan to $2,195 for a two-door phaeton, well above Buick or any but the top Chryslers, and $300 above the lowest-priced Cadillac V8.

But the Model 810 was a specialty car, not to be compared with the products of the Big Three. With its low lines (a height of 60 inches for the sedan and 58 inches for the convertibles made it the lowest full-sized American car) and striking appearance, it was a car for the individualist. Unfortunately individualists are often impatient, and many orders were canceled between the end of 1935 and the spring of 1936 when the production models were at last ready. Those who had placed firm orders got Cords for Christmas, but they were bronze models in 1/32 scale! The first production cars were troublesome, particularly in the transmission department, where they tended to shift back to neutral without warning. Even when they were working well, the semi-automatic gearshift was slower than a normal stick shift. This was a drawback on a car sold at least partly on its performance. Top speed was 92mph, or over 100mph with the supercharger offered on 1937 Cords, but acceleration through the gears was not so remarkable; rest to 60mph took 20.1 seconds (unsupercharged), an achievement that could be beaten by a Ford V8.

Model 810 output for 1936 was 1,174, a further 1,146 being made between January and August 1937. The supercharged Model 812 was an addition to the 1937 range, but prices were well up, $2,445–$2,645 for the 810 and $2,960–$3,060 for the 812s, which had longer wheelbases as well as superchargers. The Cords were the last cars of Errett Lobban's empire, but they will never be forgotten. In 1951 the New York Museum of Modern Art recognized the design as one of the ten finest examples of industrial styling of all time. With the Auburn speedster, the Cord was one of the first cars to be made in replica form; two companies offered convertible replicas powered by Chevrolet Corvair, Ford, and Chrysler V8 engines between 1964 and 1970.

▲ TWO CONVERTIBLES IN CHRYSLER'S AIRSTREAM EIGHT RANGE FOR 1936. ALTHOUGH THEY WERE CERTAINLY HANDSOME CARS, THEY WERE NOT AS LONG AND SLEEK AS THE ARTIST HAS MADE THEM OUT TO BE IN THIS DUMMY ADVERTISEMENT. BOTH WERE RARE MODELS: THE CONVERTIBLE ACCOUNTED FOR ONLY 240 SALES, THE CONVERTIBLE SEDAN FOR 362. CONVERTIBLE CHRYSLERS HAD ONE-PIECE WINDSHIELDS; THE CLOSED MODELS USED TWO-PIECE DESIGNS.

CHRYSLER ARCHIVES, MIRCO DE CET COLLECTION

B ODY STYLES — GOOD-BYE AND HELLO

The 1930s saw the disappearance of one body style and the emergence of a new one that has continued in popularity to the present day. The departure was the four-door open car, the arrival was the station wagon.

Open four-door bodies for five passengers were the norm at the beginning of the 1920s, but had become a minority taste a decade later. During the 1930s many manufacturers offered sophisticated versions of the old touring. Generally known as convertible sedans or phaetons, these had much improved weather protection, with wind-up windows. They were also often the most expensive in their ranges, which gave them an air of luxury and chic, whereas the touring had been lower priced than the sedan.

Ford offered a convertible sedan from 1935 through 1940, but not Chevrolet. The other GM divisions did, Buick from 1932 through 1941, Cadillac from 1929 through 1941, LaSalle from 1937 through 1940, Oldsmobile from 1940 through 1941, and Pontiac from 1937 through 1938. As an example, the 1941 Oldsmobile 98 phaeton cost $1,575, compared with $1,135 for the equivalent sedan, and sold only 119 units, against 22,081 sedans and total Olds output of 270,040 for the 1941 model year.

All the Chrysler divisions offered four-door convertibles, although Plymouth's convertible sedan was only available for the 1939 season, Chrysler's last. Among the independents, convertible sedans could be had from Hupmobile, Nash, Packard, and Studebaker, but never from Hudson, Graham, or Reo. The style was dead by 1942, and the only postwar offerings were from Frazer (1949–1951) and Lincoln (1961–1967).

Station wagons were also small-production, expensive vehicles but unlike convertible sedans they became more numerous during the 1930s. Nevertheless they did not come into their own until well after World War II. Right up to the outbreak of war, they were generally regarded as commercial vehicles, and were sold along with vans and pickups.

The first station wagon bodies were built by the Stoughton Wagon Company of Stoughton, Wisconsin, on Model T chassis from 1919 and on the Star from 1923. The latter was the first dealer-available woody, costing $610, but the number made was very small. Although they were not cataloged models until 1929, there were plenty of station wagon bodies on Ford chassis, mostly used by farmers, who were large-scale Ford customers. In 1929 a Model A station wagon was cataloged at $695, $170 more than a sedan, but only 5,251 were made out of a total 1,507,132 Fords built that year. The bodies were by Briggs from wood supplied by the Mengel company of Louisville, Kentucky. After 1937 the wood came from Ford's own forests at Iron Mountain in northern Michigan. Yet output remained small. In fact the original 1929 figure was not matched until 1938, when 6,012 were built, by then on the V8 chassis.

Nearly all station wagon bodies were supplied from outside in the 1930s; General Motors bought from Hercules or Ionia, Dodge from Cantrell, Plymouth from the U.S. Body & Forging Company, Packard from Cantrell and Hercules, and Willys from Mifflinburg. The numbers involved were not important enough to warrant production by the car makers themselves and, besides, the wooden construction was quite alien to firms now working largely if not entirely in steel. Only after the war, when the "woody" became a steel pressing with mock wood panels, were they made in house.

At first the station wagon went by various names such as "depot hack," "suburban," "beach wagon," or "carryall," and was used by farmers, explorers, film studios, and hotels rather than by ordinary families. Yet, by the end of the decade it was becoming more widely accepted; the author

remembers riding to school in Baltimore in a 1941 Plymouth station wagon which carried about nine kids. Apart from Cadillac, De Soto, Lincoln, and Nash, all the U.S. makers offered a woody in their range. After the war De Soto and Nash also joined the woody brigade.

COMFORT AND CONVENIENCE

It was not only in styling that the 1930s saw a revolution, but also in comfort and convenience for driver and passengers. The car of 1940 had many of the features taken for granted today, including heating and air conditioning, push-button radios, windshield washers and two-speed wipers, power-operated tops, and automatic transmissions. Air conditioning was first offered by Nash in 1938, while another heavily promoted feature of the company was a front seat that could be folded to make a comfortable double bed, offered from 1936 onward. In fact, Nash was not first with this, for Billy Durant made it an option in 1931, although there were few takers.

Car radios were first offered commercially by the Philadelphia Storage Battery Corporation in 1927 under the name Philco Transitone. Radios

were offered as regular production options by Cadillac and Pontiac in 1930, by Plymouth in 1931, by Chrysler, Dodge, and Studebaker in 1932, by Oldsmobile in 1933, and by Buick, Hudson, and Packard in 1934. In 1935 it was estimated that there were more than 1 million radio-equipped cars in the United States. By 1940 radios were available in all cars except the most basic, and push-button tuning was coming into widespread use. Pontiac offered a radio that could be removed from the car for picnics.

The power-operated top (by vacuum cylinders located behind the front seat) was pioneered not on a high-priced car but on the $895 1939 Plymouth De Luxe convertible coupe. It was later seen on 1940 De Sotos, while the 1941 Lincoln Continental and 1942 Oldsmobile featured a power top operated by dual electric motors. Power-operated windows were first seen as an option on 1941 Chrysler Crown Imperials, although some custom-bodied limousines had electric divisions between chauffeur and passenger compartments several years earlier. The industry's first power-adjusted front seats were introduced on the 1941 Lincoln Custom sedan.

Transmissions underwent some tremendous

41-9000

improvements during the last prewar decade. In 1930 not all cars had synchromesh, although this became universal during the next few years. Most gearboxes had three speeds, although there was a short-lived vogue for four among the more expensive cars in the early 1930s. This was a tribute to the "more is better" philosophy rather than a serious improvement, for the big, powerful Stutzes, Packards, and Pierce-Arrows were precisely the cars that did not need the extra ratio, having enough power and flexibility to cope with three speeds. Also, the average American driver did not want to be constantly gear-shifting, as his European counterpart, with a small, high-revving engine, was obliged to do. Nevertheless 15 makers offered four-speed transmission between 1929 and 1933, including Chrysler, Packard, Pierce-Arrow, and Stutz, as well as small firms on their last legs such as Elcar, Jordan, Kissel, and Windsor. The arrival of automatic overdrive, on the 1934 Chrysler Airflow giving an extra-high ratio without using the gearstick, marked the end of the ordinary four-speed transmission until the 1960s.

Chrysler's Warner overdrive, mounted behind the transmission, was adopted by Ford in 1948 and by GM in 1955, but earlier Fords had an alternative, the Columbia two-speed axle, which gave alternative ratios of 4.11:1 or 2.94:1. This effectively gave six forward speeds, although it was normally only used in high gear. Operation was by depressing the clutch, which actuated a vacuum-powered shift mechanism. The two-speed axle was an option costing around $100, offered on Fords between 1934 and 1948, and also on Auburns and the Franklin V12 in the early 1930s.

Another short-lived device was the freewheel, introduced by Studebaker in 1930 and within two years adopted by nearly all makers except Buick and Ford. It consisted of a small overriding clutch in the transmission which disengaged the drive, enabling the car to coast as a bicycle would.

Advantages were lower gas consumption and less wear and tear, but against these advantages, the brakes had to work harder in the absence of engine braking, which could be dangerous on long downhill stretches where the driver was most likely to freewheel. Also, the unstressed engines had a tendency to die. By 1935 freewheeling was just about obsolete.

The first steps toward automatic transmission were made by Reo with its Self-Shifter of 1933. This had two ranges, Hi and Lo, each with two speeds; shifting within each range was automatic, but between Lo and Hi shifting was manual. Acceleration in Hi was distinctly leisurely, so both ratios had to be used, and indeed it was necessary to double declutch for a rapid change. Even though the Self-Shifter was relatively cheap, adding only $80 to the cost of a Flying Cloud sedan, it did not prove popular and was dropped after 1935. Coincidentally or not, this was the year when Hudson introduced its Electric Hand, a preselector in which speeds were selected by a small lever extending from the steering column, and actuated when the clutch pedal was dipped. Shifting was by vacuum, electrically actuated. The Electric Hand was standard on Hudson Custom Eights, and a $20 option on others, less than half the cost of a Zenith radio ($44). In 1939 it gave way to a Selective Automatic Shift which, the makers claimed, allowed one to drive without ever needing to use the clutch pedal, although one was present.

True two-pedal automatic transmission did not arrive until 1940, when Oldsmobile introduced the famous HydraMatic Drive as a $75 option. GM had made a step in the same direction with its dual-range semi-automatic transmission of 1937, available on Oldsmobiles and Buicks. This was similar to the Reo Self-Shifter, although changes from one range to the other could be made without using the clutch. Use of the clutch was still necessary for starting from a standstill, though. The system was developed by Earl A. Thompson, and was offered first by the Oldsmobile Division because of the forward thinking of Olds' general manager Charles L. McCuen. The Automatic Safety Transmission, as it was called, was manufactured by Buick and was offered on Oldsmobiles from June 1937 through September 1939, and by Buick from the fall of 1937, for the

1938 season only. The cost was $80, but very few customers (probably fewer than 7 percent of all Oldsmobile and Buick buyers) chose it during the years it was on offer.

The semi-automatic had the same planetary gearsets controlled by a centrifugal governor as HydraMatic, but lacked the latter's fluid torque converter, hence the need for a clutch. When the fluid coupling, which consisted of two vaned rotors in an oil-filled enclosure with no mechanical link between them, was combined with the planetary gearsets, a proper two-pedal system became possible. Oldsmobile launched this in September 1939 on its 1940 models, and demand soon outstripped supply. Production of HydraMatics was woefully low in 1940, probably because Olds remembered the poor demand for the semi-automatic transmission; but, encouraged by public response, output was stepped up and by the beginning of the 1942 season, about 45 percent of Oldsmobiles were equipped with HydraMatic. It was also offered on 1941 and 1942 Cadillacs. The early HydraMatics were by no means trouble-free, suffering from rough and erratic shifting and a relatively short life. However, they were greatly improved during World War II, being used in armored cars, gun carriages, tanks, and in snowmobiles. As a result, GM entered the postwar era with a much better transmission, with a life of 30,000–50,000 miles between overhauls.

1956 IMPERIAL SEDAN ▼
OWNER: CARL W. REID (PHOTO NICKY WRIGHT)

THE AMERICAN AUTOMOBILE TRIUMPHANT

1945 – 1970

"To the average American, our present car and its size represent an outward symbol of prestige and well-being."

Ford Division report, 1951

WORLD WAR II HAD A MUCH greater effect on the American auto industry than World War I. Whereas automobiles continued to be turned out during 1917 and 1918, in February 1942 all passenger car production came to an end. In fact, a very limited number of cars were delivered later, as statistics show production of 139 passenger cars in 1943 and 610 in 1944, doubtless all for military or government use. The 1943 figure included 69 Hudsons, which were the last of the reserve of 1942 models. During 1941 the industry was already gearing up for war production, and in the following four years turned out an enormous quantity of material. Approximately 92 percent of scout cars and carriers, 87 percent of bombs, and 75 percent of aircraft engines were produced by the auto and truck industries.

This is not the place to list all these achievements, but among the more remarkable was Ford's production of 8,675 B-24 Liberator bombers at a specially built plant at Willow Run, near Ypsilanti, Michigan, and 57,585 Pratt & Whitney R-2800 radial engines at the River Rouge plant. Ford also built 277,896 Jeeps, nearly 50 percent of the total, and all amphibious Jeeps. Lincoln's

Detroit plant built 25,332 500bhp 32-valve twin-cam engines which powered the majority of Sherman tanks and tank-destroyers. Buick built 2,507 Hellcat tank-destroyers powered by Continental engines, and over 3 million cylinder heads for Pratt & Whitney aircraft engines. Hudson was particularly involved with aircraft, making components for B-26 Marauder bombers, P-38 Lightning fighter-bombers, and P-39 Airacobra fighters. Studebaker's specialty was vehicles, including 197,678 trucks, mostly 6 x 4 and 6 x 6, and 25,124 Weasel amphibious troop carriers.

◀ CAR-HUNGRY AMERICANS HAD A CHANCE TO SEE THE FIRST POSTWAR CARS AT THE CHICAGO AUTO SHOW HELD IN SEPTEMBER 1945. THE OLDSMOBILES SEEN HERE WERE ANNOUNCED IN JULY, ALTHOUGH PRODUCTION DID NOT GET UNDER WAY UNTIL OCTOBER. THE FASTBACK STYLING IN THE FOREGROUND, AVAILABLE ON THE MORE EXPENSIVE OLDSMOBILES IN 1942, WAS EXTENDED TO ALL MODELS FOR 1946.
OLDSMOBILE HISTORICAL CENTER

Passenger car manufacture was sanctioned on July 1, 1945. Ford was first to take advantage of this, starting its production lines on July 3 and remaining the only supplier of new cars for some time. General Motors did not start up until October and then in November was hit by a 113-day strike by the United Auto Workers Union, which saw the emergence of Walter Reuther as America's foremost labor chief. Chrysler, fearing that the strike would spread and reluctant to set the lines rolling until it could be sure of continuous production, restarted even later. Only 322 Chryslers were made by the end of the year, together with 947 De Sotos, 770 Plymouths, and 420 Dodges. The independents did better, Nash starting up in September for a year's production of 6,148, Hudson on August 30 (4,735), and Packard on October 19 (2,722). Nash, in fact, was in third position for 1945, behind Ford and Chevrolet.

The year of 1946 was difficult, with strikes and shortages of materials keeping output lower than hoped for. There was no window glass in January and again in September, while March saw a

STUDEBAKER INTRODUCED NEW BODIES THROUGH THE RANGE FOR 1953, OF WHICH THE STARLIGHT COUPES WERE THE MOST ATTRACTIVE. DESIGNED BY ROBERT E. BOURKE OF THE LOEWY STUDIOS, THEIR POPULARITY WAS EMBARRASSING FOR STUDEBAKER, WHO HAD ENVISAGED THAT SEDANS WOULD OUTSELL COUPES BY AROUND FOUR TO ONE, WHEREAS DEMAND WAS ALMOST PRECISELY THE OPPOSITE. THIS STARLIGHT COUPE SOLD FOR $1,995.

OWNER: NATIONAL AUTOMOBILE MUSEUM, RENO, NEVADA

(PHOTO NICKY WRIGHT)

shortage of door locks. Then in June hood locks disappeared, and by October there were plenty of locks but no doors. Strikes among component makers were particularly damaging because they hit production of all makes. However, by the end of the year a guaranteed minimum wage and a 40-hour week were agreed upon, and industrial disputes became fewer. Passenger car output in 1946 was 2,148,699, lower than in any year since depression-hit 1938. In 1947 and 1948 it was well over the 3 million mark, and in 1949 beat all previous records, with 5,119,466 cars made.

The pent-up demand for new cars was enormous; more than half the 26 million cars in the United States were more than ten years old and well overdue for replacement. While it would be unjust to say that *any* car sold, whatever its quality, the early postwar years were a sellers' market par excellence, and all car and truck makers flourished.

With the scramble to get back into production, it is hardly surprising that there were few novelties among the 1946 models. Without exception they were warmed-over 1942 designs with modified grilles and bits of extra chromework here and there. Plymouth boasted 50 new features and improvements over its 1942 models, but these were mostly limited to new interior trims, front bumpers that wrapped around the fenders to the wheel arches, and improved synchromesh gears. Under the hoods there were improvements, thanks to wartime experience: Ford and Mercury V8 engines had new aluminum pistons, larger and higher capacity oil pumps, nickel-chrome alloy valves, and other developments that had been tried on wartime truck engines, while GM's HydraMatic drive was

improved thanks to experience with tanks.

Ford and Mercury had new body styles in the form of a wood-paneled two-door convertible called the Sportsman. Made at Ford's Iron Mountain plant, the body consisted of mahogany panels attached to a steel inner frame. Otherwise the Sportsman was the same as the regular convertibles, although the rear fenders came from the 1941 sedan delivery, as the postwar fenders wrapped around too much and would have cut into the wooden trunk lid. The Sportsman convertibles were the most expensive of both the Ford and Mercury ranges, costing $1,982 with Ford badging and $2,263 as Mercurys. The latter were very rare, only 205 being made in 1946, but the Ford Sportsman sold 3,487 in three seasons, 1946–48.

The Sportsman was the idea of Henry Ford II (1917–1987), who took over as president of the Ford Motor Company from his grandfather in September 1945 (his father Edsel had died in 1943). The 28-year-old ex-naval ensign had a formidable task on his hands, for the company was heavily in debt — accounting procedures were so haphazard and primitive that in one department costs were estimated by weighing a pile of invoices on a scale. He also faced the hostility of his grandfather's henchman Harry Bennett. Within a few days he fired Bennett, who responded with the ungracious but undeniable comment: "You're taking over a billion-dollar organization here that you haven't contributed a damned thing to."

In February 1946 Henry II brought in a group of talented young men who had decided to hire themselves out as a ready-made management team. They included Charles (Tex) Thornton, at 32 one of the youngest colonels in the U.S. Army Air Force, and two academics, Ed Lundy from Princeton and Robert McNamara from the Harvard Business School, later to become U.S. Defense Secretary. Ten in all, they were nicknamed

STUDEBAKER BROUGHT OUT RADICALLY RESTYLED CARS IN 1946, FEATURING WRAPAROUND REAR WINDOWS ON SOME MODELS, SHORT HOODS, AND LONG TRUNKS. IN FACT ON THE ORIGINAL CHAMPION COUPE, HOOD AND TRUNK WERE OF ABOUT EQUAL LENGTH, GIVING RISE TO THE NICKNAME "COMING OR GOING STUDEBAKERS." THE BULLET-NOSE FRONT END CAME WITH THE 1950 MODELS, WHICH ALSO HAD COIL-AND-A-ARM INDEPENDENT FRONT SUSPENSION.

OWNER: JIM BABB   (PHOTO NICKY WRIGHT)

"the Whiz Kids." Together with accountant Ernest Breech, they set about turning Ford's fortunes around. This they did to a considerable extent, selling more than 1 million cars (including Lincoln and Mercury) in 1949, the first time the million mark had been passed since 1930. However, they never achieved their aim, which was to beat their great rival, General Motors.

Chrysler's equivalent to the Sportsman was the Town & Country, which was built in several models, closed and open. The 1946 catalog shows five styles, a roadster, a brougham, a two-door club coupe, a four-door sedan, and a convertible. The roadster was never built and only one brougham and seven club coupes saw the light of day, but the sedan and convertible went into production, the former mostly on the six-cylinder Windsor chassis, and the latter on the eight-cylinder New Yorker. In 1946 exactly 100 eight-cylinder sedans were made. Unlike the Ford Sportsman, which used wood strips on metal panels, the Town & Country had structured wood framing of white ash, with shaped plywood panels, and plenty of leather and Hylander wool graced the interior. This handwork was reflected in the price, $2,366 for the sedan, compared with $1,561 for a regular steel-bodied sedan, and $2,743 for the convertible, $550 more than was asked for the regular convertible.

There was little change in the years 1946 to 1948, except for price increases for 1948. The Town & Country models attracted a great deal of attention, and even if Chrysler made little profit on them their publicity value was excellent. Chryslers were restyled for 1949, and only the convertible was made in the Town & Country style, replaced by a hardtop for 1950. This had less wood in its construction, with ash framing on an all-steel body. Only 993 '49s and 698 '50s were made, and from 1951 onward the Town & Country name was used on station wagons.

1947 KAISER K-100 PINCONNING SPECIAL
TWO-DOOR SEDAN ▼ ▶
THE LOWER-PRICED CAR IN THE KAISER-FRAZER
LINE-UP, THE KAISER WAS PLANNED TO HAVE FRONT
DRIVE, BUT THIS WAS NEVER IMPLEMENTED. ONLY
FOUR-DOOR MODELS WERE OFFERED TO THE PUBLIC,
BUT THIS ONE-OFF TWO-DOOR SEDAN WAS SPECIALLY
BUILT FOR THE HANDICAPPED WIFE OF ED HUNT,
HEAD OF PRODUCTION AT KAISER-FRAZER, AND NAMED
FOR HUNT'S BIRTHPLACE, PINCONNING, MICHIGAN.
IT HAS A SWIVELING FRONT PASSENGER SEAT
TO ENABLE THE OCCUPANT TO CONVERSE WITH
REAR PASSENGERS FACE-TO-FACE.
OWNER: NATIONAL AUTOMOBILE MUSEUM, RENO, NEVADA
(PHOTO NICKY WRIGHT)

GENUINE POSTWAR CARS

Although most auto manufacturers delayed their postwar designs until 1948 or later, there were two new shapes to be seen on the streets by the end of 1946. These came from Studebaker and from the new Kaiser-Frazer organization.

When Studebaker revived the prewar Champion, it was very much a stopgap model, and only 19,275 were made between December 1945 and March 1946 when it gave way to the radical-looking "coming or going" models styled by Raymond Loewy and Virgil Exner. Loewy ran an independent design studio that had been retained by Studebaker since the 1930s. As well as the short hoods and long trunks that gave the cars their nicknames, they had wraparound rear windows and the straight-through lines from front to rear fenders that would soon become universal, although at the time these were only seen on Kaiser-Frazer cars.

The box-section Studebaker frame was designed for front or rear location of the engine but, so far as is known, no rear-engined model ever reached the prototype stage. However, air- and water-cooled flat-6s were tried before opting for the familiar 80bhp 169.6-cubic-inch Champion engine, joined by the 94bhp 226.2-cubic-inch unit from the prewar Commander. The same names were used, and both models came in four-door sedan, two-door coupe, and convertible forms. Although the Champion was compact in size, at 193 inches in length and weighing 2,600–2,875 pounds, it seated three passengers on front and rear seats thanks to the full-width styling.

The new Studebakers were launched in May 1946 as 1947 models; 1946 calendar year production was 77,567 and by 1949 this had risen to 228,402, putting Studebaker in eighth place and in the lead over other independent manufacturers. Assembly took place in eleven overseas plants, and a full manufacturing plant was opened at Hamilton,

Ontario, in 1948. Sixteen years later this would keep Studebaker production going when it had ceased in the United States. The peak year for output and workforce was 1950, when more than 23,000 workers at South Bend turned out 268,229 cars and more than 50,000 trucks. Up to 1952 the styling was little changed, apart from a pointed, missile-inspired grille in 1949. The Commander engine went up to 245.6 cubic inches and 100bhp for 1949, and independent front suspension by coils replaced the transverse leaves for 1950.

The other new cars of 1946 came from a new company, the Kaiser-Frazer Corporation, which was formed on July 23, 1945, only eight days after the two founders met for the first time. Henry J. Kaiser

(1882–1967) was a millionaire sand and gravel entrepreneur who had been chairman of the Hoover Dam project in the 1930s and whose seven shipyards had built 1,490 Liberty, Victory, and other ships during World War II. He was also a car buff who had an experimental lab at Emeryville, California. Joseph W. Frazer (1892–1971) had direct auto industry experience, having been with the Chrysler Corporation from 1924 to 1939, then served as president of Willys-Overland to 1943, after which he bought into the Graham-Paige Corporation, which had ceased car making in 1941 but still had an active plant. Their joint project would be the last attempt by an independent to challenge Detroit for a significant slice of the popular car market.

The design of the car came from Frazer, or rather from Howard Darrin and Bill Stout who worked for him, and the basic lines were established before he teamed up with Kaiser. From the Emeryville studio came two ideas that were soon abandoned, front-wheel drive and a fiberglass body. The initial idea was that an inexpensive front-drive car would be made in California under the Kaiser name, and a more expensive and conventional Frazer would be made in the Graham-Paige plant in Detroit. However, Joe Frazer decided that he needed bigger facilities than Graham-Paige could provide, so he leased the enormous 1-million-square-foot Willow Run plant where Ford had built Liberator bombers.

The front-drive Kaiser and rear-drive Frazer were shown to the public at New York's Waldorf-Astoria Hotel in January 1946, although both had to be sent there by train as neither was in a state to run. It is doubtful if the front-drive Kaiser ever ran, and it was soon dropped. When deliveries to dealers began in June, the cars were basically the same, the Frazer having more luxurious trim, a dual-choke carburetor, and overdrive; it cost $185 more than the $1,868 Kaiser Special. Both cars used a Continental flathead-6 of 226-cubic-inch displacement, which gave 100bhp and a top speed of 84mph. At first the engines were bought from Continental, but later Kaiser-Frazer made them themselves, in a former Hudson plant.

With the postwar car shortage, the slab-sided and modern-looking Kaisers and Frazers sold well to start with, 144,490 in 1947 and 181,316 in 1948. More expensive models were added in the Frazer Manhattan and Kaiser Custom, whose prices were in the $2,300–$2,746 range. The lowest-priced 1948 Kaiser cost $2,244, which put it in competition with

1950 FORD CUSTOM CONVERTIBLE ▼ ▶
FORD'S FIRST POSTWAR CARS, WHICH DEBUTED IN JUNE 1948 AS 1949 MODELS, WERE RADICALLY RESTYLED BY AN OUTSIDE TEAM HEADED BY GEORGE WALKER. FORD WAS SO PLEASED WITH THE RESULTS THAT IN 1955 WALKER BECAME CHIEF DESIGNER FOR ALL FORD COMPANIES. THE 1950 MODELS WERE WIDELY FACE-LIFTED AND QUALITY WAS IMPROVED. SIXES AND EIGHTS WERE OFFERED, BOTH IN DE LUXE AND CUSTOM SERIES. THIS V8 COUPE CONVERTIBLE COST $1,948.

OWNER: ARLEN MADLAND (PHOTO NICKY WRIGHT)

high, prewar style bodies gave way to lower, wider styles with fenders faired into the doors, while suspensions went independent even on Fords. Few cars were completely new, though, and engines remained generally unchanged, with the notable exceptions of Cadillac and Oldsmobile, who offered their valve-in-head V8s in 1949.

The 1949 Fords, announced in June 1948, were more innovative than any since the Model A replaced the T. Engineered by Harold Youngren and styled by Richard Caleal working for consultant George Walker, they had low, wide-looking bodies with straight-through lines from front to rear fenders. Although they seemed larger all round, they were fractionally shorter and narrower than the '48s, and the roof line was 3 inches lower. They were also lighter than their predecessors by up to 500 pounds. The old beam front axle with transverse leaf suspension gave way to an independent system by coil springs and wishbones; at the rear, suspension was by longitudinal leaf springs as in most other contemporary cars. The cruciform frame was replaced by a ladder type, except on the

1950 CHEVROLET STYLELINE COUPE ▲

LIKE MOST AMERICAN AUTO MAKERS, CHEVROLET INTRODUCED ITS NEW POSTWAR MODELS FOR THE 1949 SEASON, SO 1950 MODELS WERE LITTLE CHANGED. THERE WERE TWO LINES, THE STYLELINE, WITH PROJECTING TRUNK, AND THE FASTBACK FLEETLINE, MADE ONLY IN TWO- OR FOUR-DOOR SEDAN FORMS. PRICES WERE THE SAME AS FOR THE STYLELINE, $1,482 FOR A TWO-DOOR AND $1,529 FOR A FOUR-DOOR. THIS STYLELINE COUPE COST $1,498.

OWNER: BARNEY SMITH (PHOTO NICKY WRIGHT)

▼ IN 1950 THE WHITE HOUSE RENEWED ITS VEHICLE FLEET, TAKING DELIVERY OF TEN LINCOLNS, ALL ON THE 145-INCH WHEELBASE. NINE WERE LIMOUSINES WITH BODIES BY HENNEY, AND THE TENTH WAS THIS SEVEN-PASSENGER CONVERTIBLE BODIED BY DIETRICH CREATIVE INDUSTRIES OF GRAND RAPIDS, MICHIGAN. IT WAS PART OF THE WHITE HOUSE FLEET FOR 18 YEARS, SERVING PRESIDENTS TRUMAN (SEEN HERE), EISENHOWER, KENNEDY, AND JOHNSON.

FORD MOTOR COMPANY, MIRCO DE CET COLLECTION

Hudson, Mercury, and the more expensive Buicks rather than with the low-priced Ford or Chevrolet. (During the war Henry Kaiser had envisaged a sort of latter-day Model T to sell at no more than $365.) Up to 1949 only four-door sedans were offered, but then new models appeared in the form of the Frazer Manhattan four-door convertible, Kaiser Virginian hardtop, and the Kaiser Traveler utility sedan. This had a hatchback at the rear, although unlike modern one-piece hatchbacks it opened in two parts, being hinged at top and bottom. The rear seat back could be folded down to give maximum carrying space and the left rear door was welded shut. Kaiser never made a station wagon, but the Traveler offered many of its advantages, while still looking like a sedan.

Kaiser-Frazer never did as well again as in 1947, when a profit of $20 million was recorded, although output for 1948 was higher. The problem was that Detroit's big guns all had new models for 1949 and suddenly the cars from Willow Run seemed old-fashioned. Always undercapitalized, Kaiser-Frazer did not have the funds to come up with a new body style until 1951, by which time sales had dropped to 99,343. Rivals like Oldsmobile and Chrysler had new, powerful V8 engines, while K-F could never afford to replace the old Continental-designed flathead-6, which was really a prewar design. The only other company using it in 1950 was taxicab maker Checker Motors.

The 1949 model year saw genuine postwar designs from all of America's auto makers. The

1950 MERCURY COUPE ▲▼
MERCURY HAD A COMPLETELY NEW BODY AND CHASSIS IN 1949, WITH X-BRACED FRAME, INDEPENDENT FRONT SUSPENSION, AND LOWER LINES. CONSEQUENTLY, FEW CHANGES WERE MADE FOR 1950, APART FROM A NEW INSTRUMENT PANEL AND MINOR MODIFICATIONS TO THE GRILLE. A NEW MODEL IN MID-SEASON WAS THE MONTEREY COUPE WITH PADDED CANVAS OR VINYL TOP AND CUSTOM LEATHER INTERIOR. THIS IS THE STANDARD COUPE, WHICH SOLD FOR $1,980.

OWNER: ARLEN MADLAND (PHOTO NICKY WRIGHT)

TWO GENERATIONS OF BUICK STATION WAGON ▲▼
THE 1952 ROADMASTER (BELOW) STILL HARKS BACK TO THE WOODY ERA, MAKING USE OF MAHOGANY, ASH, AND BIRCH IN ITS CONSTRUCTION. THE 1964 SKYLARK SPORTWAGON (ABOVE) WAS OF ALL-METAL CONSTRUCTION, AND WAS A DISTINCTIVE DESIGN WITH ITS VISTA-DOME ROOF. IT USED A WHEELBASE 5 INCHES LONGER THAN OTHER SKYLARKS, AND CAME WITH THE OPTION OF A 155bhp 225-CUBIC-INCH V6 OR A 210bhp 300-CUBIC-INCH V8. THE ROADMASTER USED A 320-CUBIC-INCH STRAIGHT-8 ENGINE GIVING 170bhp.

ABOVE: GENERAL MOTORS BELOW: MIRCO DE CET COLLECTION

convertible, and the engine was moved 5 inches forward in the frame, which enabled the rear seats to be positioned well forward of the axle, giving a much better ride. Just about the only major components unchanged were the engines, which remained the familiar 95bhp six and 100bhp flathead V8. Ford did not adopt a valve-in-head V8 until 1954. A planned compact Ford with a small V8 engine was never made in the United States, but became the French-built Ford Vedette.

Mercury and Lincoln accompanied their sister marque with new models for 1949, using the same suspension and new bodies based on wartime-styled models by Gregorie. Mercury had a larger V8 engine of 255.4 cubic inches and 110bhp, while Lincoln abandoned its V12 in favor of a new 336.7-cubic-inch 152bhp V8. Mercurys became heavier and more expensive, taking on the role of junior Lincolns rather than senior Fords; this reinforced the decision taken by Henry Ford II in 1945 to create a Lincoln-Mercury Division.

General Motors' cars were less radically styled than Ford's, but were substantially changed in appearance. All had the wider, lower look, with straight-through lines from front to rear fenders, and low, horizontal grilles. Among the styling highlights was Buick's Riviera coupe, a hardtop styled to look like a convertible. The idea is said to have originated with Sarah Ragsdale, wife of assistant body engineer Ed Ragsdale, who drove a convertible because she liked its sporty lines but never had the top down as she said it spoiled her hairdo. Another Buick stylist, Ned Nickles, might have disputed that, as he had been working on the idea since 1945 and it was a feature of the seven Chrysler Town & Country coupe prototypes built in 1946. Nevertheless Buick was the first to put the

idea into large-scale production. There were also Cadillac and Oldsmobile hardtops, known respectively as the Coupe de Ville and Holiday.

Another characteristic of 1949 Buicks was the row of portholes just ahead of the front doors. These were Nickles' idea. He had cut them in his own 1947 Buick convertible, rigging up lights in them which flashed at increasing speed as the engine revved up. On being told that Nickles had ruined his car with these portholes, Buick's general manager Harlow Curtice asked to see them and was so impressed that he ordered them to be part of the 1949 models, three on Supers and four on Roadmasters. This became the quickest way of identifying the top model and doubtless encouraged the sales of Roadmasters. With some changes in shape, portholes were Buick features until 1958, and again on some models from 1960 into the early 1970s.

The first of the new GM bodies came from Cadillac and Oldsmobile, introduced on their 1948 ranges. Together with the 1949 Chevrolet, Buick, and Pontiac, they looked remarkably alike in

1951 OLDSMOBILE 88 SEDAN ▲▼
A NEW MODEL FOR 1949, THE OLDS 88 COMBINED THE NEW ROCKET V8 ENGINE WITH THE LIGHTWEIGHT FUTURAMIC 76 BODIES, SO WAS QUITE A PERFORMER. SIX BODIES WERE OFFERED ORIGINALLY, BUT BY 1951 THE REGULAR 88 WAS DOWN TO TWO, A TWO-DOOR AND A FOUR-DOOR SEDAN. THE SUPER 88, OF WHICH THIS IS AN EXAMPLE, WAS MADE IN FIVE STYLES, INCLUDING A HARDTOP COUPE AND A CONVERTIBLE.
OWNER: BILL GOODSENE (PHOTO NICKY WRIGHT)

1949 CADILLAC COUPE DE VILLE ▲▶
CADILLACS WERE UPDATED IN TWO STAGES BETWEEN 1947 AND 1949. NEW BODIES APPEARED FOR 1948, AND THE 1949 SEASON SAW THE TREND-SETTING OVERHEAD VALVE V8 ENGINE, WHICH GAVE 160bhp FROM A SMALLER DISPLACEMENT THAN ITS 140bhp PREDECESSOR. LARGELY ON THE STRENGTH OF THE ENGINE, THE 1949 CADILLACS WERE CHOSEN AS *MOTOR TREND* MAGAZINE'S FIRST CAR OF THE YEAR. THE SERIES 62 COUPE DE VILLE WAS A NEW STYLE FOR 1949, AND COST $3,496. ONLY 2,150 WERE BUILT, MAKING IT THE RAREST STYLE IN THE 1949 RANGE.
OWNER: LES STERLING (PHOTO NICKY WRIGHT)

1954 CHRYSLER NEW YORKER DE LUXE SEDAN ▼
IN 1954 CHRYSLER STYLING WAS STILL INFLUENCED BY KAUFMAN T. KELLER'S DEMAND FOR PLENTY OF HEADROOM. "MANY OF YOU CALIFORNIANS MAY HAVE OUTGROWN THE HABIT," HE TOLD A STANFORD UNIVERSITY AUDIENCE IN 1948, "BUT THERE ARE PARTS OF THIS COUNTRY, CONTAINING MILLIONS OF PEOPLE, WHERE BOTH THE MEN AND THE LADIES ARE IN THE HABIT OF GETTING BEHIND THE WHEEL, OR ON THE BACK SEAT, WEARING HATS." THIS 1954 NEW YORKER WAS ONE OF THE LAST "HIGH-HAT" CARS, FOR THE NEXT YEAR'S MODELS WERE STYLED BY VIRGIL EXNER, WHO GAVE CHRYSLER A LOWER APPEARANCE CALLED "THE 100 MILLION DOLLAR LOOK."
OWNER: VIRGIL MYERS (PHOTO NICKY WRIGHT)

profile, and in fact the same doors were shared by Buick, Cadillac, and Oldsmobile. The 1948 Cadillacs were the first to sport fins at the back of the rear fenders, although these were quite modest compared with later appendages. Fins became as much a Cadillac trademark as portholes were for Buick. Although Cadillac's bodies were new for 1948, their engines remained the familiar 346-cubic-inch flathead V8s that had been around since 1936.

In 1949 both Cadillac and Oldsmobile Divisions introduced their all-new valve-in-head high-compression V8 engines. Cadillac's displaced 331 cubic inches and developed 160bhp, while the Oldsmobile Rocket was slightly smaller at 303 cubic inches and 135bhp. With a compression ratio

of 7.25:1, these engines marked the beginning of the horsepower race that pushed outputs to more than 300bhp in less than ten years. Buick received its new V8 in 1953, Chevrolet and Pontiac in 1955. Pontiac replaced its venerable straight-8, which was the last engine of this layout to be made in the United States.

Chrysler Division cars were less radically restyled than their rivals, as Chrysler boss Kaufman T. Keller favored a fairly high roof line. An inveterate hat wearer, he stuck to the principle that the roof should be high enough to accommodate a man wearing a hat. "We build cars to sit in," he said, "not to piss over." The result was generally uninspired styling for the 1949 Chrysler, De Soto, Dodge, and Plymouth; the six-window sedans were

Why the New Hudson is America's "4-most" car

1 most beautiful

2 most roomy

3 most road-worthy

4 most all-round performance

New Hudson

ONLY CAR WITH THE STEP DOWN DESIGN

▲ WHETHER THE "STEP DOWN" HUDSON WAS AMERICA'S MOST BEAUTIFUL CAR IS DEBATABLE, BUT IT WAS CERTAINLY ONE OF THE MOST INNOVATIVE DESIGNS OF THE POSTWAR ERA.

MIRCO DE CET COLLECTION

replaced by four-window models with larger trunks in all four lines, although six-window eight-passenger sedans and limousines were continued in the bigger Chrysler ranges, Windsor and Crown Imperial. Dodge advertised its new models as "higher inside, lower outside, shorter outside, longer inside." The regular models were shorter by only 1.6 inches, but there was a new Wayfarer series, which was 8.2 inches shorter. A new model in the Wayfarer range was a two/three-passenger roadster in the 1930s idiom, even down to its detachable windows, although these were soon discontinued. Roadster production in 1949 was 5,420 out of a total of 298,399 Dodges made that year. Another new style was Plymouth's De Luxe Suburban, a two-door station wagon with no wood trim.

Among the independents, Hudson and Nash both had dramatically styled new models. Hudson's, announced in October 1947 as a 1948 model, featured semi-unit construction and a very low line, which gave it the nickname the "step down" Hudson. It had been planned before the war and in 1941 chief stylist Frank Spring had shown a prototype to Hudson president A. E. Barit. The conservative Barit had growled "too low," and the prototype was consigned to the roof of the Hudson plant where it rusted away for the duration of the war. In about 1946 Spring retrieved his car, smartened it up, and re-presented it to Barit, who drove it home one evening and was so delighted that he ordered it into production.

The new Hudsons were only 60 inches high, 7 inches lower than a Buick and 6 inches lower than a Chrysler, and had the lowest center of gravity of any American car. The floor dropped below the frame sides, being the lowest part of the structure. There was still a frame, although it was welded to the body, giving semi-unit construction rather than a full monocoque. The rear wheels were actually mounted inside the side members of the frame. They were big cars, 207 inches long and 77 inches wide, but had excellent roadability. The latter was praised by the British magazine, *The Motor*, which often criticized American cars for

1952 HUDSON COMMODORE EIGHT SEDAN ◀
HUDSON OFFERED FOUR LINES FOR THE 1952 SEASON: PACEMAKER, WASP AND COMMODORES SIXES, AND COMMODORE EIGHT. ALL HAD THE SAME GENERAL APPEARANCE AS THE FIRST "STEP DOWNS" OF 1948, WHICH LASTED UNTIL AFTER THE 1954 MERGER WITH NASH. AS WELL AS FOUR-DOOR SEDANS, THERE WERE COUPES AND CONVERTIBLES. COMMODORE SIXES AND EIGHTS SHARED A 124-INCH WHEELBASE AND WERE ALMOST IDENTICAL IN APPEARANCE APART FROM UPHOLSTERY, CARPETS, AND "6" OR "8" ABOVE THE FRONT WHEELS. THIS EIGHT COST $2,769. THE YEARS 1951–53 SAW HUDSON DOMINANT IN STOCK CAR RACING, WITH 105 WINS IN MAJOR NASCAR EVENTS.

OWNER: DICK GINTHER (PHOTO NICKY WRIGHT)

their soft suspension and habit of rolling on corners. Unchanged was the familiar 128bhp flathead straight-8 engine, although this was supplemented by a new 123bhp six, also a flathead. At 262 cubic inches, this had a larger displacement than the eight. Four-door sedans, two-door coupes, and convertibles were offered in both series.

Although "step down" prices were well up on those of the 1947 Hudsons, sales were up too, from just over 100,000 to 143,697 for the calendar year 1948. They dipped slightly in 1949, when Hudson was hit by several strikes, including one in August occasioned by a heatwave. The basic design of the "step down" was not changed until 1955, when the 1954 merger with Nash led to Hudsons being made at the Nash Kenosha plant. A larger engine was introduced in 1951, a 308-cubic-inch flathead-6 giving 145bhp, which enabled Hudson to dominate stock car racing for three years.

Nash's postwar car was just as striking as Hudson's, but with less satisfactory handling. Its official name was Airflyte, but it soon acquired the nickname "bathtub," due to its all-enveloping fastback styling with partial fairings over front and rear wheels. It featured full-unit construction, a curved, one-piece windshield, and a pod above the steering column that contained all the instruments, known as the Uniscope. Front seats folded back to make a double bed, as in previous Nashes. The Airflyte was available in two series, with names carried over from earlier models, the 600 and the Ambassador. The 600 rode on a 112-inch wheelbase with a small six engine of only 172.6 cubic inches, while the Ambassador had a 121-inch wheelbase and was powered by a 234.8-cubic-inch six with overhead valves. Both these engines were carried over from the 1946–48 Nashes, and were continued until 1955 when the Ambassador was given a Packard V8 engine. Because of the unit construction, there were not many body variations in the Airflyte range, only two- and four-door sedans and a two-door brougham, with no convertibles. In 1950 Nash brought out a compact car, the Rambler, to be described later in this chapter.

The only other independent, eventually to become Studebaker's partner, was Packard. The venerable Detroit company abandoned the luxury field when it sold the dies for the big 180 series to the Soviet Union, so it entered the postwar market

1947 PACKARD CLIPPER CUSTOM SUPER 8 SEDAN ▼

THE CLIPPER LINE WAS INTRODUCED IN MID-1941 AND WAS A RADICAL DEPARTURE FROM PREVIOUS PACKARD STYLING, WHICH HAD BEEN MORE CONSERVATIVE THAN OTHER DETROIT MAKES. POSTWAR PACKARDS WERE ALL CLIPPERS, AND WERE MADE IN FOUR SERIES, A SIX AND THREE EIGHTS. THE CUSTOM SUPER 8 WAS THE TOP OF THE RANGE, AND UNLIKE OTHER CLIPPERS CARRIED NO IDENTIFYING FRONT DOOR SCRIPTS; IT HAD LUXURIOUS INTERIOR TRIM, WITH SPECIAL CARPETING, RICH BROADCLOTH AND LEATHER UPHOLSTERY, AND IMITATION WOOD PANELING. THIS SEDAN COST $3,274. A BASIC CLIPPER SIX COULD BE HAD FOR $1,745.

OWNER: JOHN J. POVINELLI (PHOTO NICKY WRIGHT)

1948 CHEVROLET STATION WAGON ▲
THE TRADITIONAL "WOODY" STATION WAGON
WAS STILL PART OF THE CHEVROLET RANGE IN 1948.
THIS EIGHT-PASSENGER MODEL IN THE FLEETMASTER
SERIES WAS THE MOST EXPENSIVE CHEVROLET
THAT YEAR, AT $2,013.

(PHOTO NICKY WRIGHT)

1947 CHRYSLER TOWN & COUNTRY SEDAN ▶
THE TOWN & COUNTRY WAS MORE OF A GENUINE WOODY THAN THE FORD SPORTSMAN,
FOR THE FRAME WAS OF WHITE ASH, WITH PLYWOOD PANELS. ALTHOUGH FIVE BODY
STYLES WERE PLANNED, ONLY THE CONVERTIBLE AND THE FOUR-DOOR SEDAN WERE
PRODUCED IN ANY NUMBERS. THIS SIX-CYLINDER SEDAN WAS MADE FOR THE THREE YEARS
OF THE TOWN & COUNTRY'S LIFETIME, 1946—1948, WITH 3,994 DELIVERED. ONLY 100 EIGHT-
CYLINDER SEDANS WERE MADE, ALL OF THEM IN 1946. THIS 1947 SEDAN COST $2,713.

OWNER: BLAINE JENKINS (PHOTO NICKY WRIGHT)

1947 FORD SPORTSMAN CONVERTIBLE ◄

THE SPORTSMAN WAS HENRY FORD II's IDEA OF ADDING SOME SPICE TO THE IMMEDIATE POST-WORLD WAR II CARS, BEFORE ALL-NEW MODELS COULD APPEAR. DEVELOPED FROM BOB GREGORIE'S WARTIME SKETCHES, THE SPORTSMAN HAD WHITE ASH AN MAHOGANY PANELS OVER A STEEL FRAME. THEY ATTRACTED PLENTY OF ATTENTION AT FORD DEALERSHIPS, BUT A PRICE THAT WAS $500 MORE THAN THAT OF THE REGULAR CONVERTIBLE WAS A DETERRENT TO SALES. ONLY 1,209 SPORTSMEN WERE MADE IN 1946, 2,250 IN 1947, AND 28 IN 1948. THE COMPANION MERCURY MODEL WAS EVEN RARER, FOR ONLY 205 WERE MADE.

OWNER: BLAINE JENKINS (PHOTO NICKY WRIGHT)

1949 CROSLEY CD WAGON ▲

CROSLEY WAS THE ONLY SUCCESSFUL MAKER OF SMALL CARS IN THE POSTWAR ERA AND EVEN IT
EXPERIENCED A BAD SLUMP IN SALES IN 1949, TO ONLY 7,431 FROM 29,184 THE PREVIOUS YEAR.
THIS STATION WAGON WAS THE MOST POPULAR OF FOUR STYLES, WITH 3,803 DELIVERED.

OWNER: AUBURN-CORD-DUESENBERG MUSEUM (PHOTO NICKY WRIGHT)

THE AMERICAN AUTOMOBILE: A CENTENARY 1893 – 1993

with the middle-class Clipper, priced from $1,680 for the cheapest six to $3,047 for a Custom Super Eight sedan. Wheelbases were 120 or 127 inches, although there was an extended wheelbase model in the Super Eight series that ran to 148 inches and was available as a limousine at $4,496. For 1948 the Clippers were restyled, with longer hoods, bolder grilles, and rounded styling; like Nash's Airflyte, they earned the epithet of "bathtub" or "pregnant elephant." There were three series, Standard Eight, Super Eight, and Custom Eight, with engines of 288, 327, and 356 cubic inches respectively. With a 165bhp output, the latter was America's most powerful engine until the arrival of the 180bhp Chrysler hemi-head V8 for 1951.

Convertibles were back for the first time since 1942, and a new style in the Standard Eight range was the Station Sedan, a woody-styled car which nevertheless used mostly sedan body stampings. The only items of wood about the exterior were the bolted-on ribs over simulated woodgrain panels on the doors. These required fungus-killing treatment and regular varnishing, as did the wooden cargo deck inside, so the Station Sedan needed as much upkeep as a real woody. At $3,350 it was the most expensive Standard Eight by a wide margin, costing more than many Super Eights. It was listed through the 1950 season, after which totally new Packard bodies were introduced.

A MINOR LEAGUE REVOLT AGAINST DETROIT

In 1949 the Big Three and the major independents accounted for 19 marques, but there were, in theory, at least 40 for American car buyers to choose from. All over the country postwar euphoria saw a host of mainly small concerns making small cars. Together they made up what *Popular Mechanics* magazine called "a minor league revolt against Detroit." Not that they caused many headaches in the Motor City; with few exceptions, the newcomers were not competing in the mass-produced family car market, but catered to what turned out to be a non-existent demand for small shopping cars, or what would be called 30 years later the sub-compact class.

Typical of the smallest class was the San Diego-built Towne Shopper, a doorless open two-passenger runabout with a horizontally-opposed twin Onan engine selling at just under a dollar a pound ($595 for a 600-pound car). Others included the Airway, also from San Diego, a three-passenger sedan or two passenger coupe with aluminum and plastic body and two-cylinder engine, and the Brogan three wheeler from Rossmoyne, Ohio. Slightly larger were the Del Mar, a five-passenger convertible powered by a 162-cubic-inch Continental engine, and the Gregory, a real weirdo with a rear-mounted Continental engine driving by shaft to the front wheels.

More serious ventures which ultimately came to nothing were the Keller and Playboy. The Keller originated in San Diego in 1945 as the Bobbi-Kar, a rear-engined runabout in the Towne Shopper class, powered by a 16hp Briggs & Stratton engine. This was soon replaced by a 25hp Hercules four, and in this form it attracted the attention of ex-Studebaker sales vice-president George Keller. He convinced a group of Alabama investors that the car would be better produced in their state, where there was a lot of unemployment due to closure of wartime aircraft factories. The cars to be produced at Huntsville under the Keller name were a rear-engined convertible, essentially the four-cylinder Bobbi-Kar renamed, and a front-engined station wagon with a 49hp 162-cubic-inch Continental engine. The Huntsville plant was an assembly operation, for practically all components of the Keller were bought out; it had Ross steering, Wagner brakes, and a Carter carburetor, the transmission was the same as that in a 1941 Studebaker, the wheels were shared with the Crosley, and so on. The only parts made by Keller were the seats and the wooden station wagon body.

By September 1949 Keller Motors Corporation had signed up 1,523 dealerships, but only 18 prototypes had been made. The heart attack that killed George Keller on October 4 proved a fatal blow for the company, which had been promoted on the man rather than the car. No more Kellers were made, and finances were so tight that the Hotel Buckingham in New York was forced to sell the Keller on display in the lobby to cover outstanding bills. The design had a short further life in Belgium, where George Keller had acquired a dealership, Poelmans and Merksen of Antwerp. A few station wagons, sold under the name Pullman, were assembled at this European location.

The Playboy also started as a rear-engined convertible, with all-independent suspension as well. One prototype was built in this form, by designer Charles Thomas, but by the time he had obtained financial backing for its manufacture, the engine had moved to the front and suspension was by conventional semi-elliptic springs at the rear, although at the front it was still independent by horizontal coil springs. Backing came from Buffalo Packard dealer Louis Horwitz and service station owner Norman Richardson. They started Playboy production in the old Brunn coachbuilding plant in Buffalo, with 125 workers assembling the cars by hand. In 1948 Playboy Motor Car Corporation leased a huge former aero-engine plant at Tonawanda, New York, which was too large, just as the Brunn premises had been too small. The administration building alone offered double the space the Playboy needed.

The Playboy price was set at $985, which seemed good value compared with the Ford Super De Luxe convertible at $1,740, but this was only when comparing one convertible with another. Playboy was aiming at the bottom end of the market, regardless of body style. Here a basic Ford De Luxe six two-door sedan cost $1,212 and a similar Chevrolet $1,313. It is doubtful if Playboy could have held the price at $985, and if the $1,000 or $1,100 mark had been broached, the Playboy's price tag would have been perilously close to the Big Three, which produced much more substantial cars. However, the sale of Playboy stock was hit by the Tucker scandal, and despite plans to merge sales operations with Kaiser-Frazer, Horwitz filed for bankruptcy in July 1948. Playboy production was just 97 cars.

Crosley's postwar history was much more of a success story. Among its many wartime contracts was one to make a copper-brazed six-cylinder engine for powering generators, and Powel Crosley built a four-cylinder adaptation of this for his postwar car. It displaced only 44 cubic inches, developed 26.5bhp, and weighed only 59 pounds. Unusual was the single overhead camshaft, the first use of this on an American car since the demise of Stutz in 1935. The car had an all-new body style, with a slab-sided two-door sedan and rolltop sedan. Despite the absence of synchromesh in the three-speed transmission, the little Crosleys sold well, 4,999 in 1946 and 19,344 in 1947 when a station wagon was added. Crosley's best year was 1948, with 29,184 passenger cars sold, as well as 2,411 vans and pick-ups. Of the cars, the great majority, 23,489, were station wagons, indicating where Crosley's best market lay.

The only dark cloud on the horizon was the copper-brazed (COBRA) engine, where electrolysis was causing small holes to appear in the block, letting the cooling water escape. There was no way in which the process could be stopped, nor could the holes be repaired, so after a number of engines had been rebuilt at the factory, a switch was made to a cast-iron block (CIBA).

As the postwar sellers' market evaporated, so Crosley's sales dived to 7,431 in 1949 and 6,792 in 1950. The range was enlivened by the Hotshot, a low-built doorless two-passenger roadster on an 85-inch wheelbase, 5 inches longer than other Crosleys. Top speed was 77mph, although tuned competition versions could exceed 90mph. Special versions of the Hotshot competed at Le Mans and at Sebring, winning the Index of Performance there in 1951. In 1951 the Hotshot was joined by the Super Sport, the same car with doors and a 10:1 compression ratio. Only 2,498 sports cars were made in four seasons, 1949–52. Another new model was a small, Jeep-like vehicle with six forward and two reverse speeds, and optional dual rear wheels. Named the FarmOroad, it could be fitted with a plow or disk harrow or tow a mower. Crosley sales dwindled through 1951 and 1952, with Powel Crosley putting in $3 million of his own money, but labor costs rose more than the price he could charge for the car. This had risen from $888 in 1947 to $1,033 five years later. On July 3, 1952, Crosley closed his plant and America's most successful small car was no more. The FarmOroad design was revised by Crofton Marine Engineering of San Diego in 1959, and about 250 were sold under the name Crofton Bug.

Among all the small manufacturers who sought a place in the sun of the immediate postwar years, only one proposed a full-sized six-passenger sedan which could have mounted a serious challenge to Detroit. His name was Preston Thomas Tucker (1903–56). Having started his working life as an office boy for Cadillac engineer D. McCall White,

he went on to become a policeman, a salesman for Dodge and Studebaker, and a brewery official. During World War II he made a lot of money from a gun turret he designed, and this was the basis of the finance for his postwar car.

He had many discussions about the car with the famous race car designer Harry Miller, and when Miller died in 1943 the basic layout of the Tucker car had been decided, or so said Ben Parsons who joined Tucker in 1945 to, as he put it, "just clean up" the design. This was over-modest, for Parsons was responsible for the radical flat-6 engine and all the chassis engineering. The body was designed by former Auburn-Cord-Duesenberg stylist Alex Tremulis. Miller had suggested the rear engine location, and that it should be a flat-6; its enormous displacement (589 cubic inches) was Parsons' idea,

the theory being that it would be a really low-stressed unit turning at no more than 1,800rpm even when the car was at its maximum of 110mph. At 60mph the engine would be turning at 1,000rpm. The design was full of advanced features, including fuel injection, hemispherical combustion chambers, and hydraulic valve actuation which used columns of oil in place of cams and pushrods. The idea was that the absence of mechanical valve train would enable Parsons to design an ideal cylinder head. Unfortunately the valves wouldn't open until sufficient oil pressure had been pumped up by the engine, which clearly wouldn't start unless the valves could open. This was overcome by using the massive 24-volt battery for several seconds, but it was never satisfactory. Drive to the rear wheels was by two torque converters.

1948 TUCKER SEDAN ▼ ▶

Away from the engine, the Tucker Torpedo was no less radical, with all-independent suspension by rubber, disk brakes, seat belts, a popout windshield, and a third headlight that turned into corners. Only one chassis and one full-bodied car were made in original form, and subsequent Tuckers were more conventional, although the low (49-inch) body and cyclops headlight remained. Parsons' engine was replaced by a much smaller flat-6 made by Air Cooled Motors (formerly Franklin) of Syracuse, N.Y. Converted to water cooling, it displaced 334.1 cubic inches, about the same as a V8 Cadillac, and gave 166bhp at 3,200rpm. The torque converters gave way to a preselective transmission as used in the Cord 810; Tucker scoured junkyards to locate these for the first production cars, although later he made his own, based on the Cord design, and called them the Y-1. The seat belts went too; Tucker was strongly in favor of them but his vice-president of sales, Fred Rockelman, said that putting belts in a car implied that it was unsafe to begin with. However, the value of belts was shown when a test driver at Indianapolis rolled a Tucker several times and stepped out completely unscathed. Top speed was around 120mph, and in 1954 a Tucker out-accelerated an Oldsmobile 88, the hottest mass-produced car of the late 1940s, at the Pomona Strip, California.

For making his new car Tucker leased the world's biggest building under one roof, running to 93 acres, with two foundries and 30 to 40 separate cafeterias. Located in Chicago and even bigger than Kaiser-Frazer's Willow Run plant, this was the building that had been used by Dodge to build B-29 aircraft engines, and came with more machine tools than the whole of Switzerland. Before he could use even a fraction of this space for car production, Tucker ran into problems with the Securities Exchange Commission, the government agency that regulates the stock market. Unhappy about many of Tucker's promises, the SEC OK'd the offer of $20 million stock, but warned the public to be cautious. Tucker was also required to pay $500,000 as his first year's rent on the factory to its owners, the War Assets Administration. This wasn't too onerous as stock sold well at first, but Tucker made a great mistake in promising in September 1947 that by March 1948 he would be making 1,000 cars a day, a clear impossibility.

To obtain desperately needed cash Tucker applied for a loan to the Reconstruction Finance Corporation, a government body that helped companies to re-establish themselves after war work. The RFC asked the SEC for advice; don't do it, said the SEC, so the RFC didn't. From early 1948 things went from bad to worse for Preston Tucker; he was investigated by Michigan Senator Homer Ferguson, and suspected that Ferguson was motivated by Detroit to sabotage his efforts to establish a rival marque. The influential radio commentator Drew Pearson said that the car was a hoax, that only one had been built, out of Oldsmobile parts, and that it couldn't back up (this last accusation was true of the original prototype because fluid couplings had been used instead of the planned torque converters with reverse stators). At the time of the broadcast, Tucker had built at least eight cars, and he rushed three to Washington where he parked them outside Pearson's office. With his attorney he asked Pearson to look out of his window and retract the statement, but Pearson refused to move from his desk.

Confidence in Tucker stock, and in his car, fell, and dealers began suing him for not providing cars for them to sell. Only 51 Tuckers were ever built, and everything in the enormous factory was auctioned off in 1950, bringing in only 18 cents on the dollar. Tucker later tried to make a popular-priced car in Brazil. He died of lung cancer on December 26, 1956.

Two frequently made charges about Tucker deserve attention: that he was a fraud more interested in making money than cars, and that his woes were the result of Detroit's big guns being out to get him. In 1972 *Special-Interest Autos* magazine put the question of fraud or hoax to seven men qualified to speak on the subject, from former associates Ben Parsons and Alex Tremulis to General Motors president Ed Cole and experienced journalists John R. Bond, Maurice Hendry, and Karl Ludvigsen. No one upheld the suggestion of fraud, which had been started by Drew Pearson and others, but there was a general feeling that Tucker was sadly short of auto industry experience and that he was too enthusiastic about untried designs. Too much of his limited capital was wasted on gimmicks such as the torque converter. Also he misread the market; his car was undoubtedly way ahead of the competition, but the American public did not want what he had to offer. If the engineering and marketing might of General Motors could not make a success of the rear-engine flat-6 Corvair, what hope was there for Preston Tucker?

The suggestion that Tucker scared the daylights out of Detroit and that they resorted to underhanded methods to suppress him is equally improbable. For one thing, the late 1940s were a sellers' market and Detroit was too busy obtaining steel to meet the enormous pent-up demand for new cars to worry about a way-out design from an unknown. The Tucker was projected to sell at $2,450, so it would have been up against the Buick Roadmaster and Chrysler New Yorker, both of which appealed to traditional buyers. Kaiser-Frazer might have worried Detroit, although not for long; Tucker could hardly have cost all the Big Three executives five minutes' sleep between them.

Special-Interest Autos editor Mike Lamm summed it up as well as anyone: "Preston Tucker," he said, "was essentially a small-time promotor who'd gone big-time. He was out of his pond."

COMPACTS AND THE CONTINUING DECLINE OF THE INDEPENDENTS

In recent years the American motorist has become accustomed to a variety of sizes and ranges within each make—sub-compacts, compacts, pony cars, intermediates, and so on. Up to 1950 such variety was practically unknown; a typical make like Oldsmobile had three series, 76, 88, and 98, with two different engines, a six for the 76 and a V8 for the others, but they looked almost alike, and differences in size were very small, an extra 2.5 inches on the wheelbase and 2 inches on the front tread between the bottom and top of the range. Among the popular makes in 1950, Ford had two engines and a single wheelbase, while Chevrolet and Plymouth made do with a single engine and wheelbase.

In the 1930s several companies had tried making smaller cars, often under different names, such as Studebaker's Rockne, Buick's Marquette, and Marmon's Roosevelt, but the only one that had any lasting success was the Studebaker Champion, made from 1939, which differed in styling as well as size from the big Studebakers. Studebaker was, of course, an independent company (not part of the Big Three and not even Detroit-based), and the three small cars which emerged in the early 1950s, and of the size which would later be called "compacts," also came from independents.

Nash's Rambler was firmly supported by the company president George Mason, who reasoned

1952 ALLSTATE MODEL A-2304 SEDAN ▲▶
THE ALLSTATE WAS THE SECOND ATTEMPT BY SEARS ROEBUCK
TO MARKET ITS OWN BRAND OF AUTOMOBILE (THE FIRST
WAS THE SEARS MOTOR BUGGY OF 1908-1912).
BUILT BY KAISER-FRAZER FOR SEARS, THE ALLSTATE WAS
A HENRY J WITH A MODIFIED GRILLE AND BETTER QUALITY UPHOLSTERY,
USING SEARS' OWN BRAND OF SPARK PLUGS, BATTERIES, AND TIRES.
THE CHEAPEST ALLSTATE UNDERCUT THE HENRY J BY JUST $12, BUT
ON THE WHOLE SEARS CUSTOMERS PAID SLIGHTLY MORE
THAN THOSE WHO BOUGHT FROM K-F DEALERS.
THIS SEDAN HAS THE FOUR-CYLINDER 68bhp WILLYS ENGINE,
BUT THE 80bhp SIX WAS ALSO AVAILABLE.
OWNER: NATIONAL AUTOMOBILE MUSEUM, RENO, NEVADA (PHOTO NICKY WRIGHT)

that an independent car maker had to be different, to offer something not available from the Big Three. He also thought that the reason small cars had generally failed in America in the past was that they sold on price, and therefore marked down the owners as people of limited means. If you could get people to buy small cars because they wanted them, not because they could afford nothing else, you could capture a useful slice of the market.

This philosophy gave rise to the Rambler, regarded as a separate marque within the Nash Corporation and for which the name of a Nash predecessor made from 1902 to 1913 was revived. Launched in April 1950, it had a 100-inch wheelbase unitary construction body which bore a family resemblance to the bigger "bathtub" Nashes, with partially covered front as well as rear wheels, and was powered by the 172.6-cubic-inch 600 engine. Initially, the only model was a convertible with a price tag of $1,808; this was America's second lowest-priced convertible, after the Crosley, and cheaper than Ford or Chevrolet convertibles. It was, however, several hundred dollars above the lowest-priced Chevrolet or Ford sedan, so it escaped the label of being a cheap car. Its image was that of a chic second car for well-off suburbanites, and first year sales were an encouraging, although not spectacular, 9,330 convertibles and 1,712 station wagons (introduced in June 1950).

A "Country Club" hardtop was added to the 1951 Rambler range, and sales went up to 70,002, more than 36 percent of total Nash sales. The original Rambler never did as well again, being hit by rival compacts from Kaiser, Hudson, and Willys, and after 1955 it was dropped. However, three years later the new president George Romney relaunched the car under the name Rambler American, and this time it really was a basic automobile, offered only as a sedan and business coupe. By then George Mason was dead, and so was Nash, which had merged with Hudson in 1954 to form American Motors. All cars were called Ramblers, but the American remained the compact version and sold very well in the years 1959–61, helping Rambler into third place, behind Chevrolet and Ford, in 1960 and 1961. Its success undoubtedly influenced the Big Three into speeding up the launch of their own compact

designs in time for the 1960 auto season.

The Rambler's rivals from Kaiser, Hudson, and Willys were less stylish and aimed more at the economy market than the chic suburbanite. Henry Kaiser had dreamed of a really low-priced car, a latter-day Model T, before he launched his full-sized cars in 1946. He spoke of a target price of $385, which was quite unrealistic by any standards, but it showed that he thought a car could be sold on price alone. This was the thinking behind the Henry J, launched for 1951 as a two-door sedan on a 100-inch wheelbase (the same as the Rambler), with a choice of engines, 68bhp 134.2-cubic-inch four-cylinder or 80bhp 161-cubic-inch six. Both engines were bought from Willys, the four being that which powered the Jeep, although Kaiser did not disclose this in its publicity. The target price was $1,195 and the Henry J was not much above this when it went on sale at $1,363 for the four and $1,499 for the six.

Unfortunately a basic Ford six two-door coupe cost less than a Henry J four ($1,324) and was also a full-sized car from an established maker. Many Henry J owners complained of poor body

1950 NASH RAMBLER ▲
BORN OF PRESIDENT GEORGE ROMNEY'S BELIEF THAT INDEPENDENT AUTO MAKERS NEEDED TO OFFER SOMETHING DIFFERENT FROM THE BIG THREE IF THEY WERE TO GAIN A NICHE IN THE MARKET, THE NASH RAMBLER SHARED THE "BATHTUB" STYLING OF THE LARGER NASHES, BUT HAD A 100-INCH WHEELBASE. AT $1,808 IT WAS AMERICA'S SECOND LOWEST-PRICED CONVERTIBLE AFTER THE CROSLEY, WHICH WAS HARDLY IN THE SAME LEAGUE.
MOTOR VEHICLE MANUFACTURERS' ASSOCIATION

1953 WILLYS AERO SEDAN ▲
STYLED BY PHIL WRIGHT AND ENGINEERED BY CLYDE PATON, THE AERO WAS THE FIRST WILLYS SEDAN MADE SINCE 1942. A COMPACT IN THE RAMBLER/HENRY J MARKET, IT HAD GOOD PERFORMANCE AND FUEL ECONOMY, BUT WAS EXPENSIVE, COSTING MORE THAN A FULL-SIZE FORD OR CHEVROLET; 1953 PRICES RAN FROM $1,646 FOR A LARK TWO-DOOR SEDAN WITH 72bhp FOUR-CYLINDER L-HEAD ENGINE TO $2,157 FOR THE EAGLE HARDTOP WITH 90bhp SIX-CYLINDER F-HEAD ENGINE. THIS WAS $106 MORE THAN A CHEVROLET BEL AIR HARDTOP.
NICK GEORGANO COLLECTION

workmanship, and even of windows breaking if the doors were closed too hard. Kaiser managed to sell just over 124,000 Henry Js over a four-year period, but many people thought that his money would have been better spent on a V8 engine for the regular-sized Kaiser.

A curious venture was the Allstate, a Henry J with different grille supplied to the Sears Roebuck store chain for sale through its outlets, using Sears' own brands of tires, batteries, and spark plugs. Prices were slightly higher than for virtually the same car bought from a Kaiser-Frazer dealer, and despite the name Allstates were sold in only ten states, all in the South and Southwest. Only 2,363 were sold.

The other compacts represented two different lines of thinking: Hudson's Jet was a smaller, low-priced version of the regular Hudsons, while

Willys' Aero was a return to the passenger car field after more than a decade spent making the Jeep and its derivatives. Hudson was no stranger to smaller cars, having had a lot of success with the Essex in the 1920s and the 112 in the late 1930s. The company hoped to recreate these successes with the Jet, but was too late with its introduction, which did not happen until November 1952, with no cars reaching customers until March 1953.

By then the market was dropping, as Nash and Kaiser were discovering. The Jet was rather a dumpy-looking car, with a family resemblance to the larger "step down" Hudsons, although unfortunately the Hudson board, notably Ed Barit, wanted to step into rather than down, and the Jet had a standard height floor. Wheelbase was 105 inches and power was provided by a 202-cubic-inch L-head six which gave 104–114bhp according to carburetion and compression ratio. Although in the compact class, the Jet was wide enough to accommodate six passengers, although the rear seat legroom was strictly limited. In height it was 1 inch taller than the full-sized Hornet and Wasp. The Jet was originally offered as a four-door sedan or two-door club coupe. It was not particularly cheap, at $1,858–$1,933, but the 1954 season saw a new budget-priced Jet two-door "Family Club Sedan" at $1,621. However, the Nash-Hudson merger on May 1, 1954 put an end to the Jet, its place being taken by the Rambler which had previously been a competitor. Jet production was 21,143 in the 1953 model year, and 14,224 for 1954. As with the Henry J, the Jet was not a success for its makers. Indeed some say it killed the Hudson company. Certainly a shortage of finance prevented the development of the regular Hudson, leading to falling sales, but whether a resoundingly successful Jet would have forestalled the merger with Nash is less certain.

Production of regular passenger cars had ceased at Willys at the outbreak of World War II, during which the company became world famous for the Jeep, of which 361,000 were made between 1941 and 1945. After the war Willys continued the Jeep in modified form as the Universal, and supplemented it by a station wagon on a longer wheelbase (1946) and a sports roadster called the Jeepster (1948). Several proposals for small sedans came and went, but it was not until 1950 that

1948 WILLYS JEEPSTER ▲ ▶
THE JEEPSTER WAS PART OF WILLYS' EXTENSION OF THE JEEP RANGE INTO THE CIVILIAN MARKET, ANOTHER BEING THE STATION WAGON. DESIGNED DURING THE WAR BY BROOKS STEVENS, THE JEEPSTER WAS MADE FROM 1948 THROUGH 1951, WITH A TOTAL PRODUCTION OF 17,352. IT WAS A FUN CAR WITH FAIRLY BASIC AMENITIES, SUCH AS SIDE CURTAINS, BUT THE TOP WAS MECHANICALLY OPERATED. THIS 1948 EXAMPLE HAS A FOUR-CYLINDER ENGINE, ALTHOUGH A SIX WAS AVAILABLE FROM 1949.
OWNER: DUKE DAVENPORT (PHOTO NICKY WRIGHT)

1956 PACKARD CLIPPER SEDAN ▶
IN 1956 PACKARD PROMOTED THE CLIPPER AS A SEPARATE LINE WITH ITS OWN SCRIPT ON THE HOOD, TO DISTINGUISH IT FROM THE UPMARKET 400 AND CARIBBEAN MODELS. THE PACKARD NAME APPEARED NOWHERE ON THE CAR EXCEPT AS A TINY SCRIPT ON THE DECKLID. THERE WERE THREE LINES OF CLIPPER — DELUXE, SUPER, AND CUSTOM — ALL USING THE SAME 352-CUBIC-INCH V8 ENGINE GIVING 240 OR 275bhp. A TOTAL OF 18,482 WERE SOLD IN THE 1956 SEASON.
OWNER: JOHN MONKS (PHOTO NICKY WRIGHT)

1956 PACKARD EXECUTIVE SEDAN ▲
A NEW LINE IN MID-SEASON OF 1956, THE EXECUTIVE WAS INTENDED TO FILL THE $1,000 GAP BETWEEN THE CLIPPER CUSTOM AND THE SENIOR PACKARD LINE. MADE ONLY AS A FOUR-DOOR SEDAN OR TWO-DOOR HARDTOP, IT HAD A PACKARD GRILLE AND SIDE BODY TRIM, BUT USED CLIPPER BODY PRESSINGS AND A 352-CUBIC-INCH V8 ENGINE. THIS SEDAN COST $3,465, WHICH PLACED IT CONVENIENTLY BETWEEN THE $3,069 CLIPPER AND $4,160 PACKARD.
OWNER: ROY D. CROWE (PHOTO NICKY WRIGHT)

cubic-inch Kaiser engine, but this made for less improvement in performance than one might have imagined—better acceleration but only 1.5mph on the top speed, heavier steering, and worse handling. Sales plummeted further to 5,897 in the 1955 model year, which Kaiser-Willys halted in April. The Aero later surfaced in Brazil, where it was made from 1957 to 1964, and was then restyled by Brooks Stevens for a further lease of life as the Aero 2600. This lasted until 1972, latterly as a Ford after Ford's take-over of Willys-Overland do Brasil.

INDEPENDENTS MERGE FOR SURVIVAL

In 1929 the independents enjoyed 20 percent of the U.S. car market. In 1952 their market share had dropped to 13 percent. In 1954 it was barely over 4 percent. The output of the Big Three received a tremendous boost with the end of government controls after the Korean War, and to the beleaguered boards of America's remaining six independent auto companies, mergers seemed the only answer.

Nash Kelvinator's George Mason had approached A. E. Barit of Hudson and Alvan Macaulay of Packard as early as 1946 about a merger. Rebuffed, he tried again in 1948 and in 1951, when he outlined two mergers that eventually took place, Nash with Hudson and Studebaker with Packard. His plan was that the two groupings would then merge, giving a four-make line-up from a compact to a high-priced luxury car. Secret plans were made in 1954 for three basic bodies and major sheet metal parts, with the make and series characterized by trim. They were envisaged as 1957 models, with the Nash Rambler representing the compact, various Studebakers, Hudsons, Nashes, and the Packard Clipper in the middle, and the Packard Patrician at the top of the line. But this never happened, because Studebaker-Packard never merged with American Motors.

The birth of American Motors took place between January and March 1954. The essential aspects of the merger were worked out by Mason and Barit over a two-hour lunch in June 1953. The Hudson and Nash boards of directors agreed to a merger on January 14, 1954, and the shareholders

president Ward Canaday ordered work to start. The design he approved was by Clyde Paton, who had worked on Ford's small car that became the French Ford Vedette and who by then had his own consulting firm. The unitary body was styled by Paton's partner Phil Wright, and was made as a two-door sedan or hardtop coupe. Power came from the 161-cubic-inch six-cylinder engine which had been used in the Jeep station wagon since 1948. The car was available in two forms, an L-head giving 75bhp and an F-head giving 90bhp. Wheelbase was 108 inches and overall length 181 inches, making the Willys slightly larger than the Rambler or the Henry J.

Introduced in March 1952, the new Willys line was called the Aero, the Aero Lark having the L-head engine and the more up-market Aero Wing, Aero Ace, and Aero Eagle the F-head. The Eagle hardtop was the most expensive, at $1,979, while a Lark could be had for $1,588. The press loved the

cars, and Griff Borgeson was so delighted with the one he tested for *Motor Trend* that he bought one for his own use. He later wrote that he covered 25,000 miles without spending a cent on maintenance, averaging 20.5mpg on a 1,600-mile trip that included some flat-out runs on the Bonneville salt flats in Utah.

The only trouble with the Willys Aero was its price. Even the basic Lark was undercut by the Ford six at $1,525 and Chevrolet at $1,533. For 1953, when a four-door sedan joined the range, Willys prices went up to $1,732–$2,157. Sales were good to start with, 31,362 in 1952 and 41,814 in 1953, but the public taste was for powerful V8s rather than economy cars, and 1954 sales dived to 8,240. By this time Willys had been taken over by Kaiser-Frazer, although Willys was the more prosperous of the two firms and tried to underpin ailing Kaiser, with all car production transferred to Toledo. The only effect on the Willys Aero was availability of the 226.2-

on March 24, with American Motors officially coming into being on May 1. Packard might have been included in the group, but its president, James Nance, wanted the presidency of American Motors, which Mason would not give up. Barit, wanting to phase into retirement, was content to be a director with a four-year consulting contract. This seems to have been a wise step, for he lived another 20 years, whereas George Mason died the following October.

With debts of $30 million, Hudson had to take second position in the new corporation, and shareholders were invited to trade three Hudson shares for two in AMC. One of the largest single blocks of Hudson stock (11 percent) was held by the Netherlands Royal Family. It is likely that they sold rather than accept the swap. Although Mason stressed that Hudson had equal status with Nash, Hudson employee Don Butler said that there was a definite feeling in the styling and engineering departments that they had to adapt to Nash ways. This became evident with the 1955 models, which were basically Nashes with different grilles made alongside their former rivals in Nash plants at Kenosha and Milwaukee. Six-cylinder engines were still Hudson's, and there was a new V8 supplied by Packard. The "Hashes," as they were called, survived until the end of the 1957 season, when they and Nashes were dropped in favor of the Rambler lines.

A curiosity from American Motors was the Metropolitan, a sub-compact car on an 85-inch wheelbase which used Nash styling and a 42bhp 73-cubic-inch four-cylinder engine made by the British Austin Motor Company. Although they looked like baby Nashes, the Metropolitans were made by Austin in England, with unitary bodies by Fisher & Ludlow Ltd. They carried both Hudson and Nash badges, and cost $1,455 for a two-passenger convertible with limited rear accommodation for children or parcels. Metropolitans sold surprisingly well, 97,000 of them up to 1961, when they were discontinued. Advertised as "milady's perfect companion for shopping trips," they were also popular with American servicemen; the British historian Michael Sedgwick observed that the sight of Metropolitans in Britain tended to indicate the nearby presence of an American air base. From 1957, Metropolitans

1959 RAMBLER AMBASSADOR SEDAN ▲▼
HUDSON AND NASH DISCONTINUED THEIR FULL-SIZE CARS AFTER THEIR MERGER INTO AMERICAN MOTORS, AND FOR 1958 LAUNCHED A SINGLE CAR, THE RAMBLER AMBASSADOR. THIS HAD A 9-INCH FRONTAL EXTENSION TO THE COMPACT RAMBLER CHASSIS, AND A NEW 327-CUBIC-INCH V8 GIVING 270bhp. IT WAS MADE AS A SEDAN, STATION WAGON, AND AN UNUSUAL HARDTOP STATION WAGON, OF WHICH ONLY 294 WERE MADE IN 1958 AND 4,341 IN 1959. AMBASSADOR SALES WERE LOWER THAN THOSE OF THE SMALLER RAMBLERS.
OWNER: C. J. OWENS (PHOTO NICKY WRIGHT)

**1961 STUDEBAKER
LARK VIII REGAL
CONVERTIBLE ▲**

THE LARK WAS STUDEBAKER'S ENTRY IN
THE COMPACT FIELD, AND ANTICIPATED
THOSE OF THE BIG THREE BY A YEAR. THIS
GAVE THE SOUTH BEND COMPANY A
WELCOME BOOST IN SALES, WITH A TOTAL OF
153,823 DELIVERIES IN 1959, OF WHICH 129,950
WERE LARKS. SIX- AND EIGHT-CYLINDER ENGINES
WERE OFFERED IN LARKS, CALLED RESPECTIVELY THE
LARK VI AND VIII. THIS IS A LARK VIII CONVERTIBLE,
THE MOST EXPENSIVE 1961 STUDEBAKER AT $2,689.

OWNER: STEVE PIPER (PHOTO NICKY WRIGHT)

$5,932). The top model was the limited-production Caribbean convertible, with a 352-cubic-inch V8 engine, with two four-barrel Rochester carburetors giving 275bhp, and an overall length of 220 inches and a wheelbase of 122 inches. It was said that the Caribbean's rear deck was large enough to land a helicopter on! Similar models were made in 1956, although the Clipper was marketed as a separate line in order to reassert Packard as a luxury make. The Caribbean came as a hardtop in addition to the convertible, and refinements included twin electric radio aerials and reversible seat cushions, fabric on one side, leather on the other. For 1956, displacement and power were raised to 374 cubic inches and 310bhp.

Fine cars though the 1956 Packards were, and better made than the '55s, they were too late. The company suffered a severe blow when its body supplier, Briggs, sold out to Chrysler who, not unnaturally, vetoed the supply of bodies to a rival. Packard had to settle for a cramped body plant on Detroit's Conner Avenue, which led to supply and quality problems. In addition, Packard had lost valuable defense contracts, as had Studebaker, when the demand for military trucks dried up, and there was no money to finance new Packards. Studebaker-Packard was bought up by Curtiss-Wright in August 1956, primarily as a tax loss operation; the 1957 Packards were badge-engineered Studebakers, with this make's 289-cubic-inch V8 engine. A McCulloch supercharger, available only on the Studebaker Golden Hawk coupe, was used on all Packards, boosting power from 225 to 275bhp. Only two bodies were offered, a Town Sedan and a Country Sedan, the latter being a station wagon. Although prices were around $800 higher than those of the equivalent Studebakers, no one was fooled that they were buying a proper Packard, and only 4,809 were made. The same models were offered in 1958, plus a Packardized Studebaker Hawk coupe which cost $3,995 compared with $3,182 for the Studebaker

were sold on the British market as well.

The Studebaker-Packard merger followed close on the formation of American Motors. It was the idea of Packard's James Nance, who saw the need for diversification from his company's largely expensive cars. Studebaker seemed an attractive partner, for it not only made cars in the medium-price range, but also trucks, and had valuable defense contracts. For Studebaker the merger offered fresh capital to modernize their aging and underused plant at South Bend. The merger agreement was signed on June 22, 1954, by Nance for Packard and Paul Hoffman for Studebaker, and on October 1 the Studebaker-Packard Corporation came into existence.

The merger produced a less immediate effect on the cars than at American Motors; 1955 Packards and Studebakers continued to be distinct designs, Packard making its upper medium price Clippers ($2,586–$3,076) and luxury Senior models ($3,390–

variety. Apart from a bolt-on fiberglass grille, special features included a tire impression stamped on the rear deck, leather interior and sports car type instrumentation, and Packard emblems on the hub caps. Only 588 Hawk coupes were made, together with 2,038 other 1958 Packards, and that was the end. James Nance had already left, shortly before the Curtiss-Wright take-over.

Studebaker was working well below its plant capacity of 250,000 vehicles per year when Curtiss-Wright bought the company. Its sedans had no particular distinction, but the Hawk coupes, derived from Raymond Loewy's 1953 Starliner, had a niche market among enthusiasts, and in recent years have become significant collector cars. They were not enough to keep Studebaker afloat, however, and for 1959 the company turned to the low-priced compact idea with its Lark.

The brainchild of new president Harold E. Churchill, the Lark looked like an all-new car, which is what the stylists hoped for, although it was based on the Champion's center section, with a wraparound windshield from the 1955 Studebakers, a steering wheel from the '57s, and hardtop doors from the '58s. At 108.5 inches, the wheelbase was quite large for a compact, but very limited overhang gave a handy overall length of 175 inches. Interior space was very good, with seating for six passengers.

Two engines gave the Lark a dual character; the Lark VI was an economical budget car with a 90bhp 169-cubic-inch six-cylinder engine, while the Lark VIII had a sparkling performance with 106mph top speed, thanks to its 180bhp 259-cubic-inch V8. Two- and four-door sedans and a station wagon were offered in 1959, prices ranging from $1,925 for a VI two-door sedan to $2,590 for a VIII wagon. A convertible was added for 1960.

Thanks to the Lark, Studebaker production increased by 381 percent between 1958 and 1959, and 70 percent of the cars traded in on new Larks came from rival makes. Overall sales in 1959 totaled 153,823 units, but Studebaker could not hold this, or its tenth position, in the years that followed. The problem was twofold: imports on the one hand, and on the other new compacts from the Big Three, Corvair, Falcon, and Valiant, all of which debuted for the 1960 season. For 1961, Detroit brought out four more compacts, in a higher price range than the original cars. The Dodge Lancer, Olds F-85, Pontiac Tempest, and Buick Special competed on performance and price with the Lark VIII. Studebaker had a lot of shared dealerships with Chrysler, Ford, and GM, and when the Big Three launched their compacts dual dealers were forced to give up Studebaker. Thus Lark sales declined during the 1960s, to only 44,232 in 1964. By then the South Bend plant had closed and Studebakers were made only at the Canadian plant at Hamilton, Ontario. Production continued for a further three years, although the Lark name was dropped after 1964. Total Lark production (including the

1963 STUDEBAKER GT HAWK COUPE ▶

THE HAWK LINE DATED FROM 1956,
ALTHOUGH THE CONCEPT REALLY ORIGINATED
IN THE STARLINER COUPE OF 1953,
DESIGNED BY ROBERT G. BOURKE OF
THE LOEWY STUDIOS. THE CAR WAS
RESTYLED BY BROOKS STEVENS FOR 1962
AS THE GT HAWK, AND 1963 MODELS
CAME WITH 210bhp 289-CUBIC-INCH ENGINES
AS STANDARD. OPTIONAL WERE
THE 240bhp R1 AND 290bhp R2 ENGINES.
WITH THE LATTER, A GT HAWK
COULD EXCEED 140MPH.

OWNERS: CHUCK AND CHRIS COLLINS   (PHOTO NICKY WRIGHT)

1963 STUDEBAKER AVANTI COUPE ▼

ANOTHER DESIGN FROM THE LOEWY STUDIOS, THE AVANTI WAS QUITE UNLIKE ANY OTHER STUDEBAKER.
THE INTERIOR FEATURED FOUR SEPARATE BUCKET SEATS, AN AIRCRAFT-TYPE CONTROL PANEL, AND AMPLE CRASH
PADDING. THE BENDIX CALLIPER DISK BRAKES WERE THE FIRST OF THEIR KIND ON AN AMERICAN-BUILT CAR.

OWNER: CHRIS COLLINS   (PHOTO NICKY WRIGHT)

Canadian cars, which were lineal descendants although called Cruiser and Daytona) was 563,960, and in addition Kaiser-Illin assembled about 3,500 in Israel between 1959 and 1965. One of these was a convertible lengthened by 25 inches to make a parade phaeton for Israel's President Zalman Shazar.

Hawk coupes continued in production until the end of 1963, and there was also the strikingly different Avanti coupe. This was dreamed up by Studebaker's new president Sherwood Egbert, who replaced Churchill in February 1961, with body styling by Raymond Loewy. It had razor-edged front fenders, a jacked-up rear end, and no radiator grille, the air intakes being concealed under the front bumper. The Avanti's chassis was taken from the shorter chassis (109-inch) of the Larks and the engine was the 240bhp 289-cubic-inch V8 from the Golden Hawk. With a Paxton supercharger, power went up to 290bhp, giving a top speed of 124mph.

In order to publicize the Avanti's performance, Egbert had a special car prepared with which Andy Granatelli broke 29 stock car records at Bonneville in October 1962. The following year Granatelli returned to Bonneville with an even more powerful Avanti, whose twin-supercharged engine developed an almost unbelievable 575bhp. Little streamlining was needed since the Avanti body was so slippery,

1965 CHECKER MARATHON SEDAN ▲

AN INDEPENDENT WITH A DIFFERENCE WAS THE KALAMAZOO-BASED CHECKER MOTORS CORPORATION, FAMOUS
FOR ITS TAXICABS SINCE 1923. IN 1959 THE COMPANY LAUNCHED A VERSION OF ITS CAB FOR THE PRIVATE BUYER.
THE SAME BODY SHELL AND SIX-CYLINDER CONTINENTAL ENGINE WERE USED, AND THE INTERIOR HAD TAXI-LIKE JUMP
SEATS GIVING ACCOMMODATION TO EIGHT PASSENGERS. AN OVERHEAD VALVE VERSION OF THE ENGINE WAS OFFERED
AT NO EXTRA COST, WHICH RAISED POWER FROM 80 TO 122bhp, AND IN 1961 THIS ENGINE BECAME STANDARD
ON THE STATION WAGONS. THE TOP MODEL SUPERBA SPECIAL WAS RENAMED MARATHON IN 1961, AND FROM 1965
V8 CHEVROLET ENGINES WERE OFFERED AS ALTERNATIVES TO THE CONTINENTAL. CHECKER PASSENGER CAR
PRODUCTION WAS ALWAYS LOW, GENERALLY NOT MORE THAN 20 PERCENT OF TOTAL OUTPUT, WHICH SELDOM
EXCEEDED 6,000 UNITS PER YEAR. CHECKER BOWED OUT OF THE CAR AND TAXI FIELD IN 1982.

OWNER: JOHN R. OWEN (PHOTO NICKY WRIGHT)

1953 KAISER MANHATTAN SEDAN ▶

KAISER RECEIVED A COMPLETLEY NEW BODY FOR 1951 (ACTUALLY ANNOUNCED AS EARLY AS FEBRUARY 1950), WITH A LOWER BELT LINE THAN ANY OTHER AMERICAN CAR UP TO 1956, AND 700 SQUARE INCHES MORE GLASS THAN ITS NEAREST COMPETITOR. STYLING WAS BY HOWARD "DUTCH" DARRIN, WITH INTERIOR COLOR SCHEMES BY "COLOR ENGINEER" CARLETON B. SPENCER. AMONG STYLING FEATURES WERE THE DARRIN DIP IN THE CENTER OF THE WINDSHIELD HEADER LINE, AND A DIP IN THE REAR DOOR THAT DID AWAY WITH THE SLAB-SIDED EFFECT FOR WHICH THE EARLIER KAISERS AND FRAZERS HAD BEEN CRITICIZED. LESS INNOVATIVE WAS THE ENGINE, THE FAMILIAR OLD CONTINENTAL FLATHEAD-6. THIS 1953 MANHATTAN SEDAN RETAINED THE STYLING OF THE 1951 CARS.

OWNERS: MACK LUPEN AND DR. JOE BROMERT (PHOTO NICKY WRIGHT)

but the rear wheels were enclosed. The car was christened the Due Cento (Italian for 200) as 200mph was the top speed hoped for, but Granatelli's best figure was 196.62mph.

Unfortunately the Avanti did not move so quickly in the showrooms, largely because production problems with the fiberglass body delayed its appearance, and many who ordered an Avanti in late 1962 or early 1963 canceled and bought a Corvette instead. A total of 3,834 Avantis were built in the 1963 model year, and 809 '64s, all of which were delivered before the move to Canada. However, the Avanti didn't die, for two Studebaker-Packard dealers, Nate Altman and Leo Newman, purchased the dies, parts, and rights to the Avanti, bought a small part of the Studebaker factory, and restarted production in 1965, using 327-cubic-inch Chevrolet Corvette engines. With several changes of ownership, the Avanti is still being made at the time of writing; the original shape is little changed, although there are two styles never made by Studebaker, a convertible and a four-door sedan.

The third merger of the independents took place in April 1953, when Kaiser Industries bought Willys-Overland to form the Kaiser-Willys Sales Corporation. Kaiser sales had been falling since their peak in 1948, and the Frazer name had been dropped after the 1951 season. The Henry J and restyled 1951 Special and De Luxe kept the firm

going in the early 1950s, but the lack of a V8 engine was a growing drawback for a medium-priced car competing against such performers as the Oldsmobile 88 with 145–160bhp. The old Continental six gave only 115bhp, and there was not much Kaiser could do with it until 1954 when a McCulloch supercharger was added, boosting power to 140bhp. This was only available on the top Manhattan model, which cost nearly $300 more than the other Kaisers.

The engineering department experimented with V8 engines bought in from Oldsmobile and Cadillac, but there was no way that GM would sell such engines for production, although the corporation did let Kaiser use its HydraMatic transmission. Henry Kaiser drove a Manhattan with a Cadillac engine, although this fact was not publicized at the time.

The Willys purchase gave Kaiser a better small car than its own Henry J and also the profitable Jeep operation. (The Jeep has been an attraction for successive corporate take-overs; American Motors in 1970, Renault in 1978, Chrysler in 1987, all were lured to acquisition by the chance of getting their hands on the successful Jeep business.) The enormous Kaiser factory at Willow Run was sold to General Motors, and all car production relocated to Willys' headquarters in Toledo. Then in 1955, after only 1,000 cars had been made, Kaiser announced that it was pulling

out of the passenger car business in the United States. The majority of the 1955 models were sold to Argentina, and later in the year body dies and manufacturing equipment also went to Argentina, where the design was made for a further seven years. Latin America also received the Willys Aero, which went to Brazil and had an even longer career. Only the Jeeps in their various forms continued to issue from Toledo. Officially they were Willys Jeeps until 1963, when the maker's name became Kaiser-Jeep Corporation and Jeep became a marque in its own right. The Kaiser-Frazer Corporation was changed to Kaiser Industries Corporation and continued to be active in cement, steel, engineering, and sand and gravel, which Henry Kaiser had dealt in long before he got mixed up with automobiles.

Thus in the long run, with the exception of American Motors, mergers failed to save the independent car makers. Even AMC eventually succumbed to take-over by Chrysler, while at the time of writing even Chrysler seems none too healthy.

1956 IMPERIAL SEDAN ▲▶

ALTHOUGH THE NAME IMPERIAL HAD BEEN USED BY CHRYSLER SINCE 1924, IT DID NOT BECOME A RECOGNIZED
SEPARATE MARQUE UNTIL 1955. ENGINES AND BODIES WERE SHARED WITH LESSER CHRYSLER MODELS, BUT THE
IMPERIALS WERE DISTINGUISHED BY THEIR OWN TWO-PIECE SPLIT GRILLES AND FREE-STANDING TAILLIGHTS ABOVE THE
REAR FENDERS. THREE MODELS MADE UP THE 1956 IMPERIAL RANGE, THE FOUR-DOOR SEDAN ILLUSTRATED HERE, AND
TWO HARDTOPS, TWO- AND FOUR-DOOR VERSIONS. THERE WERE ALSO THE ENORMOUS CROWN IMPERIALS, EIGHT-
PASSENGER SEDAN AND LIMOUSINE, ON A 149.5-INCH WHEELBASE.

OWNER: CARL W. REID (PHOTO NICKY WRIGHT)

1968 CROWN IMPERIAL SEDAN ▶

IMPERIAL WAS THE TOP LINE OF CHRYSLER, AND WAS
PROMOTED TO THE STATUS OF AN INDIVIDUAL MARQUE
FROM 1955 THROUGH 1975. THE 1968 CROWN AND
LEBARON MODELS USED THE SAME 440-CUBIC-INCH V8
AS THE CHRYSLER 300 AND NEW YORKER. THIS CROWN
FOUR-DOOR HARDTOP SEDAN WAS THE MOST POPULAR,
WITH 8,492 DELIVERED; BY CONTRAST, THE TWO-DOOR
CONVERTIBLE ACCOUNTED FOR ONLY 474 DELIVERIES.
THE RAREST MODEL OF ALL WAS THE IMPERIAL
LEBARON LIMOUSINE WITH WHEELBASE STRETCHED
BY STAGEWAY OF FORT SMITH, ARKANSAS, TO 163
INCHES. FEWER THAN 12 OF THESE WERE MADE, AT
A PRICE IN EXCESS OF $12,000.

OWNER: ALLAN S. MURRAY (PHOTO NICKY WRIGHT)

V 8 ENGINES AND THE HORSEPOWER RACE

The V8 engine had been around for a long time,
but in 1946 it featured in only three makes of
American car, Cadillac, Ford, and Mercury.
Fourteen years later it was offered by every
manufacturer and was standard for larger cars. Its
rise to popularity also saw a remarkable growth in
output, popularly known as "the horsepower race."

The first of the new generation of V8s came
from Cadillac in 1949. Under development for
more than ten years, its chief novelties were
overhead valves, slightly oversquare dimensions
(3.81 x 3.63 inches), and slipper pistons, in which
the lower sides of the pistons were cut away so the
piston nested between the crankshaft
counterweights at the bottom of the stroke. This
allowed shorter connecting rods and a consequent
reduction in size and weight. The new V8 weighed
220 pounds less than its flathead predecessor, and
displaced 331 cubic inches compared with 345, yet
it gave 10bhp more, at 160. Its compression ratio
was higher, at 7.5:1, and had risen to 10.5:1 by 1959.
The engine was developed through the 1967
season, by which time it had been bored out to 429
cubic inches and gave 340bhp. Not many people
realized at the time what an important engine this
was; one who did was *Motor Trend* editor John
Bond, who chose the 1949 Cadillac as the first Car
of the Year selected by his magazine. Cadillac's
bodies had been completely restyled for 1948, with

the first of the famous fins, so the '49 Cadillac really was an all-new car compared with its predecessor of two years earlier.

Oldsmobile also came out with an overhead valve oversquare V8 for 1949, but it was smaller at 303 cubic inches and 135bhp. It was strongly influenced by the Cadillac design, and a heavier F-head V8 that Olds engineers had been working on was abandoned when they had a good look at what Cadillac was doing. The Olds was called the Rocket V8 and gave the Lansing make a change of image, with 100mph obtainable from the 98 convertible. By 1954, displacement was up to 324 cubic inches and power to 185bhp, raised to 202 for 1955.

The next important V8 engine came from Chrysler for 1951. Also an oversquare unit with the same dimensions as the Cadillac, it had hemispherical combustion chambers which gave more efficient breathing, and accounted for the extra 20bhp it yielded. The valves were inclined on either side of the combustion chamber, which necessitated four rocker shafts in place of two, and eight intake pushrods, eight exhaust pushrods, and eight intake and eight exhaust rocker arms. A conventional V8 such as Cadillac's needed 16 identical pushrods and rocker arms. The cost of making two sets of everything pushed up the price of the hemi engine to unacceptable levels, and it was eventually dropped, in 1959, but not before it had provided America with some of the most powerful and dramatic automobiles ever seen.

During the 1950s the V8 became established as the logical power unit for American cars. The straight-6 was relegated to the lowest-priced lines and the straight-8 was consigned to oblivion. Studebaker brought out a V8 in 1951, Buick, De Soto, and Dodge in 1953, Chevrolet, Hudson, Nash, Packard, Plymouth, and Pontiac in 1955. The last straight-8s were made by Packard and Pontiac in their 1954 models. Lincoln went to overhead valves in 1952, Ford and Mercury in 1954, and all the other new units also had ohv.

The adoption of V8s by Chevrolet and Plymouth sealed the success of the layout. Chevrolet's was a 265-cubic-inch unit which owed much to the '49 Cadillac, and was designed by Ed Cole and Harry Barr who had worked on the Caddy. Like its more costly sister, it had slipper pistons, but advances in manufacturing techniques made it cheaper to build. Lighter than the old six, which gave 125bhp at best, it was considerably more powerful, with 170–180bhp in 1955 and 225 in 1956. A larger 283-cubic-inch V8 was an additional option for 1957, and this gave up to 280bhp. The power race was on, even for the low-priced makes, with Ford offering a 312-cubic-inch 254bhp engine for 1957, going up to 352 cubic inches and 300bhp for 1958, while Plymouth started with a modest 177bhp from 260 cubic inches in 1955, going up to 315bhp from 350 cubic inches for 1958.

Among the larger cars, the race was between

1963 IMPERIAL HARDTOP ◄▲
THIS IS ONE OF THE LATER IMPERIALS, A DESCENDANT OF VIRGIL EXNER'S COMPLETE REDESIGN OF 1957. STYLING HAD BEEN TONED DOWN A BIT AND THE FINS HAD DISAPPEARED; 1962 IMPERIALS WERE MADE IN THREE SERIES, CUSTOM, CROWN, AND LEBARON; FOUR-DOOR HARDTOPS WERE AVAILABLE IN ALL THREE, WITH A TWO-DOOR CONVERTIBLE IN THE CROWN RANGE ALONE.

(PHOTO NICKY WRIGHT)

Cadillac and Chrysler, with the latter making the more exciting cars from 1955 onward. In that year they brought out the 300, a lowered New Yorker hardtop with grille from the top line Imperial, powered by a modified 331-cubic-inch hemi engine, with twin quadrajet carburetors, a racing type camshaft, and twin exhausts. This gave 300bhp and propelled the 4,000-pound car at 130mph. The colorful auto writer Tom McCahill pronounced it "as solid as Grant's tomb, and 130 times as fast."

The 1956 300 was the 300B, the first of the family that became known as the "letter cars," the

1957 BUICK CENTURY HARDTOP ◄
BUICKS WERE RESTYLED FOR 1957 AT A COST OF SEVERAL HUNDRED MILLION DOLLARS. BODIES WERE LOWER AND 3 INCHES LONGER. ALL '57 BUICKS USED A NEW 364-CUBIC-INCH ENGINE, WHICH GAVE 300bhp IN THE CENTURY AND ROADMASTER. AS IN PREVIOUS YEARS, THE CENTURY WAS BUICK'S PERFORMANCE MODEL, HAVING A MORE POWERFUL ENGINE IN THE RELATIVELY LIGHT SPECIAL BODY SHELL. IT COULD BE DISTINGUISHED FROM THE SPECIAL BY ITS FOUR VENTIPORTS ON THE FRONT FENDERS IN PLACE OF THREE. THIS IS THE RIVIERA TWO-DOOR HARDTOP, WHICH COST $3,270. BUICK BUILT ITS 9 MILLIONTH CAR ON NOVEMBER 7, 1956.

OWNERS: TOM AND KAREN BARNES (PHOTO NICKY WRIGHT)

1957 CHEVROLET BEL AIR HARDTOP ▼

THE 1955/57 CHEVROLETS ARE AMONG THE MOST POPULAR OF ALL CHEVYS WITH TODAY'S COLLECTORS, AND OF THESE THE '57S PROBABLY COMMAND THE GREATEST ENTHUSIASM. COMPLETELY RESTYLED AND GIVEN A NEW V8 ENGINE FOR 1955, THE '57S WERE MORE POWERFUL, WITH OPTIONAL FUEL INJECTION AND INCREASED DISPLACEMENT GIVING 283BHP, OR 1 HORSEPOWER PER CUBIC INCH. THE BEL AIR LINE WAS THE TOP OF THE RANGE AND WAS MADE IN SEVEN BODY STYLES, SEDANS, HARDTOPS, CONVERTIBLE, AND STATION WAGON. THIS TWO-DOOR HARDTOP SPORTS COUPE WAS THE SECOND MOST POPULAR BEL AIR, WITH 166,426 UNITS DELIVERED IN THE 1957 MODEL YEAR.

OWNER: BILL GOODSENE (PHOTO NICKY WRIGHT)

1957 PLYMOUTH FURY HARDTOP ▲

"SUDDENLY IT'S 1960," CLAIMED PLYMOUTH ADVERTISING IN 1957. FOR THAT YEAR PLYMOUTHS WERE COMPLETELY RESTYLED, WITH A WIDER GRILLE, QUAD HEADLIGHTS (ONE PAIR OF WHICH WERE PARKING LIGHTS), AND FINS WHICH GAVE A LOWER LOOK. MECHANICALLY, THEY WERE DISTINGUISHED BY TORSION BAR FRONT SUSPENSION. THE FURY WAS A HIGH-PERFORMANCE MODEL WITHIN THE BELVEDERE RANGE AND WAS MADE ONLY AS A TWO-DOOR HARDTOP. IT USED A 235BHP V8 ENGINE, WITH A 290BHP OPTION, AND WAS THE MOST COSTLY '57 PLYMOUTH AT $2,935. IT WAS ALSO THE LOWEST IN HEIGHT (53.4 INCHES) AND IN PRODUCTION, WITH JUST 7,438 MADE.

OWNER: BOB SCHMIDT (PHOTO NICKY WRIGHT)

1968 CHRYSLER NEW YORKER HARDTOP ▶

AS IN PREVIOUS YEARS, THE NEW YORKER FOR 1968 WAS THE TOP MODEL IN THE CHRYSLER RANGE, ALTHOUGH EXCEEDED IN PRICE AND LUXURY BY THE SEPARATE IMPERIAL LINE. THE 440-CUBIC-INCH V8 WAS THE LARGEST ENGINE CHRYSLER EVER BUILT AND GAVE 350 OR 375BHP. THERE WERE THREE MODELS IN THE NEW YORKER RANGE, OF WHICH THIS HARDTOP SEDAN WAS THE MOST EXPENSIVE, AT $4,500, AND ALSO THE MOST POPULAR, WITH 26,091 DELIVERED.

OWNER: CARL W. REID (PHOTO NICKY WRIGHT)

series going up to the 300L of 1965. The V8 was bored out to give 354 cubic inches and 340bhp, but the appearance of the 300B was similar to that of the 300 apart from slightly upswept fins. Cadillac was now up to 365 cubic inches and 305bhp, but never went in for stock car racing, as Chrysler did. In 1955 a team of 300s led by Karl Kiekhafer won 32 out of 52 NASCAR (National Association for Stock Car Auto Racing) races, taking the trophy, while in 1956 Kiekhafer's drivers took all three stock car championships. A Detroit housewife, Vicky Wood, took the Women's Speed Trial Championship in her 300B with a one-way run of 143.827mph. The 1957 300C was, like other Chryslers that year, completely restyled by Virgil Exner, and had a 392-cubic-inch engine giving 390bhp. For the first time, a convertible was made in the 300 series.

The peak of power was reached in 1962 with the 405bhp 300H, but by this time the hemi engine had been replaced by a more conventional and cheaper-to-build wedge-shaped combustion chamber. In the mid-1960s Chrysler revived the hemi design for stock car racing, and a very limited number of Plymouth and Dodge street cars were equipped with hemi engines. The 300s were never big-selling cars; total production over 11 years was only 17,007, the best single year being 1964 when 3,647 300Ks were built. Convertibles were scarcer than coupes.

Cadillac dropped out of the horsepower race

after 1958, when the more powerful version of its 365-cubic-inch engine gave a matching 365bhp. After that, although displacement went up to 390 cubic inches in 1959 and to 429 in 1964, power stayed around the 325–340bhp level. 1968 saw a new Cadillac V8 of 472 cubic inches, and the 1970 derivative of this, standard in the front-drive Eldorado, displaced 500 cubic inches, a record for a postwar American car. By then, however, the horsepower race was being contested by a very different kind of automobile, the Muscle Car, to be described later.

1958 PONTIAC BONNEVILLE HARDTOP ▲
PONTIAC FIRST USED THE NAME BONNEVILLE IN 1957 FOR A LIMITED-EDITION FUEL-INJECTED CONVERTIBLE, AND IN 1958 IT BECAME A LINE NAME INSTEAD OF A SINGLE MODEL DESIGNATION. TWO STYLES WERE OFFERED IN THE BONNEVILLE LINE, A HARDTOP KNOWN AS THE CUSTOM SPORT COUPE AND A CUSTOM CONVERTIBLE. BOTH WERE AT THE TOP OF THE PONTIAC RANGE, WITH 255 OR 285bhp STAR CHIEF V8 ENGINES AND DE LUXE STEERING WHEEL, CHROME WHEEL DISKS, AND SPECIAL UPHOLSTERY.

OWNER: JIM diGREGORIO (PHOTO NICKY WRIGHT)

1955 CHRYSLER C300 HARDTOP ▲
"AS SOLID AS GRANT'S TOMB AND 130 TIMES AS FAST," SAID TOM McCAHILL OF THE CHRYSLER 300, ALLUDING TO ITS 130mph TOP SPEED. IT WAS THE SENSATION OF 1955, WITH ITS 300bhp HEMI V8 ENGINE WITH TWIN QUADRAJET CARBURETORS, NEW YORKER NEWPORT BODY, AND IMPERIAL GRILLE. THE 300 WAS STYLED BY VIRGIL EXNER, WITH ENGINEERING BY CHRYSLER'S CHIEF ENGINEER, BOB ROGER. ONLY 1,725 WERE MADE OF THE 1955 MODEL. KNOWN AS THE C300, IT WAS FOLLOWED BY THE 300B FOR 1956 AND THE 300C FOR 1957, THE LATTER WITH NEW STYLING ALSO BY EXNER.

OWNER: OTTO ROSENBUSCH (PHOTO NICKY WRIGHT)

1958 CADILLAC ELDORADO BROUGHAM ◄
LAUNCHED IN 1957, THE ELDORADO BROUGHAM WAS A HAND-BUILT, LIMITED-EDITION VERSION OF THE SERIES 62, AND AMERICA'S FIRST COMPLETELY PILLARLESS FOUR-DOOR SEDAN. THE PRICE WAS A WHOPPING $13,074 (AN ORDINARY 1958 SERIES 62 FOUR-DOOR SEDAN COST $4,891), BUT BUYERS GOT ALL THE OPTIONS, INCLUDING DUAL FOUR-BARREL CARBURETORS AND AIR SUSPENSION. INTERIOR FITTINGS INCLUDED A DUAL HEATING SYSTEM, AIR CONDITIONING, CIGARETTE AND TISSUE DISPENSERS, AND AN ATOMIZER WITH LANVIN PERFUME. ONLY 400 BROUGHAMS WERE MADE IN 1957 AND 304 IN 1958; ALTHOUGH THE NAME SURVIVED TO 1960, LATER ELDO BROUGHAMS WERE MUCH LESS DISTINCTIVE.

OWNER: ED OBERHAUS (PHOTO NICKY WRIGHT)

1957 PONTIAC BONNEVILLE CONVERTIBLE ▲

THE YEAR 1957 WAS THE FIRST THAT PONTIAC USED THE NAME BONNEVILLE, THE UTAH SALT FLATS WHERE MANY SPEED RECORDS WERE SET. IT WAS ALSO THE FIRST YEAR FOR FUEL-INJECTED ENGINES, WHICH WERE USED EXCLUSIVELY IN THE BONNEVILLE. MADE ONLY AS A CONVERTIBLE FOR 1957, THE BONNEVILLE WAS A LUXURY SUB-SERIES OF THE STAR CHIEF CUSTOM LINE, AND ALTHOUGH IT USED THE SAME BODY PRESSINGS AS THE STAR CHIEF CONVERTIBLE IT HAD MANY EXCLUSIVE FEATURES, INCLUDING UNDERSEAT HEAT AND DEFROSTER, ELECTRIC ANTENNA, AND AN EIGHT-WAY POWER-OPERATED FRONT SEAT. ONLY 630 WERE DELIVERED AT THE HIGH PRICE OF $5,782. A REGULAR STAR CHIEF CONVERTIBLE COST $3,105.

OWNER: BARRY BALES (PHOTO NICKY WRIGHT)

1959 CADILLAC ELDORADO CONVERTIBLE ▲▶

FOR CADILLAC,1959 WAS THE YEAR OF THE FIN, WHEN TAIL ADORNMENTS REACHED THEIR PEAK OF EXTRAVAGANCE. FOR THE FIRST AND ONLY TIME THEY INCLUDED A ROCKET SHAPE COMBINED WITH THE VEE-FIN; 1960s WOULD BE LESS EXTRAVAGANT, AND BY 1965 THE FINS WOULD BE NO MORE. THIS SERIES 62 WAS THE LESS EXPENSIVE OF THE CONVERTIBLES AT $5,455. ABOVE IT WAS THE ELDORADO BIARRITZ, WITH MORE CHROME TRIM, COSTING $7,401. BOTH HAD A 390-CUBIC-INCH V8 DEVELOPING 325bhp IN THE 62 AND 345bhp IN THE ELDORADO.

(PHOTO NICKY WRIGHT)

THE NEW GENERATION AMERICAN SPORTS CAR

The sports car, roadster, speedster — call it what you will — flourished in the second and third decades of the century, and struggled into the 1930s, but after the death of the Auburn 851 in 1936, the breed went into limbo. Not for long, though, for in 1949 Californian Frank Kurtis, who had built a number of successful Indianapolis racing cars, brought out a two-passenger sports car with a fiberglass body. Engines were the customer's choice, although Ford V8s were the normal, with Cadillacs or Chryslers for richer speed freaks. Even with a Ford engine, a Kurtis cost $4,700, more than most Cadillacs and all Chryslers or Lincolns.

After building 36 cars, Kurtis sold the design to television maker Earl Muntz, who lengthened the frame so as to accommodate four passengers, standardized on a Cadillac engine, and sold his Muntz Jet for $4,450. Most Muntz Jets, of which 394 were made, had Lincoln V8 engines. Like Preston Tucker, Earl Muntz was keen on safety, and his cars featured padded dashboards, padded tops on the hardtop, and seat belts.

With its four seats the Muntz was more of a sporty convertible (or hardtop) than a sports car, but other makers soon began to cater to a growing demand. Frank Kurtis returned to the fray in 1954 with a very hot sports car with a tubular frame patterned after the Indy car that Bill Vukovitch drove to victory in 1953. It had a simple fiberglass body with a wrap-around windshield, and was sold as the 500KK in kit form, or the 500M fully built-up. With a 250bhp Cadillac V8, it was capable of 135mph, justifying Kurtis' claim that it was "guaranteed to outperform any other sports car on the road." Kurtis' manufacturing facilities were limited, and he was busy building Indy and midget race cars, so only 30 500KKs and 20 500Ms were made.

On the other side of the continent, at West Palm Beach, Florida, millionaire sportsman Briggs Swift Cunningham began

to build Chrysler-powered sports cars with the intention of winning an American victory at the Le Mans 24-Hour Race, at that time the world's premier sports car event. He had entered two Cadillacs at Le Mans in 1950, a stock Series 62 coupe and a custom two-seater which the French called "Le Monstre," and 1951 saw his Chrysler-powered C-2R open sports car with De Dion rear axle. It finished eighteenth at Le Mans, but several replicas were sold to racing enthusiasts.

Cunningham entered cars at Le Mans each year to 1955, his best place being third in 1953, but the only production cars sold for road use were the Chrysler-powered C-3s with aluminum coupe bodies by Vignale of Italy; 26 were built in 1953 and 1954, selling for the very high price of $9,000.

Numerous other sports cars appeared in the early 1950s, their makers encouraged by the successes of imports such as the MG Midget, Jaguar XK120, and Allard J2, the latter fitted with Cadillac, Mercury, or Chrysler engines when it was sold in the United States. Kaiser-Frazer built the Kaiser-Darrin 161, which had a pretty fiberglass

body styled by Howard Darrin and sliding doors. However, it was under-powered with a 90bhp Willys Six engine, and at $3,668 (more than a Corvette) was no bargain. Kaiser built only 435 in 1953-54, but then Howard Darrin bought the remaining 50 bodyshells, fitted them with Cadillac engines at his Hollywood plant, and sold them as Darrins over the next four years.

Another user of the Willys engine was Woody Woodill of Downey, California, who made about 315 Woodill Wildfire sports cars, later ones being offered in kit form, to take Ford engines and transverse spring front suspension. To demonstrate that assembly need take no more than 14 hours, Woodill once built a car in front of a TV audience. He also offered a child's version on a 63-inch wheelbase, called the Brushfire. Other entrants in the field included Brooks Stevens' Excalibur-J (1952) with a Henry J chassis and Willys engine, the Edwards America (1954–5) with a Mercury chassis and with Lincoln or Oldsmobile engines, the Multiplex (1952–4) with its Willys four or six engines, and the Ford-powered Rockefeller

1958 OLDSMOBILE SUPER 88 TWO-DOOR HARDTOP ◄
OLDSMOBILES WERE REDESIGNED FOR THE SECOND YEAR RUNNING FOR 1958, AND WERE LONGER AND MORE CHROME-LADEN THAN EVER. INNOVATIONS INCLUDED QUAD HEADLIGHTS, FEATURED BY ALL OTHER GM DIVISIONS THAT YEAR. THE SUPER 88 WAS THE MIDDLE SERIES, SHARING ITS 125.5-INCH WHEELBASE WITH THE DYNAMIC 88, AND ITS 305bhp V8 ENGINE WITH THE 98. FIVE BODY STYLES WERE OFFERED, TWO SEDANS, A HARDTOP, CONVERTIBLE, AND STATION WAGON. THIS HARDTOP HOLIDAY COUPE COST $3,262.
OWNER: DEAN ULLMAN
(PHOTO NICKY WRIGHT)

Yankee (1949–54) and Story (1950) models.

Although none of these sports cars sold in any numbers, they and, more importantly, sports car imports made the major auto firms think that maybe there was something in this hitherto ignored field. The first was Nash, whose Nash-Healey came about as a result of a shipboard meeting in 1949 between George Mason and the British sports car maker Donald Healey. Healey was on his way to Detroit to try to buy Cadillac engines in order to give his Silverstone sports car more power, and as a result of this casual meeting on board the Queen Elizabeth, he stayed with the Masons in Detroit. George Mason told him that if he failed to get Cadillac engines, he should come to him. As it happened, Cadillac was having difficulty making engines for its own use, so Healey took up Mason's offer. The stark-looking Silverstone was redesigned with an all-enveloping body and a Nash grille, and went into production at Healey's Warwick factory in 1951. Bodies were made by Panelcraft of Birmingham, so although American in design and styling, the car was fully assembled in England.

The Anglo-American Nash-Healey was soon to acquire three nationalities, for in 1952 the rather uninspired Panelcraft body was replaced by one styled and built by Pininfarina in Italy. The complicated manufacturing process went like this: engines, transmissions, and other components were shipped from the Nash plant at Kenosha to the Healey plant at Warwick, where they were mated to the Healey chassis and shipped on to the Pininfarina coachworks in Turin, Italy; from there the completed cars went direct to the United States, for Nash-Healeys were not sold in Europe. The price was a hefty $5,128 at the port of entry, although this represented no profit to Nash. What with all the shipping costs, it has been estimated that Nash lost around $9,000 on each Nash-Healey sold! No wonder production was kept low, only 506 being made between early 1951 and August 1954. However, the Nash-Healey acted as excellent bait to draw customers into showrooms to buy production Nash cars, and in this they fulfilled George Mason's original plans. They also rescued Donald Healey from possible bankruptcy, enabling him to design the Healey Hundred, which became the Austin-Healey, a much more successful and famous sports car than the Nash-Healey ever was.

THE FIRST HAND-MADE PRODUCTION MODEL OF THE CORVETTE ABOUT TO LEAVE THE LINE AT FLINT ON JUNE 10, 1953. THE FIRST 300 CARS WERE ALL IN WHITE, WHICH GAVE SOME PEOPLE THE IDEA THAT YOU COULD NOT HAVE FIBERGLASS IN ANY OTHER COLOR.

MIRCO DE CET COLLECTION

CORVETTE AND THUNDERBIRD

By the time the Nash-Healey had been laid to rest, General Motors already had a sports car in production and Ford was about to launch another. Chevrolet's Corvette was the idea of GM's styling chief Harley Earl, who envisaged a low-priced sports car for his college-age son and his friends. He began to make sketches in 1951 and, aided by a young sports car enthusiast, Bob McLean, full-size drawings were followed by a plaster mock-up. Earl originally planned a V8 engine, but owing to the popularity of the Jaguar XK120, he and McLean changed their ideas to a six.

Since 1951 General Motors had been launching its new models at an extravagant display called Motorama which toured major cities. Alongside production cars were dream cars to test out new ideas on the public. Buick, Cadillac, Oldsmobile, and Pontiac all had their dream machines, but humble Chevrolet did not, until 1953. Then it was decided to exhibit Earl's sports car as Chevy's contribution and, what is more, it was given running gear by GM's chief of engineering, Ed Cole. It was more of a functioning automobile than many other dream cars.

Cole and his team shortened the stock Chevrolet frame by 13 inches to 102 inches, and moved the engine back in the frame by 7 inches.

▲▶ GENERAL MOTORS STYLIST HARLEY J. EARL, WHO BEGAN HIS CAREER WITH THE DON LEE STUDIOS IN THE 1920S, IS PICTURED HERE WITH TWO DREAM CARS, THE BUICK LE SABRE OF 1951 (ABOVE) AND THE PONTIAC FIREBIRD III GAS TURBINE CAR OF 1959 (RIGHT). FEW OF LE SABRE'S STYLING INNOVATIONS EVER APPEARED ON PRODUCTION BUICKS, ALTHOUGH FINS BECAME FAMILIAR ON CADILLACS, AND THE CENTRAL AIR INTAKE WAS COPIED BY SEVERAL EUROPEAN CUSTOM BODY STYLISTS AND APPEARED ON AT LEAST ONE BUS. THE BIRD DESIGN ON THE PONTIAC'S HOOD WAS USED ON PRODUCTION FIREBIRDS FROM 1973 ONWARD.

GENERAL MOTORS ARCHIVES, MIRCO DE CET COLLECTION

1959 CHEVROLET CORVETTE ▲
THE '59 CORVETTE WAS LITTLE CHANGED FROM THE '58s, HAVING THE TWO FOUR-HEADLIGHT FRONT END
OF THE '58S, AND THE SCULPTURED BODY SIDES INTRODUCED IN 1956. THE BASE ENGINE WAS A 230bhp
283-CUBIC-INCH V8, BUT 245, 270, AND 290bhp COULD ALSO BE HAD. THE LATTER USED FUEL INJECTION
AND GAVE 0-60mph IN 6.6 SECONDS, WITH A TOP SPEED OF 128mph; IT COST AN ADDITIONAL $484
OVER THE LIST PRICE OF $3,875. CORVETTE PRODUCTION FOR THE 1959 SEASON WAS 9,670.

OWNER JIM DiGREGORIO (PHOTO NICKY WRIGHT)

**1953 CHEVROLET CORVETTE CONVERTIBLE
ROADSTER ▲**
THE CAR PICTURED HERE IS ONE OF THE 315 ORIGINAL
CORVETTES MADE AT FLINT BETWEEN JUNE AND
DECEMBER 1953, BEFORE PRODUCTION WAS
TRANSFERRED TO ST. LOUIS. THE FIBERGLASS BODIES
WERE ALL WHITE AND THE ENGINE WAS THE OLD
"STOVEBOLT SIX" TWEAKED UP TO 150bhp. THE
CORVETTE WAS THE BABY OF HARLEY EARL, HEAD OF
GM'S ART & COLOUR STUDIO, AND CHIEF ENGINEER ED
COLE, AND IT WAS ONLY DUE TO THEIR PLEADING THAT
THE MODEL WAS CONTINUED AFTER 1955, SINCE INITIAL
SALES WERE DISAPPOINTING. RESTYLING, GREATER
COMFORT, AND A V8 ENGINE MADE THE CORVETTE
A DIFFERENT CAR FROM 1956 ONWARD AND SALES
REALLY TOOK OFF.

OWNER: NATIONAL AUTOMOBILE MUSEUM, RENO, NEVADA

(PHOTO NICKY WRIGHT)

This meant that the driver could touch the rear wheels from his seat. The engine was a stock 235-cubic-inch Chevy six with power boosted from 115 to 150bhp thanks to triple Carter carburetors, high-lift cams, twin exhausts, and other modifications. Transmission was a two-speed Powerglide automatic, far from ideal for a sports car but the only one available that could cope with the power.

Three show cars were built, a roadster called Corvette, a fastback coupe called Corvair, and a station wagon called Nomad. The last two remained prototypes, but the Corvette was so enthusiastically received by the public that Chevrolet decided to go into limited production. The first cars came off the line at Flint in June 1953, and by the year's end 315 had been made. They had fiberglass bodies in white, which led

people to think that this was the only color you could have fiberglass in. Most of these early 'Vettes were given to VIPs or used for publicity, although a price of $3,440 was fixed. This was much more than the $1,000 college kids' car Earl had dreamed of, and made the Corvette a specialty car, nearly double the price of any other Chevrolet. One of the first private buyers was Briggs Cunningham, who gave the car to his wife.

In 1954 production was transferred to St. Louis, where it has remained ever since. Only minor improvements were made, but additional colors were introduced, Pennant Blue and Sportsman Red, although 80 percent of buyers opted for white, with red and white interiors. Of the 3,640 built in 1954, not much above 2,000 found buyers, which was disappointing after the car's rapturous reception the

year before. At the end of the season, dealers had around 1,500 Corvettes in stock. Because of this, only 674 '55 models were sold. The Corvette had fallen between two stools; the enthusiasts rejected it because of the automatic transmission and simulated knock-off wheels, while those who were used to convertibles disliked the side curtains which had to be pushed aside to gain access to the interior door handles, as there were none on the outside. Also the cars leaked water and dust. A senior, though unnamed, Chevrolet source said in the 1980s: "Quite frankly, those early 'Vettes weren't very good cars. I know they're highly praised now by collectors, but we had nothing but headaches from them, and in 1954 and 1955 it really looked like there wouldn't be any '56s."

However, Ed Cole had an ace up his sleeve, the

1967 CHEVROLET CORVETTE STING RAY COUPE ▶

THE DISTINCTIVE FASTBACK STING RAY COUPE, INTRODUCED IN 1963, IS A VERY POPULAR MODEL WITH COLLECTORS, ALTHOUGH IT WAS OUTSOLD BY THE CONVERTIBLE WHEN NEW. THE STANDARD ENGINE WAS A 300BHP V8, BUT SEVERAL MORE POWERFUL OPTIONS WERE AVAILABLE, UP TO THE L-71 TRI-CARB WHICH GAVE 435bhp FROM 427 CUBIC INCHES. A THREE-SPEED MANUAL TRANSMISSION WAS STANDARD, BUT ONLY 1.9 PERCENT OF BUYERS CHOSE IT; 88 PERCENT WENT FOR THE FOUR-SPEED MANUAL, AND 10.1 PERCENT FOR THE POWERGLIDE AUTOMATIC TRANSMISSION.

OWNERS: SKIP AND KATHY MARKETTI (PHOTO NICKY WRIGHT)

1969 CHEVROLET CORVETTE STINGRAY CONVERTIBLE ▲

CORVETTES WERE RESTYLED FOR 1968 WITH A MORE AERODYNAMIC FRONT END AND A NEW TUNNELBACK COUPE REPLACING THE SPLIT-WINDOW FASTBACK. ALTHOUGH THE WHEELBASE WAS THE SAME, 98 INCHES, OVERHANG MADE THE NEW CORVETTE 7 INCHES LONGER. THE STING RAY NAME WAS DROPPED, BUT REAPPEARED FOR 1969 AS ONE WORD, STINGRAY. POWER STEERING WAS AN INCREASINGY POPULAR OPTION, UP FROM 13.7 PERCENT IN 1965 TO 59.2 PERCENT IN 1969.

(PHOTO NICKY WRIGHT)

V8 engine which powered all Corvettes from 1956 onwards. This 265-cubic-inch overhead valve unit gave 195bhp in its mildest 1955 form, and up to 225bhp in 1956. Combined with a three-speed manual transmission, this made the Corvette into a more serious sports car, reinforced in 1957 when the V8, enlarged to 283 cubic inches, gave 220–283bhp, the latter the psychologically and promotionally valuable figure of 1 horsepower per cubic inch. Corvette sales increased to 3,467 in the 1956 season, 6,339 in 1957, and 9,168 in 1958. By 1960, sales were well into five figures, where they have remained ever since.

Belgian-born and Russian-educated Zora Arkus-Duntov was the man really responsible for the Corvette's success, working on the improved suspension of the '56 model, and introducing fuel injection and four-speed transmission options on the '57. Whereas the original Corvette had taken 11 seconds to reach 60mph, the '57 fuelie did it in 5.7 seconds, a respectable figure for a sports car even today; 240 fuel-injected 1957 Corvettes were made, as many buyers just did not want that amount of performance, or to pay the additional $675.

By 1962 the Corvette engine was up to 327 cubic inches and a maximum of 360bhp. Then, in the following year came the Sting Ray, which, apart from its engine, was an all-new car. The body was completely restyled, and in addition to the roadster there was a striking split-window fastback coupe. Suspension was all-independent, by coil springs at the front (from the stock passenger cars) and by transverse leaf springs and lower wishbones at the rear. The wheelbase was 4 inches shorter, rear tread 2 inches narrower, and frontal area reduced by 1 square foot. Front/rear weight distribution was 48/52 compared with 53/47 for previous Corvettes. Ride and handling were significantly improved, with the most powerful engine option giving 360bhp and a top speed of 147mph.

Chevrolet now had a sports car which could compare well with European competition, at the quite reasonable price of $4,037 for the roadster and $4,252 for the coupe. Sting Ray sales were well up on previous Corvettes, at 21,513, divided equally between the open and closed models. The Sting Ray was steadily developed during its five-year lifespan, notably in 1965 when disk brakes were fitted and a 396-cubic-inch engine was the largest option. This grew again to 427 cubic inches in 1966, when maximum output was 425bhp. This gave 0–60mph in around 5 seconds and a

theoretical top speed with the 3.08:1 rear axle of 170mph. Most powerful of all was the L88 competition coupe with aluminum cylinder head, four-barrel carburetor, and a compression ratio of 12.5:1. This developed 560bhp. Only 20 Corvettes used this engine. No price was quoted, but the 435bhp tri-carb engine cost $947 above the standard coupe price of $4,663.

The Sting Ray name was discontinued for the 1968 Corvettes, to be revived by the single word, Stingray, for 1969. Stingrays were roomier, longer, and heavier than their predecessors, and their styling lasted up to 1983. Engine size and power were drastically reduced, though, the 1982 models having just one 350-cubic-inch unit giving 200bhp.

Ford's Thunderbird was made in larger numbers than the Corvette, but only for the first three years of its life could it really be considered a sports car. Thereafter it grew into a four-passenger personal convertible. The idea of a two-passenger sports car had been around at Ford for some time, but only crystallized when Chevrolet showed the Corvette at the GM Motorama in February 1953. It

was the work of a team acting under Ford design director, Franklin Q. Hershey, and encouraged by general manager Lewis D. Crusoe. A mock-up remarkably similar to the production Thunderbird was shown at the January 1954 Detroit Auto Show, and the cars began to come off the assembly lines on September 9, 1954.

Although it was compared to the Corvette in having two seats, the Thunderbird was a very different car in other ways. Hershey shunned the Corvette's crude side curtains for proper roll-up windows, used conventional steel instead of fiberglass for the body, and installed a larger and more powerful V8 engine. This gave it a better performance than the Corvette, 112 as against 107mph top speed, and 0–60 in 9.3 seconds as against the 11 seconds needed by the Corvette. No wonder it sold well, for it performed better without the sports car crudities of the Corvette. At $2,944, it was $496 less than its GM rival. More of a conventional American car than a European imitation, it shared the Corvette's 102-inch wheelbase, yet its substantial rear overhang gave it 18 inches more length. At 3,850 pounds curb weight, it was 730 pounds heavier. Sales of the first model year were 16,155, nearly four and a half times the Corvette's figures.

Impressive though they were for the first year of a new model, Thunderbird's sales figures were not good enough for divisional general manager Robert McNamara, who thought that a popular car

1956 FORD THUNDERBIRD CONVERTIBLE ◄
THE THUNDERBIRD WAS SEEN AS A RIVAL TO THE CORVETTE AS IT WAS A TWO-PASSENGER CAR, BUT FROM THE START IT WAS LARGER AND MORE POWERFUL, WITH ALL THE CREATURE COMFORTS THAT THE FIRST CORVETTES LACKED, SUCH AS WIND-UP WINDOWS INSTEAD OF SIDE CURTAINS. THE TOP WAS POWER-OPERATED, WITH THE OPTION OF A DETACHABLE HARDTOP. OUTPUT FROM THE V8 ENGINE WAS NEARLY 200bhp, 50bhp MORE THAN THE CORVETTES, YET THE T-BIRD COST $496 LESS. UNLIKE THEIR SUCCESSORS, THE EARLY T-BIRDS WERE RACED; JOE FERGUSON WON THE 1955 PRODUCTION SPORTS CAR CLASS AT DAYTONA, BEATING AUSTIN HEALEYS AND PORSCHES.

OWNER: NATIONAL AUTOMOBILE MUSEUM, RENO, NEVADA

(PHOTO NICKY WRIGHT)

1959 FORD THUNDERBIRD CONVERTIBLE ◄
FOR 1958 THE THUNDERBIRD WAS REDESIGNED AS A
FOUR-PASSENGER CONVERTIBLE, LOSING WHATEVER
CLAIMS IT MIGHT HAVE HAD TO BE A SPORTS CAR. THE
WHEELBASE WAS LENGTHENED FROM 102 TO 113 INCHES
AND THE ENGINE WAS A NEW 352-CUBIC-INCH V8 GIVING
300bhp. THIS CONVERTIBLE SOLD FOR $3,979. THERE
WAS ALSO A HARDTOP AT $3,696 WHICH PIONEERED
THE SQUARE-CUT FORMAL-LOOK BODY LATER USED
ON OTHER FORD MODELS.
OWNER: DR. ROSS BEWLEY (PHOTO NICKY WRIGHT)

T WO CURIOSITIES FROM FORD—
EDSEL AND CONTINENTAL MARK II
By the mid-1950s Ford had come a long way from
their parlous postwar state, thanks to Ernest
Breech, the "Whiz Kids," and, not least, Henry
Ford II. However, the company still lagged behind
General Motors, by 1,187,033 cars in 1954, and
Breech felt Ford needed more marques to match
the five offered by GM. The middle price class was
catered to by three GM marques, Pontiac,
Oldsmobile, and Buick; Ford had only Mercury, so
a new marque was planned that would bracket
Mercury at either end, giving a wide spread of
models and engines.

The new project was christened the E-car (for
Experimental) and was to be all new, with its own
engines and body shells. Ford engineers soon
realized that this would be too expensive, so
existing Ford and Mercury bodies were used, Ford
in the lower-priced Ranger and Pacer models,
Mercury for the more expensive Corsair and
Citation. Two engines were offered, both from the
new family of overhead valve V8s, a 361-cubic-inch
which was not used by either Ford or Mercury, and
a 410-cubic-inch from the middle of the Mercury
range. If the bodies and engines were familiar, a
note of distinction had to be sounded somewhere,
and this was in the grille, a vertical shape when all
contemporaries were horizontal, and generally
likened to a horse collar. It was certainly unusual,
but whether it conveyed the right messages is
another matter.

The naming of the new car caused more

should seat at least four passengers. His attitude
highlighted a fundamental difference between the
thinking behind Corvette and Thunderbird. The
Corvette was intended to earn publicity for GM
through a performance image, not to make money.
For McNamara, every automobile carrying the
Ford name was expected to make money.

Work on a four-passenger Thunderbird went
ahead in 1955, and for the 1958 season the two-
passenger car was dropped. It had not been greatly
changed, although a 312-cubic-inch engine was an
option for 1956, and for 1957 this came in three
versions, 245, 270, or 285bhp. These were
introduced to counter the greatly improved and
more powerful Corvettes that were coming on the
market. There were also the McCulloch
supercharged versions giving 300–340bhp, of which
only 208 were made; 300bhp was probably the
maximum output from a customer car, with 340
being reserved for the T-birds that Ford entered in

NASCAR racing during the 1950s.

The four-passenger Thunderbird which
debuted for 1958 was a different car, 11 inches
longer in wheelbase and 20 inches longer overall.
Styling was closer to that of other Fords, although
no T-bird was as distinctive as the Corvette was
from regular Chevrolets. The four-passenger
convertible or hard-top, known as the Square Bird
or Big Bird, was a great success, selling nearly
38,000 in its first year, nearly double the Little
Bird's best figure, and going on to 90,843 in 1960. It
lost whatever sporting image it had in the mid-
1960s, when a four-door sedan was made, but by
the late 1980s the T-bird was again a performance
car, with a turbocharger from 1984 to 1988, and then
a supercharger.

1958 EDSEL CITATION HARDTOP ▲

THE CITATION WAS THE TOP MODEL OF EDSEL, SHARING THE BODY OF THE CORSAIR BUT WITH MORE DELUXE TRIM AND
INTERIORS. BOTH THE CITATION AND THE CORSAIR HAD MERCURY-BASED BODIES ON A 124-INCH WHEELBASE EXCLUSIVE
TO EDSEL. ASSEMBLED IN THE MERCURY FACTORY AT WAYNE, MICHIGAN, THEY WERE KNOWN INTERNALLY AS EMs
(EDSEL MERCURY) TO DISTINGUISH THEM FROM THE LOWER-PRICED FORD-DERIVED EFs. THIS CITATION TWO-DOOR
HARDTOP COUPE SOLD 2,535 UNITS IN THE 1958 MODEL YEAR, AT A PRICE OF $3,535.

OWNER: MIKE SAYER (PHOTO NICKY WRIGHT)

1961 LINCOLN CONTINENTAL FOUR-DOOR CONVERTIBLE ▲

THIS STRIKING CAR MARKED A RETURN TO THE FOUR-DOOR CONVERTIBLE STYLE LAST SEEN IN THE 1930s. IT WAS A BIG CAR, 212.4 INCHES LONG AND WEIGHING 5,215 POUNDS, BUT SHORTER THAN THE MASSIVE 1960 PREMIERE AND CONTINENTAL MARK V. THERE WERE ONLY TWO STYLES IN THE 1961 LINCOLN RANGE, THE CONVERTIBLE AND A SEDAN WITH SIMILAR LINES. THE CONVERTIBLE COST $6,713, MAKING IT AMERICA'S MOST EXPENSIVE CAR IN 1961, APART FROM THE LIMITED-PRODUCTION CADILLAC 75 LIMOUSINE. IT WAS IN AN EXTENDED VERSION OF THE 1961 CONTINENTAL THAT PRESIDENT KENNEDY WAS RIDING WHEN HE WAS ASSASSINATED IN NOVEMBER 1963.

OWNER: BLAINE JENKINS (PHOTO NICKY WRIGHT)

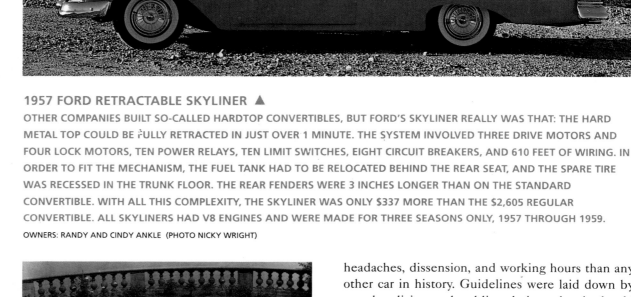

1957 FORD RETRACTABLE SKYLINER ▲

OTHER COMPANIES BUILT SO-CALLED HARDTOP CONVERTIBLES, BUT FORD'S SKYLINER REALLY WAS THAT: THE HARD METAL TOP COULD BE FULLY RETRACTED IN JUST OVER 1 MINUTE. THE SYSTEM INVOLVED THREE DRIVE MOTORS AND FOUR LOCK MOTORS, TEN POWER RELAYS, TEN LIMIT SWITCHES, EIGHT CIRCUIT BREAKERS, AND 610 FEET OF WIRING. IN ORDER TO FIT THE MECHANISM, THE FUEL TANK HAD TO BE RELOCATED BEHIND THE REAR SEAT, AND THE SPARE TIRE WAS RECESSED IN THE TRUNK FLOOR. THE REAR FENDERS WERE 3 INCHES LONGER THAN ON THE STANDARD CONVERTIBLE. WITH ALL THIS COMPLEXITY, THE SKYLINER WAS ONLY $337 MORE THAN THE $2,605 REGULAR CONVERTIBLE. ALL SKYLINERS HAD V8 ENGINES AND WERE MADE FOR THREE SEASONS ONLY, 1957 THROUGH 1959.

OWNERS: RANDY AND CINDY ANKLE (PHOTO NICKY WRIGHT)

1957 CONTINENTAL MARK II COUPE ▲

MARKETED AS A SEPARATE MARQUE FROM LINCOLN, WHICH THE FIRST CONTINENTAL HAD NEVER BEEN, THE MARK II HAD TOTALLY FRESH STYLING AND A NEW CHASSIS DIPPED BETWEEN FRONT AND REAR AXLES TO GIVE PLENTY OF HEADROOM WITHOUT A HIGH ROOF LINE. THE ENGINE WAS THE STANDARD LINCOLN V8, ALTHOUGH EACH UNIT WAS SELECTED FROM THE ASSEMBLY LINE AND INDIVIDUALLY BALANCED. ALL 2,989 PRODUCTION MARK IIs WERE COUPES, ALTHOUGH A SOLITARY CONVERTIBLE WAS MADE FOR MRS. WILLIAM CLAY FORD, WHOSE HUSBAND HEADED THE CONTINENTAL DIVISION.

LEFT, OWNER: PETE GARBE (PHOTO NICKY WRIGHT); RIGHT, FORD ARCHIVES, MIRCO DE CET COLLECTION

headaches, dissension, and working hours than any other car in history. Guidelines were laid down by merchandising and public relations that it should have two or three syllables, be clear and distinct, and not be prone to obscene double-entendres or translate into anything objectionable. Some of the suggestions made were later adopted as model names, including Citation, Pacer, and Ranger, but the marque name was still unchosen. Advertising agents Foote, Cone & Belding came up with a list of 6,000 names; project chief Dick Krafve exclaimed, "My God, we don't want six thousand names, we only want one," which left FC & B distinctly crestfallen, although presumably they collected their fee just the same.

One who would not accept a fee ("My fancy would be inhibited by acknowledgment in advance of performance") was Brooklyn poet Marianne Moore, whom market research manager David Wallace contacted with a request for suitable names. He recalled that an entertaining

THE AMERICAN AUTOMOBILE: A CENTENARY 1893–1993

correspondence ensued, but none of Miss Moore's suggestions was remotely suitable. They included "The Intelligent Whale" (after a pioneer submarine shaped like a sweet potato), "Resilient Bullet," "Mongoose Civique," "Taper Racer," "Taper Acer," and as a final fling "Utopian Turtletop." Miss Moore never received a fee, but eventually $25 worth of red roses were dispatched to her, with the message "Merry Christmas to our favorite Turtletopper."

As David Wallace recalled, the final choice of name went to the man with the most power, Ernest Breech, who was deputizing for Henry Ford, vacationing in the Bahamas. "Why don't we call it Edsel?" he asked, and when told that Ford family members had expressed their distaste for their father's name to be spinning on countless hubcaps across the nation, he replied "Don't worry about that; I'll take care of Henry."

And so the new car was launched as the Edsel on September 4, 1957, with a TV spectacular starring Bing Crosby with Frank Sinatra as principal guest. This was a significant event in itself, as it marked Crosby's rather belated transition from radio to TV. The trouble was that, after all the hype swallowed and propagated by such wide-selling magazines as *Time* and *Life*, it was not a new car in the sense that the Corvette or Thunderbird were. Apart from its curious grille, its

chief innovation was push-button gear selection in the center of the steering wheel. There were 13 models in four series on three wheelbases, 116 (station wagons), 118, and 124 inches. In addition to the wagons there were two- and four-door sedans, hardtops, and convertibles. Prices ran from $2,519 for a two-door Ranger sedan, a little above the Ford Fairlane 500 on the same wheelbase but with a smaller engine, to $3,801 for a Citation convertible, $317 less than a Mercury Park Lane convertible. Compared with rivals from other groups, these prices were lower than De Soto or Oldsmobile, about on a par with Pontiac, and slightly higher than Dodge.

Although Krafve was given a small assembly plant devoted exclusively to Edsels, most of them rolled off the same lines as Fords and Mercurys, which was logical as they used basically the same bodies and chassis. The trouble was that Edsel was a separate division at first, so Krafve had to pay the Ford or Mercury divisions for every Edsel they

made. If they had been genuine outside suppliers he could have refused to accept a defective car, but as it was he could only complain. There was plenty to complain about. Edsel production was squeezed in at the end of each hour of Ford work, with the inevitable lowering of quality associated with rushed work. Despite McNamara's efforts to rectify matters, dealers and buyers began to see Edsels as being of inferior quality to Fords or Mercurys.

Worse than quality control, which was rectified as time went on, was the shift in American car-buying patterns. During the years when the Edsel was being developed, medium-sized cars accounted for about 40 percent of the market, but by the end of 1957 this had dropped to 25 percent, the balance being taken up by economy cars such as the Rambler American and by imports, which quadrupled between 1956 and 1958. It is debatable whether the Edsel was the right car for any time; certainly the late 1950s were the wrong time. Another factor was the dealer network. Of 2,400 dealers selling Edsels, only 118 had exclusive franchises; the rest were shared with Mercury, or even De Soto, which was not a Ford product at all. With cars in that price range becoming harder to sell, it is not surprising that dealers pushed the well-known makes rather than the newcomer.

Even before the end of 1957 it was evident that the Edsel was not selling well enough to sustain a separate division, so in January 1958 it was merged with Lincoln-Mercury to form the M-E-L Division, which also had responsibility for selling small imports from British and German Ford factories. Edsel production for the 1958 model year was 63,110, putting it in twelfth place. Mercury, in contrast, made 133,271 cars. To break even, Ford

needed to sell 650 Edsels a day; for the first ten days the daily average was 409, but then it dropped to around 300.

The Edsel range was cut for the 1959 season to three lines, Ranger, Corsair, and station wagons; only one 120-inch wheelbase was offered, and a 145bhp six joined the V8s as a sop to the economy market. Production slipped to 44,891, and for 1960 the horse collar grille was dropped. This may have deprived comedians of jokes, although most of them had found other sources of humor after the first few months anyway, but it robbed the Edsel of any individuality. The new horizontal grille looked rather like last year's Pontiac, while the bodies were mildly restyled Fords. Only 2,846 '60 Edsels

were made, and production ended on November 19, 1959. Customers who had already placed their orders for Edsels were given a $300 voucher toward the purchase of any other Ford product. The Edsel venture is said to have lost Ford more than $250 million, and gave the language a new word for failure.

Ford's other new marque of the 1950s was the Continental Mark II, a response to Lincoln dealers who were asking for a new Continental to replace the much-loved V12 coupes and convertibles that had gone out of production in 1948. Market research indicated that there were some 250,000 to 300,000 families in the United States whose disposable incomes would justify spending $10,000 on a car. At the time of the survey, the most expensive domestic product was the Cadillac Series 75 imperial sedan at $5,643. Some imports such as Rolls-Royce and Ferrari cost over $10,000, but their sales amounted to no more than 200 units a year. The Continental was going to be a gamble, but Ford was willing to take it, and set up a separate division under Henry's younger brother, 26-year old William Clay Ford.

Several body designs were put forward, and the chosen one was by John Reinhart. It was a low, wide four-passenger coupe with no family resemblance to the contemporary Lincoln, which made it a more distinctive design than the former Continentals. A spare wheel motif was molded into the rear deck and actually held the spare wheel. Bodies were not made by Ford's usual supplier, Briggs, but by Mitchell-Bentley of Ionia, Michigan. The Continental Mark II was a big car, 218.5 inches long and weighing 4,825 pounds. The engine was Lincoln's new 368-cubic-inch V8 which developed 285bhp. Experiments had been made with fuel injection, which would have given increased power, but the budget would not allow it.

The Continental Mark II was launched in June 1955 as a 1956 model, the model year running for fifteen months. The price was just under the envisaged $10,000, at $9,695, but customers did not flock to the showrooms. Of the estimated 250,000 families who could have afforded one, only 1,325 actually paid up. The Mark II cost more than twice as much as a Lincoln Premiere ($4,601), but it was clearly not twice the car. Few changes were made for 1957, although power went up to 300bhp, and

1964 FORD FALCON SPRINT HARDTOP ▼
UNDER THE GUIDANCE OF LEE IACOCCA THE FALCON BEGAN TO CHANGE FROM PLAIN-JANE COMPACT TO MUSCLE CAR IN 1963, WHEN V8 POWER WAS AVAILABLE FOR THE FIRST TIME. THE SPRINT WAS THE HIGH-PERFORMANCE VERSION OF THE FALCON FUTURA, AND CAME IN TWO-DOOR HARDTOP AND CONVERTIBLE FORMS, ALL WITH 260-CUBIC-INCH V8 ENGINES. MOST SPRINTS HAD BUCKET SEATS, ALTHOUGH 626 CONVERTIBLES WERE DELIVERED WITH BENCH SEATS.
OWNER: MIKE MYERS (PHOTO NICKY WRIGHT)

production was discontinued on May 13 that year. The total number made was 2,989, plus 23 prototypes, for an overall figure of 3,012. Among the prototypes was a solitary convertible by Derham. Made in 1956 and updated to 1957 specifications, it became the property of Mrs. William Clay Ford. It is estimated that Ford lost $1,000 on each Mark II sold, but at least this was better than Cadillac's estimated loss of $10,000 on each of its Eldorado Brougham rivals to the Continental.

Continental was retained as a separate marque for 1958, but the car was really a de luxe Lincoln with similar styling to other Lincolns, and sold for a more modest $5,800–$6,200. For 1959 it was absorbed into the Lincoln range. A separate Continental series was revived in 1968 with the Mark III, but it was not so distinctive as the Mark II and is generally regarded as a model of Lincoln.

THE SIXTIES: COMPACTS, PONY CARS AND MUSCLE CARS

While independents such as Kaiser, Studebaker, and American Motors built smaller cars in the 1950s, the Big Three left well enough alone until the very end of the decade. The subject was being thought about, though, and two compact designs rejected by Detroit went on to successful careers abroad. These were a Chevrolet tested in four- and six-cylinder form, which inspired the Australian Holden of 1948, and the 1945 compact Ford, which became the French Ford Vedette, also in 1948. Chevrolet began tooling in 1946 for a compact car to be called the Cadet and built in Cleveland, only to drop it because regular-sized Chevies were selling so well.

It was not until October 1959 that the Big Three launched their compacts, and a very diverse trio they turned out to be. Ford's Falcon was the most conventional, using regular Ford engineering with simple, unadorned styling, Chevrolet's Corvair was the most unorthodox with its rear-mounted flat-6 air-cooled engine, while Chrysler's Valiant was front-engined but had completely fresh styling, a tilted engine, and unitary construction. The impetus to bring them out came from the 1958 season, which had been poor for large cars but very successful for the compact Rambler American. The standard size American car had been growing over the previous

few years, so that the 1960 Ford Fairlane stretched 214 inches from bumper to bumper, 16 inches longer than its counterpart of 1954. The Falcon was only 181 inches long, yet offered as much interior space as the regular '54 Fords.

In 1957/58 Fords had been offered in two wheelbases, 116 inches for the Custom line and 118 inches for the Fairlanes. The larger cars had sold better, and 1959, when all Fords rode on a 118-inch wheelbase, was one of the very rare years when Ford outsold Chevrolet. This led the company to favor a two-pronged attack, with its large Fairlane and a considerably smaller car, the Falcon. This used a new 144-cubic-inch 90bhp six-cylinder engine which contained 120 fewer parts than its predecessor. Transmission was three-speed manual, with two-speed Fordomatic optional for an extra $180. Four bodies were offered, two- and four-door sedans, and equivalent station wagons, at prices from $1,912 to $2,287. These were about $300 lower than a six-cylinder Fairlane and more than $700 below the top line V8 Galaxie.

The Falcon may have looked dull in its specification and appearance, but it sold better than the other two compacts, with 435,676 units in its first year. This represented nearly 50 percent of all Ford sales. Within the next few years the Falcon became more exciting, with convertibles and V8

engines from 1963. This was largely the idea of Lee Iacocca, who took over the presidency of Ford in 1960 from the more conservative Robert McNamara. The Falcon was dropped after 1970, but it sired numerous famous Fords, including the Mustang, Comet, and Maverick. At the time of writing it is still being made in Argentina, complete with 1962 styling.

The Corvair had a longer gestation than the Falcon, and it needed it, considering its radical design. Robert Benzinger, who was in charge of engine design, said: "We started with probably about the blankest piece of paper we'd had in a long time." The flat-6 engine was the basis of the design, around which the rest of the car grew. Its layout was possibly inspired by the similarly designed Continental engine that powered the

M42 tank, for Chevrolet's general manager Ed Cole had supervised tank production at Cadillac during the Korean War. Also Cole's private Beechcraft Bonanza used a flat-6. Another factor was the growing success on the U.S. market of Volkswagen, which also featured a rear-mounted air-cooled horizontal engine.

Cole was never a man to shy away from innovation, and the Corvair certainly had the kind of innovations never seen before on a mass-production American car. Up to then no one had seriously questioned the dogma that an automobile must have its engine up front, vertically mounted and water-cooled, driving the rear wheels. The Corvair upset all that, and threw in all-round independent suspension by coil springs as well. The Tucker had several of the Corvair's features, but was hardly an example to follow. Ed Cole wanted the Corvair to be as different as possible from regular Chevrolets, so as not to steal sales from them. He saw it competing against the Rambler and Studebaker Lark, and against the VW and other imports. In fact, because the Corvair appealed to enthusiasts who liked a car that was sporty and fun to drive, it became something of a niche car before the end of its run, but that was not how its creator saw it at the start.

The 140-cubic-inch flat-6 had an aluminum block and separate cylinder barrels. A four-cylinder engine was considered briefly, and would have been much simpler to make, but a 140-cubic-inch four would have been unacceptably rough; apart from Jeep, which was not a regular passenger car, no other American auto maker was offering a four in 1959. In its original form, the Corvair engine gave 80 or 95bhp according to the number of carburetors. Transmission was three-speed manual with floor shift (very unusual at that time), or a two-speed Powerglide. A four-speed manual was optional on the Monza coupe, which came onto the market in May 1960. Initial Corvair bodies were a four-door sedan and two-door coupe. With no tunnel for the drive shaft, they could be full six-passenger automobiles and unusually low as well. Height was 51.5 inches, 3 inches lower than a Falcon. Prices were $1,984–$2,049 for the coupe and $2,038–$2,103 for the sedan, the higher prices being for the De Luxe 700 Series, which accounted for many more sales than the basic 500 Series. The

1961 CHEVROLET CORVAIR MONZA SEDAN ▲
THE MONZA NAME WAS FIRST USED FOR A SPORT COUPE VERSION OF THE CORVAIR, BUT FOR 1961 THERE WAS A MONZA SEDAN WITH BUCKET SEATS, FRONT ARM RESTS, CARPETING, BACK-UP LIGHTS, AND MANY OTHER FEATURES EITHER NOT AVAILABLE ON THE LESSER CORVAIRS OR ONLY AT EXTRA COST. THREE-SPEED MANUAL TRANSMISSION WAS STANDARD, BUT A FOUR-SPEED FLOOR TRANSMISSION WAS A $65 OPTION, WHILE A THREE-SPEED AUTOMATIC COST $157 EXTRA. IN THE BACKGROUND IS A MONZA CONVERTIBLE.
OWNER: LEE ROWE (PHOTO NICKY WRIGHT)

more powerful Monza coupe was priced at $2,265.

First year sales of the Corvair were 250,007, not much over half the Falcon's figure, but well ahead of the Valiant's 182,274. The Corvair received the best press reports, and the editors of *Motor Trend* named it their Car of the Year in April 1960. For 1961 a station wagon was added, and in addition there was the Greenbriar, a forward-cab six-door sports wagon also made in half-ton panel delivery and pick-up form.

April 1962 saw important changes in the Corvair range. The Lakewood station wagon was dropped because it was facing heavy competition from the conventional Falcon-like Chevy II which had arrived the previous fall. This simple car, which used Chevrolet's first four-cylinder engine since

1928, was an acknowledgment that GM could not rely on the unorthodox Corvair to challenge the Falcon and Valiant as basic transportation. With the Chevy II taking that role, at prices slightly below those of the Corvair, the latter was pushed into the role of a sporty car for the enthusiast. The station wagon was withdrawn, but in its place came the first Corvair convertible, the Monza, offered with a turbocharger which raised power from 90 to 150bhp. This was the world's first use of a turbocharger in a production car, although it differed from most later designs in that the turbo was mounted between the carburetor and intake manifold, drawing air through the carb, whereas modern turbos blow air into the carb or fuel injection system. The turbo version was called the Monza Spyder, and cost an extra $317.45, this being part of a package that included a heavy-duty clutch, four-speed transmission, and strengthened suspension.

The Monza Spyder soon attracted a cult following, but it had two serious drawbacks. Like all early turbos, there was a lag of up to 2 seconds between flooring the accelerator and any reaction from the engine, which took some getting used to. Once going, though, the Spyder was brisk, with 0–60mph taking 9.7 seconds compared with a snail-like 23.2 seconds for the original 80bhp Corvair. The other problem was handling with a high proportion of weight in the rear. Original weight distribution was to be 40/60 front/rear, but when the spare tire was moved from under the hood this went up to 37/63. Tire pressures were critical; the makers recommended 15psi at the front and 26psi at the rear, and these inflations, combined with the heavy-duty suspension, made for pretty good handling. Not every driver bothered too much about tire pressures, though.

For 1964 the Spyder became a standard model instead of an option package, and displacement went up to 164 cubic inches. With the turbo, power was now 180bhp and top speed 114mph. The convertible price was $2,811 — expensive for a Corvair, but more than $1,200 below a Corvette. The Monza was considered the poor man's equivalent to the Corvette. Indeed, for nimbleness and sense of driver control, it was more enjoyable than the more powerful front-engined car. All Corvairs were restyled for 1965, but by then sales were dropping. From a peak of 329,632 in 1961 they fell to 207,114, in 1964, and the restyling only lifted them slightly to 237,056 for 1965. Thereafter they dropped rapidly, to 103,745 in 1966, 27,253 in 1967, and only 6,000 in 1969, the last Corvair leaving the line on May 14 that year.

Much has been written about the death of the Corvair, the blame being laid on Ralph Nader. A crusading young lawyer (who didn't hold a driver's license), Nader published an article in *The Nation* magazine in November 1965 entitled "The Corvair Story." This formed the first chapter of his book *Unsafe at any Speed*, which came out the same month. His charges were that the swing axle, under the severe lateral forces produced by cornering, tended to lift the rear wheels of the car so that both wheels leaned outward, the angle increasing from

an acceptable 4° to a dangerous10° or 11°. The wheels tucked under in an instant causing rollover. Maurice Olley, an ex-Rolls-Royce GM engineer, had warned of this when he saw the swing axle designs before the Corvair project was launched, but his warnings were ignored. He had studied European cars with rear engines and swing axles, such as the Volkswagen Beetle and Renault Dauphine, and pronounced them "a poor bargain." The Corvair was heavier than either of these, with a higher proportion of weight at the rear. There were certainly a number of one-car accidents involving Corvairs, including the one which cost comedian Ernie Kovacs his life. Nader pointed out that GM could easily have afforded safety research, as their net income as a percentage of sales was 10.2 percent (Ford, 5.6 percent) and their return on

invested capital was 20.4 percent (Ford 11.3 percent).

Nader certainly influenced some Corvair owners to shop elsewhere for their next car, but his book was not crucial. The problem was that the complex Corvair was not as profitable as more conventional Chevrolets. As early as May 1965, when Nader was still at his typewriter, word went down the line to stop further development on the Corvair, just to do enough to satisfy Federal smog and safety requirements. The Mustang, which debuted in April 1964, was the biggest threat to the Corvair, for its wide hood could accommodate any size of V8 engine. The Corvair flat-6 could not be enlarged much without a complete redesign, and when a 283-cubic-inch V8 was tried the handling was so terrible that the idea was quickly forgotten.

1972 PLYMOUTH DUSTER ◄
THE DUSTER WAS A NEW PLYMOUTH FOR 1970, AIMED AT THE FORD MAVERICK MARKET. IN BASIC FORM, IT WAS AN ECONOMY COMPACT, ALTHOUGH THERE WAS A PERFORMANCE VERSION, THE 340, WITH 275BHP V8 ENGINE. WONDER HOW MANY CARS THIS CUTESY AD SOLD?
CHRYSLER CORPORATION

Many special versions of the Corvair were made, including three which were regarded as separate makes. John Fitch's Phoenix of 1966 was a two-passenger convertible with a body built in Italy by Intermeccanica. It had an electrically operated rear window and a removable metal roof panel that could be stowed in the trunk. A tuned engine gave 170bhp without the need for a turbocharger. The really high-performance Corvairs were called Yenko Stingers. Built by Don Yenko of Canonsburg, Pennsylvania, they came in several degrees of performance, the hottest having an engine bored out to 176 cubic inches and giving 240bhp. About 130 Stingers were made between 1965 and 1969, and they won many races, the last in 1973, four years after Corvair production ended.

The most bizarre of all Corvair conversions was the Lost Cause, offered by former mayor of Louisville, Kentucky, Charles Peaslee Farnsley. Using a 1963 four-door sedan, he had Derham do some customizing of the bodywork and equipped the interior with such delights as altimeter, compass, picnic hamper, lap robes, matching luggage, and vermeil mint julep cups. If you dared sip your mint julep at 115mph, a John Fitch conversion was available to provide this speed. Even without the Fitch conversion, the cost was $19,600, more than eight times that of a regular Corvair sedan.

The third competitor for the compact market was Chrysler's Valiant, which appeared on October 29, 1959 — 27 days after the Corvair. Built by Dodge and sold mainly by Plymouth dealers, it was considered a separate brand for the 1960 season only, after which it became a Plymouth. A new Plymouth-DeSoto-Valiant Division was created, and the Valiant was promoted as "Nobody's kid brother — this one stands on its own four tires." It was certainly different, with totally fresh styling dominated by a rectangular grille and sculptured rear end with simulated spare wheel cover molded into the trunk lid. The spare wheel actually lived under the trunk floor, but the effect was stylish, recalling the Continental Mark II.

The Valiant's engine was a 170-cubic-inch overhead valve six tilted at 30° to allow a lower hood. It gave 110bhp, or 148bhp with a four-barrel carburetor, and featured alternator ignition, not used by Plymouth. Two bodies were offered initially, a four-door sedan and a station wagon called the Suburban. The latter was made in two versions, with two or three rows of seats; the third row, for two passengers, was rear-facing. Like the other compacts, the Valiants came with a three-speed manual transmission as standard, with a two-speed automatic as a $172 option. Prices were $2,033 for a basic sedan and $2,546 for a de luxe nine-passenger Suburban; although listed as a nine-passenger, the rear seat of the de luxe Suburban would not comfortably accommodate more than two adults, whereas the larger Plymouth Suburban was a genuine nine-passenger car.

The Valiant changed little until 1963, when it lost its distinctive styling in favor of a blander look somewhat reminiscent of a Rambler. A convertible was offered and a 225-cubic-inch six was an alternative engine. The 1964 Valiant-based Barracuda coupe was hastily developed to meet the Mustang challenge. Upon learning that Ford was working on a sporty car based on the Falcon, Chrysler set to work on a rival. Having less money and time, for the Mustang project was well advanced before the rumors started, Chrysler could not afford an all-new body, so used the regular Valiant shell back to the windshield, and grafted onto it a two-door coupe with an enormous wraparound rear window; this was the Barracuda's most distinctive feature — with an area of 2,070 square inches, it was the largest piece of glass ever used in an automobile. A choice of three engines was offered, the 170 or 225-cubic-inch sixes, and a new 180bhp 273-cubic-inch V8.

As a Mustang rival, the Barracuda was a pony car, while installation of the larger V8s put it in the muscle car category, to be considered later. Meanwhile the Valiant sedans, convertibles, and Suburbans were continued as the lowest-priced Plymouth line up to 1976. Some were very plain-Jane cars in styling and performance, but in 1971 you could have a 275bhp 340-cubic-inch V8 in your Valiant Duster coupe.

The 1960 compacts catered well for the low-priced market, but the buyer who wanted a little more style and performance in a small package got nothing from the Big Three. He did not have long to wait, however, for the 1961 season saw three new cars from Buick, Oldsmobile, and Pontiac, as well as the Valiant-related Dodge Lancer. The GM cars were very interesting, for while they shared the same basic bodies, they incorporated plenty of technical innovation in engines and transmissions. Somewhat larger than the Big Three compacts, they rode on 112-inch wheelbases.

The Buick Special and Oldsmobile F-85 appeared in the first week of October 1960, with the Pontiac Tempest following on November 3. Buick and Oldsmobile shared a 215-cubic-inch V8 with aluminum blocks and cylinder heads, but the engines were not identical. Output was the same, at 155bhp, but combustion chamber differences gave the Buick slightly better torque. Pontiac, on the other hand, used a 194.5-cubic-inch four which was essentially half of the big 389 V8. More than 120 parts were common to both engines, with only 16 non-common parts, including the fuel pump. Standard output was 110bhp, but higher compression ratios and four-barrel carbs gave 120, 130, 140, or 155bhp, and the Buick V8 was also available in the Tempest, though only 2 percent of buyers chose it in the first season. The Tempest's transmission was unconventional, with a curved driveshaft driving to a rear axle mounted three-speed manual transmission. The shaft was arched just under 3 inches at its center (if the arch were a

1961 PONTIAC TEMPEST SEDAN ▲▼

THE TEMPEST WAS THE LEAST CONVENTIONAL OF GM'S SECOND GENERATION OF COMPACTS, WHICH INCLUDED THE BUICK SPECIAL AND OLDSMOBILE F-85. THE ENGINE WAS A 194.5-CUBIC-INCH FOUR, EFFECTIVELY HALF OF PONTIAC'S 389 V8, AND THE TRANSMISSION WAS VIA A CURVED DRIVESHAFT TO A THREE-SPEED MANUAL GEARBOX LOCATED ON THE REAR AXLE. WITH FIRST SEASON SALES OF OVER 100,000, THE TEMPEST BEAT ITS RIVALS FROM BUICK AND OLDSMOBILE.

PONTIAC MOTOR DIVISION, GENERAL MOTORS (PHOTO NICKY WRIGHT)

segment of a complete circle, it would have had a diameter of 73 feet) and absorbed much of the torsional vibration associated with a four-cylinder engine.

Although it had the same body as Olds and Buick, the Tempest had a strong Pontiac appearance thanks to its divided grille. Sedans, coupes, and station wagons were available, and Tempest sales were the best of the three makes, at 100,783. For comparison, the Buick Special sold 86,868 and the Olds F-85 59,674.

For 1962, a 198-cubic-inch cast-iron V6 joined the V8 in the Buick, and convertibles were added to all three ranges. From Spring 1962 to summer 1963, the Olds F-85 was offered with a turbocharger similar to that of the Corvair; 215bhp from 215 cubic inches allowed Olds to boast of

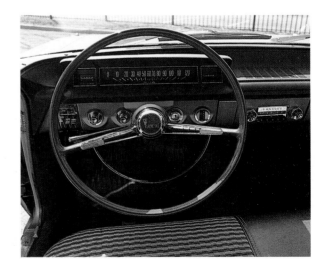

being the first U.S. manufacturer to offer 1 horsepower per cubic inch. However, Chevrolet had achieved this with the 1957 Corvette, and the turbo Corvair gave a better ratio, 150bhp from 145 cubic inches. An advantage of the Olds turbo was that it incorporated a wastegate, in effect a safety valve which "blew off" when pressure threatened to damage the engine. To combat build-up of carbon deposits in the cylinders, Olds injected a 50-50 mixture of methyl alcohol and water between the carburetor and turbocharger, calling the mixture "turbo rocket fluid." However, it was found that at the top end of the speed range, acceleration faded away, so that a Jetfire was slower than a four-barrel carb non-turbo car. The Jetfire, made as a two-door coupe only, was dropped after 9,607 had been made.

Fine engine though it was, the aluminum V8 proved uneconomical to make, so it was dropped after the 1963 season. It was subsequently sold to Rover in England, where it featured in Rover cars, Range Rovers, Morgan, and TVR sports cars. In its place came the cast-iron V6 in both Buicks and Oldsmobiles, although larger V8s were also available, 300 cubic inches in the Buick and 330 in the Olds F-85 Cutlass. The Pontiac Tempest lost its four in favor of a 215-cubic-inch six, and there were also V8 options. The cars were growing in size, and were called intermediates rather than compacts. The year 1964 was the first in which Pontiac used the magic letters GTO (Gran Turismo Omologato, or homologated Grand Touring), which were to appear on the company's powerful muscle cars.

1964½ FORD MUSTANGS ▲▶
THE FIRST SERIES MUSTANGS ARE CALLED 1964½ MODELS, AS THEY WERE INTRODUCED IN MID-SEASON, APRIL 17, 1964, SEVEN MONTHS LATER THAN OTHER 1964 FORDS. A COMPACT CAR WITH A VARIETY OF CHARACTERS FROM TAME TO FIERCE ACCORDING TO THE ENGINE FITTED, THE MUSTANG WAS DETROIT'S GREATEST SUCCESS OF THE 1960s. AT ONE TIME THERE WERE 15 ORDERS FOR EVERY AVAILABLE MUSTANG AND DEALERS TOOK TO AUCTIONING OFF THE CARS THEY HAD. THE FIRST MUSTANG WAS GIVEN THE TIFFANY AWARD FOR EXCELLENCE IN AMERICAN DESIGN, THE ONLY TIME AN AUTOMOBILE HAS BEEN SO HONORED. SEEN HERE ARE THE FIRST SEASON CONVERTIBLE AND COUPE.

CONVERTIBLE OWNER: BILL GOOSENE (PHOTO NICKY WRIGHT)
COUPE: FORD ARCHIVES, MIRCO DE CET COLLECTION

PONY CARS AND MUSCLE CARS

The 1960s saw a widening of American car ranges that has continued up to the present day. In the early 1950s there was generally one body shell made in traditional models such as sedan, coupe, convertible, and station wagon, and more often than not, only one engine. By the end of the decade there were usually several engine options from a humble six to a powerful V8, but only one size of car on a single wheelbase. Then came the compacts which grew into intermediates, and two new types emerged, the personal two-door four-passenger coupe and the high-performance machine which resulted from installing the most powerful V8 from the full size range in an intermediate body shell. The former were nicknamed "pony cars," while a powerful engine in an intermediate sedan body shell was called a "muscle car."

The first of the pony cars was the Ford Mustang; doubtless the name was derived from that of the Mustang, although the word pony was appropriate to their size and nimbleness. Interestingly, the term "pony car," used to designate a comparatively small sporty car, was current in the United States back in the 1920s. Some historians have called the Mustang the most significant American car of the 1960s; certainly it captured the trends of the decade, a brilliant piece of market identification as successful as the Edsel was disastrous.

Although many people were responsible for its design, the Mustang owed its existence to one man, Lee Iacocca. The Pennsylvania-born son of an Italian immigrant, Iacocca became a Ford salesman in Allentown, and vowed that he would be a Ford vice-president by his 35th birthday. He didn't quite make it, although 18 days after the birthday Henry Ford II invited him to become Vice-President of Cars and Trucks, with overall responsibility for Lincoln-Mercury as well as Ford. This was in January 1965, by which time the Mustang had been on the market for nearly a year.

If the Mustang idea had any ancestors, the two-passenger Thunderbird and the Corvair Monza were among them. Ever since the "baby 'bird" had been dropped, Ford customers and dealers had been calling for a replacement, while the bucket-seated Monza accounted for 76 percent of all Corvair sales. Iacocca was devoted to the philosophy of Thinking Young and had been responsible for Ford's re-entry into NASCAR events as well as dropping a V8 engine into the Falcon. He saw the growing purchasing power of the young and of women. The postwar baby boomers were coming up to driving age by the mid-1960s and were increasingly likely to want a car different from that of their parents. Women had traditionally influenced their menfolk in the choice of a car, but were now actually buying cars for themselves, particularly young, professional women such as teachers, accountants, and doctors. In Iacocca's mind it all added up to the need for an individually styled car, smaller than the regular models but without the family sedan image of the existing compacts.

A lot of market research figures have been published concerning the expected growth of the 15–29 year old sector of the market, its preference for sporty cars, floor shifts, and so on, and these have been given as the impetus for the Mustang project. However, according to Donald Frey, Iacocca's manager of product planning, most of the encouraging market research figures came after the project was under way. "They made it all up afterward — somebody did — in order to sanctify the whole thing. The market research that you read of is a bunch of bull."

The original Mustang prototype had a German-built Ford V4 engine mounted transversely behind the driver and passenger. It was tested at Watkins Glen by racing driver Dan Gurney, who loved it, as did the rest of the racing fraternity. However, Iacocca knew that a car that pleased the racing buffs would never sell in the volume he wanted, so it was abandoned. The car that came to the market in April 1964 was a front-engined coupe or convertible

with a long hood and a relatively short passenger compartment that seated four. Iacocca saw to it that it covered as wide a market as possible, with five engines, six transmissions, three suspension packages, three brake systems, three wheel sizes, and many other options in the comfort and performance fields. This blanket market coverage was later used in the Anglo-German Ford Capri, although not with such a wide range of options.

Mustang engines in the first year were a 101bhp 171-cubic-inch six, a 260-cubic-inch V8 (164bhp), and three variations of the 289 V8, giving 210, 220, and 271bhp. Only 26.9 percent of customers chose the six, but this rose to 41.7 percent the following year. In view of the supposed preference of the young for floor-shift manual transmissions, it is surprising to find that in the first year 49.2 percent of Mustangs were sold with automatic transmission, rising to 62.6 percent on the 1965 models, and to 90.4 percent by 1973.

The Mustang's target price was $2,500, but Ford managed to start at $2,368 for the base six-cylinder coupe. The V8 options added between $75 and $442.60, while four-speed manual transmission was an extra $75.80. Thus a Mustang with the most powerful V8 engine and all the handling and performance options could cost over $3,850, but this fitted perfectly with Iacocca's aim. The young, economy-minded schoolteacher could buy a Mustang for $2,368, while the speed enthusiast could also be a Mustang customer. This reasoning certainly worked, for more than 100,000 Mustangs were sold in the first four months of production, while the first 24 months accounted for over 1 million. For 1965, the six went up to 200 cubic inches, front disk brakes were available (at $58), and a fastback coupe joined the hardtop and convertible. Power options went up over the next few years to keep pace with competition from Plymouth's

Barracuda and Chevrolet's Camaro. For 1968 there were seven engine choices, from a 115bhp six to a 390bhp 427-cubic-inch V8. The most powerful Mustangs were the Boss 429s of 1969, which developed 375bhp in standard form, and up to 515bhp when tuned for Trans Am racing.

Distinctive Mustangs, although not the most powerful, were those assembled by Carroll Shelby and marketed as a separate make from 1965 through 1970. The first 100 were built in Ford's San Jose, California, plant and had a number of Shelby-requested modifications. These included the hi po (high power) 289 engine with stronger con rods and crankshaft, and a Shelby-designed camshaft. The engines were delivered to Shelby's plant near Los Angeles airport, where they were further developed, with four-barrel Holley carburetor and improved exhaust manifolding. Handling was improved by stiffer anti-roll bars, new steering arms, and modified suspension. The

1970 FORD MUSTANG BOSS 302 COUPE ▲▶

NAMED FOR ITS ENGINE DISPLACEMENT, THE BOSS 302 WAS A HIGH-PERFORMANCE MUSTANG LAUNCHED IN MID-1969 AS A ROAD-GOING VERSION OF THE TRANS AM RACING MUSTANGS. OUTPUT WAS RATED AT 290bhp, BUT 350bhp WAS A MORE REALISTIC FIGURE. MADE ONLY IN COUPE FORM, THE 302s HAD SPECIAL STRIPING, A FRONT "CHIN" SPOILER, AND DISTINCTIVE REAR WINDOW LOUVERS. STANDARD EQUIPMENT INCLUDED HEAVY-DUTY SPRINGS, FOUR-SPEED MANUAL TRANSMISSION, AND POWER-ASSISTED FRONT DISK BRAKES; 1,934 BOSS 302s WERE MADE IN 1969 AND 6,318 IN 1970.

OWNERS: TOM AND CAROL PODEMSKI (PHOTO NICKY WRIGHT)

rear seat was replaced by a shelf, and a fiberglass hood took the place of the metal one. Externally the Shelby Mustangs were distinguished by a thin blue stripe running between front and rear wheel arches, incorporating the letters GTO 350, and two wide blue stripes running from the front of the hood over the top and down the rear deck. In standard form a GT 350 gave 306bhp, but Carroll Shelby soon brought out the Competition version with 350bhp. About 25 of these were sold, and they became SCCA (Sports Car Club of America) "B" Production Class champions in 1966 and 1967.

GT 350 production was only 562 in 1965, but the next year 2,378 were made, including 936 bought by Hertz Rent-A-Car. Hirers had to be aged over 25 with a clean license; rates were $17 a day and 17 cents a mile. Most of the Hertz cars except the very earliest had automatic transmissions, whereas the regular GT 350 came with a four-speed manual.

In 1967 the GT 350 was joined by the GT 500, which offered such refinements as a rear seat, air conditioning, and power steering and brakes. To cope with the additional weight the 429-cubic-inch engine was used, and performance was similar to that of the smaller cars. The luxury/GT package with seating for four seemed to appeal more than the stark 350, and 1967 sales of the GT 500 were 2,950, nearly double the 1,175 350s sold. Late that year Shelby lost the lease on the Los Angeles airport site, and later Shelby Mustangs were built in the Ford plant. Problems with insurance, emission, and safety regulations, common to all high-performance cars, brought Shelby production to an end in 1970.

We have seen that Plymouth's Barracuda began

as a hastily produced rival to the Mustang, but in its early days it was not offered with such a wide variety of options. Stirred into action by the challenge of the Mustang, Pontiac GTO, and Oldsmobile 4-4-2, Plymouth offered a 235bhp V8 for $146 extra in the 1965 Barracuda and enhanced its sporting character by an all-synchro four-speed transmission with Hurst floor gearshift. For 1967 the Barracuda was restyled to distance it from the prosaic Valiant, and three bodies were offered, fastback and notchback coupes, and a convertible. The body was 11/2 inches wider, which meant that the hood could accommodate the 383-cubic-inch V8 giving 280 or 325bhp. A year later the fabulous 425bhp 426 hemi engine could be had in the Barracuda, although very few were so equipped and those mostly for drag racing.

The years 1970 and 1971 were the last for the big-engined Barracudas, when a wide range was offered. The car had been nicknamed the 'Cuda, and for 1970 this became the official name for the high-performance versions, carried in script on the

rear end. Models included the AAR 'Cuda, named for the All-American Racers developed for Dan Gurney and the Plymouth Trans Am team. This used the 290bhp 340-cubic-inch V8, but 'Cudas could be had with a 383, 440, or 426 hemi engine. The 440 was less powerful than the 426, as it did not have the hemi head, but still delivered 390bhp. It was known as the six-pack, from its three two-barrel carburetors; 0–60mph took 5.9 seconds, pretty impressive for a 3,720-pound car. Nor was it very expensive. Base price for a 440 six-pack was $3,414, but this could be inflated by options such as power steering and brakes. Singer Richard Carpenter bought a 440 six-pack with every possible option except air conditioning, not available on the 440 as there was no space under the hood for the compressor, and paid $4,400.

With Ford and Chrysler offering increasingly powerful pony cars, GM had to get in on the act too, which it did in 1967 with the Chevrolet Camaro and Pontiac Firebird. When the Mustang first appeared, GM management was not very

1968 CHEVROLET CAMARO SS CONVERTIBLE ◄ ▲

THE CAMARO WAS GM'S ANSWER TO FORD'S PHENOMENALLY SUCCESSFUL MUSTANG, AND FOLLOWED THE SAME PHILOSOPHY OF A SPORTY FOUR-PASSENGER CAR WITH A WIDE RANGE OF ENGINES, IN THIS CASE FROM A 140bhp SIX TO A 350bhp V8. THE LETTERS SS INDICATE A SPORT PACKAGE; THIS INCLUDED STIFFER SPRINGS AND SHOCK ABSORBERS, WIDER TIRES, DISK BRAKES, AND A MODIFIED HOOD WITH EXTRA SOUND INSULATION.

(PHOTO NICKY WRIGHT)

1969 PONTIAC FIREBIRD TRANS AM COUPE ▲▶
THE FIREBIRD WAS PONTIAC DIVISION'S VERSION OF THE
CAMARO, AND USED THE SAME SHEET METAL, WITH ITS
OWN DISTINCTIVE FRONT END. ENGINES WERE NOT
SHARED WITH THE CAMARO, BEING PONTIAC UNITS
FROM A 165bhp SIX TO A 325bhp V8. THE TRANS AM
VERSION WAS INTRODUCED IN MARCH 1969 AND
FEATURED A 345bhp ENGINE, HEAVY-DUTY THREE-SPEED
MANUAL GEARBOX, AEROFOIL ON THE REAR DECK, AND
FULL-LENGTH BODY STRIPES ON HOOD, TOP, AND REAR
DECK. THIS IS A RARE CAR, AS ONLY 607 TRANS AMS
WERE MADE IN 1969. IT WAS PRICED AT $3,556,
WHILE A REGULAR FIREBIRD COUPE COST $2,831.

OWNER: KEITH WILSON (PHOTO NICKY WRIGHT)

interested, thinking that it had a good competitor in the Corvair Monza. However, by the time the Mustang had sold 100,000 cars in four months, rethinking was suggested, and a program was hurriedly set in motion which resulted in the Camaro for the 1967 season. It was in many ways a similar concept to the Mustang, being a hardtop coupe or convertible with two standard engines, a 230-cubic-inch six and a 327-cubic-inch V8. The latter could be had in various models from 210 to 325bhp, and another option was the 350bhp 396-cubic-inch V8. The six-cylinder coupe was priced just $5 above the Mustang at $2,466, while the V8s were up to $70 more.

While the F-car, as it was called before being named Camaro, was being developed by Chevrolet, GM reasoned that it could sell more pony cars through two divisions than one (Ford was already doing the same with the Mustang-based Mercury Cougar) and that the second model should come from Pontiac. This was a logical choice, for

Pontiac already had a sporty image with the GTO, and its General Manager John Z. DeLorean was performance-minded and had recently submitted proposals for a two-passenger sports car. This was killed off by the Pontiac F-car, on which work started only six months before the Camaro's debut in September 1966. It was to have been called the Banshee, a name Pontiac had used for some of its show cars, but when an ad agency did a dictionary check and found that a banshee (a spirit in Irish folklore) foretold a death in the family, a hasty search for other names began. Firebird, which had also been used for General Motors prototypes, was ultimately chosen.

The Firebird used the same sheet metal as the Camaro for all major body panels, but managed a distinctive front end appearance by adding a large grille/bumper ahead of the fender, common to both models. Engines were Pontiac's own, a 165bhp 230-cubic-inch six and V8s of 326 and 400 cubic inches, giving 250–285 and 350bhp. The latter

breached GM's internal rule that power should not exceed a ratio of 10 pounds/horsepower, so the 350 was reduced to 325bhp by a small metal tab in the throttle linkage. Once the car had been sold with a limit of 325bhp, there was nothing GM or anyone else could do to prevent those tabs being removed. Ride characteristics were better on the Firebird, which had different spring rates and two adjustable traction bars connecting the rear axle to the floorpans rather than the Camaro's one.

The Firebird was launched in mid-season on February 23, 1967. Prices were about $200 higher than the Camaro right through the range. Both cars were soon given high-performance models, the Camaro Z/28 appearing in December 1966 and the Firebird Trans Am in March 1969. Both were suitable for street or track, and won many races in the Trans Am series. These were started in 1966 by the Sports Car Club of America for sedans in two classes, up to 2.5 liters (152.5 cubic inches) and up to 5 liters (305 cubic inches). The small class was dominated by foreign cars such as Alfa Romeo, but the larger was just right for the pony cars, and promoted much rivalry between Mustangs, Camaros, Firebirds, Barracudas, Challengers, and AMC Javelins. Z/28s took 18 out of the 25 races in 1967, and won the class championships in 1968 and 1969, while the Trans Am was third in the 1969 series. Both cars had 302-cubic-inch engines, the largest permitted under SCCA rules.

Street Z/28s and Trans Ams could be had with larger engines, up to 400 cubic inches. Only 697 Trans Ams were built in 1969, and of these precisely eight were convertibles. These were the only convertible Trans Ams ever built. The next Firebirds were not introduced until February 1970, which led to them being called 1970½ models. They had restyled bodies with lower, meaner lines, and six engines from a 155bhp six to a 345bhp V8. With the latter, 0-60mph took only 5.4 seconds.

1967 AMERICAN MOTORS MARLIN COUPE ▶
THE MARLIN WAS AMC'S ENTRY INTO THE MUSTANG/CAMARO PERSONAL CAR MARKET, BUT IT MET WITH MUCH LESS SUCCESS THAN THESE. ORIGINALLY STYLED THE RAMBLER MARLIN IN 1965, IT WAS A FASTBACK COUPE DERIVED FROM THE RAMBLER CLASSIC SEDAN ON A 112-INCH WHEELBASE. THE 1967 MARLIN WAS LONGER AND BETTER LOOKING, BEING BASED ON THE 118-INCH AMBASSADOR, BUT SALES WERE SLUGGISH: ONLY 4,547 IN 1966 AND 2,545 IN 1967. ENGINE OPTIONS WERE A 145bhp SIX AND V8s OF 235 OR 280bhp, AND SPORTY ITEMS SUCH AS FOUR-SPEED MANUAL TRANSMISSION, BUCKET SEATS, AND TACHOMETER WERE ALSO AVAILABLE.

(PHOTO NICKY WRIGHT)

1961 PONTIAC BONNEVILLE CONVERTIBLE ▲
PONTIAC'S TRANSFORMATION FROM A STAID "AUNTIE" CAR TO AN AUTO HIGH IN PERFORMANCE AND STYLE WAS ALMOST COMPLETE BY 1961. A LARGE CAR ON A 123-INCH WHEELBASE WITH AN OVERALL LENGTH OF 217 INCHES, THE BONNEVILLE WAS PONTIAC'S TOP LINE. THREE BODIES WERE OFFERED, SEDAN, HARDTOP, AND CONVERTIBLE, OF WHICH THE CONVERTIBLE WAS THE MOST COSTLY AT $3,905. THE CUSTOM SAFARI STATION WAGON WAS A SEPARATE SERIES. THE BASE ENGINE WAS A 303bhp 389-CUBIC-INCH V8, WITH THE 348bhp TRI-POWER V8 AS AN OPTION.

OWNER: BARRY BALES   (PHOTO NICKY WRIGHT)

1964 FORD GALAXIE 500 SEDAN ▲
THE FULL-SIZE FORDS WERE COMPLETELY RESTYLED FOR 1964 WITH A MORE COMPLEX GRILLE AND SCULPTURED LOWER BODY PANELS. THE BASE MODEL WAS THE CUSTOM, FOLLOWED BY THE GALAXIE AND GALAXIE XL, THE LATTER WITH FLOOR TRANSMISSION, BUCKET SEATS, AND OTHER SPORTY APPURTENANCES. AVAILABLE ENGINES COULD BE ANYTHING FROM A 138bhp SIX THROUGH FIVE V8s, TOPPED BY THE 425bhp 427-CUBIC-INCH UNIT THAT POWERED THE SUCCESSFUL NASCAR RACERS.

OWNER: JEFFREY HODDER   (PHOTO NICKY WRIGHT)

THE AMERICAN AUTOMOBILE: A CENTENARY 1893 – 1993

1954 LINCOLN CAPRI CUSTOM COUPE ◀

LINCOLN'S RACING PROGRAM PRECEDED THAT OF FORD BY THREE YEARS, AND WAS CONCENTRATED ON THE CARRERA PANAMERICANA, A 1,938-MILE RACE ACROSS THE OFTEN UNMADE ROADS OF MEXICO. LINCOLNS TOOK THE FIRST FOUR PLACES IN THE PRODUCTION CAR CLASS IN NOVEMBER 1952 AND 1953, AND THE FRIST TWO PLACES IN 1954. THIS CAPRI COUPE, DRIVEN BY RAY CRAWFORD, WAS THE WINNER, FOLLOWED BY WALT FAULKNER. CADILLACS TOOK THE NEXT TWO PLACES.

OWNER: NATIONAL AUTOMOBILE MUSEUM, RENO, NEVADA

(PHOTO NICKY WRIGHT)

1964 DODGE POLARA 500 HARDTOP ▲

INTRODUCED IN 1960, THE POLARA WAS THE TOP MODEL OF DODGE, AND IN 1964 WAS AVAILABLE IN FOUR BODY STYLES, SEDAN, HARDTOP SEDAN, HARDTOP COUPE, AND CONVERTIBLE. THE POLARA 500 WAS A SPECIAL TRIM OPTION WITH BUCKET SEATS, "SPORTS INTERIOR TRIM," AND EXTERIOR IDENTIFICATION NAMEPLATES. A VERY SMALL NUMBER OF POLARA 500S, OF WHICH THIS IS ONE, WERE FITTED WITH THE 426 HEMI ENGINE, GIVING 415 OR 425bhp ACCORDING TO COMPRESSION RATIO.

OWNER: JIM DONALDSON (PHOTO NICKY WRIGHT)

The front air dam and rear spoilers on the Trans Am were made of fiberglass, and were developed not in a wind tunnel but by running on a dry lake. The Trans Am name has been retained for the top model of Firebird up to the present day.

American Motors was not going to be left out of the pony car field, and in 1966 sorely needed a change from its "sound and sensible" image. The answer was the Javelin, launched in September 1967. It had a new four-passenger coupe body with a choice of three existing AMC engines, a 232-cubic-inch six, and 290 or 343 V8s, the latter with four-barrel carburetor and dual exhausts. Heavy-duty suspension, front disk brakes, and wide tires made it a good performer, with a top speed approaching 120mph. At $2,482 for the six and $2,588 for the smaller V8, the Javelin was lower in price than the Mustang, Camaro, or Barracuda. Unlike its rivals, it was never offered in convertible form.

First year sales for the Javelin were 55,124, quite encouraging for an independent car maker, but after that they dropped instead of climbing. By 1972 sales were down to 26,184, and although they recovered to over 27,000 in the next two years, AMC dropped the Javelin at the end of 1974 because it could not meet Federal bumper standards without a drastic redesign.

From mid-1968 to the end of the 1970 season, there was a shorter companion to the Javelin called the AMX. Unique among pony cars in that it seated only two passengers, it was 12 inches shorter in wheelbase. To reinforce its sporty image the AMX was not available with the six-cylinder engine; the 225bhp 343 V8 was standard, with optional 280bhp 343 and 315bhp 390 V8s. Richard

Teague, vice-president of styling at AMC, recalled that the AMX gave the Corvettes a really hard time in local races, and feels that with a little more time for development and styling improvements, it could have been a great car; not a big seller, but a useful addition to AMC's prestige. Unfortunately sales were very modest, only 6,725 in 1968 and 8,293 in 1969. AMC president William Luneburg complained that it was cluttering up the line, and killed it at the end of 1970. Total production of AMXs was 19,134, and of Javelins 236,379.

1968 PONTIAC GTO COUPE ▲▼

OFTEN CITED AS THE FIRST OF THE MUSCLE CARS,
THE GTO WAS A GOOD EXAMPLE OF THE OLD FORMULA
OF LARGE ENGINE IN MID-SIZED BODYSHELL. THE GTO
BEGAN LIFE IN 1964 AS A SUB-MODEL OF THE TEMPEST,
BUT BY THE TIME THIS 1968 COUPE WAS BUILT IT
WAS A LINE OF ITS OWN, AND ONE OF THE MOST
EXCITING OF ALL PONTIACS. FOUR ENGINE OPTIONS
WERE OFFERED, FROM 265 TO 366bhp, THE MORE
POWERFUL HAVING FOUR-JET CARBURETION AND
10.75:1 COMPRESSION RATIOS. COUPES WERE BY FAR
THE MOST POPULAR, WITH 77,704 DELIVERED,
COMPARED WITH 9,980 CONVERTIBLES.

OWNER: BARRY BALES (PHOTO NICKY WRIGHT)

MUSCLE CARS

Precise definitions are seldom accurate, but it is generally considered that two-door purpose-built coupes like the Mustang and Camaro are "pony cars," no matter how powerful their engines, while intermediates or full-size cars with the same engines under the hood are "muscle cars." Competition has reinforced the distinction, for pony cars competed in SCCA Trans Am races, while muscle cars ran in the NASCAR events. These dated back to 1947 when dirt track races were held for stock production sedans and coupes. Purpose-built tracks which became banked oval superspeedways followed, mostly in the Southeastern states which were the birthplace and spiritual home of stock car racing.

During the 1950s auto makers began to develop cars for NASCAR events, encouraged by the slogan "The sedan that wins on Sunday sells on Monday." Plymouth began supporting NASCAR in 1949, Dodge in 1953, Ford in 1955, and Pontiac in 1957. Their regular sedans became increasingly powerful, so it is not easy to say where or when the muscle car breed began. The Pontiac Tempest GTO of 1964 is often cited as the first, but what about the Chevrolet Impala SS 409, the Pontiac Grand Prix 421, the Ford Galaxie 500 XL, all cars of 1962 or 1963, and all delivering more than 400bhp? They were production cars, but their ancestors were the tuned and lowered custom cars of the 1950s, the first fruits of the marriage between youth culture and the automobile.

Some of the customs were purely performance cars, hot rods designed for straight-line acceleration, while others were styling exercises of which the peak was represented by the creations of George Barris. Most were something of both, for to gain the admiration of the pack, you needed Go as well as Show. A new car culture emerged in the late 1950s, riding on the back of growing national prosperity and youth independence. The car had always been an important status symbol for the family, but now the young wanted something quite different from their parents. Some went for foreign sports cars, but these were always expensive, and too small. Youth culture flourished in groups rather than exclusive couples; if your friends were temporarily carless you could take six of them around in your Galaxie, which you certainly couldn't do in an MG or Jaguar XK120. And if you wanted privacy with your girlfriend, the Galaxie was also fine, and a lot warmer and more comfortable than the MG.

The hot rod and custom car movement began, like so many trends, in California, but by 1960 had spread to virtually every town across the nation.

The growing suburbs, with miles rather than blocks between home and school, shops, restaurants, and drive-in movie houses, made the need for personal transportation ever more important. The car and its nurture soon became a way of life for millions of Americans between the ages of 15 and 25. As Dave Emanuel said: "The entire legacy of human interaction could be experienced from the front seat of a one-and-a-half ton three hundred horsepower womb. Heroes and villains, damsels in distress and gallant knights, courtesans, jesters, and pretenders could all play out their roles as the wombs rolled from stoplight to drive-in to parking lot."

Music, too, took up the theme. Groups such as the Beach Boys and Jan and Dean came up with "Little Deuce Coupe," "Shutdown," "409," "Dead-man's Curve," and "Little GTO," a best seller from the never-heard-from-again group Ronnie and the Daytonas. Dave Emanuel again: "The religion of the automotive sub-culture was now complete. It had its own icons, high priests, rubric, argot, and finally, its very own hymns."

Despite the popularity of hopped-up full-size sedans and coupes, the market welcomed the Pontiac GTO with wild enthusiasm. It was the idea of John DeLorean and his team and followed the age-old theme of a big engine in a small body. The engine was the 389-cubic-inch V8 from the Pontiac's Catalina/Bonneville line in 325 or 348bhp versions, and the body was the Tempest coupe. This had grown somewhat from its launch as a compact for 1961, but was still 17 inches shorter than the full-size Pontiacs. To round out the sporting specification,

1970 DODGE CHALLENGER R/T COUPE ▲

THE CHALLENGER WAS DODGE'S ANSWER TO THE MUSTANG AND THE CAMARO, AND WAS A SMALLER COMPANION TO THE CHARGER MUSCLE CAR. A NEW MODEL FOR 1970, IT WAS OFFERED AS A HARDTOP OR CONVERTIBLE, WITH TWO REGULAR ENGINE OPTIONS, A 145bhp SLANT-6 AND A 230bhp V8. THERE WERE SIX OTHER OPTIONS UP TO THE FORMIDABLE 425bhp 426 HEMI. R/T REPRESENTS ROAD/TRACK, AND WAS APPLIED TO THE HIGHER-PERFORMANCE CHALLENGERS WITH 383 OR LARGER V8 ENGINES. 1970 CHALLENGER OUTPUT WAS 83,032 CARS, OF WHICH 60 PERCENT HAD THE STANDARD V8 AND 26 PERCENT OPTIONAL V8s; 14.4 PERCENT WERE SIXES.

OWNER: LARRY BELL (PHOTO NICKY WRIGHT)

the GTO had a four-speed floorshift transmission and beefed-up suspension and brakes. It nearly didn't happen at all, for DeLorean knew that the GM hierarchy would not approve the idea, so he went ahead quietly. "When the corporation management got wind of the car shortly before it was introduced, it was mad. But the GTO was too late in its development to be stopped."

As we have seen, the letters GTO stood for Gran Turismo Omologato, the designation used by Ferrari for the cars it had manufactured in sufficient numbers to be homologated for production car racing. As might have been expected, sports cars enthusiasts objected to the use of the hallowed letters on a mass-produced American car, but as *Car & Driver* pointed out, the Pontiac could beat the Ferrari in a straight line, and with NASCAR suspension, even on corners. "The Ferrari costs at least $20,000; with every conceivable option on a GTO it would be difficult to spend more than $3,800. That's a bargain."

Strictly speaking, the GTO was an option package on the Tempest Le Mans for 1964 and 1965, becoming a line in its own right in 1966. Sales

were 32,450 the first year, 75,352 the second, and 96,946 the third. Research revealed that the average age of a GTO buyer was 25.7 years, compared with 43.3 years for all other new car buyers; that 30 percent were living with their parents (6 percent of all new car buyers); that 60 percent had attended college (46 percent of all new car buyers); and that 43 percent were unmarried. Roughly the same figures probably applied to purchasers of the GTO's rivals, which sprang up between 1965 and 1970.

Chevrolet and Oldsmobile responded to the GTO with the Chevelle SS-396 and the Cutlass 4-4-2, both of which had intermediate body shells with powerful V8 engines. Output started at 375bhp in the Chevrolet and 290 in the Olds, but quickly went up to 425bhp in the 1966 SS-396 and 390bhp in the 1968 4-4-2. This designation signified four-on-the-floor transmission, four-barrel carb, and dual exhausts. The ultimate 4-4-2 was the Hurst/Olds of 1968; this began as a special for gearbox manufacturer George Hurst, but was offered as a limited production model prepared by Lansing industrialist John Demmer. He received the 4-4-2s from the Olds assembly line, and in his own workshops fitted the Hurst four-speed transmission or HydraMatic with Hurst floor shifter, and high-performance cylinder heads which gave 390bhp from the 455-cubic-inch engine. Only 515 Hurst/Olds were made in 1968, all coupes, and 906 in 1969. No convertibles received the Hurst treatment, and indeed convertible muscle cars were generally few and far between. The GTO was made in a special version called The Judge in 1969; of 6,833 made, only 108 were convertibles.

Convertibles were never offered on the Chrysler Corporation's muscle cars, which were some of the most dramatic of all. Dodge's Charger began in 1965 as a fastback coupe derived from the mid-sized Coronet, and was available with the usual choice of engines from a relatively mild 230bhp 318-cubic-inch V8 to a blistering 425bhp from the 426 hemi V8. This remarkable engine was developed for NASCAR events in 1964 and was so successful that NASCAR stipulated that all engines should be available in production cars. Because of this, Dodge and Plymouth took a year out from NASCAR racing in 1965 and came up with the "street hemi" for 1966, used in the Charger,

1970 DODGE CHARGER RT/SE HEMI COUPE ◄

CHRYSLER CORPORATION'S HEMI ENGINES OF
THE 1960s WERE THE SECOND GENERATION OF THIS
DESIGN, AND WERE ALWAYS LIMITED EDITIONS.
THIS RT/SE (*ROAD & TRACK,* SPECIAL EDITION)
COUPE IS VERY RARE, ONLY FOUR HAVING BEEN MADE
IN 1970. THE 426 STREET HEMI POWER UNIT COST
AN ADDITIONAL $618 OVER THE $3,711 PRICE
OF THE CHARGER WITH 400 ENGINE. THE SE PACKAGE
INCLUDED SPECIAL EXTERIOR AND INTERIOR TRIM,
AND WAS NOT CONCERNED WITH PERFORMANCE.
PROBABLY THE MOST FAMOUS CHARGER R/T WAS
"THE GENERAL LEE," THE FOUR-WHEELED STAR
OF THE "DUKES OF HAZZARD" TV SERIES.
THE WHOLE STOCK CAR RACING SCENE GREW UP
IN THE COUNTRY DISTRICTS OF THE SOUTHEASTERN
UNITED STATES, TYPIFIED BY HAZZARD COUNTY.

OWNER: STEVE WITMER (PHOTO NICKY WRIGHT)

1974 PLYMOUTH ROAD RUNNER 440 COUPE ►

1974 SAW THE END OF BOTH THE HIGH-PERFORMANCE
PLYMOUTH LINES, BARRACUDA AND SATELLITE,
THE ROAD RUNNER BEING A MEMBER OF THE
SATELLITE FAMILY. THE STANDARD ENGINE
IN THE ROAD RUNNER WAS A 318-CUBIC-INCH V8
GIVING ONLY 170bhp, ALTHOUGH THE 440 WAS
AN OPTION. EVEN THIS DEVELOPED ONLY 275bhp,
COMPARED WITH 390bhp FOUR YEARS EARLIER.
THE ROAD RUNNER WAS IDENTIFIED BY THE STRIPES,
POWER BULGE ON THE HOOD, AND CARTOON BIRD
EMBLEM ON THE VERTICAL PART OF THE STRIPE,
JUST BEHIND THE WINDOWS. IT WAS PRICED AT $3,545,
AND 11,555 WERE MADE IN THE 1974 SEASON.

OWNER: GILMORE CAR MUSEUM, KALAMAZOO, MICHIGAN

(PHOTO NICKY WRIGHT)

Plymouth Belvedere, and Satellite, and later in the Barracuda, Road Runner, and GTX. The fastback Charger gave way to a notchback design for 1968, of which the muscle version was the Charger R/T (Road/Track), available with the 426 hemi or the larger but less powerful (375bhp) 440-cubic-inch V8. Along with other sporting Dodges such as the Super Bee, Dart GTS, and Coronet R/T, it came with bumble bee stripes running round the rear deck and on the quarter panels. These cars were collectively known as Dodge's Scat Pack. The Charger was the most performance-oriented, with stiffer springs and shock absorbers, and larger front disk brakes than its stablemates. When *Road & Track* editors tested an automatic version they

1964 AND 1971 BUICK RIVIERA COUPES ◄▼▲►

ONE OF THE MOST IMPORTANT POSTWAR BUICKS, THE RIVIERA ORIGINATED IN A BILL MITCHELL PROJECT TO REVIVE THE LASALLE. MITCHELL TOOK OVER FROM HARLEY EARL AS GM's STYLING CHIEF IN 1958, AND PENNED A FRESHLY STYLED PERSONAL SPORT COUPE WHICH WENT INTO PRODUCTION AS A SEPARATE BUICK LINE FOR 1963. IT REMAINED A SEPARATE LINE, MADE ONLY AS A HARDTOP COUPE, THROUGH THE 70s. BY 1971 THE WHEELBASE HAD INCREASED FROM 117 TO 122 INCHES, AND MITCHELL HAD GIVEN IT A VERY DRAMATIC BOATTAIL REAR DECK; SOME THOUGHT IT THE MOST BEAUTIFUL CAR TO APPEAR IN YEARS, WHILE OTHERS HATED IT. THE 455-CUBIC-INCH V8 ENGINE GAVE 315 OR 345bhp.

OWNER: ED BEHLE (PHOTO NICKY WRIGHT)

recorded a top speed of 156mph and 0–60mph in 4.8 seconds, a figure hardly equaled by any of today's supercars from Lamborghini or Ferrari. However, Chrysler had reservations about the hemi's longevity; the normal five-year or 50,000-mile warranty was reduced to 12 months or 12,000 miles for any car equipped with the hemi engine, and even then only if the engine had not been modified in any way.

Plymouth's hemi-powered cars were the Road Runner and GTX coupes. The former was named after the cartoon bird, whose "beep-beep" call was imitated by the car's horn. The GTX was similar in appearance, but more luxuriously equipped, hence the $3,355 price, $459 above the Road Runner. The 426 hemi was an option in both cars, but few were fitted compared with the 383 or 440 engines. The most dramatic-looking Road Runners were the

Superbirds of 1970. These were replicas of the NASCAR racers, with extended streamlined noses and large rear stabilizers. Regulations dictated that Plymouth build half as many of these cars as the total number of dealers, so 1,920 were made. The hand-built Superbird was priced at $4,298, while a regular Road Runner coupe cost $3,204. There was a very similar-looking Dodge, the Charger Daytona, of which 505 were made in the 1969/70 season.

For the muscle car, 1970 was the high point. After that the pony cars took over briefly as the favorite choice of performance-minded youngsters. Then the whole scene changed. Environmental pressures forced power-reducing controls on engine design and the oil crisis intervened. In some cases the names lingered on lesser cars, such as the Barracuda (to 1974), BD Charger (to 1978), and the 4-4-2 to the present day. Only the Firebird, Camaro, and Corvette survived the 1970s, to receive a new lease of life and power in the next decade.

1991 CHEVROLET CAPRICE SEDAN ▼

CHEVROLET DIVISION, GENERAL MOTORS (PHOTO NICKY WRIGHT)

CHAPTER SEVEN

THE AMERICAN AUTOMOBILE AT BAY

1970 – 1992

"Americans are fat and happy, but that doesn't mean America is
finished. When it gets tough they will straighten out."
Lee Iacocca, chairman of Chrysler, 1988

1979 AMC PACER LIMITED STATION WAGON ▲

THE PACER WAS LAUNCHED IN 1975 AS A COMPETITOR FOR FORD'S PINTO AND CHEVROLET'S VEGA, ALTHOUGH AT
$3,299 IT WAS MORE EXPENSIVE THAN EITHER. THE PLANNED POWER UNIT WAS A GM-BUILT WANKEL ROTARY ENGINE,
BUT WHEN THIS WAS DROPPED THE PACER HAD TO USE A RELATIVELY HEAVY AMC-BUILT SIX, WHICH DAMAGED
PERFORMANCE AND ECONOMY. BY 1979, WHEN THIS STATION WAGON WAS MADE, A 304-CUBIC-INCH V8 WAS AN
ALTERNATIVE TO THE SIX. THIS LIMITED WAGON COST A HEFTY $6,189 WITH THE SIX-CYLINDER ENGINE, AND $6,589
WITH THE V8. THE PACER WAS DROPPED AFTER THE 1980 SEASON.

OWNER: EBER SCHMUCKER (PHOTO NICKY WRIGHT)

THE AMERICAN AUTOMOBILE: A CENTENARY 1893 – 1993

THE PAST TWO DECADES have been more traumatic for the American auto industry than anything that went before. The Depression of the 1930s saw a more drastic drop in production, but it was a worldwide phenomenon. America still turned out more than twice as many cars as its nearest rival (Britain), and the Depression bottomed out within three years, after which there was a cautious climb to renewed prosperity. There are few signs of such a climb back today. American complacency, Arab self-assertiveness, and Japanese drive and ingenuity have wrought mighty and irreversible changes in the American auto scene.

In 1970 the industry was riding high, with production of more than 6.5 million passenger cars, more than double that of its nearest rival, Japan. Luxury cars such as the Cadillac Eldorado had the world's largest engine at 500 cubic inches and Chrysler's Hemi 426 was the world's most powerful at 425bhp. When John Q. Public bought a Ford, Chevrolet, or Pontiac (or almost any other make), he knew he was buying an American-designed and American-built car and giving employment to American workers. Twenty years later a Ford Festiva was a Korean-built Japanese Mazda design, a Chevrolet Turbo Sprint was a Japanese-built Suzuki, and a Pontiac Le Mans was a German-designed Opel Kadett built in Korea. The best-selling American-built model in 1989 and 1990 was a Honda Accord.

Ever since 1906, when France fell from its commanding position, America had built more cars than any other nation, and even in 1970 there was no reason to suppose that this position would change. America was the natural leader, and although exports were not as large as they had been in the 1920s and 1930s, U.S. companies made cars throughout Europe, Latin America, and Australia. No foreign companies were building cars on American soil.

IMPORTS AND THE AMERICAN RESPONSE

Until well into the 1950s the imported car was a grace note on the American scene, not an important economic factor. Before World War II imports were largely confined to luxury cars such as Mercedes, Minerva, Renault, and Rolls-Royce, although there were some improbable imports such as Fiat's tiny 500 Topolino (Mickey Mouse); 434 were sold in 1938/39, making it the best-selling imported car. Almost every corner of the world wanted American cars, but America had no need of the products of the rest of the world.

In the early postwar years imports meant sports cars, first MG Midgets, then Allard J2s, which were fitted with American engines, and Jaguar XK120s. The first family car to make any impact on the U.S. market was the Volkswagen Beetle, early examples

1977 FORD PINTO HATCHBACK ▲
THE PINTO, FORD'S ENTRY IN THE SUBCOMPACT FIELD, WAS LAUNCHED IN SEPTEMBER 1970, EIGHT DAYS AFTER ITS RIVAL THE CHEVROLET VEGA. IT WAS MADE AS A TWO-DOOR SEDAN OR THREE-DOOR HATCHBACK, WITH THE CHOICE OF 98.6- OR 122-CUBIC-INCH FOUR ENGINES, THE LATTER WITH SINGLE OVERHEAD CAM GIVING 100bhp. AFTER 1973 DISPLACEMENT WENT UP TO 122 AND 140 CUBIC INCHES, ALTHOUGH POWER WAS DOWN TO 80 AND 82bhp RESPECTIVELY, THANKS TO EMISSION CONTROLS. FROM 1975 YOU COULD HAVE A 103bhp PINTO, BUT IT NEEDED A 170-CUBIC-INCH V6 TO DELIVER THIS POWER. THE PINTO GAVE WAY TO THE ESCORT IN 1981.

OWNER: HERSCHEL CLIZER (PHOTO NICKY WRIGHT)

▼ THE SUBCOMPACTS WERE THE AMERICAN INDUSTRY'S RESPONSE TO THE SUCCESS OF SMALL EUROPEAN AND JAPANESE IMPORTS, AND THE FIRST ON THE SCENE WAS THE GREMLIN FROM AMERICAN MOTORS. MAKING ITS DEBUT ON APRIL 1, 1970, IT WAS A STUBBY LITTLE COUPE ON A 96-INCH WHEELBASE. STANDARD ENGINE WAS A 232-CUBIC-INCH SIX, WITH A 258-CUBIC-INCH SIX OPTIONAL. FOR 1972, WHEN THIS MODEL WAS MADE, A 304-CUBIC-INCH V8 WAS ALSO OFFERED.

AMERICAN MOTORS

but were badly hit by the compact cars from 1960 onward. Who wanted a 55bhp four-cylinder Vauxhall station wagon for $2,367 when he could get an 85bhp six-cylinder Ford Falcon station wagon for $2,287? From 1961 Vauxhalls were available on a special order basis only, and not many orders materialized.

The Japanese made a very hesitant start. The first Toyotas reached the West Coast in 1957, against the wishes of designer Kenya Yakamura, who felt that Toyota was not ready to challenge the U.S. market. Ford's Donald Frey tried a Toyota and pronounced it to be "a piece of junk." By U.S. standards, Toyotas were poorly made and so underpowered that they could not accelerate safely when joining freeways. You had to be pretty desperate to take on a Toyota dealership.

Robert Krause of Schnecksville, Pennsylvania, lost his Dodge and Plymouth agency when the main distributor switched to Ford in 1959. Needing something to sell, he took on a franchise for the Toyopet Crown Custom, purchasing six of the 65bhp 88-cubic-inch four-door sedans, plus $800 worth of parts, special tools, and a small sign. Selling Toyopets was no bed of roses; people asked if they were made of beer cans, and once on the

1987 CHEVROLET CHEVETTE FIVE-DOOR HATCHBACK ▼
GENERAL MOTORS' FIRST WORLD CAR, THE CHEVETTE, WAS MADE FROM 1976 THROUGH 1987 YET CHANGED LITTLE, SO THIS LAST SEASON'S MODEL IS NOT GREATLY DIFFERENT FROM THE FIRST. THE FIVE-DOOR VERSION, WITH A 97.3-INCH WHEELBASE, WAS MADE FROM 1978. ENGINES WERE ORIGINALLY 84- OR 97-CUBIC-INCH FOURS; THE LATTER UNIT WAS STANDARDIZED FROM 1978. THE LOWEST-PRICED CHEVETTE WAS THE VERY BASIC SCOOTER THREE-DOOR AT $2,899 IN 1976, BUT MOST BUYERS PREFERRED TO PAY AN EXTRA $200 FOR THE BETTER-EQUIPPED STANDARD MODEL. FUEL ECONOMY WAS A GREAT FEATURE OF THE CHEVETTE, AT 35mpg IN HIGHWAY USE.

CHEVROLET DIVISION, GENERAL MOTORS

of which reached these shores in 1949. Sales were negligible the first year, but in 1950 New York dealer Max Hoffmann managed to move 157 of the funny little foreign cars. In 1954 the figure had jumped to 6,343, and VW chief Heinz Nordhoff was able to describe the Beetle as the symbol of German recovery. In 1955, 35,581 Volkswagens found buyers in the United States; the 500,000th was sold in June 1960 and the 5 millionth in September 1971. In 1962 there were 687 VW dealers across the nation.

Although the most successful of the foreign imports, the Volkswagen was not the only small foreign car to change the ingrained habits of American drivers. Renault, Simca, and Fiat all sold in reasonable numbers in the late 1950s, leading to total imports of 100,000 in 1956, which doubled in 1957 and again in 1958. Buick dealers started selling Opel Olympias from GM's German factory in 1957, and Pontiac did the same with British-built Vauxhalls from 1958. These sold well for a while,

THE VEGA WAS CHEVROLET'S CANDIDATE IN THE SUBCOMPACT FIELD, AND WAS MADE FROM 1970 THROUGH 1977. OF THE 1,988,933 BUILT, 3,508 HAD A TWIN-CAM 16-VALVE ALUMINUM CYLINDER HEAD DESIGNED BY COSWORTH ENGINEERING, THE BRITISH COMPANY FAMED FOR ITS 3-LITRE DFV V8, WHICH POWERED MANY FORMULA 1 RACE CARS. FUEL SUPPLY WAS BY BENDIX ELECTRONIC FUEL INJECTION CONTROLLED BY A COMPUTER LOCATED IN THE GLOVEBOX. UNFORTUNATELY THE "COSVEG" NEVER DEVELOPED ENOUGH POWER TO MATCH THE EXPECTATIONS RAISED BY ITS "GO FASTER" STRIPES, WIDE RADIAL TIRES, ANTIROLL BARS FRONT AND REAR, AND CAST ALUMINUM WHEELS. PERFORMANCE WAS LITTLE BETTER THAN A VOLKSWAGEN RABBIT. THE "COSVEG" WAS PRODUCED FOR THE 1975 AND 1976 SEASONS ONLY.

OWNER: NATIONAL AUTOMOBILE MUSEUM, RENO, NEVADA (PHOTO NICKY WRIGHT)

road they suffered broken valves at 55–60mph and seized overdrives after 300 miles. Krause sold 12 cars his first year, but stayed with Toyota. He was still with them in 1990, having one of the oldest Toyota franchises in the country. He describes it as "the next best thing to owning a McDonalds."

The Japanese studied the U.S. industry very carefully. In the early 1950s Eiji Toyoda of Toyota spent three months at Ford, remarking when he left: "I realize this is the way to produce perfect cars. Toyota has much to learn here. . . Because we are such a little company, we managers have to be involved in all the manufacturing areas."

Before long Japanese engineers began to see ways in which they could improve on American techniques. Take, for example, the design of stamping machines. In America machines tended to make the same parts for weeks at a time, which led to stockpiling. This meant that capital was tied up for a long time. The Japanese were determined to turn materials into money as soon as possible, so Toyota's production manager Taiichi Ohno developed machines that could be changed easily, making 100 units of one shape, then turning to another. Such changes took up to three hours in Detroit, hence the reluctance to make frequent changes, but Ohno got them down to a few minutes. The enormous capital investment for such machinery was met by low-cost loans from the Japan Development Bank and the World Bank.

Other Japanese firms moved into the U.S. market, Datsun with its Bluebird in 1960, Mitsubishi with the Colt, sold by Dodge from 1971, and Honda with the Civic from 1973. These and, more important, Volkswagen prompted Detroit to move into a still smaller market than had been attempted hitherto, the "sub-compact" sector. True to its custom of innovation, American Motors was first in this field with the Gremlin, announced as a mid-season model on April 1, 1970. It rode on a 96-inch wheelbase and from the doors forward was similar to the compact-sized Hornet. The rear end was very short, with a sharply sloping fastback and very little overhang. Two- and four-passenger models were available, the latter with a fold-down rear seat. The standard engine was a 323-cubic-inch six, also used in the Hornet, Javelin, and Matador, but a larger six of 258 cubic inches was an option.

Despite controversial styling, which meant that a sizable minority of potential buyers couldn't stand it, the Gremlin sold well enough, 26,000 in the half season to September. Stylist Richard A. Teague maintained that it needed to look different. "Nobody would have paid it any attention if it had looked like one of the Big Three."

In September 1970 the Big Two had answers to the Gremlin. Chevrolet's Vega debuted on September 10 and Ford's Pinto eight days later. Chrysler's planned sub-compact never appeared, but instead the British Hillman Avenger was imported and sold under the name Plymouth Cricket. The Pinto and the Vega were generally similar, with two-door sedan bodies on wheelbases of 94.2 and 97 inches respectively. Both ranges included a station wagon, the Pinto's not until 1972. The Pinto was another of Lee Iacocca's babies and took less than three years from original conception to showroom. Both engines were European-built fours, a British 75bhp 98.6-cubic-inch unit with pushrod overhead valves, or a German 100bhp 122-cubic-inch with single overhead camshaft. The Vega was more American in content, with a specially designed 140-cubic-inch four with cogged belt drive to the single overhead camshaft, made in 90 or 110bhp forms. The Pinto cost $1,919–$2,062 compared with the Vega's $2,090–$2,328.

In its first season the Pinto outsold the Vega by 352,402 to 269,905, and continued to do so until the Vega was dropped after 1977. Neither model was free from problems, the Pinto suffering severe criticism with regard to safety, and the Vega dogged by body rust, rough engines, oil leaks, and cylinder head warping. The Vega also suffered from something of an identity crisis, as the Corvair had done. Intended as a mass-market low-price sedan, it acquired the image of a sporty small car for a specialty market, an image reinforced by its hatchback coupe. In 1975 there was an overtly sporting model, the Cosworth-Vega, which used a 16-valve twin-overhead cam engine developed by the British firm Cosworth Engineering Ltd. Ironically, Cosworth was famed mainly for its work with Ford in the 3-liter engine used in countless Formula One racing cars, and in the 16-valve four of today's Cosworth Sierra Sapphire 144mph sedans.

Cosworth's involvement with GM was not a happy one. The development time was very long, for John DeLorean had planned a Cosworth engine

for the Vega in 1969, more than twelve months before the car was launched, yet the Cosworth-Vega did not come onto the market until May 1975. By then emission controls had seriously eroded the engine's power. The first development engines of 1971 gave 180bhp, which augured really dramatic performance, but the production engine of 1975 gave no more than 110bhp and 0–60mph in 12.3 seconds was on a par with the Volkswagen Rabbit, hardly the BMW rival that Chevrolet anticipated. The Cosworth's price was much higher than the Rabbit, though, at $5,916, and nearly double that of the regular Vega hatchback. The youth market at which the car was aimed either couldn't afford the price or preferred to pay another $900 and buy a Corvette. GM planned to sell 5,000 Cosworth-Vegas per year, but only managed 3,508 in two seasons; 1,500 unused engines were scrapped.

The Vega stayed in the Chevrolet range until 1977, but in 1976 it was supplanted at the lower-priced end by the Chevette. This was GM's first world car, and was soon made in five different countries, Brazil, the United States, Britain, Germany, and Japan. Called a Chevette in the first three countries, in Germany it was the Opel Kadett and in Japan the Isuzu Gemini. It was a

▼ BUILDING, REPAIRING, AND IMPROVING ROADS WENT ON ALL THROUGH THE 1970s, AS IN PREVIOUS DECADES. THESE PHOTOS SHOW M-84 AT SAGINAW, MICHIGAN, BEFORE AND AFTER REPAIRS THAT TOOK PLACE IN THE FALL OF 1975.
MICHIGAN DEPARTMENT OF HIGHWAYS

1990 CADILLAC FLEETWOOD SEDAN ▲▶
FLEETWOOD HAD BEEN CADILLAC'S "CAPTIVE" COACHBUILDERS SINCE THE LATE 1920s AND THE NAME WAS USED FOR
MANY POSTWAR CLOSED MODELS, ESPECIALLY THE LONG-WHEELBASE LIMOUSINES. THE 1990 FLEETWOOD SEDAN WAS
A FRONT-DRIVE C-BODY CAR WITH A 272.5-CUBIC-INCH FUEL-INJECTED V8 ENGINE GIVING 185bhp. IN THE BACKGROUND
ARE EARLIER CADILLACS OF (LEFT TO RIGHT) 1939, 1946, 1954, 1967, AND 1976.

CADILLAC DIVISION, GENERAL MOTORS

conventional small car (94.3-inch wheelbase) in the European mold, with a front engine, rear drive, and unit body construction, and was originally made in three-door hatchback form only. A five-door on a 97.3-inch wheelbase arrived for 1978. Two four-cylinder engines were offered, an 85-cubic-inch 52bhp and a 98-cubic-inch 60bhp. These were more conventional than the Vega's, with iron cylinder blocks in place of aluminum, although they used the cogged rubber belt for driving the overhead camshaft.

The Chevette sold for a modest $2,899 in its stripped Scooter form, although most customers preferred to pay an extra $199 for the more fully equipped version. Chevrolet geared up for 275,000 Chevettes in 1976, but actually sold only 187,817. The first impact of the oil shortage was receding and Americans were turning to larger cars again. In the long term, though, the Chevette was a success, selling 451,161 units in 1980 and 433,600 in 1981, when a diesel option was added. But it never reached these figures in later years, when it was overtaken by more advanced front-drive small cars such as Ford's Escort and various imports. The

1990 CHEVROLET BLAZER 4 X 4 STATION WAGON ▲▼

THE RUGGED 4 X 4 WITH GOOD CROSS-COUNTRY ABILITY WAS A POPULAR MODEL WITH ALL AMERICAN MANUFACTURERS FROM THE 1960s. THEY FOLLOWED THEIR REGULAR COUSINS IN REDUCTION IN SIZE IN THE EARLY 1980s, AND CHEVROLET'S SMALLER BLAZER S JOINED THE BIGGER BLAZER IN SEPTEMBER 1982. IT WAS MADE THROUGH 1990 WITH A 262-CUBIC-INCH V6 ENGINE IN TWO- AND FOUR-DOOR MODELS.

CHEVROLET DIVISION, GENERAL MOTORS

conceived by Ford's powertrain research group in Dearborn, but was engineered for production in Europe, where there was more experience in small displacement four-cylinder engines. Like the Chevette, the Escort engine had a cast-iron block with aluminum intake manifolds and crossflow heads. Combustion chambers were hemispherical, as in the Chrysler muscle cars of the 1960s although nobody made much fuss about it. The engine had a 97.6-cubic-inch displacement, giving 65bhp, and this was upped to 72 or 88bhp for 1983, and to 120bhp on the turbo version of 1984.

Transmission was four-speed automatic, with a five-speed manual arriving for 1983. Escort bodies were similar in appearance to the European varieties, three-door hatchbacks or four-door station wagons, with a five-door hatchback coming in 1982. Mercury equivalents at slightly higher prices were called Lynx. The Escort convertible and high-performance XR3, both popular models in Europe, were never made in the United States.

For 1982 a new coupe derived from the Escort appeared, under the name EXP. Ford's first two-seater since the original Thunderbird, it used the same wheelbase and engines as the Escort, but new body panels disguised the hatchback's appearance completely. However, it did not sell too well. Everyone realized that it was just a re-skinned Escort costing around $1,000 more. The EXP lasted until 1988, but a companion Mercury, the LN7, did not survive beyond 1983.

The Escort was Ford's best-selling model in the United States for several years, but profit margins on each car were very low and for a while it was a net drain on company resources. For 1990 Ford decided to shop abroad for the Escort's replacement. Still called an Escort, the new model launched in mid-season was a rebodied Mazda 323

Chevette soldiered on into 1987, when only 46,208 were made, but by then the sub-compact end of the Chevrolet range had been taken over by the three-cylinder Sprint, actually a Japanese-built Suzuki Swift. For 1989 the Sprint was rebadged as a Geo Metro, part of the Geo range which was a subdivision of Chevrolet. Other Geos were the imported Spectrum (Isuzu) and Tracker (Suzuki 4x4), and the California-built Toyota-designed Nova.

Ford continued the Pinto through the 1980 season, by which time 3,150,313 had been made. A 170-cubic-inch V6 engine originating from Ford's German division was an optional alternative to the four from 1975 through 1979. Styling evolved

gradually, but the round-backed body of 1980 was clearly recognizable as the same design that had appeared in the fall of 1970. A Mercury version called the Bobcat appeared in 1975. Costing around $400 more than the equivalent Pintos, Bobcats were better trimmed and were distinguished by what the auto editors of *Consumer Guide* called "a pretentious little stand-up grille." Like the Pinto, the Bobcat survived to the end of the 1980 season.

For 1981 Ford replaced the Pinto with its own world car, the Escort. This was a new design with transverse-mounted engine driving the front wheels, although the Escort name had been carried on rear-drive British and German Fords since 1968. Code-named Erika, the new small Ford was with a 116-cubic-inch Ford four in the base model, and a 110-cubic-inch twin cam Mazda four in the GT. The latter gave 127bhp. Despite the fact that the engineering work was done in Japan, the new Escort program still cost Ford $2 billion. No wonder more and more American auto makers are sharing their new models with foreign firms.

Chrysler's sub-compacts were all foreign-based from 1970 onward. From 1971 through 1977 they relied on imports, the Hillman Avenger-based Plymouth Cricket from 1971 through 1973, and various Mitsubishi designs sold as Plymouth Arrow or Dodge Colt from 1971 through 1977. For 1978 Chrysler launched the Dodge Omni and Plymouth Horizon, very similar front-drive five-door hatchbacks with styling based on that of the European Chrysler Horizon. Unlike the Cricket and Colt, the Horizon and Omni were made in the United States and had U.S.-designed four-cylinder 104.7-cubic-inch engines based on a Volkswagen unit. For 1979 Chrysler followed Ford in offering a sporty-looking coupe derived from its sub-compact. Known as the Dodge 024 or Plymouth TC3, it was 2½ inches shorter in wheelbase and offered 2+2 seating at an extra cost of up to $400 above the hatchback. In 1982, however, Plymouth offered Miser models of both designs at an identical $5,299. In 1983 the 024 and TC3 became the Charger and Turismo, and were continued until 1989. The Omni/Horizon hatchbacks lasted until December 1989, after which they were replaced by Chrysler-distributed Mitsubishis and the Dodge Shadow/Plymouth Sundance sedans. These, introduced in 1986, were 2 inches shorter in wheelbase, but increased overhang gave them greater overall length than the Horizon.

DESIGNED IN WASHINGTON?

Until the late 1960s car design was largely dictated by two interests, consumers on the one hand and manufacturers' accountants on the other. Engineers and stylists juggled with what they perceived to be consumer tastes and the limitations imposed by accounts and general management. Sometimes they got public taste wrong, as with the Chrysler Airflow. Often they had to bow to financial necessity and abandon cherished technical advances. Then, suddenly, a third factor loomed: the bureaucrats in Washington, whose dictates alarmed engineers and accountants alike.

It is hardly an exaggeration to say that in the 1960s much of the decision-making power passed from Detroit to Washington. By setting standards for fuel consumption, exhaust emissions, and safety the legislators mandated whole new fields of

1980 CADILLAC SEVILLE SEDAN ▲

ONE OF THE CARS OFFERED WITH A DIESEL ENGINE FROM 1978 TO 1985 WAS THE SEVILLE. IT WAS THE FIRST CADILLAC TO BE BUILT TO COMPETE WITH AN IMPORTED CAR IN THE INTERMEDIATE SIZE, THE MERCEDES-BENZ 450. ALTHOUGH CONSIDERABLY SMALLER THAN ANY OTHER CADILLAC, WITH A WHEELBASE OF 114.3 INCHES (THE DE VILLE AND CALAIS WERE 130 INCHES), IT WAS MORE EXPENSIVE THAN ANY BUT THE ENORMOUS 75 SEDAN AND LIMOUSINE. THE 1975 PRICE OF A SEVILLE WAS $12,479, AND THIS CONSIDERABLY RESTYLED 1980 MODEL SOLD FOR $20,477. THE RAZOR-EDGE STYLING OF THE REAR BODYWORK WAS REMINISCENT OF SOME CUSTOM BODIES ON PRE-WORLD WAR II ROLLS-ROYCES, AND GAVE THE SECOND GENERATION SEVILLES MORE DISTINCTION THAN THE ORIGINAL SEDANS. THE STYLE LASTED THROUGH 1985; AFTER THIS THE SEVILLE NAME WAS CARRIED BY A NEW FRONT-DRIVE SEDAN, WHICH SHARED A 108-INCH WHEELBASE WITH THE ELDORADO.

OWNERS: BRENT AND NANCY STEWART (PHOTO NICKY WRIGHT)

research into engine design, bumpers, seat belts, air bags, and so on.

Concern about exhaust emissions first surfaced in California, specifically in Los Angeles where the combination of sunshine and exhausts produced notorious smogs, so endangering the health of young children and susceptible elderly people that they were advised not to go out of doors on some days. In 1988, even after two decades of anti-pollution regulation, there were 75 such days, leading to more drastic decisions such as banning gasoline-burning vehicles from the city by 2007. Martin Wachs, professor of urban planning at UCLA, doubted whether this was possible, but said that at least by setting such a goal, people's minds would be concentrated on the problem.

The main preoccupation of the legislators was to reduce the amount of hydrocarbons, carbon monoxide and oxides of nitrogen being emitted in exhausts. The most effective way of doing this was by catalytic converter, familiarly known as a cat. An uncontrolled engine produces 84 grams per milliliter of carbon monoxide; this has been reduced to 3.4gm/ml under current federal regulations, with a target figure of 1.7gm/ml for the year 2000. The equivalent figures for hydrocarbon emissions are 10.6gm/ml unrestricted, 0.41gm/ml current, and 0.125gm/ml for 2000, showing how effective a cat can be. Two drawbacks exist, however: the cat converts unwelcome emissions into water, carbon dioxide, and nitrogen, and carbon dioxide is considered to be the main element in the greenhouse effect leading to global heating. Also the effectiveness of a cat decreases with use; according to the Environmental Protection Agency (EPA), after 50,000 miles a cat might be letting virtually untreated gases through. To control this would require regular compulsory exhaust check-

ups; these are already available on a voluntary basis, and are especially popular in Los Angeles.

Emission control began in California in the mid-1960s with the PCV (positive crankcase ventilation) valve. In 1973 came mandatory exhaust gas recirculation to control nitrogen oxide emissions. Coupled with lower compression ratios, this led to drastic reductions in power output, especially from large engines. A 460-cubic-inch Lincoln engine gave 365bhp in 1971, but only 224bhp a year later, and 202bhp in 1976. Dramatic engines like the 426 Hemi were dropped altogether after 1971, and Chrysler's 440 fell from 385bhp in 1971 to a miserable 195 in 1977, after which it ceased to be made.

Up to the 1950s America had produced all the oil she needed, but a massive increase in consumption in the next decade was not accompanied by increased output, so the country became more dependent on imported oil, most of which came from the Arab countries. The Arab-Israeli war of 1973 led to an enormous price increase and a reduction in supplies to countries thought to be favorable to Israel. When the oil companies offered a 15 percent increase in price the producers demanded 70 percent and got it, together with a 5 percent reduction in output.

The immediate effect of the gas shortage was a downturn in sales of large cars. Worst hit were large-sized, medium-priced cars such as Mercury, whose model year production of Monterey/Marquis models fell from 184,346 to 88,593 between 1973 and 1974. At one point the St. Louis plant was shut down completely, since the daily supply of cars far exceeded requirements for the rest of the model year. Although nothing could be done immediately, there was a noticeable downsizing of large cars during the late 1970s, both in engine displacement and overall length. The 1977 Cadillac De Ville sedan was 8.5 inches shorter in wheelbase than the previous year's, and 900 pounds lighter. By 1981 it had lost a further 200 pounds, and the 1985 models were shorter by another 10.7 inches.

This was the era when fuel consumption, never a great concern to makers of larger cars, began to interest the U.S. government. In 1976 the Energy Conservation and Oil Policy Act was passed, mandating Corporate Average Fuel Economy (CAFE) for all manufacturers. The initial level for 1978 was 18 miles per gallon, and by 1992 it had risen to 27.5mpg. This is an average figure for all models, and auto makers can apply credits from the three previous years or the next projected three. However, there are strict penalties, $5 per 0.1mpg

1986 CHRYSLER LEBARON CONVERTIBLE ▶
CHRYSLER WAS THE FIRST MAJOR U.S. COMPANY TO ABANDON THE CONVERTIBLE, IN 1970 — BUT ALSO THE FIRST TO REINSTATE A RAGTOP IN ITS RANGE, AND THIS WAS OFFERED FROM 1982. THE LEBARON WAS BASED ON THE K-CAR FRAME, AND WAS AVAILABLE WITH 135-CUBIC-INCH CHRYSLER OR 156-CUBIC-INCH MITSUBISHI ENGINES, BOTH FOUR-CYLINDER UNITS. THE MOCK WOODY BODY PANELS RECALLED CHRYSLER'S TOWN & COUNTRY CONVERTIBLES OF THE 1940s, AND WERE ALSO SEEN ON A STATION WAGON. AT $17,595, THIS TOWN & COUNTRY CONVERTIBLE WAS THE MOST EXPENSIVE CHRYSLER OF 1986, APART FROM THE VERY LIMITED PRODUCTION LIMOUSINE.
CHRYSLER CORPORATION

diesel fuel had been used in European trucks since the early 1930s, and were offered in a Mercedes-Benz passenger car in 1936. America was slow to take to the diesel engine, even in heavy trucks, and there were no diesel passenger cars until 1978 when Oldsmobile offered a 350-cubic-inch diesel which shared dimensions with the equivalent gas engine, although block, heads, crankshaft, and pistons were all modified. Fuel economy was 25 percent better than with the gasoline engine, but there was a penalty in price ($735–$895) and power was 50bhp down at 120bhp.

For 1979 Olds offered a 260-cubic-inch V8 diesel as well as the 350, and from 1982 a 262-cubic-inch V6. Olds made all the diesels for GM, and the same units were offered by Buick, Cadillac, Chevrolet, and Pontiac. However, the drawbacks of low specific output, noisy running, and slow cold-weather starting damped down the diesel engine's popularity, and after the fuel crisis passed sales

shortfall, multiplied by the number of cars produced. Imports are calculated separately in CAFE figures; any car with less than 75 percent local content is considered foreign-made. This has led to the ridiculous situation of Ford loading its standard-size Crown Victoria and Mercury Marquis with non-U.S. content components so that the high consumption of these cars can be factored out of

the domestic CAFE. Today there is also a Gas Guzzler Tax on the car's list price, triggered at anything below 22.5mpg. In 1986 the revenue from this tax was $116.8 million.

Another approach to fuel economy and pollution was the use of alternative fuels, particularly diesel for the former, unleaded gasoline and methanol for the latter. Compression ignition engines burning

dropped. GM offered its last diesels in 1985, although Ford listed a small four-cylinder unit in the Escort, Tempo, and Mercury Lynx from 1984 through 1987, and a turbocharged diesel in the 1984/85 Lincolns. In 1991 the only diesels on the U.S. market were in imports, the Volkswagen Jetta and Mercedes-Benz 190. The attraction of diesel in cutting carbon dioxide emissions has not yet made an impact in the United States, although diesel cars are being built in growing numbers in Europe.

Tetraethyl lead (TEL) was added to gasoline in the 1920s as a remedy for knocking and pinking in the long and shallow combustion chambers of side-valve engines. It was added without arousing much comment until the 1960s, when the growing use of cats made it essential to remove it, because it rapidly destroys the elements of a cat. Even so-called unleaded gasoline contains a very small amount of TEL, but the proportion was limited by the EPA to 0.4 grams per gallon, reduced to 0.2gm/g in December 1986 and to 0.1gm/g in September 1988. Leaded fuel was still available, but in decreasing amounts, and by 1989 some larger urban areas were completely without it.

Methanol is a high octane fuel produced from coal or natural gas which produces little in the way of hydrocarbons, so it is not a smog creator, although it is high in carbon dioxide output. At the end of the 1980s Ford and GM both offered engines adapted to run on methanol as well as gasoline, or a mixture of the two. Expectations are

that by 1993 at least 100,000 variable fuel cars, light trucks, and buses will be made per year. Two gas companies, Arco and Chevron, plan to offer methanol from many of their outlets.

The other area in which Washington played an increasing part in auto design was safety. For years it had been an accepted axiom in the auto industry that safety doesn't sell cars. Some manufacturers had made half-hearted gestures in the safety direction — Chrysler rolled Airflows in public to demonstrate the rigidity of their unitary bodies and Muntz installed seat belts in its 1952 convertibles. The main theme of Ralph Nader's *Unsafe at any Speed*, published in 1965, was that the industry did not make use of available technology in the service of safety. He complained that Buick was indifferent to failures of its power brake system, and that Cadillac did nothing to modify its fins until several pedestrians and cyclists had been impaled on them. There may have been some truth in his accusations against the Corvair, but the Pinto almost certainly involved more painful deaths and payouts by its makers than the Corvair ever did.

In May 1972 California housewife Lily Gray pulled out onto a freeway in her new Pinto, the engine died, and before she could restart, another car rear-ended her. The fuel tank, crushed between the rear bumper and axle, burst, filling the car with gasoline vapor which exploded. Lily died soon afterward and her passenger, 13-year-old Richard Grimshaw, was so badly burned that he spent the

rest of his teenage years in operating theaters where surgeons made heroic attempts to rebuild his face.

Over the next few years, at a conservative estimate, 59 Pinto drivers and passengers died in the same way as Lily Gray. The problem was that, in order to keep the weight below 2,000 pounds, Ford engineers had eliminated rear subframe members on the car, leaving the gas tank more vulnerable than on heavier cars. Also the Pinto had a filler neck that was very likely to be ripped out in a collision, pouring fuel into the passenger compartment.

The cost of economizing on safety was high. In the case of Richard Grimshaw vs. the Ford Motor Company the judge awarded Grimshaw $3.5

1988 CHEVROLET CAVALIER RS COUPE ▶

THE CHEVROLET CAVALIER, ONE OF GM's J-CAR FAMILY,
WAS LAUNCHED FOR 1982 AS A MONZA REPLACEMENT.
LIKE ITS SISTERS IT HAD A TRANSVERSELY MOUNTED
FOUR-CYLINDER ENGINE DRIVING THE FRONT WHEELS,
AND IN ITS CHEVROLET GUISE A CHOICE OF FOUR
BODIES: TWO- AND FOUR-DOOR SEDANS, THREE-DOOR
HATCHBACK COUPE, AND FIVE-DOOR STATION WAGON.
A FIVE-SPEED MANUAL TRANSMISSION AND FUEL
INJECTION CAME WITH THE 1983 MODELS, AND THE V6-
POWERED Z24 CONVERTIBLE AND HATCHBACK FOR 1985.
THIS 1988 RS COUPE COST $9,175.

CHEVROLET DIVISION, GENERAL MOTORS

million in compensation and $125 million in punitive damages. On appeal the latter were reduced to $3 million, but the case still cost Ford $6.5 million, plus interest. This was substantial, as the case was not finally settled until March 1986, when Grimshaw was 27 years old. Numerous other cases followed, including one in which Ford was charged with reckless homicide, the first time any auto maker had been accused of a criminal offense. The company was finally cleared, but the affair did not make pretty headlines, particularly when Henry Ford II's contemptuous views about safety became known.

The Pinto's frame was duly strengthened, at a cost of an extra 600 pounds weight. The Pinto saga concentrated the minds of auto makers on the safety question, and by the mid-1970s federal legislation dictated bumper height and front/rear end deformation after 30mph collisions. A decade later, side impact standards were also set, for a vehicle traveling at 15mph being struck by one traveling at 30mph. There was a brief fashion for safety features to be combined in special cars called Experimental Safety Vehicles (ESV). In June 1970 Secretary of Transportation John Volpe offered multi-million dollar incentives to build such cars, which had to be capable of withstanding 10mph front and rear impacts with no damage to the bumpers, and 50mph impacts without injury to passengers. Some of the results were quite grotesque, for example a front bumper which extended automatically by 12 inches when the car's speed exceeded 25mph. GM's contribution had interior padding to give protection at impact speeds

1991 CHEVROLET CAVALIER Z24 TWO-DOOR SEDAN ◀ ▶

THE CAVALIER FIRST APPEARED IN CHEVY'S 1982 RANGE,
AS ONE OF THE INTERNATIONAL J-CARS OFFERED (FOR
THE FIRST TIME FOR ANY MODEL) BY ALL FIVE GM
DIVISIONS, AS WELL AS IN BRITAIN, GERMANY, AND
AUSTRALIA. IMPROVEMENTS DURING THE DECADE
INCLUDED A FIVE-SPEED MANUAL TRANSMISSION FOR
1983, A CONVERTIBLE AND NEW FRONTAL STYLING FOR
1984, AND THE Z24 "MINI-MUSCLE CAR" FOR 1985. THIS
HAD A 173-CUBIC-INCH V6 ENGINE GIVING 125bhp. THE
1991 Z24 SEEN HERE HAD A LARGER V6 OF 189 CUBIC
INCHES, SPORT SUSPENSION, AND FIVE-SPEED
TRANSMISSION AS STANDARD.

CHEVROLET DIVISION, GENERAL MOTORS

1990 PONTIAC SUNBIRD LE CONVERTIBLE ▼▶

SUNBIRD WAS PONTIAC'S VERSION OF THE J-CAR, ALTHOUGH IT WAS CALLED THE J-2000 UNTIL 1984 WHEN IT BECAME THE 2000 SUNBIRD, AND THEN PLAIN SUNBIRD. THE CONVERTIBLE RETURNED TO THE RANGE IN 1984 AND WAS STILL MADE IN 1990, ALONG WITH A FOUR-DOOR SEDAN AND TWO-DOOR COUPE. THE ENGINE WAS A 121-CUBIC-INCH FOUR THAT GAVE 95bhp, OR 165bhp IN TURBO FORM.

PONTIAC DIVISION, GENERAL MOTORS (PHOTO NICKY WRIGHT)

up to 30mph, after which airbags took over. The downside of all these ESVs was their greatly increased weight. In the wake of the fuel crisis they were all quietly forgotten.

Two safety devices that did make it into production were seat belts and airbags. The former were first seen on Nash and Muntz cars in 1952, and by 1970 active belts (which the wearer had to put on) were standard equipment in all new cars, as they were virtually everywhere else in the world. Compulsory belt-wearing took longer to be applied, dating from 1971 in the Australian state of Victoria, and spreading throughout Europe, West and East, during the 1980s. In America a good many states mandated the wearing of belts, and manufacturers were required to install passive belts, which fitted automatically. This regulation was to have been mandatory by 1990, but the

deadline has been extended to 1994.

The airbag was a supplementary device which inflated within about 40 milliseconds of a collision, and protected the driver from impact on the steering column and windshield. Ideal in a head-on collision, an airbag is only helpful within a range of 30° on either side, and of no use at all in a side-impact collision. There were fears that the great increase in pressure might blow out windows or rupture passengers' eardrums, although neither of these eventualities has actually happened. A number of Mercurys were fitted with airbags for the Allstate Insurance Company as early as 1974, and airbags were offered by Oldsmobile for several years from 1974, proving to be one of the least popular options in the accessory book. By the late 1980s they were seen on a number of models by the Big Three. Usually for the driver only, bags have been offered for the front passenger on a few cars, but not yet for passengers in the back.

One of the casualties of the growing safety movement, and also of a preference for air conditioning and stereo systems, was that

quintessential American dream car, the convertible. Chrysler made its last ragtop in 1970, and associates Dodge and Plymouth in 1971. The last convertible from the Ford Motor Company was a Mercury Cougar XR-7, which left the line on July 7, 1973. GM carried on somewhat longer, Buick, Chevrolet, Oldsmobile to the end of the 1975 season, and Cadillac to 1976. The day the last Cadillac convertible came down the line — Wednesday, April 21, 1976 — was a sad one, marking not only the end of the famous Eldorado convertible, but of all U.S. convertible production.

The factory was besieged with orders for the last convertible, and produced 200 identical "last" cars, painted white with white tops, leather upholstery, and wheel covers. Prices quickly shot up (and as quickly came down later), and many were the Eldorado coupes that lost their tops to earn their owners a few more bucks. The actual last car was retained by Cadillac for its historical collection.

Although there did not seem to be sufficient demand for the big manufacturers to continue making convertibles, clearly some people still wanted them, and within a year custom firms began to fill the gap. Convertibles Inc. of Lima, Ohio, offered an Eldorado convertible for $6,500 above the list price of a coupe, and American Custom Coachworks of Beverly Hills, California, made an open-top version of the new downsized Coupe de Ville. This retailed for $37,000, while a coupe cost only $9,810. The following year American Custom Coachworks offered a wider range of convertible Cadillacs, on two- and four-door models, while another firm made an open-top Seville. One of the best-known of the conversion firms, Hess & Eisenhardt, famed for ambulances and funeral cars, made more than 300 converted Coupe de Villes in 1978 and 1979. They sold for $29,000 and were marketed through 60 Cadillac dealers.

By the early 1980s the customizers were working not only on Cadillacs but on Lincolns, Pontiacs, Buicks, and other makes. Even the compact Pontiac Phoenix was offered in convertible form by American Custom Coachworks from 1980. This tempted Detroit back into the market, and Chrysler, the first corporation to abandon the ragtop, was the first to return, offering two convertibles in the compact LeBaron line for 1982. This was the decision of Lee Iacocca, who moved from Ford to Chrysler in 1978. Convertibles were also offered on the companion Dodge 400.

Once Chrysler had given the lead, others followed. Cadillac brought back the Eldorado convertible for 1984, while two of GM's J-cars, the Chevrolet Cavalier and Pontiac Sunbird, were made in convertible form from 1984. The Chevrolet Corvette had a convertible in 1986 and the Camaro in 1987. Lowest-priced of all the new generation convertibles, at $10,295, was American Motors' Alliance of 1985. This was actually a French-designed Renault, made in closed form as the Alliance sedan and Encore hatchback, but the French never got a convertible.

1985 BUICK REGAL GRAND NATIONAL COUPE ▲
THE REGAL WAS A REAR-DRIVE COUPE MADE FROM 1978 TO 1987, AND ITS T-TYPE WAS ONE OF THE SPORTIER BUICKS WITH STRONGER CHASSIS AND SUSPENSION, AND FAT TIRES. THE GRAND NATIONAL WAS A LOW-PRODUCTION COMMEMORATIVE MODEL NAMED FOR THE NASCAR GRAND NATIONAL RACES, AND WAS MADE FROM MID-1982 THROUGH 1987. T-TYPE AND GRAND NATIONALS HAD A TURBOCHARGED 321-CUBIC-INCH V6 ENGINE GIVING 200bhp. ONLY 2,102 GRAND NATIONALS WERE MADE IN 1985, OUT OF TOTAL REGAL PRODUCTION OF 124,546.
OWNER: PAT JANISCH (PHOTO NICKY WRIGHT)

S TANDARDIZATION: LATTER-DAY LETTER CARS

Bodies began to be standardized before World War II, but in the past 20 years standardization has extended to engines and transmissions as well. In the 1980s there was much less difference between a Buick, Pontiac, or Oldsmobile J-car than between a Buick J and a Buick H. Toward the end of the decade models more individual to a particular marque began to appear, Buick's Reatta for example, and Chevrolet's Beretta and Corsica.

In the early 1970s GM's production was already highly standardized. All bodies were produced by Fisher Body Division; Chevrolet shared the A-body (Chevelle) and B-body (Impala) with all but Cadillac, the X-body (Nova) with Oldsmobile and Pontiac, the F-body (Camaro) with the Pontiac

Firebird, and so on. Other components were also shared as it was uneconomical for each division to make its own. Thus Oldsmobile was responsible for steering design (the actual gears and linkages were made by Saginaw), Buick for brakes (made by Delco-Moraine), Chevrolet for front suspension, and Pontiac for rear suspension. A similar situation obtained at Chrysler, where four bodies and seven engines were combined to make up 35 models of Chrysler, Dodge and Plymouth.

As the cost of new models escalated, it became necessary to share designs more thoroughly, and this was typified by GM's J-cars introduced for 1982. In the United States the J-cars were aimed at the quality small imports, particularly the Honda Accord, but the design was international, also made in Britain as the Vauxhall Cavalier, in Germany as

ANNOUNCED IN MARCH 1987 AS 1988 MODELS, THE CORSICA AND BERETTA BROKE WITH RECENT GENERAL MOTORS CUSTOM IN HAVING NO EQUIVALENTS IN OTHER GM DIVISIONS. THEY HAD A NEW PLATFORM ON A 103.4-INCH WHEELBASE, AND USED COMPONENTS FROM J- AND N-CARS, INCLUDING INDEPENDENT COIL FRONT SUSPENSION WITH McPHERSON STRUTS, AND FRONT DISK/REAR DRUM BRAKES. ENGINES ALSO CAME FROM THE J-CAR RANGE, A 90bhp 121-CUBIC-INCH FOUR OR A 120/135bhp 173-CUBIC-INCH V6. THEY WERE PRICED AT AROUND $1,500–$2,000 ABOVE EQUIVALENT CAVALIERS, BUT SOLD VERY WELL. IN 1991 THEY WERE STILL AMONG THE MOST SUCCESSFUL CHEVROLETS.

CHEVROLET DIVISION, GENERAL MOTORS

the Opel Ascona, and in Australia as the Holden Camira. For the first time all five GM divisions used a single design, known as the Buick Skyhawk, Chevrolet Cavalier, Oldsmobile Firenza, and Pontiac J-2000. Cadillac was rather cagey about its J-car, calling it Cimarron by Cadillac rather than a Cadillac Cimarron. No Cadillac badge featured on the car.

All J-cars rode on a common wheelbase of 101.2 inches, but body variations allowed for slight differences in overall length, from 169.4 inches for the Pontiac and Chevrolet hatchback copies to 175.3 inches for the station wagons offered by all but Cadillac. Engines were 112- or 121-cubic-inch fours giving 84 or 98bhp. The smaller was an overhead cam unit built by GM in Brazil, while the larger had pushrod overhead valves and was made by Chevrolet. The overhead cam engine was turbocharged from 1984, and enlarged to 121 cubic inches in 1987, when the 150bhp turbo engine was dropped. All engines were transversely mounted and drove the front wheels.

J-car prices ran from $6,966 for the base Cavalier coupe to $12,131 for the Cimarron. As one would expect, the Chevrolet sold the best, more than 270,000 in the 1982 model year, rising to more than 462,000 for 1984. It was followed by Pontiac, Buick, Oldsmobile, and Cadillac, whose Cimarron managed only 25,968 for 1982, and fell thereafter, whereas other J-cars improved their sales. The

1991 CHEVROLET BERETTA COUPE ►▼

THE BERETTA COUPE, LAUNCHED IN MARCH 1987, CONTINUED TO BE INDIVIDUAL
TO CHEVROLET, REVERSING THE EARLIER GM TREND TOWARD SHARING
MODELS BETWEEN ALL THE DIVISIONS. ALTHOUGH 8½ INCHES LONGER
THAN THE CAVALIER, THE BERETTA WAS NEVERTHELESS CLASSED
AS A COMPACT. ENGINES WERE A 140bhp V6 OR A MORE
POWERFUL, ALTHOUGH SMALLER, 180bhp TWIN-CAM
FOUR. BERETTAS WERE MADE AT THEIR OWN
PLANT AT WILMINGTON, DELAWARE.

CHEVROLET DIVISION, GENERAL MOTORS

Cimarron was aimed at younger, affluent buyers who had never entered a Cadillac showroom before, but such buyers were not taken in by a car which wasn't all that different from a Buick Skyhawk, yet sold for $4,200 more than a Skyhawk with all options. The Cimarron had a few exclusive features such as the leather upholstery and, from 1983, a sliding glass "Astroroof," but these were clearly not enough, and Cimarron sales skidded down to 6,454 in 1988, its last year. One advantage for Cadillac was that the modest fuel consumption of the Cimarron helped its CAFE figures until new downsized models could be made.

The J-cars were gradually improved over the years, with a convertible coming to the Cavalier and J-2000 Sunbird in 1984, and V6 engines in some models from 1986. Cavalier and Sunbird were still being made in 1992. There were numerous other "letter cars" in the 1980s. GM's first front-drive designs were the X-cars launched in mid-1979 as the Buick Skylark, Chevrolet Citation, Oldsmobile Omega, and Pontiac Phoenix. They featured transverse 151-cubic-inch 90bhp four-cylinder engines built by Pontiac, with a 173-cubic-inch 115bhp V6 optional on most models. Bodies included three- and five-door hatchbacks, and two-door coupes. In August 1985 the X-cars gave way to the N-cars — Buick Skylark, Oldsmobile Cutlass, and Pontiac Grand Am — with slightly more powerful four- and six-cylinder engines.

Chevrolet's individual cars, not shared with any other division, were the Beretta coupe and Corsica sedan which debuted in March 1987. Although they employed a new body platform of 103.4-inch wheelbase, their engineering owed much to the J- and N-cars, notably the suspension. The standard engine was the Cavalier's 90bhp four, but the 120/135bhp V6 was an option. Corsica and Beretta found a useful niche in the import-dominated market for more individual smaller cars; in 1988 they were the second and third best-selling Chevrolets after the Cavalier, with 291,163 Corsicas and 275,098 Berettas finding buyers.

Chrysler had been famous for its "letter cars" in the 300 series of the 1950s, but its offerings 30 years later were less interesting. Smallest was the L-car, the European-designed Dodge Omni/Plymouth Horizon sub-compact hatchback, then came the K-car, badged as a Chrysler LeBaron, Dodge Aries, and Plymouth Reliant. Made as a sedan, coupe, and station wagon, with a convertible in the LeBaron range, it was a compact car on a 100.1-inch wheelbase, with a choice of Chrysler-built 135-cubic-inch or Mitsubishi-built 156-cubic-inch fours under the hood. The K-platform was used for a

wide variety of cars, from the sporty coupes badged as Chrysler Lasers or Dodge Daytonas, through the Chrysler GTS/Dodge Lancer five-door hatchback, which had an H-body on a K-platform, to the Executive sedan and limousine with wheelbase stretched to 124.3 or 131.3 inches. The latter cost $26,318 in 1985, when you could get a LeBaron sedan for $9,309.

Even more expensive was the Chrysler TC by Maserati, a two-passenger convertible on a shortened version of the K-platform, using the 135-cubic-inch four with a 16-valve twin cam head designed and made by the famous Italian firm in which Chrysler acquired a minority interest in 1984. The turbocharged engine gave 200bhp, but despite disk brakes all round it did not handle as well as a $30,000 car should, and sales were slow. Later models had a 183-cubic-inch V6 engine and automatic transmission in place of the five-speed manual of the first. Production was phased out early in 1991.

Other Chryslers of the 1980s were the P-body replacements for the Omni/Horizon, which debuted in 1987 and ran alongside the older designs for a while. They were badged as Dodge Shadow and Plymouth Sundance. There was also the K-car replacement, the A-body Chrysler Saratoga/Dodge Spirit/Plymouth Acclaim. The big rear-drive Fifth Avenue, the last of what had been the standard models, was dropped for 1990, making Chrysler the only one of the Big Three to offer an all-front-drive range.

Over at Ford the most important model of the 1980s was the mid-sized Taurus, also badged as a Mercury Sable, originally known as the DN5 project (D for the class of car, N for North America). Launched for 1986, its development dated back to 1979 and involved study of all domestic, European, and Japanese cars in the same class. The result was

1980 PONTIAC FIREBIRD TRANS-AM COUPE ▲▶
PONTIAC BROUGHT OUT A TENTH ANNIVERSARY FIREBIRD FOR 1979, AND THE 1980 MODELS WERE LITTLE CHANGED. THE 1979/80 CARS WERE CHARACTERIZED BY THE BOLDER FRONTAL AIR DAM, WITH SEPARATE COMPARTMENTS FOR THE FOUR HEADLIGHTS, BUT THE BODY WAS CARRIED OVER FROM THE 1976 MODELS. THE FIREBIRD MOTIF ("THE CHICKEN") HAD CHANGED CONSIDERABLY SINCE ITS INTRODUCTION IN 1973, GETTING LARGER WINGS AND BREATHING FIRE FROM ITS MOUTH. ALTHOUGH IT WAS THE MOST EXPENSIVE, THE TRANS-AM WAS THE MOST POPULAR FIREBIRD IN 1980. THE 301-CUBIC-INCH V8 COULD BE HAD WITH TURBOCHARGER, WHICH RAISED POWER FROM 140 TO 210BHP.
PONTIAC MOTOR DIVISION, GENERAL MOTORS
(PHOTO NICKY WRIGHT)

the most aerodynamic American sedan ever made, with a drag coefficient of 0.33 for the Taurus and 0.32 for the slightly longer and sleeker Sable. Even the station wagon achieved 0.35. Engine options were a 88bhp 153-cubic-inch four or a 140bhp 182-cubic-inch V6, both new engines specially developed for the new cars.

With an investment of more than $3 billion, the DN5 project was crucial for Ford, which had lost $1 billion a year for two years in a row. Fortunately the new cars were a runaway success; in spite of a shortened season (they were launched on December 26, 1985), sales of the 1986 Taurus reached 236,362 and the Sable 95,638. The 1987 Taurus was the best-selling Ford (beating the Escort by just seven cars to reach 374,772), while Sable sales totaled 121,313. In 1989 the Taurus was the best-selling American-designed car, though just beaten to first place by the Honda Accord. The 1989 season included a high-performance Taurus called the SHO (Super High Output), with a Yamaha-engineered 24-valve V6 engine with single camshaft to each bank of cylinders. This developed 220bhp and propelled the six-passenger sedan to 60mph in 7 seconds. Features included disk brakes all round and larger antiroll bars. The SHO sold for $19,739, more than $4,000 above the price of a Taurus LX sedan.

INDIVIDUALITY FIGHTS BACK

But the auto scene wasn't all standardization in the 1980s. There were several models individual to particular makes, such as the Pontiac Fiero, Cadillac Allante, and Buick Reatta, while evergreens like the Corvette, Camaro, Firebird, and Mustang carried on, gaining fresh performance and power by the end of the decade. There was also a growing fashion for 1930s-styled neo-classics and replica cars.

Once a staid "schoolteacher's car," Pontiac had a performance image from the mid-1960s, and the

Firebird was a hot performer 20 years later. In 1973 the first of the firebird motifs, familiarly known as "the chicken," was seen on the hood. At first opposed by GM's Bill Mitchell, the motif soon became inseparably associated with the Firebird Trans Am. In 1989 the most powerful engine option in the Firebird was a 225bhp V8. However, the lower-priced two-passenger sports car was an attraction which would not go away, and a mid-engined Firebird concept car was built as early as 1971. Locating the engine behind the driver gave the best handling characteristics for a sports car, but

1987 FORD TAURUS SEDAN ▲

FORD'S MOST IMPORTANT CAR OF THE 1980s, THE TAURUS WAS LAUNCHED FOR 1986 AND INCORPORATED A COMPLETELY FRESH AERODYNAMIC BODY, AND NEW FOUR-CYLINDER AND V6 ENGINES. BODIES WERE LIMITED TO TWO, A FOUR-DOOR SEDAN AND A FIVE-DOOR STATION WAGON. THEY SHARED McPHERSON STRUT AND COIL FRONT AND REAR SUSPENSION; BUT WHEREAS THE SEDAN HAD PARALLEL CONTROL ARMS AT THE REAR THE WAGON USED TWIN ARMS, WHICH WERE MORE SUITABLE FOR THE WIDE VARIATION OF LOAD WEIGHT CARRIED BY THIS CATEGORY OF CAR. THE HIGH-PERFORMANCE SHO TAURUS CAME IN 1989, AND IMPROVEMENTS FOR 1991 INCLUDED SEQUENTIAL FUEL INJECTION AND AN ELECTRONICALLY CONTROLLED FOUR-SPEED AUTOMATIC TRANSMISSION ON ALL MODELS BUT THE SHO.

FORD MOTOR COMPANY

1983 PONTIAC FIERO COUPE ▶ ▼
EXTERNALLY, THE MID-ENGINED FIERO WAS A
COMPLETELY NEW CAR, ALTHOUGH IT USED
THE TRANSVERSE ENGINE AND TRANSMISSION FROM
GM's X-CARS, SUCH AS THE PONTIAC PHOENIX.
FRONT SUSPENSION CAME FROM THE CHEVETTE. THE
FIRST NEW VOLUME PRODUCTION TWO-PASSENGER
CAR FROM DETROIT SINCE THE ORIGINAL FORD
THUNDERBIRD, THE FIERO USED THE SAME BASIC
LAYOUT AS THE FIAT X1/9 AND THE TOYOTA MR2.
IT WAS NOT SO LONG LIVED AS THESE IMPORTED
CARS, HOWEVER, FOR IT WAS DROPPED AFTER FIVE
SEASONS. GOVERNMENT-MANDATED RECALLS AND
A GREAT INCREASE IN INSURANCE PREMIUMS FOR
SPORTS CARS HASTENED ITS DEMISE. THE FIERO
WAS ANNOUNCED AS A 1984 MODEL;
THIS IS A 1983 PROTOTYPE.
PONTIAC MOTOR DIVISION, GENERAL MOTORS
(PHOTO NICKY WRIGHT)

finding a suitable drive train was a problem, and
Pontiac could not afford to engineer one from
scratch. Then, in 1980, came the X-car, with
transverse engine and front drive, which could be
adapted to a mid-engined rear-drive sports car.
This was the essence of the Fiero, largely
developed for Pontiac by Turkish-born Hilki
Aldikacti, head of Pontiac's Advanced Engineering.

The Fiero had a spaceframe chassis to which
plastic body panels were attached, and rode on a
short wheelbase of 93.4 inches. The engine was the
151-cubic-inch cast-iron block four known as the
"Iron Duke," and transmission also came from the
X-cars. The Chevette's front suspension was used.
Although the Fiero looked a sporty little thing, the
public realized that it used many components from
standard sedans, and this, coupled with a none-too-
inspiring top speed of 97mph, prevented it from
being the sales success that Pontiac hoped for.

Even at the modest base price of $7,999, Fiero
sales disappointed, although the first year (1984)
was quite promising at 136,840. They dropped to
76,371 in 1985 and to 46,581 in 1987, despite the
option of the 173-cubic-inch V6 engine which
pushed top speed up to 112mph. A series of engine
fires in 1984 models prompted a government-
ordered recall of 20 percent of that year's
production, and this was followed by a sudden
increase in insurance rates for two-passenger sports

1990 CADILLAC ALLANTE ◀ ▶
THE ALLANTE WAS CADILLAC'S ATTEMPT TO RE-
ESTABLISH ITSELF AS AN EXCLUSIVE CAR, AFTER A
PERIOD WHEN THE MAKE BECAME INCREASINGLY
SIMILAR TO OTHER GM MODELS. BASED ON A
SHORTENED ELDORADO FRAME, THE ALLANTE HAD
A TWO-PASSENGER BODY BUILT BY PININFARINA IN
ITALY AND MATED TO THE FRAMES, WHICH WERE THEN
FLOWN BACK TO DETROIT IN SPECIALLY CONVERTED
BOEING 747s. THE ORIGINAL 1987 MODELS GAVE MANY
PROBLEMS, PARTICULARLY WITH THE HARD-TO-RAISE
TOP, WHICH WAS PRONE TO LEAK WATER. BY 1990
THE ALLANTE WAS MUCH IMPROVED, BUT SALES
STILL DISAPPOINTED.

OWNER: ED OBERHAUS (PHOTO NICKY WRIGHT)

cars. It was all too much for the Fiero, which registered only 26,402 sales in 1988, and GM announced that there would be no 1989 Fieros.

A measure of the imported car threat was that a number of new American models were aimed directly at competing with imports rather than domestic cars. One such was Cadillac's Allante two-passenger convertible with which the makers hoped to dent sales of Mercedes-Benz's 560SL convertible. The car had an Eldorado frame shortened from 108 to 99.4 inches and a 249-cubic-inch V8 engine tuned to give 170bhp. The frames were flown out to Pininfarina in Turin, Italy, where the convertible bodies were built in a separate plant from Pininfarina's other activities. The complete cars were then flown back to Detroit for drive train installation and final finishing. Specially equipped Boeing 747s were used for this operation, dubbed "the longest production line in the world."

The Allante's exotic origins were reflected in its price, $54,000, well over double that of an Eldorado convertible. It was difficult to justify such a price differential except in terms of exclusiveness. In 1973 the staff of *Automobile Quarterly* commented: "We know the real reason why people buy Eldorados, and logic has nothing to do with it. This is status, conspicuous consumption, a highly visible declaration of what its owner thinks of himself, and what he would like other people to think about him. But it's a free country, and everybody has the right to make a fool of himself." No doubt they would have said the same about the Allante.

Cadillac hoped to sell 4,000 Allantes in 1987, but managed only 1,651, and 2,569 of the 1988 models. The large stock of unsold cars meant that, unlike the Mercedes, the Allante depreciated as soon as it left the showroom. Also there were criticisms of water leaks, squeaks and rattles, horns that didn't work, and heaters that worked too well — a sorry catalog of woe for America's most expensive domestic car. For 1989 engine displacement went up to 273 cubic inches, giving 200bhp, and so did the price, to $57,183. The 1993 Allante promised to be a much improved car, with the new 32-valve Northstar V8 engine giving 290bhp, and with four-speed automatic transmission and improved brakes, steering and suspension. The price was now $65,000, but this was still $30,000 below the rival Mercedes-Benz.

Another two-passenger car, this time exclusive to Buick, was the Reatta, introduced for the 1988 season. It was based on a shortened Riviera platform with a 98.5-inch wheelbase. Also from the Riviera came the 231-cubic-inch V6 engine, transmission, suspension, brakes, steering, and instrument panel. The Reatta's novelty lay in its

body, which gave it the character of a mature sporty car likely to appeal to America's aging baby boom generation now around 40 years old. By no means cheap at $25,000, it was conceived by Buick as a "halo car," enhancing the corporate image and luring into showrooms buyers who might place an order for a more prosaic sedan or station wagon. The cars were hand-assembled at the Reatta Craft Center in Lansing, Michigan. Sales never reached the Center's capacity of 25,000 a year, and little more than 20,500 were made between October 1987 and May 1991, when the Reatta was discontinued. The plant was to be used for the manufacture of GM's Impact electric car.

Chevrolet's Corvette was little changed in the 1970s, apart from inevitable reductions in engine size and power. These reached a low point in 1975 when the only engine was a 350-cubic-inch V8 giving 190 or 210bhp. Five years earlier there had been a 454-cubic-inch giving 465bhp. The last convertible Corvette for 11 years came in 1975. Yet despite its aging body and emasculated engine it became more popular than ever in the late 1970s, with a record 53,807 sales in 1979.

Officially there was no 1983 Corvette, for the completely revised car that appeared in March was classed as a 1984 model. The body was restyled with much smoother lines; there was a forward-opening alligator hood and a hatchback rear window; the frame was a Lotus-like backbone chassis welded to an upper birdcage for added strength; and the body was of fiberglass, like all previous Corvettes. A convertible returned to the range in 1986, engineered by the American Sunroof Corporation of Bowling Green, Ohio, which also aided GM with the J-car convertibles and American

Motors with the Alliance.

The next big step in Corvette development came for 1989 with the LT5 engine. This had the same displacement, 350 cubic inches, as existing engines, but was a completely new design with shorter bore and longer stroke, twin camshafts for each bank of cylinders, and four valves per cylinder. Developed by GM's recent acquisition, Lotus of Norfolk, England, the LT5 developed 385bhp yet delivered up to 22.5mpg and complied with all current emission regulations. An unusual feature was the "granny switch" by which the secondary ports could be deactivated so that only three valves were working in each cylinder. The second intake valve moved but did not admit any mixture to the combustion chamber. The switch was operated by a key.

The ZR1 also featured Selective Ride Control (optional on lesser Corvettes) and a six-speed manual transmission which shifted automatically at light throttle openings (below 35 percent) and low speed (12–19mph). This gave better fuel consumption, which helped Chevrolet with their CAFE figures, but most Corvette owners were likely to floor the throttle, in which case the automatic shift did not come into effect. The ZR1 was a limited edition Corvette, and the first season's production was not expected to exceed 1,500, out of a total Corvette output of about 27,000. Its price was around $60,000, as against $31,545 for a regular coupe. The sticker price for a ZR-1 in 1991 was $64,138, but recession-hit dealers were offering it for around $13,000 below this figure. The 1992 sales are likely to be hit further by the greatly improved regular Corvette, the LT1. Although still with only two valves per cylinder, the engines had greatly improved breathing, giving 300bhp. Prices started at only $33,635.

NEO-CLASSICS AND REPLICAS

In 1964 stylist Brooks Stevens was working as a consultant for Studebaker. In order to liven up its image he built a two-passenger roadster styled after the 1930 Mercedes-Benz SSK, using a Lark Daytona chassis and an Avanti V8 engine. The car was scheduled to debut on the Studebaker stand at the New York Show in April 1964, but before it reached the show Studebaker vetoed it on the grounds that a replica classic did not fit the common sense image that it was trying to project. Stevens and his sons found themselves with a car and nowhere to show it, so they hired a small stand of their own.

Christened Excalibur after a sports car Stevens had built in the early 1950s, the car was a hit, and in August 1964 the Stevens formed SS Automobiles in Milwaukee to build it commercially. One of the first orders came from Chevrolet dealer Jerry Allen, the show organizer who had found Stevens his last-minute stand. He wanted 12 cars, but as a Chevy dealer with showrooms on the ground floor of New York's General Motors building he could hardly sell a car with a Studebaker engine. "One day the

directors are going to stop off at my showroom out of curiosity on their way to lunch, and I'm going to have my ass kicked. Couldn't you put a Chevrolet engine in it?"

This wasn't too difficult as Stevens was friendly with GM's Ed Cole, and all production Excaliburs were Chevrolet-powered. The Studebaker chassis, however, was used up to 1969. Bodies were originally of hammered aluminum, later of fiberglass. Stevens could not obtain the burnished outside exhaust pipes in the United States, but managed to track down the German firm that had made them for the original Mercedes, and placed an order.

As production did not begin until August 1964, the first Excaliburs were 1965 models; 56 cars were sold at a price of $7,250, followed by 90 in 1966, when a four-passenger phaeton with full fenders and running boards was added. A new 111-inch chassis came in 1970, and the standard engine went up from 327 to 350 cubic inches. By then competitors had appeared. Oklahoma schoolteacher Glenn Pray began building replicas of the Cord 810 in ⅘th size of the original, powered by a Corvair engine. The necessary restyling was done by the car's original designer, Gordon Buehrig. After he had sold 91 Cords, Pray decided that the Auburn 851 speedster would be a better-selling replica, so he sold the Cord project to another Oklahoma company, which made a few more Cord 810s powered with Ford or Chrysler V8 engines.

The Auburn proved to be a better proposition,

not only for Pray but for numerous other companies who jumped on the bandwagon. Pray's Auburn-Cord-Duesenberg Company stayed in business into the 1980s, by which time at least four other companies had offered Auburn speedsters, one making a four-passenger dual-cowl model which Auburn itself never built. Most used Ford V8 running gear, though one was based on a VW Beetle frame!

The Auburns were full-size replicas, quite difficult to distinguish from the originals. Soon numerous other companies began to offer similar replicas of classics such as the Duesenberg Model J and SSJ, the 1934 Ford V8 roadster (the Canadian-built Timmis), and the 1932 Packard (Second Chance). Postwar sports cars also came in for the replica treatment, notably the Cobra (by far the most popular, with around 20 companies worldwide

making replicas), Mercedes-Benz 300SL gull-wing, and original Corvette and Thunderbird. These are intentional replicas, whereas the Excalibur was never such a close copy of the Mercedes, and became less so as the years passed.

The Excalibur was really the first of the neo-classics, a breed that proliferated from the late 1970s onward. Most were not based on any real classic but aimed to recapture the style of the 1930s continental luxury coupe — long, long hood, sweeping fenders, shallow windshield, relatively small two-passenger coupe body. Some had side-mounted spare wheel covers and/or outside exhausts, although these were strictly ornamental, with a conventional exhaust system under the floor and a spare wheel at the rear.

One of the first neo-classics, after Excalibur, was the Clenet built in Goleta, California, by

French-born Alain Clenet. This used a center section from an MG Midget, with a very long hood and exhaust pipes emerging under the fenders. The hood seemed long enough to house a straight-12 or at least a straight-8, but in fact there was just a compact Lincoln V8. Behind the tiny two-passenger convertible body was a small trunk and a separate spare wheel cover. The price when the Clenet was introduced in 1976 was $83,000, high enough, but not a top price for a neo-classic, which could go as high as $130,000.

Most neo-classics seemed to emanate from either California or Florida, where most of their customers were to be found. One cannot imagine many canny Vermonters investing in Clenets or Zimmer Golden Spirits! The Golden Spirit, made by a mobile home manufacturer from Pompano Beach, was the best-known Florida neo-classic. The recipe was to take a Mustang coupe, chainsaw the monocoque in half, and add in an extension to give an extra 3 feet at the front. The floor, doors, window glass, and roof of the center section were retained, and a period body in fiberglass was built around them. Looking at the long, low coupe, one would never guess its Mustang origins, but it was clearly less of an original car than the Excalibur, which had its own ladder chassis.

For $90,000 the Golden Spirit owner got a luxurious interior, with walnut fascia, Italian leather upholstery, and Bohemian crystal vases in the rear compartment. For such a high-priced car, the Golden Spirit sold quite well, about 1,400 between 1980 and 1988, but then the firm got into difficulties, turned to making an expensive customized Pontiac Fiero called the Quicksilver, and nearly went out of business, although the Golden Spirit was revived in 1990.

Bankruptcies and changes of name and ownership were frequent in the neo-classic world. The Clenet disappeared in 1982, reappearing a few years later as the Roaring Twenties. The Scepter sports car was made at Goleta by the Scepter Motor Car Company, then went out of production, only to reappear as the Gatsby Griffin from San Jose, one of a range of neo-classics offered by Gatsby Coachworks. Most neo-classics were two-door coupes or convertibles, but four-door sedans were made by Excalibur (from 1988) and Zimmer, among others, and there were a few stretched

1991 CHEVROLET CAMARO Z-28 COUPE ◄▼
THE Z-28 DESIGNATION WAS FIRST USED FOR THE TOP
MODEL OF CAMARO IN 1983, DROPPED FOR 1988, AND
REVIVED FOR 1991. HOT CAMAROS IN THE LATE 1980s
WERE DESIGNATED Z-IROC, FOR THE INTERNATIONAL
RACE OF CHAMPIONS IN WHICH THEY COMPETED. THE
1991 CARS SPORTED A TALLER REAR WING, BOLDER-
LOOKING ALLOY WHEELS, AND A CHOICE OF 230 OR
245bhp V8s. THE LATTER WAS ONLY AVAILABLE
WITH AUTOMATIC TRANSMISSION.
CHEVROLET DIVISION, GENERAL MOTORS (PHOTO NICKY WRIGHT)

limousines in neo-classic style, by Baroque from
Omaha, Nebraska, and Excalibur. Most of the
breed used the largest available V8 engine,
although power was inevitably down compared
with 1976. However, the Knudsen Baroque used a
turbocharged Buick V6 and the Spartan from San
Marcos, California, took its engine and central body
section from the Nissan 300X.

There was inevitably a heavy mortality among
neo-classic manufacturers; of the 40 or so models
announced between 1976 and 1990, only 5 were
listed for 1992. Excalibur went bankrupt in 1986,
but the company was taken over by the Acquisition
Company of Illinois, which continued the range
and later added the sedan and limousine.

A specialty car which falls neither into the
replica or neo-classic category is the Avanti,
continued after the demise of Studebaker by two
former dealers, Leo Newman and Nathan Altman.
Like Excalibur, they turned to Chevrolet power,
using the 327-cubic-inch V8 until 1969, when it was
enlarged to 350 cubic inches. They gradually
upgraded the Avanti's equipment, with electric

THE AMERICAN AUTOMOBILE: A CENTENARY 1893–1993

1990 CHEVROLET CORVETTE ZR-1 ▲ ▼ ▶
POWER AND PERFORMANCE RETURNED TO THE
CORVETTE WITH THE ZR-1, A LIMITED PRODUCTION CAR
THAT HAD A COMPLETELY NEW LOTUS-DESIGNED 32-
VALVE FOUR-CAM V8 ENGINE. KNOWN AS THE LT-5, THIS
ENGINE GAVE 385bhp FROM 350 CUBIC INCHES,
COMPARED WITH 240–245bhp FROM THE REGULAR L69
ENGINE. THE LT5 POWER UNIT WAS ENGINEERED TO FIT
THE EXISTING CORVETTE CHASSIS WITHOUT ALTERATION,
BUT THE ZR-1 COULD BE RECOGNIZED BY SQUARED-UP
TAILLIGHTS AND A WIDER BODY BEHIND THE DOORS TO
ACCOMMODATE THE FATTER TIRES.

CHEVROLET DIVISION, GENERAL MOTORS (PHOTO NICKY WRIGHT)

window lifts, optional leather trim, and tinted
windshield, while colors could be anything the
customer wanted. This lifted prices from the
original $6,550 ($1,100 more than the Studebaker-
built Avanti) to $18,995 by 1980. Inflation
contributed to this increase, of course, but the
Avanti's makers deliberately pushed it into a higher
class to compete with the Cadillac Eldorado.

The 1980s saw two changes of ownership, in
1982 and 1985, and a move to Youngstown, Ohio,
which marked the end of car making in South
Bend. The original Avanti shape was continued
with hardly any change, and was still made in 1991,
but two new models were introduced, a convertible
in 1985 and a four-door sedan in 1989. At the end of
1990 Avanti was in deep trouble, with complaints
over unpaid bills from dealers, suppliers and its
advertising agency, and 80 percent of its workforce
laid off.

1977 AVANTI II COUPE ▲

AFTER STUDEBAKER MOVED PRODUCTION TO CANADA IN 1963, THE AVANTI DESIGN WAS CONTINUED BY LEADING
STUDEBAKER DEALERS LEO NEWMAN AND NATHAN ALTMAN. THE STUDE ENGINE WAS REPLACED BY A CHEVROLET V8.
THE BASE PRICE IN 1977 WAS $13,195, BUT THIS WAS FREQUENTLY INCREASED BY OPTIONS SUCH AS HURST FOUR-SPEED
FLOOR TRANSMISSION, AIR CONDITIONING, POWER STEERING, LEATHER TRIM, AND MANY OTHER FEATURES. KNOWN AS
THE AVANTI II UNTIL 1981, IT BECAME PLAIN AVANTI AFTER A CHANGE OF OWNERSHIP. CONVERTIBLE AND FOUR-DOOR
SEDAN VERSIONS WERE ADDED IN 1985 AND 1989.

OWNER: DAN KUHL (PHOTO NICKY WRIGHT)

▼ IN 1980 MOLONEY COACHBUILDERS OFFERED A
LIMOUSINE DERIVED FROM THE CADILLAC SEVILLE, WITH
A 42-INCH EXTENSION. IN THE BACKGROUND ARE TWO
OTHER MOLONEY OFFERINGS, FLEETWOOD BROUGHAMS
EXTENDED BY 45 INCHES.

MOLONEY COACHBUILDERS, (PHOTO WALTER McCALL)

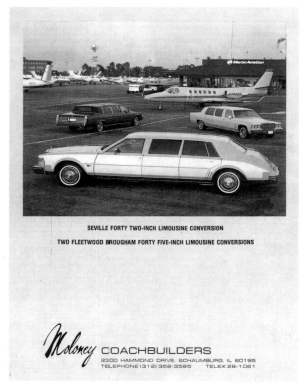

THE STRETCHED LIMOUSINE

The 1980s saw a boom in both the quantity and size of limousines built on lengthened standard chassis. The basic idea had been around since the early 1920s, when stretched Cadillacs and Pierce-Arrows were often used on bus routes that did not warrant full-size buses. Later, six- and even eight-door limousines were built for airport and hotel work, but they were relatively utilitarian vehicles, with no luxuries. The typical stretched limo that began to appear at the end of the 1970s had only four doors, with a fixed panel between front and rear doors behind which were located the bar, tape and compact disk player, cellular telephone, radio, and TV, all essential amenities in such cars. Instead of the forward-facing jump seats of the old style limousine, there were now rear-facing seats that

were just as luxurious as those opposite.

The usual base for limo conversions has been the Cadillac Fleetwood Brougham and the Lincoln Town Car, although some smaller front-drive models have been given similar treatment, their advantage being that there is no need to extend the drive shaft. However, they lack the dignity of the traditional rear-drive Cadillacs and Lincolns which are the favorite for hire work. It is the growth of private hire that has given such a boost to the stretched limo trade, for many hire companies offer such cars, giving Hollywood-style luxury for little more than double the price of a regular cab. Production doubled to 5,000 between 1983 and 1984, and has run at around 6,000 a year since then.

One of the first companies to offer luxury limousine conversions was A.H.A. (Andrew Hotten

Associates) of Brampton, Ontario, which began stretching Lincolns in 1977, later working on Buick Electra, Cadillac, Chrysler, and Mercedes-Benz chassis platforms. For those who wanted a compact limousine, a Honda Accord or Volvo 264 would be stretched. A.H.A.'s boss Andrew Hotten has the world's largest collection of classic Lincolns. Other specialists in this field were American Custom Coach of Beverly Hills, Armbruster of Fort Smith, Arkansas, Bradford Coach Works of Boca Raton, Florida, Hess & Eisenhardt of Cincinnati, Ohio, Moloney of Schaumberg, Illinois, National Coach of Port Sanilar, Michigan, and O'Gara of Simi Valley, California. The latter builds presidential Lincolns and specializes in armored bodywork.

A typical stretch involved adding a center section of 36 or 42 inches, extending a Lincoln

1987 LINCOLN TOWN CAR LIMOUSINE ▲

THE LINCOLN TOWN CAR HAS BEEN THE MOST POPULAR BASE FOR STRETCH LIMOUSINES. THEY WERE SUPPLIED IN
ORDINARY FORM TO THE COACHBUILDER BUT WITH A DELETE TRIM OPTION. THIS WAS DONE SO THAT, IN ADDITION TO
STRETCHING THE FRAME, THE COACHBUILDER COULD ADD HIS OWN INTERIOR TRIM. THE COMPANY RESPONSIBLE FOR
THIS LIMOUSINE WAS NOT IDENTIFIED IN THE LINCOLN CATALOG, BUT IT COULD WELL BE A.H.A. OR BRADFORD.

LINCOLN-MERCURY DIVISION, FORD MOTOR COMPANY

**1988 CHEVROLET SPRINT
METRO HATCHBACK** ◄
AS A REPLACEMENT FOR THE AGING CHEVETTE,
CHEVROLET IMPORTED THE SUZUKI SWIFT WITH
61-CUBIC-INCH THREE-CYLINDER ENGINE, THE FIRST
THREE-CYLINDER CAR TO BE SOLD ON THE U.S. MARKET
SINCE BEFORE WORLD WAR I. AT $5,995 IT WAS ONE OF
THE LOWEST-PRICED CARS AVAILABLE, BUT CHEVROLET
DEALERSHIPS FOUND THEM DIFFICULT TO SELL. FOR 1989
A SUBDIVISION CALLED GEO WAS FORMED, AND THE
SPRINT WAS RENAMED GEO METRO.

CHEVROLET DIVISION, GENERAL MOTORS

Town Car wheelbase from 117.3 to 153.3 or 159.3 inches, giving an overall length of up to 261 inches. For those who wanted such things, more extensive stretching could be done. When the length became too great to be reasonably supported on four wheels, the makers added an extra axle at the rear. Several New York hire companies offered six wheelers by the end of the 1980s, overall length running to more than 300 inches. In Los Angeles (where else?) Ed Tillman had an eight-wheeled Lincoln with a floorplan stretched by 83 inches and a swimming pool (actually no bigger than a large bath) where the trunk would normally be. The ultimate in long cars is probably a 26-wheeled 100-foot creation by Jay Ohrburg of Burbank, California, containing not only a swimming pool with a diving board, but also a king-size water bed. It is powered by two Cadillac engines.

HOW AMERICAN IS AN AMERICAN CAR?

Up to the 1970s it was taken for granted that a car bearing any of the well-known names would be an American design built in America. However, the situation has changed greatly in the past decade, largely because the enormous cost of retooling for a new model can be bypassed if an already-developed foreign design is used instead. The first American Ford Escort was an international car engineered in Europe as well as the United States, while the second, introduced in 1990, was engineered in Japan by Mazda. In 1988 cars badged as Fords, Lincolns, and Mercurys came from five different countries: Korea (Ford Festiva), Mexico (Mercury Tracer), Canada (Mercury Topaz and Grand Marquis, Ford Tempo and Crown Victoria), Germany (Merkur), and the United States (Ford Escort, Tempo, Taurus, Mustang, Thunderbird, Mercury Topaz, Sable and Cougar, all Lincolns). A sixth country was added in 1990, when Mercury started selling the Australian-built Capri sports car, although the poor-selling German-made Merkur was dropped.

Mercury had a tradition of selling imported cars, beginning in 1970 with the European Ford Capri

coupe. This was a junior Mustang in conception, with a variety of engines from tame to hot, but the one Mercury sold started with a British-sourced 97.6-cubic-inch four-cylinder engine. Although introduced in mid-1970 as a 1971 model, sales during the calendar year 1970 were 17,300, a record for an import in its first year. For 1972 the engine range was extended to include a 122-cubic-inch four and a 158.6-cubic-inch V6 billed as "the sexy European in a more passionate version." In 1971 Mercury dealers began selling an even more passionate European, the Italian-built mid-engined De Tomaso Pantera, offered with a choice of three Ford V8s up to 330bhp. U.S. sales were discontinued after 1974, although the same design was still being built in Italy in 1992.

The Capri, on the other hand, continued to sell well, its V6 engine being shared with the Mustang from 1974. Another example of international cooperation was that while the American-built Mercury Bobcat used engines from Lima, Ohio, those in the Canadian Bobcat were sourced to a Ford plant in Brazil. Capri imports ended in 1977 when the name went on a hatchback coupe that shared a body with the Ford Mustang. However, Lincoln-Mercury dealers had another import to sell in 1985, the German-built Merkur, the "hot" model of the European Ford Sierra range. A slippery three-door hatchback coupe with grille-less front end and biplane spoiler at the rear, the Merkur XR4Ti was powered by a 140-cubic-inch turbocharged four similar to that used in the Thunderbird and Cougar. Selling for $16,361, the Merkur (German for Mercury) was predicted to be a great success. "I've never seen a vehicle attract as

much attention as the XR4Ti in America," enthused Egon Goegel, Ford's European chief engineer for vehicle development in Europe.

In May 1987 the three-door hatchback was joined by a five-door model called the Merkur Scorpio powered by a 177-cubic-inch V6. Riding on a 108.7-inch wheelbase, this was classed as a mid-sized car, whereas the XR4Ti was a compact. Neither sold as well as was hoped, probably because they were high-priced, and the Scorpio in particular had little to offer that could not be found on the roomier Taurus and Sable for less money.

GM's foreign involvement, after the

importation of Vauxhalls and Opels in the 1960s and 1970s, has centered on Japan. (The Chevette, although a foreign design, was built in the United States.) In 1971 GM acquired a 34.2 percent stake in Isuzu, which resulted in the Japanese company's light pickup being sold in the United States as the Chevrolet LUV (Light Utility Vehicle) from March 1972 through the 1982 season. By the mid-1980s it was evident that the rear-drive Chevette was coming to the end of its career; for its replacement, the three- or five-door front-drive hatchback called the Swift, Chevrolet went to Suzuki. In its 61-cubic-inch three-cylinder form, the Swift was sold

1988 CHEVROLET NOVA, TURBO SPECTRUM, AND TURBO SPRINT ▲

CHEVROLET'S THREE SMALL CARS FOR 1988: THE TWIN-CAM NOVA SEDAN (FOREGROUND) WAS A TOYOTA DESIGN BUILT IN CALIFORNIA BY NUMMI; THE SPECTRUM (CENTER) AND SPRINT (BACKGROUND) WERE BUILT IN JAPAN, THE SPECTRUM BY ISUZU AND THE SPRINT BY SUZUKI. THE LATTER HAD A FOUR-CYLINDER TURBOCHARGED ENGINE GIVING 101bhp AND A TOP SPEED OF 105mph. FOR 1989 THESE CARS WERE RENAMED GEO PRIZM, GEO SPECTRUM, AND GEO METRO.

CHEVROLET DIVISION, GENERAL MOTORS

GEO WAS A NEW BRAND NAME FOR 1989, A
SUBDIVISION OF CHEVROLET THAT COVERED THE
CALIFORNIA-BUILT NOVA (GEO PRIZM), AND THE
IMPORTED SUZUKI SPRINT (GEO METRO) AND SAMURAI
(GEO TRACKER). THE STORM WAS A 1990 ADDITION TO
THE GEO RANGE, BEING A REBADGED ISUZU IMPULSE
2 + 2 COUPE WITH 125bhp 16-VALVE TWIN-CAM FOUR
ENGINE. A COMPETITOR FOR THE HONDA CRX, THE
STORM WAS 18 INCHES LONGER THAN ITS RIVAL, ABOUT
EQUAL IN PRICE ($11,650), AND SOMEWHAT INFERIOR IN
PERFORMANCE. STYLING WAS CONTROVERSIAL AND
COMMENTS VARIED FROM "...REALLY TURNS HEADS" TO
"AT BEST, UNUSUAL LOOKING, AT WORST, ODD."

GEO DIVISION, CHEVROLET

on the U.S. market as the Chevrolet Sprint. In 1986
the twin cam 16-valve turbocharged Turbo Sprint
appeared. It was joined by the Isuzu-built
Chevrolet Spectrum and the Nova, a rebadged
Toyota Corolla built by a joint GM-Toyota
operation called NUMMI (New United Motor
Manufacturing Company Inc.) at Fremont,
California.

Although all three were good cars, sales were
slower than anticipated. One reason was that
buyers of Hondas, Nissans, and the like were used
to purchasing fully equipped cars, whereas the
traditional Chevy dealer offered a base model with
a long list of options. Chevrolet General Manager
Jim Perkins observed: "Generally speaking, the
people who look at and buy these cars are a little
different from those we would see in a Chevrolet
dealership."

To set up a new dealer network in competition
with Chevrolet's nearly 5,000 locations was clearly
out of the question, so GM compromised with a
new brand name which they called Geo. This was a
sub-division of Chevrolet, and all Chevy dealers
had the opportunity to add Geo cars to their line.
Two of the three Chevrolets were renamed, the
Sprint becoming the Geo Metro and the Nova the
Prizm. Another model was added, the Suzuki
Samurai 4x4 light cross-country vehicle, which
became the Geo Tracker. Geo models debuted in
1989. Later additions to the range included a Metro
convertible and the Storm, a GT coupe derived
from the Isuzu Impulse. The Metro is the most
frugal car on the U.S. market and the lowest-priced,
at $5,995 undercutting the Ford Festiva by $500. At
around $10,000, the Metro convertible is the lowest-
priced open-top car currently on the U.S. market.

Chrysler took a 15 percent stake in Mitsubishi
in 1970, which led to the latter's Colt small cars
being sold under the Dodge Colt name from 1971.

In 1978 Chrysler sold 25 percent of all Mitsubishi's
passenger car output. Starting in 1982, Mitsubishi
engines were alternatives in the K-cars, Chrysler
LeBaron, Dodge Aries, and Plymouth Reliant, and
have been continued in subsequent models up to
the present.

In 1988 Chrysler and Mitsubishi set up a joint
factory at Normal, Illinois, under the name
Diamond Star. The product was a very sleek sports
coupe with a choice of four-cylinder engines from a
110bhp 109.7-cubic-inch single cam to a 195bhp
122-cubic-inch twin cam turbocharged engine, five-
speed manual transmission, and full-time four-
wheel drive on the top GSX models. Mechanical
elements were designed and built by Mitsubishi
and the body by Chrysler, and the cars were
marketed under three names with only minor
differences, Mitsubishi Eclipse, Eagle Talon, and
Plymouth Laser. The Mitsubishi models sold the
best, according to Lee Iacocca, because Americans
have an inferiority complex about American-brand
cars in the sporty field. Prices were very close, from
around $10,800 for the base model two-wheel drive
to $13,400 for a turbo model, with an extra $3,600
for four-wheel drive.

For 1990 the Mitsubishi models were joined by
the V6-powered Dodge Stealth, a close cousin of
the Mitsubishi 3000GT/HSX. This was a more

1978 DODGE ASPEN COUPE ◄

INTRODUCED FOR 1976, THE ASPEN WAS A COMPACT: A
SLIGHTLY LARGER, ROOMIER, AND HEAVIER VERSION OF
THE DART, MUCH AS FORD'S GRANADA WAS OF THE
MAVERICK. ORIGINALLY MADE AS A SEDAN, COUPE OR
WAGON IN SEVERAL SERIES, THE ASPEN WAS DOWN TO
THREE MODELS BY 1978. THIS COUPE CAME ON A 108.7-
INCH WHEELBASE; THE FOUR-DOOR SEDAN AND WAGON
WERE 4 INCHES LONGER. THE ASPEN'S TWIN IN THE
PLYMOUTH RANGE WAS THE VOLARE, AND BOTH CARS
WERE SUBJECT TO MASSIVE RECALLS TO THE FACTORIES
BECAUSE OF POOR QUALITY CONTROL AND RUSTING.
THEY WERE MADE THROUGH THE 1980 SEASON, AFTER
WHICH THEY WERE REPLACED BY THE DODGE
ARIES/PLYMOUTH RELIANT.

(PHOTO NICKY WRIGHT)

sophisticated and expensive car, with steering as well as drive to all four wheels, and a twin-turbocharged engine giving 280bhp. Much of the mechanical content came from the Mitsubishi Galant sedan, which is not made in the United States. A Stealth was selected as the 1991 Indianapolis Pace Car, a choice seen by some as a symbol of America's automotive decline. Bill Osos, director of the United Auto Workers' Union Region 3, said: "I think it's morally wrong to use a 100 percent Japanese-built car right here in the heart of Indiana. It's a slap in the face of the American auto worker." As a result of this and other protests, the Stealth was replaced by a Dodge V10 Viper driven by Carroll Shelby.

Other American-badged Mitsubishis were the Dodge and Plymouth Colts, both small hatchbacks with four-wheel drive at the top of the range, selling from $6,995 to $14,700.

The only other major American car maker, American Motors, also came under foreign influence when the French Renault company began to buy into AMC in 1978. Renault eventually acquired 46.9 percent of the stock, and in 1982 gave AMC an entry in the sub-compact market with its four-cylinder sedans and hatchbacks, badged as Alliance and Encore. AMC's president in 1983 was a Renault man, Jose Dedeurwaerder, and the Renault-based cars were soon outselling the American-designed four-wheel drive Eagles by ten to one. Jeeps still remained the most profitable part of AMC's business, and it was interest in Jeep

which led Chrysler to acquire AMC for $600 million in 1987. Chrysler discontinued the old Eagle designs but set up a new Jeep-Eagle Division which made the Renault 21-based Eagle Premier and Eagle Talon coupe as part of the Diamond Star program.

Foreign penetration into U.S. car manufacturing has been very deep. In fact it is almost impossible to quantify the exact American content of models such as those described here. Foreign auto companies are also manufacturing under their own name in the United States. This trend began with Volkswagen setting up a plant in New Scranton, Pennsylvania, in 1978 to make Rabbits, the American name for the Golf. The first to start, VW was also the first, and so far the only, company to abandon U.S. manufacture, giving up in 1988 after serious problems with quality control. Honda opened its plant at Marysville, Ohio, in 1983, the same year that Nissan started production at

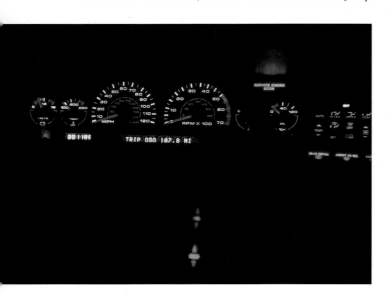

1991 OLDSMOBILE 98 TOURING SEDAN ◄▲►
THE NUMBER 98 HAS LONG INDICATED THE TOP MODEL OF OLDSMOBILE, SINCE 1941 IN FACT, AND THE 50TH ANNIVERSARY OF THE NAME BROUGHT A LARGE FRONT DEIVE SEDAN WITH GENERAL MOTORS' C-BODY AND A 231-CUBIC-INCH 170BHP V6 ENGINE. ALTHOUGH IN THE SAME SIZE CATEGORY AS BUICK'S PARK AVENUE, THE 98 DID NOT SHARE A SINGLE BODY PANEL WITH ITS COUSIN FROM FLINT. THE OLDSMOBILE'S SUSPENSION IS FIRMER THAN THE BUICK'S. THE BASE PRICE FOR THE TOURING SEDAN WAS $28,595.

OLDSMOBILE DIVISION, GENERAL MOTORS (PHOTO NICKY WRIGHT)

Smyrna, Tennessee. Mazda began its operations at Flat Rock, Michigan, in 1985, and Toyota at Georgetown, Kentucky, in 1988. Not only did these factories build cars for the U.S. market, they also started exporting U.S.-built Japanese cars to Japan. Diamond Star shipped its first 3,000 Eclipse coupes in November 1989, and in 1990 Toyota began building right-hand-drive Camry sedans for export. These operations reduced to some extent the trade imbalance between the United States and Japan, brought about by the enormous volume of imports from Japan, not only of cars but of electrical goods, televisions, videos, and cameras.

In 1990 Honda took an important step toward becoming a fully-fledged domestic manufacturer, with the introduction of its Accord station wagon. This was styled by Honda's research and development facility at Torrance, California, and engineered at Marysville. Engines were built at Honda's other Ohio plant, at Anna. The 134-cubic-inch all-aluminum 16-valve unit was also used in Accord sedans and coupes. Production for 1991 was set at 30,000–35,000 cars: 10,000 earmarked for export, 5,000 to Japan and 5,000 to Europe — the first time a U.S.-made Japanese car has been exported other than to Japan. Honda's marketing in the United States has been double-pronged, the Ohio-built Civic and Accord being sold under the Honda name, and the higher-priced Legend sedan and coupe and NSX sports car carrying the Acura name and being sold by a different dealer network. The same strategy is employed by Nissan and Toyota, whose Infiniti and Lexus luxury sedans are marketed quite separately from their lower-priced cars. The Lexus even uses a different advertising agency from Toyota.

Korea is also making inroads into the North American market, with Hyundai having a Canadian plant at Bromont, Quebec, whose cars are sold in the United States through Chrysler/Eagle dealers. GM's Korean arm, Daewoo, builds the Opel Kadett-based Pontiac LeMans compact sedan and coupe, and has considered marketing its cars in the United States under its own name.

TROUBLED DECADE, AND
THE WAY AHEAD

The American auto industry took a real battering at the beginning of the 1980s. In the wake of the fuel consumption regulations that reduced the appeal of the traditional big American car, imports surged ahead, particularly those from Japan. Domestic production, which had been 9.7 million in 1973, dropped to little over 6 million in 1980, the year in which America took second place to Japan in overall production. And between 1978 and 1982 32 manufacturing and assembly plants across the nation closed. In 1987 imports accounted for 3,197,000 cars, 31.1 percent of the total sold in the United States.

The relative decline of American car makers vis-à-vis the Japanese began in the 1960s, when American confidence slipped into complacency, and the Japanese were exerting themselves to build up an industry from nothing. The cost-accounting dominance of men like Ford's Whiz Kids led to a short-sighted policy where year-end profits were the sacred cow and capital investment which would lower those profits was severely discouraged. Thus both new machine tools and research and development were starved of funds. By the early 1980s Japan's level of automation was double that of America. Of course high profits and low investment suited the American work force. Executives' annual profits-linked bonuses

FORD WORLD HEADQUARTERS AT DEARBORN, MICHIGAN. IN THE FOREGROUND IS A PROBE, FORD'S JOINT VENTURE WITH MAZDA. THE SPORTY-LOOKING COUPES ARE MADE AT MAZDA'S FLAT ROCK, MICHIGAN, PLANT, AND COME WITH A 133-CUBIC-INCH FOUR OR 182-CUBIC-INCH V6 UNIT. FORD HAD SOLD 341,000 BY MID-1991.

(PHOTO MIRCO DE CET)

sometimes exceeded their salaries, and blue collar workers, in the late 1970s, took home 60 percent more than the average industrial wage. Each year would bring a substantial rise in their standard of living, wouldn't it?

Ford entered the 1980s in bad shape; between June 1979 and the end of 1981 its white-collar workforce was cut by a quarter, and the blue-collar payroll was reduced from 190,000 to 115,000. Personal differences between Henry Ford II and Lee Iacocca led to the latter's departure in August 1978, and Henry himself stepped down from the three-man "office of chief executives" on October 1, 1980. His brother, William Clay Ford, and

Donald Petersen stepped up to take the vacant places, and Philip Caldwell, who was already there, made up the third. Caldwell had made a great success with Ford trucks and, although unkindly described as "uncharismatic" and "a gray, cold-blooded bean counter," he did the same with the whole company, achieving profits of $187 million in 1984 after three years of serious losses.

Iacocca moved to Chrysler and had much the same success there. When he took over, U.S. passenger car sales were only 1.25 million, and the 1978 loss was $208 million. The introduction of the K-cars achieved a turnaround, putting Chrysler in profit again in 1983. Since then the corporation has had several milestones — the reintroduction of the convertible, the purchase of American Motors and Lamborghini in 1987, and the Diamond Star joint venture with Mitsubishi from 1988.

By the end of the decade Chrysler was in a healthier position than it had been at the beginning, but as the smallest of the Big Three it was still vulnerable in a world difficult for all Detroit car makers. In 1989 the corporation was forced to sell $300 million worth of Mitsubishi

shares to cover losses, and a year later was trying to divest itself of the Technologies Group and other non-automotive businesses. There were rumors, strongly denied by vice-president Bob Lutz, that Lamborghini would have to be sold, and a merger with Fiat was discussed. One growth field for Chrysler was exports, particularly to Europe, where American cars have been little represented in recent years. The medium-sized Chrysler Saratoga and LeBaron went to France, Switzerland, Germany, and other markets at prices somewhat below the similar-sized BMW 5 Series. The 1990 export sales, including Jeep products, were 41,000, with an anticipated 55,000 for 1991. In December 1990 California billionaire Kirk Kerkorian bought nearly 10 percent of Chrysler stock, which led to rumors of a takeover. However, it seems more likely that he was simply investing in stock that was very low ($12.25 compared with $48 in 1987) and could only move upward.

General Motors also had a roller coaster ride in the 1980s, rising from a poor start to record sales in 1984/85, when it had three makes in the top five best sellers, Chevrolet in first place, Oldsmobile in third, and Pontiac in fifth. GM also made its mistakes, particularly in the Cadillac Division, where the V-8-6-4 engine, which could be run with a varying number of cylinders according to driving conditions, flopped after one season. A good idea, it was too complex to be reliable and brought many customer complaints. The automated Hamtramck body plant, where Cadillac Sevilles, Olds Toronados, and Buick Rivieras were made, gave a lot of trouble to start with (robots painted each other instead of the cars). Cadillac suffered from a severe loss of image, having too little to distinguish it from other GM products. The Allante was an attempt to rectify this but has not been a marked success so far. However, GM increased its market share in 1990 to 35.7 percent, 0.5 per cent up on 1989.

Although GM's small car imports in the Geo range sold quite well, they made very little profit. In order to meet the imports head on, a new division making an all-new car was announced in 1983, with production slated to start in the summer of 1990. Named Saturn in tribute to the rocket that carried America to the moon, it was located in a new 2,450-acre complex at Spring Hill, Tennessee. Unlike GM plants which work in collaboration with

1988 CHEVROLET ASTRO CL ◄

VARIOUSLY CALLED THE PEOPLE CARRIER OR MPV
(MULTIPURPOSE VEHICLE) THE HIGH-ROOF, SHORT-HOOD
DESIGN COMBINED THE VIRTUES OF A STATION WAGON
AND A VAN. MPVs WERE BUILT IN EUROPE AND JAPAN
FROM THE EARLY 1980s, AND THE LAYOUT APPEARED IN
THE UNITED STATES IN 1984 WITH THE DODGE CARAVAN.
THIS WAS FOLLOWED BY THE CHEVROLET ASTRO FOR
1985 AND THE FORD AEROSTAR FOR 1986. THE ASTRO
USED A STANDARD V6 ENGINE AND REAR DRIVE, AND
CAME IN PANEL VAN OR STATION WAGON FORM. THE CL
PACKAGE INCLUDED CUSTOM STEERING WHEEL, WHEEL
TRIM RINGS, AUXILIARY LIGHTING, CIGAR LIGHTER, AND
CARPETS. IN FIVE-PASSENGER FORM IT COST $9,359.

CHEVROLET DIVISION, GENERAL MOTORS

others, using engines from one source, transmissions from another, and steering gears from a third, Spring Hill is a complete producer, with its own foundry, body-stamping shop, and paint, interior and general assembly shops. No components are shared with other GM cars, although, surprisingly, 65 percent of the Saturn's content comes from outside suppliers. Bought-in items include spark plugs, seats, and tires, which the auto industry traditionally buys from specialists.

Working conditions at Saturn are above average for the industry, including complete air conditioning throughout the complex, electrically powered tools rather than air-driven ones, and less demarcation between management and workforce. Taking a lead from the NUMMI plant at Fremont, California, which is said to have the best quality control of any GM installation, there is less dependence on robots than in some Detroit plants.

The Saturn is a generally conventional car made

in sedan and coupe forms, with two 116-cubic-inch four-cylinder engines, a single cam developing 85bhp and a twin cam giving 123bhp. The sedan's wheelbase is 104.2 inches, identical to the Honda Accord and Toyota Camry. Construction is a pressed steel spaceframe and steel top and hood, with doors and side panels of molded plastic screwed to the frame.

Saturn marketing is new, too, with one dealer for each of 250 geographical areas, who sells only Saturns. He may handle other cars, but only from a different location. Saturn stresses a high degree of customer friendliness, with as much prominence being given to service as to sales. Market research has shown that many customers feel intimidated in car showrooms and have a low level of trust in salespeople. Initial sales were to be confined to

1990 PONTIAC TRANS SPORT MPV ◄

ONE OF A GENERAL MOTORS FAMILY OF MPVs THAT INCLUDED THE
CHEVROLET LUMINA AND OLDSMOBILE SILHOUETTE, THE TRANS
SPORT HAD A 191-CUBIC-INCH FUEL-INJECTED V6 MOUNTED
TRANSVERSELY UNDER THE SHORT HOOD AND DRIVING THE FRONT
WHEELS. DESPITE ITS NAME IT WAS NOT PARTICULARLY SPORTING:
"MORE TRANS THAN SPORT" AS *AUTOWEEK* MAGAZINE REPORTED.
THERE WAS A SINGLE DOOR ON THE DRIVER'S SIDE, TWO ON THE
PASSENGER SIDE, WITH SEATING FOR FIVE OR SEVEN.

PONTIAC DIVISION, GENERAL MOTORS

1991 SATURN SEDAN AND COUPE ▲ ▶

PRODUCTS OF AN ALL-NEW GM DIVISION LOCATED IN TENNESSEE, THE SATURN MODELS WERE DESIGNED TO MEET
IMPORTS SUCH AS THE HONDA ACCORD AND TOYOTA CAMRY HEAD-ON. IT WAS OFFERED IN FOUR MODELS:
THE BASE SL AND BETTER-TRIMMED SL1 SEDANS (BACKGROUND) WITH SINGLE-CAM FOUR-CYLINDER ENGINES; THE
SL2 SEDAN (RIGHT FOREGROUND) WITH TWIN-CAM ENGINE; AND THE SC COUPE (LEFT FOREGROUND), ONLY
AVAILABLE IN TWIN-CAM FORM. ALL HAD TRANSVERSE ENGINES DRIVING THE FRONT WHEELS. IN THE EXPLODED
DRAWING, THE DETACHABLE HOOD AND TOP PANELS ARE OF STEEL, THE BODY SIDE, FRONT AND REAR PANELS
OF MOLDED DENT-RESISTANT POLYMER PLASTIC.

SATURN CORPORATION

California, the prime market for imported cars, and to the home state of Tennessee. Production started up on July 31, 1990, and dealers received their first sedans in December. In February 1991, 50 percent of the 3,000 Saturns made up to that date were subject to recall because of possibly faulty seat recliners. However, overall 1991 sales were encouraging, at nearly 75,000. Saturn was ranked first among 24 small cars in a J. D. Power customer satisfaction survey. A station wagon was added to the range in 1992. Exports to Canada began in 1991, and entry into the Japanese market is planned for the mid-1990s.

An interesting recent development has been the revival of the traditional large rear-drive V8 sedan, which even as recently as 1988 seemed doomed to extinction. The genre was gradually marginalized in the ranges of all Big Three manufacturers. GM offered only station wagons in the Buick, Oldsmobile, and Pontiac lines, and production was among the lowest of any of its models. Chrysler kept alive the Fifth Avenue and its sisters the Dodge Diplomat and Plymouth Grand Fury because their development costs had

long since been amortized, and big cars generally make more profit than small ones. They, and equivalents from Ford and Chevrolet, were popular with taxi operators and police forces.

However, a wider market for a large six-passenger car clearly still existed, and so, despite concern over CAFE figures, Chevrolet brought out a completely restyled Caprice for 1990. Launched in January as a 1991 model, it preserved the 305-cubic-inch V8 engine and rear drive via automatic transmission that dated back to 1976, but it was clothed in a new aerodynamic body. A large car at 214 inches overall length and weighing 3,935 pounds, it gave neither sparkling performance nor a taut ride, yet it clearly struck a chord with the American public. To the amazement of European commentators, who referred to its "Moby Dick school of styling," the Caprice was named Car of the Year by *Motor Trend* magazine.

At the end of 1990 other GM divisions followed Chevrolet; Oldsmobile announced the Custom Cruiser eight-passenger station wagon, and Buick revived the Roadmaster name, unused since 1958, for a similar wagon. A Roadmaster sedan joined it

in spring 1991, powered by a larger engine of 348 cubic inches. The wagons were really big, with 87 cubic feet of cargo space, yet prices were quite reasonable, around $18,000 for a fully equipped Caprice to $25,000 for a Buick Roadmaster. Cadillac continued its old-style Brougham, which used the same platform as the Roadmaster/Caprice, but a restyle was announced for 1993.

Over at Ford there was a similar revival of the large car, with the Crown Victoria and Mercury Grand Marquis completely restyled to look like grown-up versions of the Taurus/Sable. Unlike the GM cars, the Fords had new engines as well, 281-cubic-inch overhead cam V8s giving 190 or 210bhp with dual exhausts. These were 40 and 50bhp better than the larger pushrod V8s in the previous big Fords. Prices started at $19,200 for the Crown Victoria. Careful choice of components enabled these Fords to be classed as imports, having just over 25 percent imported parts. Thus their fuel consumption could be averaged with more economical Ford imports such as the Festiva and Mercury Capri.

Despite all these new models, the outlook for the American auto industry at the beginning of 1992 is not encouraging. The recession began to hit in the second half of 1990, and overall U.S. production of cars and light trucks was down on 1989. Yet the Japanese, both with imports and transplants, mostly registered an increase on 1989. Mitsubishi's sales jumped by 29.6 percent, Toyota's by 15.1 percent, and Honda's by 9.2 percent. For the second year running, the Honda Accord was the best-selling model, beating the Taurus by more than 100,000 units, while Chrysler only just held onto third place, selling only 6,000 more cars than Honda. The Accord again registered first place in 1991. In 1990 the domestic car makers had 60 percent of the market, with the Japanese taking 27.5 percent and European imports 12.5 percent. In January 1991 the Big Three temporarily closed 24 of 62 main plants, laying off 62,000 workers. A year later GM announced closure of 21 U.S. plants over the next four years.

In order to boost sales in a market where cars are a fairly expensive item, more expensive relative to family income than at any time in the last two decades, almost all dealers offered discounts on the list price. This applied not only to domestic models

1991 CHEVROLET CAPRICE SEDAN ▲ ▶
ONE OF GENERAL MOTORS' NEW GENERATION OF FULL-
SIZE, REAR-DRIVE CARS, THE 1991 CAPRICE WAS BASED
ON A WIDENED VERSION OF THE 1990 CHASSIS, WITH AN
ALL-NEW BODY WHOSE DRAG COEFFICIENT WAS ONLY
0.33, COMPARED WITH 0.41 FOR THE 1990 SEDAN.
OVERALL LENGTH WAS NEARLY 18 FEET AND TRUNK
VOLUME 20.4 CUBIC FEET. OTHER CARS IN THE SAME
FAMILY WERE THE BUICK ROADMASTER SEDAN AND
OLDSMOBILE CUSTOM CRUISER STATION WAGON.

CHEVROLET DIVISION, GENERAL MOTORS

(PHOTO NICKY WRIGHT)

but to supposed popular imports such as the Lexus luxury sedan, officially priced at $38,000 but available for $30,400 to a determined bargainer. Discounting may help to move cars, but it is no way to make profits. Even the sticker price, which hardly anybody pays, represents a loss to manufacturers. In 1989 it was estimated that GM lost around $1,200 per car on average, Chrysler $1,000, and Ford $800. In 1990 GM lost $1.6 billion and Ford $519 million, although Chrysler recorded a $31 million profit. Even more depressing was 1991. July–September losses were $1.1 billion for GM, $574.4 million for Ford, and around $82 million for Chrysler. Analysts predicted that overall 1991 losses might be the worst in the history of the industry. One of the victims was Roger Penske's

1991 CHEVROLET CAPRICE SEDAN ▲◀

THE CAPRICE AND ITS SISTER, THE BUICK ROADMASTER, MARKED A RETURN TO THE TRADITIONAL FULL-SIZE, REAR-DRIVE AMERICAN AUTOMOBILE, AND GM'S COMMITMENT TO SUCH CARS WAS UNDERLINED BY BRAND-NEW BODIES THAT WERE CLEARLY PLANNED TO HAVE SEVERAL YEARS OF LIFE. PRICES BEGAN AT JUST UNDER $16,000, AND BUYERS GOT A LOT OF CAR FOR THEIR MONEY. AN UPGRADED F41 SUSPENSION PACKAGE WENT SOME WAY TO ELIMINATING THE WALLOW ASSOCIATED WITH THESE CARS. CHEVROLET OFFERED POLICE AND TAXI PACKAGE VERSIONS OF THE CAPRICE, THE LATTER PRICED AT $19,283.

CHEVROLET DIVISION, GENERAL MOTORS (PHOTO NICKY WRIGHT)

1992 FORD CROWN VICTORIA AND MERCURY MARQUIS SEDANS ◄▼
FORD AND MERCURY COMPLETELY MODERNIZED THEIR LARGE REAR-DRIVE CARS FOR 1992, THE NEW MODELS BEING ANNOUNCED IN DECEMBER 1990. STYLING BORE A CLOSE FAMILY RESEMBLANCE TO THE FORD TAURUS AND MERCURY SABLE, AND THERE WAS A NEW ENGINE IN THE MODULAR OVERHEAD-CAM V8. THIS WAS 37 POUNDS LIGHTER THAN ITS PREDECESSOR, YET GAVE 40bhp MORE IN SINGLE EXHAUST FORM AND 50bhp WITH TWIN EXHAUSTS. THE ALL-NEW ALUMINUM CYLINDER HEAD ACCOUNTED FOR PART OF THE WEIGHT REDUCTION, AIDED BY ALUMINUM PISTONS AND INTAKE MANIFOLD. NOT SO MUCH "CARS FOR THE SHUFFLEBOARD SET" AS THEIR PREDECESSORS HAD BEEN, THE NEW BIG FORDS HAD GREATLY IMPROVED RIDE AND HANDLING.

FORD MOTOR COMPANY

huge Cadillac-Buick-Chevrolet dealership in Manhattan, which closed in the spring of 1991.

Recession apart, much of the malaise in the American auto industry stems from a massive loss of confidence on the part of the American car-buying public. At one time, enthusiasm and snobbery were the main motives for buying imported cars, but over the past decade or so, budget-minded drivers worried about every cent of repair and running costs, and trade-in values, have been the main customers for foreign cars. A 1988 survey of customer satisfaction put the top U.S. car (Cadillac) in fifteenth place, beaten by Acura, Range Rover, and Mercedes-Benz (first, second, and third respectively), and also by such minor imports as Daihatsu and Hyundai. However, at least Cadillac beat Volkswagen! The Acura has been so reliable that a dealer complained that he could make no money in his service department. "These cars just do not break. You know, we said that in the beginning, too, and everyone thought it was because the cars were brand new. Well, they can't say that any more, and we still don't have any service business." In 1991 Japan again topped the list, the Lexus gaining 146 points, but U.S. makes were much higher. Cadillac was second with 140 points and Lincoln fourth with 136.

Yet industry leaders see several gleams of hope. Lee Iacocca thinks that hard times will concentrate the American mind on efficiency and quality:

1992 BUICK ROADMASTER STATION WAGON ▲

BUICK REVIVED THE ROADMASTER NAME, DORMANT SINCE 1958, FOR THE NEW FULL-SIZE SEDAN AND STATION
WAGON. THE BUICK WAGON SHARED PLATFORM AND 305-CUBIC-INCH V8 ENGINE WITH CHEVROLET'S CAPRICE
AND OLDS' CUSTOM CRUISER, WHILE THE SEDAN HAD A LARGER ENGINE. THE WAGON WAS DESCRIBED BY
ROAD & TRACK AS "DECIDEDLY UNTRENDY, WITH ITS FLOATING RIDE AND VINYL WOODGRAIN APPLIQUÉ," BUT
ITS ACCOMMODATION FOR EIGHT PASSENGERS AND 87 CUBIC FEET OF CARGO SPACE CLEARLY APPEALED
TO MANY AMERICANS TIRED OF SHOEBOX-SIZED COMPACTS.

BUICK DIVISION, GENERAL MOTORS (PHOTO NICKY WRIGHT)

◀▼ TWO OF THE MOST INTERESTING CONCEPT CARS OF RECENT YEARS WERE THE ZIG (LEFT) AND ZAG (BELOW) FROM FORD WITH STYLING BY GHIA. BASED ON A FIESTA FLOORPAN SHORTENED BY 6 INCHES, THEY WERE RESPECTIVELY A TWO-PASSENGER ROADSTER AND A MINIVAN. GHIA STRESSED THAT OTHER STYLES COULD BE HAD ON THE SAME FLOORPAN: THREE- OR FIVE-DOOR SEDANS OR A STATION WAGON. A SARICH-DESIGNED TWO-CYCLE ENGINE WAS A PLANNED POWER UNIT, AS WERE ELECTRIC MOTORS.

MIRCO DE CET COLLECTION

"When it gets tough they will straighten out." This applies just as much to the parts industry, which has to compete with imported parts when supplying to transplants like U.S.-built Hondas and Toyotas. Iacocca sees hope here, too. The annual Detroit Auto Shows have become increasingly important for new "concept cars," which reach the marketplace within a few years, just as Japanese concept cars have been doing. Pontiac's Trans Sport multipurpose vehicle was a concept in 1986 and in the showrooms four years later. Buick's Essence concept of 1989 became a reality with the 1991 Park Avenue Ultra, described by international journalist Peter Robinson as "one of the most promising of American cars." With radical ideas like two-stroke engines and electric motors now actually powering running cars, Detroit seems more in the engineering vanguard that it has been for many years. Let us hope that Henry Ford, Alfred Sloan, and Walter Chrysler can rest in peace, in the knowledge that their legacies will continue to flourish.

1992 FORD TAURUS ▲◄

ALTHOUGH THE 1992 TAURUS AND SABLE REPRESENT THE BIGGEST SINGLE MODEL YEAR CHANGE SINCE THEIR INTRODUCTION, PROGRESS HAS BEEN EVOLUTIONARY RATHER THAN DRAMATIC. BODY PANELS ARE ALL NEW APART FROM THE DOORS, YET APPEARANCE IS NOT RADICALLY CHANGED. SUSPENSION AND TIRES ARE SOFTER, GIVING A SMOOTHER RIDE. ON THE ENGINE SIDE, THE FOUR HAS BEEN DROPPED, LEAVING TWO PUSHROD V6 AND THE TWIN-CAM 24-VALVE V6 USED IN THE HIGH-PERFORMANCE SHOW MODEL.

FORD MOTOR COMPANY

1930 RUXTON ROADSTER ▼

CHAPTER EIGHT

OLD BANGERS TO BLUE CHIP INVESTMENTS

"I warn you that in ten years most of you guys will be standing
outside the hobby, looking in."
Parke-Bernet spokesman, 1962

save cars from the scrappers, and some newspapers demanded that the cars be barred from the streets as dangerous old wrecks. Sometimes there was justification for this, for the meticulous care for authenticity and safety that characterizes nearly all old car lovers today was not so evident 50 years ago. Old tire sizes were unobtainable until the Firestone Company stepped in to make replicas after World War II, so bald tires were frequently seen at early meets.

The AACA formed its first regional chapter in 1945, in northern Illinois, followed by Cleveland. By 1960 more than 80 chapters spanned the United States and Canada, with more than 9,000 members. Two big meets were held each year, Spring and Fall, and the latter seemed to attract the most entrants. Held at the Devon (Pennsylvania) Horse Show Grounds from 1946 through 1953, meets grew too large when more than 200 cars were entered, so a move was made to the stadium at Hershey, home town of the famous chocolate bars. The first Hershey Meet took place in October 1954, and the Fall Meet has been held there annually ever since and now occupies a vast area outside the stadium. The swap meet, in which parts, literature, photographs, and phonograph records as well as cars change hands, occupies far more space than the car show.

Meanwhile other clubs had been formed. The second was the Horseless Carriage Club of America headquartered in Downey, California, which began in November 1937. Formed by automotive engineer and designer of a teardrop three-wheeled car, W. Everett Miller, it had a number of active women members from the start, including Miller's

I N JANUARY 1931 THE Philadelphia Automobile Trade Association, which organized the annual auto show in the city, was looking for inexpensive publicity to spice up the unveiling of new models in Convention Hall. Someone suggested inviting owners of early cars to come along, the definition of "early" being 25 or more years old. The number of owners who turned up has not been traced, but the occasion was considered enough of a success to be repeated annually.

The Antique Automobile Derby, as it was called, attracted more entries each year, and by 1936 at least 40 cars rallied to Philadelphia from points which had to be 25 or more miles away. The contestants were not too happy, though, as they received little prize money and were regarded as

comic relief by the public and the show organizers. In 1935 two of the participants, Ted Fiala and Frank Abramson, suggested the formation of a club for old car enthusiasts, and in November 1935 this became a reality as the Antique Automobile Club of America, with 14 paid-up members (annual dues $1). This was the second such organization in the world, the first being Britain's Veteran Car Club formed in November 1930.

Membership grew only slowly in the pre-war years, but among the club's supporters was pioneer automobilist Charles Duryea, who donated a mimeograph machine to the club in 1938. By 1944, there were 400 paid-up members. The war saw many antique cars melted down in the scrap drive, but this also gave an impetus to enthusiasts to save what they could. Although they had a lot of fun at meets, they were labeled unpatriotic for trying to

wife Katherine, who suggested the club name, Margaret Lewerenz, and Doris Twohy. They encouraged the wearing of period costume at meets, although this has always been a controversial subject. Some enthusiasts feel it introduces a carnival atmosphere unsuited to the serious use of old cars. The HCCA flourished after the war, and has 27 regions across the United States and one in New Zealand.

The third national club was formed in the Boston area in December 1938, under the name Veteran Motor Car Club of America. This had 107 members by 1940, and in 1949 acquired the cars belonging to the Larz Anderson estate at Brookline, Massachusetts. They also had the use of the Coach House on the estate, whose mansion is modeled after the Château de Chaumont in France, as club headquarters.

▲ A 1935 AUBURN 851 CONVERTIBLE AMONG OTHER PRODUCTS OF THE AUBURN-CORD-DUESENBERG GROUP AT MEADOWBROOK IN 1991.

(PHOTO NICKY WRIGHT)

CLUBS FOR LATER CARS

Prior to World War II, collector interest was confined to cars made before 1920. Model Ts were just acceptable if they had brass radiators (pre-1917), but later ones were of no interest. The loss to the scrapman of so many expensive cars of the 1920s alerted enthusiasts to the idea that collectible cars did not have to be Brass-Age antiques. Immediately after World War II a number of big old Lincolns, Cadillac V16s, Pierce-Arrows, and Rolls-Royces came out of hibernation. Many of them were quickly sold by their well-heeled owners as soon as new cars became available, and they were snapped up by young enthusiasts for a few hundred dollars. Keith Marvin, later a founder member of the Automobilists of the Upper Hudson Valley, bought his first Rolls-Royce, a 1930 Phantom I, for $500 in 1946. Giants of the 1920s could be had for less than this. In 1953 autobook publisher George Dammann was able to buy a 1936 Lincoln V12 Brunn Brougham in reasonable shape for $10.

The Classic Car Club of America (CCCA) was founded late in 1951. At the 1952 International Motor Sport Show in New York City, a 1931 Cadillac V16 displayed by a CCCA member attracted so much attention that club membership

rose from around 20 to almost 90 before the show closed. The club's definition of a classic was a car of recognized quality made between 1925 and 1942. Definitions of "recognized quality" were not always easy to establish, but certain makes were accepted unconditionally for all models. These included Cord, Duesenberg, duPont, Mercer, Pierce-Arrow, and Stutz, as well as foreign makes such as Alfa-Romeo, Bugatti, Isotta-Fraschini, Rolls-Royce, and others. For some other makes, the club was more selective. Most Packards were allowed, but not the

120s or 110s. The big Lincolns and Continentals were accepted, but not the Zephyr. The acceptance of the Continental necessitated a date extension to 1948, as the postwar cars were essentially the same as the prewar ones. No Chevrolets, Fords, Oldsmobiles, or Pontiacs were admitted — unless with custom coachwork and a special application had been made — and among Buicks, only the 90 or Limited series from 1931 to 1942. Classics are ideal tour cars. The CCCA, with its 27 regions, organizes regular long-distance journeys, with some

▲ POST-WORLD WAR II CARS AT A MEET AT THE SLOANE MUSEUM, FLINT, MICHIGAN, IN 1991. IN THE FOREGROUND ARE A 1953 STUDEBAKER AND A 1951 CHEVROLET.

(PHOTO MIRCO DE CET)

◄ ANOTHER CORNER OF THE SLOANE MUSEUM MEET; IN THE FOREGROUND, A CORVETTE, BEHIND IT A CUSTOMIZED 1939 CHEVROLET AND BEYOND THAT A DE TOMASO PANTERA.

(PHOTO MIRCO DE CET)

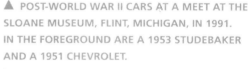

▶ A PRISTINE EXAMPLE OF A 1956 MERCURY CONVERTIBLE AT MEADOWBROOK.

(PHOTO NICKY WRIGHT)

or one-model clubs. In fact there are clubs for almost every make one can think of, from the prestigious Auburn-Cord-Duesenberg Club to the King Midget and Eshelman Registry. There are at least 23 Ford clubs as well as separate ones for Mustangs and Thunderbirds. At first only the two-passenger T-Birds were thought worth collecting, but soon a club for the four-passenger "Square

◀ RICHARD KUGHN IS A LEADING CAR COLLECTOR WHO ALSO HAS A MAGNIFICENT COLLECTION OF LIONEL MODEL TRAINS. HERE HE IS DRIVING HIS 1935 AUBURN PHAETON.

(PHOTO NICKY WRIGHT)

▼ A 1937 CORD 812 SEDAN.

(PHOTO NICKY WRIGHT)

members driving hundreds of miles to the start of the event. Like the other clubs mentioned, the CCCA publishes a fine magazine, *The Classic Car*.

By the late 1960s it was felt that humbler cars of the classic period should be recognized. By then there were many one-make clubs which catered to Ford V8s, Chevys, and Plymouths, but an umbrella organization for all cars made between 1928 and 1948, the Contemporary Historical Vehicle Association, was formed in 1967. Then, in 1971, came the Indianapolis-based Milestone Car Society "For the Great Post-war Cars." Founded by historian Richard M. Langworth, it covered a later period still, 1945 through 1967 (recently extended to 1972). American and foreign cars are eligible, and are selected by a committee, of which the author has the honor to be a member. Names are put forward by club members, who are usually owners of the cars they propose; if they achieve sufficient votes in five areas, Styling, Engineering, Performance, Innovation, and Craftsmanship, they are admitted. Among more than 170 Certified Milestones in 1992 were early postwar cars such as Chrysler Town & Country, Frazer Manhattan, and Tucker, and recent ones have included Ford Mustang Boss 302, Plymouth Roadrunner, and Pontiac GTO.

Nearly all the domestic makes in the Classic and Milestone clubs also have their own one-make

Birds" appeared as well. There are also clubs for trucks, motorcycles, and foreign cars, so that the total currently listed — and it is changing all the time — is around 550.

▲ THIS GATHERING OF WOODIES AT MEADOWBROOK SHOWS SOME UNUSUAL CARS. ON THE LEFT IS A 1941 CADILLAC WITH A CUSTOM BODY, POSSIBLY BY BOHMAN & SCHWARTZ (CADILLAC NEVER CATALOGED A STATION WAGON). ON THE RIGHT IS A 1941 PACKARD WHICH WAS CATALOGED, THOUGH FEW WERE MADE. VISIBLE IN THE BACKGROUND BETWEEN THEM IS A 1941 OR '42 CHRYSLER.

(PHOTO NICKY WRIGHT)

THE COLLECTORS

The backbone of the old vehicle movement is the individual enthusiast who owns one or two cherished cars, but some enthusiasts have a great many more and a few are collectors on a grand scale. The first big collector was probably Henry Ford, who began amassing cars in the early 1920s, along with a great many other pieces of American rural life, particularly plows and other items of farm equipment, which went to make up the Henry Ford Museum and Greenfield Village. The historical complex opened on October 21, 1929, with Thomas Alva Edison, Orville Wright, and President Hoover on hand for the celebrations. Among highlights of the car collection were

Sylvester Roper's pioneer steamer of 1863, Ford's first quadricycle of 1896 and his massive 999 racer of 1903, and cars associated with personalities, such as Charles Lindbergh's Franklin and President Taft's 1912 Baker Electric.

Another pioneer collector, in a very different mold from Henry Ford, was Detroit entrepreneur (coal and coke, asphalt paving, excavating) Barney Pollard, whose collection eventually totaled over 1,000 cars. He acquired the first, a 1910 Cadillac, in 1938, but the real volume came during World War II, when two or three car carriers would come in daily. This continued after the war, when old cars would be brought in on back hauls from delivering new cars all over the country. The cars were

stacked vertically in sheds and remained thus until Pollard began to sell them off, starting in 1976. About 40 remain to this day in the Pollard family. They are now well housed in purpose-built accommodation.

Henry Austin Clark Jr., one of the great figures of the old car world, bought his first antique, a 1915 Ford Model T, in 1937 when he was a freshman at Harvard. By the outbreak of World War II, when he went into the Navy, he had acquired five more antiques, and has subsequently owned more than 400 vehicles. He was one of the first to appreciate the interest and fun in collecting old trucks, buses, and fire engines. In 1948 he opened the Long Island Automotive Museum at Southampton.

◀ A 1935 CADILLAC V16 TOWN CAR NEXT TO THE 1941 STATION WAGON.

(PHOTO NICKY WRIGHT)

Another collector who eventually opened a museum was Briggs Cunningham, whose assembly of mostly sporting machines opened at Costa Mesa, California, in the 1960s. Early collectors who saved countless cars from the crusher included D. Cameron Peck of Chicago and opera singer James Melton, who had more than 100 cars by 1946, which he displayed in a museum.

The best known collector of them all, and founder of the world's largest auto museum, was Reno casino owner William Fisk Harrah. Beginning in 1948 with a Model T Ford and a two-cylinder Maxwell, Harrah amassed an enormous collection before he opened to the public. Within a few years he had around 1,400 cars, trucks, and fire engines, of which 1,100 were on display. Countless makes, both domestic and foreign, were represented. Among the highlights were more than 100 Fords (at least one for every year from 1903 to 1951) and more than 50 each of Franklin and Packard, two of Bill Harrah's favorite makes. He personally tested every car before it went on display, and his restoration workshops and library were world famous. Unfortunately he left no instructions about the fate of his collection after his death, which occurred in June 1978. There were plans to disperse the collection completely, and objectors to this took their appeals as far as President Reagan.

Eventually a series of sales was arranged to bring the collection down to more manageable proportions. These took place in 1984 and 1985, and a nucleus of about 225 cars was rehoused in downtown Reno. The collection is now known as the National Automobile Museum, which has made available for photography many of the cars illustrated in this book.

As well as broad spectrum collectors there are many who specialize in one make or model. Their dedication is amazing. Everitt White of Middletown, Wisconsin, had 150 Corvairs in the late 1970s, although about 50 were parts cars and others were bought and sold as part of his used car business. Don Schneider of Mansfield, Ohio, had 60 Corvairs, mostly 1964–66 models, which were part of a permanent collection. Pennsylvania farmer Hugh Lesley must have the world's largest collection of Edsels, with about 150 at the last count. One way to economize on space is to collect small cars. Paul Gorrell of Burlington, Iowa, restricts himself to Crosleys, of which he has 41, as well as a few King Midgets. He can haul four of these small cars on a trailer behind a van, with a fifth on the van roof, and even squeeze a sixth inside. He has nearly every body style and color Crosley built, and at least three of each year.

Some one-make names may have physical origins. Milwaukee Buick dealer Wally Rank was knocked out cold at the age of three by a Pierce-Arrow. Although he made a full recovery, he says he cannot see a Pierce-Arrow today without wanting to buy it. His last total was 18. One of the most specialized collections is that of Dick de Vecchi of San Lorenzo, California. He has concentrated on 1941 Chevrolets and now has seven, one of every style Chevy offered for that year, including a sedan delivery. Is he content? Not quite. He would like the one-and-only 1941 convertible sedan, a car built up by another enthusiast from two sedans and two convertibles.

A one-year collection which earned its keep was that of the Santa Ynez, California, airport rental fleet, all of which were 1958 Chevrolets. Most were sedans, with a few wagons and a Bel Air hardtop. They were active in 1978, but it is not known if you can still rent a 1958 Chevy at Santa Ynez today.

THE PROFESSIONALS

For many years the old car hobby was just that, a pastime that provided hundreds of happy hours of tinkering and driving for enthusiasts. Nobody made any money out of it, the reverse in fact, although when prices were low, it was more costly in time than in dollars and cents. However in

▼ 1957 PONTIAC BONNEVILLE CONVERTIBLE WITH FUEL INJECTION ENGINE — A PRIZE WINNING CAR.

(PHOTO NICKY WRIGHT)

famous international auction houses such as
Sotheby's and Christies from London. Sotheby's
worked in conjunction with the New York house of
Parke-Bernet, but the best known purely American
company is the Indiana-based Kruse Classic
Auction Company. Well known for real estate and
farm equipment auctions, Kruse made headlines in
January 1973 when it sold an armor-plated
Mercedes-Benz limousine from the Adolf Hitler
stables for $153,000. The following year a
Duesenberg Model J broke the $200,000 barrier,
and in 1979 Christie's sold the Hitler Mercedes-
Benz for $400,000. Throughout the 1980s Kruse
held around 40 auctions annually across the United

the past 30 years or so a growing number of people
have made satisfactory livings out of restoring,
dealing in, and auctioning collector cars of all ages.

The first important American auction took
place in May 1962, when the Wallace C. Bird
collection of classic cars was sold by O'Reilly
Brothers on Long Island. Nine cars realized
$37,850, and the prices of $5,300 for a Duesenberg,
$3,700 for a Hispano-Suiza, and $1,850 for a Bugatti
Type 43 were regarded as very high at the time. An
observer from Parke-Bernet predicted that this was
only the beginning; "Friend, I would advise you to
buy your heart's desire now. I warn you that in ten
years most of you guys will be standing outside the
hobby looking in."

He was right. Prices soon escalated. But even
modest hobbyists were not excluded, for rising
prices meant that the capital value of even a small
collection appreciated accordingly. By the late
1960s a Mercer 35 Raceabout was fetching $45,000,
and during the next decade the importance of old
cars was validated by the entry into the field of

States. Kruse auctions more than 13,000 cars annually, representing more than 75 percent of all collector cars offered for sale in the United States. Including property auctions, their annual volume of sales approaches $1 billion. The current U.S. auction record is the $6.5 million paid by Jerry Moore for a Bugatti Royale in 1986. This car later changed hands privately for $8.1 million, the new owner being pizza king Tom Monaghan. The Bugatti joined his collection of 20 Ferraris, 20 Rolls-Royces, and 28 Duesenbergs.

If one adds to the auctioneers the dealers and professional restorers of old cars, the cars of yesteryear are certainly a multi-million dollar industry, yet for all those who earn a living from it, there are far more who put money into one of the fastest growing hobbies of the late twentieth century.

BIBLIOGRAPHY

Among my reference books, some have been constant and indispensable companions, in particular:

The Standard Catalog of American Cars 1805–1942 by Beverly Rae Kimes and Henry Austin Clark Jr.; Krause Publications, 1989

The Standard Catalog of American Cars 1946–1975 by The Editors of Old Cars publications; Krause Publications, 1982

Fifty Years of American Automobiles from 1939 by The Auto Editors of *Consumer Guide*, 1989

Also the magnificent series of one-make books published by Crestline Publishing, Sarasota, Florida

Seventy Years of Buick by George Dammann, 1973

Cadillac and La Salle by Walter McCall, 1982

Seventy Years of Chrysler by George Dammann, 1974

The Dodge Story by Thomas A. McPherson, 1976

The History of Hudson by Don Butler, 1982

The Cars of Lincoln and Mercury by George Dammann and James K. Wagner, 1987

Seventy Five Years of Oakland and Pontiac by John Gunnell, 1982

The Cars of Oldsmobile by Dennis Casteele, 1981

The Plymouth and De Soto Story by Don Butler, 1979

Many other books consulted include:

American Automobile Manufacturers by John B. Rae, Chilton, Philadelphia, 1959

American Cars, 1930–1942 by James H. Moloney, Crestline, Sarasota, Florida 1977

The American Car Since 1775 by the Editors of *Automobile Quarterly*, New York, 1971

The American Rolls-Royce by Arthur W. Soutter, Mowbray, Providence, Rhode Island, 1976

Automania — Man and the Motorcar by Julian Pettifer and Nigel Turner, Collins, London, 1984

The Automobile and American Culture edited by David L. Lewis and Laurence Goldstein, University of Michigan Press, 1983

Automobiles of America Wayne State University Press, Detroit, 1962

Beetle — the Chronicles of a People's Car by Hans-Rudiger Etzold, Haynes, England, 1988

Cars of Canada by Hugh Durnford and Glenn Baechler, McClelland & Stewart, Toronto, 1973

Cars of 1923 by Keith Marvin and Arthur Lee Homan, Automobilists of the Upper Hudson Valley, Troy, N.Y., 1957

Cars of the 1930s by Michael Sedgwick, B.T. Batsford Ltd, London, 1970

Chevrolet, 1911–1985 by the Auto Editors of *Consumer Guide*, 1984

The Classic Cord by Dan R. Post, Dan Post Publications, Arcadia, California, 1952

The Complete Handbook of Automobile Hobbies edited by Beverly Rae Kimes, Princeton Publishing Inc, Princeton, N.J., 1981

Duesenberg — the Pursuit of Perfection by Fred Roe, Dalton Watson, London, 1982

Encyclopedia of American Cars, 1945–1970 by Richard M. Langworth, Beekman House, New York, 1980

The Fabulous Firebird by Michael Lamm, Lamm-Morada Press, Stockton, California 1979

Fit for the Chase — Cars and the Movies by Raymond Lee, A.S. Barnes & Co, New York, 1969

Ford, 1903–1984 by the Auto Editors of *Consumer Guide*, 1984

Ford, the Dust and the Glory by Leo Levine, Collier-Macmillan, Toronto, 1968

Ford, the Men and the Machine by Robert Lacey, Heinemann, London, 1986

The Great Old Cars, Where Are They Now? by Stanley K. Yost, The Wayside Press, Mendota, Illinois, 1960

Last Onslaught on Detroit by Richard M. Langworth, Automobile Quarterly Publications, New York, 1975

The Motor Car, 1945–1956 by Michael Sedgwick, B.T. Batsford Ltd, London, 1979

Pierce-Arrow by Marc Ralston, A.S. Barnes & Co, New York, 1980

A Record of Motor Racing, 1984–1908 by Gerald Rose, Motor Racing Publications, Abingdon, England, 1949

Rolls-Royce in America by John Webb de Campi, Dalton Watson, London, 1975

The Shell Book of Firsts by Patrick Robertson, Ebury Press, London, 1974

Standard Catalog of Light Duty Trucks edited by John Gunnell, Krause Publications, Iola, Wisconsin, 1987

The Studebaker Century by Asa E. Hall and Richard M. Langworth, Dragonwyck Publishing, Contoocook, New Hampshire, 1983

They Don't Build Cars Like They Used To by Stanley K. Yost, The Wayside Press, Mendota, Illinois, 1963

Turbo — an A to Z of turbocharged cars by Graham Robson, Apple Press, London, 1988

Unsafe at any Speed by Ralph Nader, Grossman Publishers, New York, 1965

US Military Wheeled Vehicles by Fred Crismon, Crestline, Sarasota, Florida, 1983

The VW Beetle by Jonathan Wood, Motor Racing Publications, London, 1983

What was the McFarlan? by Keith Marvin and Alvin J. Arnheim, published privately, 1967

World Guide to Automobiles by Nick Baldwin, Nick Georgano, Brian Laban and Michael Sedgwick, Orbis, London, 1987

Magazines consulted include:

Antique Automobile, Autocar & Motor, Automobile Quarterly, The Upper Hudson Valley Automobilist, Autoweek, Bulb Horn, Car, Car & Driver, Motor Trend, Road & Track, the Society of Automotive Historians Journal and Automotive History Review, Special Interest Autos, Top Wheels

INDEX

Figures in *italics* refer to captions to illustrations.

17, 18, 29; Charles E. 13, 14–15, 274

Earl, Harley J. 87, 107, 113, 194, *194*, 195, *195*, *222*
Eclipse (steam) 24
Edsel *see* Ford
Edwards America 193
Elcar 128, 157
Electric Vehicle Co. 25, 39
Electrobat 16, *16*, 25
Elmore 44
EMF (Everitt-Metzger-Flanders Co.) 45, 47. *See also* Studebaker
Erskine 129. *See also* Studebaker
Essex 80, 87–88, *88*, 129, 178. *See also* Hudson
Ewing 44
Excalibur-J *see* Stevens, Brooks
Exner, Virgil 162, *167*, *189*, *191*

Fageol 56
Flanders 45. *See also* Studebaker
Fleetwood (coachbuilder) 104, 112, *127*, 130, 131, *131*, *132*, *133*, 144. *See also under* Cadillac
Flint 89, 91
Ford 17, *18*, 33–34, *41*, 42, 44, 47, 52, 91, 94, 106, 120, 155, 157, 160, 173, 176, 177, *177*, 180, 187, 189, 202, 210, 211, 216, 227, 237, 240, 241, 250, 262, *262*, 265, 276; **999** 33, *33*; Aerocar 36; Bronco *42*, *76*; Comet 203; concept cars *270*; Crown Victoria 236, *268*; Edsel 198, *199*, 201–2, 281; Escort 227, 231, 232, 237, 245, 256; EXP 232; Fairlane 201, 203; Falcon 183, *202*, 203, 204, *206*, 209, 228; Galaxie 203, *213*, 217; Granada *259*; Limited II *233*; Maverick 203, *205*, *259*; Model A 34, *78*, 81, *81*, 83–85, 87, 90, 121, 129, 144, 146, 154, 164; Model B 34–36, 49, 87, 121; Model C 34; Model K 34, 36, 49, 55, 81; Model N *34*, 36, 37; Model R 37; Model S 37; Model T 32, 36, *36*, 37–39, *38*, 45, 48, 49, 56, *60*, 65, 66, 80–81, *81*, 83, *83*, 84, *84*, 85, 88, 89, 99, 113, 124, 125, 141, 154, 164, 177, 280, 281; Mustang 203, 205, 206, 207, *208*, 209–11, *210*, *211*, 213, 215, 245, 251, 256, 278, *282*; Pinto *226*, *227*, 230, 232, 237–38; Probe *262*; Quadricycle 18, 280; Skyliner *143*, *200*; Sportsman 161, *170*, 171; station wagons 154, *155*; Taurus 244, 245, *245*, *246*, 256, 257, 265, *268*, *271*; Tempo 237, 256; Thunderbird 197, *197*, 198, *198*, 201, 209, 232, 247, 251, 256, 278; Torino *233*; V8s 33, 104, 116, 121, *121*, 123, 124, 125, 129, 137, 153, *163*, 166, 192, 251, 278
Ford, Edsel 18, 81, 83, 85, 105–6, 125, 134, 137, 141, 161
Ford, Henry 17, 18, *18*, 19, *19*, 24, 29, 32–33, *33*, 34, *34*, 36, 37, 38, 39, *39*, 42, 45, 48, 49, 66, 81–83, 84, 85, 89, 102, 105–6, 121, 124-25, 134, 161, 270, 280; Henry Ford Co. 33; Henry Ford Museum 280
Ford, Henry, II 161, 166, *171*, 198, 201, 202, 209, 238, 262
Ford, William Clay 202, 262
Franklin *52*, 55, 57, 63, 70, 112, *117*, 133, 135, 157, 280, *281*
Frazer 164, 186, 278; Frazer, Joseph W. 163. *See also* Kaiser-Frazer
Fritchle (electric) 71
Frontenac 48, 91
F.R.P. 94, 104. *See also* Porter

Gardner 128
Garford Co. 45
Gatsby Griffin (Scepter) 251
Gearless (steam) 111
General Motors (GM) 40, *40*, 42–44, *42*, 46, 47, 48, 49, 59, 81, 85, 87, 88, 90, *90*, 91, 94, 107, 112, 113, 123, 125, 126, 130, *131*, 144, 149, 154, 155, 157, 160, 161, 166, 175, 183, 186, 193, 194, *194*, 195, 197, 198, 204, 205, 207, *207*, 211–12, *222*, *228*, 230, 236, *237*, 238, 240, 241, 242, *242*, 246, 247, 249, 250, 259,

260, *260*, 262–63, 265, 266, *266*, *267*
Geo 232, 257, 259, *259*, 262
Glover (five-wheeler) 68
GM *see* General Motors
Gordon Diamond *68*
Graham 128–29, 154; Graham brothers 128; Graham-Paige 128, 163
Green Bay (steam) 11, 13, 21
Gregorie, Bob 137, 141, 166, *171*
Gregory 173
Greyhound (cyclecar) 65

HAL 59
Hanson 94
Harrah, William Fisk 280; Harrah collection *see* National Automobile Museum
Hayes Body Co. 127, 146, 147
Haynes *14*, *52*, *53*, 92; Haynes-Apperson 15, *15*; Haynes, Elwood P. *14*, 15, 45, *53*
Heine-Velox 107, 108; Heine, Gustav Otto 107
Henry J. *see* Kaiser-Frazer
Hershey, Franklin Quick 114, *120*, 197
Hess & Eisenhardt (coachbuilder) 241, 254
Hewitt 57
Holbrook (coachbuilder) 108, 112, *112*, 116, 142
Holsman (buggy) 63, 65; Holsman, Henry 63
Homer-Laughlin 59
Honda 68, 92, 260, 263, *264*, 265, 268
Hood (steam) 24
Horseless Carriage Club of America (HCCA) 274, 275
Hudson 59, 73, 80, 110, 128, 130, *130*, 154, 155, 160, 163, 164, 168, 169, 177–78, 180, 181, *181*, 189; Commodore 168; Eight 129, *129*, 157; Hornet 178; Jet 178; Model 20 *44*; Pacemaker *168*; Super Six 87; Wasp *168*, 178
Hupmobile *44*, *46*, 128–29, *128*, 154; Hupp, Robert 46

Iacocca, Lee *202*, 203, 209, 230, 241, 259, 262, 268–69, *270*
Imp (cyclecar) *64*
Impact (electric) 249
Imperial *see under* Chrysler
Ingram Hatch (kerosene) 68; Ingram, Joseph 68
International Harvester (I.H.C.) 29, 63, 65, *66*
Isuzu 257, 259, *259*

Jackson 59
Jeep *42*, 90, 144, 147, 160, *178* 186, 204, 260, 262. *See also* American Motors Corp.; Chrysler; Willys
Jeffery *42*. *See also* Nash
J.I. Case Co. *11*, 13. *See also* Case
Jordan 73, 96, 97, *97*, 110, 128, 157; Jordan, Ned *42*, 97, *97*
Judkins (coachbuilder) 55, 105, 108, 112, 116, 135, 142, 143, 144

Kaiser, Henry J. 163, 164, 177, 186
Kaiser-Frazer 47, 129, 162, 173, 175, *176*, 203; Henry J. *176*, 177, *177*, 178, 180, 186, 193; K-100 *162*; Kaiser-Darrin 193; Manhattan *186*; Special 163; Traveler 164; Virginian 164
Kaiser-Jeep Corp. 186; Kaiser-Willys Sales Corp. 186
Kearns (highwheeler) 63
Keller 173; Keller, George 173
Kenworthy 108; Kenworthy, Cloyd Y. 107–8
Kiblinger (highwheeler) 63
King 92, 104; King, Charles Brady 17–18, *19*, 45
King Midget 278, 281
Kissel 96, 97, 110, 128, 129, 157
Knox 39
Knudsen, William S. 29, 85
Kurtis 192–93; Kurtis, Frank 192–93

Laconia (cyclecar) 65
Lambert 15; Lambert, John William 15
LaSalle 87, 88–89, *105*. 106–7, 110, 113, 126, 131, 137, 154, *222*
LeBaron (coachbuilder) 112, *113*, *114*, 116, 133, 134, *135*, *136*, 142, 143, *187*, *189*, 241. *See also* under Chrysler
Leland: Henry 19, 31, 33, 34, *34*, 104–6; Wilfred 104–6
Lincoln 104–6, 124, 133, 134, *135*, 142, 154, 160, *164*, 166, *169*, 189, 192, 193, 200, 209, 235, 237, 241, 251, 268, 276; Continental 139, 141, *141*, 144, 155, *200*, 201, 202–3, 206, 276; Custom 141, 155; K Series 143–44; Premiere 202; Touring *112*, Town Car 254–56, *255*; V12 125, 130, 131, 134–35, *137*, 139, 276; Zephyr 125, 135, 137, 139, 141, *141*, 148, 152, 276
Littlemac 144
Locke (coachbuilder) 101, 108, 112, *112*, 116, 142
Locomobile 23–24, *23* (steam); 25, 31, 39, 69, 70, 91, 104,106, 109, 112, 113, *117*; Model 48 57, 99; Model 90 99–100; Sportif 57
Loewy Studios *161*, *184*; Loewy, Raymond 162, 183, 184
Long Island Automotive Museum 280
Lozier 55

MacDonald (steam) 111
McFarlan 99, 102–3, 104
McKay (steam) 21
McNamara, Robert 161, 197–98, 201, 203
Malcomson, Alexander Young 33, 34, *34*, 36
Marathon Six 147
Marion 95
Marmon 39, 96, 110, 113, 130, 131–33, 176; Marmon, Colonel Howard C. 131
Mason 48, 108; Mason, Arthur 48. *See also* Duesenberg
Mason, George 176–77 180, 181, 194
Maxim (electric) 24–25; Maxim, Hiram Percy 24
Maxwell 74, 94, 116, 281; Maxwell-Briscoe 39, 42, 45, *45*, 46, 47; Maxwell-Chalmers 47; Maxwell, Jonathan D. 44, 45, *45*, 47
Mayfair 39
Mazda 68, 92, 232–33. *262*
Mercer 47, 94–95, *95*, 96, *96*, 104, 276, 282
Mercury 85, 124, 125, 144, 164, 166, *171*, 187, 189, 193, 198, *199*, 202, 209, 236, 237, *276*; Bobcat 232, 256; Cougar 212, 240, 256; Grand Marquis 256, 265; LN7 232; Lynx 232; Marquis 235; Monterey 165, 235; Park Lane 201; Sable 244, 245, 256, 257, 265, *268*; Sportsman 161; Topaz 256; Tracer 256
Metz *66*; Metz, Charles *66*
Milburn (electric) 71
Milestone Car Society 278
Minerva 45, 112
Mitchell 39, 92
Mitsubishi 259, 260, 262, 265
Mobile (steam) *8*, *22*, 23–24, *23*, 46, 70
Model T *see* Ford
Moloney (coachbuilder) 254, *254*
Moon 29, 98, 128, 129
Mors 32
Mueller-Benz 16, 17
Multiplex 193
Muntz 193, 237, 240; Muntz, Earl 192–93
Murphy, Walter M. (coachbuilder) 108, 109, 112, *113*, 114, 116, 130, 133, 135, 142
Murray Corp. (coachbuilder) 128, *136*

Nader, Ralph 205, 237
Nance, James 181, 182, 183
Napier 55, 58, 75
Nash *42*, 92, 123, 128, 154, 155, 160, 168, *181*, 189, 240;

ACKNOWLEDGMENTS

Nick Georgano would like to thank the numerous people who helped in the research for this book, especially Keith Marvin and Beverly Rae Kimes, who answered a barrage of queries with kindness and good humour. Also Lynda Springate and her staff at the Library of the National Motor Museum, Beaulieu, Hampshire, England.

Others who helped include Charles L. Betts Jr., James T. Billings Public Relations Director of Kruse International, Homer D. Brown, Christopher Foster, Jack Heald, Wade Hoyt, editor of *MoTor* magazine, Linda Huntsman, Research Librarian at the National Automobile Museum, Reno, Nevada, Richard Langworth, Professor David Lewis of the University of Michigan, Walter McCall, G. Marshall Naul, and Barney C. Pollard.

Nicky Wright would like to thank the following museums and people for the special help they gave:
  Auburn-Cord-Duesenberg Museum, Auburn, Indiana
  Gilmore Car Museum, Kalamazoo, Michigan
  Jim Ransom
  National Automobile Museum, (William F. Harrah
    Foundation), Reno, Nevada
  Western Reserve Historical Society, Cleveland, Ohio

He would also like to thank: Chris Anderson, Harvey Anderson, Tom & Karen Barnes, Patricia Beck, Jim Bell, Larry Bell, Russ Bell, Steve & Evelyn Benn, Mr. & Mrs. James Beversdorf, Dan Blakely, Rod Butler, Dell Casters, Dick Choler, Randy Daniels, Jonathan Day, Fuji Film, Ira Gamble, Dick Ginther, Bill Goodsene, William Goodwin, Steven C. Graham/A-C-D Museum, Mrs. Cynthia Haines, Charles Hilton, Biff Hitzeman, Dave Holcombe, Blaine Jenkins & Phil, Robert A. Jordan, Rod Lungstrom, Bob MacMillam, Skip Marketti, Mike Myers, Lee Muzzila, National Motor Museum, Beaulieu, England, Nikon Cameras, Pentax Cameras, Scott Pirsak, Gene Povinelli, George Sanders, Barney Smith, Less Sterling, Unique Color Lab, Ft. Wayne, Indiana, Gary & Sharon Vick, Tim Woods

Mirco De Cet would like to thank the following people and organizations for their help with picture research: Helen Gray at Ford Motor Co. Public Relations dept. Dearborn, Michigan. The Henry Ford Museum, Dearborn, Michigan. Linda Busse at the MVMA, Detroit, Michigan. Helen Early and James Walkinshaw at the Oldsmobile History Center, Lansing, Michigan. Lawrence Gustin at Buick Motor Div. Public Relations Dept., Flint, Michigan. Richard Scharchburg at the GMI Archives, Flint, Michigan.

TREASURY OF LITERATURE

OUT OF THIS WORLD

SENIOR AUTHORS

ROGER C. FARR
DOROTHY S. STRICKLAND

AUTHORS

RICHARD F. ABRAHAMSON
ELLEN BOOTH CHURCH
BARBARA BOWEN COULTER
BERNICE E. CULLINAN
MARGARET A. GALLEGO
W. DORSEY HAMMOND
JUDITH L. IRVIN
KAREN KUTIPER
DONNA M. OGLE
TIMOTHY SHANAHAN
PATRICIA SMITH
JUNKO YOKOTA
HALLIE KAY YOPP

SENIOR CONSULTANTS

ASA G. HILLIARD III
JUDY M. WALLIS

CONSULTANTS

ALONZO A. CRIM
ROLANDO R. HINOJOSA-SMITH
LEE BENNETT HOPKINS
ROBERT J. STERNBERG

HARCOURT BRACE & COMPANY

Orlando   Atlanta   Austin   Boston   San Francisco   Chicago   Dallas   New York
Toronto   London

Acknowledgments continue on page 622, which constitutes an extension of this copyright page.

Acknowledgments
For permission to reprint copyrighted material, grateful acknowledgment is made to the following sources:
Alurista: "address" from *Floricanto en Aztlán* by Alurista. Copyright © 1971 by Aztlán Publications, UCLA.
Atheneum Publishers, an imprint of Macmillan Publishing Company: From *From the Mixed-up Files of Mrs. Basil E. Frankweiler* by E. L. Konigsburg. Copyright © 1967 by E. L. Konigsburg. From *Beetles, Lightly Toasted* by Phyllis Reynolds Naylor. Text copyright © 1987 by Phyllis Reynolds Naylor.
Avon Books: Cover illustration from *S. O. R. Losers* by Avi. Copyright © 1984 by Avi Wortis.
Bradbury Press, an Affiliate of Macmillan, Inc.: Cover illustration from *Her Seven Brothers* by Paul Goble. Copyright © 1988 by Paul Goble. Cover photograph by Lyn Topinka from *Volcano: The Eruption and Healing of Mount St. Helens* by Patricia Lauber. Cover photograph courtesy of United States Department of the Interior, U. S. Geological Survey, David A. Johnston Cascades Volcano Observatory, Vancouver, Washington. From *Hatchet* by Gary Paulsen. Text copyright © 1987 by Gary Paulsen. Cover illustration by Pat Cummings from *Mariah Loves Rock* by Mildred Pitts Walter. Illustration copyright © 1988 by Pat Cummings.
Brandt & Brandt Literary Agents, Inc.: "Johnny Appleseed" from *A Book of Americans* by Stephen Vincent Benét and Rosemary Carr Benét. Text copyright 1933 by Rosemary and Stephen Vincent Benét; copyright renewed © 1961 by Rosemary Carr Benét.
Carolrhoda Books, Inc., Minneapolis, MN: Cover photograph from *Space Challenger: The Story of Guion Bluford* by Jim Haskins and Kathleen Benson. Cover photograph courtesy of the National Aeronautics and Space Administration. Cover illustration from *Song of the Chirimia* by Jane Anne Volkmer. Copyright © 1990 by Carolrhoda Books, Inc.
Cobblehill Books, an affiliate of Dutton Children's Books, a division of Penguin Books USA Inc.: Cover illustration by Elton C. Fax from *Take a Walk in Their Shoes* by Glennette Tilley Turner. Illustration copyright © 1989 by Elton C. Fax.
Crown Publishers, Inc.: Cover illustration by Mary Rayner from *Babe: The Gallant Pig* by Dick King-Smith. Illustration copyright © 1983 by Mary Rayner.
Delacorte Press, a division of Bantam Doubleday Dell Publishing Group, Inc.: Cover illustration by Richard Lauter from *The War with Grandpa* by Robert Kimmel Smith. Illustration copyright © 1984 by Richard Lauter.
Dell Books, a division of Bantam Doubleday Dell Publishing Group, Inc.: From *Tornado! Poems* by Arnold Adoff, illustrated by Ronald Himler. Text copyright © 1976, 1977 by Arnold Adoff; illustrations copyright © 1977 by Ronald Himler. Cover photograph by Franke Keating from *Walter Warthog* by Betty Leslie-Melville. Copyright © 1989 by Betty Leslie-Melville.
The Dille Family Trust: "Tiger Men of Mars" Buck Rogers® cartoon from *The Collected Works of Buck Rogers in the 25th Century.* © 1929–1967, 1969, 1993 by The Dille Family Trust. Color added to original illustrations with permission.
Dover Publications, Inc.: Text and illustrations from *The American Revolution: A Picture Sourcebook* by John Grafton. Copyright © 1975 by Dover Publications, Inc.
Farrar, Straus & Giroux, Inc.: From *A Wrinkle in Time* by Madeleine L'Engle. Text copyright © 1962 by Madeleine L'Engle Franklin; text copyright renewed © 1990 by Crosswicks, Ltd.; cover illustration copyright © 1979 by Leo and Diane Dillon. From *Whose Side Are You On?* by Emily Moore. Text copyright © 1988 by Emily Moore. Adapted from *The Green Book* by Jill Paton Walsh, cover illustration by Peter Catalanotto. Text copyright © 1982 by Jill Paton Walsh; cover illustration copyright © 1986 by Peter Catalanotto.
Harcourt Brace & Company: From *In for Winter, Out for Spring* by Arnold Adoff, illustrated by Jerry Pinkney. Text copyright © 1991 by Arnold Adoff; illustrations copyright © 1991 by Jerry Pinkney. Cover illustration by Paul Bacon from *Teammates* by Peter Golenbock. Illustration copyright © 1990 by Paul Bacon. From *The Bells of Christmas* by Virginia Hamilton, illustrated by Lambert Davis. Text copyright © 1989 by Virginia Hamilton; illustrations copyright © 1989 by Lambert Davis. From *The Riddle of Penncroft Farm* by Dorothea G. Jensen. Text copyright © 1989 by Dorothea G. Jensen. From *Monarchs* by Kathryn Lasky Knight, photographs by Christopher G. Knight. Text copyright © 1993 by Kathryn Lasky Knight; illustrations copyright © 1993 by Christopher G. Knight. From *Slabs of the Sunburnt West* by Carl Sandburg. Copyright 1922 by Harcourt Brace & Company; copyright renewed 1950 by Carl Sandburg. "La Bamba" from *Baseball in April and Other Stories* by Gary Soto. Text copyright © 1990 by Gary Soto. Originally published in *Fiction Network.* Illustrations from *Many Moons* by James Thurber, illustrated by Marc Simont. Illustrations copyright © 1990 by Marc Simont. Cover illustration by Louis Slobodkin from *Many Moons* by James Thurber. Copyright 1943 by James Thurber, renewed 1971 by Helen Thurber. *New Providence: A Changing Cityscape* by Renata von Tscharner, Ronald Lee Fleming and The Townscape Institute, illustrated by Denis Orloff and The Townscape Institute. Text copyright © 1987 by Renata von Tscharner, Ronald Lee Fleming and The Townscape Institute, Inc.; illustrations copyright © 1987 by The Townscape Institute, Inc. and Denis Orloff. From *Pride of Puerto Rico: The Life of Roberto Clemente* by Paul Robert Walker. Text copyright © 1988 by Harcourt Brace & Company. Pronunciation Key from *HBJ School Dictionary*, Third Edition. Text copyright © 1990 by Harcourt Brace & Company.

continued on page 622

TREASURY OF LITERATURE

Dear Reader,

When you think of your world, what do you see? Your neighborhood? Your school? The planet Earth? What do you think life is like for people beyond your world? The literature in this anthology will take you out of your own world and into the lives of people from all corners of the globe and all corners of the imagination.

Begin by taking a look at the strange world of America as seen through the eyes of Shirley Temple Wong, who has moved to America from China. Then play baseball with young Roberto Clemente in his world of the Barrio San Antón in Puerto Rico. Later, you can run through the fields of the flat, golden land of the Kansas prairie and then join Thomas Small as he explores a house that was once a station on the Underground Railroad.

You may find yourself wiping your brow as you experience—with Bird Wing and her mother—the hottest day on record in the Sonoran Desert. Keep reading, and you'll want to button your coat as you journey to the snowy world of a Vermont farm to help the Lacey family tap sugar maple trees. Finally, in a unit about flights, you will rocket into space with astronaut Sally Ride and have the chance to look back at the "sparkling blue oceans and bright orange deserts" of Earth.

Join us as we travel around the block, around the world, and beyond the solar system. As you visit these exciting places, keep your eyes open for people with experiences and feelings just like your own. Keep your mind open, too, and try to see each world through their eyes. We hope that these literary travels may return you to your world with new insights, interests, and delights.

Sincerely,
The Authors

OUT OF THIS WORLD

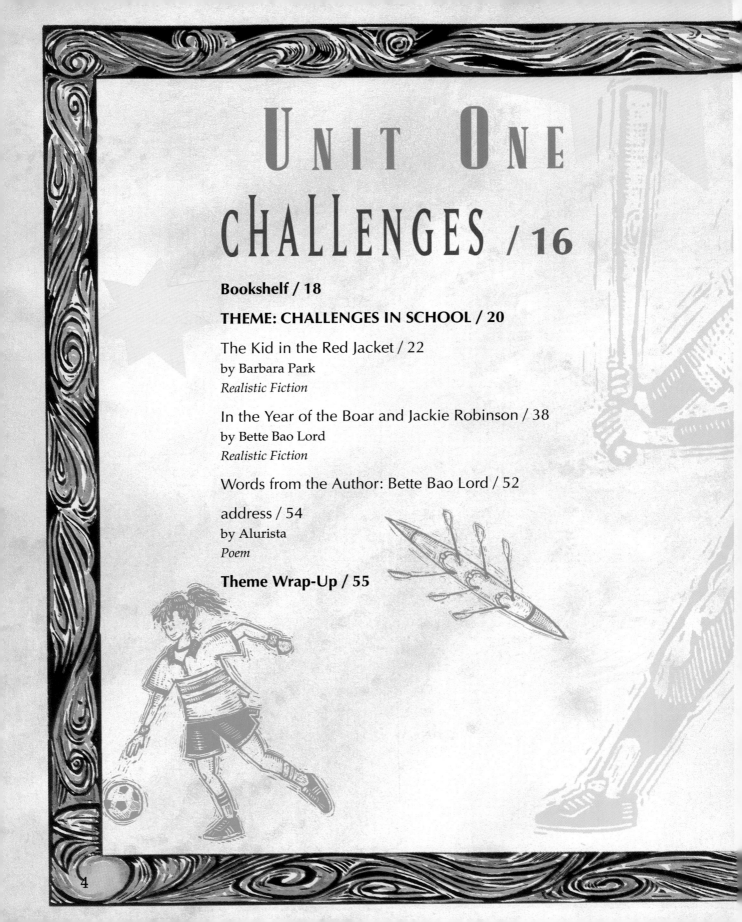

UNIT ONE
cHaLLenges / 16

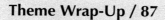

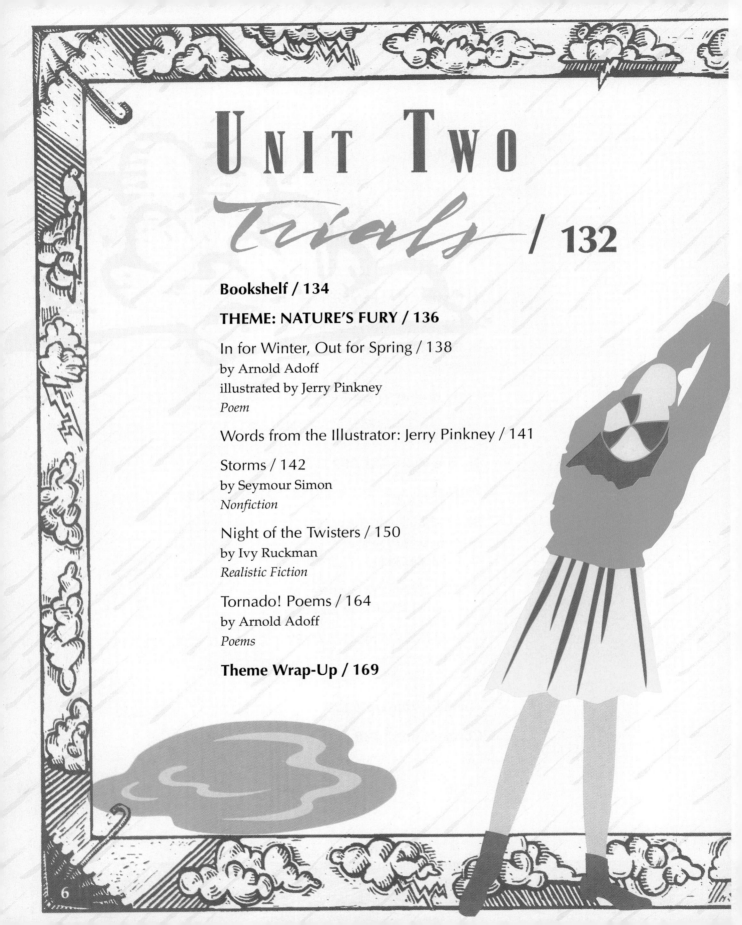

UNIT TWO
Trials / 132

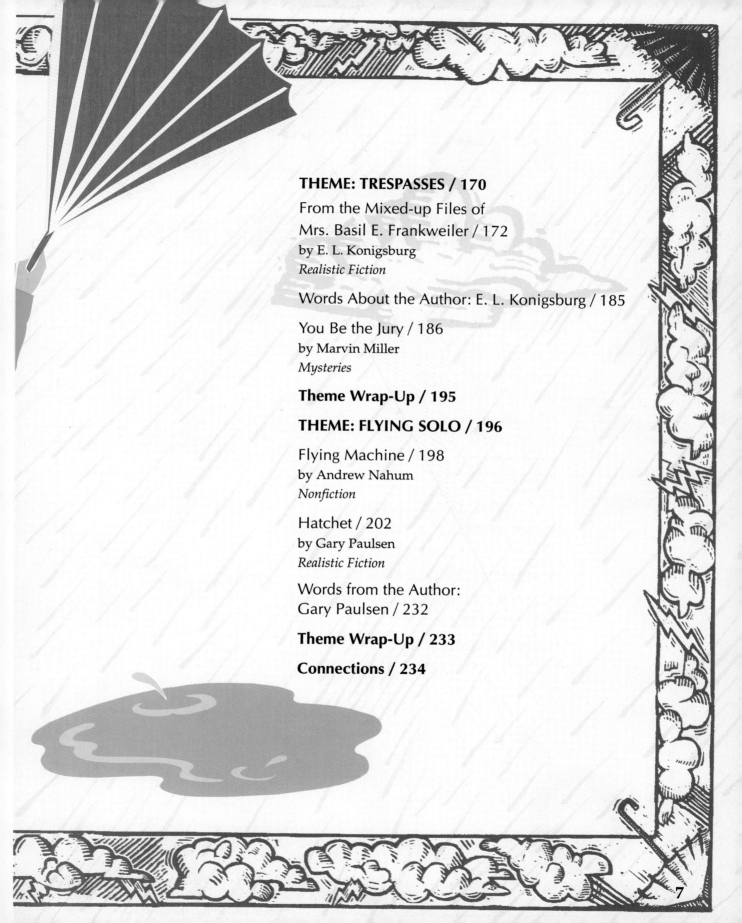

UNIT THREE

YESTERYEAR / 236

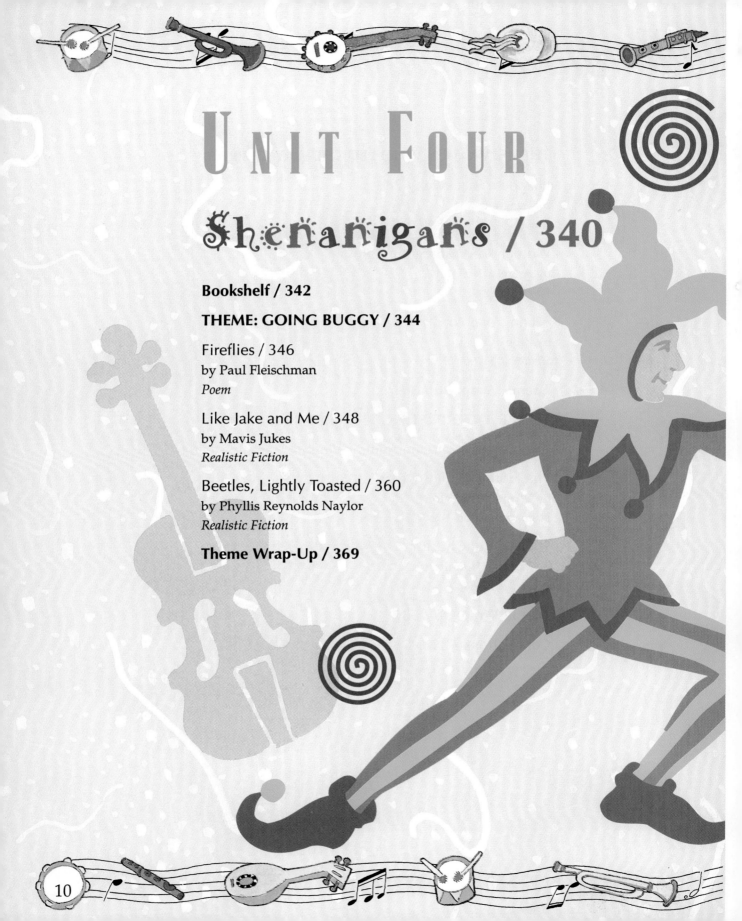

UNIT FOUR

Shenanigans / 340

UNIT FIVE

Lifelines / 424

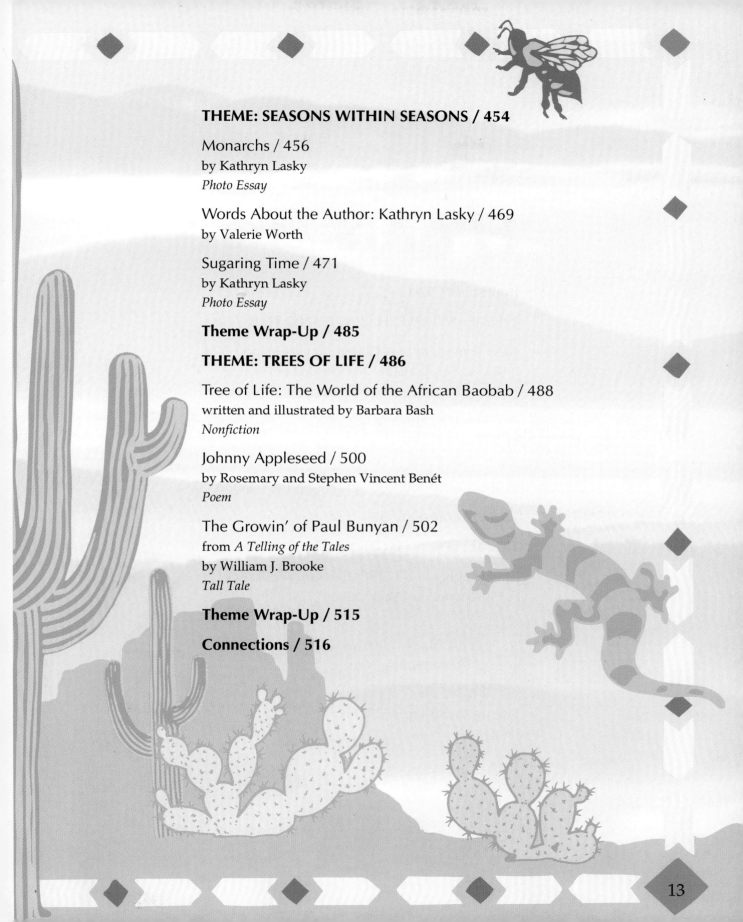

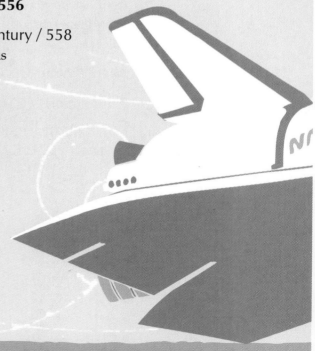

Unit Six

Flights / 518

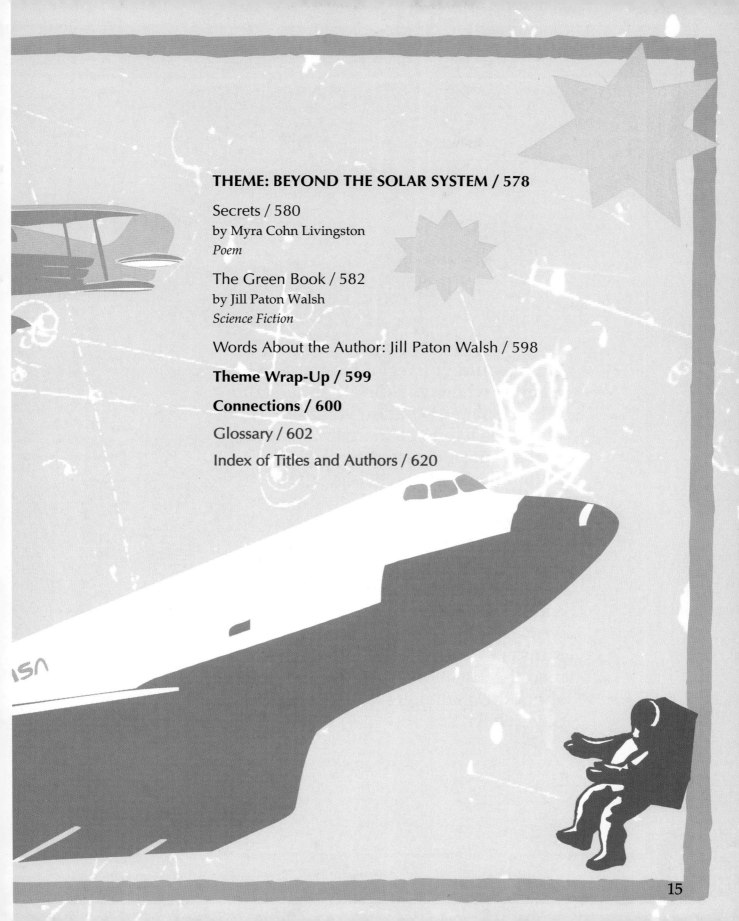

UNIT ONE

CHALLENGES

How would you feel if you moved to a country where you didn't understand the language? What do you think it would be like to be in Spain, Mexico, or the Philippines and to play an unfamiliar sport such as jai alai[hī´lī] for the very first time? These are the kinds of challenges that face some of the characters in this unit. Read about a young girl from China who finds herself in the middle of a strange game called *stickball*. Step into the shoes of a woman from Maine who travels to Kansas to join a new family. As you read the selections in this unit, think about the challenges you face from day to day.

THEMES

BOOKSHELF

THE KID IN THE RED JACKET

by Barbara Park

Howard and his family move to a new home 1,000 miles away, where everything is different and where no one knows his name.

Children's Choice, SLJ Best Books of the Year, Parents' Choice

Harcourt Brace Library Book

TEAMMATES

by Peter Golenbock

In 1947, a great social change came to American sports. Jackie Robinson became the first African American baseball player to be signed by a major league team—the Brooklyn Dodgers.

NCSS Notable Trade Book in the Field of Social Studies

Harcourt Brace Library Book

MARIAH LOVES ROCK

by Mildred Pitts Walter

Mariah loves rock music and is eagerly looking forward to the big concert. But the arrival of her half-sister might ruin everything.

Award-Winning Author

DEAR MR. HENSHAW

by Beverly Cleary

Leigh Botts writes a letter to his favorite author, Mr. Henshaw. When the famous author writes back, Leigh finds himself drawn into sharing more and more about his life.

Newbery Medal, SLJ Best Books of the Year

THE FACTS AND FICTIONS OF MINNA PRATT

by Patricia MacLachlan

As she plays her many roles in life—the daughter, the sister, the friend, the musician—Minna Pratt struggles to sort out the facts from the fictions.

ALA Notable Book

THEME

Challenges in School

→

Have you ever been the "new kid" in a school? How did you deal with the many challenges that faced you? The following selections describe new kids who are determined to meet their challenges head-on.

CONTENTS

The Kid in the Red Jacket

When Howard's parents decide to move to Rosemont, Massachusetts, Howard is reluctant to go. He doesn't want to be a new kid, on a new block, in a new school.

As the school year begins, Howard is anxious to make friends. Unfortunately, the only person who befriends him is Molly Vera Thompson, his pesky six-year-old neighbor.

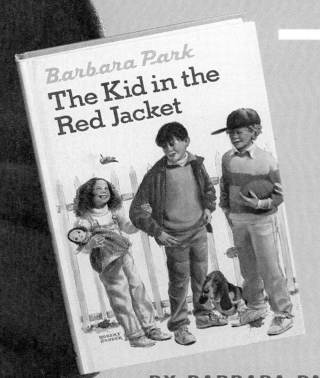

BY BARBARA PARK

ILLUSTRATED BY MICHAEL GARLAND

23

On my second day at school, believe it or not, I walked there with Molly Vera Thompson.

I was about halfway down the street when I first heard her.

"Hey! Hey, you! Howard Jeeper! Wait up! It's Molly Vera Thompson!"

I knew this was going to happen. I just knew it. But even though I had begged and begged for someone to drive me, both Mom and Dad had refused.

"One reason we bought this house was so that you could walk," my father informed me. "The exercise will be good for you."

"Hey, I said! Hold it!" she shouted again.

Two girls walking on the other side of the street started to laugh.

What was I supposed to do? If I didn't stop, she'd just keep shouting her head off. And if I ran, she'd run after me. Finally, I bent down, pretended to tie my shoe, and waited for her to catch up. The way I figured it, walking to school with a first-grader is bad enough, but being chased by one to school is even worse.

"That was close!" she yelled, running up behind me. "For a minute there I didn't think you heard me or something!"

Why was she still shouting? I was standing right next to her.

"Shhh!" I ordered. "Not so loud."

Molly's voice got quieter as she looked around us. "Why? Is someone listening?"

"Only the whole world."

Molly just shrugged her shoulders and fell into step as I started walking again. We had only gone a couple of yards when she wrinkled up her nose and started to giggle.

"This is fun, isn't it, Howard Jeeper?"

I started walking a little faster.

"Hey! How's the weather up there?" she called, looking up at me. Then she started laughing like it was the funniest thing anyone had ever said.

I didn't answer. What was I supposed to say? Cloudy, with a chance of rain?

"Hey!" she persisted. "What's wrong? Cat got your tongue this morning?" Her legs hurried faster and faster, trying to keep up with me. "That's what my nonny says to me sometimes. 'Cat got your tongue, young lady?' she'll say. It means that you're being quiet."

"Yeah, right," I responded. I wasn't paying attention, of course. All I wanted to do was get to school before anyone saw the two of us together.

"Hey! Why are we walking so fast? Are we in a hurry?"

"Nope," I answered simply. "I always walk this fast. That's why you probably shouldn't walk with me. It's probably not good for a little kid like you."

"No. It's okay," she replied, huffing and puffing beside me. "I like to walk fast. It kind of bobs you up and down, doesn't it? See how fast my legs are going?"

Suddenly I started to run. I just didn't want to be with her anymore, that's all. I knew she couldn't catch me. And since I was getting closer to the playground, I couldn't risk the embarrassment of what she might do when we got there.

This time Molly didn't even try to keep up. As soon as I started to sprint, she stopped to watch me go.

I didn't feel guilty, either. Maybe I should have, but I didn't. Only a few more yards and I would be across the street, heading toward the gate of the playground. Alone. I was just about ready to breathe a sigh of relief when I heard it.

Still on the sidewalk where I left her, Molly had cupped her hands around her mouth like a megaphone and was shouting in the loudest voice I ever heard: *Hey, Howard Jeeper! Why're you running? Do you have to go to the potty?*

I wanted to die. I didn't stop running until I got inside the building. I know the whole playground must have heard. I tried not to look at anyone's face as I ran, but I could hear people laughing, so I'm sure they heard. They probably even heard on playgrounds in Russia.

The bell hadn't rung yet when I got to my classroom, but there were already three kids sitting down. One of them was the girl who sits in front of me. She didn't say hi or anything, but as it turned out, she was the first one in my class to talk to me. After I sat down, she turned around and asked if I would mind getting my big feet off the back of her chair.

"They're not big," I answered.

It wasn't much of a conversation, but when you're desperate, you appreciate almost anything.

At lunch, I sat by myself again. Only this time I picked a seat next to the wall so I could sort of blend in with the bricks.

As I started to eat I realized that a lot of the guys in my class were sitting at the next table. And since I was blending in with the wall pretty good, I could watch them without being too obvious. The guy I watched the most was this kid named Pete. I guess I was sort of scouting him out to see what kind of friend he'd make. Scouting is what they do in professional sports. It's a sporty word for spying.

I thought Pete might be someone I could like. I had noticed him on the soccer field. He was pretty athletic, you could tell that. And he wasn't a ball hog. Pete was the kid who had passed me the ball right before I took my big shot.

The good thing about Pete was that when my kick didn't go in, he didn't start swearing or anything. When you get to be my age, swearing comes pretty easily, especially when someone blows a chance for a goal.

The other kid that I couldn't help noticing was this guy named Ollie. You could tell that he was the wise-guy type. He was real loud, and he talked a lot, and practically everything that came out of his mouth was a joke. He seemed like the kind of kid that grownups can't stand but kids sort of admire. The thing is, to be a wise guy in class takes guts. Kids admire guts. Adults don't. It's that simple.

When Ollie sat down, he took one look inside his lunch bag and held his nose. Then, without saying a word, he stood up and threw the whole thing into the garbage can. Back at the table, someone asked him what his mother had packed.

Ollie was still holding his nose. "Something dead and a cookie."

It really cracked me up. Something dead and a cookie. I was sitting all by myself, but I laughed out loud.

After that some kid threw Ollie an orange to eat. Instead of peeling it, he put the whole thing right into his mouth. It must have hurt his mouth to stretch it that far, but that's the great thing about wise guys. When it comes to acting stupid, they know no limit.

Anyway, when Ollie was standing there with that orange in his mouth, even Pete cracked up. You could tell by the expression on his face that he thought Ollie was acting like an idiot, but he still thought it was funny. Even quiet guys like Pete enjoy a good idiot once in a while.

It might sound dumb, but after lunch I felt like I knew the guys in my class a little better. I guess that's why at recess I hung around the group that was getting ready to play soccer. I was sure somebody would pick me. Maybe they'd pick me last, but I'd get picked. It's sort of this unwritten rule every kid knows. If you're standing there to play, somebody's got to pick you, even if you stink.

Just like the day before, Pete and this kid Joe were the captains. Pete picked me before Joe did. I didn't get chosen first or anything; but I wasn't last, either. A kid with his ankle in a cast was last. Still, it felt good when Pete chose me. All of a sudden

he just looked over at me and said, "I'll take the kid in the red jacket."

It's funny. I used to think that being called something like that would really bother me. But the weird thing was, being

called the kid in the red jacket hardly bothered me at all. Let's face it, after a couple of days of not being called anything, almost any name sounds good.

My father gave me some advice. He's tried this kind of thing before, but it's never worked out too well. The trouble is, most of the time his advice is about stuff he doesn't know how to do. Like during basketball season, he'll tell me how to shoot a lay-up. Then he'll shoot a lay-up and miss. It's hard to take advice like that.

"Horn in," he said one night at dinner. I was explaining how much I hated to eat lunch alone, and he looked right up from his pork chop and said, "Horn in."

"Er, horn in?" I repeated, confused. I guess it must be one of those old-time expressions they don't use much anymore.

"Sure. Be a little pushy. Stand up for yourself," he went on. "You can't wait for the whole world to beat a path to your door."

"Beat a path to my door?" I asked again. Another old-time expression, I think.

"That means you can't wait for everyone else to come to you, son," he explained. "Sometimes you've just got to take the bull by the horns."

"Oh geez. Not more horns," I groaned.

"Bull by the horns," repeated Dad. "Haven't you ever heard that before? It means you've got to get right in there and take charge. If you don't want to eat alone, then sit right down at the lunch table with the rest of them. Just walk up there tomorrow, put your lunch on the table, and say, 'Mind if I join you, fellas?' That's all there is to it."

I didn't say anything, but kids just don't go around talking like that. If a kid came up to a bunch of guys eating lunch and said, "Mind if I join you, fellas?" the whole table would fall on the floor laughing.

Still, I knew what Dad was getting at. I think it's something all new kids learn sooner or later. Even if you're the shy type, you have to get a little bold if you want to make any friends. You have to say hi and talk to people, even if it makes you nervous. Sometimes you even have to sit down at a lunch table without being invited. You don't have to say, "Mind if I join you, fellas?" though. I'm almost positive of that.

I have to admit that the "horning in" part worked out pretty well. The next day at lunch I took a deep breath, sat down at the table with the other guys, and started eating. That was that. No one seemed to mind, really. They hardly even stared.

After that it got easier. Once kids have seen you at their table, it's not as hard to accept you the next time. Then pretty soon they figure that you must belong, or you wouldn't be sitting there every day.

I'm not saying that after horning in I automatically started to love Rosemont, Massachusetts. All I mean is, the more days that passed, the less I felt like an outsider. I guess you'd say stuff started feeling more familiar. Like at school, if a stranger had asked me for directions, I could have steered him to all the

water fountains and lavatories. For some reason, knowing your lavatories sort of gives you a feeling of belonging.

I guess moving to a new school is like anything else you hate. Even though you can't stand the thought of it, and you plan to hate it for the rest of your life, after you've been doing it for a while, you start getting used to it. And after you start getting used to it, you forget to hate it as much as you'd planned. I think it's called adjusting. I've given this some thought, and I've decided that adjusting is one of those things that you can't control that much. It's like learning to like girls. It sort of makes you nauseous to think about it, but you know it's going to happen.

Did you feel Howard's day at school was miserable, funny, or both? Explain your answer.

What is Howard's problem in the story?

At what point does Howard begin to feel accepted by his classmates? How do you know?

What do you think is the worst experience Howard has? Explain your choice.

WRITE   Do you think Howard goes about making friends in the right way? Write a friendly letter to Howard that gives him your advice on making friends.

BY BETTE BAO LORD
ILLUSTRATED BY AMY HILL

IN THE YEAR OF THE BOAR AND JACKIE ROBINSON

LEAVING YOUR HOMELAND, CHINA, AND BEGINNING SCHOOL IN THE UNITED STATES CAN BE A VERY TRYING EXPERIENCE. IN 1947, SHIRLEY TEMPLE WONG MUST FACE MANY CHALLENGES, INCLUDING A CONFRONTATION WITH MABEL, THE STRONGEST GIRL IN THE FIFTH GRADE. BUT SHIRLEY KEEPS TRYING AND DISCOVERS A NEW FRIEND, A LOVE OF BASEBALL, AND THE EXCITEMENT AMERICANS WERE EXPERIENCING OVER A VERY SPECIAL TEAM—THE BROOKLYN DODGERS.

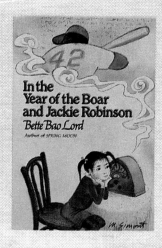

In the Year of the Boar and Jackie Robinson
Bette Bao Lord
Author of SPRING MOON

MAY

When the sides were chosen, Mabel pointed to a spot by the iron fence. "Shirley, you play right field. If a ball comes your way, catch it and throw it to me. I'll take care of the rest."

"Where you be?"

"I'm the pitcher."

"Picture?"

"Ah, forget it. Look for me, I'll be around."

Resisting the temptation to bow, Shirley headed for her spot.

Mabel's picture was something to see. First, hiding the ball, she gave the stick the evil eye. Then, twisting her torso and jiggling a leg, she whirled her arm around in a most impressive fashion, probably a ritual to shoo away any unfriendly spirits, before speeding the ball furiously into the hands of squatting Joseph.

Once in a great while, the stick got a lucky hit, but the Goddess Kwan Yin was again merciful and sent the ball nowhere near the fence.

After the change of sides, Mabel stood Shirley in place and told her she would be first to hit. Shirley would have preferred to study the problem some more, but was afraid to protest and lose face for her captain. Standing tall, with her feet together, stick on her shoulder, she waited bravely. Dog Breath had a ritual of his own to perform, but then, suddenly, the ball was coming her way. Her eyes squeezed shut.

"Ball one!" shouted the umpire.

"Good eye!" shouted Mabel.

Shirley sighed and started to leave, but was told to stay put.

Again the ball came. Again her eyes shut.

"Ball two!"

"Good eye!" shouted the team. "Two more of those and you're on."

Shirley grinned. How easy it was!

Sure enough, every time she shut her eyes, the ball went astray.

"Take your base," said the umpire.

Mabel came running over. "Stand on that red bookbag until someone hits the ball, then run like mad to touch the blue one. Got it?"

"I got."

Mabel then picked up the stick and with one try sent the ball flying. In no time, Shirley, despite her pigeon toes, had dashed to the blue bookbag. But something was wrong. Mabel was chasing her. "Go. Get going. Run."

Shirley, puzzled over which bookbag to run to next, took a chance and sped off. But Mabel was still chasing her. "Go home! Go home!"

Oh no! She had done the wrong thing. Now even her new friend was angry. "Go home," her teammates shouted. "Go home."

She was starting off the field when she saw Joseph waving. "Here! Over here!" And off she went for the green one. Just before she reached it, she stumbled, knocking over the opponent who stood in her way. He dropped the ball, and Shirley fell on top of the bag like a piece of ripe bean curd.

Her teammates shouted with happiness. Some helped her up. Others patted her back. Then they took up Mabel's chant.

"Hey, hey, you're just great
Jackie Robinson crossed the plate.
Hey, hey, you're a dream
Jackie Robinson's on our team."

Mabel's team won. The score was 10 to 2, and though the Chinese rookie never got on base again or caught even one ball, Shirley was confident that the next time . . . next time, she could. And yes, of course, naturally, stickball was now her favorite game.

On Saturday, Mabel taught her how to throw—overhand. How to catch—with her fingers. How to stand—feet two shoes apart. How to bat—on the level.

On Sunday, Mabel showed her how to propel herself on one skate at a time, then pulled her about on both until Shirley had learned how to go up and down the street without a fall.

Until that day, Shirley had never really understood something Grandfather had told her many times. "Things are not what they seem," he had said. "Good can be bad. Bad can be good. Sadness can be happiness. Joy, sorrow.

"Remember always the tale of Wispy Whiskers, who did not cry when his beautiful stallion ran away. All his neighbors, though, were certain that it was a sign from heaven of his ill fortune.

"Later, when the stallion returned leading a herd of wild horses, he did not boast of his newfound wealth. This time his neighbors were equally certain that it was a sign from heaven of his good fortune.

"Later still when his son broke his leg taming one of the mares, the wise man did not despair. Not even when behind his back all his neighbors spread the terrible rumor that anyone with even one droplet of Wispy Whiskers' blood was forever cursed by the gods.

"And in the end, only his son lived. For the sons of all the inconstant neighbors, being sound of body, were forced into military service and one by one perished in a futile battle for a greedy emperor."

How wise Grandfather was, Shirley thought. Only he could have foreseen how two black eyes would earn her the lasting friendship of the tallest, and the strongest, and the fastest girl in all of the fifth grade.

JUNE

It was almost summer. An eager sun outshone the neon sign atop the Squibb factory even before the first bell beckoned students to their homerooms. Now alongside the empty milk crates at Mr. P's, brown paper bags with collars neatly rolled boasted plump strawberries, crimson cherries and Chiquita bananas. The cloakroom stood empty. Gone, the sweaters, slickers and galoshes.

At the second bell, the fifth grade, as always, scrambled to their feet. As always, Tommy O'Brien giggled, and each girl checked her seat to see if she was his victim of the day. Susie Spencer, whose tardiness could set clocks, rushed in, her face long with excuses. Popping a last bubble, Maria Gonzales tucked her gum safely behind an ear while Joseph gave an extra stroke to his hair.

Finally Mrs. Rappaport cleared her throat, and the room was still. With hands over hearts, the class performed the ritual that ushered in another day at school.

Shirley's voice was lost in the chorus.

"I pledge a lesson to the frog of the United States of America, and to the wee puppet for witches' hands. One Asian, in the vestibule, with little tea and just rice for all."

"Class, be seated," said Mrs. Rappaport, looking around to see if anyone was absent.

No one was.

"Any questions on the homework?"

All hands remained on or below the desks, etched with initials, new with splinters, brown with age.

"In that case, any questions on any subject at all?"

Irvie's hand shot up. It was quickly pulled down by Maria, who hated even the sound of the word "spider." Spiders were all Irvie ever asked about, talked about, dreamed about. How many eyes do spiders have? Do spiders eat three meals a day? Where are spiders' ears located?

By now, everyone in the fifth grade knew that spiders come with no, six, or eight eyes. That spiders do not have to dine regularly and that some can thrive as long as two years without a bite. That spiders are earless.

Since Irvie was as scared of girls as Maria was of spiders, he sat on his hands, but just in case he changed his mind, Maria's hand went up.

"Yes, Maria?"

"Eh . . . eh, I had a question, but I forgot."

"Was it something we discussed yesterday?"

"Yeah, yeah, that's it."

"Something about air currents or cloud formation, perhaps?"

"Yeah. How come I see lightning before I hear thunder?"

"Does anyone recall the answer?"

Tommy jumped in. "That's easy. 'Cause your eyes are in front, and your ears are off to the side." To prove his point, he wiggled his ears, which framed his disarming smile like the handles of a fancy soup bowl.

Laughter was his reward.

"The correct answer, Maria," said Mrs. Rappaport, trying not to smile too, "is that light waves travel faster than sound waves."

Shirley raised her hand.

"Yes?"

"Who's the girl Jackie Robinson?"

Laughter returned. This time Shirley did not understand the joke. Was the girl very, very bad? So bad that her name should not be uttered in the presence of a grown-up?

Putting a finger to her lips, Mrs. Rappaport quieted the class. "Shirley, you ask an excellent question. A most appropriate one. . . ."

The Chinese blushed, wishing her teacher would stop praising her, or at least not in front of the others. Already, they called her "teacher's dog" or "apple shiner."

"Jackie Robinson," Mrs. Rappaport continued, "is a man, the first Negro to play baseball in the major leagues."

"What is a Negro, Mrs. Rappaport?"

"A Negro is someone who is born with dark skin."

"Like Mabel?"

"Like Mabel and Joey and . . ."

"Maria?"

"No, Maria is not a Negro."

"But Maria is dark. Darker than Joey."

"I see what you mean. Let me try again. A Negro is someone whose ancestors originally came from Africa and who has dark skin."

"Then why I'm called Jackie Robinson?"

Mrs. Rappaport looked mystified. "Who calls you Jackie Robinson?"

"Everybody."

"Then I'll have to ask them. Mabel?"

"'Cause she's pigeon-toed and stole home."

The teacher nodded. "Well, Shirley, it seems you are not only a good student, but a good baseball player."

There, she'd done it again! The kids would surely call her "a shiner of apples for teacher's dog" next. Shirley's unhappiness must have been obvious, because Mrs. Rappaport evidently felt the need to explain further.

"It is a compliment, Shirley. Jackie Robinson is a big hero, especially in Brooklyn, because he plays for the Dodgers."

"Who is dodgers?" Shirley asked.

That question, like a wayward torch in a roomful of firecrackers, sparked answers from everyone.

"De Bums!"

"The best in the history of baseball!"

"Kings of Ebbets Field!"

"They'll kill the Giants!"

"They'll murder the Yankees!"

"The swellest guys in the world!"

"America's favorites!"

"Winners!"

Mrs. Rappaport clapped her hands for order. The girls quieted down first, followed reluctantly by the boys. "That's better. Participation is welcome, but one at a time. Let's do talk about baseball!"

"Yay!" shouted the class.

"And let's combine it with civics too!"

The class did not welcome this proposal as eagerly, but Mrs. Rappaport went ahead anyway.

"Mabel, tell us why baseball is America's favorite pastime."

Pursing her lips in disgust at so ridiculous a question, Mabel answered. "'Cause it's a great game. Everybody plays it, loves it and follows the games on the radio and nabs every chance to go and see it."

"True," said Mrs. Rappaport, nodding. "But what is it about baseball that is ideally suited to Americans?"

Mabel turned around, looking for an answer from someone else, but to no avail. There was nothing to do but throw the question back. "Whatta ya mean by 'suits'?"

"I mean, is there something special about baseball that fits the special kind of people we are and the special kind of country America is?" Mrs. Rappaport tilted her head to one side, inviting a response. When none came, she sighed a sigh so fraught with disappointment that it sounded as if her heart were breaking.

No one wished to be a party to such a sad event, so everybody found some urgent business to attend to like scratching, slumping, sniffing, scribbling, squinting, sucking teeth or removing dirt from underneath a fingernail. Joseph cracked his knuckles.

The ticking of the big clock became so loud that President Washington and President Lincoln, who occupied the wall space to either side of it, exchanged a look of shared displeasure.

But within the frail, birdlike body of Mrs. Rappaport was the spirit of a dragon capable of tackling the heavens and earth. With a quick toss of her red hair, she proceeded to answer her own question with such feeling that no one who heard could be so unkind as to ever forget. Least of all Shirley.

"Baseball is not just another sport. America is not just another country. . . ."

If Shirley did not understand every word, she took its meaning to heart. Unlike Grandfather's stories which quieted the warring spirits within her with the softness of moonlight or the lyric timbre of a lone flute, Mrs. Rappaport's speech thrilled her like sunlight and trumpets.

"In our national pastime, each player is a member of a team, but when he comes to bat, he stands alone. One man. Many opportunities. For no matter how far behind, how late in the game, he, by himself, can make a difference. He can change what has been. He can make it a new ball game.

"In the life of our nation, each man is a citizen of the United States, but he has the right to pursue his own happiness. For no matter what his race, religion or creed, be he pauper or president, he has the right to speak his mind, to live as he wishes within the law, to elect our officials and stand for office, to excel. To make a difference. To change what has been. To make a better America.

"And so can you! And so must you!"

Shirley felt as if the walls of the classroom had vanished. In their stead was a frontier of doors to which she held the keys.

"This year, Jackie Robinson is at bat. He stands for himself, for Americans of every hue, for an America that honors fair play.

"Jackie Robinson is the grandson of a slave, the son of a sharecropper, raised in poverty by a lone mother who took in ironing and washing. But a woman determined to achieve a better life for her son. And she did. For despite hostility and injustice, Jackie Robinson went to college, excelled in all sports, served his country in war. And now, Jackie Robinson is at bat in the big leagues. Jackie Robinson is making a difference. Jackie Robinson has

50

changed what has been. And Jackie Robinson is making a better America.

"And so can you! And so must you!"

Suddenly Shirley understood why her father had brought her ten thousand miles to live among strangers. Here, she did not have to wait for gray hairs to be considered wise. Here, she could speak up, question even the conduct of the President. Here, Shirley Temple Wong was somebody. She felt as if she had the power of ten tigers, as if she had grown as tall as the Statue of Liberty.

If you were playing baseball, would you like to have Shirley Temple Wong on your team? Why or why not?

Many of our American words and customs seem strange to Shirley Temple Wong. What are some of the things that Shirley does not understand?

Why do you think Shirley is thrilled by Mrs. Rappaport's speech about America, baseball, and Jackie Robinson?

WRITE   Imagine that you are about to spend a year in a school in China. Make a list of questions you would ask Shirley Temple Wong about her former country and its schools.

Words from the Author:

Bette Bao Lord

Some of the parts of the story you read are true and others are made up, but the feelings Shirley Temple Wong has were very much my own.

I was eight when I came to America, and I didn't know a word of the language. As I say in *In the Year of the Boar and Jackie Robinson*, the conversation in the classroom sounded "like gargling water" to me. But one of the miracles of childhood is that you can do things that adults cannot. One of them is that you can learn languages easily. I learned English in a surprisingly short time. And I made friends and I learned about baseball. It was a very special year.

At first, I tried writing about that special year of my life as autobiography. But it wasn't right. I sounded like an adult looking back, which of course, I was. I thought the story worked much better when a young girl was telling it.

Another problem in writing the book for an adult audience was that adults don't believe much in the American Dream anymore. But I think children know that the American Dream of success is still possible. I know it. It happened to me. I came from China, and when I grew up, I married the American ambassador to China. And look at Jackie Robinson. He's still a symbol of the American Dream. That's why people remember him.

Jackie ROBINSON
BROOKLYN DODGERS

I've written a number of adult books, but *In the Year of the Boar and Jackie Robinson* is the book I enjoyed writing more than any other. After you write an adult book, you get letters about it for perhaps a year after it comes out. But hardly a week goes by when I do not get a letter about *In the Year of the Boar and Jackie Robinson*. One of the biggest thrills about writing a children's book is getting those letters. It's like a dividend.

AWARD-WINNING
AUTHOR

I get many letters from immigrant children. It's interesting, because I think these children share the same experience I had. They are lonely in a new school, and it's difficult for them to make friends. They like the book because it's funny, but it speaks to them, too. One thing I'd like children to know is that their diversity enriches the group. I couldn't have written this book if I wasn't different! You can be different in any number of ways, but it is important to remember that those differences are what make you special.

Dodgers

address

from *Floricanto en Aztlán*

by Alurista

illustrated by Buster O'Connor

address _____

occupation _____

age _____

marital status _____

   perdone . . .   *pardon . . .*
      yo me llamo pedro   *my name is pedro*

telephone _____

height _____

hobbies _____

previous employers _____

   perdone . . .   *pardon . . .*
      yo me llamo pedro   *my name is pedro*
      pedro ortega   *pedro ortega*

zip code _____

i.d. number _____

classification _____

rank _____
   perdone . . . mi padre era   *pardon . . . my father was*
     el señor ortega   *señor ortega*
     (a veces don josé)   *(sometimes called don josé)*

race _____

Challenges in School

How are the challenges faced by Howard and Shirley alike? How are Shirley's problems in school different from Howard's?

WRITER'S WORKSHOP

What experiences have you or a schoolmate had that were similar to those described in the selections? Make a list of these experiences. Then choose the one that is the most similar to Howard's or Shirley's, and write a short paragraph about it.

Writer's Choice

Howard and Shirley face similar challenges in school. What other challenges in school might a character face? Choose an idea and write about it. Share your idea in some way with your classmates.

THEME

Challenges at Home

Kids everywhere experience disappointments and setbacks. Whether it's a bad report card in New York or a lost baseball game in Puerto Rico, it's not easy to go home afterward.

CONTENTS

Whose Side Are You On?

by Emily Moore
illustrated by Thomas Hudson

Report-Card Day

Whose Side Are You On?
= Emily Moore =

THE CLOCK on the teacher's desk ticked away. Just fifteen minutes to go, I thought, as I shifted nervously in my seat. If only it had snowed hard enough for school to be closed, I could be anywhere else but here, sitting at my desk, waiting for my report card. I dreaded getting it because my grades for the first marking period had been lousy compared to last year. It wasn't my fault, though. Everything was so much harder in sixth grade, especially my teacher, Mrs. Stone.

The sound of jangling bracelets brought me back to the chalky smell of the classroom and to the sight of Mrs. Stone standing over my desk.

"Barbra," she said in her metallic voice, "if you're ready to join us, I'll now distribute report cards."

I gulped so loud that the kids around me heard and started giggling. Mrs. Stone shook her head and walked to the front of the room, undoing the rubber band binding the packet of report cards. She began to give them out. I sat on my hands, anxiously waiting for her to get to me. Mrs. Stone had promised that in the second marking period she was going to be even tougher than before. I didn't see how. She was hard enough on me the first time.

Several kids whooped and hollered when they opened their cards. Mrs. Stone smiled at my best friend, Claudia. She patted my other friend, Patricia, on the shoulder and said, "Nice work."

Finally it was my turn. From across the room, Claudia made an A-okay sign at me. I drew in my breath and opened the card.

Tears came to my eyes when I saw my grades. I never dreamed it would be this bad! Not one *Excellent*. In my favorite subject, reading, Mrs. Hernandez only gave me a *Satisfactory*. But that wasn't the worst of it. In math, Mrs. Stone gave me a *U*. *Unsatisfactory* is the nice word for *failed*. I couldn't believe that Mrs. Stone had actually flunked me! I felt a thump on my back and jerked around.

Nosy Kim was grinning at me. Kids called her Gumdrop because she ate a lot of candy and was fat. "Show me your report card; I'll show you mine." She stuck her report card in my face.

I pushed her hand away.

"What did you get?" she whined.

"Leave me alone, Gumdrop," I snapped.

I stuffed my report card into my schoolbag before anyone else asked to see it, and as soon as Mrs. Stone dismissed us, I took off down the block.

"Barbra, wait up!" Claudia called, walking with Patricia.

"Got to go," I called back, as if I had to get someplace fast.

Since we all lived in the River View Co-ops, I went in the opposite direction. As I ran up the snow-slicked street, my

unzipped boots flapped against my legs. I didn't stop to zip them or to swipe at my tear-stained eyes. I kept running until I passed Harlem Hospital.

Out of breath, I stopped and opened the report card again. There it was—a fat, red *U*—the first one of my life. It made me feel like a real failure. Nobody in my family had ever failed at anything before. I couldn't bring this report card home. What was I going to do?

Then I saw the solution to my problem: a trash can on the corner. The sign tacked on it said *Throw It Here*. So I did. A feeling of lightness came over me. I twirled around, holding my mouth open to catch snowflakes. The next moment, a snowball splattered against my back, making me stumble

forward. "Hey!" I said out loud, and looked around to see who threw it.

The street was empty except for a woman in a fur coat hurrying along and two old men talking in the doorway of Patricia's father's barbershop on 138th Street. I was sure it couldn't have been any of them. Then I saw the real culprit peer up from behind a car and duck down again. I should have known.

"What's the big idea, T.J.?" I yelled, marching over to him.

T.J. was tall, with gleaming black eyes and deep, round dimples. Even though he was twelve, a year older than me, he was in Mrs. Stone's class, too. A long time ago, he told me that the reason he got left back in first grade was that his teacher said he wasn't mature enough to be promoted to second grade. She was probably right.

He opened his mouth wide, pretending to be astonished.

"Don't play innocent," I said. "You hit me."

"You're hallucinating."

"Then why were you trying to hide?"

"I dropped some money." He poked around in the snow. I could tell it was all a big act by the way he kept looking up, grinning that sneaky, crooked grin of his.

"Why weren't you in school today?" I asked.

"Playing hookey," he said sarcastically.

"Seriously."

He took an Oreo cookie from his pocket, waved it in my face, then popped it into his mouth whole. I walked away, disgusted.

"If you must know," he said, tagging after me, "I was getting Pop's asthma medicine and the newspaper." Pop was his grandfather, whom he lived with.

"All day?" Not that I was complaining. In school I sat next to him. It was a relief that he was absent and could not pester me, for a change.

He hitched his old green knapsack on his shoulders, ignoring my question. "Weren't we supposed to get report cards?" he asked.

"What of it?"

"How did you do?"

"Why does everybody care how I did?"

He made tsk-tsking noises. "That bad, huh?"

"Good as yours, I bet."

He stuck out his pinky and thumb. I knew better than to bet with T.J. He'd always done well in school. He never failed math or anything else. He may have been immature, but he certainly was smart.

Turning up my nose at him, I glanced away and saw a garbage truck stop in front

of the trash can. A second later, I realized the terrible thing that was about to happen. I had to get that report card back before it got dumped in the trash for real.

"Stop!" I shouted.

"I'm not doing anything," T.J. said.

I waved him off and ran back to the trash can. "Wait! Stop," I called again, but the sanitation man paid no attention. He picked up the can and shook the contents into the garbage chute in the back of the truck. He climbed inside the cab. The driver put the truck into gear. The truck rumbled away and disappeared around the corner. My report card was on its way to the city dump.

What had I been thinking? My mother was going to be mad enough about my grades, let alone a thrown-away report card. I stamped my foot and kicked over the can. Without a word, T.J. righted it and gave me a strange look.

"Well, I know you're dying to ask me what's wrong," I said.

"Here," he said, offering me a cookie from his pocket.

"No, thanks." I loved Oreos, but I didn't trust T.J. The last time he offered me ice cream, it was a Dixie cup filled with mushed-up peas and mashed potatoes. Besides, I was in no mood to eat now. I sniffed and crossed the street.

He kept walking with me toward my building on Harlem River Drive. The River View Co-ops took up the entire square block from 139th to 140th Streets and from Fifth Avenue to the Drive. The buildings were red and beige brick and were built around an inner courtyard. I lived in building number 4, which faced the Drive and the East River. From halfway down the block, I heard the swishing sound of traffic on the Drive.

"Come on, take it," he said gently. "It will make you feel better."

"Nothing could make me feel better." But the thought of the bittersweet chocolate and sweet, creamy center made my mouth water. "Okay," I finally said. "I'll take one, thanks."

I bit into the cookie and almost broke my tooth. It wasn't a cookie at all, but a wooden disk made to look like one. T.J. bent over, laughing.

I threw the fake cookie at him and pushed through the doors of my building's lobby. "I hate you, Anthony Jordan Brodie!" I'd never fall for one of his tricks again.

"Can't you take a joke?" he called after me.

I turned around, sticking my tongue between my teeth, and gave him a loud, sloppy raspberry.

Wishful Thinking

I DUMPED my books on the kitchen counter and poured myself a glass of ice-cold chocolate milk, hoping it would make the burning in my stomach go away. It only gave me the chills. I stomped upstairs to where our bedrooms were. All the second-floor apartments in our co-op were duplexes.

The door to my brother Billy's room was slightly opened. His baseball and swimming trophies were lined up on his dresser, along with his comb, brush, and cologne bottle in the shape of a steam engine. He loved trains. The Tyco train set he'd received for Christmas took up much of the floor space in his room. Pushing the door open a bit more, I could see the brown report-card envelope leaning up against his mirror like another trophy on display.

"Hey," he said, glancing up from his homework. "What took you so long to get home?"

"I bumped into you-know-who. The pain." I told him about T.J.'s trick and finished by saying, "I felt like smashing his face in the snow."

But Billy only laughed. "He likes you. That's what grownups always say about kids teasing each other."

"They sure don't know anything about me and T.J."

"If you say so," he said and reached into the old, battered briefcase that had belonged to Daddy when he was a reporter. Daddy died in a plane crash when we were four years old. Billy's named after him.

Billy pulled his protractor out of the briefcase. He carefully measured angles and made calculations. While I was still struggling with division and word problems, he was doing geometry. It was hard to believe we were twins. I was ten minutes older; he was ten times smarter—which is why I was in a regular sixth-grade class and he was in the IGC, the class for "intellectually gifted children."

I pushed aside his blue plaid curtains. The snow continued to fall

thick and steady. How I hoped school would be closed tomorrow. Hmmph! Fat chance! I let the curtain fall back in place and went to my own room. After changing into old jeans, I got out my schoolbooks and worked on my homework until it was almost dinnertime.

Passing Billy's room on my way downstairs, I heard his trains chugging around the track. He'd be in for it when Ma saw he hadn't set the table. But as I entered the kitchen, I was surprised to see the yellow dishes on top of the daisy-patterned place mats. Billy had even made a tossed salad. Everything was ready for when Ma came home in a few minutes. Now I would be the only one she'd scold.

When I heard her at the door, I figured it was best to try to be extra nice. I kissed her hello and helped her off with her coat. "Let me take that," I said, putting her briefcase on the lacquered parson's table next to the coat closet.

"My, what did I do to get such treatment?" She pulled off her hat and ran her fingers through her short, curly hair.

"You work hard, and I'm sure you're tired."

She sank down on the sofa. "It's worth it." I put her boots in the bathroom to dry.

She sat with her eyes closed for a while, then got up and stretched. "After I change, I'll warm up the leftover turkey and gravy for sandwiches."

However, instead of going up to her room, she went into Billy's. I tried to hear what they were saying, but the sound of the trains drowned out their voices. All I could do was hope for two things—that Ma did not notice the brown envelope on Billy's dresser and that Billy didn't start blabbing.

In any case, report cards would have to come up during supper, the time when important family discussions took place. Usually, the first thing Ma did once we sat down to eat was to ask us about school. But tonight she started telling us about what happened to her at Citibank, where she is a manager.

65

"I got a promotion," she said. "It's now official. I'm a vice president."

"Wow!" Billy said. "That's just one step from president."

"It's many steps away, but it's exactly what I've been working toward. It will mean longer hours," she said and then gave us some other details about her new job.

"More money, too?" Billy asked.

She nodded. "Most definitely."

"Oh, Ma, that reminds me," said Billy.

I knew he was going to tell her about his report card. In the excitement of Ma's news, I had almost forgotten about it. My heart began to beat faster.

"Ma," Billy said, "I'm going to need a new baseball uniform. My old one is too small."

"No problem," Ma said, then faced me. "Are you all right? You're awfully quiet."

"I'm okay."

"You sure?" Ma ate a forkful of salad.

"Uh-huh." I pushed my plate to one side. All this suspense took away my appetite.

"Is something wrong with your food?" Ma asked.

"Big lunch," I said, getting up from the table.

"It's almost eight hours since lunch."

"I ate a big snack, too."

Ma told me to sit back down. "You know the rules. We eat as a family."

Rules, rules. Rules made me sick. I propped my elbows on the table, but one look from Ma and I began to eat slowly. Billy was cutting his sandwich into bite-size pieces. Whoever heard of eating a sandwich with a knife and fork, even if it was a sloppy kind of sandwich? Everything about him was so proper and right. He would never even think of throwing away his report card, let alone do it.

"Can I go upstairs now?" I asked after forcing down the last of my turkey sandwich.

Ma put her hand to my forehead. "What's the matter?"

"Nothing."

"You call T.J. nothing?" asked Billy, with a silly grin on his face.

"He's such a pain," I said, grateful to him for changing the subject.

"The way you and T.J. needle each

other," Ma said, shaking her head. "It's . . ."

"It's his fault," I said, cutting her off. "Like when he put that caterpillar down my back."

"That was last summer at the Labor Day picnic," said Billy, as if a few months made a difference. "And the caterpillar was made from a pipe cleaner and yarn."

"It wiggled like it was real. I thought I was going to die."

"Oh, Barbra," Ma said. "You're exaggerating."

"He's always bugging me, Ma."

"You know what they say." Billy was hinting again about T.J. liking me. I kicked at him under the table.

Ma ate some more salad. "Anyway, I've invited his grandfather and him to dinner Friday night," Ma said.

I nearly jumped out of my seat. "Oh, no. You didn't!"

"Since T.J.'s mom is still away, it's probably lonely for him."

"So what," I blurted out.

She gave me a look and I knew I had said the wrong thing. So I quickly said, "I don't feel well. May I be excused?"

Ma drew in a long sigh. "Go on."

I ran up the stairs to my room, shut the door, and got ready for bed, even though it was way before my bedtime. Going to sleep was the only way out of my mess. Why, oh, why did I ever do such a stupid thing?

I hugged Brown Bear close until he was all squished up. Ever since I was a little girl, hugging him always comforted me. Just as I was falling asleep, I heard the click of my door.

Ma came into the room. She stood over me a long time before sitting down on the edge of my bed. When she turned on the lamp, my eyelids fluttered, but I kept my eyes squeezed shut.

Brushing down my bangs, she said, "Whatever is bothering you, you can tell me. I'll understand."

I looked up at her. This is silly, I thought. Sooner or later she's going to find out. I should just get it over with. I sat up and finally told her about how Mrs. Stone failed me in math.

"No wonder you're upset. But, honey, I'll see that you get help. And I suspect it's not as bad as you make out."

"It's worse."

"Let me see." She held out her hand.

I looked down. "You can't." Twisting the blanket around, I said, "See, there was this trash can, and a sign. Then T.J. hit me with a snowball and I forgot all about it. Then a garbage truck came . . ."

"Talk plainly, Barbra."

"I threw my report card in a trash can."

She didn't say anything.

"I tried to get it back," I rushed on to explain, "but I was too late. The garbage man wouldn't listen."

She sat there, not saying a word. The change in her expression was like what happened to that Dr. Jekyll in the movie. One minute he looked like a regular person and then the next he looked real mean and evil.

"How could you do such a thing?" she said in such a quiet voice I got goose pimples.

"It was an accident. I never meant to throw it away. Not really. But that T.J. . . ."

"Don't blame him," she said.

While my voice was high and shrieky, Ma stayed quietly angry.

"In a way, it's kind of funny. Don't you think?" I looked at her hopefully, but she was not amused.

"It wasn't on purpose!" I said.

"Wasn't it?" she asked. "You never think. And now look what's happened."

"I was so upset. I never got a *U* before, and I was scared of what you would say."

"I'm disappointed in you." She got up and left. I threw Brown Bear across the room. He could stay in that corner forever.

After a while, Ma came back into

68

the room with a long, white envelope in her hand. She laid it on the dresser. "Give this to Mrs. Stone. She'll write you another report card, and I'll talk to her tomorrow at the parent-teacher's conference." She saw Brown Bear in the corner, picked him up, and put him on my chair. "You're grounded. You won't have any special privileges."

"Forever?" I asked in a panic.

"Let me finish. No special privileges until your math grades improve."

That may as well be forever, I thought, as she closed the door behind her.

Good News and Bad

FIRST THING the next morning, Mrs. Stone asked for the signed report cards. I pulled Ma's letter halfway out of my schoolbag, but I didn't have the nerve to give it to her in front of the whole class.

"Do I have them all?" Mrs. Stone asked, waving the packet in the air. I wondered if she could feel that one was missing. Sometime later, in private, I would give the letter to her. Until then, I would just act normally. I put my homework on my desk to be collected, then went to sharpen my pencils. On my way back to my seat, I noticed the envelope on the floor. It must have fallen from my schoolbag. Before I could get it, Kim picked it up.

"Give me that," I said, reaching for the envelope.

She hid it behind her back, all the while chomping on something—a gooey gumdrop, no doubt. "Mrs. Stone's name is written on it."

"It's mine."

Kim bit her lip as if thinking it over. Meanwhile, Mrs. Stone noticed, "Kim, bring that up here."

If Mrs. Stone read that letter aloud, I'd be the laughingstock of the whole, entire sixth grade. And all because of Gumdrop. I'd fix her but good. I stuck my foot out into the aisle, but she stepped over it without tripping.

"Thank you, Kim." Mrs. Stone opened the envelope. "And empty your mouth," she added, not even looking at Kim as she spat a wad of gum into the trash can.

Over the rim of her glasses, Mrs. Stone glanced at me as she read the letter. After she finished, she called me to her desk.

"Why do you need another report card?" Mrs. Stone asked in a low voice.

"The letter explains it."

She showed me the letter. Ma requested another report card without any explanation. How could she have done this to me?

"Well, Barbra," Mrs. Stone said. Her head bobbed, showing her impatience.

"I lost it." I swallowed and went on. "I, um, reached into my schoolbag to give it to my mother, you know, um, to sign. And it wasn't there."

She gave me a long, hard look to see if I was really telling the truth. "Why wasn't it in your schoolbag?"

"It was, but . . ." I shifted uneasily, then asked, "Will you give me another one?"

The bell rang for first period and Mrs. Stone said, "Barbra will stay behind. The rest of you may go to your reading classes." She went into the hall to ask her reading group to wait outside.

On her way out with Patricia, Claudia whispered, "We'll wait by the water fountain."

The last person to leave was T.J. At the door, he brushed his two pointer fingers together and said, "Shame, shame."

I threw an ink eraser at him just as Mrs. Stone was coming back. She scolded me, then made me pick it up.

"Do you have a problem, Anthony?" Mrs. Stone asked T.J.

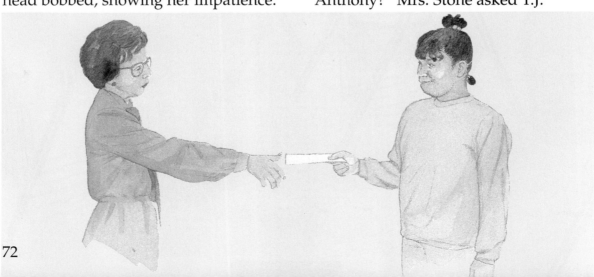

"No, ma'am," he said and hiked out of the room fast.

I knew what Mrs. Stone was going to say—I'd heard it before. "You have to try harder. Don't say you can't." And that's just what she said, adding, "Until you change your attitude, you will continue to do poorly. Losing your report card is an example of your carelessness." With that, she slipped Ma's letter into her roll book and told me to go to reading.

By now, only a few kids were straggling through the hall, but as they promised, Claudia and Patricia were waiting by the water fountain. I hurried to meet them.

Ever since this past summer when Patricia moved into River View, she, Claudia, and I were together every chance we got. Claudia was the lucky one, because she and Patricia both lived in building number 6 and went to the same ballet school. Ma refused to pay for lessons for me on account of what happened last year. She had signed me up and after three lessons I begged her to let me stop. Even though I promised not to drop out this time, she wouldn't let me take them.

"What did Mrs. Stone say?" asked Patricia.

"Gave me a lecture. I lost my report card," I said, trying to sound nonchalant.

"Anybody can lose a report card," said Claudia.

"True," I said and crossed my fingers, hoping they would never find out about the dumb thing I had done.

Would you like to read more about Barbra? Explain why or why not.

Why is what Barbra did with her report card so shocking to her mother?

How does Barbra feel about what she did? What does that tell you about her?

Do the characters in the story seem real to you? Explain why or why not.

WRITE   Barbra's mother will be meeting Mrs. Stone at a parent-teacher conference. Write a brief dialogue of their discussion. Include what they think should be done to help Barbra improve her grades.

PRIDE OF PUERTO RICO

by Paul Robert Walker

illustrated by Harvey Chan

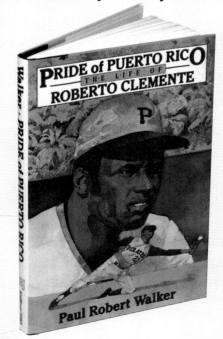

Roberto closed his eyes and imagined himself in the great stadium of San Juan. There were men on first and third with two outs in the bottom of the ninth. His team was losing, 5–3. A double would tie the game. A home run would win it. Everything depended on him.

He stepped confidently into the batter's box and took two level practice swings. Then he cocked his bat and waited for the pitch. The white ball came toward him in slow motion, its seams spinning clearly in the air. His bat was a blur as he whipped it around and smashed the ball over the left-field fence!

"Clemente!" cried a voice behind him. "Are you playing or dreaming?"

Roberto opened his eyes and stared seriously at the boy who had spoken. "I am playing," he said.

It was a warm tropical evening in Puerto Rico. Roberto Clemente was playing with a group of boys on a muddy field in Barrio San Antón. It was nothing at all like the great stadium in San Juan. There were bumps and puddles, and the outfield was full of trees. The bat in Roberto's hand was a thick stick cut from the branch of a guava tree. The bases were old coffee sacks. The ball was a tightly-knotted bunch of rags.

The boys on the field were black and white and many shades of brown. They shouted at each other in Spanish, encouraging their teammates, taunting their opponents. This was an important game between the boys of Barrio San Antón and a team from Barrio Martín Gonzalez.

Eight-year-old Roberto Clemente was one of the youngest and smallest boys on the field. As he stepped up to the plate, the thick guava stick felt very heavy in his hands. It was a great honor to represent his neighborhood. Everything depended on him.

Roberto looked over at third base, where his brother Andrés stood waiting to score. He looked at first, where another boy waited impatiently, hoping to score the tying run. Then he took a deep breath, cocked his bat and waited for the pitch.

The big ball of rags arched toward him as if it were in slow motion. Roberto swung with all his strength, but instead of sailing over the left-field fence, the ball rolled weakly back to the mound. The pitcher fielded it easily and threw to first for the final out. The game was over. San Antón had lost by a score of 5–3. Roberto stood alone while the other players left the field. He could feel tears trickling down his cheeks, and he was ashamed to cry in front of the older boys. His brother Andrés called to him from a few feet away. "Momen!" he said. "Are you going to stand there all night? It's time for supper."

"You go ahead," said Roberto. "I promised to meet Papá."

Roberto was the youngest of seven children in the Clemente family. There were six boys and one girl. When he was very little, Roberto's sister Rosa called him "Momen." It didn't mean anything in particular. It was just a made-up word, but to his family Roberto was always Momen.

Roberto's father, Don Melchor Clemente, worked as a foreman in the sugar fields. Sugar was the most important crop for the people of Puerto Rico. At harvest time, the sharp green stalks of sugar cane stood twice as tall as a man.

From sunrise to sunset, the men of Barrio San Antón worked in the fields, cutting the thick stalks of cane with their sharp machetes. It was hard, back-breaking work and the pay was $2.00 per week.

Don Clemente was more fortunate than most. As a foreman, he earned $4.00 a week. He and his wife, Doña Luisa, also ran a small store, selling meat and other goods to the workers on the sugar plantation. There was no money for luxuries like real baseballs and bats, but there was always plenty of rice and beans on the Clemente family table.

As he walked down the dirt road between the tall fields of sugar cane, Roberto thought about the game. He had failed his team. Perhaps he was not good enough to play with the bigger boys. Perhaps he would never be good enough. Once again he could feel the tears in his eyes.

It was late in the evening now, and the sun was setting over the fields like a great orange ball of fire. Roberto reached a high point in the road and looked for his father. Suddenly his tears disappeared. There, above the tall stalks of cane sat Don Melchor Clemente, riding slowly on his paso fino horse.

"Papá! Papá! Wait for me!"

Roberto ran through the cane field to where his father was riding. Don Melchor reached down and helped Roberto climb into the saddle behind him. Don Melchor Clemente was very proud to own such a fine horse. And Roberto was proud to ride behind his father.

"So, Momen," Don Melchor said as they rode home through the fields, "you come at last. I thought you had forgotten."

"Forgive me, Papá," said Roberto. "I was playing baseball."

"Ah, and how was the baseball?"

Roberto was silent for a moment. He thought again of the weak ground ball that ended the game for Barrio San Antón. He did not want to tell his father of his failure, but he knew that Don Melchor Clemente was a man who accepted only the truth. Finally he took a deep breath and spoke. "I lost the game, Papá."

"Hmmm," Don Melchor said. "That is very interesting." Father and son continued to ride in silence. Then Don Melchor spoke again. "I do not know very much about this baseball," he said. "But I know that there are many players on a team. I do not understand how one small boy can lose the game."

"But, Papá," said Roberto, "I was our only hope. I could have been the hero. Instead I was the last man out. The other boys will never ask me to play again."

They were out of the sugar fields now and riding slowly down the red dirt road that ran through Barrio San Antón. Don Melchor looked straight ahead as he guided his horse toward home. His words were strong and clear in the evening air.

"Momen," he said, "I want you to listen very carefully. Perhaps the other boys will ask you. Perhaps they will not. It does not matter. There are other boys and other teams, but there is only one life. I want you to be a good man. I want you to work hard. And I want you to be a serious person."

Don Melchor stopped his horse in the road. They were only a few hundred yards from home now, and Roberto could clearly see the wood and concrete house set in a grove of banana trees. Barrio San Antón lay on the outskirts of the city of Carolina. To the west was the capital city of San Juan. To the east were the cloud-covered slopes of El Yunque, barely visible in the fading light.

"Remember who you are," Don Melchor said. "Remember where you come from. You are a Jíbaro.[1] Like me. Like my

---

[1] hē'bä·rō'

father and my father's father. We are a proud people. Hundreds of years ago, we went into the mountains because we refused to serve the Spanish noblemen. In the wilderness, we learned to live off the land. Now, even in the sugar fields, we do not forget what we have learned."

"A man must be honest. He must work for what he needs. He must share with his brothers who have less. This is the way of the Jíbaro. This is the way of dignity." Don Melchor paused for a moment. It was dark now, and supper was waiting. "Do you understand, my son?" he asked.

Roberto thought carefully about his father's words. Then he spoke, quietly but firmly. "Yes, Papá," he said, "I understand."

Señora Cáceres stood behind her wooden desk and watched her new students file into the room. "You may choose your own seats," she said. "But remember, that will be your seat for the whole semester."

It was the first day of school at Vizcarrondo High School in the city of Carolina. Señora Cáceres waited until the students were settled into their seats before beginning the lesson.

"Today we will try to speak in English," she said. "I know that will be difficult for many of you, but the only way to improve is to practice. Now, who can tell me something about the history of Puerto Rico?"

Several students eagerly raised their hands. Señora Cáceres pointed to a pretty girl in the front row. The girl stood up and spoke in careful English.

"Puerto Rico was discovered by Christopher Columbus in 1493. He claim the island for Spain. The first governor was Ponce de León."

"Very good," said Señora Cáceres as the girl sat down. "And when did Puerto Rico become part of the United States?"

Again the same students raised their hands. Señora Cáceres looked around the room. Roberto sat in the very last row, his eyes staring at the floor. He had studied English in grammar school, but, like most of his friends, he could not really use it in conversation.

"Come now," said Señora Cáceres. "You'll never learn unless you try it."

Very slowly, Roberto raised his hand. Señora Cáceres smiled and pointed to the back row. As Roberto stood up and began to answer, he kept his eyes cast down toward the floor. His voice was very quiet. "We . . . become . . . United States . . . 1898," he said. "We are American . . . cities."

A few of the students laughed at Roberto's poor pronunciation. Señora Cáceres smiled and gently corrected him. "Citizens," she said. "We are American citizens."

As Roberto took his seat, Señora Cáceres noticed a group of girls giggling and whispering in the corner. "Yes," she thought, "this quiet one is a very handsome boy."

Señora Cáceres soon discovered that her quiet student was not so shy on the playing field. Roberto was the greatest athlete in the history of Vizcarrondo High School. He was not only a star on the baseball diamond; he also excelled in track and field. He could throw the javelin 190 feet, triple-jump 45 feet, and high-jump over 6 feet. Many people hoped that Roberto would represent Puerto Rico in the Olympic Games. But despite his success in track and field, baseball was his greatest love.

Bam! Bam! Bam!

Roberto stood on the muddy field in Barrio San Antón with a broomstick in his hands. Next to the boy on the pitcher's mound was a pile of old tin cans. Roberto and his friends were using the tin cans for batting practice. According to the rules,

Roberto could bat until the pitcher struck him out. The rest of the boys had to wait in the field for their turn at bat.

Frowning in frustration, the pitcher reached down and picked up another tin can. Once again, he leaned back and tried to fire the can past Roberto at the plate. Bam! Once again, Roberto smashed the can into the outfield.

"Hey, Clemente!" yelled a boy at shortstop. "Why don't you give someone else a chance to bat?"

Roberto smiled seriously and shrugged his shoulders. "First you must strike me out," he said.

On the dirt road that ran along the field, Señor Roberto Marín leaned against his car and watched carefully. It was almost sunset, but he could still see the boys clearly in the twilight. Señor Marín was a man who loved baseball, and he was always looking for new talent. As part of his job with the Sello Rojo Rice Company, he was putting together an all-star softball team to represent the company in a big tournament in San Juan.

"*Caramba!*" said Señor Marín. "That boy can really hit those cans." Señor Marín walked across the field to Roberto. "Who are you?" he asked.

"I am Momen," Roberto replied.

"Well, I tell you, Momen. Why don't you come over to Carolina and try out for my softball team? I think we can use you."

The next day, Roberto rode his bicycle into Carolina to try out for the softball team. It was only a couple of miles from Barrio San Antón to the field in Carolina, but it was a big step for Roberto. He was only a freshman in high school. Most of the other players were much older.

"Don't worry," said Señor Marín, "if you can hit a softball like you hit those tin cans, you'll do all right."

Roberto waited patiently at the plate as the softball sailed toward him in the evening air. At the last moment, he whipped his bat around and smashed the ball into right field. Señor Marín smiled with satisfaction. I know a ballplayer when I see one, he thought.

For the next two years, Roberto played for the Sello Rojo softball team. At first he played shortstop, but Señor Marín decided he would be better in the outfield. Soon Roberto was entertaining the softball fans of Carolina and San Juan with his brilliant catches and powerful arm.

Although softball was his favorite game, Roberto also played hardball in the San Juan youth league. When he was sixteen, he played for the Ferdinand Juncos team in the Puerto Rican amateur league. Here the competition was stronger, and the quality of the players was similar to the Class-A minors in the professional leagues of the United States.

One day, Don Melchor came to watch his son. Roberto's father knew very little about baseball. Unfortunately, Roberto's teammates did not hit very well that day. Time after time, they struck out or grounded weakly to the infielders. But when Roberto came to bat, he smashed a long home run and ran at full speed around the bases.

After the game, Roberto approached his father proudly. "Tell me, Papá," he said, "how did you like the baseball?"

"Very interesting," Don Melchor replied. "But no wonder you are always tired! The other players just run to first base and walk back to the dugout. You run all the way around the bases!"

Don Melchor smiled slightly at his own joke. Then his face turned serious. "Momen," he said, "perhaps someday you will run to the major leagues."

What did you like or not like about this story?

What special qualities did people see in young Roberto Clemente?

Roberto was very upset that he had lost the baseball game. Why didn't his father seem to care about that at all?

WRITE   Don Melchor gave his son Roberto advice for leading a good life. What other positive qualities and values do you think are important for leading a good life? Write a paragraph describing these qualities and values and providing examples to support your opinion.

Challenges at Home

Think about Barbra's and Roberto's problems. How did talking to their parents help them resolve their problems?

WRITER'S WORKSHOP

Roberto Clemente became a famous baseball player. Imagine that Barbra becomes a famous mathematician and you are asked to write her biography. Write a paragraph or two about the lost report card incident and how it affected Barbra's career.

Writer's Choice

You have seen how the theme Challenges at Home can be expressed through a work of fiction and a work of nonfiction. Think about what this theme means to you. Then think of a way to express your thoughts, and share them with others.

THEME

Understanding Others

America is a huge country, with many types of land and people. Consider the seacoast of Maine and the prairie in Kansas. They are like two different worlds. What might happen when people from these two different worlds meet? Is it possible they could learn from each other?

CONTENTS

Sarah

PLAIN AND TALL

by
Patricia MacLachlan

Illustrations by
Gary Aagaard

Sarah, Plain and Tall
Patricia MacLachlan

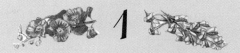

1

"Did Mama sing every day?" asked Caleb. "Every-single-day?" He sat close to the fire, his chin in his hand. It was dusk, and the dogs lay beside him on the warm hearthstones.

"Every-single-day," I told him for the second time this week. For the twentieth time this month. The hundredth time this year? And the past few years?

"And did Papa sing, too?"

"Yes. Papa sang, too. Don't get so close, Caleb. You'll heat up."

He pushed his chair back. It made a hollow scraping sound on the hearthstones, and the dogs stirred. Lottie, small and black, wagged her tail and lifted her head. Nick slept on.

I turned the bread dough over and over on the marble slab on the kitchen table.

"Well, Papa doesn't sing anymore," said Caleb very softly. A log broke apart and crackled in the fireplace. He looked up at me. "What did I look like when I was born?"

"You didn't have any clothes on," I told him.

"I know that," he said.

"You looked like this." I held the bread dough up in a round pale ball.

"I had hair," said Caleb seriously.

"Not enough to talk about," I said.

"And she named me Caleb," he went on, filling in the old familiar story.

"*I* would have named you Troublesome," I said, making Caleb smile.

"And Mama handed me to you in the yellow blanket and said . . ." He waited for me to finish the story. "And said . . .?"

I sighed. "And Mama said, 'Isn't he beautiful, Anna?'"

"And I was," Caleb finished.

Caleb thought the story was over, and I didn't tell him what I had really thought. He was homely and plain, and he had a terrible holler and a horrid smell. But these were not the worst of him. Mama died the next morning. That was the worst thing about Caleb.

"Isn't he beautiful, Anna?" Her last words to me. I had gone to bed thinking how wretched he looked. And I forgot to say good night.

I wiped my hands on my apron and went to the window. Outside, the prairie reached out and touched the places where the sky came down. Though winter was nearly over, there were patches of snow and ice everywhere. I looked at the long dirt road that crawled across the plains, remembering the morning that Mama had died, cruel and sunny. They had come for her in a wagon and taken her away to be buried. And then the cousins and aunts and uncles had come and tried to fill up the house. But they couldn't.

Slowly, one by one, they left. And then the days seemed long and dark like winter days, even though it wasn't winter. And Papa didn't sing.

Isn't he beautiful, Anna?

No, Mama.

It was hard to think of Caleb as beautiful. It took three whole days for me to love him, sitting in the chair by the fire, Papa washing up the supper dishes, Caleb's tiny hand brushing my cheek. And a smile. It was the smile, I know.

"Can you remember her songs?" asked Caleb. "Mama's songs?"

I turned from the window. "No. Only that she sang about flowers and birds. Sometimes about the moon at nighttime."

Caleb reached down and touched Lottie's head.

"Maybe," he said, his voice low, "if you remember the songs, then I might remember her, too."

My eyes widened and tears came. Then the door opened and wind blew in with Papa, and I went to stir the stew. Papa put his arms around me and put his nose in my hair.

"Nice soapy smell, that stew," he said.

I laughed. "That's my hair."

Caleb came over and threw his arms around Papa's neck and hung down as Papa swung him back and forth, and the dogs sat up.

"Cold in town," said Papa. "And Jack was feisty." Jack was Papa's horse that he'd raised from a colt. "Rascal," murmured Papa, smiling, because no matter what Jack did Papa loved him.

I spooned up the stew and lighted the oil lamp and we ate with the dogs crowding under the table, hoping for spills or handouts.

Papa might not have told us about Sarah that night if Caleb hadn't asked him the question. After the dishes were cleared and washed and Papa was filling the tin pail with ashes, Caleb spoke up. It wasn't a question, really.

"You don't sing anymore," he said. He said it harshly. Not because he meant to, but because he had been thinking of it for so long. "Why?" he asked more gently.

Slowly Papa straightened up. There was a long silence, and the dogs looked up, wondering at it.

"I've forgotten the old songs," said Papa quietly. He sat down. "But maybe there's a way to remember them." He looked up at us.

"How?" asked Caleb eagerly.

Papa leaned back in the chair. "I've placed an advertisement in the newspapers. For help."

"You mean a housekeeper?" I asked, surprised.

Caleb and I looked at each other and burst out laughing, remembering Hilly, our old housekeeper. She was round and slow and shuffling. She snored in a high whistle at night, like a teakettle, and let the fire go out.

"No," said Papa slowly. "Not a housekeeper." He paused. "A wife."

Caleb stared at Papa. "A wife? You mean a mother?"

Nick slid his face onto Papa's lap and Papa stroked his ears.

"That, too," said Papa. "Like Maggie."

Matthew, our neighbor to the south, had written to ask for a wife and mother for his children. And Maggie had come from Tennessee. Her hair was the color of turnips and she laughed.

Papa reached into his pocket and unfolded a letter written on white paper. "And I have received an answer." Papa read to us:

"Dear Mr. Jacob Witting,

"I am Sarah Wheaton from Maine as you will see from my letter. I am answering your advertisement. I have never been married, though I have been asked. I have lived with an older brother, William, who is about to be married. His wife-to-be is young and energetic.

"I have always loved to live by the sea, but at this time I feel a move is necessary. And the truth is, the sea is as far east as I can go. My choice, as you can see, is limited. This should not be taken as an insult. I am strong and I work hard and I am willing to travel. But I am not mild mannered. If you should still care to write, I would be interested in your children and about where you live. And you.

"Very truly yours,

"Sarah Elisabeth Wheaton

"P.S. Do you have opinions on cats? I have one."

No one spoke when Papa finished the letter. He kept looking at it in his hands, reading it over to himself. Finally I turned my head a bit to sneak a look at Caleb. He was smiling. I smiled, too.

"One thing," I said in the quiet of the room.

"What's that?" asked Papa, looking up.

I put my arm around Caleb.

"Ask her if she sings," I said.

2

Caleb and Papa and I wrote letters to Sarah, and before the ice and snow had melted from the fields, we all received answers. Mine came first.

Dear Anna,

Yes, I can braid hair and I can make stew and bake bread, though I prefer to build bookshelves and paint.

My favorite colors are the colors of the sea, blue and gray and green, depending on the weather. My brother William is a fisherman, and he tells me that when he is in the middle of a fogbound sea the water is a color for which there is no name. He catches flounder and sea bass and bluefish. Sometimes he sees whales. And birds, too, of course. I am enclosing a book of sea birds so you will see what William and I see every day.

Very truly yours,
Sarah Elisabeth Wheaton

Caleb read and read the letter so many times that the ink began to run and the folds tore. He read the book about sea birds over and over.

"Do you think she'll come?" asked Caleb. "And will she stay? What if she thinks we are loud and pesky?"

"You *are* loud and pesky," I told him. But I was worried, too. Sarah loved the sea, I could tell. Maybe she wouldn't leave there after all to come where there were fields and grass and sky and not much else.

"What if she comes and doesn't like our house?" Caleb asked. "I told her it was small. Maybe I shouldn't have told her it was small."

"Hush, Caleb. Hush."

Caleb's letter came soon after, with a picture of a cat drawn on the envelope.

Dear Caleb,

My cat's name is Seal because she is gray like the seals that swim offshore in Maine. She is glad that Lottie and Nick send their greetings. She likes dogs most of the time. She says their footprints are much larger than hers (which she is enclosing in return).

Your house sounds lovely, even though it is far out in the country with no close neighbors. My house is tall and the shingles are gray because of the salt from the sea. There are roses nearby.

Yes, I do like small rooms sometimes. Yes, I can keep a fire going at night. I do not know if I snore. Seal has never told me.

Very truly yours,
Sarah Elisabeth

"Did you really ask her about fires and snoring?" I asked, amazed.

"I wished to know," Caleb said.

He kept the letter with him, reading it in the barn and in the fields and by the cow pond. And always in bed at night.

One morning, early, Papa and Caleb and I were cleaning out the horse stalls and putting down new bedding. Papa stopped suddenly and leaned on his pitchfork.

"Sarah has said she will come for a month's time if we wish her to," he said, his voice loud in the dark barn. "To see how it is. Just to see."

Caleb stood by the stall door and folded his arms across his chest.

"I think," he began. Then, "I think," he said slowly, "that it would be good—to say yes," he finished in a rush.

Papa looked at me.

"I say yes," I told him, grinning.

"Yes," said Papa. "Then yes it is."

And the three of us, all smiling, went to work again.

The next day Papa went to town to mail his letter to Sarah. It was rainy for days, and the clouds followed. The house was cool and damp and quiet. Once I set four places at the table, then caught myself and put the extra plate away. Three lambs were born, one with a black face. And then Papa's letter came. It was very short.

Dear Jacob,

I will come by train. I will wear a yellow bonnet. I am plain and tall.

Sarah

"What's that?" asked Caleb excitedly, peering over Papa's shoulder. He pointed. "There, written at the bottom of the letter."

Papa read it to himself. Then he smiled, holding up the letter for us to see.

Tell them I sing was all it said.

3

Sarah came in the spring. She came through green grass fields that bloomed with Indian paintbrush, red and orange, and blue-eyed grass.

Papa got up early for the long day's trip to the train and back. He brushed his hair so slick and shiny that Caleb laughed. He wore a clean blue shirt, and a belt instead of suspenders.

He fed and watered the horses, talking to them as he hitched them up to the wagon. Old Bess, calm and kind; Jack, wild-eyed, reaching over to nip Bess on the neck.

"Clear day, Bess," said Papa, rubbing her nose.

"Settle down, Jack." He leaned his head on Jack.

And then Papa drove off along the dirt road to fetch Sarah. Papa's new wife. Maybe. Maybe our new mother.

Gophers ran back and forth across the road, stopping to stand up and watch the wagon. Far off in the field a woodchuck ate and listened. Ate and listened.

Caleb and I did our chores without talking. We shoveled out the stalls and laid down new hay. We fed the sheep. We swept and straightened and carried wood and water. And then our chores were done.

Caleb pulled on my shirt.

"Is my face clean?" he asked. "Can my face be *too* clean?" He looked alarmed.

"No, your face is clean but not too clean," I said.

Caleb slipped his hand into mine as we stood on the porch, watching the road. He was afraid.

"Will she be nice?" he asked. "Like Maggie?"

"Sarah will be nice," I told him.

"How far away is Maine?" he asked.

"You know how far. Far away, by the sea."

"Will Sarah bring some sea?" he asked.

"No, you cannot bring the sea."

The sheep ran in the field, and far off the cows moved slowly to the pond, like turtles.

"Will she like us?" asked Caleb very softly.

I watched a marsh hawk wheel down behind the barn.

He looked up at me.

"Of course she will like us." He answered his own question. "We are nice," he added, making me smile.

We waited and watched. I rocked on the porch and Caleb rolled a marble on the wood floor. Back and forth. Back and forth. The marble was blue.

We saw the dust from the wagon first, rising above the road, about the heads of Jack and Old Bess. Caleb climbed up onto the porch roof and shaded his eyes.

"A bonnet!" he cried. "I see a yellow bonnet!"

The dogs came out from under the porch, ears up, their eyes on the cloud of dust bringing Sarah. The wagon passed the fenced field, and the cows and sheep looked up, too. It rounded the windmill and the barn and the windbreak of Russian olive that Mama had planted long ago. Nick began to bark, then Lottie, and the wagon clattered into the yard and stopped by the steps.

"Hush," said Papa to the dogs.

And it was quiet.

Sarah stepped down from the wagon, a cloth bag in her hand. She reached up and took off her yellow bonnet, smoothing back her brown hair into a bun. She was plain and tall.

"Did you bring some sea?" cried Caleb beside me.

"Something from the sea," said Sarah smiling. "And me." She turned and lifted a black case from the wagon. "And Seal, too."

Carefully she opened the case, and Seal, gray with white feet, stepped out. Lottie lay down, her head on her paws, staring. Nick leaned down to sniff. Then he lay down, too.

"The cat will be good in the barn," said Papa. "For mice."

Sarah smiled. "She will be good in the house, too."

Sarah took Caleb's hand, then mine. Her hands were large and rough. She gave Caleb a shell—a moon snail, she called it—that was curled and smelled of salt.

"The gulls fly high and drop the shells on the rocks below," she told Caleb. "When the shell is broken, they eat what is inside."

"That is very smart," said Caleb.

"For you, Anna," said Sarah, "a sea stone."

And she gave me the smoothest and whitest stone I had ever seen.

"The sea washes over and over and around the stone, rolling it until it is round and perfect."

"That is very smart, too," said Caleb. He looked up at Sarah. "We do not have the sea here."

Sarah turned and looked out over the plains. "No," she said. "There is no sea here. But the land rolls a little like the sea."

My father did not see her look, but I did. And I knew that Caleb had seen it, too. Sarah was not smiling. Sarah was already lonely. In a month's time the preacher might come to marry Sarah and Papa. And a month was a long time. Time enough for her to change her mind and leave us.

Papa took Sarah's bags inside, where her room was ready with a quilt on the bed and blue flax dried in a vase on the night table.

Seal stretched and made a small cat sound. I watched her circle the dogs and sniff the air. Caleb came out and stood beside me.

"When will we sing?" he whispered.

I shook my head, turning the white stone over and over in my hand. I wished everything was as perfect as the stone. I wished that Papa and Caleb and I were perfect for Sarah. I wished we had a sea of our own.

 4

The dogs loved Sarah first. Lottie slept beside her bed, curled in a soft circle, and Nick leaned his face on the covers in the morning, watching for the first sign that Sarah was awake.

No one knew where Seal slept. Seal was a roamer.

Sarah's collection of shells sat on the windowsill.

"A scallop," she told us, picking up the shells one by one, "a sea clam, an oyster, a razor clam. And a conch shell. If you put it to your ear you can hear the sea." She put it to Caleb's ear, then mine. Papa listened, too. Then Sarah listened once more, with a look so sad and far away that Caleb leaned against me.

"At least Sarah can hear the sea," he whispered.

Papa was quiet and shy with Sarah, and so was I. But Caleb talked to Sarah from morning until the light left the sky.

"Where are you going?" he asked. "To do what?"

"To pick flowers," said Sarah. "I'll hang some of them upside down and dry them so they'll keep some color. And we can have flowers all winter long."

"I'll come, too!" cried Caleb. "Sarah said winter," he said to me. "That means Sarah will stay."

Together we picked flowers, paintbrush and clover and prairie violets. There were buds on the wild roses that climbed up the paddock fence.

"The roses will bloom in early summer," I told Sarah. I looked to see if she knew what I was thinking. Summer was when the wedding would be. *Might* be. Sarah and Papa's wedding.

We hung the flowers from the ceiling in little bunches. "I've never seen this before," said Sarah. "What is it called?"

"Bride's bonnet," I told her.

Caleb smiled at the name.

"We don't have this by the sea," she said. "We have seaside goldenrod and wild asters and woolly ragwort."

"Woolly ragwort!" Caleb whooped. He made up a song.

"Woolly ragwort all around,
Woolly ragwort on the ground.
Woolly ragwort grows and grows,
Woolly ragwort in your nose."

Sarah and Papa laughed, and the dogs lifted their heads and thumped their tails against the wood floor. Seal sat on a kitchen chair and watched us with yellow eyes.

We ate Sarah's stew, the late light coming through the windows. Papa had baked bread that was still warm from the fire.

"The stew is fine," said Papa.

"Ayuh." Sarah nodded. "The bread, too."

"What does 'ayuh' mean?" asked Caleb.

"In Maine it means yes," said Sarah. "Do you want more stew?"

"Ayuh," said Caleb.

"Ayuh," echoed my father.

After dinner Sarah told us about William. "He has a gray-and-white boat named *Kittiwake*." She looked out the window. "That is a small gull found way off the shore where William

fishes. There are three aunts who live near us. They wear silk dresses and no shoes. You would love them."

"Ayuh," said Caleb.

"Does your brother look like you?" I asked.

"Yes," said Sarah. "He is plain and tall."

At dusk Sarah cut Caleb's hair on the front steps, gathering his curls and scattering them on the fence and ground. Seal batted some hair around the porch as the dogs watched.

"Why?" asked Caleb.

"For the birds," said Sarah. "They will use it for their nests. Later we can look for nests of curls."

"Sarah said 'later,'" Caleb whispered to me as we spread his hair about. "Sarah will stay."

Sarah cut Papa's hair, too. No one else saw, but I found him behind the barn, tossing the pieces of hair into the wind for the birds.

Sarah brushed my hair and tied it up in back with a rose velvet ribbon she had brought from Maine. She brushed hers long and free and tied it back, too, and we stood side by side looking into the mirror. I looked taller, like Sarah, and fair and thin. And with my hair pulled back I looked a little like her daughter. Sarah's daughter.

And then it was time for singing.

Sarah sang us a song we had never heard before as we sat on the porch, insects buzzing in the dark, the rustle of cows in the grasses. It was called "Sumer Is Icumen in," and she taught it to us all, even Papa, who sang as if he had never stopped singing.

> *"Sumer is icumen in,*
> *Lhude sing cuccu!"*

"What is sumer?" asked Caleb. He said it "soomer," the way Sarah had said it.

"Summer," said Papa and Sarah at the same time. Caleb and I looked at each other. Summer was coming.

"Tomorrow," said Sarah, "I want to see the sheep. You know, I've never touched one."

"Never?" Caleb sat up.

"Never," said Sarah. She smiled and leaned back in her chair. "But I've touched seals. Real seals. They are cool and slippery and they slide through the water like fish. They can cry and sing. And sometimes they bark, a little like dogs."

Sarah barked like a seal. And Lottie and Nick came running from the barn to jump up on Sarah and lick her face and make her laugh. Sarah stroked them and scratched their ears and it was quiet again.

"I wish I could touch a seal right now," said Caleb, his voice soft in the night.

"So do I," said Sarah. She sighed, then she began to sing the summer song again. Far off in a field, a meadowlark sang, too.

5

The sheep made Sarah smile. She sank her fingers into their thick, coarse wool. She talked to them, running with the lambs, letting them suck on her fingers. She named them after her favorite aunts, Harriet and Mattie and Lou. She lay down in the field beside them and sang "Sumer Is Icumen in," her voice drifting over the meadow grasses, carried by the wind.

She cried when we found a lamb that had died, and she shouted and shook her fist at the turkey buzzards that came from nowhere to eat it. She would not let Caleb or me come near. And that night, Papa went with a shovel to bury the sheep and a lantern to bring Sarah back. She sat on the porch alone. Nick crept up to lean against her knees.

After dinner, Sarah drew pictures to send home to Maine. She began a charcoal drawing of the fields, rolling like the sea rolled. She drew a sheep whose ears were too big. And she drew a windmill.

"Windmill was my first word," said Caleb. "Papa told me so."

"Mine was flower," I said. "What was yours, Sarah?"

"Dune," said Sarah.

"Dune?" Caleb looked up.

"In Maine," said Sarah, "there are rock cliffs that rise up at the edge of the sea. And there are hills covered with pine and spruce trees, green with needles. But William and I found a sand dune all our own. It was soft and sparkling with bits of mica, and when we were little we would slide down the dune into the water."

Caleb looked out the window.

"We have no dunes here," he said.

Papa stood up.

"Yes we do," he said. He took the lantern and went out the door to the barn.

"We do?" Caleb called after him.

He ran ahead, Sarah and I following, the dogs close behind.

Next to the barn was Papa's mound of hay for bedding, nearly half as tall as the barn, covered with canvas to keep the rain from rotting it. Papa carried the wooden ladder from the barn and leaned it against the hay.

"There." He smiled at Sarah. "Our dune."

Sarah was very quiet. The dogs looked up at her, waiting. Seal brushed against her legs, her tail in the air. Caleb reached over and took her hand.

"It looks high up," he said. "Are you scared, Sarah?"

"Scared? Scared!" exclaimed Sarah. "You bet I'm not scared."

She climbed the ladder, and Nick began to bark. She climbed to the very top of the hay and sat, looking down at us. Above, the stars were coming out. Papa piled a bed of loose hay below with his pitchfork. The light of the lantern made his eyes shine when he smiled up at Sarah.

"Fine?" called Papa.

"Fine," said Sarah. She lifted her arms over her head and slid down, down, into the soft hay. She lay, laughing, as the dogs rolled beside her.

"Was it a good dune?" called Caleb.

"Yes," said Sarah. "It is a fine dune."

Caleb and I climbed up and slid down. And Sarah did it three more times. At last Papa slid down, too, as the sky grew darker and the stars blinked like fireflies. We were covered with hay and dust, and we sneezed.

In the kitchen, Caleb and I washed in the big wooden tub and Sarah drew more pictures to send to William. One was of Papa, his hair curly and full of hay. She drew Caleb, sliding down the hay, his arms like Sarah's over his head. And she drew a picture of me in the tub, my hair long and straight and wet. She looked at her drawing of the fields for a long time.

"Something is missing," she told Caleb. "Something." And she put it away.

"'Dear William,'" Sarah read to us by lantern light that night. "'Sliding down our dune of hay is almost as fine as sliding down the sand dunes into the sea.'"

Caleb smiled at me across the table. He said nothing, but his mouth formed the words I had heard, too. *Our dune.*

 6

The days grew longer. The cows moved close to the pond, where the water was cool and there were trees.

Papa taught Sarah how to plow the fields, guiding the plow behind Jack and Old Bess, the reins around her neck. When the chores were done we sat in the meadow with the sheep, Sarah beside us, watching Papa finish.

"Tell me about winter," said Sarah.

Old Bess nodded her head as she walked, but we could hear Papa speak sharply to Jack.

"Jack doesn't like work," said Caleb. "He wants to be here in the sweet grass with us."

"I don't blame him," said Sarah. She lay back in the grass with her arms under her head. "Tell me about winter," she said again.

"Winter is cold here," said Caleb, and Sarah and I laughed.

"Winter is cold everywhere," I said.

"We go to school in winter," said Caleb. "Sums and writing and books," he sang.

"I am good at sums and writing," said Sarah. "I love books. How do you get to school?"

"Papa drives us in the wagon. Or we walk the three miles when there is not too much snow."

Sarah sat up. "Do you have lots of snow?"

"Lots and lots and lots of snow," chanted Caleb, rolling around in the grass. "Sometimes we have to dig our way out to feed the animals."

"In Maine the barns are attached to the houses sometimes," said Sarah.

Caleb grinned. "So you could have a cow to Sunday supper?"

Sarah and I laughed.

"When there are bad storms, Papa ties a rope from the house to the barn so no one will get lost," said Caleb.

I frowned. I loved winter.

"There is ice on the windows on winter mornings," I told Sarah. "We can draw sparkling pictures and we can see our breath in the air. Papa builds a warm fire, and we bake hot biscuits and put on hundreds of sweaters. And if the snow is too high, we stay home from school and make snow people."

Sarah lay back in the tall grasses again, her face nearly hidden.

"And is there wind?" she asked.

"Do you like wind?" asked Caleb.

"There is wind by the sea," said Sarah.

"There is wind here," said Caleb happily. "It blows the snow and brings tumbleweeds and makes the sheep run. Wind and wind and wind!" Caleb stood up and ran like the wind, and the sheep ran after him. Sarah and I watched him jump over rock and gullies, the sheep behind him, stiff legged and fast. He circled the field, the sun making the top of his hair golden. He collapsed next to Sarah, and the lambs pushed their wet noses into us.

"Hello, Lou," said Sarah smiling. "Hello, Mattie."

The sun rose higher, and Papa stopped to take off his hat and wipe his face with his sleeve.

"I'm hot," said Sarah. "I can't wait for winter wind. Let's swim."

"Swim where?" I asked her.

"I can't swim," said Caleb.

"Can't swim!" exclaimed Sarah. "I'll teach you in the cow pond."

"That's for cows!" I cried.

But Sarah had grabbed our hands and we were running through the fields, ducking under the fence to the far pond.

"Shoo, cows," said Sarah as the cows looked up, startled. She took off her dress and waded into the water in her petticoat. She dived suddenly and disappeared for a moment as Caleb and I watched. She came up, laughing, her hair streaming free. Water beads sat on her shoulders.

She tried to teach us how to float. I sank like a bucket filled with water and came up sputtering. But Caleb lay on his back and learned how to blow streams of water high in the air like a whale. The cows stood on the banks of the pond and stared and stopped their chewing. Water bugs circled us.

"Is this like the sea?" asked Caleb.

Sarah treaded water.

"The sea is salt," said Sarah. "It stretches out as far as you can see. It gleams like the sun on glass. There are waves."

"Like this?" asked Caleb, and he pushed a wave at Sarah, making her cough and laugh.

"Yes," she said. "Like that."

I held my breath and floated at last, looking up into the sky, afraid to speak. Crows flew over, three in a row. And I could hear a killdeer in the field.

We climbed the bank and dried ourselves and lay in the grass again. The cows watched, their eyes sad in their dinner-plate faces. And I slept, dreaming a perfect dream. The fields had turned to a sea that gleamed like sun on glass. And Sarah was happy.

7

The dandelions in the fields had gone by, their heads soft as feathers. The summer roses were opening.

Our neighbors, Matthew and Maggie, came to help Papa plow up a new field for corn. Sarah stood with us on the porch, watching their wagon wind up the road, two horses pulling it and one tied in back. I remembered the last time we had stood here alone, Caleb and I, waiting for Sarah.

Sarah's hair was in thick braids that circled her head, wild daisies tucked here and there. Papa had picked them for her.

Old Bess and Jack ran along the inside of the fence, whickering at the new horses.

"Papa needs five horses for the big gang plow," Caleb told Sarah. "Prairie grass is hard."

Matthew and Maggie came with their two children and a sackful of chickens. Maggie emptied the sack into the yard and three red banty chickens clucked and scattered.

"They are for you," she told Sarah. "For eating."

Sarah loved the chickens. She clucked back to them and fed them grain. They followed her, shuffling and scratching primly in the dirt. I knew they would not be for eating.

The children were young and named Rose and Violet, after flowers. They hooted and laughed and chased the chickens, who flew up to the porch roof, then the dogs, who crept quietly under the porch. Seal had long ago fled to the barn to sleep in cool hay.

Sarah and Maggie helped hitch the horses to the plow, then they set up a big table in the shade of the barn, covering it with a quilt and a kettle of flowers in the middle. They sat on the porch while Caleb and Matthew and Papa began their morning of plowing. I mixed biscuit dough just inside the door, watching.

"You are lonely, yes?" asked Maggie in her soft voice.

Sarah's eyes filled with tears. Slowly I stirred the dough. Maggie reached over and took Sarah's hand.

"I miss the hills of Tennessee sometimes," she said.

Do not miss the hills, Maggie, I thought.

"I miss the sea," said Sarah.

Do not miss the hills. Do not miss the sea.

I stirred and stirred the dough.

"I miss my brother William," said Sarah. "But he is married. The house is hers now. Not mine any longer. There are three old aunts who all squawk together like crows at dawn. I miss them, too."

"There are always things to miss," said Maggie. "No matter where you are."

I looked out and saw Papa and Matthew and Caleb working. Rose and Violet ran in the fields. I felt something brush my legs and looked down at Nick, wagging his tail.

"I would miss you, Nick," I whispered. "I would." I knelt down and scratched his ears. "I miss Mama."

"I nearly forgot," said Maggie on the porch. "I have something more for you."

I carried the bowl outside and watched Maggie lift a low wooden box out of the wagon.

"Plants," she said to Sarah. "For your garden."

"My garden?" Sarah bent down to touch the plants.

"Zinnias and marigolds and wild feverfew," said Maggie. "You must have a garden. Wherever you are."

Sarah smiled. "I had a garden in Maine with dahlias and columbine. And nasturtiums the color of the sun when it sets. I don't know if nasturtiums would grow here."

"Try," said Maggie. "You must have a garden."

We planted the flowers by the porch, turning over the soil and patting it around them, and watering. Lottie and Nick came to sniff, and the chickens walked in the dirt, leaving prints. In the fields, the horses pulled the plow up and down under the hot summer sun.

Maggie wiped her face, leaving a streak of dirt.

"Soon you can drive your wagon over to my house and I will give you more. I have tansy."

Sarah frowned. "I have never driven a wagon."

"I can teach you," said Maggie. "And so can Anna and Caleb. And Jacob."

Sarah turned to me.

"Can you?" she asked. "Can you drive a wagon?"

I nodded.

"And Caleb?"

"Yes."

"In Maine," said Sarah, "I would walk to town."

"Here it is different," said Maggie. "Here you will drive."

Way off in the sky, clouds gathered. Matthew and Papa and Caleb came in from the fields, their work done. We all ate in the shade.

"We are glad you are here," said Matthew to Sarah. "A new friend. Maggie misses her friends sometimes."

Sarah nodded. "There is always something to miss, no matter where you are," she said, smiling at Maggie.

Rose and Violet fell asleep in the grass, their bellies full of meat and greens and biscuits. And when it was time to go, Papa and Matthew lifted them into the wagon to sleep on blankets.

Sarah walked slowly behind the wagon for a long time, waving, watching it disappear. Caleb and I ran to bring her back, the chickens running wildly behind us.

"What shall we name them?" asked Sarah, laughing as the chickens followed us into the house.

I smiled. I was right. The chickens would not be for eating.

And then Papa came, just before the rain, bringing Sarah the first roses of summer.

8

The rain came and passed, but strange clouds hung in the northwest, low and black and green. And the air grew still.

In the morning, Sarah dressed in a pair of overalls and went to the barn to have an argument with Papa. She took apples for Old Bess and Jack.

"Women don't wear overalls," said Caleb, running along behind her like one of Sarah's chickens.

"This woman does," said Sarah crisply.

Papa stood by the fence.

"I want to learn how to ride a horse," Sarah told him. "And then I want to learn how to drive the wagon. By myself."

Jack leaned over and nipped at Sarah's overalls. She fed him an apple. Caleb and I stood behind Sarah.

"I can ride a horse, I know," said Sarah. "I rode once when I was twelve. I will ride Jack." Jack was Sarah's favorite.

Papa shook his head. "Not Jack," he said. "Jack is sly."

"I am sly, too," said Sarah stubbornly.

Papa smiled. "Ayuh," he said, nodding. "But not Jack."

"Yes, Jack!" Sarah's voice was very loud.

"I can teach you how to drive a wagon. I have already taught you how to plow."

"And then I can go to town. By myself."

"Say no, Papa," Caleb whispered beside me.

"That's a fair thing, Sarah," said Papa. "We'll practice."

A soft rumble of thunder sounded. Papa looked up at the clouds.

"Today? Can we begin today?" asked Sarah.

"Tomorrow is best," said Papa, looking worried. "I have to fix the house roof. A portion of it is loose. And there's a storm coming."

"We," said Sarah.

"What?" Papa turned.

"*We* will fix the roof," said Sarah. "I've done it before. I know about roofs. I am a good carpenter. Remember, I told you?"

There was thunder again, and Papa went to get the ladder.

"Are you fast?" he asked Sarah.

"I am fast and I am good," said Sarah. And they climbed the ladder to the roof, Sarah with wisps of hair around her face, her mouth full of nails, overalls like Papa's. Overalls that *were* Papa's.

Caleb and I went inside to close the windows. We could hear the steady sound of hammers pounding the roof overhead.

"Why does she want to go to town by herself?" asked Caleb. "To leave us?"

I shook my head, weary with Caleb's questions. Tears gathered at the corners of my eyes. But there was no time to cry, for suddenly Papa called out.

"Caleb! Anna!"

We ran outside and saw a huge cloud, horribly black, moving toward us over the north fields. Papa slid down the roof, helping Sarah after him.

"A squall!" he yelled to us. He held up his arms and Sarah jumped off the porch roof.

"Get the horses inside," he ordered Caleb. "Get the sheep, Anna. And the cows. The barn is safest."

The grasses flattened. There was a hiss of wind, a sudden pungent smell. Our faces looked yellow in the strange light. Caleb and I jumped over the fence and found the animals huddled by the barn. I counted the sheep to make sure they were all there, and herded them into a large stall. A few raindrops came, gentle at first, then stronger and louder, so that Caleb and I covered our ears and stared at each other without speaking. Caleb looked frightened and I tried to smile at him. Sarah carried a sack into the barn, her hair wet and streaming down her neck. Papa came behind, Lottie and Nick with him, their ears flat against their heads.

"Wait!" cried Sarah. "My chickens!"

"No, Sarah!" Papa called after her. But Sarah had already run from the barn into a sheet of rain. My father followed her. The sheep nosed open their stall door and milled around the barn, bleating. Nick crept under my arm, and a lamb, Mattie with the black face, stood close to me, trembling. There was a soft paw on my lap, then a gray body. Seal. And then, as the thunder pounded and the wind rose and there was the terrible crackling of lightning close by, Sarah and Papa stood in the barn doorway, wet to the skin. Papa carried Sarah's chickens. Sarah came with an armful of summer roses.

Sarah's chickens were not afraid, and they settled like small red bundles in the hay. Papa closed the door at last, shutting out some of the sounds of the storm. The barn was eerie and half lighted, like dusk without a lantern. Papa spread blankets around our shoulders and Sarah unpacked a bag of cheese and bread and jam. At the very bottom of the bag were Sarah's shells.

Caleb got up and went over to the small barn window.

"What color is the sea when it storms?" he asked Sarah.

"Blue," said Sarah, brushing her wet hair back with her fingers. "And gray and green."

Caleb nodded and smiled.

"Look," he said to her. "Look what is missing from your drawing."

Sarah went to stand between Caleb and Papa by the window. She looked a long time without speaking. Finally, she touched Papa's shoulder.

"We have squalls in Maine, too," she said. "Just like this. It will be all right, Jacob."

Papa said nothing. But he put his arm around her, and leaned over to rest his chin in her hair. I closed my eyes, suddenly remembering Mama and Papa standing that way, Mama smaller than Sarah, her hair fair against Papa's shoulder. When I opened my eyes again, it was Sarah standing there. Caleb looked at me and smiled and smiled until he could smile no more.

We slept in the hay all night, waking when the wind was wild, sleeping again when it was quiet. And at dawn there was the sudden sound of hail, like stones tossed against the barn. We stared out the window, watching the ice marbles bounce on the ground. And when it was over we opened the barn door and walked out into the early-morning light. The hail crunched and melted beneath our feet. It was white and gleaming for as far as we looked, like sun on glass. Like the sea.

9

It was very quiet. The dogs leaned down to eat the hailstones. Seal stepped around them and leaped up on the fence to groom herself. A tree had blown over near the cow pond. And the wild roses were scattered on the ground, as if a wedding had come and gone there. "I'm glad I saved an armful" was all that Sarah said.

Only one field was badly damaged, and Sarah and Papa hitched up the horses and plowed and replanted during the next two days. The roof had held.

"I told you I know about roofs," Sarah told Papa, making him smile.

Papa kept his promise to Sarah. When the work was done, he took her out into the fields, Papa riding Jack who was sly, and Sarah riding Old Bess. Sarah was quick to learn.

"Too quick," Caleb complained to me as we watched from the fence. He thought a moment. "Maybe she'll fall off and have to stay here. Why?" he asked, turning to me. "Why does she have to go away alone?"

"Hush up, Caleb," I said crossly. "Hush up."

"I could get sick and make her stay here," said Caleb.

"No."

"We could tie her up."

"No."

And Caleb began to cry, and I took him inside the barn where we could both cry.

Papa and Sarah came to hitch the horses to the wagon, so Sarah could practice driving. Papa didn't see Caleb's tears, and he sent him with an ax to begin chopping up the tree by the pond for firewood. I stood and watched Sarah, the reins in her hands, Papa next to her in the wagon. I could see Caleb standing by the pond, one hand shading his eyes, watching, too. I went into the safe darkness of the barn then, Sarah's chickens scuttling along behind me.

"Why?" I asked out loud, echoing Caleb's question.

The chickens watched me, their eyes small and bright.

The next morning Sarah got up early and put on her blue dress. She took apples to the barn. She loaded a bundle of hay on the wagon for Old Bess and Jack. She put on her yellow bonnet.

"Remember Jack," said Papa. "A strong hand."

"Yes, Jacob."

"Best to be home before dark," said Papa. "Driving a wagon is hard if there's no full moon."

"Yes, Jacob."

Sarah kissed us all, even my father, who looked surprised.

"Take care of Seal," she said to Caleb and me. And with a whisper to Old Bess and a stern word to Jack, Sarah climbed up in the wagon and drove away.

"Very good," murmured Papa as he watched. And after a while he turned and went out into the fields.

Caleb and I watched Sarah from the porch. Caleb took my hand, and the dogs lay down beside us. It was sunny, and I remembered another time when a wagon had taken Mama away. It had been a day just like this day. And Mama had never come back.

Seal jumped up to the porch, her feet making a small thump. Caleb leaned down and picked her up and walked inside. I took the broom and slowly swept the porch. Then I watered Sarah's plants. Caleb cleaned out the wood stove and carried the ashes to the barn, spilling them so that I had to sweep the porch again.

"I *am* loud and pesky," Caleb cried suddenly. "You said so! And she has gone to buy a train ticket to go away!"

"No, Caleb. She would tell us."

"The house is too small," said Caleb. "That's what it is."

"The house is not too small," I said.

I looked at Sarah's drawing of the fields pinned up on the wall next to the window.

"What is missing?" I asked Caleb. "You said you knew what was missing."

"Colors," said Caleb wearily. "The colors of the sea."

Outside, clouds moved into the sky and went away again. We took lunch to Papa, cheese and bread and lemonade. Caleb nudged me.

"Ask him. Ask Papa."

"What has Sarah gone to do?" I asked.

"I don't know," said Papa. He squinted at me. Then he sighed and put one hand on Caleb's head, one on mine. "Sarah is Sarah. She does things her way, you know."

"I know," said Caleb very softly.

Papa picked up his shovel and put on his hat.

"Ask if she's coming back," whispered Caleb.

"Of course she's coming back," I said. "Seal is here." But I would not ask the question. I was afraid to hear the answer.

We fed the sheep, and I set the table for dinner. Four plates. The sun dropped low over the west fields. Lottie and Nick stood at the door, wagging their tails, asking for supper. Papa came to light the stove. And then it was dusk. Soon it would be dark. Caleb sat on the porch steps, turning his moon snail shell over and over in his hand. Seal brushed back and forth against him.

Suddenly Lottie began to bark, and Nick jumped off the porch and ran down the road.

"Dust!" cried Caleb. He climbed the porch and stood on the roof. "Dust, and a yellow bonnet!"

Slowly the wagon came around the windmill and the barn and the windbreak and into the yard, the dogs jumping happily beside it.

"Hush, dogs," said Sarah. And Nick leaped up into the wagon to sit by Sarah.

Papa took the reins and Sarah climbed down from the wagon.

Caleb burst into tears.

"Seal was very worried!" he cried.

Sarah put her arms around him, and he wailed into her dress. "And the house is too small, we thought! And I am loud and pesky!"

Sarah looked at Papa and me over Caleb's head.

"We thought you might be thinking of leaving us," I told her. "Because you miss the sea."

Sarah smiled.

"No," she said. "I will always miss my old home, but the truth of it is I would miss you more."

Papa smiled at Sarah, then he bent quickly to unhitch the horses from the wagon. He led them to the barn for water.

Sarah handed me a package.

"For Anna," she said. "And Caleb. For all of us."

The package was small, wrapped in brown paper with a rubber band around it. Very carefully I unwrapped it, Caleb peering closely. Inside were three colored pencils.

"Blue," said Caleb slowly, "and gray. And green."

Sarah nodded.

Suddenly Caleb grinned.

"Papa," he called. "Papa, come quickly! Sarah has brought the sea!"

We eat our night meal by candlelight, the four of us. Sarah has brought candles from town. And nasturtium seeds for her garden, and a book of songs to teach us. It is late, and Caleb is nearly sleeping by

his plate and Sarah is smiling at my father. Soon there will be a wedding. Papa says that when the preacher asks if he will have Sarah for his wife, he will answer, "Ayuh."

Autumn will come, then winter, cold with a wind that blows like the wind off the sea in Maine. There will be nests of curls to look for, and dried flowers all winter long. When there are storms, Papa will stretch a rope from the door to the barn so we will not be lost when we feed the sheep and the cows and Jack and Old Bess. And Sarah's chickens, if they aren't living in the house. There will be Sarah's sea, blue and gray and green, hanging on the wall. And songs, old ones and new. And Seal with yellow eyes. And there will be Sarah, plain and tall.

Do you think Sarah is brave? Explain why or why not.

How does Sarah help the Witting family? How do the Wittings help Sarah?

What is the importance of singing in this story?

Would you enjoy living in Anna and Caleb's time and place? Explain why or why not.

WRITE   Sarah first writes to Jacob to ask about his children and about the place where they live. Write a list that describes the place where you live. Note the appearance, the weather, and the plants and animals.

Patricia MacLachlan

Descriptions of the prairie in *Sarah, Plain and Tall* are vivid, vibrant, and true because the author, Patricia MacLachlan, knows the prairie well. MacLachlan, who was born in Cheyenne, Wyoming, says that for her "the western landscape has always been a powerful force . . . fueling mind and imagination."

That lively imagination began in childhood when MacLachlan—an only child—invented characters she wished to be. She was encouraged to read by her parents, who were teachers, so she filled her world with characters from books as well as from her imagination. With such a vivid imagination and strong love of reading, writing stories should have followed naturally.

Yet the only story the author remembers writing as a child was a school assignment at age eight. The story was to be about a pet and had to have "a beginning, a middle, and an ending." Her teacher was not impressed with the story she turned in on a three-by-five card: *My cats have names and seem happy. Often they play. The end.* The young author was discouraged enough to write in her diary: "I shall try not to be a writer."

MacLachlan did indeed "try not to be a writer." Following in her parents' footsteps, she became an English teacher. But her powerful imagination and her love for books proved too strong a combination to resist. In her thirties, Patricia MacLachlan began to write novels with proper beginnings, middles, and endings. Now she shares her talent and experience in creative writing workshops that she conducts for adults and children.

Much of the action in *Sarah, Plain and Tall* comes from MacLachlan's imagination, but the basic story idea is factual. When Patricia was a child, her mother told her about "the real Sarah, who came from the coast of Maine to the prairie to become a wife and mother." Building on that fact, MacLachlan crafted a simple but fine story that expresses the importance of family—a theme that runs through many of her books. She has received several awards for *Sarah, Plain and Tall*, among them the 1986 Newbery Medal. The little girl who tried not to be a writer grew up to distinguish herself in that profession.

Kansas Boy

Illustrations by Davy Liu

This Kansas boy who never saw the sea
Walks through the young corn rippling at his knee
As sailors walk; and when the grain grows higher
Watches the dark waves leap with greener fire
Than ever oceans hold. He follows ships,
Tasting the bitter spray upon his lips,
For in his blood up-stirs the salty ghost
Of one who sailed a storm-bound English coast.
Across wide fields he hears the sea winds crying,
Shouts at the crows — and dreams of white gulls flying.

Ruth Lechlitner

Understanding Others

What character traits might the boy in "Kansas Boy" and Sarah Wheaton have in common?

Writer's Workshop

Imagine that you, like Caleb or Anna, want a certain person to visit you. Think about who it is, where he or she lives, and why you want the person to visit you. Then write a letter to persuade that person to come.

Writer's Choice   What can we do to

understand people who are different from us? Perhaps you could give some advice. Perhaps you could tell what you have done to understand such a person. Write your response and share it in some way.

CONNECTIONS

MULTICULTURAL CONNECTION

Imported Ball Games

A ballplayer sprints across a walled court similar to a handball court. He leaps forward and catches a ball in a scoop called a *cesta* and flings the ball back at the wall at a speed well over 100 miles per hour.

He's playing *jai alai* (pronounced hī´lī), named by the Basque people of Spain and France. This name has been used in the Americas since jai alai came to Cuba in 1900. In Spain the game is called *pelota* (pronounced pā•lō´ta), meaning "ball."

Although the Basques may have improved jai alai, they may not have been its inventors. Some historians believe that the game was first played by the Aztecs in Mexico and that Spanish explorer Hernando Cortés carried it back to Spain more than 400 years ago.

Like jai alai, many of the games enjoyed in the Americas have come from other countries. With your classmates, list some games you enjoy. Then, on your own, research one or more of them. Write a report that describes the origin and rules of each game. You and your classmates can publish your reports in a games encyclopedia.

SOCIAL STUDIES CONNECTION

Guard the Chief!

Games and sports have always helped young people prepare for life. Find out what games Native American children played to develop important survival skills. Teach one to your classmates. Then, with a group, create a bulletin board on Native American games.

Southern Ute schoolchildren play *Nia-Kup,* "The Hand Game"

HEALTH CONNECTION

Fit for Living

Playing sports and games can make people healthier. Research how activity affects such physical functions as digestion, muscle tone, and circulation. Find out which physical activities are most beneficial and which are least beneficial. Share what you learn in a health newsletter.

UNIT TWO

Trials

Trials can mean different things to
different people. Trials can happen
in front of hundreds of spectators
or, as in trials held in many Native
American nations, in front of only
two participants and a judge. Maybe
the most challenging trials are those
that involve only one—a person
standing alone while being tested
by nature. As you read the selections
in this unit, compare the many
types of trials that people face.
Which experiences have you shared?
Which can you learn from?

THEMES

BOOKSHELF

STORMS

by Seymour Simon

Spectacular photographs illustrate some of nature's most extreme moments–including hurricanes, lightning strikes, and tornadoes.

Award-Winning Author

Harcourt Brace Library Book

ANNO'S HAT TRICKS

by Akihiro Nozaki and Mitsumasa Anno

If you like brainteasers, then hold on to your hat! Enter the world of the hatter. To solve his puzzles, you must learn how to think like a computer.

Outstanding Science Trade Book for Children

Harcourt Brace Library Book

BOAT GIRL

by Bernard Ashley

How will Kim cope with being the only refugee and the only Vietnamese in her London school?

BORIS

by Jaap ter Haar

Boris and Nadia struggle to survive as their home city of Leningrad is bombed during World War II.
Award-Winning Author

SONG OF THE CHIRIMIA

by Jane Anne Volkmer

Illustrations based on Mayan stone carvings accompany this colorful folktale from Guatemala, told in both Spanish and English.

T H E M E

Nature's Fury

Have you ever been frightened by lightning, pounded by hailstones, or snowed in by high drifts? If so, then you, like the people in these selections, know what it is like to face nature's fury.

C O N T E N T S

137

FROM

In for Winter, Out for Spring

by Arnold Adoff
illustrated by Jerry Pinkney

My Brother Aaron Runs Outside To Tell Us There Is A Severe
                                                    Thunder
                                                    Storm
                                                    Warning

Just Announced On The Radio While We Were Out
                                            U n d e r

A Perfectly Blue Sky
We Know How Fast The   Weather Can Change   How
                         Fast Those Storms   Can
                         Blow Across These   Corn
                         Fields   Every   Spring

We Bring   Our   Books
And Toys Inside And
Listen To The   Noon
                  News
Between   The   Soup
And   Sandwiches
And
Try   To Only   Think
        A b o u t
        Our Lunch

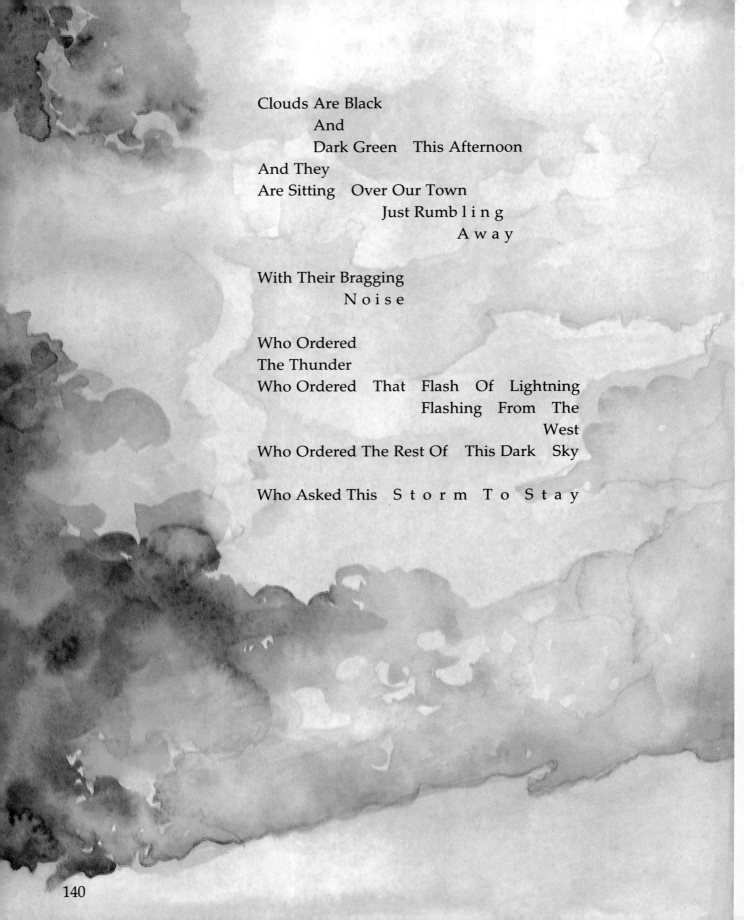

Clouds Are Black
    And
    Dark Green   This Afternoon
And They
Are Sitting   Over Our Town
        Just Rumb l i n g
           A w a y

With Their Bragging
      N o i s e

Who Ordered
The Thunder
Who Ordered   That   Flash   Of   Lightning
        Flashing   From   The
           West
Who Ordered The Rest Of   This Dark   Sky

Who Asked This S t o r m T o S t a y

Words from the Illustrator: Jerry Pinkney

People often think that an author and an illustrator work together on a book, but this is rarely the case. Usually, the author writes the book, and then the illustrator takes over. The situation with *In for Winter, Out for Spring* was a little different, though. I often run into Arnold Adoff, so for the first time I was working with an author I knew. While there was no discussion of how I would illustrate the book, Arnold did send me a tape of him reading the poems. That added a great deal to my interpretation.

After reading a manuscript, I draw small sketches called thumbnails. In these I sketch the situations that I think are the most interesting. Then I put together a dummy. This is a mock copy of the book showing the characters I plan to use. I send the dummy to the publisher, and if everyone agrees, I go ahead and hire the models for the characters.

With Arnold's poetry, I had a lot of images I could have chosen to illustrate. In the excerpt you read, for instance, I could have drawn more of the storm. But I had been looking for an opportunity to put the mother, the daughter, and the son in the same picture, and this seemed like a good place to do it. More than anything else, I wanted to emphasize the family aspect of this book.

AWARD-WINNING
AUTHOR

STORMS

SEYMOUR SIMON

MORROW

We live at the bottom of a blanket of air called the atmosphere. The atmosphere is always moving, sometimes slowly, other times quickly and violently. These changes in the atmosphere are called the weather. We call the violent changes storms.

Thunderstorms are the most powerful electrical storms in the atmosphere. In twenty minutes, a single thunderstorm can drop 125 million gallons of water and give off more electrical energy than is used in a large city during an entire week.

143

Lightning is an electrical discharge within a thunderstorm. As a thunderstorm develops, the clouds become charged with electricity. Scientists are still not sure exactly what causes this to happen. But they do know that as much as 100 million volts build up in the lower part of a thunderhead, and the temperature of a single bolt of lightning reaches 50,000 degrees F. within a few millionths of a second. That's almost five times greater than the temperature at the sun's surface.

Lightning flashes when the voltage becomes high enough for electricity to leap across the air from one place to another. Lightning can spark within the cloud, from one cloud to another, from ground to cloud, or from cloud to ground.

Thunder is the sound given off by the explosive expansion of air heated by a lightning stroke. When lightning is close, thunder sounds like a single, sharp crack. From farther away, thunder sounds like a growling or rumbling noise. Thunder usually can be heard easily from six or seven miles away, and even from twenty miles away on a quiet day.

Light is about a million times faster than sound, so you see a lightning bolt almost instantly, but the sound of thunder takes about five seconds to travel one mile. This makes it possible for you to judge the distance of a lightning stroke by timing how long it takes you to hear the thunder.

Count the number of seconds between the flash and the thunder. (You can count seconds by counting slowly in this way: and a one and a two and a three and a four and a five, and so on.) Divide the number of seconds by five. The number you get is the number of miles away the lightning struck.

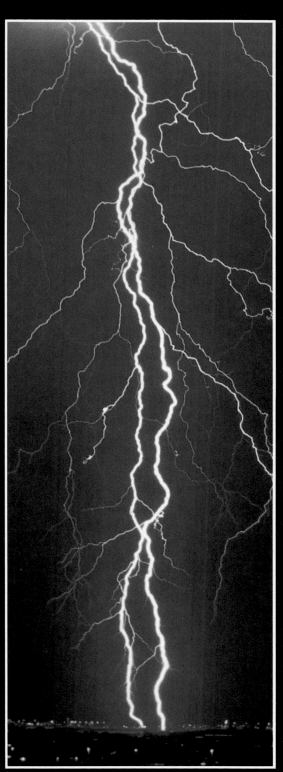

Sometimes a thunderstorm gives birth to a tornado. The wind blows hard and trees bend. Heavy rains or hailstones fall. Lightning and thunder rip the dark sky, and a howling roar like hundreds of jet planes fills the air.

Spinning winds inside the thunderstorm begin forming a funnel-shaped cloud that reaches downward to the ground. When it contacts the earth, an explosion of flying dirt turns the tornado dark.

This remarkable series of photos shows the life of a tornado in hours, minutes, and seconds.

As the spinning winds pick up speed, the tornado grows larger and larger. The funnel skips across the ground, sometimes setting down, sometimes bouncing upward, and then touching down again, leaving semicircular marks on the ground like the hoofprints of giant horses. The funnel moves forward at speeds averaging thirty miles per hour, but some tornadoes travel at more than sixty miles per hour.

Like the hose of an enormous vacuum cleaner, the tornado picks up loose materials and whirls them aloft. In less than fifteen minutes, the funnel cloud becomes clogged with dirt and air and can no longer suck up any more. The cloud becomes lighter in color as less dirt is swept aloft. As the tornado begins to lag behind the parent thunder-head, it narrows and finally vanishes altogether.

The twisting winds of a tornado whirl around the funnel at speeds of 200 miles an hour or more. Houses may be knocked down and blown apart by the wind. Then the tornado picks up the pieces, along with chairs, tables, and beds, and carries them away.

If you know a tornado is coming, go indoors, but stay away from windows. In a house, the safest place is in the cellar. Get under a table or under the stairs. If there is no cellar, go to a closet or a small room in the middle of the house. Cover yourself with a blanket or heavy towels to protect against flying glass.

Tornadoes sometimes do strange things. Once a car with two people inside was lifted to a height of 100 feet, then deposited right side up without injuring the passengers. Another tornado lifted a train locomotive from one track, spun it around in midair, and then set it down on another track facing the opposite direction.

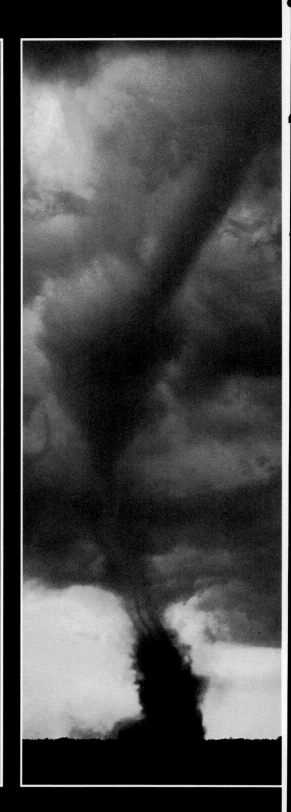

HURRICANE ALICIA
7PM CDT AUG 17 1983

There are many ancient myths about storms. The early Norsemen believed that Thor was the god of thunderstorms. They thought that lightning struck when Thor threw his mighty hammer and thunder rumbled when his chariot struck storm clouds.

Nowadays, radar, satellites, and computers keep track of storms and help scientists forecast their behavior. But the more scientists learn about storms, the more complicated they find them to be. Storms still arouse our sense of awe and wonder.

Do you agree with Seymour Simon that storms "arouse our sense of awe and wonder"? Why or why not?

What are some of the dangerous things that can happen during a thunderstorm?

According to the selection, what is one thing that ancient myths and modern technology have in common?

WRITE   What would you do if you knew a tornado was coming? Write a set of directions telling what to do and what not to do during a tornado.

Night

of

the

Twisters

CHILDREN'S CHOICE

by Ivy Ruckman
illustrated by Jeffrey Terreson

The night of June 4, 1980, is a dark and stormy one in Grand Island, Nebraska. Some people are even predicting a tornado. Dan is at home with his mother and his baby brother Ryan. Unafraid of the gathering storm, Dan's friend Arthur has come over to watch a comedy on TV.

Mom's forehead puckered as she walked away. I knew what was on her mind. We were both wishing Dad was home.

We watched TV another few minutes, but I couldn't get into it like before. Not that I was scared, exactly. I'd been through dozens of tornado watches in my life and nothing ever happened, though a barn roof got rearranged over in Clay Center one year. Every spring, practically, we have to "hit for the cellar," as Grandpa puts it. But when a tornado watch changes to a warning, and when the siren starts . . . well . . . that's when things aren't so mellow anymore.

"Shouldn't you call your mother, Arthur?" Mom said to him after trying the phone again. "I'm not sure she'd want you to stay here tonight."

"Oh, Mom!" I groaned. (There I was, thinking the sun rose and set on me.)

"Wait, I'd better call Goldie first," she said. "Someone should run over and check on Mrs. Smiley. When she turns that hearing aid down . . ."

After a while she hung up again. "Doesn't anybody stay home?" she muttered.

By then I was standing in the kitchen doorway, trying to tell her Aunt Goldie had probably gone bowling.

"Who you calling now?" I asked instead. Her attacks on the phone were suddenly more interesting than what was happening in living color on the nineteen-inch screen.

"Mrs. Smiley. Ssssh . . ."

"She's trying to finish a needlepoint cushion for the Presbyterians," Arthur piped up from the sofa.

"Yeah," I whispered in Mom's face, remembering, "and I'm supposed to tell you not to forget she's coming Friday for you to fix her hair."

All the while Mom was waving her hand for us to be quiet, so I backed away.

Next thing I knew she was at the hall closet, putting her red Windbreaker on over her jeans and Hastings College T-shirt.

"She doesn't answer," she said. "I'm driving over there to make sure she has her TV on. I won't be long. Now listen, both of you."

We listened. She was using a very firm voice.

"I want you to take this flashlight"—she got it off the shelf and handed it to me—"and a blanket and put them in the downstairs bathroom. I want you to do it *this minute!*" I nodded, trying the flashlight to make sure it worked.

"If the siren starts, get Ryan and go downstairs. Don't wake him up if you can help it, all right?"

Arthur's eyes got big listening to Mom. He told me once they never go to the basement during windstorms. That figures. They moved here from California, what do they know? Ever hear of a tornado in good old CA?

Mom went to get a blanket.

"I'll be right back," she told us, hooking her purse on her shoulder. "I'm sure nothing's going to happen, but we have to be prepared, right? Your father would have a fit if we ignored the siren."

She smiled and waved her car keys at us as she left, barely squeezing out before the door slammed shut again.

"Whooeeeee!" Arthur exclaimed. "Sounds like my bull-roarer outside!"

I hurried downstairs with the emergency stuff and set it on the bathroom counter. Minerva went with me, scurrying across my feet on the steps, acting the way she does when she wants attention.

I picked her up by the middle, smoothed down her stripes, and balanced her on the glass door of the shower. Usually

153

she'll do a tightrope act for me, but she only yowled and jumped off. After giving me her mean jungle look, she sat down to dig at her ear.

"You got a flea in there?" I asked, bending to give her a good scratching.

She didn't like that, either.

Upstairs, Arthur was hooting and hollering again. I decided I was missing all the good parts, so I hurried up the two short flights of steps, with Minerva dashing ahead of me.

Sometime in there, in the middle of all that comedy on the screen, the siren began. Now, *that* is a very sobering sound. It's unlike anything else, having its own built-in chill factor.

I thought of Mom first. She'd hear it and come back, I told myself.

Then I thought of Dad and how far the farm was from town. They wouldn't even hear the siren out there.

In half a second, I was at the phone, dialing 555-2379.

Four rings. Then I heard Grandma's voice.

"Grandma!" I shouted into the phone. "Where have you been? There's a tornado just north of G.I. The siren's going, can you hear it?"

A voice said something, but it sounded so far away.

"Talk louder, Grandma! I can't hear you."

The voice faded away entirely. I wasn't even sure it was Grandma's now.

"There's a tornado coming! Can you hear me?"

Finally, there wasn't anything on the line but the sound of another phone ringing very faintly, as if it were in New York or someplace far away. I couldn't figure it out.

By then, Arthur was standing next to me. I was just about to hand him the phone when, abruptly, the siren stopped. It didn't taper off, it just quit, as if someone snipped it with scissors. Except for the TV, everything around us suddenly seemed very still.

"Hey," he said, raising his eyebrows, "they changed their minds."

155

I hung up the phone. I didn't know what was happening.

"Maybe they got their weather signals crossed," he suggested happily. "They could, you know. I read a book once about that happening, where this whole fleet of fishing boats put out to sea . . ." he rattled on.

I ran to the door, thinking I might see Mom pulling into the driveway, but no luck.

"It's quit blowing," I called over my shoulder to Arthur.

Sure enough, the wind had died down. Maybe the storm wouldn't amount to anything after all.

That nice comforting thought had hardly entered my mind when the siren blared forth again. With a jolt, I remembered what Mom had told us to do.

"We always turn on the radio," Arthur said, already on his way to the kitchen. "You want me to? I'll get the weather station."

I was hardly listening. I hurried down the bedroom hallway to Ryan's room at the end. I hated like everything to get him up. He'd cry. I knew he'd wake up and cry. Without Mom, Arthur and I would have him screaming in our ears the whole time.

When I saw him in his crib, peacefully sleeping on the side of his face, his rear end in the air, I just didn't have the heart to wake him up. I'd wait a minute or two. Mom would be back. Anyway, it's blowing over, I told myself, it won't last.

Quietly, I closed the door behind me.

That's when the lights started flickering.

In the hallway, I practically had a head-on with Arthur, who was coming at me real fast. The look on his face scared me.

"There's no . . . there's no . . ."

"*What?*"

"There's no radio reception anymore. It just went dead! This guy . . . He kept saying, 'Tornado alert, tornado alert!' Then it went dead."

We rushed back to the living room. The TV was flashing these big letters that filled the entire screen: CD . . . CD . . . CD . . .

157

"What's it mean?" Arthur cried.

"Civil Defense Emergency!" I whirled around. "I'm getting Ryan!"

The lights flickered again.

At the same time we heard these really strange sounds that stopped us in our tracks. They were coming from the bathroom and the kitchen. Sucking sounds. The drains were sucking! I felt this awful pulling in my ears, too, as if there were vacuums on both sides of my head.

"I've got to go home!" Arthur cried all of a sudden, bolting for the door.

I ran after him. "You're not—you can't!" I grabbed the back of his T-shirt, hauled him around, and pushed him toward the stairs. "Get *down* there. I have to get Ryan! Now *go!*"

I don't know what I'd have done if he hadn't minded me. We were catching the fear from each other, and even though the siren was screaming on and off again, so I didn't know what it was telling us, I knew we had to take cover fast.

The lights went out for good just before I reached Ryan's room. I smashed face first into Ryan's butterfly mobile. That's how I knew I was at the crib. I felt for him, got my hands under his nightshirt and diaper, rolled him over. I lifted him, but we didn't get far. He was caught in the mobile, his arm or his head . . . I couldn't see . . . I couldn't get him loose. . . .

"Mom!" I yelled, though I knew she wasn't there.

I tried to lay him down again, but he was so tangled, part of him was still up in the air. He started to cry.

"Wait, Ryan, I'll get you out!" But I couldn't.

Finally, holding him with my left arm, I climbed onto the side of the crib. My right hand followed the string up the mobile, way up to the hook. I yanked it loose. The whole thing came crashing down on top of us as I jumped backward off the crib.

The plastic butterfly poking me was poking Ryan, too, but I didn't care. The tornado was close, and I knew it. Both my ears had popped, and I had this crazy fear that those drains, sucking like monsters now, would get us if the storm didn't.

Arthur was at the bottom of the stairs, waiting. Thank God he'd found the flashlight! I jumped the last half-flight to the floor.

"Hurry!" I screamed. I swung into the doorway of the bathroom, with Arthur right behind me. We crouched under the towel rack.

"Shine it here, on Ryan," I gasped. "He's caught in this thing." By now Ryan was kicking and screaming, and his eyes were big in the light.

Once we got the mess of strings free of Ryan's sweaty nightshirt, Arthur kicked the mobile against the wall by the toilet.

"I have to go home!" he cried. "They won't go to the basement. Mama never does."

The beam of light bounced around the blackness of the bathroom as Arthur scrambled to his feet, but I grabbed and held on to him.

"You can't go! It's here! Can't you feel it?"

The siren quit again as I pulled him back down and threw my leg over him. The flashlight clattered to the floor and rolled away from us.

We heard it next. The lull. The deadliest quiet ever, one that makes you think you might explode. The heat in that room built until I couldn't get my breath.

Then I began to hear noises. A chair scraping across the kitchen floor upstairs.

"Your mom's back!" Arthur said, pushing at my leg.

I knew it wasn't my mother moving the chair.

The noises got worse. It seemed as if every piece of furniture was moving around up there . . . big, heavy things, smashing into each other.

A window popped.

Crash! Another.

Glass, shattering—everywhere—right next to us in the laundry room.

I pulled a towel down over Ryan and held him tight. If he was still crying, I didn't know it because I was *feeling* the sucking this time. It was like something trying to lift my body right up off the floor.

Arthur felt it, too. "Mother of God!" He crossed himself. "We're going to die!"

Ten seconds more and that howling, shrieking tornado was upon us.

"The blanket!" I screamed at Arthur's ear.

He pulled it down from the countertop and we covered ourselves, our hands shaking wildly. I wasn't worrying about my mom then or my dad or Mrs. Smiley. Just us. Ryan and Arthur and me, huddled together there on the floor.

The roaring had started somewhere to the east, then came bearing down on us like a hundred freight trains. Only that twister didn't move on. It stationed itself right overhead, making the loudest noise I'd ever heard, whining worse than any jet. There was a tremendous crack, and I felt the wall shudder behind us. I knew then our house was being ripped apart. Suddenly chunks of ceiling were falling on our heads.

We'll be buried! was all I could think.

At that moment, as plain as anything above that deafening roar, I heard my dad's voice: *The shower's the safest place.*

I didn't question hearing it. Holding Ryan against me with one arm, I began crawling toward the shower stall. I reached back and yanked at Arthur's shirt. Somehow we got inside with the blanket. Another explosion, and the glass shower door shattered all over the bathroom floor.

We pulled the blanket over our heads and I began to pray. Out loud, though I couldn't hear my own voice: "God help us, God help us." I said it over and over, into Ryan's damp hair, my lips moving against his head. I knew Arthur was praying, too, jammed there into my side. I could feel Ryan's heart beating through his undershirt against mine. *My* heart was thanking God for making me go back for him, but not in words. Outside those places where our bodies touched, there was nothing but terror as the roar of that tornado went on and

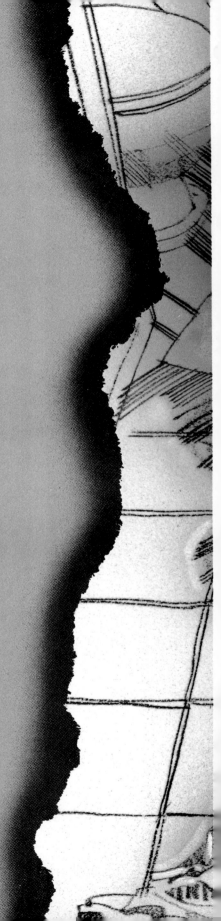

161

on. I thought the world was coming to an end, *had* come to an end, and so would we, any minute.

Then I felt Ryan's fat fingers close around one of mine. He pulled my hand to his mouth and started sucking on my finger. It made me cry. The tears ran down my cheeks and onto his head. With the whole world blowing to pieces around us, Ryan took my hand and made me feel better.

Afterward, neither Arthur nor I was able to say how long we huddled there in the basement shower.

"A tornado's forward speed is generally thirty to fifty miles an hour," the meteorologist had told us.

Our tornado's forward speed was zero. It parked right there on Sand Crane Drive. Five minutes or ten, we couldn't tell, but it seemed like an hour. Roaring and humming and shrieking, that twister was right on top of us. I'll never be that scared again as long as I live. Neither will Arthur.

How did you feel while you read the story?

What problems does Dan face in the story?

At the beginning of the selection, Dan and Arthur are not very worried about the approaching storm. What events lead them to realize that they are in great danger?

The story does not say that the boys are cold during the tornado. Why do they cover themselves with a blanket?

WRITE Think about Dan's behavior throughout the selection. How would you react in the same situation? Write a report that praises some of Dan's actions and criticizes others.

FROM
TORNADO!
POEMS BY ARNOLD ADOFF
ILLUSTRATED BY RONALD HIMLER

Poet Arnold Adoff lived through the fury of a tornado strike in his home near Xenia, Ohio. In these poems, he describes how the people rose up on the day after and went on with their lives.

CHILDREN'S CHOICE

in the morning

the sky is blue
and it is school
again

hungry
hungry hurry
up

at our school

the skylights have big holes
through their glass panes
there is glass all over
all the floors

it is a day for wearing shoes
even on the mats

164

the firemen start yelling

get away from there
these
buildings
can fall
at any time

will have to be
knocked
down as soon as the people
move their things away

one girl is carrying
her winter coat
her boots
out to a truck

one boy is playing
where
his
house had been
is not

you can see

a broken house
a street of broken
houses
a broken baby doll
in the boards

dogs and cats
are
sniffing
hungry
and
cows are strolling
down the
street

the woman

is telling about the wind

it was not just the wind
and the pressure
on your back
on your head
you couldn't get up
you couldn't
move

but the wind was full of dirt
and sand and filth and rocks
so many bits of
glass
and heavy things

heavy things
in the
air

momma says

that's why
the funnel
cloud
is
black

not the
color
of
the
wind

but dirt and boards
and trees
and stone

daddy says

there will be
storms for many springs
for many summers

momma says
we can be tougher
than some thunder
noise
some flash

grandma
says
the last time one came
through here was fifty
years ago and i can
wait another fifty
for the next

brother says

it never seems to rain
in a quiet way out here
just water
for the garden
and the corn fields
when they get dry

just wet
no
wind
it never seems to rain
in a quiet
way

i say
that's right
good
night

and anyway

no
old
tornado

i don't care
how
bad

is stronger
than the
people on the land

168

Nature's Fury

According to the selections and poems, what impact can a tornado have on people's lives?

WRITER'S WORKSHOP

Not all parts of the country experience tornadoes, but people everywhere know nature's fury firsthand. For example, people who live in some coastal states are familiar with hurricanes, while people living in northern states are prepared for ice storms. What sorts of weather emergencies have you experienced? Write a descriptive paragraph about a severe storm or other weather condition you have lived through.

Writer's Choice   Storms are a part of nature.

What are your feelings about nature's fury now that you have read these selections? Respond in your own way. Share your feelings with your classmates.

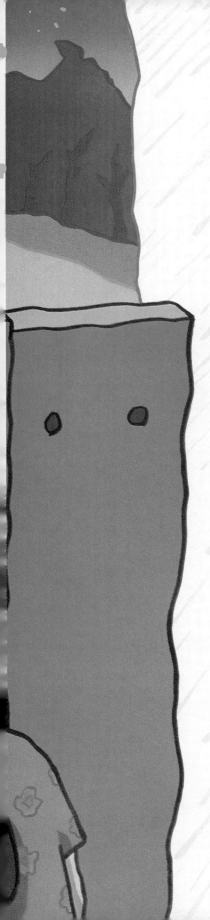

T H E M E

Trespasses

There are boundaries that can be seen—such as locked doors—and boundaries that cannot be seen—such as laws. When the characters in these selections cross those boundaries, they trespass.

C O N T E N T S

From the Mixed-up Files of Mrs. Basil E. Frankweiler

NEWBERY MEDAL

LEWIS CARROLL
SHELF AWARD

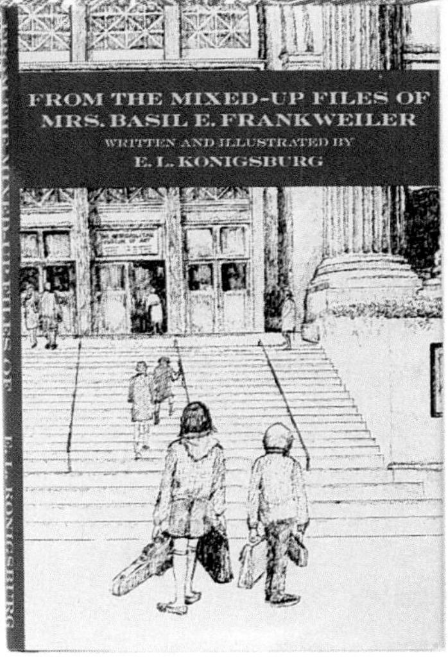

FROM THE MIXED-UP FILES OF
MRS. BASIL E. FRANKWEILER
WRITTEN AND ILLUSTRATED BY
E. L. KONIGSBURG

**Written and illustrated
by
E. L.
Konigsburg**

Claudia has a goal—to make her family appreciate her more. She also has a plan—to run away, temporarily, so that they'll all have a chance to miss her.

Problem 1: Where can she go that is nearby, safe, and interesting?
Solution: The Metropolitan Museum of Art in New York City

Problem 2: How can she finance such an adventure?
Solution: Bring along her penny-wise younger brother Jamie as treasurer

In the following account, written by Mrs. Basil E. Frankweiler to a lawyer named Saxonberg, Claudia sets her plan in motion.

AS SOON AS THEY REACHED THE SIDEWALK, JAMIE made his first decision as treasurer. "We'll walk from here to the museum."

"Walk?" Claudia asked. "Do you realize that it is over forty blocks from here?"

"Well, how much does the bus cost?"

"The bus!" Claudia exclaimed. "Who said anything about taking a bus? I want to take a taxi."

"Claudia," Jamie said, "you are quietly out of your mind. How can you even think of a taxi? We have no more allowance. No more income. You can't be extravagant any longer. It's not my money we're spending. It's *our* money. We're in this together, remember?"

"You're right," Claudia answered. "A taxi is expensive. The bus is cheaper. It's only twenty cents each. We'll take the bus."

"*Only* twenty cents each. That's forty cents total. No bus. We'll walk."

"We'll wear out forty cents worth of shoe leather," Claudia mumbled. "You're sure we have to walk?"

"Positive," Jamie answered. "Which way do we go?"

"Sure you won't change your mind?" The look on Jamie's face gave her the answer. She sighed. No wonder Jamie had more than twenty-four dollars; he was a gambler and a cheapskate. If that's the way he wants to be, she thought, I'll never again ask him for bus fare; I'll suffer and never, never let him know about it. But he'll regret it when I simply collapse from exhaustion. I'll collapse quietly.

"We'd better walk up Madison Avenue," she told her brother. "I'll see too many ways to spend *our* precious money if we walk on Fifth Avenue. All those gorgeous stores."

She and Jamie did not walk exactly side by side. Her violin case kept bumping him, and he began to walk a few steps ahead of her. As Claudia's pace slowed down from what she was sure was an accumulation of carbon dioxide in her system (she had not yet learned about muscle fatigue in science class even though she was in the sixth grade honors class), Jamie's pace quickened. Soon he was walking a block and a half ahead of her. They would meet when a red light held him up. At one of these mutual stops Claudia instructed Jamie to wait for her on the corner of Madison Avenue and 80th Street, for there they would turn left to Fifth Avenue.

She found Jamie standing on that corner, probably one of the most civilized street corners in the whole world, consulting a compass and announcing that when they turned left, they would be heading "due northwest." Claudia was tired and cold at the tips; her fingers, her toes, her nose were all cold while the rest of her was perspiring under the weight of her winter clothes. She never liked feeling either very hot or very cold, and she hated feeling both at the same time. "Head due northwest. Head due northwest," she mimicked. "Can't you simply say turn right or turn left as everyone else does? Who do you think you are? Daniel Boone? I'll bet no one's used a compass in Manhattan since Henry Hudson."

Jamie didn't answer. He briskly rounded the corner of 80th Street and made his hand into a sun visor as he peered down the street. Claudia needed an argument. Her internal heat, the heat of anger, was cooking that accumulated carbon dioxide. It would soon explode out of her if she didn't give it some vent. "Don't you realize that we must try to be inconspicuous?" she demanded of her brother.

"What's inconspicuous?"

"Un-noticeable."

Jamie looked all around. "I think you're brilliant, Claude. New York is a great place to hide out. No one notices no one."

"Anyone," Claudia corrected. She looked at Jamie and found him smiling. She softened. She had to agree with her brother. She was brilliant. New York was a great place, and being called brilliant had cooled her down. The bubbles dissolved. By the time they reached the museum, she no longer needed an argument.

As they entered the main door on Fifth Avenue, the guard clicked off two numbers on his people counter. Guards always

count the people going into the museum, but they don't count them going out. (My chauffeur, Sheldon, has a friend named Morris who is a guard at the Metropolitan. I've kept Sheldon busy getting information from Morris. It's not hard to do since Morris loves to talk about his work. He'll tell about anything except security. Ask him a question he won't or can't answer, and he says, "I'm not at liberty to tell. Security.")

By the time Claudia and Jamie reached their destination, it was one o'clock, and the museum was busy. On any ordinary Wednesday over 26,000 people come. They spread out over the twenty acres of floor space; they roam from room to room to room to room to room. On Wednesday come the gentle old ladies who are using the time before the Broadway matinee begins. They walk around in pairs. You can tell they are a set because they wear matching pairs of orthopedic shoes, the kind that lace on the side. Tourists visit the museum on Wednesdays. You can tell them because the men carry cameras, and the women look as if their feet hurt; they wear high heeled shoes. (I always say that those who wear 'em deserve 'em.) And there are art students. Any day of the week. They also walk around in pairs. You can tell that they are a set because they carry matching black sketchbooks.

(You've missed all this, Saxonberg. Shame on you! You've never set your well-polished shoe inside that museum. More than a quarter of a million people come to that museum every week. They come from Mankato, Kansas, where they have no museums and from Paris, France, where they have lots. And they all enter free of charge because that's what the museum is: great and large and wonderful and free to all. And complicated. Complicated enough even for Jamie Kincaid.)

No one thought it strange that a boy and a girl, each carrying a book bag and an instrument case and who would normally be in school, were visiting a museum. After all, about a thousand school children visit the museum every day. The guard at the entrance merely stopped them and told them to check their cases and book bags. A museum rule: no bags, food, or umbrellas. None that the guards can see. Rule or no rule, Claudia decided it was a good idea. A big sign in the checking room said NO TIPPING, so she knew that Jamie couldn't object. Jamie did object, however; he pulled his sister aside and asked her how she expected him to change into his pajamas. His pajamas, he explained, were rolled into a tiny ball in his trumpet case.

Claudia told him that she fully expected to check out at 4:30. They would then leave the museum by the front door and within five minutes would re-enter from the back, through the door that leads from the parking lot to the Children's Museum. After all, didn't that solve all their problems? (1) They would

177

be seen leaving the museum. (2) They would be free of their baggage while they scouted around for a place to spend the night. And (3) it was free.

Claudia checked her coat as well as her packages. Jamie was condemned to walking around in his ski jacket. When the jacket was on and zippered, it covered up that exposed strip of skin. Besides, the orlon plush lining did a great deal to muffle his twenty-four-dollar rattle. Claudia would never have permitted herself to become so overheated, but Jamie liked perspiration, a little bit of dirt, and complications.

Right now, however, he wanted lunch. Claudia wished to eat in the restaurant on the main floor, but Jamie wished to eat in the snack bar downstairs; he thought it would be less glamorous, but cheaper, and as chancellor of the exchequer, as holder of the veto power, and as tightwad of the year, he got his wish. Claudia didn't really mind too much when she saw the snack bar. It was plain but clean.

James was dismayed at the prices. They had $28.61 when they went into the cafeteria, and only $27.11 when they came out still feeling hungry. "Claudia," he demanded, "did you know food would cost so much? Now, aren't you glad that we didn't take a bus?"

Claudia was no such thing. She was not glad that they hadn't taken a bus. She was merely furious that her parents, and Jamie's too, had been so stingy that she had been away from home for less than one whole day and was already worried about survival money. She chose not to answer Jamie. Jamie didn't notice; he was completely wrapped up in problems of finance.

"Do you think I could get one of the guards to play me a game of war?" he asked.

"That's ridiculous," Claudia said.

"Why? I brought my cards along. A whole deck."

Claudia said, "*Inconspicuous* is exactly the opposite of that. Even a guard at the Metropolitan who sees thousands of people every day would remember a boy who played him a game of cards."

Jamie's pride was involved. "I cheated Bruce through all second grade and through all third grade so far, and he still isn't wise."

"Jamie! Is that how you knew you'd win?"

Jamie bowed his head and answered, "Well, yeah. Besides, Brucie has trouble keeping straight the jacks, queens, and kings. He gets mixed up."

"Why do you cheat your best friend?"

"I sure don't know. I guess I like complications."

"Well, quit worrying about money now. Worry about where we're going to hide while they're locking up this place."

They took a map from the information stand, for free. Claudia selected where they would hide during that dangerous time immediately after the museum was closed to the public and before all the guards and helpers left. She decided that she would go to the ladies' room, and Jamie would go to the men's room just before the museum closed. "Go to the one near the restaurant on the main floor," she told Jamie.

"I'm not spending a night in a men's room. All that tile. It's cold. And, besides, men's rooms make noises sound louder. And I rattle enough now."

Claudia explained to Jamie that he was to enter a booth in the men's room. "And then stand on it," she continued.

"Stand on it? Stand on what?" Jamie demanded.

"You know," Claudia insisted. "Stand on it!"

"You mean stand on the toilet?" Jamie needed everything spelled out.

"Well, what else would I mean? What else is there in a booth in the men's room? And keep your head down. And keep the door to the booth very slightly open," Claudia finished.

"Feet up. Head down. Door open. Why?"

"Because I'm certain that when they check the ladies' room and the men's room, they peek under the door and check only to see if there are feet. We must stay there until we're sure all the people and guards have gone home."

"How about the night watchman?" Jamie asked.

Claudia displayed a lot more confidence than she really felt. "Oh! there'll be a night watchman, I'm sure. But he mostly walks around the roof trying to keep people from breaking in. We'll already be in. They call what he walks, a cat walk. We'll learn his habits soon enough. They must mostly use burglar alarms in the inside. We'll just never touch a window, a door, or a valuable painting. Now, let's find a place to spend the night."

They wandered back to the rooms of fine French and English furniture. It was here Claudia knew for sure that she had chosen the most elegant place in the world to hide. She wanted to sit on the lounge chair that had been made for Marie Antoinette or at least sit at her writing table. But signs everywhere said not to step on the platform. And some of the chairs had silken ropes strung across the arms to keep you from even trying to sit down. She would have to wait until after lights out to be Marie Antoinette.

At last she found a bed that she considered perfectly wonderful, and she told Jamie that they would spend the night there. The bed had a tall canopy, supported by an ornately carved headboard at one end and by two gigantic posts at the other. (I'm familiar with that bed, Saxonberg. It is as enormous and fussy as mine. And it dates from the sixteenth century like mine. I once considered donating my bed to the museum, but Mr. Untermyer gave them this one first. I was somewhat relieved when he did. Now I can enjoy my bed without feeling guilty because the museum doesn't have one. Besides, I'm not that fond of donating things.)

Claudia had always known that she was meant for such fine things. Jamie, on the other hand, thought that running away from home to sleep in just another bed was really no challenge at all. He, James, would rather sleep on the bathroom floor, after all. Claudia then pulled him around to the foot of the bed and told him to read what the card said.

Jamie read, "Please do not step on the platform."

Claudia knew that he was being difficult on purpose; therefore, she read for him, "State bed—scene of the alleged murder of Amy Robsart, first wife of Lord Robert Dudley, later Earl of . . ."

Jamie couldn't control his smile. He said, "You know, Claude, for a sister and a fussbudget, you're not too bad."

Claudia replied, "You know, Jamie, for a brother and a cheapskate, you're not too bad."

Something happened at precisely that moment. Both Claudia and Jamie tried to explain to me about it, but they couldn't quite. I know what happened, though I never told

them. Having words and explanations for everything is too modern. I especially wouldn't tell Claudia. She has too many explanations already.

What happened was: they became a team, a family of two. There had been times before they ran away when they had acted like a team, but those were very different from *feeling* like a team. Becoming a team didn't mean the end of their arguments. But it did mean that the arguments became a part of the adventure, became discussions not threats. To an outsider the arguments would appear to be the same because feeling like part of a team is something that happens invisibly. You might call it *caring*. You could even call it *love*. And it is very rarely, indeed, that it happens to two people at the same time— especially a brother and a sister who had always spent more time with activities than they had with each other.

They followed their plan: checked out of the museum and re-entered through a back door. When the guard at that entrance told them to check their instrument cases, Claudia told him that they were just passing through on their way to meet their mother. The guard let them go, knowing that if they went very far, some other guard would stop them again. However, they managed to avoid other guards for the remaining minutes until the bell rang. The bell meant that the museum was closing in five minutes. They then entered the booths of the rest rooms.

They waited in the booths until five-thirty, when they felt certain that everyone had gone. Then they came out and met. Five-thirty in winter is dark, but nowhere seems as dark as the Metropolitan Museum of Art. The ceilings are so high that they fill up with a lot of darkness. It seemed to Jamie and Claudia that they walked through miles of corridors. Fortunately, the corridors were wide, and they were spared bumping into things.

At last they came to the hall of the English Renaissance. Jamie quickly threw himself upon the bed forgetting that it was only about six o'clock and thinking that he would be so exhausted that he would immediately fall asleep. He didn't.

He was hungry. That was one reason he didn't fall asleep immediately. He was uncomfortable, too. So he got up from bed, changed into his pajamas and got back into bed. He felt a little better. Claudia had already changed into her pajamas. She, too, was hungry, and she, too, was uncomfortable. How could so elegant and romantic a bed smell so musty? She would have liked to wash everything in a good, strong, sweet-smelling detergent.

As Jamie got into bed, he still felt uneasy, and it wasn't because he was worried about being caught. Claudia had planned everything so well that he didn't concern himself about that. The strange way he felt had little to do with the strange place in which they were sleeping. Claudia felt it, too. Jamie lay there thinking. Finally, realization came.

"You know, Claude," he whispered, "I didn't brush my teeth."

Claudia answered, "Well, Jamie, you can't always brush after every meal." They both laughed very quietly. "Tomorrow," Claudia reassured him, "we'll be even better organized."

It was much earlier than her bedtime at home, but still Claudia felt tired. She thought she might have an iron deficiency anemia: tired blood. Perhaps, the pressures of everyday stress and strain had gotten her down. Maybe she was light-headed from hunger; her brain cells were being robbed of vitally needed oxygen for good growth and, and . . . yawn.

She shouldn't have worried. It had been an unusually busy day. A busy and unusual day. So she lay there in the great quiet of the museum next to the warm quiet of her brother and allowed the soft stillness to settle around them: a comforter of quiet. The silence seeped from their heads to their soles and into their souls. They stretched out and relaxed. Instead of oxygen and stress, Claudia thought now of hushed and quiet words: glide, fur, banana, peace. Even the footsteps of the night watchman added only an accented quarter-note to the silence that had become a hum, a lullaby.

They lay perfectly still even long after he passed. Then they whispered good night to each other and fell asleep. They were quiet sleepers and hidden by the heaviness of the dark, they were easily not discovered.

(Of course, Saxonberg, the draperies of that bed helped, too.)

Would you have stayed with Claudia in the museum? Why or why not?

How do you know that Claudia is familiar with the museum?

Describe Claudia's personality. Describe Jamie's personality. Why do they make a good team for their adventure?

Why do Claudia and Jamie visit the French and English furniture section of the museum?

WRITE   What do you think will happen in the morning? Write a short description of what you think will happen next. Include some dialogue between Claudia and Jamie.

E. L. KONIGSBURG

Author E. L. (Elaine) Konigsburg got the idea for *From the Mixed-up Files of Mrs. Basil E. Frankweiler* from three experiences. Two of them were reading experiences. "I read in the *New York Times* that the Metropolitan Museum of Art in New York City had bought a statue for $225. At the time of the purchase they did not know who had sculpted it, but they suspected it had been done by someone famous."

"Shortly after that article appeared in the paper, I read a book about the adventures of some children, who, upon being sent by ship from their island home to England, were captured by pirates. In the company of the pirates, the children became piratical themselves."

The third thing that happened was a picnic that Mrs. Konigsburg went on with her husband and three children in Yellowstone Park. There were no outdoor tables or chairs, so the family had to eat their salami and bread and chips and chocolate milk crouching slightly above the ground. "Then," she says, "the complaints began: the milk was getting warm, and there were ants over everything, and the sun was melting the icing on the cupcakes. I thought to myself, that if my children ever left home they would never become barbarians even if they were captured by pirates. They would want at least all the comforts of home plus a few extra dashes of elegance." She began thinking of places where they might go and decided the only place they would possibly run away to would be the Metropolitan Museum of Art.

You Be the Jury

by **Marvin Miller**

illustrated by **Harvey Chan**

◆

Ladies and Gentlemen of the Jury:

This court is now in session. My name is Judge John Denenberg. You are the jury, and the trials are set to begin.

You have a serious responsibility. Will the innocent be sent to jail and the guilty go free? Let's hope not. Your job is to make sure that justice is served.

Read each case carefully. Study the evidence presented and then decide:

Innocent or Guilty?

Both sides of the case will be presented to you. The person who has the complaint is called the *plaintiff*. He has brought the case to court.

The person being accused is called the *defendant*. He is pleading his innocence and presents a much different version of what happened.

IN EACH CASE, THREE PIECES OF EVIDENCE WILL BE PRESENTED AS EXHIBITS A, B, AND C. EXAMINE THE EXHIBITS VERY CAREFULLY. A *CLUE* TO THE SOLUTION OF EACH CASE WILL BE FOUND THERE. IT WILL DIRECTLY POINT TO THE INNOCENCE OR GUILT OF THE ACCUSED.

Remember, each side will try to convince you that his version is what actually happened. BUT YOU MUST MAKE THE FINAL DECISION.

◆ ✦ ◆

◆ The Case of the Wrong Bag ◆

LADIES AND GENTLEMEN OF THE JURY:

A person who is found with stolen property is not necessarily a thief.

Keep this in mind as you go over the facts in this case. Since we are in criminal court today, the State is the accuser. In this case, the State, represented by the district attorney, has accused John Summers of robbing Kay's Jewelry Store. John Summers, the defendant, has pleaded innocent and claims that his arrest is a mistake.

The State called the owner of Kay's Jewelry Store as its first witness. She has testified as follows:

"My name is Wendy Kay, and I own Kay's Jewelry Store in Martinville. I was working alone in the store on Wednesday afternoon, December 2, when a man walked in. It was exactly 3:30. I noticed the time because I had just put a new collection of diamond watches from Switzerland on display. I noticed the man because he had a handkerchief over his face. I thought that was odd until I also noticed the outline of a gun projecting from his pocket. That's when I got scared."

The man ordered Wendy Kay to empty a case of jewels and all the store's cash into a black bag. The robbery took only minutes, and the thief escaped on foot.

At four o'clock the next afternoon, John Summers entered the lobby of the Bristol Hotel and walked over to the luggage checkroom. He pointed to a black bag, which the bellman gave him. As he handed the bellman a tip, a hotel detective noticed that Summers's bag matched the description of the bag used in the jewelry store robbery. He arrested Summers and called the police.

When the police opened the bag and emptied its contents, a look of shock and surprise spread over Summers's face. Inside was the stolen jewelry.

John Summers was dumbfounded. He claimed he had pointed to the wrong bag in the hotel checkroom. This bag was not his, he said, but an identical twin belonging to someone else. His own bag contained a blue toothbrush and underwear, and it was locked.

The police returned to the luggage checkroom and questioned the bellman. The man thought there might have been two bags in the checkroom, although a second black bag was nowhere to be found.

EXHIBIT A is a picture of the bag and jewelry. John Summers claims that he checked an identical bag and that he mistakenly picked up this bag from the luggage room.

The State has drawn your attention to the shape of this bag, its handle, and lock. The State submits that this is an unusual-looking bag, and that it is very unlikely, if not impossible, that another bag looking just like it would be checked into the same hotel on the same day.

The State also presented EXHIBIT B, a list of the contents of John Summers's pockets at the time he was arrested. His wallet contained $710 in cash, a sizable sum for a person spending only one night in town. The State alleges that the $710 in Summers's wallet is the money stolen from the jewelry store.

No gun was found in Summers's pocket. The State claims a simple explanation. John Summers robbed Kay's Jewelry Store by pretending the object in his pocket was a gun. In reality, it was only his pointed finger.

On the basis of all this evidence, John Summers was accused of the jewelry store robbery.

John Summers has given the following testimony:

"My visit to Martinville was supposed to be a simple overnight trip. Every year around this time, the Martinville Museum has its annual art sale, and I wanted to buy a painting. I just started collecting art last year. I may not know a lot about art, but I know what I like. I've already got two of those pictures of the sad-looking kids with the big eyes. But this time I wanted something really stupendous to go over the sofa in the living room. Maybe something with some purple in it to match the drapes. I saved up more than eight hundred bucks to buy a painting this trip."

Summers's schedule was easy to reconstruct. He arrived by bus on Wednesday morning and checked into the Bristol Hotel. The Museum opened at noon. Mr. Summers was one of the first persons to enter the Museum. He spent the entire afternoon there. But to his disappointment, he could not find any artwork he liked.

EXHIBIT C is a torn Museum ticket stub for the day in question. The Museum hours were noon to four o'clock. The robbery of Kay's Jewelry Store took place at 3:30. While there was no witness who can testify he saw John Summers in the museum the entire time, the stub shows he indeed visited the Museum.

When the Museum closed, John Summers went back to his hotel, disappointed his trip was in vain. The following day, he checked out of the hotel at noon. Since his bus did not leave until later that day, Summers locked his black bag, checked it in the hotel's luggage checkroom, and went sightseeing. Later he returned to pick up his bag, and he was promptly arrested.

John Summers claims that he is the victim of an unfortunate coincidence.

LADIES AND GENTLEMEN OF THE JURY: You have just heard the Case of the Wrong Bag. You must decide the merit of the State's accusation. Be sure to carefully examine the evidence in EXHIBITS A, B, and C.

Did John Summers rob Kay's Jewelry Store? Or had he indeed picked up the wrong bag?

(The jury's verdict appears on page 194.)

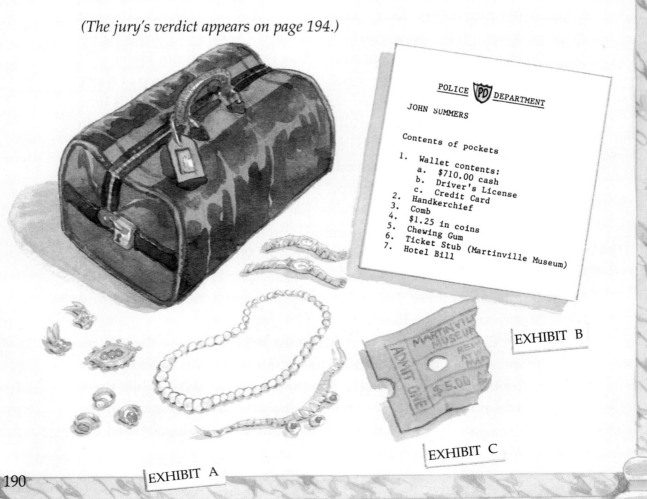

POLICE **PD** DEPARTMENT

JOHN SUMMERS

Contents of pockets

1. Wallet contents:
   a. $710.00 cash
   b. Driver's License
   c. Credit Card
2. Handkerchief
3. Comb
4. $1.25 in coins
5. Chewing Gum
6. Ticket Stub (Martinville Museum)
7. Hotel Bill

EXHIBIT B

EXHIBIT C

EXHIBIT A

◆ The Case of the Power Blackout ◆

LADIES AND GENTLEMEN OF THE JURY:

A company that provides a public service, such as a power company, has special responsibilities. When the service fails, the company is responsible for any damages that may happen.

Keep this in mind as you decide the case before you today. Mel Mudd, the plaintiff and owner of Mudd's Diner, claims that a power failure lasted sixteen hours and he was unable to serve his customers. Mr. Mudd wants to be paid for this lost business. Allied Utilities, the defendant, is a power company that provides electricity and gas to the people in Fairchester County. Allied Utilities admits to the power failure. But it claims to have repaired it three hours after it was reported.

Mel Mudd has given the following testimony:

"My name is Mudd. I'm the owner of Mudd's Diner. On Thursday, February 16 at 9:30 P.M., just as I was about to close up for the night, the lights went out. Do you know that old joke: Where was Thomas Edison when the lights went out? Well, the answer is: In the dark. And that's exactly where I was, too. I immediately called the power company and was assured the power would be restored promptly."

Mr. Mudd returned to his diner the following morning, opened the back door and flipped on the light switch. The room was totally dark.

He telephoned the power company several times, and each time the line was busy. After posting a "closed" sign on the front of the diner, Mudd returned to the back room and tried to telephone the company again. The line was still busy.

Mr. Mudd kept phoning the utility company and after two hours finally got through. The company told him they had fixed the problem the night before, but they promised they would send a repairman right away.

It took two hours for the repairman to arrive. By that time, Mr. Mudd had turned away the noon lunch crowd.

The repairman again checked the outside cable. He tightened the couplings but found nothing to indicate further repairs were needed. When the repairman went back to the diner to report his findings, the lights were on in the back room.

Mr. Mudd insisted the second visit was necessary to repair the lost power because the work had not been done properly the night before. He telephoned Allied Utilities and told them he planned to sue the company for lost business. A supervisor arrived at the diner in five minutes.

EXHIBIT A shows the lost business at Mudd's Diner during the time Mudd claims he had no power. You will note on that day he had only $146.35 in business. Entries for other days show he usually had up to $450.00 worth of business. This is the amount Mudd seeks from the utility company— $450.00.

Mel Mudd was extremely angry when the supervisor arrived at the back room of the diner. The man assured Mudd the power failure had been fixed the night before. Mudd strongly disagreed.

Allied Utilities enters as EXHIBIT B the repair work-order for the diner. This is a record kept for each customer complaint. You will note that the first call came in at 9:35 P.M. The repair order shows that the power failure lasted only three hours during the time the diner was closed. Power was claimed to have been restored by 12:36 A.M.

The company also enters EXHIBIT C, a photograph of the back room that was taken shortly after the supervisor arrived. You will note that the supervisor is holding up a light bulb. He had found it in a wastebasket in the diner's back room. Tests have shown this bulb is burned out and no longer in working order.

The company contends that while its repairman was outside checking the power the second time, Mudd somehow realized he may have been mistaken about the power failure.

The light in the back room had failed to go on because of a burned-out bulb. Mr. Mudd then replaced the bulb with a new one but said nothing to the company so he could sue them for lost business. Allied Utilities refuses to pay the money Mel Mudd has requested.

LADIES AND GENTLEMEN OF THE JURY: You have just heard the Case of the Power Blackout. You must decide the merit of Mel Mudd's claim. Be sure to carefully examine the evidence in EXHIBITS A, B, and C.

Should Allied Utilities pay Mr. Mudd for the income he lost during the power failure? Or did Mudd know that the power had been restored?

(The jury's verdict appears on page 194.)

EXHIBIT A

| DATE | GROSS RECEIPTS WEEK OF FEB. 12 | | | |
	BREAKFAST 6-11	LUNCH 11-5	DINNER 5-9	TOTAL
2/12	93.25	116.42	170.52	380.15
2/13	123.60	88.25	225.80	437.45
2/14	85.25	116.45	248.20	450.00
2/15	47.55	93.85	286.45	427.95
2/16	48.12	106.75	254.25	408.12
2/17	—	20.22	126.25	146.55
2/18	94.45	123.22	204.20	421.85

WEEKLY TOTAL - $2,673.25

EXHIBIT C

DATE	TIME	NAME	ADDRESS	REPAIR MAN	DIS. TIME	COMP. TIME
2/16	7:12p	B.ROPER	186 CHEW ST.	8	7:30p	7:50p
2/16	7:26p	G.MORRISON	S.POINT ST.	17	8:10p	8:55p
2/16	8:17p	K.SPENCER	274 8th ST.	15	8:30p	9:58p
2/16	8:42p	B.SEATED	26 BLAIR AVE	8	9:30p	10:15p
2/16	9:35p	M.MUDD	15 SOUTH ST.	17	10:43p	12:36p
2/16	9:55p	R.LEMON	7 W. POINT	9	10:55p	11:30p
2/16	10:30p	H.RUBIN	19 2nd AVE	8	11:15p	11:35p
2/16	10:40p	D.CLARK	40 TOMS RD.	15	12:00p	12:20p

ALLIED UTILITIES TELEPHONE LOG

EXHIBIT B

◆ The Case of the Wrong Bag ◆

John Summers claimed that the bag he stored in the checkroom was *locked*. But the contents of his pockets in EXHIBIT B showed he had no key. Summers was lying. He had indeed robbed Kay's Jewelry Store, and the bag with the jewelry was his.

◆ The Case of the Power Blackout ◆

EXHIBIT C shows the back room of Mudd's Diner after the supervisor arrived. An empty glass with ice cubes is on a table. If the electricity was out until shortly before the supervisor got there, it would have been impossible for Mudd to have used ice cubes in the drink. When Mudd realized he had ice, he knew the power had been restored the night before. This was confirmed when he replaced the burned-out light bulb. However, he had already turned away his lunchtime customers, so he said nothing to the supervisor so he could illegally sue the power company.

When you were acting as the jury, did you guess the right verdicts? Explain why or why not.

What are the similarities and the differences in the cases of John Summers and Mel Mudd?

Why was it important to note that John Summers did not have a key in his pocket?

No light came on when Mel Mudd flipped the switch, so he closed his restaurant. If you had been Mel, what would you have done?

WRITE   What would you do to find out whether someone was innocent or guilty of a crime? Write a list of steps you might follow.

Trespasses

To trespass can mean "to go beyond a boundary." How are Claudia, John Summers, and Mel Mudd all guilty of trespassing?

WRITER'S WORKSHOP

Do you think you could have persuaded one of the characters in these selections not to do what he or she did? Write a persuasive paragraph giving strong reasons that could change one character's mind. Use facts from the story to bolster your case.

Writer's Choice   In these selections,
people commit different types of trespasses. What do you think about their actions? Write down your thoughts, and think of a way to present them.

T H E M E

Flying Solo

Imagine that you are left alone in a small airplane. You don't know how to fly, but the plane seems to be able to fly itself. The problem is that it doesn't know how to land, and neither do you.

C O N T E N T S

197

FLYING MACHINE

WRITTEN BY ANDREW NAHUM

ENCLOSED COCKPITS had to await the development of safety glass in the late 1920s. Until then, pilots sat in the open, exposed to howling winds, freezing cold, and damp—with nothing more to protect them than a tiny windshield and warm clothes. Naturally, comfort was a low priority in these open cockpits, and they were very basic and functional in appearance. There were few instruments, and engine gauges were just as often on the engine itself as in the cockpit. The layout of the main flight controls became established fairly early on, with a rudder bar at the pilot's feet for turning and a control column, or "joy stick," between the knees for diving, climbing, and banking. Some early planes had a wheel rather than a joy stick, but it served the same purpose. This basic layout is still used in light planes today.

By the 1930s, the joy stick had become the standard form of control, and even the simplest planes, like this De Havilland Tiger Moth, had a range of basic instruments. The whole cockpit was functional and basic, with none of the comforts light planes usually have today, such as carpets, molded seats, and heaters.

Turn indicator

Small windshield

Notice saying that aerobatic maneuvers may be performed

Engine rev counter

Compass

Airspeed indicator

Altimeter

Joy stick

Notice reminding the pilot that the plane can cruise at 94 mph (150 kmh) but will stall if flown slower than 45 mph (72 kmh)

Lever to close landing/takeoff slats on the wing during aerobatic maneuvers

Engine oil pressure gauge

Rudder bar

Throttle

Landing and
taxi light
switches

Engine starting
controls

Engine data such
as fuel flow, torque
(the force turning
the turbines), and
turbine
temperature

Battery-powered,
stand-by main
flight instruments,
enabling the pilot
to land safely in
case of complete
electrical failure

Navigation
computer
equipment

Engine
speed
control
(throttle)

Indicators for brakes and
hydraulic systems

THE FLIGHT DECK of a modern jetliner looks dauntingly complicated, with its array of switches, dials, and displays for such
things as engine condition, hydraulics, navigational aids, and
so on, not to mention the basic flight controls. Increasingly,

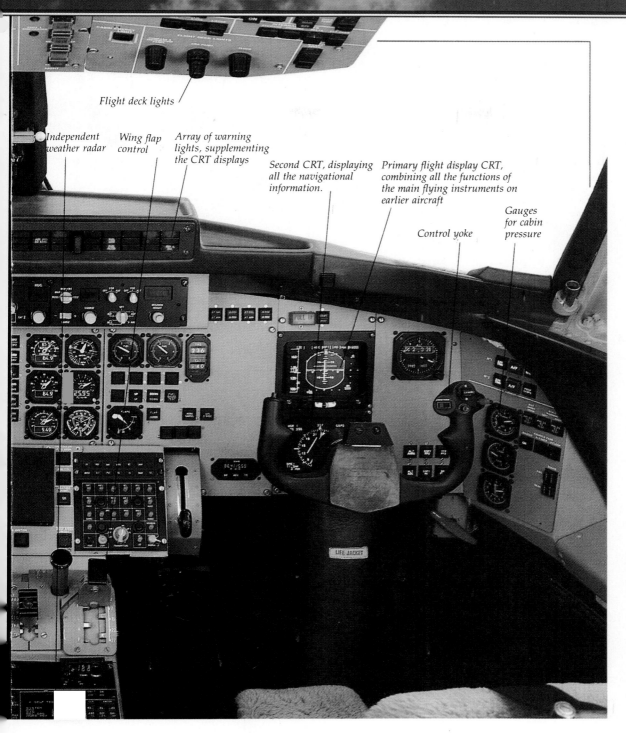

Flight deck lights

Independent
weather radar

Wing flap
control

Array of warning
lights, supplementing
the CRT displays

Second CRT, displaying
all the navigational
information.

Primary flight display CRT,
combining all the functions of
the main flying instruments on
earlier aircraft

Control yoke

Gauges
for cabin
pressure

LIFE JACKET

however, computers are taking over certain functions, and the
mass of dials is being replaced by neat screens called CRTs (for
"cathode ray tube"), on which the pilot can change the
information displayed at the flick of a button.

NEWBERY HONOR
ALA NOTABLE
BOOK

HATCHET

Hatchet
GARY PAULSEN

WRITTEN BY GARY PAULSEN
ILLUSTRATED BY MARK REIDY

Brian is flying 7,000 feet above the Canadian wilderness on the way to visit his father. Brian is enjoying his first flight in a small plane, until the unthinkable happens.

The pilot sat large, his hands lightly on the wheel, feet on the rudder pedals. He seemed more a machine than a man, an extension of the plane. On the dashboard in front of him Brian saw dials, switches, meters, knobs, levers, cranks, lights, handles that were wiggling and flickering, all indicating nothing that he understood and the pilot seemed the same way. Part of the plane, not human.

When he saw Brian look at him, the pilot seemed to open up a bit and he smiled. "Ever fly in the copilot's seat before?" He leaned over and lifted the headset off his right ear and put it on his temple, yelling to overcome the sound of the engine.

Brian shook his head. He had never been in any kind of plane, never seen the cockpit of a plane except in films or on television. It was loud and confusing. "First time."

"It's not as complicated as it looks. Good plane like this almost flies itself." The pilot shrugged. "Makes my job easy."

He took Brian's left arm. "Here, put your hands on the controls, your feet on the rudder pedals, and I'll show you what I mean."

Brian shook his head. "I'd better not."

"Sure. Try it . . ."

Brian reached out and took the wheel in a grip so tight his knuckles were white. He pushed his feet down on the pedals. The plane slewed suddenly to the right.

"Not so hard. Take her light, take her light."

Brian eased off, relaxed his grip. The burning in his eyes was forgotten momentarily as the vibration of the plane came through the wheel and the pedals. It seemed almost alive.

"See?" The pilot let go of his wheel, raised his hands in the air and took his feet off the pedals to show Brian he was actually flying the plane alone. "Simple. Now turn the wheel a little to the right and push on the right rudder pedal a small amount."

Brian turned the wheel slightly and the plane immediately banked to the right, and when he pressed on the right rudder pedal the nose slid across the horizon to the right. He left off on the pressure and straightened the wheel and the plane righted itself.

"Now you can turn. Bring her back to the left a little."

Brian turned the wheel left, pushed on the left pedal, and the plane came back around. "It's easy." He smiled. "At least this part."

The pilot nodded. "All of flying is easy. Just takes learning. Like everything else. Like everything else." He took the controls back, then reached up and rubbed his left shoulder. "Aches and pains—must be getting old."

Brian let go of the controls and moved his feet away from the pedals as the pilot put his hands on the wheel. "Thank you . . ."

But the pilot had put his headset back on and the gratitude was lost in the engine noise and things went back to Brian looking out the window at the ocean of trees and lakes. The burning eyes did not come back, but memories did, came flooding in. The words. Always the words.

Divorce.

The Secret.

Fights.

Split.

The big split. Brian's father did not understand as Brian did, knew only that Brian's mother wanted to break the marriage apart. The split had come and then the divorce, all so fast, and the court had left him with his mother except for the summers and what the judge called "visitation rights." So formal. Brian hated judges as he hated lawyers. Judges that leaned over the bench and asked Brian if he understood where he was to live and why. Judges who did not know what had really happened. Judges with the caring look that meant nothing as lawyers said legal phrases that meant nothing.

In the summer Brian would live with his father. In the school year, with his mother. That's what the judge said after looking at papers on his desk and listening to the lawyers talk. Talk. Words.

Now the plane lurched slightly to the right and Brian looked at the pilot. He was rubbing his shoulder again and there was the sudden smell of body gas in the plane. Brian turned back to avoid embarrassing the pilot, who was obviously in some discomfort. Must have stomach troubles.

So this summer, this first summer when he was allowed to have "visitation rights" with his father, with the divorce only one month old, Brian was heading north. His father was a mechanical engineer who had designed or invented a new drill bit for oil drilling, a self-cleaning, self-sharpening bit. He was working in the oil fields of Canada, up on the tree line where the tundra started and the forests ended. Brian was riding up from New York with some drilling equipment—it was lashed down in the rear of the plane next to a fabric bag the pilot had called a survival pack, which had emergency supplies in case they had to make an emergency landing—that had to be specially made in the city, riding in a bushplane with the pilot named Jim or Jake or something who had turned out to be an all right guy, letting him fly and all.

Except for the smell. Now there was a constant odor, and Brian took another look at the pilot, found him rubbing the shoulder and down the arm now, the left arm, letting go more gas and wincing. Probably something he ate, Brian thought.

His mother had driven him from the city to meet the plane at Hampton where it came to pick up the drilling equipment. A drive in silence, a long drive in silence. Two and a half hours of sitting in the car, staring out the window just as he was now staring out the window of the plane. Once, after an hour, when they were out of the city she turned to him.

"Look, can't we talk this over? Can't we talk this out? Can't you tell me what's bothering you?"

And there were the words again. Divorce. Split. The Secret. How could he tell her what he knew? So he had remained silent, shook his head and continued to stare unseeing at the countryside, and his mother had gone back to driving only to speak to him one more time when they were close to Hampton.

She reached over the back of the seat and brought up a paper sack. "I got something for you, for the trip."

Brian took the sack and opened the top. Inside there was a hatchet, the kind with a steel handle and a rubber handgrip. The head was in a stout leather case that had a brass-riveted belt loop.

"It goes on your belt." His mother spoke now without looking at him. There were some farm trucks on the road now and she had to weave through them and watch traffic. "The man at the store said you could use it. You know. In the woods with your father."

Dad, he thought. Not "my father." My dad. "Thanks. It's really nice." But the words sounded hollow, even to Brian.

"Try it on. See how it looks on your belt."

And he would normally have said no, would normally have said no that it looked too hokey to have a hatchet on your belt. Those were the normal things he would say. But her voice was thin, had a sound like something thin that would break if you touched it, and he felt bad for not speaking to her. Knowing what he knew, even with the anger, the hot white hate of his anger at her, he still felt bad for not speaking to her, and so to humor her he loosened his belt and pulled the right side out and put the hatchet on and rethreaded the belt.

"Scootch around so I can see."

He moved around in the seat, feeling only slightly ridiculous.

She nodded. "Just like a scout. My little scout." And there was the tenderness in her voice that she had when he was small, the tenderness that she had when he was small and sick, with a cold, and she put her hand on his forehead, and the burning came into his eyes again and he had turned away from her and looked out the window, forgotten the hatchet on his belt and so arrived at the plane with the hatchet still on his belt.

Because it was a bush flight from a small airport there had been no security and the plane had been waiting, with the engine running when he arrived and he had grabbed his suitcase and pack bag and run for the plane without stopping to remove the hatchet.

So it was still on his belt. At first he had been embarrassed but the pilot had said nothing about it and Brian forgot it as they took off and began flying.

More smell now. Bad. Brian turned again to glance at the pilot, who had both hands on his stomach and was grimacing in pain, reaching for the left shoulder again as Brian watched.

"Don't know, kid . . ." The pilot's words were a hiss, barely audible. "Bad aches here. Bad aches. Thought it was something I ate but . . ."

He stopped as a fresh spasm of pain hit him. Even Brian could see how bad it was—the pain drove the pilot back into the seat, back and down.

"I've never had anything like this . . ."

The pilot reached for the switch on his mike cord, his hand coming up in a small arc from his stomach, and he flipped the switch and said, "This is flight four six . . ."

And now a jolt took him like a hammerblow, so forcefully that he seemed to crush back into the seat, and Brian reached for him, could not understand at first what it was, could not know.

And then knew.

Brian knew. The pilot's mouth went rigid, he swore and jerked a short series of slams into the seat, holding his shoulder now. Swore and hissed, "Chest! Oh God, my chest is coming apart!"

Brian knew now.

The pilot was having a heart attack. Brian had been in the shopping mall with his mother when a man in front of Paisley's store had suffered a heart attack. He had gone down and screamed about his chest. An old man. Much older than the pilot.

Brian knew.

The pilot was having a heart attack and even as the knowledge came to Brian he saw the pilot slam into the seat one more time, one more awful time he slammed back into the seat and his right leg jerked, pulling the plane to the side in a sudden twist and his head fell forward and spit came. Spit came from the corners of his mouth and his legs contracted up, up into the seat, and his eyes rolled back in his head until there was only white.

Only white for his eyes and the smell became worse, filled the cockpit, and all of it so fast, so incredibly fast that Brian's mind could not take it in at first. Could only see it in stages.

The pilot had been talking, just a moment ago, complaining of the pain. He had been talking.

Then the jolts had come.

The jolts that took the pilot back had come, and now Brian sat and there was a strange feeling of silence in the thrumming roar of the engine—a strange feeling of silence and being alone. Brian was stopped.

He was stopped. Inside he was stopped. He could not think past what he saw, what he felt. All was stopped. The very core of him, the very center of Brian Robeson was stopped and stricken with a white-flash of horror, a terror so intense that his breathing, his thinking, and nearly his heart had stopped.

Stopped.

Seconds passed, seconds that became all of his life, and he began to know what he was seeing, began to understand what he saw and that was worse, so much worse that he wanted to make his mind freeze again.

He was sitting in a bushplane roaring seven thousand feet above the northern wilderness with a pilot who had suffered a massive heart attack and who was either dead or in something close to a coma.

He was alone.

In the roaring plane with no pilot he was alone.

Alone.

For a time that he could not understand Brian could do nothing. Even after his mind began working and he could see what had happened he could do nothing. It was as if his hands and arms were lead.

Then he looked for ways for it not to have happened. Be asleep, his mind screamed at the pilot. Just be asleep and your eyes will open now and your hands will take the controls and your feet will move to the pedals—but it did not happen.

The pilot did not move except that his head rolled on a neck impossibly loose as the plane hit a small bit of turbulence.

The plane.

Somehow the plane was still flying. Seconds had passed, nearly a minute, and the plane flew on as if nothing had happened and he had to do something, had to do something but did not know what.

Help.

He had to help.

He stretched one hand toward the pilot, saw that his fingers were trembling, and touched the pilot on the chest. He did not know what to do. He knew there were procedures, that you could do mouth-to-mouth on victims of heart attacks and push their chests—C.P.R.—but he did not know how to do it and in any case could not do it with the pilot, who was sitting up in the seat and still strapped in with his seatbelt. So he touched the pilot with the tips of his fingers, touched him on the chest and could feel nothing, no heartbeat, no rise and fall of breathing. Which meant that the pilot was almost certainly dead.

"Please," Brian said. But did not know what or who to ask. "Please . . ."

The plane lurched again, hit more turbulence, and Brian felt the nose drop. It did not dive, but the nose went down slightly and the down-angle increased the speed, and he knew that at this angle, this slight angle down, he would ultimately fly into the trees. He could see them ahead on the horizon where before he could see only sky.

He had to fly it somehow. Had to fly the plane. He had to help himself. The pilot was gone, beyond anything he could do. He had to try and fly the plane.

He turned back in the seat, facing the front, and put his hands—still trembling—on the control wheel, his feet gently on the rudder pedals. You pulled back on the stick to raise the plane, he knew that from reading. You always pulled back on the wheel. He gave it a tug and it slid back toward him easily.

Too easily. The plane, with the increased speed from the tilt down, swooped eagerly up and drove Brian's stomach down. He pushed the wheel back in, went too far this time, and the plane's nose went below the horizon and the engine speed increased with the shallow dive.

Too much.

He pulled back again, more gently this time, and the nose floated up again, too far but not as violently as before, then down a bit too much, and up again, very easily, and the front of the engine cowling settled. When he had it aimed at the horizon and it seemed to be steady, he held the wheel where it was, let out his breath—which he had been holding all this time—and tried to think what to do next.

It was a clear, blue-sky day with fluffy bits of clouds here and there and he looked out the window for a moment, hoping to see something, a town or village, but there was nothing. Just the green of the trees, endless green, and lakes scattered more and more thickly as the plane flew—where?

He was flying but did not know where, had no idea where he was going. He looked at the dashboard of the plane, studied the dials and hoped to get some help, hoped to find a compass, but it was all so confusing, a jumble of numbers and lights. One lighted display in the top center of the dashboard said the number 342, another next to it said 22. Down beneath that were dials with lines that seemed to indicate what the wings were doing, tipping or moving, and one dial with a needle pointing to the number 70, which he thought—only thought—might be the altimeter. The device that told him his height above the ground. Or above sea level. Somewhere he had read something about altimeters but he couldn't remember what, or where, or anything about them.

Slightly to the left and below the altimeter he saw a small rectangular panel with a lighted dial and two knobs. His eyes had passed over it two or three times before he saw what was written in tiny letters on top of the panel. TRANSMITTER 221 was stamped in the metal and it hit him, finally, that this was the radio.

The radio. Of course. He had to use the radio. When the pilot had—had been hit that way (he couldn't bring himself to say that the pilot was dead, couldn't think it), he had been trying to use the radio.

Brian looked to the pilot. The headset was still on his head, turned sideways a bit from his jamming back into the seat, and the microphone switch was clipped into his belt.

Brian had to get the headset from the pilot. Had to reach over and get the headset from the pilot or he would not be able to use the radio to call for help. He had to reach over . . .

His hands began trembling again. He did not want to touch the pilot, did not want to reach for him. But he had to. Had to get the radio. He lifted his hands from the wheel, just slightly, and held them waiting to see what would happen. The plane flew on normally, smoothly.

All right, he thought. Now. Now to do this thing. He turned and reached for the headset, slid it from the pilot's head, one eye on the plane, waiting for it to dive. The headset came easily, but the microphone switch at the pilot's belt was jammed in and he had to pull to get it loose. When he pulled, his elbow bumped the wheel and pushed it in and the plane started down in a shallow dive. Brian grabbed the wheel and pulled it back, too hard again, and the plane went through another series of stomach-wrenching swoops up and down before he could get it under control.

When things had settled again he pulled at the mike cord once more and at last jerked the cord free. It took him another second or two to place the headset on his own head and position the small microphone tube in front of his mouth. He had seen the pilot use it, had seen him depress the switch at his belt, so Brian pushed the switch in and blew into the mike.

He heard the sound of his breath in the headset. "Hello! Is there anybody listening on this? Hello . . ."

He repeated it two or three times and then waited but heard nothing except his own breathing.

Panic came then. He had been afraid, had been stopped with the terror of what was happening, but now panic came and he began to scream into the microphone, scream over and over.

"Help! Somebody help me! I'm in this plane and don't know . . . don't know . . . don't know . . ."

And he started crying with the screams, crying and slamming his hands against the wheel of the plane, causing it to jerk down, then back up. But again, he heard nothing but the sound of his own sobs in the microphone, his own screams mocking him, coming back into his ears.

The microphone. Awareness cut into him. He had used a CB radio in his uncle's pickup once. You had to turn the mike switch off to hear anybody else. He reached to his belt and released the switch.

For a second all he heard was the *whusssh* of the empty air waves. Then, through the noise and static he heard a voice.

"Whoever is calling on this radio net, I repeat, release your mike switch—you are covering me. You are covering me. Over."

It stopped and Brian hit his mike switch. "I hear you! I hear you. This is me . . . !" He released the switch.

"Roger, I have you now." The voice was very faint and breaking up. "Please state your difficulty and location. And say *over* to signal end of transmission. Over."

Please state my difficulty, Brian thought. God. My difficulty. "I am in a plane with a pilot who is—who has had a heart attack or something. He is—he can't fly. And I don't know how to fly. Help me. Help . . ." He turned his mike off without ending transmission properly.

There was a moment's hesitation before the answer. "Your signal is breaking up and I lost most of it. Understand . . . pilot . . . you can't fly. Correct? Over."

Brian could barely hear him now, heard mostly noise and static. "That's right. I can't fly. The plane is flying now but I don't know how much longer. Over."

". . . lost signal. Your location please. Flight number . . . location . . . ver."

"I don't know my flight number or location. I don't know anything. I told you that, over."

He waited now, waited but there was nothing. Once, for a second, he thought he heard a break in the noise, some part of a word, but it could have been static. Two, three minutes, ten minutes, the plane roared and Brian listened but heard no one. Then he hit the switch again.

"I do not know the flight number. My name is Brian Robeson and we left Hampton, New York headed for the Canadian oil fields to visit my father and I do not know how to fly an airplane and the pilot . . ."

He let go of the mike. His voice was starting to rattle and he felt as if he might start screaming at any second. He took a deep breath. "If there is anybody listening who can help me fly a plane, please answer."

Again he released the mike but heard nothing but the hissing of noise in the headset. After half an hour of listening and repeating the cry for help he tore the headset off in frustration and threw it to the floor. It all seemed so hopeless. Even if he did get somebody, what could anybody do? Tell him to be careful?

All so hopeless.

He tried to figure out the dials again. He thought he might know which was speed—it was a lighted number that read 160—but he didn't know if that was actual miles an hour, or kilometers, or if it just meant how fast the plane was moving through the air and not over the ground. He knew airspeed was different from groundspeed but not by how much.

Parts of books he'd read about flying came to him. How wings worked, how the propellor pulled the plane through the sky. Simple things that wouldn't help him now.

Nothing could help him now.

An hour passed. He picked up the headset and tried again—it was, he knew, in the end all he had—but there was no answer. He felt like a prisoner, kept in a small cell that was hurtling through the sky at what he thought to be 160 miles an hour, headed—he didn't know where—just headed somewhere until . . .

There it was. Until what? Until he ran out of fuel. When the plane ran out of fuel it would go down.

Period.

Or he could pull the throttle out and make it go down now. He had seen the pilot push the throttle in to increase speed. If he pulled the throttle back out, the engine would slow down and the plane would go down.

Those were his choices. He could wait for the plane to run out of gas and fall or he could push the throttle in and make it happen sooner. If he waited for the plane to run out of fuel he would go farther—but he did not know which way he was moving. When the pilot had jerked he had moved the plane, but Brian could not remember how much or if it had come back to its original course. Since he did not know the original course anyway and could only guess at which display might be the compass—the one reading 342—he did not know where he had been or where he was going, so it didn't make much difference if he went down now or waited.

Everything in him rebelled against stopping the engine and falling now. He had a vague feeling that he was wrong to keep heading as the plane was heading, a feeling that he might be going off in the wrong direction, but he could not bring himself to stop the engine and fall. Now he was safe, or safer than if he went down—the plane was flying, he was still breathing. When the engine stopped he would go down.

So he left the plane running, holding altitude, and kept trying the radio. He worked out a system. Every ten minutes by the small clock built into the dashboard he tried the radio with a simple message: "I need help. Is there anybody listening to me?"

In the times between transmissions he tried to prepare himself for what he knew was coming. When he ran out of fuel the plane would start down. He guessed that without the propellor pulling he would have to push the nose down to keep the plane flying—he thought he may have read that somewhere, or it just came to him. Either way it made sense. He would have to push the nose down to keep flying speed and then, just before he hit, he would have to pull the nose back up to slow the plane as much as possible.

It all made sense. Glide down, then slow the plane and hit. Hit.

He would have to find a clearing as he went down. The problem with that was he hadn't seen one clearing since they'd started flying over the forest. Some swamps, but they had trees scattered through them. No roads, no trails, no clearings.

Just the lakes, and it came to him that he would have to use a lake for landing. If he went down in the trees he was certain to die. The trees would tear the plane to pieces as it went into them.

He would have to come down in a lake. No. On the edge of a lake. He would have to come down near the edge of a lake and try to slow the plane as much as possible just before he hit the water.

Easy to say, he thought, hard to do.

Easy say, hard do. Easy say, hard do. It became a chant that beat with the engine. Easy say, hard do.

Impossible to do.

He repeated the radio call seventeen times at the ten-minute intervals, working on what he would do between transmissions. Once more he reached over to the pilot and touched him on the face, but the skin was cold, hard cold, death cold, and Brian turned back to the dashboard. He did what he could, tightened his seatbelt, positioned himself, rehearsed mentally again and again what his procedure should be.

When the plane ran out of gas he should hold the nose down and head for the nearest lake and try to fly the plane kind of onto the water. That's how he thought of it. Kind of fly the plane onto the water. And just before it hit he should pull back on the wheel and slow the plane down to reduce the impact.

Over and over his mind ran the picture of how it would go. The plane running out of gas, flying the plane onto the water, the crash—from pictures he'd seen on television. He tried to visualize it. He tried to be ready.

But between the seventeenth and eighteenth radio transmissions, without a warning, the engine coughed, roared violently for a second and died. There was sudden silence, cut only by the sound of the windmilling propellor and the wind past the cockpit.

Brian pushed the nose of the plane down and threw up.

Going to die, Brian thought. Going to die, gonna die, gonna die—his whole brain screamed it in the sudden silence.

Gonna die.

He wiped his mouth with the back of his arm and held the nose down. The plane went into a glide, a very fast glide that ate altitude, and suddenly there weren't any lakes. All he'd seen since they started flying over the forest was lakes and now they were gone. Gone. Out in front, far away at the horizon, he could see lots of them, off to the right and left more of them, glittering blue in the late afternoon sun.

But he needed one right in front. He desperately needed a lake right in front of the plane and all he saw through the windshield were trees, green death trees. If he had to turn—if he had to turn he didn't think he could keep the plane flying. His stomach tightened into a series of rolling knots and his breath came in short bursts . . .

There!

Not quite in front but slightly to the right he saw a lake. L-shaped, with rounded corners, and the plane was nearly aimed at the long part of the L, coming from the bottom and heading to the top. Just a tiny bit to the right. He pushed the right rudder pedal gently and the nose moved over.

But the turn cost him speed and now the lake was above the nose. He pulled back on the wheel slightly and the nose came up. This caused the plane to slow dramatically and almost seem to stop and wallow in the air. The controls became very loose-feeling and frightened Brian, making him push the wheel back in. This increased the speed a bit but filled the windshield once more with nothing but trees, and put the lake well above the nose and out of reach.

For a space of three or four seconds things seemed to hang, almost to stop. The plane was flying, but so slowly, so slowly . . . it would never reach the lake. Brian looked out to the side and saw a small pond and at the edge of the pond some large animal—he thought a moose—standing out in the water. All so still looking, so stopped, the pond and the moose and the trees, as he slid over them now only three or four hundred feet off the ground—all like a picture.

Then everything happened at once. Trees suddenly took on detail, filled his whole field of vision with green, and he knew he would hit and die, would die, but his luck held and just as he was to hit he came into an open lane, a channel of fallen trees, a wide place leading to the lake.

The plane, committed now to landing, to crashing, fell into the wide place like a stone, and Brian eased back on the wheel and braced himself for the crash. But there was a tiny bit of speed left and when he pulled on the wheel the nose came up and he saw in front the blue of the lake and at that instant the plane hit the trees.

There was a great wrenching as the wings caught the pines at the side of the clearing and broke back, ripping back just

outside the main braces. Dust and dirt blew off the floor into his face so hard he thought there must have been some kind of explosion. He was momentarily blinded and slammed forward in the seat, smashing his head on the wheel.

Then a wild crashing sound, ripping of metal, and the plane rolled to the right and blew through the trees, out over the water and down, down to slam into the lake, skip once on water as hard as concrete, water that tore the windshield out and shattered the side windows, water that drove him back into the seat. Somebody was screaming, screaming as the plane drove down into the water. Someone screamed tight animal screams of fear and pain and he did not know that it was his sound, that he roared against the water that took him and the plane still deeper, down in the water. He saw nothing but sensed blue, cold blue-green, and he raked at the seatbelt catch, tore his nails loose on one hand. He ripped at it until it released and somehow—the water trying to kill him, to end him—somehow he pulled himself out of the shattered front window and clawed up into the blue, felt something hold him back, felt his windbreaker tear and he was free. Tearing free. Ripping free.

But so far! So far to the surface and his lungs could not do this thing, could not hold and were through, and he sucked water, took a great pull of water that would—finally—win, finally take him, and his head broke into light and he vomited and swam, pulling without knowing what he was, what he was doing. Without knowing anything. Pulling until his hands caught at weeds and muck, pulling and screaming until his hands caught at last in grass and brush and he felt his chest on land, felt his face in the coarse blades of grass and he stopped, everything stopped. A color came that he had never seen before, a color that exploded in his mind with the pain and he was gone, gone from it all, spiraling out into the world, spiraling out into nothing.

Nothing.

Brian opened his eyes and screamed.

For seconds he did not know where he was, only that the crash was still happening and he was going to die, and he screamed until his breath was gone.

Then silence, filled with sobs as he pulled in air, half crying. How could it be so quiet? Moments ago there was nothing but noise, crashing and tearing, screaming, now quiet.

Some birds were singing.

How could birds be singing?

His legs felt wet and he raised up on his hands and looked back down at them. They were in the lake. Strange. They went down into the water. He tried to move, but pain hammered into him and made his breath shorten into gasps and he stopped, his legs still in the water.

Pain.

Memory.

He turned again and sun came across the water, late sun, cut into his eyes and made him turn away.

It was over then. The crash.

He was alive.

The crash is over and I am alive, he thought. Then his eyes closed and he lowered his head for minutes that seemed longer. When he opened them again it was evening and some of the sharp pain had abated—there were many dull aches—and the crash came back to him fully.

Into the trees and out onto the lake. The plane had crashed and sunk in the lake and he had somehow pulled free.

He raised himself and crawled out of the water, grunting with the pain of movement. His legs were on fire, and his forehead felt as if somebody had been pounding on it with a hammer, but he could move. He pulled his legs out of the lake and crawled on his hands and knees until he was away from the wet-soft shore and near a small stand of brush of some kind.

Then he went down, only this time to rest, to save something of himself. He lay on his side and put his head on his arm and closed his eyes because that was all he could do now, all he could think of being able to do. He closed his eyes and slept, dreamless, deep and down.

There was almost no light when he opened his eyes again. The darkness of night was thick and for a moment he began to panic again. To see, he thought. To see is everything. And he could not see. But he turned his head without moving his body and saw that across the lake the sky was a light gray, that the sun was starting to come up, and he remembered that it had been evening when he went to sleep.

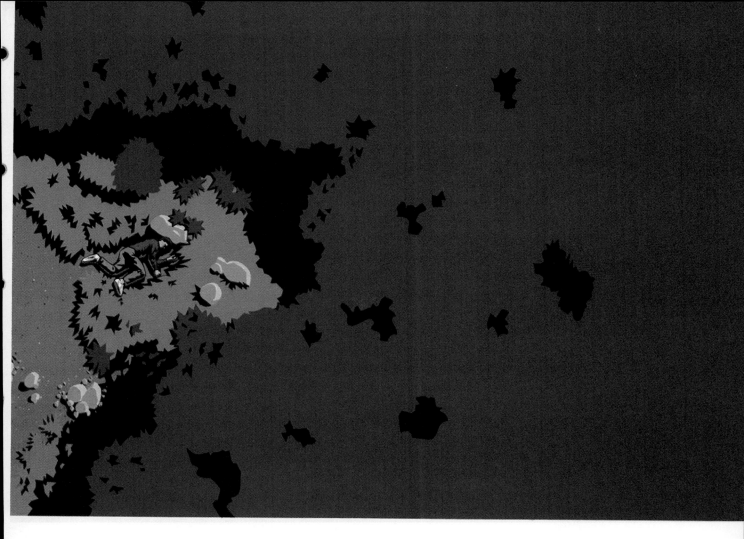

"Must be morning now . . ." He mumbled it, almost in a hoarse whisper. As the thickness of sleep left him the world came back.

He was still in pain, all-over pain. His legs were cramped and drawn up, tight and aching, and his back hurt when he tried to move. Worst was a keening throb in his head that pulsed with every beat of his heart. It seemed that the whole crash had happened to his head.

He rolled on his back and felt his sides and his legs, moving things slowly. He rubbed his arms; nothing seemed to be shattered or even sprained all that badly. When he was nine he had plowed his small dirt bike into a parked car and broken his

ankle, had to wear a cast for eight weeks, and there was nothing now like that. Nothing broken. Just battered around a bit.

His forehead felt massively swollen to the touch, almost like a mound out over his eyes, and it was so tender that when his fingers grazed it he nearly cried. But there was nothing he could do about it and, like the rest of him, it seemed to be bruised more than broken.

I'm alive, he thought. I'm alive.

Do you think that a teenager like Brian could actually do what he does in this story? Why or why not?

What are the problems that Brian Robeson faces in this story?

Why wouldn't air traffic controllers or any other authorities know the real path of Brian's flight?

What personal qualities does Brian exhibit in the selection? How do these qualities help him to survive?

WRITE Imagine that it is your job to contact Brian's father about the accident. Write down the message that you would leave for him.

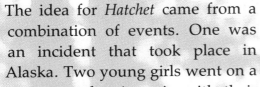

The idea for *Hatchet* came from a combination of events. One was an incident that took place in Alaska. Two young girls went on a boating trip with their father. The boat began to leak, so he put the girls off on an island, telling them he'd come back as soon as he could. But he took ill, and he couldn't get right back. The girls didn't even have a hatchet! He expected they would be dead by the time he got back. Living on seaweed, and using an old piece of tarp for shelter, the girls somehow survived. I was very interested in that story because I've lived off the land, too. There was a time in my life when I got by with gardening, trapping, and hunting.

Most of the things that happen in the book have happened to me, too. I've been in a forced landing of a small plane, so I know about that kind of fear. I also know what it means to depend on yourself to survive. I wanted to write a book about young people being self-sufficient, on all levels—emotional, intellectual, physical. I decided to take a basically urban boy, put him in a hostile environment, and then see what happened.

When you're writing, there's no substitute for personal experience. When I realized that writing isn't just something I do, but is what I am, things changed for me. Like the storytellers of long ago, I'm the person who puts an animal skin on his back, dances around the fire, and tells what the hunt was like.

AWARD-WINNING
AUTHOR

Flying Solo

What feelings and ideas about life might Brian share with the author who created him, Gary Paulsen?

WRITER'S WORKSHOP

Imagine what it would be like to fly a plane, drive a bus, or ride a wild horse without really knowing how. Think of a character who must do something he or she has never done before. Write a short story about the adventure. Tell the story in the first person, using words such as *I*, *me*, and *mine*.

Writer's Choice

What do you think about the theme Flying Solo? Write down your ideas, and think of a way to share them with friends.

CONNECTIONS

Multicultural Connection

Courts of a Different Order

Every society has written or unwritten laws and a system for enforcing those laws. The early Native Americans had a very efficient and just system. Wrongdoers were brought before tribal leaders, who were usually a council of elders, warriors, or religious heads. The council's goal was not to hand out punishments but to settle the case in a way that satisfied both sides.

This idea of justice lives on in modern tribal courts on Indian reservations. Such courts deal mostly with disputes between people.

The Oglala Sioux Court is a good example. It has one chief judge and three other judges, all elected by the tribal council, and one "special judge" who must have legal training. Lawyers seldom appear. The judges' good sense and their knowledge of tribal law enable them to hand down fair decisions.

Imagine a problem that might come before a tribal court. With a group, create a dramatic skit in which you try a case and settle it in a way that satisfies both parties.

234

Social Studies Connection

Tracking Down Facts About Different Ways of Life

Indian reservations are governed much as states are. With a group, find out about some of the differences between life on and off Indian reservations. Share your findings in an oral report.

Science/Literature Connection

Ancient Mysteries

There were some natural mysteries the Indians of ancient times couldn't solve. So they made up "why" stories, similar to the myths of the Greeks and Romans, to explain nature's riddles. Read and summarize an Indian "why" story. Then write a scientific explanation of the condition or event the story is about.

UNIT THREE

YESTERYEAR

*A people without history
is like the wind on the buffalo grass.*
—a Sioux saying

How did General George Washington command his troops in battle? Why did free African-American men and women risk their lives for others in the Underground Railroad? Who were the Chinese pioneers of the American West? Historians such as Ruthanne Lum McCunn seek answers to such questions. You too can find out about America's history by being curious and asking your own questions. As you read the selections in this unit, see how many of your questions are answered.

THEMES

BOOKSHELF

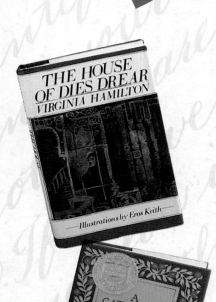

THE HOUSE OF DIES DREAR

by Virginia Hamilton

Thomas and his family move into a house with a long history of danger as a stop on the Underground Railroad. Thomas soon begins to wonder if the "danger" part is over.

Edgar Allan Poe Award
Harcourt Brace Library Book

A GATHERING OF DAYS

by Joan W. Blos

What was it like to live in the United States 160 years ago? Share the daily life and struggles of thirteen-year-old Catherine Hall of New Hampshire in the 1830s.

Newbery Medal
Harcourt Brace Library Book

TAKE A WALK IN THEIR SHOES

by Glennette Tilley Turner

The stories of fourteen great African Americans are told, first in short biographies and then in dramatic skits that allow you to "walk in their shoes."

Notable Trade Book in the Field of Social Studies

LINCOLN: A PHOTOBIOGRAPHY

by Russell Freedman

Photographs and drawings depict the life of Abraham Lincoln and the many faces of the American Civil War.

Newbery Medal, Notable Trade Book in the Field of Social Studies

HER SEVEN BROTHERS

by Paul Goble

This Cheyenne legend explains the origin of the constellation that we call "The Big Dipper."

Children's Choice, Teachers' Choice

THEME

EARLY AMERICA

When you think about the early days of the United States of America, what pictures come to mind? The following selections may provide you with new pictures, including some seen through the eyes of children who were there when it all began.

CONTENTS

241

The Sign of the Beaver

Elizabeth George Speare

Winner of the Newbery Award for both *The Witch of Blackbird Pond*
and *The Bronze Bow*

The Sign of the Beaver

by Elizabeth George Speare

Illustrations by Tom Ricks

Father has gone back to Massachusetts to fetch the rest of the family, leaving Matt alone to guard their cabin. When Matt stumbles into a swarm of bees, he is rescued by an Indian chief and his grandson. The chief will accept no reward, but he will allow Matt to teach his grandson, Attean, how to read English. Attean hates the idea of learning from Matt and quickly reverses their roles of student and teacher.

When they came upon a row of short tree stumps, birch and aspen cut off close to the ground, Matt's heart gave a leap. Were there settlers nearby? Or Indians? There was no proper clearing. Then he noticed that whoever had cut the trees had left jagged points on each one. No axe would cut a tree in that way. He could see marks where the trees had been dragged along the ground.

243

In a few steps the boys came out on the bank of an unfamiliar creek. There Matt saw what had happened to those trees. They had been piled in a mound right over the water, from one bank to the other. Water trickled through them in tiny cascades. Behind the piled-up branches, a small pond stretched smooth and still.

"It's a beaver dam!" he exclaimed. "The first one I've ever seen."

"*Qwa bit*," said Attean. "Have red tail. There beaver wigwam." He pointed to a heap of branches at one side, some of them new with green leaves still clinging. Matt stepped closer to look. Instantly there was the crack of a rifle. A ring of water rippled the surface of the pond. Near its edge a black head appeared for just a flash and vanished again in a splutter of bubbles.

Attean laughed at the way Matt had started. "Beaver make big noise with tail," he explained.

"I thought someone had shot a gun," Matt said. "I wish I had my rifle now."

Attean scowled. "Not shoot," he warned. "Not white man, not Indian. Young beaver not ready."

He pointed to a tree nearby. "Sign of beaver," he said. "Belong to family."

Carved on the bark, Matt could make out the crude figure of an animal that could, with some imagination, be a beaver.

"Sign show beaver house belong to people of beaver," Attean explained. "By and by, when young beaver all grown, people of beaver hunt here. No one hunt but people of beaver."

"You mean, just from that mark on the tree, another hunter would not shoot here?"

"That our way," Attean said gravely. "All Indian understand."

Would a white man understand? Matt wondered. He thought of Ben with his stolen rifle. It wasn't likely Ben would respect an Indian sign. But he must remember to warn his father.

When it seemed the beaver did not intend to show itself again, the two boys climbed back up the bank. At the row of stumps, Attean halted and signaled for Matt to go ahead.

"Show way to cabin," he ordered.

All Matt's suspicions came rushing back. Did Attean intend to sneak off behind his back and leave him to find his own way home?

"Is this some kind of trick?" he demanded hotly.

Attean looked stern. "Not trick," he said. "Matt need learn."

To Matt's relief, he took the lead again. After a short distance he stopped and pointed to a broken stick leaning in the direction of the creek. A little farther on there was a small stone set against a larger one. Not far away a tuft of dried grass dangled from a branch of a small tree.

"Indian make sign," Attean said. "Always make sign to tell way. Matt must same. Not get lost in forest."

Now Matt remembered how Attean had paused every so often, sometimes to break off a branch that hung in their path, once to nudge aside a stone with the toe of his moccasin. He had done these things so quickly that Matt had paid no mind. He saw now that Attean had carefully been leaving markers.

"Of course," he exclaimed. "But my father always made blazes on the trees with his knife."

Attean nodded. "That white man's way. Indians maybe not want to show where he go. Not want hunters to find beaver house."

So there were secret signs. Nothing anyone following them would notice. It would take sharp eyes to find them, even if you knew they were there.

"Matt do same," Attean repeated. "Always make sign to show way back."

Matt was ashamed of his suspicions. Attean had only meant to help him. If only he didn't have to be so superior about it.

As though Attean sensed that Matt was disgruntled, he stopped, whipped out his knife, and neatly sliced off two shining gobs of dried sap from a nearby spruce. He grinned and held out one of them like a peace offering. "Chaw," he ordered. He popped the other piece into his mouth and began to chew with evident pleasure.

Gingerly, Matt copied him. The gob fell to pieces between his teeth, filling his mouth with a bitter juice. He wanted to spit it out in disgust, but Attean was plainly enjoying the stuff, so he stubbornly forced his jaws to keep moving. In a moment the bits came together in a rubbery gum, and the first bitterness gave way to a fresh piney taste. To his surprise, it was very good. The two boys tramped on, chewing companionably. Once more, Matt acknowledged to himself, Attean had taught him another secret of the forest.

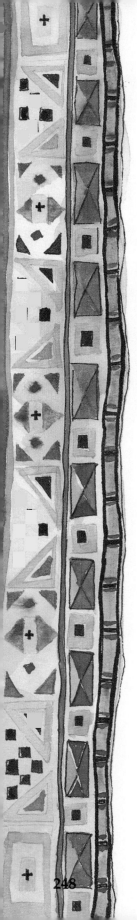

I MUST HAVE A BOW, MATT DECIDED ONE MORNING. He was envious of the bow Attean often carried behind his shoulder, and of the blunt arrows he tucked into his belt. Only the day before, Matt had watched him swing it suddenly into position and bring down a flying duck. Attean had picked up the dead bird carefully and carried it away with him. No doubt the Indians would find some use for every scrap of bone and feather. Matt knew by now that Attean never shot anything just for the fun of it. With a bow and a little practice, Matt thought now, he might get a duck for himself. It would be a fine change from his usual fish.

He had no doubt he could shoot with a bow. In fact he had made them years ago back in Quincy. He and his friends had played at Indians, stalking each other through the woods and whooping out from behind trees. They had even practiced half-earnestly at shooting at a target. How could he have known that someday he would have need of such a skill?

He cut a straight branch, notched it at either end, and stretched tight a bit of string his father had left. Arrows he whittled out of slender twigs. But something was definitely wrong. His arrows wobbled off in odd directions or flopped on the ground a few feet away. He was chagrined when next morning Attean came walking out of the woods and surprised him at his practice.

Attean looked at the bow. "Not good wood," he said at once. "I get better."

He was very exacting about the wood he chose. He searched along the edge of the clearing, testing saplings, bending slender branches, discarding one after another, till he found a dead branch of ash about the thickness of his three fingers. He cut a rod almost his own height and handed it to Matt.

"Take off bark," he directed, and squatted down to watch while Matt scraped the branch clean. Then, taking it in his hands again, he marked off several inches in the center where

Matt's hand would grip the bow. "Cut off wood here," he said, running his hand from center to ends. "Make small like this." He held up one slim finger.

Matt set to work too hastily. "Slow," Attean warned him. "Knife take off wood too fast. Indian use stone."

Under the Indian's critical eye, Matt shaved down the branch, paring off the thinnest possible shavings. The slow work took all his patience. Twice he considered the task finished, but Attean, running his hand along the curve of the bow, was not satisfied till it was smooth as an animal bone.

"Need fat now," he said. "Bear fat best."

"Will this do?" Matt asked, bringing out a bowl of fish stew he had left cooling on the table. Carefully, with a bit of bark, Attean skimmed off the drops of oil that had risen to the surface. He rubbed the oil from one end of the bow to the other

249

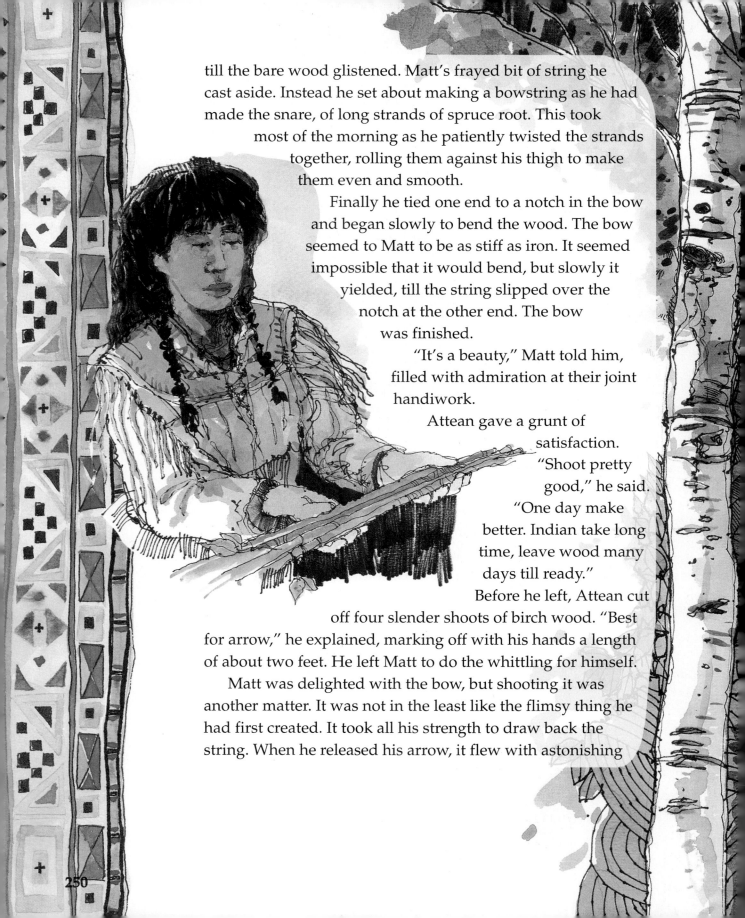

till the bare wood glistened. Matt's frayed bit of string he cast aside. Instead he set about making a bowstring as he had made the snare, of long strands of spruce root. This took most of the morning as he patiently twisted the strands together, rolling them against his thigh to make them even and smooth.

Finally he tied one end to a notch in the bow and began slowly to bend the wood. The bow seemed to Matt to be as stiff as iron. It seemed impossible that it would bend, but slowly it yielded, till the string slipped over the notch at the other end. The bow was finished.

"It's a beauty," Matt told him, filled with admiration at their joint handiwork.

Attean gave a grunt of satisfaction. "Shoot pretty good," he said. "One day make better. Indian take long time, leave wood many days till ready."

Before he left, Attean cut off four slender shoots of birch wood. "Best for arrow," he explained, marking off with his hands a length of about two feet. He left Matt to do the whittling for himself.

Matt was delighted with the bow, but shooting it was another matter. It was not in the least like the flimsy thing he had first created. It took all his strength to draw back the string. When he released his arrow, it flew with astonishing

250

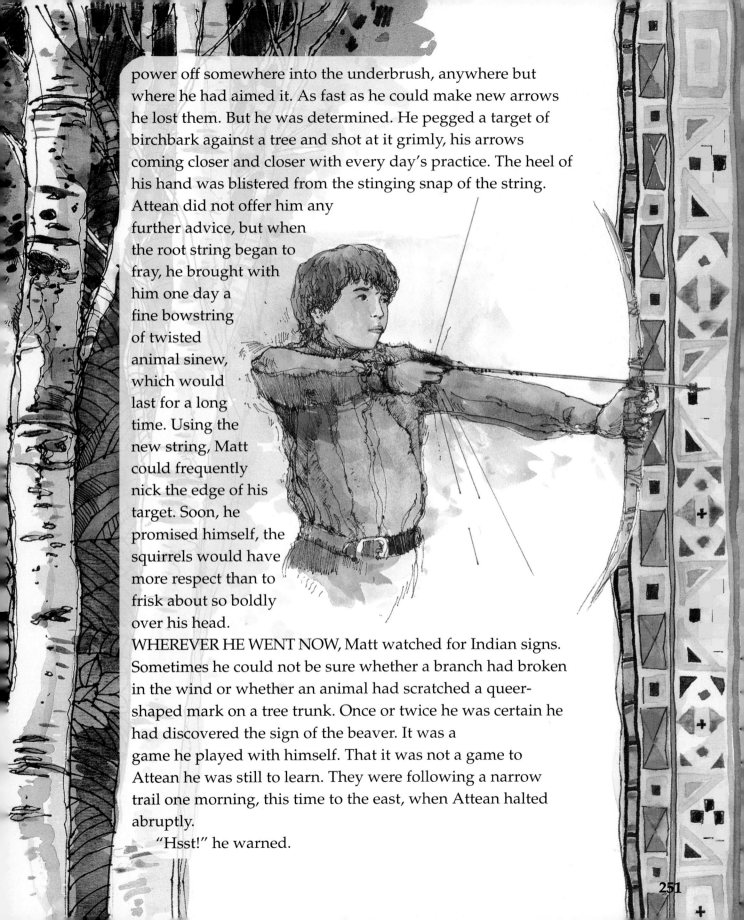

power off somewhere into the underbrush, anywhere but where he had aimed it. As fast as he could make new arrows he lost them. But he was determined. He pegged a target of birchbark against a tree and shot at it grimly, his arrows coming closer and closer with every day's practice. The heel of his hand was blistered from the stinging snap of the string. Attean did not offer him any further advice, but when the root string began to fray, he brought with him one day a fine bowstring of twisted animal sinew, which would last for a long time. Using the new string, Matt could frequently nick the edge of his target. Soon, he promised himself, the squirrels would have more respect than to frisk about so boldly over his head.

WHEREVER HE WENT NOW, Matt watched for Indian signs. Sometimes he could not be sure whether a branch had broken in the wind or whether an animal had scratched a queer-shaped mark on a tree trunk. Once or twice he was certain he had discovered the sign of the beaver. It was a game he played with himself. That it was not a game to Attean he was still to learn. They were following a narrow trail one morning, this time to the east, when Attean halted abruptly.

"Hsst!" he warned.

251

Off in the brush Matt heard a low, rasping breathing and a frantic scratching in the leaves. The noise stopped the moment they stood still. Moving warily, the boys came upon a fox crouched low on the ground. It did not run, but lay snarling at them, and as he came nearer, Matt saw that its foreleg was caught fast. With a long stick Attean pushed aside the leaves and Matt caught the glint of metal.

"White man's trap," said Attean.

"How do you know?" Matt demanded.

"Indians not use iron trap. Iron trap bad."

"You mean a white man set this trap?" Matt thought of Ben.

"No. Some white man pay for bad Indian to hunt for him. White man not know how to hide trap so good." Attean showed Matt how cleverly the trap had been hidden, the leaves and earth mounded up like an animal burrow with two half-eaten fish heads concealed inside.

The fox watched them, its teeth bared. The angry eyes made Matt uncomfortable. "We're in luck to find it first," he said, to cover his uneasiness.

Attean shook his head. "Not beaver hunting ground," he said. "Turtle clan hunt here." He pointed to a nearby tree. On the bark Matt could just make out a crude scar that had a shape somewhat like a turtle. He was indignant.

"We found it," he said. "You mean you're just going to leave it here because of a mark on a tree?"

"Beaver people not take animal on turtle land," Attean repeated.

"We can't just let it suffer," Matt protested. "Suppose no one comes here for days?"

"Then fox get away."

"How can he get away?"

"Bite off foot."

Indeed, Matt could see now that the creature had already gnawed its own flesh down to the bone.

"Leg mend soon," Attean added, noting Matt's troubled face. "Fox have three leg beside."

"I don't like it," Matt insisted. He wondered why he minded so much. He had long ago got used to clubbing the small animals caught in his own snares. There was something about this fox that was different. Those defiant eyes showed no trace of fear. He was struck by the bravery that could inflict such pain on itself to gain freedom. Reluctantly he followed Attean back to the trail, leaving the miserable animal behind.

"It's a cruel way to trap an animal," he muttered. "Worse than our snares."

"*Ehe*," Attean agreed. "My grandfather not allow beaver people to buy iron trap. Some Indian hunt like white man now. One time many moose and beaver. Plenty for all Indians and

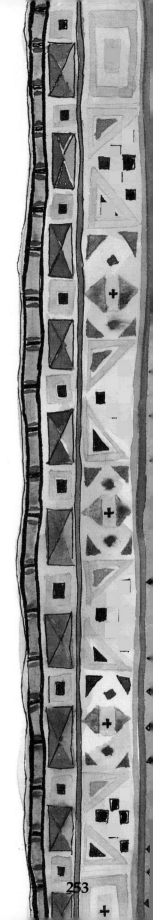

for white man too. But white man not hunt to eat, only for skin. Him pay Indian to get skin. So Indian use white man's trap."

Matt could not find an answer. Tramping beside Attean he was confused and angry as well. He couldn't understand the Indian code that left an animal to suffer just because of a mark on a tree. And he was fed up with Attean's scorn for white men. It was ridiculous to think that he and Attean could ever really be friends. Sometimes he wished he could never see Attean again.

Even at the same moment, he realized that this was really not true. Even though Attean annoyed him, Matt was constantly goaded to keep trying to win this strange boy's respect. He would lie awake in the night, staring up at the chinks of starlight in the cabin roof, and make up stories in which he himself, not Attean, was the hero. Sometimes he imagined how Attean would be in some terrible danger, and he, Matt, would be brave and calm and come swiftly to the rescue. He would kill a bear unaided, or a panther, or fend off a rattlesnake about to strike. Or he would learn about an enemy band of Indians sneaking through the forest to attack the place where Attean was sleeping, and he would run through the woods and give the alarm in time.

In the morning he laughed at himself for this childish daydreaming. There was little chance he would ever be a hero, and little chance too that Attean would ever need his help. Matt knew that the Indian boy came day after day only because his grandfather sent him. For some reason the old man had taken pity on this helpless white boy, and at the same time

he had shrewdly grasped at the chance for his grandson to learn to read. If he suspected that Attean had become the teacher instead, he would doubtless put a stop to the visits altogether.

Matt knew he ought to feel grateful for Attean's teaching. Every day Attean taught him some new thing—a plant like an onion that he could drop into his cooking pot to make his stew more tasty—a weed with a small orange flower and a milky juice in its stem that took away the sting of insect bites or poison ivy—a plant with brownish flowers and roots bearing a string of nutlike bulbs that thickened his stew and made it more nourishing. He had pointed out plants that Matt must never eat, no matter how hungry he might be. He had even shown Matt how to improvise a rain cape in a sudden rain by quickly punching a hole through the center of a wide strip of birchbark and making a cone of bark for his head.

The only thing that Matt could teach him, Attean was set against learning. For Attean the white man's signs on paper were *piz wat*—good for nothing.

Nevertheless, Matt noticed that in spite of himself Attean had learned something from the white boy. He was speaking the English tongue with greater ease. Perhaps he was not aware himself how differently he spoke. He picked up new words readily. Sometimes he used them with that odd humor that Matt was beginning to recognize. Matt knew that Attean was mocking when some of his own favorite expressions came solemnly out of the Indian's mouth.

"Reckon so," Attean would say. "Rain come soon, by golly." Sometimes he even took a fancy to a word out of *Robinson Crusoe*. He especially liked the sound of *verily*.

255

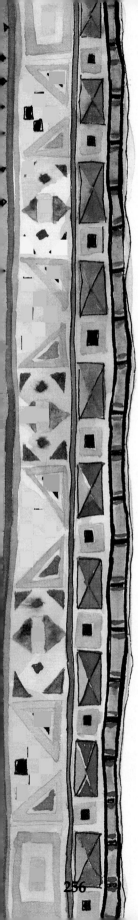

In return, Matt liked to try out Indian words. They were not hard to understand but impossible to get his tongue around. He didn't think he could ever quite get them right, but he could see that though it amused Attean when he tried, it also pleased him.

"*Cha kwa*—this morning," Matt might say, "I chased a *kogw* out of the corn patch." He wouldn't add that he had wasted an arrow and watched the porcupine waddle off unharmed.

Perhaps, after all, those lessons hadn't been entirely wasted.

Which character do you like better, Matt or Attean? Explain your answer.

What does Matt learn from Attean? How does it help him?

What about Attean annoys Matt?

What character traits help Matt succeed in living in the forest? Find events in the story that show these traits.

WRITE   Everyone needs some help adapting to new situations. What would you tell a new person in your neighborhood that would make life easier for him or her? Write a list of neighborhood survival skills that you think are important.

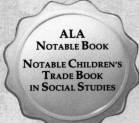

POEMS SELECTED BY

VIRGINIA DRIVING HAWK SNEVE

To American Indians, the spoken word was sacred. Children
listened to their grandparents tell stories, recite ceremonial
prayers and chants, and sing lullabies and other tribal songs.
The children grew up remembering the music and knew that the
act of speaking words gave life to Native American stories, songs,
and prayers. Words were chosen carefully and rarely wasted.

Sun, Moon, Stars

Sun, moon, stars,
You that move in the heavens,
Hear this mother!
A new life has come among you.
Make its life smooth.

(from an Omaha ceremony for the
newborn)

My Horse, Fly Like a Bird

My horse, fly like a bird
To carry me far
From the arrows of my enemies,
And I will tie red ribbons
To your streaming hair.

(adapted from a Lakota warrior's
song to his horse)

DANCING

SELECTED BY
VIRGINIA
DRIVING HAWK SNEVE
WITH ART BY
STEPHEN GAMMELL

POEMS ◆ OF ◆ AMERICAN ◆ INDIAN ◆ YOUTH

TEEPEES

AN AMERICAN
SOLDIER

The American Revolution: A Picture Sourcebook

by John Grafton

A BRITISH GRENADIER

JOIN, or DIE.

This cartoon of a rattlesnake cut in segments representing parts of America with the legend "Join, or Die" was designed by Benjamin Franklin at the time of the Albany Congress of 1754. (The issue then was joint action with regard to the Indians, not the British.)

INDIANS AND THE FRONTIER:
MOHAWK CHIEF JOSEPH BRANT
The main area of Indian activity during the Revolutionary period was western New York and Pennsylvania, where the Six Nations of the Iroquois and their British allies battled American settlers and villages.

GEORGE WASHINGTON

THE HESSIANS IN THE REVOLUTION

During the period from 1776 to 1783 as many as 17,000 German mercenary soldiers—primarily from the state of Hesse-Cassel, thus the name Hessians—fought for the British in America.

A HESSIAN GRENADIER

THE BATTLE OF THE BRANDYWINE

American forces at the battle of Brandywine Creek. In the late summer of 1777, the British Commander Howe landed with his army from New York at the northern tip of Chesapeake Bay, fifty miles from his objective, Philadelphia. Washington met Howe at the Brandywine on September 11 and suffered a tactical defeat largely through insufficient knowledge of the terrain. Later that month the British army occupied Philadelphia, driving the American Congress first to Lancaster and then to York. Washington attacked the British at their main base, Germantown, on October 4 and nearly won a major victory before being forced back.

THE BOSTON MASSACRE

A contemporary broadside gives evidence of popular reaction to the Boston Massacre. The list of victims, of course, includes the last name of Crispus Attucks, a black man killed by the British.

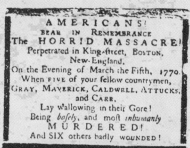

AMERICANS!
BEAR IN REMEMBRANCE
The HORRID MASSACRE!
Perpetrated in King-street, Boston,
New-England,
On the Evening of March the Fifth, 1770.
When FIVE of your fellow countrymen,
GRAY, MAVERICK, CALDWELL, ATTUCKS,
and CARR,
Lay wallowing in their Gore!
Being basely, and most inhumanly
MURDERED!
And SIX others badly WOUNDED!

West Branch

Brandy wine Creek

Buck Run

The Riddle of Penncroft Farm

by Dorothea Jensen

TEACHERS' CHOICE

In the fall of 1777, in the midst of the
American Revolution, Philadelphia has been
taken over by George Washington's patriot
forces. Many farmers in that area are
Tories, colonists who side with the British.

Geordie's father, a stout Tory, is outraged when
his oldest son, Will, leaves to fight for the patriot cause.
He is angered further when the Continental Congress
decrees that apples cannot be exported to England. In
response, he sends Geordie to Philadelphia to try to
peddle their farm goods.

———

illustrated by Gary Lippincott
map by Michelle Nidenoff

Big Elk Creek

Red Clay Creek

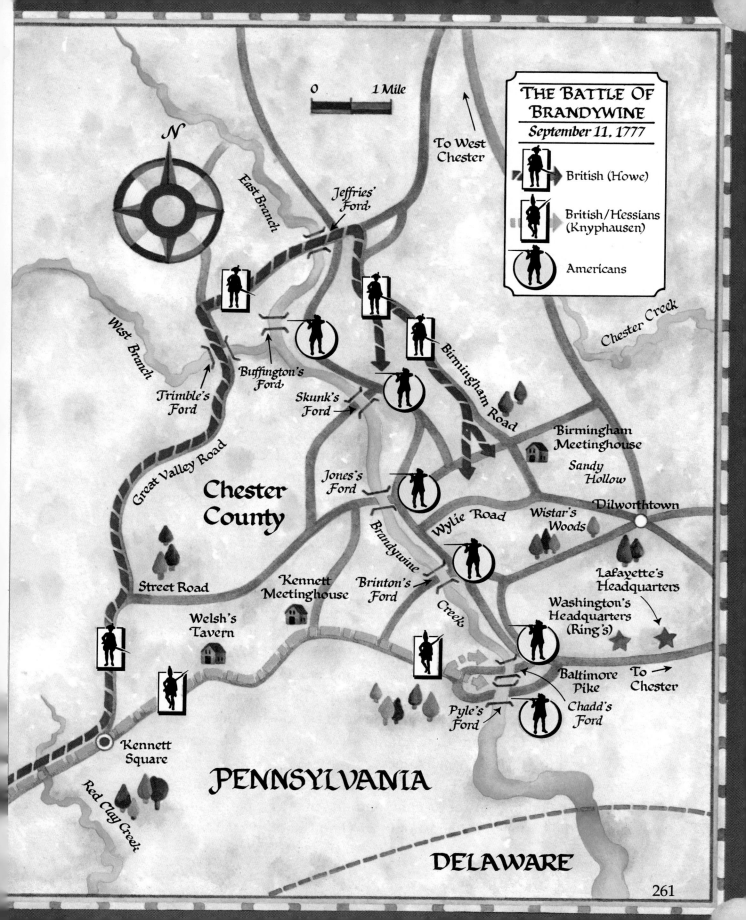

$\mathcal{S}$ince the British columns blocked the road going west, I was forced to turn east, toward Chadd's Ford. Soon I came in sight of Kennett Meetinghouse. I could see that the Friends were assembled for midweek meeting, and I stopped to warn them that the British were not far behind me. What a waste of precious time! They thanked me for the warning but went calmly on with their meeting as if I had never interrupted, even though shots were now ringing out behind me on the road.

I hunkered down on the seat and looked desperately about for a place to turn off the main road. To my great relief, I found a lane that headed north. It was barely more than wheel ruts in the dirt, but at least 'twas clear of trees—and soldiers. Seemingly oblivious to my fears, Daisy and Buttercup ambled along at their regular snail's pace, despite my shaking the reins to urge them faster. Such efforts only delayed me further, for one of the reins snapped. It took the better part of an hour to mend. Thus, it was past noon before I reached Street Road and turned east toward Jones's Ford, several miles upstream from Chadd's Ford, where the Americans were waiting for the British attack.

Crossing at Jones's Ford was not easy—I had to pick my way around felled logs in the stream, and an American patrol stopped me on the east side for questioning. When I said I'd seen troops at

Welsh's but none since, the captain nodded. "Just what Major Spear reported. I don't know what that blind fool Colonel Bland saw going up to the fork, but it surely wasn't redcoats[1]! Now you'd best get along, boy," he said.

Mystified, I got along. Then, toiling up a steep slope, I heard rolling, distant thunder. I looked at the sky. It was cloudless— even the morning fog had burned away under the bright, hot sun. Again the rumbling rent the air, and this time I knew 'twas no thunderclap but the firing of guns, louder than I'd ever heard. I stopped the wagon to listen closely, trying to decide where the ominous sound was coming from. Panic rose in my chest until I could scarcely catch my breath. Instinctively, I reached into my pocket and brought out my lucky piece. The small, lead grenadier[2] in the red-painted tunic stood on my palm, aiming down his long musket. Clutching the toy, I made a childish wish that it could tell me what to do.

But a much larger and less silent figure decided my course of action. I heard a peculiar muttering in the woods nearby—a string of oaths. Without stopping to think, I raised up my lead soldier to throw at the mutterer. Then I saw his face: it belonged to Squire Thomas Cheyney, a swarthy, thickset man who had been a friend of my father's before the war had set them at odds. As the squire thrashed his way through the bushes with his riding crop, he scowled and swore like a madman. When he spotted me, his mouth opened into a perfect O of astonishment.

"Why, Geordie, what are you doing here?" he gasped.

"Been delivering perry[3] at Welsh's."

"Then your horses are fresh?" he inquired eagerly.

"If you want to call them that. Slowest nags in creation."

---

[1]British soldiers
[2]soldier
[3]pear cider

"At least they're not lame," he said with disgust. "I had to leave *my* infernal mount tied to a stile and was nearly caught by the redcoats! Give me a hand up, lad. We must hurry."

"What do you mean?" I asked, helping him up beside me.

"Why, we must warn Washington about this flanking action!"

"Flanking action?" I echoed, still not understanding.

"Aye. Ten thousand British are crossing the two branches of the Brandywine north of the fork, guided by the Tory Galloway. I saw them myself! They'll come down Birmingham Road behind the American line and fall upon the Continentals[4] from the rear. And by the cannon fire coming from the south, I judge Howe has sent some troops to make Washington believe that *that* is where the main attack will come."

"Aye, troops under Knyphausen[5] are moving against Chadd's."

Cheyney pounded his fist down on the seat. "I thought so! 'Tis the same trick Howe used to win at Long Island! I tried to warn General Sullivan of this, but he thought I was exaggerating! Well, at least the fool gave me a pass to Washington's headquarters. I'll need your wagon."

My expression must have resembled one of the idiots the Hessian[6] thought me to be, for the squire said, more kindly, "If you're too feared to come, wait here for me. I'll be back as soon as I can."

"Father will flay me if I help the Continentals, but . . ." Suddenly I thought of my brother, Will. I couldn't let him be taken by surprise. "Aye, I'm going with you!" I blurted out.

"That's a brave lad!" the squire cried. He seized the reins and whipped up the horses until they ran as if wolves were nipping at their hooves.

* * * * *

---

[4] American soldiers
[5] British/Hessian officer who had questioned Geordie earlier and thought him an "idiot"
[6] German soldier fighting for the British

As it turned out, Squire Cheyney and I didn't get far before the road along the creek grew too crowded with American troops for our wagon to pass. Nothing daunted, Cheyney said we must leave the wagon on Wylie Road and ride the three miles overland to Ring's house, Washington's headquarters near Chadd's Ford. With growing misgivings, I helped unhitch the team and conceal the wagon in the woods, and soon we were up on Daisy and Buttercup's bare backs, trotting over the rough ground. I clutched Buttercup's reins and mane for dear life as I followed Squire Cheyney up and down the steep wooded hills, more than once nearly sliding backwards off Buttercup's rump or forward over his head. Cheyney, all unheeding, allowed branches to whip behind him into my face; they stung like the very devil.

As we came out of the trees on the hill behind Ring's house and paused to get our bearings, I quickly forgot my stinging face, for I could hear the sharp staccato of musketry coming from Brandywine Creek below. The thought that Will might be the target made me sick with fear.

Cheyney glanced at me. "Never heard muskets before, boy?" he asked brusquely, gathering up his reins.

I shuddered. "Not trained on men. And not when one of those men might be my brother, and he could be shot from the back."

"We'll prevent that if we get through in time! And Ring's is just below!" the squire cried, goading the winded Daisy into a gallop down the hill. As we reached the stone wall behind Washington's headquarters, a line of Continentals blocked our way. One grabbed Daisy's bridle and barked, "Don't you know there's a battle brewing? This is no place for farmers!"

"Don't be daft, sir!" Cheyney roared. "We've a pass from Sullivan to deliver urgent information to General Washington."

He held out a piece of paper. After the guard read it, he quickly motioned us on. Cheyney chirruped his horse down the hill, with mine wheezing along behind. We stopped beside the well. Dismounting, the squire sprinted around the side of the house and I scuttled behind him to the wide front door.

Two brawny sentries brought us both to a halt. Squire Cheyney, glaring at them, simply hallooed through the doorway in a voice Knyphausen likely could hear above the booming cannon beyond the Brandywine. I caught my breath, not only because my brother's life hung in the balance, but also because I was to see the man many revered as a god—and my father reviled as the devil.

My suspense lasted but a trice.[7] A dignified figure in a buff-and-blue uniform appeared before us—General Washington.

Broad-shouldered, taller than anyone I'd ever seen, he regarded us through icy blue eyes. "There had better be an excellent reason for this interruption, sir," he exclaimed.

After all his sprinting and bellowing, Cheyney had little breath for speech. He panted like a landed fish for several long moments. Then, finally, he gasped out, " 'Tis the British, ten thousand strong, crossing upstream to attack from behind."

Washington narrowed his eyes, looked us over as if we stank of barn muck, and motioned us into the house.

---

[7]an instant

"I heard some such nonsense from Colonel Bland, but later reports proved this false," he said, frowning. "Local sources have assured me there is no ford above the fork that's close enough to offer a serious threat. No, it's here at Chadd's Ford that the British attack will come, and here at the Brandywine is where we'll hold them!" In an undertone, he added, "Indeed we must: no other obstacles lie 'twixt Howe and Philadelphia save the Schuylkill River—at the very doors of the city!"

The squire could barely contain his outrage. "Local sources!" he spluttered. "I *am* a local source. And a local source most loyal to your efforts! Don't you know that most of the farmers who've stayed nearby, in Howe's path, are neutrals or Tories who want to throw dust in your eyes?" His voice squeaked with fury, and with despair I perceived that he sounded too much like a bedlamite[8] to be taken seriously.

Washington dismissed Cheyney's words with a wave of his hand. "And why should I not think *you* are doing the same? Nay, I choose to believe the word of an innocent youth before that of a man puffed full of Tory guile!"

"Tory guile?!" Cheyney squawked, as ruffled as a fighting cock.

"Yes, an innocent such as this lad here."

Suddenly I felt pride and glory swelling within me. As puffed up as any guileful man, I stepped forward and gazed up expectantly at that lofty, grave countenance.

"Aye, this lad," repeated Washington. "Now confound the boy, where'd he get to? . . . Ned—Ned Owens?"

"Here, Excellency." As we stood in the corridor, I could see a pudgy boy standing at a sideboard in the room to the right. In one hand he held a meat pasty; in the other, a pewter tankard. Juice from one or the other was dribbling down his cheeks. Crestfallen, I watched him wipe his mouth on his sleeve.

"Have you heard what this man says, Owens?"

---

[8]insane person

"Aye, sir. And it be lies. I've been up and down the Brandy-wine—all the way north to the fork—and there's nary a ford you've not covered with patrols." He leveled a look at me that was brimming over with self-importance. 'Twas this barefaced conceit that gave me back my tongue.

"But the British crossed *above* the fork, at *Jeffries'* Ford!" I exclaimed. "The squire saw them, and I *know* him to be true to the patriot cause. Redcoats in the *thousands* will be coming south down Birmingham Road, behind you to the east! Don't let them flank your troops, sir. My brother, Will, is a Continental, and I couldn't bear . . ."

I shall never know why—'twas probably a storm of nerves after all I'd been through and my fears for Will—but then and there I burst into tears. No man would have done so, but 'tis likely my sobs did more than any man's vows (and surely more than Cheyney's dismayed howls) to convince Washington of the truth.

For a long moment those cool blue eyes took my measure. Just then an aide dashed into the room and thrust some papers into Washington's hand. From what he said, it appeared they were reports verifying all that Squire Cheyney and I had told the general. Washington immediately ordered word sent to Sullivan to meet the column advancing on his rear. After the aide's departure, the general buckled on his sword. As he did so, he asked, "What's your name, lad?"

"Geordie."

"We need drummer boys, Geordie. Join us, as Owens here has done." He threw these words over his shoulder as he strode from the room. Jealously, I glanced at Owens. How much I wanted to take up the drum—and how impossible that I do so!

Squire Cheyney cleared his throat. "Well done, Geordie." He mopped his brow with a handkerchief. "We'd best head back north to Wylie Road. 'Twill be safe enough—the main battle will surely be to the east, where the redcoats are."

We hurried outside, but before we could mount, one of Washington's aides sped up the path and stopped the squire.

"Go along with the courier and show Sullivan the way to Birmingham Road!" He cast a disparaging look at Daisy. "That nag will not be quick enough. Come, I'll find another for you."

Squire Cheyney handed me Daisy's reins with a warning to waste no time, then rushed away with the aide. By this time the gunfire was quickening, making Buttercup as skittish as an unbroken filly. I was still trying to get up on her when General Washington himself emerged from the house, calling for a guide to lead him to Birmingham Road.

I half hoped and half feared that I would be that guide, but instead his aides brought up an elderly man from the neighborhood, Mr. Joseph Brown. Old Mr. Brown made every possible excuse not to go, but in the end was convinced at swordpoint where his duty lay. When he protested his lack of a horse, one of Washington's aides dismounted from his own fine charger.

As Brown reluctantly climbed into the saddle, Washington sat impatiently on his own beautiful white horse. The instant the frightened farmer was in place, Washington snapped a whip at the rump of the reluctant guide's horse, which leapt into a gallop. The general followed, spurring his own mount until its nose pushed into the leader's flank like a colt suckling its mother. Even this didn't satisfy Washington, who cracked his whip and shouted, "Push along, old man, push along!" Spellbound, I watched the two race up the hill across the golden fields, jumping the fences as they came to them. I had never seen such horsemanship—superb on the part of the general, dreadful on the part of Mr. Brown. Behind them ran a ragged line of soldiers, rucksacks[9] bobbing as they sped over the uneven ground.

After the two mismatched leaders disappeared over the brow of the hill, I managed to get on Buttercup and take hold of Daisy's bri-

---

[9]backpacks

dle. It took very little urging to hasten the two frightened horses north, away from the sound of gunfire. By the time I got back to my wagon, my hands were too shaky for my fingers to work properly, and it took ages to harness the team. At the very moment I climbed to the seat and took up the reins, the valley behind me exploded with artillery fire. Terrified, Daisy and Buttercup reared in their traces. Up and up they went, pawing the smoke-filled air. Then they plunged back to the ground, landing at a dead run. For a few breathless moments I simply clung to the reins, pulling for all I was worth, but the horses were too panic-stricken to feel the bits sawing at their mouths. My arms ached from the effort, and I eased off to recover some strength for another try. *Perhaps my horses bolting might be a blessing in disguise,* I thought. It would surely get me away from the Brandywine much faster than their usual pace. Then I realized where we were headed: due east toward Birmingham Road, where the British and Americans were about to clash in battle.

With strength born of fear, I reached for the brake, only to have the lever break off in my hand. Clutching the reins, I shut my eyes and prayed. At the sound of gunfire, my eyes flew open once more. Up the hill to my left were two lines of soldiers. At the top of the ridge, one line raised their muskets in unconscious mimicry of the toy soldier in my pocket. Their tall caps were as pointed as my little grenadier's; their tunics as scarlet. But my toy had never spat forth puffs of smoke or blazes of fire as did the muzzles glinting in the sun. My eyes shifted down to the target below: the second line of soldiers, whose black cockaded hats proclaimed them Continentals. Under my horrified gaze, this American line wavered and broke, some few soldiers staying to return fire, but most wheeling in confusion toward the road down which my team was bolting.

As the wagon careened down the dusty lane, I glimpsed still, crumpled figures, their coats turning red with blood, lying in the field where the American line had stood. The thought that Will might be bleeding to death under the hot September sun made me steer my winded team into a thick copse of beech trees to consider what to do. 'Twas lucky I did, else I'd never have heard it—the faint but unmistakable sound of Will's whistle. I shook my head, thinking I must be imagining things. Then it came again more clearly from the thicket ahead.

I shot off the wagon seat and hurtled into the woods, crashing through underbrush in the manner of an animal fleeing a forest fire. My lips puckered soundlessly in the vain effort to whistle back. "Will! Where are you?" I finally called hoarsely.

Through the leaves, a gleam of pallid skin told me I'd found him. Will lay at the base of a beech tree looking much as he did napping in our orchard after a dip in our pond on a hot summer day. But the dark red daubs on his leg came from no pond.

"Geordie! I thought my eyes were playing tricks on me, seeing you pull up in our wagon. But when I whistled and you looked startled as a deer, I knew 'twas really you. Trust you to be in Wistar's Woods just when things got hot." Managing a feeble grin, he tried to sit up. Then, his face contorted with pain, and he fell back with a groan that tore at my heart.

"Don't you worry, Will," I said with a confidence I was far from feeling. "I'm taking you home."

"Nay," Will said weakly. "If the lobsterbacks[10] catch you . . ."

"Hush, you great booby. I still have some perry in the wagon; I can bribe my way through the whole British army with you safely hidden under the hay. You look as if you could use a cupful." I ran to the wagon and fetched a tin cup full of perry for him. Will's hands shook so much I had to help him hold the cup, but the strong cider appeared to strengthen him a little.

With every moment, the sounds of battle crept closer. In my distraction, I noticed that golden leaves were sifting down upon us, but it was early for the trees to be shedding so much of their foliage. An odd buzzing sound drew my attention. I looked up and

---

[10]British soldiers

saw the cause of the early autumn: deadly grapeshot whizzing back and forth through the trees cutting down the leaves as it had cut down the young men in the field.

Frantically, I ripped off my shirt and tore it in two. As gently as I could, I wrapped one half around Will's wounded leg. It was agony for both of us, but I had to staunch the bleeding, else he'd die before I even got him into the wagon. If I could get him that far. He was at least a foot taller than I, and heavier by several stone.[11] Without daring to think of the impossibility of my task, I knotted the other piece of shirt round Will's wrists, slipped them over my head, and started to crawl for the wagon, dragging my brother beneath me. He cried out so piteously that I froze, but a burst of artillery fire shook the earth beneath me and I lunged forward convulsively. I don't know if Will struck his head or fainted, but suddenly he went slack, his dead weight bringing me down on top of him so abruptly that my face hit the ground. Everything swirled in a dizzy spiral.

It was the blood streaming down my own face that spurred me back into action. I clawed wildly to lift myself enough to give Will air. Then, slowly we inched forward to the wagon, stopped behind it, and I gently eased my head out from Will's hands. Leaving him below, I jumped up on the wagon and fixed the slats down at their loading angle. Grabbing the rope of the loading pulley, I tied it to Will's wrist and grasped the other end. Though I strained and heaved with every ounce of strength I possessed, I couldn't budge him.

Will's eyes flickered open and he moaned.

"Will," I cried. "Can you crawl any? I can't pull you. . . ."

But Will fell back senseless once more.

I was in such despair that I didn't hear anyone approaching until I saw him standing next to me—a man in a scarlet jacket with little wings on the shoulders and a tall helmet of black fur. Even without it, he was the tallest man I'd ever seen, that British grenadier.

---

[11]British unit of weight equal to 14 pounds

Without a word, we stared at each other. Then he drew one arm over his face to wipe the sweat out of his eyes. I didn't move, though I could feel the blood dripping down my own face and the sting of the sweat running into the cuts on my cheek.

His eyes flicked over me and then down to Will and the telltale cockade on his hat.

"My brother," I said, and opened my palms to him in appeal.

Still silent, the grenadier set down his musket and swung the pack off his back to the ground with a loud thud that showed how very heavy it was. Then he gathered Will up in his arms and carefully laid him down upon the wagon bed.

"Be that drink?" he asked, jutting his chin toward the barrel of perry.

I nodded my head, speechless.

"I could use a bit o' drink. Seventeen miles I've marched since dawn. Seventeen miles in all this heat. 'Tis enough to kill a man, even without the efforts of this lot." He jerked his thumb at Will.

I swarmed up the slats, filled a cup, and thrust it at him. The soldier drained it in one gulp and held the cup out for more. I hastily obliged. After downing the second cupful, he picked up his pack and musket.

"Thankee, lad," he growled, and plunged back into the woods before I could thank him in return.

I had no time to ponder what had happened. The sounds of muskets were all around me in the woods, and the next redcoat to come upon us might not be so helpful. Quickly, I replaced the slats across the wagon and flung myself back on the seat. Even in my hurry, I felt an uncomfortable lump under my breeches.

It was my lead soldier. I took him up in my hand and gazed at it. After the flesh-and-blood grenadiers I'd seen in the field and in the forest, the toy seemed different. With all the force that remained to me, I threw it down to the ground and left it behind me on the Brandywine battlefield.

I turned southeast past Sandy Hollow, joining a trickle of Continentals fleeing toward Dilworthtown. I slaked their thirst with the perry, while it lasted. The poor fellows deserved it.

It was midnight by the time we came up our lane. By great good fortune my father, exhausted by his harvest work, was sleeping too soundly to hear us arrive, but my mother's ear was sharpened with worry. She soon rushed out of the house, lantern in hand. As she stood there, the wind swirled her long white shift about her ankles and sent her long brown hair, loosened for bed, flying about her head.

"Geordie, I thought thee'd never get home!" she cried when she saw me.

"There was a battle at Brandywine, Mother. I found . . . "

"Geordie, thee knows I don't believe in bloodshed . . . no matter what the cause," she cut in. "It's bad enough to have thy brother run away and break thy father's heart, but now thee, too. . . ." Her voice faltered as she followed my mute gesture toward the wagon bed. "It's Will! Oh, Geordie, he isn't dead?"

"No, but grievously wounded."

Mother felt Will's forehead, then quickly looked over his wounds, murmuring under her breath all the while. "Ever since Will ran away, thy father has said he would treat him like the traitor he is should he return. I must think what's best to do." She pressed her hands to her head as if that would untangle her thoughts. Then, with an air of decision, she told me we would hide Will in Grampa's Folly.

This was a secret room my grandfather had insisted Father build into the barn foundation. Grampa had a fear of Indian raids and wanted a refuge handy in case of attack. Of course, there had never been any Indian raids—in fact, the only raids I heard about were the other way around. The Indians in our part of the colony had always been peaceful farmers. Indeed, they had taught the settlers the best ways to till the soil.

Now, however, we were heartily glad of Grandfather's stubbornness. The two of us managed to get Will to the barn, open the hidden door, and put him down on a pile of straw.

Will's eyes fluttered open. "Water," he murmured, then his eyelids closed once more.

Mother and I looked at each other, jubilant at this proof that he still lived. I ran for the spring, she for the herb garden to gather lamb's ear leaves to bandage and soothe his wounds.

It was not easy over the next few weeks to care for Will and keep Father ignorant of his presence in the barn. During that time I confided to my gentle Quaker mother the tale of how I had come to find Will in the beech grove. Though horror-struck by the dangers I had run and the sights I had seen, she conceded that my action had surely saved my brother's life.

Reports sifted in about the outcome of the Brandywine battle that had engulfed me and wounded Will. I heard that the American divisions, lacking the training to wheel and face the redcoats coming up behind them, had ended up dangerously separated from each other. Attempts to close the gap resulted in even more confusion—so much so that some Continentals had even fired on their own advance lines. As for the men pelting across the fields behind Washington and Mr. Brown, they had fought valiantly, but finally had had to retreat in disarray.

Still, 'twas said that Washington's men were not downcast by their defeat, especially since the British were too exhausted by their long day's march to pursue them. For a fortnight after Brandywine, the Continentals had done their best to keep Howe from crossing the Schuylkill, but to no avail. By late September, the British occupied Philadelphia.

Father was delighted, but Mother and I scarcely cared about the capture of the capital (if it could be called such after Congress had fled), for Will was safe at home again.

Would you like to have lived in Geordie's time? Explain why or why not.

What does Geordie learn about himself and his feelings about war?

Why does Geordie throw away his toy grenadier when he drives from the battlefield?

WRITE   Imagine that you are Geordie and that Father discovers you have hidden Will in the barn. What would you say? Write a note to Father to explain your actions.

EARLY AMERICA

Do you think Matt could do what Geordie does? Do you think Geordie could live in the forest as Matt does? Explain why you think as you do.

WRITER'S WORKSHOP

Attean teaches Matt valuable skills for living in the forest. Geordie uses skills such as hitching up a team and driving a wagon to go to Philadelphia. What skills could you teach someone? Write a paragraph that teaches someone your skill.

Writer's Choice
In early America, young people were often left on their own to do important jobs. What do you think about life in early America? Respond in your own way. Share your writing with your classmates.

THEME

WOMEN WHO LED THE WAY

Throughout American history, men and women have had to fight to win their freedoms. Names of leaders such as George Washington and Abraham Lincoln are well known to us, but what are the names of some of the women who led the way? The following selections may help you find out.

CONTENTS

ELIZABETH BLACKWELL

from INDEPENDENT VOICES ▪ by EVE MERRIAM

What will you do when you grow up,
nineteenth-century-young-lady?
Will you sew a fine seam and spoon dappled cream
under an apple tree shady?

Or will you be a teacher
in a dames' school
and train the little dears
by the scientific rule
that mental activity
may strain
the delicate female brain;
therefore let
the curriculum stress music, French, and especially
etiquette:
teach how to set
a truly refined banquet.
Question One:
What kind of sauce
for the fish dish,
and pickle or lemon fork?
Quickly, students,
which should it be?

Now Elizabeth Blackwell, how about you?
Seamstress or teacher, which of the two?
You know there's not much else that a girl can do.
Don't mumble, Elizabeth. Learn to raise your head.

"I'm not very nimble with a needle and thread.
"I could teach music—if I had to," she said,
"But I think I'd rather be a doctor instead."

"Is this some kind of joke?"
asked the proper menfolk.
"A woman be a doctor?
Not in our respectable day!
A doctor? An M.D.! Did you hear what she said?
She's clearly and indubitably out of her head!"

"Indeed, indeed, we are thoroughly agreed,"
hissed the ladies of society all laced in and prim,
"it's a scientific fact a doctor has to be a him.
"Yes, sir,
"'twould be against nature
"if a doctor were a her."

282

Hibble hobble bibble bobble
widdle waddle wag
tsk tsk
   twit twit
      flip flap flutter
          mitter matter mutter
moan groan wail and rail
  Indecorous!
       Revolting!!
        A scandal
          A SIN

their voices pierced the air like a jabbing hat-pin.
But little miss Elizabeth wouldn't give in.

To medical schools she applied.
In vain.
And applied again
and again
and again
and one rejection offered this plan:
why not disguise herself as a man?
If she pulled back her hair, put on boots and pants,
she might attend medical lectures in France.
Although she wouldn't earn a degree,
they'd let her study anatomy.

Elizabeth refused to hide
her feminine pride.
She drew herself up tall
(all five feet one of her!)
and tried again.
And denied again.
The letters answering no
mounted like winter snow.

Until the day
when her ramrod will
finally had its way.
After the twenty-ninth try,
there came from Geneva, New York
the reply
of a blessed
Yes!
Geneva,
Geneva,
how sweet the sound;
Geneva,
Geneva,
sweet sanctuary found. . . .

. . . . and the ladies of Geneva
passing by her in the street
drew back their hoopskirts
so they wouldn't have to meet.

Psst, psst,
hiss, hiss
this sinister scarlet miss.
Avoid her, the hoyden, the hussy,
lest we all be contaminated!
If your glove so much as touch her, my dear,
best go get it fumigated!

When Elizabeth came to table,
their talking all would halt;
wouldn't so much as ask her
please to pass the salt.

In between classes
without a kind word,
Elizabeth dwelt
like a pale gray bird.

In a bare attic room
cold as a stone,
far from her family,
huddled alone

studying, studying
throughout the night
warming herself
with an inner light:

don't let it darken,
the spark of fire;
keep it aglow,
that heart's desire:

the will to serve,
to help those in pain—
flickered and flared
and flickered again—

until
like a fairy tale
(except it was true!)
Elizabeth received
her honored due.

The perfect happy ending
came to pass:
Elizabeth graduated . . .
. . . at the head of her class.

And the ladies of Geneva
all rushed forward now to greet
that clever, dear Elizabeth,
so talented, so sweet!

Wasn't it glorious
she'd won first prize?

Elizabeth smiled
with cool gray eyes

and she wrapped her shawl
against the praise:

how soon there might come
more chilling days.

Turned to leave
without hesitating.

She was ready now,
and the world was waiting.

Women in Washington

by Angela de Hoyos

First there was a teacher, then a lawyer, then a doctor . . . and the career fields for women in America continued to grow. Today, women's opportunities are unlimited, due to the leadership of people such as Elizabeth Blackwell. The following portraits show six women who were and are leaders in their fields in our nation's capital, Washington, D.C.

FRANCES PERKINS   (April 10, 1880–May 14, 1965)
Secretary of Labor

In 1933, Frances Perkins was appointed the first female member of the Cabinet, the group of official advisers to the president. As Secretary of Labor during the hard times of the Great Depression, Perkins helped to pass laws such as the Federal Emergency Relief Act and the Social Security Act. These laws led to programs that are still in effect and helping people today.

JEANNETTE RANKIN   (June 11, 1880–May 18, 1973)
Congresswoman

In 1917, Jeannette Rankin from Montana became the first woman ever elected to the House of Representatives. Jeannette Rankin firmly believed in world peace. She was the only member of Congress to vote against the entry of the United States into both World War I and World War II. Of her first antiwar vote she said, "It was the most significant thing I ever did."

HELEN THOMAS   (August 4, 1920–)
White House Bureau Chief

In 1974, Helen Thomas became the first woman to serve as the White House Bureau Chief for a major news service, the United Press International. This honor came after working for more than thirty years as a reporter. Thirteen of those years had been spent in the White House, which she calls "the most exciting place in the world." In 1976, the *World Almanac* named Helen Thomas as one of the most influential women in America.

SANDRA DAY O'CONNOR   (March 26, 1930–)
Supreme Court Justice

In 1981, Sandra Day O'Connor was nominated to fill a vacant position on the Supreme Court of the United States. Sandra Day O'Connor was a successful lawyer, state senator, and judge from Arizona. Her appointment was approved unanimously, making one of her fondest dreams come true: to be "remembered as the first woman who served on the Supreme Court."

DR. ANTONIA NOVELLO   (August 23, 1944–)
Surgeon General of the United States

In 1990, Dr. Antonia Novello became the first female Surgeon General, the highest-ranking officer in the United States Public Health Service. Dr. Antonia Novello, who was born in Puerto Rico, suffered from a serious birth defect throughout her childhood. This condition required frequent surgery and was not corrected until she was eighteen years old. She decided to become a doctor then, saying " . . . no other person is going to wait eighteen years."

SHARON PRATT KELLY   (January 30, 1944–)
Mayor of Washington, D.C.

In January of 1991, Sharon Pratt Kelly was sworn in as the first woman mayor of Washington, D.C. During her campaign, she wore a pin in the shape of a shovel, the symbol of her promise to clean up the city. Sharon Pratt Kelly began her career as a successful lawyer. She is also the first woman and the first African American to serve as national treasurer of the Democratic Party.

ONCE UPON AMERICA

A Long Way to Go

BY ZIBBY ONEAL

ILLUSTRATED BY MICHAEL DOOLING

A LONG
WAY TO GO
by
ZIBBY ONEAL

*In 1917, Lila's proper family was scandalized by Grandmama,
who wore a yellow chrysanthemum and spoke out for the right
of women to vote. Lila, however, admired her grandmother's
courage and tried to imitate her. Lila decided to prove to her
friend Mike that women can do whatever men can do,
including selling newspapers on the street corner.*

illustrated by
SHELDON GREENBERG

AWARD-WINNING
AUTHOR

"Now let's see you sell," Mike said, but he didn't wait to watch. Instead he began running after customers, waving papers, shouting, "Read all about the big fire in Brooklyn! Read about the flames forty feet high!"

Lila pulled a paper from the bag and looked at it. She couldn't see where he was getting all that. The paper didn't say a thing about flames. It didn't really say much about the fire. That was what he meant by imagination, she guessed, but it didn't seem quite fair to fool people that way.

She ran her eyes down the front page. The bond speech. The fire. But then she saw, down at the bottom of the page, not taking much space, a small article headed, SUFFRAGISTS REFUSE TO EAT. Lila read as fast as she could. There were suffragists in jail in Washington who wouldn't eat a bite. They said they'd rather starve than do without the vote. The paper called it a hunger strike.

Lila's eyes widened. This was news. This was something interesting. And, besides, it was true. She pulled a few more papers from her bag and stood herself right in the middle of the sidewalk. "Suffragists starving to death!" she yelled. "Read all about it!"

To her amazement, someone stopped to buy a paper. She tried again. "Read all about the ladies starving to death in Washington!" And, again, someone stopped.

"Crazy women," the man said, but he paid her and didn't seem to think it was strange at all to see a girl selling papers.

Lila felt encouraged. Over and over she waved her papers at people walking past. She shouted her headline until she was hoarse, but it felt good to be hoarse, to be shouting and running.

"President making women starve!" she cried. "They won't eat till they get to vote!" Anything she said seemed to work. People bought papers. Maybe they would have bought them anyway, thought Lila. She didn't know, but she didn't care. She was too busy selling. In no time, her bag was empty.

She hadn't had time to think about Mike, but now, bag empty, she turned around to look for him. He was leaning against a lamppost, watching her. "I sold them all," she said breathlessly.

"I noticed."

"Here's the money." She fished the change and a few bills from her pocket.

"You keep it."

"No. Why?"

"You earned it."

"But I didn't do it for that. You take the money. I just did it to show you I could."

"Yeah. Well." Mike kicked the lamppost with the toe of his shoe. "I guess you showed me."

There were things that Lila felt like saying, but she decided not to say them. Instead she picked up the empty canvas bag and slung it over her shoulder. Together they started back the way they had come.

* * * * *

"Lila, you've told me all about it three times."

She had. She couldn't help it. Saturday afternoon was like a story she didn't want to finish, like a book of beautiful colored pictures that she couldn't bear to close.

291

"Oh, I liked it all so much, but I'm not going to tell anyone else about it. Just you." Lila looked out the window at the sunlight on the fence around the park. "I wish girls could sell papers," she said a little sadly. "I mean all the time."

"There are more and more things that girls can do. Think of all the jobs women have now that there's a war on. When I was your age we didn't dream of working in offices and factories."

"That's women. I mean girls." And then, "Do you think that if women could vote, they'd let girls sell papers?"

Grandmama laughed. "I don't know. I suppose there'd be a better chance of that happening."

"Then I'm a suffragist," Lila said. "I *thought* I was, but now I'm sure."

"That's fine."

Lila frowned. "But what can I do?"

"Believe that women have rights the same as men."

That wasn't what Lila had in mind. She wanted action. She wanted to shout headlines, run around yelling. "I could give speeches," she said. She imagined herself standing on a wooden box speaking to crowds in the street. It would be a lot like selling papers.

But Grandmama only laughed again. "You're still too young to make speeches."

"But I want to do *something*. It's no use just sitting around believing things."

Grandmama looked thoughtful. "Well, there's a suffragist parade a week or so before the state election. We're going to march up Fifth Avenue all the way from Washington Square to Fifty-ninth Street."

"With signs?" said Lila. "And banners?"

"Oh, yes, and music, too. We're going to make people notice us."

"Would you take me?"

"Well, I was thinking—"

Lila sat up straight. "I'm coming."

"But not without permission you aren't. Not unless your mama and papa agree."

"I'll make them agree," said Lila, though she had no idea how she'd do that.

"Well, I'll try to help you," Grandmama said. "At least I'll mention the parade."

Lila sat quietly in church with her hands in her lap. She played nicely with George until lunchtime, rolling his ball to him over and over though this was the most boring game in the world. She sat straight at the table and ate all of her lunch, though that included beets. Really, Lila thought, she was being so perfect it was hard to see how Mama and Papa could say no.

But that was what Papa said. While they were waiting for dessert, Grandmama brought up the parade. She did it in a kind of offhanded way, as if it were something she'd only just remembered. "And I think Lila would like to march, too," she said. Lila looked down at her napkin and crossed her fingers. But Papa said no.

It was such a small word, no, but it seemed to Lila that it was the biggest word in her life. So many nos. She felt tears of disappointment prickling in her eyes. She couldn't look up.

When, after lunch, Papa said, "Come on, Lila, it's time for our Sunday walk," Lila felt like saying, "No!" She didn't want to go for a walk with her father. She felt too mad and disappointed. All the same, she went to get her coat, because a little girl didn't say no to her father.

"Which way shall we walk?" he asked her when they were standing on the pavement.

"I don't care." And she didn't. She didn't care at all.

"What about Fifth Avenue then?"

Lila had known he'd choose that. Papa liked walking along Fifth Avenue, looking at the new motorcars pass by. One day, he said, he thought he might buy one.

And so they walked over to Fifth Avenue. Lila was wearing her best coat again and clean white gloves because Papa liked her to look like a lady when they went walking. But her hands felt crowded in the gloves and her shoulders felt crowded in her coat. She felt crowded all over.

At the corner of Fifth Avenue, they turned and walked north, past banks and office buildings, past shops and department stores. Usually Lila liked looking into the department store windows, but today they didn't seem exciting. Fifth Avenue was dull.

"Has the cat got your tongue?" Papa said.

"No. I'm thinking."

"About important things?"

"I was thinking about the parade. It's going to come right up this street."

"Lila, you must forget the parade."

But how could she? She couldn't stop thinking about it, even though the thinking made her sad.

They waited to cross the street while a car passed. "That's a Pierce Arrow," Papa said. "It's really something, isn't it?"

Lila nodded. She supposed so.

"Maybe when George is older we'll buy one like that. He can learn to drive it."

"What about me?"

"Oh, you'll be a beautiful grown lady by then. You can ride in the back and tell George where to take you. You'll have all kinds of pretty clothes to wear. We'll go shopping for things like the dress in that window."

Lila glanced at the dress in the shop window. She had to admit it was pretty. She wondered why she didn't like it more, and then she knew. It looked like the kind of dress that was for sitting around doing nothing.

"I'd rather learn how to drive a motorcar," she said. "I'd rather be *doing* something."

Papa didn't understand. "There'll be plenty for you to do. Tea dances and parties and all that sort of thing."

"Those aren't the things I want to do."

"No? What then?"

"Oh!" Lists of things came tumbling into Lila's head. She wanted to march in the parade, turn cartwheels, walk on her hands, roll her stockings down. She wanted to run and yell, sell papers—but that was not what Papa meant. He meant later, when she was grown-up. What did she want to do *then*? Lila closed her eyes and squeezed them tight. "I want to vote," she said.

The words were out before she knew she was going to say them, but suddenly they seemed just right. "I want to be able to vote same as George."

When she opened her eyes, Papa was looking at her. "That's what you want more than anything?"

Lila nodded. She dug her fists into her pockets and looked up at Papa bravely. "It's what Grandmama says. Girls are people, too. They have rights. It isn't fair the way it is. Billy Ash says he's smarter than me just because he's a boy. But I'm the one who gets all *A*'s, not him. So why should he be allowed to vote and not me? Why should George if I can't? It's not fair, Papa. It's not fair to girls."

Lila paused for breath, but she couldn't stop talking. "When I grow up, I want to be just like Grandmama. I want to make things fair for everyone. That's why I want to march in the parade—to show people that's what I think. And if they put me in jail for marching, then I just won't eat, like the ladies in Washington."

Then Lila stopped. She didn't have anything else to say.

"Well," said Papa, "that was quite a speech."

Lila couldn't tell what he was thinking. His face was very serious. She wondered if he would stop loving her now because of all she'd said. She wondered if he'd already stopped. She waited for him to say something more, but he said nothing at all. He took her hand and they kept on walking.

Lila's feet slapped along beside him. It was too late now to take it back, and, anyway, she couldn't take it back without lying. She'd said what she meant. But Papa wasn't saying anything at all. He was looking straight ahead as if he had forgotten all about her, as if he didn't know she was there any more.

Lila felt hollow in the middle. She bit the insides of her cheeks to keep from crying. On the way home, she counted cracks in the sidewalk.

When they reached the corner of Twenty-first Street and were almost home, Papa said, "How did you happen to know about those women in Washington, the ones who aren't eating? Did Grandmama tell you?"

Lila shook her head, still counting cracks. "No," she said. "I read it in the paper."

"Did you really? For heaven's sake." Lila could have sworn, if she hadn't known better, that he sounded proud of her.

After supper, she had her bath and watched Katie Rose laying out her clothes for school the next day. The same old stockings. The same old dress. Lila sighed. Everything was the same old thing again, except that now it would be different with Papa. She climbed out of the tub and wrapped herself in a towel. She went into her room to put on her nightgown.

And that was when Grandmama came in. She had a funny, puzzled sort of expression. "It looks as if we'll be going to the parade together," she said.

Lila paused. The damp ends of her hair swung against her shoulders. "What?"

"Your father says you may go."

"With you? To the parade?" Lila felt as if she couldn't take it all in so fast.

"That's what he says."

"But why?"

Grandmama shrugged. "I don't know what you said to him on that walk, but you must have said something."

Lila swallowed. He had called it a speech. She had made a speech and he'd listened! A bubble of happiness began to rise inside her. He had listened and it was all right. She grinned at Grandmama. She dropped her towel. And then right there, in the middle of her bedroom, stark naked, she turned a cartwheel.

Do you think Lila is right to question her father's decision? Why or why not?

What is Lila's problem in this story? How does she solve it?

As they walk along Fifth Avenue, Lila tells Papa about the things she wants to do in her life. What are some of these things?

The author says Lila feels crowded in her gloves and coat. Why do you think she feels that way?

WRITE Imagine that you are a newspaper headline writer. Write headlines that describe what might happen to Mike, to Lila, to Grandmama, and to Papa.

WOMEN WHO LED THE WAY

What do the selections reveal about obstacles in the paths of women who wanted to do something different? What qualities helped the women overcome these obstacles?

WRITER'S WORKSHOP

Eve Merriam chose Elizabeth Blackwell as the subject of her poem. Choose a woman whom you admire, and write a poem about her. The woman may be from the past or may be alive today. Tell what she has done that makes you admire her. Use words that will make other people feel as you do.

Writer's Choice
What do you think of the women in these selections? Plan a way to respond to the theme Women Who Led the Way. Then carry out your plan.

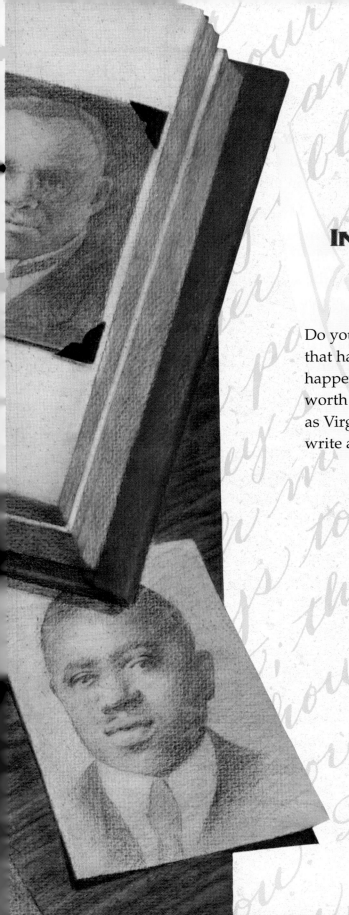

THEME

INTERPRETING THE PAST

Do you ever think about the vast amount of history that has gone before you? Every event that has ever happened is a part of history, but not every event is worth writing about. Think about how authors such as Virginia Hamilton decide what is important to write about when they interpret the past.

CONTENTS

AN INTERVIEW

with the

AUTHOR:
Virginia Hamilton

AWARD-WINNING
AUTHOR

Writer Ilene Cooper had the opportunity to talk with Virginia Hamilton about two of her novels: *The House of Dies Drear* and *The Bells of Christmas.* This is what Virginia Hamilton had to say about interpreting the past for her readers.

COOPER: You write about history from both historical and personal points of view. In your work they often blend together, don't they?

HAMILTON: My personal history does enhance my fiction. In *The House of Dies Drear,* I started with the town history as well as the stories that I heard growing up. For one thing, my grandfather, a fugitive from slavery, had come north to Ohio. The area where I live in Ohio had been a station on the Underground Railroad. Because of that there were many houses in my town that had hidden rooms and secret passages. In fact, here in Yellow Springs is the Octagon House, one of the few buildings left that was designed specifically to hide slaves. The eight corners of the house were made into little cubbyholes that could be used as hiding places. I knew all this and found it fascinating. Enough so that when I started writing *The House of Dies Drear,* I called on what I knew. In the first chapter, when the family is traveling north, they are using one of the same routes that the fugitives had used a century before. Though you don't know that from reading the book, I called on that information to make it historically correct.

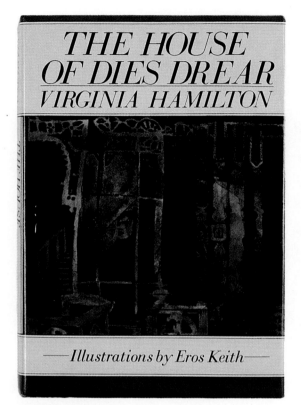

THE HOUSE OF DIES DREAR
VIRGINIA HAMILTON

—— *Illustrations by Eros Keith* ——

COOPER: Where did you get the idea for *The Bells of Christmas*?

HAMILTON: One of my editors said to me, "You've never done a Christmas book." The idea appealed to me greatly because of the stories I had heard growing up about the way my mother's family spent the holiday. There were sleighs and sleigh bells, big snows, and lots of family around.

COOPER: So that was personal history. Did you research facts for the story as well?

HAMILTON: Oh, yes. I'm lucky enough to live near the National Road. I've often used aspects of the National Road in books. The Midwest was opened up by people using that road, and so that became a part of the story. I also wanted a big snow in my book. I began researching the newspapers from one hundred years or so back to see what year there was a huge snowfall at Christmas. I couldn't find one! I was dying. Finally, I found one; you see, it is very important to me that details be historically correct. I would never say in a book that there was a snow during a particular year if there wasn't one.

COOPER: Can we say that when the story is historical, you still inject some of your personal history, and when the story is personal, you still make sure the facts are correct?

HAMILTON: Yes, I'm lucky enough to have a personal history to draw on *and* an area to draw on that is important to our country's history. I used to say it was serendipity that helped me find material. Now I believe that all of the things a writer needs are out there waiting; you just have to be able to recognize them.

The House of Dies Drear

by Virginia Hamilton

Illustrations by Scott Scheidly

Thomas Small and his family have just moved into a fascinating old house—a house that was once a stopover for runaway slaves along the Underground Railroad.

Thomas is eager to explore the old house. He quickly discovers a wood button hidden in the design of the front door. When he presses the button, it reveals a tunnel under the front porch. Thomas's further exploration is interrupted, however, by two children and a big black horse.

"I think you children just better get off my father's land," said Thomas. He stepped off the porch. "Part of the Underground Railroad must be under these steps. I've got work to do."

"There's no train tracks down there," said Pesty. "There never was none that I ever seen."

But Thomas was not stopping for them. The boy stood up, eyeing Thomas seriously now. Pesty backed the horse off so Thomas could kneel down by the hole.

"You fixing to go down under there? You want some company?" asked the boy.

"You'd just better get out of here," said Thomas, not looking at him. "I don't need any of your help."

"Well, I reckon that's true as far as it goes," said the boy. "But I suspect you'll be needing me later."

"We'll come back after a while to see how you come out," said the child on the horse. And then she and the boy fell into more laughter.

"Naw," said the boy laughing. "Naw, Pesty, you can't come back today. You are all ready for bed in your pajamas, and after supper I'm going to lock you up so you can't bother this here new boy. How you like Pesty's pretty night clothes, new boy? She likes to wear red because Mr. Pluto told her red was the best color. Mr. Pluto likes red because it is the color of fire, and he is the keeper of fire. Pesty is the keeper's helper!" The boy laughed and laughed.

Thomas was excited at having met such odd children. But he hid his feelings from them by turning calmly away. "You get out of here," he said, "before I call my father!"

"Oh, we're going," said the boy. "And I'm M. C. Darrow, the youngest."

"I don't really care who you are," said Thomas right back at him. "I am Thomas Small, the oldest son of my father."

"But you can just call me Mac," said M. C. Darrow. "Everybody calls me Mac, even Mr. Pluto, when I let him get close enough."

Thomas didn't say anything. Lying flat on his stomach, he looked into the hole; his head and shoulders disappeared inside. It was then he lost his grip and fell head first into thin, black air. He landed some five feet down, on damp sod that smelled like a mixture of yellow grass and mildew. All the breath was knocked out of him. He lay there unable to move or think for at least ten seconds, until air seeped back into his lungs. Otherwise he seemed not to have hurt himself. He could hear Pesty and M. C. Darrow going away. Mac was talking quietly to the child. Then Thomas couldn't hear them anymore.

There was gray light filtering down from the opening of the steps to where Thomas lay, and he could see that he was at the edge of a steep stairway cut out of rock. The stairs were wet; he could hear water dripping down on them from somewhere.

"I could have rolled down those steps," he whispered. Mac Darrow and Pesty must have known there was a drop down to where Thomas now lay. But they hadn't told him. "They are not friends then," said Thomas softly. He cautioned himself to be more careful.

I was showing off, he thought. I hurried and I fell. That was just what they'd wanted.

"Move slowly. Think fast," Thomas whispered. "Keep in mind what's behind and look closely at what's in front."

Thomas always carried a pencil-thin flashlight, which he sometimes used for reading in the car. He sat up suddenly and pulled out the flashlight. It wasn't broken from the fall, and he flicked it on. He sat in a kind of circle enclosed by brick walls. In some places, the brick had crumbled into powder, which was slowly filling up the circle of sod.

That will take a long time, thought Thomas. He looked up at the underside of the veranda steps.

Thomas got to his feet and made his way down the rock stairway into

darkness. At the foot of the stairs was a path with walls of dirt and rock on either side of it. The walls were so close, Thomas could touch them by extending his arms a few inches. Above his head was a low ceiling carved out of rock. Such cramped space made him uneasy. The foundation of the house had to be somewhere above the natural rock. The idea of the whole three-story house of Dies Drear pressing down on him caused him to stop a moment on the path. Since he had fallen, he hadn't had time to be afraid. He wasn't now, but he did begin to worry a little about where the path led. He thought of ghosts, and yet he did not seriously believe in them. "No," he told himself, "not with the flashlight. Not when I can turn back . . . when I can run."

And besides, he thought, I'm strong. I can take care of myself.

Thomas continued along the path, flickering his tiny beam of light this way and that. Pools of water stood in some places. He felt a coldness, like the stream of air that came from around the button on the oak door-frame. His shoes were soon soaked. His socks grew cold and wet, and he thought about taking them off. He could hear water running a long way off. He stopped again to listen, but he couldn't tell from what direction the sound came.

"It's just one of the springs," he said. His voice bounced off the walls strangely.

Better not speak. There could be tunnels leading off this one. You can't tell what might hear you in a place like this.

Thomas was scaring himself. He decided not to think again about other tunnels or ghosts. He did think for the first time of how he would get out of this tunnel. He had fallen five feet, and he wasn't sure he would be able to climb back up the crumbling brick walls. Still, the path he walked had to lead somewhere. There had to be another way out.

Thomas felt his feet begin to climb; the path was slanting up. He walked slowly on the slippery rock; then suddenly the path was very wide. The walls were four feet away on either side, and there were long stone slabs against each wall. Thomas sat down on one of the slabs. It was wet, but he didn't even notice.

"Why these slabs?" he asked himself. "For the slaves, hiding and running?"

He opened and closed a moist hand around the flashlight. The light beam could not keep back the dark. Thomas had a lonely feeling, the kind of feeling running slaves must have had.

And they dared not use light, he thought. How long would they have to hide down here? How could they stand it?

Thomas got up and went on. He placed one foot carefully in front of the other on the path, which had narrowed again. He heard the faint sound of movement somewhere. Maybe it was a voice he heard, he couldn't be sure. He swirled the light around over the damp walls, and fumbled it. The flashlight slid out of his hand. For a long moment, he caught and held it between his knees before finally dropping it. He bent quickly to pick it up and stepped down on it. Then he accidentally kicked it with his heel, and it went rattling somewhere over the path. It hit the wall, but it had gone out before then. Now all was very dark.

"It's not far," Thomas said. "All I have to do is feel around."

He felt around with his hands over smooth, moist rock; his hands grew cold. He felt water, and it was icy, slimy. His hands

trembled, they ached, feeling in the dark, but he could not find the flashlight.

"I couldn't have kicked it far because I wasn't moving." His voice bounced in a whisper off the walls. He tried crawling backward, hoping to hit the flashlight with his heels.

"It's got to be here . . . Papa?" Thomas stood, turning toward the way he had come, the way he had been, crawling backward. He didn't at all like walking in the pitch blackness of the tunnel.

"I'll go on back," he said. "I'll just walk back as quick as I can. There'll be light coming from the veranda steps. I'll climb up that wall and then I'll be out of this. I'll get Papa and we'll do it together."

He went quickly now, with his hands extended to keep himself from hitting the close walls. But then something happened that caused him to stop in his tracks. He stood still, with his whole body tense and alert, the way he could be when he sensed a storm before there was any sign of it in the air or sky.

Thomas had the queerest notion that he was not alone. In front of him, between him and the steps of the veranda, something waited.

"Papa?" he said. He heard something.

The sound went, "Ahhh, ahhh, ahhh." It was not moaning, nor crying. It wasn't laughter, but something forlorn and lost and old.

Thomas backed away. "No," he said. "Oh please!"

"Ahhh, ahhh," something said. It was closer to him now. Thomas could hear no footsteps on the path. He could see nothing in the darkness.

He opened his mouth to yell, but his voice wouldn't come. Fear rose in him; he was cold, freezing, as though he had rolled in snow.

"Papa!" he managed to say. His voice was a whisper. "Papa, come get me . . . Papa!"

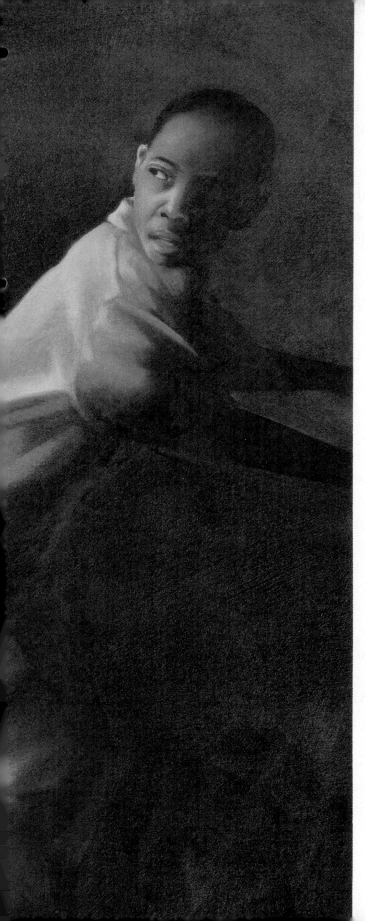

"Ahhhh." Whatever it was, was quite close now. Thomas still backed away from it, then he turned around, away from the direction of the veranda. He started running up the path, with his arms outstretched in front of him. He ran and ran, his eyes wide in the darkness. At any moment, the thing would grab him and smother his face. At any time, the thing would paralyze him with cold. It would take him away. It would tie him in one of the tunnels, and no one would ever find him.

"Don't let it touch me! Don't let it catch me!"

Thomas ran smack into a wall. His arms and hands hit first; then, his head and chest. The impact jarred him from head to foot. He thought his wrists were broken, but ever so slowly, painful feeling flowed back into his hands. The ache moved dully up to the sockets of his shoulders. He opened and closed his hands. They hurt so much, his eyes began to tear, but he didn't seem to have broken anything.

Thomas felt frantically along the wall. The wall was wood. He knew the feel of it right away. It was heavy wood, perhaps oak, and it was man made, man hewn. Thomas pounded on it, hurting himself more, causing his head to spin. He kept on, because he knew he was about to be taken from behind by something ghostly and cold.

"Help me! It's going to get me!" he called. "Help me!"

Thomas heard a high, clear scream on the other side of the wall. Next came the sound of feet scurrying, and then the wall slid silently up.

"Thomas Small!" his mother said. "What in heaven's name do you think you are doing inside that wall!"

"I see you've found yourself a secret passage," said Mr. Small. "I hadn't thought you'd find that button by the front door so soon."

Mr. Small, with Billy and Buster, was seated at the kitchen table. They were finishing supper. Mr. Small smiled at Thomas, while the twins stared at him with solemn eyes.

Mrs. Small stood directly in front of Thomas and then stepped aside so that he could take a few steps into the kitchen. Thomas glanced behind him at the tunnel, a gaping space carved out of the comfortable kitchen. He saw nothing at all on the path.

He sat down beside his father. There was the good smell of food hanging in the air. The twins seemed full and content.

"You knew about that tunnel, Papa?" Thomas said. He felt discouraged, as though he'd been tricked.

"If anyone came unexpectedly to the front door," said Mr. Small, "the slaves could hide in the tunnel until whoever it was had gone. Or, if and when the callers began a search, the slaves could escape through the kitchen or by way of the veranda steps."

It's not any fun, Thomas thought. Not if he already knows about it.

"Thomas, you frightened me!" Mrs. Small said. She had recovered enough to take her eyes from the tunnel and sit down beside Thomas at the table.

"Goodness, yelling like that all of a sudden," she said. "I didn't know what it was." She jumped up, remembering Thomas hadn't eaten, and quickly fixed his plate. Then she seated herself as before.

"Yes, why were you calling for help, Thomas?" asked Mr. Small. "You really made your mama scream."

Thomas bent down to take off his shoes and socks. A pool of water stood dark and brackish on the linoleum. "There was something there," he said.

Mrs. Small looked at him hard. Without a word, she got up and disappeared down the long hall from the kitchen toward the front of the house. When she returned, she carried a pair of Mr. Small's socks and Thomas's old tennis shoes.

"This is all I could find," she said to Thomas. She fairly flung the shoes and socks into his lap. Then she cleaned up the pool of water.

"There was something on that path," Thomas said. "It was coming after me as sure as I'm sitting here."

"You shouldn't make up stories like that," his mother said, "not even as a joke."

"There was something there." His voice quivered slightly, and the sound of that was enough to tell Mr. Small that Thomas wasn't joking.

"Then what was it?" asked Mr. Small. He watched Thomas closely.

"I don't know," Thomas said. "I didn't see anything."

His father smiled. "It was probably no more than your fear of the dark and strange surroundings getting the best of you."

"I heard something though," Thomas said. "It went 'ahhh, ahhh' at me and it came closer and closer."

Mrs. Small sucked in her breath. She looked all around the kitchen, at the gaping hole and quickly away from it. The kitchen was large, with a single lamp of varicolored glass

hanging from the ceiling on a heavy, black chain. Her shadow, along with Thomas's, loomed long and thin on a far wall.

"Thomas, don't make up things!" his father said sternly.

"I'm not, Papa!" There was a lump in Thomas's throat. He gripped the table and swallowed a few times. He had to find just the right words if ever his father was to believe him.

His hands rose in the air. They began to shape the air, to carve it, as though it were a pretty piece of pine. "It was like no other voice," he began. "It wasn't a high voice or a low voice, or even a man's voice. It didn't have anything bad in it or anything. I was just in its way, that's all. It had to get by me and it would have done anything to get around me along that path."

"I forbid you to go into that tunnel again!" whispered Mrs. Small. She was afraid now, and even Mr. Small stared at Thomas.

Mr. Small seemed to be thinking beyond what Thomas had told them. "You say you saw nothing?" he asked.

"I thought I heard somebody moving around," Thomas said, "but that could have been you all in here. Or maybe it was the kids, come back to scare me."

"Kids?" said Mr. Small.

"The Darrow children," Thomas said. "I mean that youngest Darrow boy and that little girl he calls Pesty that lives with them although she doesn't really belong to them. She came riding around the house in her pajamas on this big horse, and M. C. Darrow was hanging on the horse's tail. He was trying to get the horse to stop, but it wouldn't. Only Pesty could stop that big horse, and she was so little, too."

"What in the world . . ." said his father.

"Thomas, if you don't stop it!" warned Mrs. Small.

"Mama, it's the truth!" said Thomas. "There were these children, I'm not making it up! I can't help it if this is the craziest place we've ever lived in!"

"All right now," said Mr. Small. "Start over and take it slowly. You say there were children here?"

"Yes, they came from around the house just after I found the button and moved the steps." Then Thomas told all about Pesty, the horse and Mac Darrow. He even managed to make his father and mother understand that the children had been playing with him, toying with him, as if he were the object of a game.

"They were not friends," Thomas said finally. "They let me fall under those steps."

"No, they weren't, if they did let you fall," said his mother, "but maybe they didn't know about that drop down."

"No," said Mr. Small, "they probably knew, but I would guess they had no real intention of causing Thomas harm. It was their joke on the 'new boy.' It wasn't a very nice joke and it was a joke that might have not worked at all. They were playing with you, Thomas, to find out what you knew. They must have thought you knew more than they did. After all, you came from far away to live in a house that no child in his right mind in these parts would dare enter. I would think that by now you are pretty famous all over town."

"I see," said Thomas. "Because I dared go into 'Mr. Pluto's tunnel'!"

"Yes," his father said.

"It wasn't a human voice I heard," Thomas said. "It wasn't alive."

They all fell silent for a moment. Then Mr. Small asked, "And you're sure you heard nothing more than that sighing?"

"That's all," Thomas said. "It just kept coming at me, getting closer."

Mr. Small got up and stood at the tunnel opening. He went into the long hall after a few seconds and came back with a flashlight. "I'll go with you," Thomas said.

"I'd rather you stayed here. I'll only be a minute," said his father.

Mr. Small was gone less than a minute. Thomas and his mother waited, staring into the tunnel opening, flooded with

the light from the kitchen. A few feet beyond the opening, the kitchen light ended in a wall of blackness. They could see the light from Mr. Small's flashlight darting here and there along the ceiling of the tunnel until the path descended.

Mr. Small returned by way of the veranda steps. His white shirt was soiled from scaling the brick wall. As he came into the kitchen, muddying the floor as Thomas had, he was thoughtful, but not at all afraid.

He walked over to a high cabinet on the opposite wall from the tunnel. Beneath it, a small panel in the wall slid open at his touch. The panel had been invisible to the eye, but now revealed what seemed to be a jumble of miniature machinery. Mr. Small released a lever. The tunnel door slid silently down, and the patterned wallpaper of the kitchen showed no trace of what lay hidden behind it. Lastly, Mr. Small removed a mechanism of some kind from the panel and put it in his pocket.

"Did you see anything?" Thomas asked him. "Did you find my flashlight?"

"I didn't see anything," Mr. Small said, "and I didn't hear any sighing."

"Well, that's a relief," said Mrs. Small. "Goodness, if you'd found somebody . . . I'm sure my nerves would just give way."

"Your flashlight must have fallen in a crack," said Mr. Small. "I couldn't find it. Oh, yes, I removed the control from the panel. Without it, a giant couldn't raise that tunnel door."

"But you said there wasn't anything in the tunnel," said Thomas.

"That's so, but I don't want you wandering around in there," his father said. "The walls and ceiling are dirt and rock. There hasn't been a cave-in that I know of in a century, yet I think it best we don't take chances. I also removed the gears that control the front steps."

All he had to do was tell me not to go into the tunnel, Thomas thought. Give me a good reason and I wouldn't go . . . he knows that's all he has to do. He saw something or he heard something, and he's not going to tell anybody!

Undaunted, Thomas will continue to investigate the mysteries of his historic new house—mysteries from days long ago and mysteries in the present day—in The House of Dies Drear *and its sequel,* The Mystery of Drear House.

Would you like to read more about the house of Dies Drear? Why or why not?

How do Thomas's feelings change as he explores the tunnel? What causes the change?

What kind of person is Thomas? Give examples from the story to support your answer.

What does Thomas think was in the tunnel? What do you think was in the tunnel? Explain your answer.

WRITE   Thomas is fascinated by the history of the old house he lives in. Think of a place that fascinates you. Write a paragraph or two to explain what attracts you to this place.

VIRGINIA HAMILTON

THE BELLS OF CHRISTMAS

ILLUSTRATED BY LAMBERT DAVIS

324

The Bells of CHRISTMAS

ALA Notable Book

by **Virginia Hamilton**

illustrated by **Lambert Davis**

It is Christmastime in 1890. Jason Bell, his sister Lissy, and his brother Bob are waiting for their relatives, who are traveling down the National Road in Ohio.

The National Road, a part of American history, is the way west for the pioneers. It is also a part of the Bells' family history because it is the place where Papa lost his leg in an accident.

Lissy smiled and looked happy as she could be. Well, it was Christmas, and to me it felt like she was less of a bother as the day wore on.

We broke out of the trees, away from the patches of cattails, and stood a few feet off the Road.

"Ah, me!" I exclaimed.

"Ah, me!" said copy-cat Lissy.

"That makes the three of us—ah, me!" said Bob.

All was a sight to see on this Great Day. On the National Road!

And bells. Bells! No, not my relative Bells, not yet!

But bells, sets of three or five attached to the collars around horses' necks. Sometimes there was a whole string of bells tied to horses' harnesses. As the horses of a team moved, guided by the driver holding the reins, the bells sounded *jing-jing, jing-a-ling!* up and down the Road. And *ching, ching-aling.*

"Never in my life!" said I.

"Never in my life!" said Lissy.

Bob laughed. "Then feast your eyes!" said he. "This is the best part of a deep-snow day."

The snow kept on snowing, all over us and everything. Horses, teams of two and four, pulled sleighs! And the sleighs were full of laughing, talking, shouting Christmas folks. Whole families sometimes, if a sleigh was large enough. Whole families out for a sleigh ride before the favorite, Great Day supper.

The sky emptied its heart out. I knew I would hear the scudding sound of sleigh runners gliding through snow even in my dreams. And the muffley clip-clop of teams as snow deepened on the Road.

"Bob, will our sleigh work—can we sleigh ride?" I asked.

"Yes! Yes!" shouted Melissy. "Let's go before the snow stops!"

"This snow won't stop, Lissy, not for a good while," Bob said. "We'll sleigh ride when the relatives get here."

The snowfall and the sleigh bells must have heard him. For all at once there was a shout down the Road. We all turned as a four-horse team pulling a large, covered sleigh swung into view. The riders had spied me and Bob and Lissy before we spied them.

"Ho-ho!" shouted Bob.

"Ho-ho-ho-o-o!" came the return call.

"Bells!" I shouted. "It's Uncle Levi!"

"They're here!" shouted Lissy.

We jumped up and down for joy.

The horses came on, decorated with harness bells. They trotted briskly and snorted loudly at the driver's directions.

The covered sleigh top was homemade and fashioned to look like an old Conestoga wagon top.

Oh, it was a sight, that sleigh of merry Bells. "Tisha! Tisha!" we called out.

"You look like pioneers!" I hollered.

And they all waved and laughed and shouted, "Merry Christmas, Bells!"

"Same to you!" I called.

"Jason! Lissy! Bob! Jason! Jason! Merry Christmas!" called Tisha.

Then they were with us. Tisha was just the prettiest girl! She wore a hooded cloak of dark wool and a skirt with back drapery.

"You look all new!" I told her, gaping. "Haven't seen you in *so* long!"

"And you!" she said, eyes big and wide. "Jason, you look thirteen!"

Uncle Levi and Aunt Etta Bell gave hugs all around. The older brothers, Anthony and Chester, and cousin Sebella, took in Christmas packages.

The best gifts for the younger relatives had been exchanged. But there were some few gifts, such as Jason's from Tisha, and goods for the best meal, that had come with the Bells on this Great Day.

My present for Tisha was waiting for her under the tree.

"My pa has brought his grand surprise for Uncle James," whispered Tisha. "Remember, I said it was a secret, and I can't tell."

"Yes," I said. And I wondered all over again what it could be.

"You'll be surprised," she said.

Then brother Bob and Chester, my oldest Bell cousin, took Lissy, me, and Tisha for a sleigh ride. Just a short one. For the team was tired and needed tending to.

"Oh, now!" I said to Tisha. We were settled under the blanket, and we were a grand sight through the snow on our lane by the National Road. "How are you—shall we stop for Matthew?"

We did stop for him. We talked excitedly about everything as we neared his house. Tisha called from the sleigh: "Here, Matthew. I've come to get you!"

The door of Matthew's house flew open. Matthew sprang out so quickly he fairly slid halfway to us.

"Ah, gee! A fine sleigh this is, is it new?" he asked, climbing in next to Tisha. I was on her other side. Lissy sat in the front seat between Bob and Chester, listening to their eager talk.

"Poor Matthew! I suppose you've forgotten me as well as this sleigh. Now then, shall we ride, or shall we take you back before you forget where you came from?" she asked.

Matthew sat grinning from ear to ear. But his tongue was tied. Speechless.

"We ride! We glide!" I said. Matthew stole glances at Tisha. She looked just perfect, I thought. I was proud she was my relative and here for the Great Day.

"Aunt Lou Rhetta made this wonderful cloak," Tisha was telling Matthew, about Mama. "There's no other like it," said Tisha.

"It looks so nice on you, too," said Matthew, shyly.

I smothered a laugh so as not to disturb their talk.

"And this muff my ma found for me. I put it to my face when my nose gets cold," said Tisha. "I declare, I no longer can feel my feet!"

Matthew looked ready to wrap her feet in the blanket and run to the fire with them.

I grinned and looked away. I knew Bob and Chester smiled as Lissy chattered about the snow making her a white cloak with a hood, like Tisha's.

Soon we headed back, and in no time we were home. The house was a supper house, full of smells of good food—a mixture of sauces and meats and desserts. The spicy-sweet scent of pumpkin pie rode high above everything. My big brothers Ken and Samuel were here now with their families. The house was just full to bursting with relatives. Tisha and I circled the tree. I gave her the present I had picked out for her.

"Oh!" she exclaimed. "I did hope for a toilet set!" It had a brush, a comb, and a mirror. "It's so pretty, thank you, Jason."

She gave me a pocketknife of quality, and I praised it highly and showed Matthew.

"That's the finest I've seen," he said. Shyly, he handed Tisha his gift for her.

"I adore presents at Christmas," she said, and opened it. It was a bracelet with charms upon it. Quite pretty, too, and Tisha was delighted.

"Matthew, you weren't to spend a great lot of money, don't you know," she told him. But I could tell Tisha was pleased. Matthew had saved for months.

Then he went home for his supper. I thought he might refuse altogether to leave Tisha's side. "You can come back for pie," she said.

"I will," said Matthew.

Oh, but Christmas lasted long on its Great Day! I was filling up with it, and each sweet morsel of it was the best yet.

Mama received wonderful bead necklaces from Aunt Etta. She presented Aunt Etta with a silk umbrella. Aunt Etta loved it. She and Tisha and I went outside to open it. We three got under the umbrella.

Large flakes of snow came streaming down upon it as we stood there, shivering.

Papa gave his brother, Uncle Levi, a spokeshave, a cutting tool with a blade set between two handles. Uncle Levi was pleased.

We all waited eagerly to see what Uncle Levi would give to Papa. But they took Papa's present and went into the sitting room. They were gone a short while. And in that time, we children helped out. We moved tables, spread tablecloths, and arranged chairs for supper. Tisha and I placed the plates and silverware.

* * * * *

When Papa and Uncle Levi made their appearance, we were all back in the parlor. Mama had herded us there to sing carols. We had finished a sweet "Silent Night" when in came Papa, empty-handed. I couldn't see the present. It had been wrapped in a big box, too. Uncle Levi didn't have it either. What had happened to it?

Everybody stared at the two of them. Papa cut quite a figure in his Christmas suit. As he walked toward all of us and the tree, he held onto Uncle Levi's shoulder.

"Well, I declare," said Aunt Etta Bell. "Lou Rhetta, it sure is a wonder!" And she smiled brightly at Mama and all around. Mama looked Papa up and down and then, she, too, broke into a smile. "It's a wonder, indeed!" she said.

"And takes some getting use to, I'll wager," said cousin Chester Bell.

My brother Bob nodded agreement. "Papa will get used to it as quick as you please, if I know him," he said.

Well, I wondered! I gazed at my papa and he looked just like my papa, which he was. It was Christmas, with everybody and Tisha and oh, so many new things and goings on. That was the wonder, that I could see anything atall.

"What in the world is everybody talking about?" I asked.

"Yes, what are you all talking . . ." Lissy began.

I cut her off. "Hush up!" I said. I did not like being left out of things.

Papa smiled at me and said, "Calm down, son." He took his hand from Uncle Levi's shoulder.

"Now," said Papa, "come see what your Uncle Levi made me."

There was silence as I came up close to Papa. Lissy was right behind me with her walking doll. Everybody else crowded around. To my surprise, Papa raised his pant leg.

"Just look," said Papa. "Two true feet!"

I bent near with my hands on my knees. Well, it was a shock! Sure enough, where once there had been only the tip of a peg leg, there was now a shoe. And I hadn't noticed atall. And in Papa's stocking in the shoe was a foot. It matched the foot he'd always had. Attached to the foot was an ankle and then a leg. Not a peg leg atall. It was a wonder, all right.

"Knock on it, Jason," said Papa. And I did. I knocked on the leg, and it was wood. Very gently, I touched it with my fingers, and it was smooth oak, turned and made perfect by a master carver. It looked true, like the one that was real.

I shook my head, it was so hard to believe. "Is it a mechanical thing?" I asked Uncle Levi, for I knew he had made it.

"In some ways it is," said he. "There are wonders going on in mechanics."

"The foot moves up and down, like any foot," said Papa, "and it walks comfortable. For now, I will wear Levi's fine 'mechanical thing' on special occasions, such as this Great Day."

We all applauded wildly.

"You should both take a bow," said brother Bob. And they did. Uncle Levi and Papa bowed, holding onto each other for support. Each swept his free arm back in a grand gesture. They gave us a swell stage bow.

"It's a great wonder," I said, "to have a mechanical leg and foot. Papa, you look just like everybody!"

The grown-ups laughed at that. I was not too embarrassed. Tisha knew what I meant. So did Papa. It was a good son that wanted his papa to be just like folks. Oh, I liked him fine in his wheel-a-chair or on his peg leg. He was only different to me because he was such a fine carpenter and woodworker. But his two true feet did look the marvel. And then I just swelled up with pride at my papa and Uncle Levi.

"I'm glad of you both!" I couldn't help saying. "What true brothers you are!" And then Papa put his arm around me. And it was me and Uncle Levi who helped him to the dining room, and then into his wheel-a-chair, off his new leg for a while.

Well, it was a wonderful Christmas, 1890. A Great Day.

What feeling did you get from this story as you read it?

What are some of the things that make the Christmas of 1890 so memorable for Jason?

What do the Bells think of family celebrations? How can you tell?

WRITE   Think of a past holiday that is as memorable to you as this holiday is to Jason. Write a narrative paragraph telling about this holiday.

INTERPRETING THE PAST

What do "The House of Dies Drear" and "The Bells of Christmas" have in common? How do these stories reflect the interests and beliefs of Virginia Hamilton?

WRITER'S WORKSHOP

There are many places around the country that were important in our history. Picture a place, such as the Drear house or the National Road, that might call up memories of the past. As you imagine the place, make notes on what you see in your mind. Try to recall the history connected to the place. Then use your notes to write a short story involving the place's past. Write a story about the people who lived at that time. A drawing might help your audience visualize the place as they read your story.

Writer's Choice   What do you think about explaining history through a fictional story? Write down your ideas on the subject. Then think of a way to share your ideas.

南 西 東 冬 春 夏 秋

Connections

Multicultural Connection

Keeping Our Yesteryears Alive

What picture comes to your mind when you hear the word *pioneers*? You should have a vision of men, women, and children of every age and race.

Years ago, one San Francisco teacher decided that not enough people were aware of the contributions of Chinese American pioneers. Ruthanne Lum McCunn also felt that she could understand how the pioneers felt living in a new country because she had spent her own childhood in Hong Kong.

To share the fascinating stories of Chinese Americans, McCunn wrote a book for young readers called *An Illustrated History of the Chinese in America*. Since that book was published, she has become a full-time writer and historian. Besides a folktale called *Pie Biter*, she has written three more books about America's Chinese heritage.

Use research books and other materials to make a classroom display that highlights the contributions of Chinese pioneers and their descendants.

March Fong Eu,
California
Secretary of State

子 英 孝 情 友 愛 美

Social Studies/Art Connection

Our Past Is Many People

From what parts of the world did the people who settled in your community come? How did they contribute to the history of your region? Find the answers to these questions, and then work with classmates to create a mural that reflects your community heritage.

Music Connection

Songs That Save the Past

In addition to books, songs keep our history and heritage alive. With a group, find two songs about political or social events that took place between 1750 and 1950. If the songs are in another language, you should provide a translation. Before singing the songs, tell your classmates why these songs were popular.

Judge Thomas Tang,
State Bar of Arizona

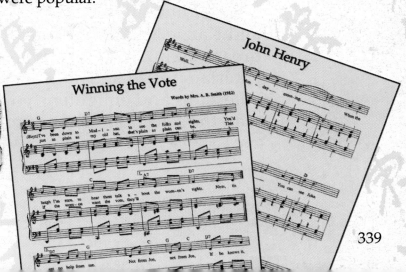

Winning the Vote

John Henry

UNIT FOUR 4

Shenanigans

O once upon a time in Arkansas,
An old man sat in his little cabin door,
And fiddled a tune that he lik'd to hear,
A jolly old tune that he'd play by ear.
                    —an American folk song

Entertainers seem to speak in a universal language, a language to which people all over the world can respond. How might a television newscaster such as Ed Bradley go about sharing world events with an audience of millions? Do you ever wonder how writers such as Gary Soto and Kazue Mizumura consistently dream up images and adventures that entertain readers? Think about what entertains and enlightens you as you read the selections in this unit.

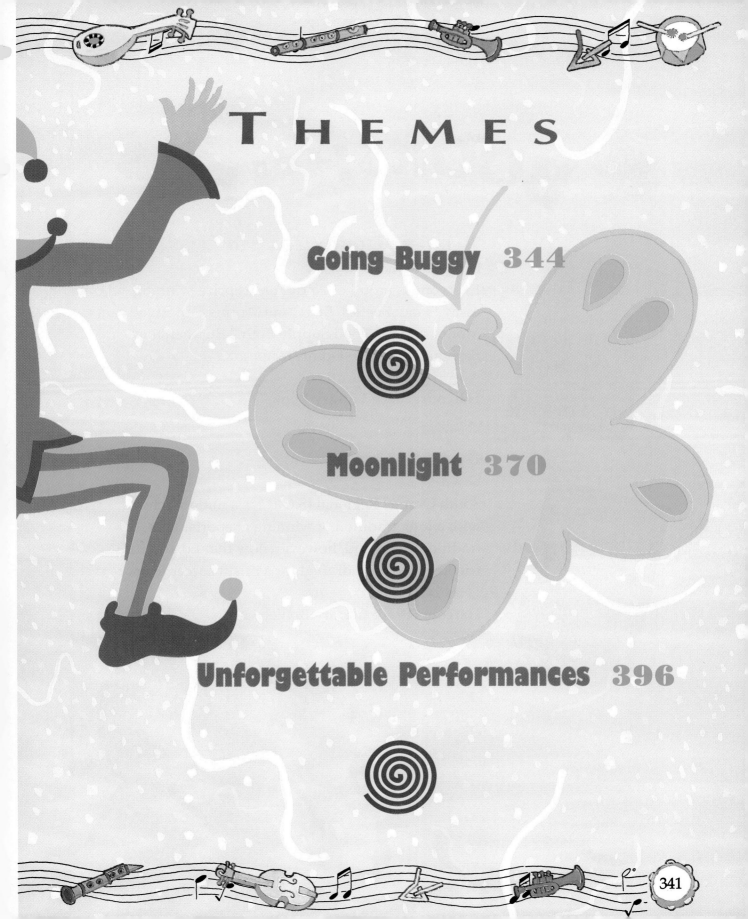

THEMES

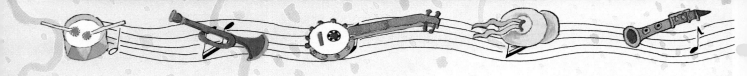

BOOKSHELF

BEETLES, LIGHTLY TOASTED

by Phyllis Reynolds Naylor

Everyone is proud of Andy for his prize-winning essay "How Beetles, Bugs, and Worms Can Save Money and the Food Supply Both." But then they find out how he tested his recipes.

Award-Winning Author

Harcourt Brace Library Book

S.O.R. LOSERS

by Avi

South Orange Regional (S.O.R.) is a middle school with a long tradition of winning at sports. That tradition could end, however, now that Ed and his friends have been drafted for a misfit soccer team.

Parents' Choice

Harcourt Brace Library Book

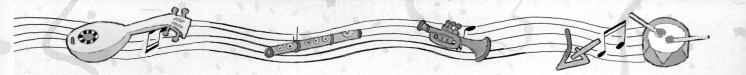

BABE: THE GALLANT PIG

by Dick King-Smith

Babe, the new pig at Farmer Hogget's, finds ways to help out on the farm and to avoid becoming a meal.

ALA Notable Book,

Boston Globe-Horn Book Honor Book

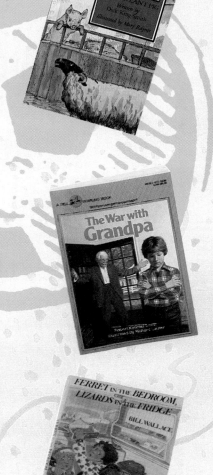

THE WAR WITH GRANDPA

by Robert Kimmell Smith

When Peter is forced to give up his room to his grandfather, he decides to declare war. It is a decision that Peter soon comes to regret.

Award-Winning Author

FERRET IN THE BEDROOM, LIZARDS IN THE FRIDGE

by Bill Wallace

All Liz wants to do is lead a normal life. But Liz's dad works with some strange and unusual animals, and he keeps bringing his work home.

Children's Choice

T H E M E

Going Buggy

How do you feel about bugs? They share the planet with us, yet we usually try to avoid them. The following selections are based upon some encounters between people and insects.

C O N T E N T S

JOYFUL
NOISE

Poems for Two Voices

PAUL FLEISCHMAN

illustrated by Eric Beddows

·F·I·R·E·F·L·I·E·S·

from Joyful Noise: Poems for Two Voices
by Paul Fleischman
illustrated by Eric Beddows

Light	Light
	is the ink we use
Night	Night
is our parchment	
	We're
fireflies	fireflies
flitting	flickering
fireflies	flashing
glimmering	
	fireflies
glowing	gleaming
Insect calligraphers	
practicing penmanship	Insect calligraphers
	copying sentences
Six-legged scribblers	Six-legged scribblers
of vanishing messages,	
	fleeting graffiti
Fine artists in flight	Fine artists in flight
adding dabs of light	
	bright brush strokes
Signing the June nights	Signing the June nights
as if they were paintings	as if they were paintings
	We're
flickering	fireflies
fireflies	flickering
fireflies.	fireflies.

LIKE JAKE AND ME

by Mavis Jukes · pictures by Lloyd Bloom

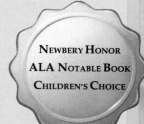

THE RAIN HAD STOPPED. The sun was setting. There were clouds in the sky the color of smoke. Alex was watching his stepfather, Jake, split wood at the edge of the cypress grove. Somewhere a toad was grunting.

"Jake!" called Alex.

Jake swung the axe, and wood flew into the air.

"Jake!" Alex called again. "Need me?" Alex had a loose tooth in front. He moved it in and out with his tongue.

Jake rested the axe head in the grass and leaned on the handle. "What?" he said. He took off his Stetson hat and wiped his forehead on his jacket sleeve.

Alex cupped his hands around his mouth. "Do . . . you . . . need . . . me . . . to . . . help?" he hollered. Then he tripped over a pumpkin, fell on it, and broke it. A toad flopped away.

Jake adjusted the raven feather behind his hatband. "Better stay there!" he called. He put his hat back on. With powerful arms, he sunk the axe blade into a log. It fell in half.

"Wow," thought Alex. "I'll never be able to do that."

Alex's mother was standing close by, under the pear tree. She was wearing fuzzy woolen leg warmers, a huge knitted coat with pictures of reindeer on the back, and a red scarf with the name *Virginia* on it. "I need you," she said.

Alex stood up, dumped the pumpkin over the fence for the sheep, and went to Virginia.

"I dropped two quarters and a dime in the grass. If I bend down, I may never be able to get up again," she said. Virginia was enormous. She was pregnant with twins, and her belly blocked her view to the ground. "I can't even see where they fell."

"Here!" said Alex. He gave her two quarters. Then he found the dime. He tied her shoe while he was down there.

"Thanks," said Virginia. "I also need you for some advice." She pointed up. "Think it's ready?"

One of the branches of the pear tree had a glass bottle over the end of it. Inside were some twigs and leaves *and* two pears. In the spring, Virginia had pushed the bottle onto the branch, over the blossoms. During the summer, the pears had grown and sweetened inside the bottle. Now they were fat and crowding each other.

The plan was that when the pears were ripe, Virginia would pull the bottle from the tree, leaving the fruit inside. Then she'd fill the bottle with pear nectar and trick her sister, Caroline. Caroline would never guess how Virginia got the pears into the bottle!

"Shall we pick it?" asked Virginia.

"Up to you!" said Alex.

Months ago, Virginia had told him that the pears, and the babies, would be ready in the fall. Alex looked away at the hills. They were dusky gray. There were smudges of yellow poplars on the land. Autumn was here.

Alex fiddled with his tooth. "Mom," he asked, "do you think the twins are brothers or sisters?"

"Maybe both," said Virginia.

"If there's a boy, do you think he'll be like Jake or like me?"

"Maybe like Jake *and* you," said Virginia.

"Like Jake *and* me?" Alex wondered how that could be possible.

"Right," said Virginia.

"Well, anyway," said Alex, "would you like to see something I can do?"

"Of course," she said.

Alex straightened. Gracefully he lifted his arms and rose up on his toes. He looked like a bird about to take off. Then he lowered his arms and crouched. Suddenly he sprang up. He spun once around in midair and landed lightly.

Virginia clapped. "Great!"

Alex did it again, faster. Then again, and again. He whirled and danced around the tree for Virginia. He spun until he was pooped. Jake had put down the axe and was watching.

"Ballet class!" gasped Alex. "Dad signed me up for lessons, remember?"

"Of course I remember," said Virginia. "Go show Jake!"

"No," panted Alex. "Jake isn't the ballet type."

"He might like it," said Virginia. "Go see!"

"Maybe another time," said Alex. He raced across the field to where Jake was loading his arms with logs. "Jake, I'll carry the axe."

"Carry the axe?" Jake shook his head. "I just sharpened that axe."

Alex moved his tooth with his tongue and squinted up at Jake. "I'm careful," he said.

Jake looked over at the sheep nosing the pumpkin. "Maybe another time," he told Alex.

Alex walked beside him as they headed toward the house. The air was so cold Jake was breathing steam. The logs were stacked to his chin.

Virginia stood under the pear tree, watching the sunset. Alex ran past her to open the door.

Jake thundered up the stairs and onto the porch. His boots were covered with moss and dirt. Alex stood in the doorway.

"Watch it!" said Jake. He shoved the door open farther with his shoulder, and Alex backed up against the wall. Jake moved sideways through the door.

"Here, I'll help you stack the wood!" said Alex.

"Watch it!" Jake came down on one knee and set the wood by the side of the woodstove. Then he said kindly, "You've really got to watch it, Alex. I can't see where I'm going with so big a load."

Alex wiggled his tooth with his tongue. "I just wanted to help you," he said. He went to Jake and put his hand on Jake's shoulder. Then he leaned around and looked under his Stetson hat. There was bark in Jake's beard. "You look like a cowboy in the movies."

352

"I have news for you," said Jake. "I *am* a cowboy. A real one." He unsnapped his jacket. On his belt buckle was a silver longhorn steer. "Or was one." He looked over at Alex.

Alex shoved his tooth forward with his tongue.

"Why don't you just pull out that tooth?" Jake asked him.

"Too chicken," said Alex. He closed his mouth.

"Well, everybody's chicken of something," said Jake. He opened his jacket pocket and took out a wooden match. He chewed on the end of it and looked out the windows behind the stove. He could see Virginia, still standing beneath the tree. Her hands were folded under her belly.

Jake balled up newspaper and broke some sticks. He had giant hands. He filled the woodstove with the wadded paper and the sticks and pushed in a couple of logs.

"Can I light the fire?" Alex asked.

"Maybe another time," said Jake. He struck the match on his rodeo belt buckle. He lit the paper and threw the match into the fire.

Just then Alex noticed that there was a wolf spider on the back of Jake's neck. There were fuzzy babies holding on to her body. "Did you know wolf spiders carry their babies around?" said Alex.

"Says who?" asked Jake.

"My dad," said Alex. He moved his tooth out as far as it would go. "He's an entomologist, remember?"

"I remember," said Jake.

"Dad says they only bite you if you bother them, or if you're squashing them," said Alex. "But still, I never mess with wolf spiders." He pulled his tooth back in with his tongue.

"Is that what he says, huh," said Jake. He jammed another log into the stove, then looked out again at Virginia. She was gazing at the landscape. The hills were fading. The farms were fading. The cypress trees were turning black.

"I think she's pretty," said Alex, looking at the spider.

"I do, too," said Jake, looking at Virginia.

"It's a nice design on her back," said Alex, examining the spider.

"Yep!" said Jake. He admired the reindeer coat, which he'd loaned to Virginia.

"Her belly sure is big!" said Alex.

"It has to be big, to carry the babies," said Jake.

"She's got an awful lot of babies there," said Alex.

Jake laughed. Virginia was shaped something like a pear.

"And boy! Are her legs woolly!" said Alex.

Jake looked at Virginia's leg warmers. "Itchy," said Jake. He rubbed his neck. The spider crawled over his collar.

"She's in your coat!" said Alex. He backed away a step.

"We can share it," said Jake. He liked to see Virginia bundled up. "It's big enough for both of us. She's got to stay warm." Jake stood up.

"You sure are brave," said Alex. "I like wolf spiders, but I wouldn't have let that one into my coat. That's the biggest, hairiest wolf spider I've ever seen."

Jake froze. "Wolf spider! Where?"

"In your coat getting warm," said Alex.

Jake stared at Alex. "What wolf spider?"

"The one we were talking about, with the babies!" said Alex. "And the furry legs."

"Wolf spider!" Jake moaned. "I thought we were talking about Virginia!" He was holding his shoulders up around his ears.

"You never told me you were scared of spiders," said Alex.

"You never asked me," said Jake in a high voice. "Help!"

"How?" asked Alex.

"Get my jacket off!"

Alex took hold of Jake's jacket sleeve as Jake eased his arm out. Cautiously, Alex took the jacket from Jake's shoulders. Alex looked in the coat.

"No spider, Jake," said Alex. "I think she went into your shirt."

355

"My shirt?" asked Jake. "You think?"

"Maybe," said Alex.

Jake gasped. "Inside? I hope not!"

"Feel anything *furry* crawling on you?" asked Alex.

"Anything *furry* crawling on me?" Jake shuddered. "No!"

"Try to get your shirt off without squashing her," said Alex. "Remember, we don't want to hurt her. She's a mama."

"With babies," added Jake. "*Eek!*"

"And," said Alex, "she'll bite!"

"Bite? Yes, I know!" said Jake. "Come out on the porch and help me! I don't want her to get loose in the house!"

Jake walked stiffly to the door. Alex opened it. They walked out onto the porch. The sky was thick gray and salmon colored, with blue windows through the clouds.

"Feel anything?" asked Alex.

"Something . . ." said Jake. He unsnapped the snaps on his sleeves, then the ones down the front. He opened his shirt. On his chest was a tattoo of an eagle that was either taking off or landing. He let the shirt drop to the floor.

"No spider, back or front," reported Alex.

They shook out the shirt.

"Maybe your jeans," said Alex. "Maybe she got into your jeans!"

"Not my *jeans!*" said Jake. He quickly undid his rodeo belt.

"Your boots!" said Alex. "First you have to take off your boots!"

"Right!" said Jake. He sat down on the boards. Each boot had a yellow rose and the name *Jake* stitched on the side. "Could you help?" he asked.

"Okay," said Alex. He grappled with one boot and got it off. He checked it. He pulled off and checked the sock. No spider. He tugged on the other boot.

"You've got to pull harder," said Jake, as Alex pulled and struggled. "Harder!"

The boot came off and smacked Alex in the mouth. "Ouch!" Alex put his tongue in the gap. "Knocked my tooth out!" He looked in the boot. "It's in the boot!"

"Yikes!" said Jake.

"Not the spider," said Alex. "My tooth." He rolled it out of the boot and into his hand to examine it.

"Dang," said Jake. "Then hurry up." Alex dropped the tooth back into the boot. Jake climbed out of his jeans and looked down each leg. He hopped on one foot to get the other sock off.

"She won't be in your sock," said Alex. "But maybe—"

"Don't tell me," said Jake. "Not my shorts!"

Alex stared at Jake's shorts. There were pictures of mallard ducks on them. "Your shorts," said Alex.

"I'm afraid to look," said Jake. He thought he felt something creeping just below his belly button.

"Someone's coming!" said Alex. "Quick! Give me your hat! I'll hold it up and you can stand behind it."

"Help!" said Jake in a small voice. He gave Alex the hat and quickly stepped out of his shorts. He brushed himself off in the front.

"Okay in the back," said Alex, peering over the brim of the hat.

Jake turned his shorts inside out, then right side in again. No spider. When he bent over to put them on, he backed into his hat, and the raven feather poked him. Jake howled and jumped up and spun around in midair.

"I didn't know you could do ballet!" said Alex. "You dance like me!"

"I thought I felt the spider!" said Jake. He put on his shorts.

"What on *earth* are you doing?" huffed Virginia. She was standing at the top of the stairs, holding the bottle with the pears inside.

"We're hunting for a spider," said Jake.

"Well!" said Virginia. "I like your hunting outfit. But aren't those *duck*-hunting shorts, and aren't you cold?"

"We're not hunting spiders," explained Jake. "We're hunting *for* a spider."

"A big and hairy one that *bites!*" added Alex.

"A wolf spider!" said Jake, shivering. He had goose bumps.

"Really!" said Virginia. She set the bottle down beside Jake's boot. "Aha!" she cried, spying Alex's tooth inside. "Here's one of the spider's teeth!"

Alex grinned at his mother. He put his tongue where his tooth wasn't.

Jake took his hat from Alex and put it on.

"Hey!" said Virginia.

"What?" said Jake.

"The spider!" she said. "It's on your hat!"

"Help!" said Jake. "Somebody help me!"

Alex sprang up into the air and snatched the hat from Jake's head.

"Look!" said Alex.

"Holy smoke!" said Jake.

There, hiding behind the black feather, was the spider.

Alex tapped the hat brim. The spider dropped to the floor. Then off she swaggered with her fuzzy babies, across the porch and into a crack.

Jake went over to Alex. He knelt down. "Thanks, Alex," said Jake. It was the closest Alex had ever been to the eagle. Jake pressed Alex against its wings. "May I have this dance?" Jake asked.

Ravens were lifting from the blackening fields and calling. The last light had settled in the clouds like pink dust.

Jake stood up holding Alex, and together they looked at Virginia. She was rubbing her belly. "Something is happening here," she told them. "It feels like the twins are beginning to dance."

"Like Jake and me," said Alex. And Jake whirled around the porch with Alex in his arms.

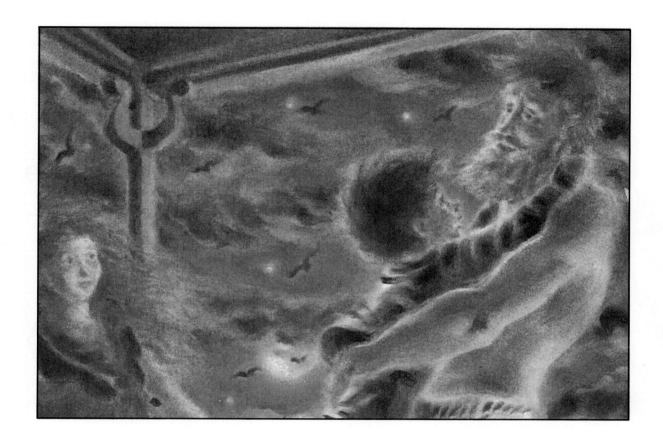

Do you think Jake should have allowed Alex to help with the chores? Why or why not?

How does Jake change from the beginning to the end of the story?

Why doesn't Alex want to show Jake what he learned at his ballet class?

WRITE The incident with the wolf spider brings Jake and Alex closer together. Write a journal entry telling about a meaningful or funny experience you shared with a family member or a friend.

BEETLES, LIGHTLY TOASTED

by Phyllis Reynolds Naylor

After weeks of preparing and testing his bug recipes, Andy entered the Roger B. Sudermann Contest. Andy felt confident that his essay about using beetles, bugs, and worms as food was good enough to win first prize.

illustrated by Katy Farmer

ON JUNE 4, TWO DAYS BEFORE SCHOOL WAS OUT, Mrs. Haynes' class sat waiting as Luther Sudermann's car pulled up outside the window. As they watched him shake hands with the principal, the teacher said, "No matter who wins the contest, I want you to know that I read all the essays myself before I sent them to Mr. Sudermann, and I think that every one of them was good. *All* of you who entered the contest deserve to feel proud of what you've done."

There were footsteps in the hall, then the principal came in, followed by a gray-haired man in a blue suit. His eyes seemed to take in the whole room at once, and he smiled as the principal introduced him. Then he sat down on the edge of Mrs. Haynes' desk and looked the students over.

"I was disappointed," he said, "that only nine of you decided to enter my contest this year, but I'm delighted with those who did. It just goes to show that imagination is alive and well in these United States, and if the future of our country depends on people like you, then we're in good hands."

The principal beamed.

Mr. Sudermann went on to talk about his son Roger when he was alive, and how Roger was always building something or taking it apart.

"If something broke around the house, Roger would say, 'Maybe I can fix it, Dad,' and when he saw something new, he'd say, 'Show me how it works.' He was intellectually curious—always tried to improve things, make them a little better." Mr. Sudermann bowed his head for a moment and stared at the floor. "Needless to say, I miss him," he told the class, "but through this contest, I can keep the idea of him alive—I can keep his imagination going, and reward others who show the same inventiveness as Roger."

Andy had never known anything about Roger Sudermann before, and could almost see the boy that Mr. Sudermann was talking about. He was wondering, too, if *he* ever died young, what his dad would say about *him*. That Andy was imaginative? Helpful? Open to new ideas?

"To the nine of you who entered my contest," Mr. Sudermann went on, "I want you to know that I have read your essays carefully—some of them several times. I narrowed my choice down to five, then four, then three, and I had a very hard time narrowing it down to two. But once I had eliminated all but two, I simply could go no further, and so—for the first time in the history of the Roger B. Sudermann Contest—I am declaring two winners this year, and each will receive a check for fifty dollars. The two winning essays were: 'Saving Energy When You Cook,' by Jack Barth, and 'How Beetles, Bugs, and Worms Can Save Money and the Food Supply Both,' by Andy Moller. Would you two boys come up here, please?"

The class began to clap as Andy, swallowing, stood up and moved numbly to the front of the classroom beside Jack. The teacher and principal were clapping too.

Mr. Sudermann shook both boys' hands. "I saw a little of my son in what each of you boys wrote," he said, "and I know that if Roger were alive, he'd want to be your friend. You have both shown the spirit of initiative and creativity that Mrs. Sudermann and I so admire, and on June 10, I am going to feel very honored to shake your hands again on the steps of the library."

"Thank you," said Jack.

"Thank you," said Andy, barely audible.

The principal walked Mr. Sudermann back out to his car again, and Mrs. Haynes beamed at Jack and Andy.

"Read their essays out loud!" someone said.

"Yes!" said the others.

"Isn't it lucky that I made copies?" Mrs. Haynes smiled, and took them out of her drawer. Andy stared down at his feet.

Mrs. Haynes read Jack's essay first. Everybody laughed when she read the part about the hamburgers almost catching fire under the hood of the car. The class clapped when the essay was over, and Mrs. Haynes said she was looking forward to cooking fish in her dishwasher. Then she picked up Andy's essay.

When it was clear that Andy was talking about *eating* beetles, bugs, and worms, there were gasps.

"Oh, gross!" someone giggled.

"Eeeyuuk!" said somebody else.

Andy saw Sam look over at him nervously and smile. He tried to smile back but his face felt frozen. When Mrs. Haynes read about using little bits of beetles, lightly toasted, in brownies, the room suddenly got very quiet. And when at last she finished reading, nobody clapped. Sam started to, then stopped. Mrs. Haynes looked around, puzzled.

"Wasn't that a good essay, class?" she said. "I suppose it might take some getting used to, but there is really no reason why we can't use insects as a source of protein."

Dora Kray raised her hand. "What if somebody gives you a brownie with beetles in it and doesn't tell you?"

The teacher thought about it. "Well, I think everyone has the right, certainly, to know what he's eating, but . . ." She looked around, puzzled. "Andy wouldn't do . . ." She stopped.

The room was embarrassingly quiet, and Mrs. Haynes didn't quite know what to do. Finally she asked everyone to take out his arithmetic book, and she started the morning's lesson.

"Listen, they had to find out sooner or later," Sam said to Andy at recess when the others walked by without talking to him. "Heck, they'll get over it. They'll forget."

"Go on and play kickball with them," Andy said. "I don't want them mad at you, too."

It was one of the most horrible days Andy had ever spent. Whenever the other students walked by his desk, they either looked the other way or glared at him. Jack, strangely, spoke to him on the bus going home, but no one else did. Andy didn't know just how he was going to tell his family. He was relieved, when he reached the house, that Mother had forgotten what day it was, and she and Aunt Wanda were busily putting up pints of strawberry jam.

In a matter of minutes, however, the phone rang and it was Aunt Bernie, telling Mother that both Jack and Andy had won the contest together, and Mother said she would call her back later, that the preserves were boiling.

"For heaven's sake, Andy, you didn't even tell us," Mother said, turning back to the stove. "How wonderful!"

Andy faked a smile.

"You're going to have to tell us all about it at supper," she went on. "Won't your dad be pleased, though?"

"What did you write about?" Aunt Wanda asked, pouring a pitcherful of sugar into the pot of boiling berries.

"Oh, saving money on groceries," Andy said.

"Well, I'll be glad to hear how to do that!" Mother told him.

Andy went out in the barn and began shoveling out the stalls. The whole fifth-grade class was mad at him, and he couldn't much blame them. In another hour or so, the entire family would be angry, too. He didn't see how saying that he was sorry would help. What was done was done, and no one would ever forget it.

At supper that evening, Dad had no sooner asked the blessing than Mother said, "Andy has some good news tonight. Tell them, Andy."

Andy swallowed. His cheeks felt as though they would crack if he tried to make them smile once more. "I was one of the winners of the Roger B. Sudermann Contest," he said. "There were two winners this year, and Jack was the other one."

"Isn't that marvelous?" said Mother. "Did Mr. Sudermann come to school and announce the winners himself?"

Andy told them about the little speech Mr. Sudermann had given the class, glad to turn the attention away from himself. He said how Luther Sudermann had told them that Roger was always inventing things, trying to find out how something worked.

"He *was* the boy who came to school as a TV set!" Lois said suddenly. "I remember now! He was wearing this box with knobs, and his face was where the screen would be. When you turned one knob, he gave you a dog food commercial, and when you turned the other one, he shut up."

"Well!" said Andy's father. "We'll have to read that essay you wrote. What was it about?"

"Saving money on groceries," said Aunt Wanda. "I'd certainly like to know how Andy knows anything about that."

"What did you call your essay?" Wendell asked, reaching for another slice of beef.

Andy took a deep breath and put down his fork. " 'How Beetles, Bugs, and Worms Can Save Money and the Food Supply Both,' " he said.

The family stared at him.

"How can they do *that?* " asked Mother.

Andy's face felt flushed. His tongue seemed to be swelling. "You eat them," he said.

"*Eat* them?" cried Lois.

Andy continued staring down at his hands. "I wrote to a man at the University and he told me how to fix them."

"*Safely?* " said Mother.

Andy nodded.

"Did you *try* it?" she asked.

"I cooked them," Andy said, not quite answering.

Suddenly no one was eating.

"What . . . did . . . you . . . cook?" came Aunt Wanda's voice, slow and steady.

Andy closed his eyes. "Brownies . . .," he said.

He heard Wendell cough.

"Deep-fried worms . . ."

The family seemed to have stopped breathing.

"And . . . grubs in egg salad."

"Egg salad!" Lois leaped up, tipping over her chair. "Not *my* egg salad!"

Andy didn't answer.

A long, piercing shriek filled the kitchen, rattling the walls. "Arrrrggggggh!" Lois lunged for the sink, stuck her mouth under the faucet and turned the water on full force. "Yauuugghh!" she screamed again, gargling and screeching, both at the same time.

"Andy," said Aunt Wanda, and her voice was like lead weights. "Did you touch my Okra Surprise?"

Andy couldn't answer that either, and continued staring down at his lap. And at that very moment, the phone rang.

Andy got up from the table and answered the phone because he needed an excuse to leave. If he could have sailed out the window and over the treetops, he would have done so gladly. A ringing telephone was the next best thing. It saved him from simply getting up from the table and going upstairs to his room, which was what he was about to do anyway.

"Could I speak to Andy Moller, please?" said a man's voice at the other end.

"I'm Andy."

"Good! This is Frank Harris, a photographer from the *Bucksville Gazette.* Mr. Sudermann told me about you winning the essay contest—you and another boy—and we'd like to get a photo of the winners."

It was what Andy had been waiting for for two years—the reason he had entered the contest. Now, the last thing in the world he wanted was his picture in the *Bucksville Gazette,* but there was no way he could get out of it.

"You're the one who wrote about beetles and bugs, aren't you?" the photographer asked.

"Yes . . ."

"Well, what Mr. Sudermann has in mind, see, is a photo of you right there on the steps of the library eating one of those meals you wrote about."

Should Andy have told his classmates and his family about the ingredients he used before they ate his dishes?

What is Andy's problem in the story?

Why doesn't anyone in the classroom applaud after Mrs. Haynes reads Andy's essay?

How would you react if you were in Andy's class and realized you had eaten one of his brownies?

WRITE Put yourself in Andy's place. Decide whether Andy should accept or back down from the challenge of eating one of his dishes on the steps of the library. Write a statement from Andy explaining why he will accept or decline.

Going Buggy

Insects play a big part in the outcomes of both "Like Jake and Me" and "Beetles, Lightly Toasted." How do insects make life better for Alex and worse for Andy?

Writer's Workshop

Andy wrote a letter to a university, asking for information on the food value of insects. Think of a topic for which you need some expert information. Decide who could give you that information, and write a business letter making your request.

Writer's Choice
What do you think of the theme Going Buggy now that you have read these selections? Respond to the theme in your own way, and write about your response to it. Share your feelings with your classmates.

THEME

Moonlight

The same moon shines down upon us all with the same light. Yet each person looks back at the moon with different thoughts and different feelings.

CONTENTS

MOON

from *Flower Moon Snow: A Book of Haiku*
written and illustrated by Kazue Mizumura

Following me all along the road,
The moon came home
With me tonight.

Coming home late,
Only my moonlit shadow
Dances on the street.

Again and again,
The wind wipes away the clouds
And shines up the moon.

Clink!
An iced branch falls.
I see the shattered moonlight
Scatter at my feet.

The party is over.
The moon in the swimming pool
Is all alone.

Many Moons

by JAMES THURBER

Illustrated by MARC SIMONT

ONCE UPON A TIME, in a kingdom by the sea, there lived a little Princess named Lenore. She was ten years old, going on eleven. One day Lenore fell ill of a surfeit of raspberry tarts and took to her bed.

The Royal Physician came to see her and took her temperature and felt her pulse and made her stick out her tongue. The Royal Physician was worried. He sent for the King, Lenore's father, and the King came to see her.

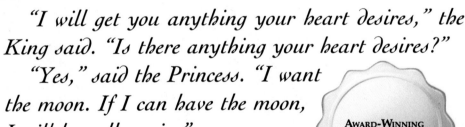

"I will get you anything your heart desires," the King said. "Is there anything your heart desires?"

"Yes," said the Princess. "I want the moon. If I can have the moon, I will be well again."

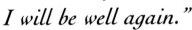

AWARD-WINNING AUTHOR

375

Now the King had a great many wise men who always got for him anything he wanted, so he told his daughter that she could have the moon. Then he went to the throne room and pulled a bell cord, three long pulls and a short pull, and presently the Lord High Chamberlain came into the room.

The Lord High Chamberlain was a large, fat man who wore thick glasses which made his eyes seem twice as big as they really were. This made the Lord High Chamberlain seem twice as wise as he really was.

"I want you to get the moon," said the King. "The Princess Lenore wants the moon. If she can have the moon, she will get well again."

"The moon?" exclaimed the Lord High Chamberlain, his eyes widening. This made him look four times as wise as he really was.

"Yes, the moon," said the King. "M-o-o-n, moon. Get it tonight, tomorrow at the latest."

The Lord High Chamberlain wiped his forehead with a handkerchief and then blew his nose loudly. "I have got a great many things for you in my time, your Majesty," he said. "It just happens that I have with me a list of the things I have got for you in my time." He pulled a long scroll of parchment out of his pocket.

"Let me see, now." He glanced at the list, frowning. "I have got ivory, apes, and peacocks, rubies, opals, and emeralds, black orchids, pink elephants, and blue poodles, gold bugs, scarabs, and flies in amber, hummingbirds' tongues, angels' feathers, and unicorns' horns, giants, midgets, and mermaids, frankincense, ambergris, and myrrh, troubadours, minstrels, and dancing women, a pound of butter, two dozen eggs, and a sack of sugar—sorry, my wife wrote that in there."

"I don't remember any blue poodles," said the King.

"It says blue poodles right here on the list, and they are checked off with a little check mark," said the Lord High Chamberlain. "So there must have been blue poodles. You just forget."

378

"Never mind the blue poodles," said the King. "What I want now is the moon."

"I have sent as far as Samarkand and Araby and Zanzibar to get things for you, your Majesty," said the Lord High Chamberlain. "But the moon is out of the question. It is 35,000 miles away and it is bigger than the room the Princess lies in. Furthermore, it is made of molten copper. I cannot get the moon for you. Blue poodles, yes; the moon, no."

The King flew into a rage and told the Lord High Chamberlain to leave the room and to send the Royal Wizard to the throne room.

The Royal Wizard was a little, thin man with a long face. He wore a high red peaked hat covered with silver stars, and a long blue robe covered with golden owls. His face grew very pale when the King told him that he wanted the moon for his little daughter, and that he expected the Royal Wizard to get it.

"I have worked a great deal of magic for you in my time, your Majesty," said the Royal Wizard. "As a matter of fact, I just happen to have in my pocket a list of the wizardries I have performed for you." He drew a paper from a deep pocket of his robe. "It begins: 'Dear Royal Wizard: I am returning herewith the so-called philosopher's stone which you claimed—' no, that isn't it." The Royal Wizard brought a long scroll of parchment from another pocket of his robe. "Here it is," he said. "Now, let's see. I have squeezed blood out of turnips for you, and turnips out of blood. I have produced rabbits out of silk hats, and silk hats out of rabbits. I have conjured up flowers, tambourines, and doves out of nowhere, and nowhere out of flowers, tambourines, and doves. I have brought you divining rods, magic wands, and crystal spheres in which to behold the future. I have compounded philters, unguents, and potions, to cure heartbreak, surfeit, and ringing in the ears. I have made you my own special mixture of wolfbane, nightshade, and eagles' tears, to ward off witches, demons, and things that go bump in the night. I have given you seven-league boots, the golden touch, and a cloak of invisibility—"

"It didn't work," said the King. "The cloak of invisibility didn't work."

"Yes, it did," said the Royal Wizard.

"No, it didn't," said the King. "I kept bumping into things, the same as ever."

"The cloak is supposed to make you invisible," said the Royal Wizard. "It is not supposed to keep you from bumping into things."

"All I know is, I kept bumping into things," said the King.

The Royal Wizard looked at his list again. "I got you," he said, "horns from Elfland, sand from the Sandman, and gold from the rainbow. Also a spool of thread, a paper of needles, and a lump of beeswax—sorry, those are things my wife wrote down for me to get her."

"What I want you to do now," said the King, "is to get me the moon. The Princess Lenore wants the moon, and when she gets it, she will be well again."

"Nobody can get the moon," said the Royal Wizard. "It is 150,000 miles away, and it is made of green cheese, and it is twice as big as this palace."

The King flew into another rage and sent the Royal Wizard back to his cave. Then he rang a gong and summoned the Royal Mathematician.

The Royal Mathematician was a bald-headed, nearsighted man, with a skullcap on his head and a pencil behind each ear. He wore a black suit with white numbers on it.

"I don't want to hear a long list of all the things you have figured out for me since 1907," the King said to him. "I want you to figure out right now how to get the moon for the Princess Lenore. When she gets the moon, she will be well again."

"I am glad you mentioned all the things I have figured out for you since 1907," said the Royal Mathematician. "It so happens that I have a list of them with me."

He pulled a long scroll of parchment out of a pocket and looked at it. "Now, let me see. I have figured out for you the distance between the horns of a dilemma, night and day, and A and Z. I have computed how far is Up, how long it takes to get to Away, and what becomes of Gone. I have discovered the length of the sea serpent, the price of the priceless, and the square of the hippopotamus. I know where you are when you are at Sixes and Sevens, how much Is you have to have to make an Are, and how many birds you can catch with the salt in the ocean—187,796,132, if it would interest you to know."

"There aren't that many birds," said the King.

"I didn't say there were," said the Royal Mathematician. "I said if there were."

"I don't want to hear about seven hundred million imaginary birds," said the King. "I want you to get the moon for the Princess Lenore."

"The moon is 300,000 miles away," said the Royal Mathematician. "It is round and flat like a coin, only it is made of asbestos, and it is half the size of this kingdom. Furthermore, it is pasted on the sky. Nobody can get the moon."

The King flew into still another rage and sent the Royal Mathematician away. Then he rang for the Court Jester.

The Jester came bounding into the throne room in his motley and his cap and bells, and sat at the foot of the throne.

"What can I do for you, your Majesty?" asked the Court Jester.

"Nobody can do anything for me," said the King mournfully. "The Princess Lenore wants the moon, and she cannot be well till she gets it, but nobody can get it for her. Every time I ask anybody for the moon, it gets larger and farther away. There is nothing you can do for me except play on your lute. Something sad."

"How big do they say the moon is," asked the Court Jester, "and how far away?"

"The Lord High Chamberlain says it is 35,000 miles away, and bigger than the Princess Lenore's room," said the King. "The Royal Wizard says it is 150,000 miles away, and twice as big as this palace. The Royal Mathematician says it is 300,000 miles away, and half the size of this kingdom."

The Court Jester strummed on his lute for a little while. "They are all wise men," he said, "and so they must all be right. If they are all right, then the moon must be just as large and as far away as each person thinks it is. The thing to do is find out how big the Princess Lenore thinks it is, and how far away."

"I never thought of that," said the King.

"I will go and ask her, your Majesty," said the Court Jester. And he crept softly into the little girl's room.

The Princess Lenore was awake, and she was glad to see the Court Jester, but her face was very pale and her voice very weak.

"Have you brought the moon to me?" she asked.

"Not yet," said the Court Jester, "but I will get it for you right away. How big do you think it is?"

"It is just a little smaller than my thumbnail," she said, "for when I hold my thumbnail up at the moon, it just covers it."

"And how far away is it?" asked the Court Jester.

"It is not as high as the big tree outside my window," said the Princess, "for sometimes it gets caught in the top branches."

"It will be very easy to get the moon for you," said the Court Jester. "I will climb the tree tonight when it gets caught in the top branches and bring it to you."

Then he thought of something else. "What is the moon made of, Princess?" he asked.

"Oh," she said, "it's made of gold, of course, silly."

The Court Jester left the Princess Lenore's room and went to see the Royal Goldsmith. He had the Royal Goldsmith make a tiny round golden moon just a little smaller than the thumbnail of the Princess Lenore. Then he had him string it on a golden chain so the Princess could wear it around her neck.

"What is this thing I have made?" asked the Royal Goldsmith when he had finished it.

"You have made the moon," said the Court Jester. "That is the moon."

"But the moon," said the Royal Goldsmith, "is 500,000 miles away and is made of bronze and is round like a marble."

"That's what you think," said the Court Jester as he went away with the moon.

The Court Jester took the moon to the Princess Lenore, and she was overjoyed. The next day she was well again and could get up and go out in the gardens to play.

But the King's worries were not yet over. He knew that the moon would shine in the sky again that night, and he did not want the Princess Lenore to see it. If she did, she would know that the moon she wore on a chain around her neck was not the real moon.

So the King sent for the Lord High Chamberlain and said, "We must keep the Princess Lenore from seeing the moon when it shines in the sky tonight. Think of something."

The Lord High Chamberlain tapped his forehead with his fingers thoughtfully and said, "I know just the thing. We can make some dark glasses for the Princess Lenore. We can make them so dark that she will not be able to see anything at all through them. Then she will not be able to see the moon when it shines in the sky."

This made the King very angry, and he shook his head from side to side. "If she wore dark glasses, she would bump into things," he said, "and then she would be ill again." So he sent the Lord High Chamberlain away and called the Royal Wizard.

"We must hide the moon," said the King, "so that the Princess Lenore will not see it when it shines in the sky tonight. How are we going to do that?"

The Royal Wizard stood on his hands and then he stood on his head and then he stood on his feet again.

"I know what we can do," he said. "We can stretch some black velvet curtains on poles. The curtains will cover all the palace gardens like a circus tent, and the Princess Lenore will not be able to see through them, so she will not see the moon in the sky."

The King was so angry at this that he waved his arms around. "Black velvet curtains would keep out the air," he said. "The Princess Lenore would not be able to breathe, and she would be ill again." So he sent the Royal Wizard away and summoned the Royal Mathematician.

"We must do something," said the King, "so that the Princess Lenore will not see the moon when it shines in the sky tonight. If you know so much, figure out a way to do that."

The Royal Mathematician walked around in a circle, and then he walked around in a square, and then he stood still. "I have it!" he said.

"We can set off fireworks in the gardens every night. We will make a lot of silver fountains and golden cascades, and when they go off, they will fill the sky with so many sparks that it will be as light as day and the Princess Lenore will not be able to see the moon."

The King flew into such a rage that he began jumping up and down. "Fireworks would keep the Princess Lenore awake," he said. "She would not get any sleep at all and she would be ill again." So the King sent the Royal Mathematician away.

When he looked up again, it was dark outside and he saw the bright rim of the moon just peeping over the horizon. He jumped up in a great fright and rang for the Court Jester. The Court Jester came bounding into the room and sat down at the foot of the throne.

"What can I do for you, your Majesty?" he asked.

"Nobody can do anything for me," said the King mournfully. "The moon is coming up again. It will shine into the Princess Lenore's bedroom, and she will know it is still in the sky and that she does not wear it on a golden chain around her neck. Play me something on your lute, something very sad, for when the Princess sees the moon, she will be ill again."

The Court Jester strummed on his lute. "What do your wise men say?" he asked.

"They can think of no way to hide the moon that will not make the Princess Lenore ill," said the King.

The Court Jester played another song, very softly. "Your wise men know everything," he said, "and if they cannot hide the moon, then it cannot be hidden."

The King put his head in his hands again and sighed.

Suddenly he jumped up from his throne and pointed to the windows. "Look!" he cried. "The moon is already shining into the Princess Lenore's bedroom. Who can explain how the moon can be shining in the sky when it is hanging on a golden chain around her neck?"

The Court Jester stopped playing on his lute. "Who could explain how to get the moon when your wise men said it was too large and too far away? It was the Princess Lenore. Therefore the Princess Lenore is wiser than your wise men and knows more about the moon than they do. So I will ask *her*." And before the King could stop him, the Court Jester slipped quietly out of the throne room and up the wide marble staircase to the Princess Lenore's bedroom.

The Princess was lying in bed, but she was wide awake and she was looking out the window at the moon shining in the sky. Shining in her hand was the moon the Court Jester had got for her. He looked very sad, and there seemed to be tears in his eyes.

"Tell me, Princess Lenore," he said mournfully, "how can the moon be shining in the sky when it is hanging on a golden chain around your neck?"

The Princess looked at him and laughed. "That is easy, silly," she said. "When I lose a tooth, a new one grows in its place, doesn't it?"

"Of course," said the Court Jester. "And when the unicorn loses his horn in the forest, a new one grows in the middle of his forehead."

"That is right," said the Princess. "And when the Royal Gardener cuts the flowers in the garden, other flowers come to take their place."

"I should have thought of that," said the Court Jester, "for it is the same way with the daylight."

"And it is the same way with the moon," said the Princess Lenore. "I guess it is the same way with everything." Her voice became very low and faded away, and the Court Jester saw that she was asleep. Gently he tucked the covers in around the sleeping Princess.

But before he left the room, he went over to the window and winked at the moon, for it seemed to the Court Jester that the moon had winked at him.

Who is your favorite character in the story? What qualities make this character likable?

Why are the King and his advisers in such an uproar?

How does Princess Lenore's opinion about the moon differ from the opinions of the King's advisers?

Why is the King still worried on the day after the Princess gets the moon?

WRITE   The Lord High Chamberlain, the Royal Wizard, the Royal Mathematician, and the Royal Goldsmith all provide information about the moon. Compile a list of your own imaginary "facts" about the moon.

Words from the ILLUSTRATOR:

MARC SIMONT

I first met James Thurber and his family when they moved to Cornwall, Connecticut, during the late 1940s. *Many Moons* had already been written. It was illustrated by Louis Slobodkin and had won the Caldecott Medal.

A few years ago, when Mrs. Thurber was asked about doing a newly illustrated edition, she had qualms. But she and her family finally decided to do it. Since I had illustrated other James Thurber books, *The Wonderful O* and *The Thirteen Clocks,* she asked me to do this one.

Usually, I don't like to meet the authors of the books I'm illustrating. They have their own ideas, and it creates conflicts. But James Thurber was my friend before he was my collaborator. We had talked about various things in *Many Moons* before I ever knew that I would one day illustrate it.

Some people have asked me how I felt about reillustrating a book that is so famous. To tell you the truth, when I illustrate a book, I decide to make it all my own, my personal interpretation of the story. Yes, I was interested in seeing how Louis Slobodkin had done it, but in no way did his work affect my vision, which was quite different. There are some things I like about Slobodkin's version, but his *Many Moons* had no impact on my own. When it comes to an artist's vision, every artist is in a different world.

Moonlight

Think about the descriptions of the moon in the story and in the poetry. Explain how they are alike and how they are different.

WRITER'S WORKSHOP

The Court Jester finds a way to give the Princess the moon. If the Princess's ideas about the moon had been impossible to fulfill, however, he would have had to persuade her not to desire the moon. What reasons might he have given her? Write a paragraph giving reasons the Court Jester could use to convince the Princess that she does not need the moon.

Writer's Choice   Moonlight affects people
in different ways. How does moonlight affect you? Respond in your own way. Plan a way to share your writing.

THEME

Unforgettable Performances

Have you ever performed before a large audience? Or even before an audience of one? If so, you probably learned what the characters in these selections learned: You just never know what might happen!

CONTENTS

397

Oliver Hyde's DISHCLOTH CONCERT

from

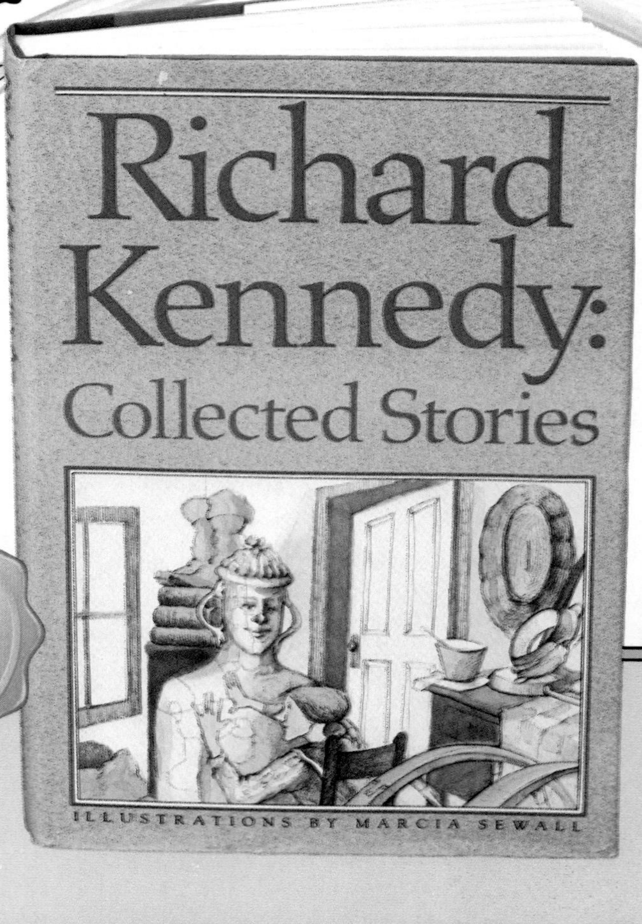

Richard Kennedy: Collected Stories

ILLUSTRATIONS BY MARCIA SEWALL

CHILDREN'S CHOICE

by Richard Kennedy
illustrated by Marcia Sewall

Now maybe it's sad and maybe it's spooky, but there was a man who lived just out of town on a scrubby farm and no one had seen his face for years. If he was outside working, he kept his hat pulled down and his collar turned up, and if anyone approached him he ran up the hill to his house and shut himself inside. He left notes pinned to his door for a brave errand boy who brought him supplies from town. The people asked the boy what he heard up there in that tomblike house when he collected the notes and delivered the supplies. "Darkness and quietness," said the boy. "I hear darkness and quietness." The people nodded and looked at the boy. "Aren't you afraid?" The boy bit his lip. "A fellow has to make a living," he said.

Sometimes the children would come out of town and sing a little song up at the house and then run away. They sang:

"The beautiful bride of Oliver Hyde,
Fell down dead on the mountainside."

Yes, it was true. The man was full of grief and bitterness. He was Oliver Hyde, and his young bride's wagon had been washed into a canyon by a mudslide and it killed her, horse and all. But that was years ago. The children sang some more:

"Oliver Hyde is a strange old man,
He sticks his head in a coffee can,
And hides his face when there's folks about,
He's outside in, and he's inside out."

It was too bad. Oliver used to have many friends, and he played the fastest and sweetest fiddle in the county. And for the few short weeks he was married his playing was sweeter than ever. But on the day his wife was buried he busted his fiddle across a porch post, and now he sat cold, dark, and quiet on his little hill. No one had visited him for years. There was a reason. You shall see.

One day a man came from the town and walked up the hill toward Oliver's house. He was carrying a fiddle case. Two or three times he stopped and looked up at the house and shook his head, as if trying to free himself from a ghost, and continued on. He arrived at the porch steps. All the window shades were pulled down and it was dead quiet inside. The three porch steps creaked like cats moaning in their dreams, and the man knocked on the door. For a little bit it was quiet, then there was the sound of a chair being scooted across the floor. A voice said, "Come in."

The man opened the door a crack and peeked inside.

"Oliver?" he said. "It's me, Jim." No answer. Jim opened the door farther and put a foot inside. It was dark, and smelled stale. Jim opened the door all the way.

Off in a corner where the light didn't touch sat a figure in a chair, perfectly upright, with his hands on his knees like a stone god, as still and silent as a thousand years ago. The head was draped completely with a dishcloth. Not a breath ruffled the ghost head.

Jim swallowed and spoke. "Haven't seen you around lately, Oliver." No answer.

People used to visit Oliver for a while after his beautiful bride fell down dead on the mountainside, but this is how it was—Oliver sitting in the dark with a dishcloth over his head, and he never spoke to them. It was too strange. His friends stopped visiting.

All Jim wanted was a single word from Oliver—yes or no.

He had a favor to ask. He was Oliver's oldest friend. He moved inside.

"Sue's getting married, Oliver," he said. No answer. "You remember my little girl, Sue? She's all growed up now, Oliver, and mighty pretty, too." For all the notice he got, Jim might just as well have been talking to a stove. He cleared his voice and went on. "The reason I came, Oliver, was to ask you to come and play the fiddle for us at the dance. We was the best friends, and I don't see how I can marry off Sue without you being there to fiddle for us. You can just say yes or no, Oliver."

Now Oliver wasn't dead himself yet, so he still had feelings, and Jim had been his best friend. They had played and fought together, fished and hunted, and grown up together. So Oliver hated to say "No" just flat out like that, so he said instead, "No fiddle." Jim was prepared for that, and he laid the fiddle case down on the floor and flipped it open.

"Here, I brought a fiddle, Oliver. Porky Fellows was happy to make a lend of it."

Oliver felt trapped now. He was silent for a long time, then finally he said, "Tell you what. I can't wear this dishcloth on my head and fiddle, but if everyone else wears a dishcloth I'll come."

Jim was quiet for a long time, but at last he said, "All right, Oliver, I'll ask if they'll do it. The dance is tomorrow night at Edward's barn. I'll leave the fiddle here, and if I don't come back to pick it up, then you got to come to the dance and fiddle for us. I got your promise."

Oliver smiled under his dishcloth. They'd be fools to agree to that. You can't have any fun with a dishcloth over your head.

"So long, Oliver," Jim said. Oliver didn't answer. Jim went back on down the hill.

Oliver took the dishcloth off. The fiddle was laying in the light of the open door. He sucked a whisker and looked at it. Oliver knew the fiddle, and it was a good fiddle. He wondered if it was in tune and wanted to pick it up, but he let it lay there. His foot was tapping, and he slapped his knee to make it stop. He laughed to himself and muttered, "Them donkeys—what do they know?" Then he got up and moved around the little house on his dreary business.

The sun went down and the shadow of the fiddle case stretched across the floor. Oliver's eyes kept landing on the

fiddle, and he stepped over the shadow when he crossed that way. It looked to him like the bow had new horsehair on it. But it didn't make any difference to him. He figured he'd never be playing on that fiddle, and he never touched it.

Next morning Oliver watched down the hill for Jim to come and tell him the deal was off and to get the fiddle. Noon came. Oliver ate some beans. Afternoon came on. Jim didn't show. Oliver began to get mad. He was mad that he had ever made the promise. It started to get dark. "Those cluckheads!" Oliver said, pulling the window shut. "They can't dance with dishcloths on their heads, or drink punch, either. They'll have a rotten time."

But a promise is a promise.

Finally he decided it was time to put his hat and coat on. "They tricked me," Oliver grumbled, "but I got a trick for them, too. They'll be sorry I came to their party." It wasn't a great trick Oliver had in mind, but just a miserable little one to make sure nobody could have any fun while he was there. He figured they'd ask him to leave shortly. He wouldn't even bother to take off his hat and coat.

He headed down the hill with the fiddle and into the little town. He entered Edward's barn with his hat pulled down and his collar turned up. It was dark except for two bare, hanging light bulbs, one over the center of the barn and one at the end where a sort of stage was built up. Oliver had played at shindigs there many times. He kept his head down, and only from the corners of his eyes could he see all the people sitting around the walls. "Lord, it's awfully dark," Oliver thought to himself, "and quiet. I figure they know that's the way I like it." He got under the light bulb that hung over the stage and took out the fiddle.

He tuned down to a fretful and lonesome sound, and then he played.

Of course he knew they were all looking for happy dancing tunes, so first off he played a slow and sad tune about a man who was walking down a long road that had no ending and was gray all about, and the man was looking forward to being dead because it might be more cheerful. Nobody danced, naturally, and didn't clap either when Oliver finished it. "That's just right," Oliver thought. "I'll give them a wretched time." And he started on another.

The second tune he played was even slower and sadder, about a man who thought his heart was a pincushion and it seemed to him that everyone was sticking pins and needles into it, and it was hurtful even to listen to it. Nobody danced, and nobody even moved to the punch bowl to get their spirits up. "Now they're sorry I came," Oliver thought. Still, he had played that last tune especially sweet, and he expected that someone might have clapped a little just for that, even if it was sad.

Oliver looked out a little under his hat as he retuned a bit. He tried to see Jim. He ought to come up and say hello at least, not just let him stand there completely alone. And he wondered where the other musicians were. Four people were sitting down off to the right of the stage. That would be them. Oliver considered it would be nice to have a little slide guitar on these slow ones, sort of mournful played, and a mouth harp and mandolin would fit in nice. "Naw! This is just the way I want it. One more gloomy song and they'll ask me to leave."

So then he played another, this one about a man who had a wife that just recently moved to heaven, and how roses grew all over her tombstone even in the winter. Oliver was halfway through that before he remembered that he'd played that tune at his own wedding party. He pulled up short a bit then, but kept on playing it out, and a tear rolled down his cheek. Well, nobody could see. He wiped his eyes when he was finished.

Nobody clapped and nobody moved, just sat against the dark walls perfectly still. Among the dark figures was a lighter shape. Probably the bride in her white gown. Oliver remembered how lovely and happy his bride had been, and he felt a little mean when he thought about that, giving out such sad tunes.

He spoke out loud, the first words that were spoken since he came in. "Well, I guess you're all ready for me to leave now, and I will. But first I want to play just one happy tune for the bride, and so you can dance, and then I'll go." Then he did play a happy one, a fast one, carrying on with fiddling lively enough to scramble eggs. But nobody got up to dance, and when he was finished nobody moved or made a sound.

"Look here," Oliver said. "I reckon you can't dance with those dishcloths over your heads, I forgot about that. So take 'em off. I'll give you another dancing tune, then I'll go." And then he went into another, as sweet and light and fast as any-

one ever could, something to get even a rock up and dancing,
but nobody moved. And when he was finished they all sat
silent with the dishcloths still on their heads.

"Come on," Oliver said. "Take those things off your heads.
You other fellows get up here with your music and help me
out. Let's have some dancing, drink some punch, let's get
alive now." He stomped his foot three times and threw into a
tune that would churn butter all by itself. But the other four
musicians sat perfectly still, and so did everybody else, and
Oliver was standing there under the light bulb in silence when
he finished the tune.

He stood there with his head down, understanding things, and how it felt to be on the other side of the darkness and silence when all you wanted was some sign of life to help out. Then he leaned over and put the fiddle in the case and closed it. He said one last thing, then walked out from under the light toward the door. "Okay," he said. "That's a hard lesson, but I got it."

When he opened the door he bumped into someone sitting next to it against the wall, and the fellow fell off his chair. Oliver put a hand down to help him up. But the fellow just lay there. Oliver touched him. "What's this?" He felt around, then shoved back his hat for a look. It was a sack of grain he'd knocked over. And the next person sitting there was a sack of grain, too. And the next was a bale of hay.

Oliver walked completely around the barn. All the people were sacks of grain and bales of hay sitting against the dark walls, and the bride was a white sack of flour. The four musicians sitting off to the right of the stage were four old saddles setting on a rail.

When Oliver came around to the door again he heard music. He stepped outside and looked down the street. A barn down near the end was all lit up, and lots of people were moving about. He went back up on the stage, got the fiddle, and headed down the street.

Jim was standing by the door. "Waiting for you, Oliver," he said. "We're just getting under way—come on in." When he led Oliver inside everyone became quiet, first one little group of people, then another, until at last everyone was silent and looking at Oliver. The bride and groom were holding hands. Jim made a motion and everyone headed for a chair against the walls. They all took out dishcloths to put over their heads.

"Edward's got himself a new barn, huh?" Oliver said.

"Yeah," said Jim. "I guess you didn't know that. Uses the old one to store stuff. I shoulda told you."

"It's all right," Oliver said. He looked up on the stage. Four musicians were sitting there with dishcloths over their heads. Then Jim took out a large dishcloth. Oliver touched him on the arm.

"Never mind that. And everyone else, too. Just be regular and dance. I'll fiddle for you."

Jim slapped him on the back and shouted out the good news. Oliver went up on the stage. Someone got him a mug of punch. The musicians tuned up. Oliver took off his hat and dropped it, and tossed his coat on a chair. They lit into a fast, happy tune. They danced and played and sang half the night.

Ah, they had a wonderful time. Oliver included.

If Oliver Hyde were your friend, would you have asked him to play at a wedding? Explain your answer.

Oliver Hyde intends to play only sad songs when he gets to Edward's barn. Why does he change his mind while he is performing?

Do you think Oliver Hyde has the right to behave as he does? Explain why you feel as you do.

Why, in the end, does Oliver Hyde tell the wedding guests to take off the dishcloths?

WRITE   If this story were a fable, it would have a moral, or lesson. Write your own moral for this story.

LA BAMBA

from Baseball in April and Other Stories

BEST BOOKS FOR YOUNG ADULTS

by Gary Soto

illustrated by David Diaz

anuel was the fourth of seven children and looked like a lot of kids in his neighborhood: black hair, brown face, and skinny legs scuffed from summer play. But summer was giving way to fall: the trees were turning red, the lawns brown, and the pomegranate trees were heavy with fruit. Manuel walked to school in the frosty morning, kicking leaves and thinking of tomorrow's talent show. He was still amazed that he had volunteered. He was going to pretend to sing Ritchie Valens's "La Bamba" before the entire school.

hy did I raise my hand? he asked himself, but in his heart he knew the answer. He yearned for the limelight. He wanted applause as loud as a thunderstorm, and to hear his friends say, "Man, that was bad!" And he wanted to impress the girls, especially Petra Lopez, the second-prettiest girl in his class. The prettiest was already taken by his friend Ernie. Manuel knew he should be reasonable, since he himself was not great-looking, just average.

Manuel kicked through the fresh-fallen leaves. When he got to school he realized he had forgotten his math workbook. If the teacher found out, he would have to stay after school and miss practice for the talent show. But fortunately for him, they did drills that morning.

During lunch Manuel hung around with Benny, who was also in the talent show. Benny was going to play the trumpet in spite of the fat lip he had gotten playing football.

"How do I look?" Manuel asked. He cleared his throat and started moving his lips in pantomime. No words came out, just a hiss that sounded like a snake. Manuel tried to look emotional, flailing his arms on the high notes and opening his eyes and mouth as wide as he could when he came to *"Para bailar la baaaaammmba."*

After Manuel finished, Benny said it looked all right, but suggested Manuel dance while he sang. Manuel thought for a moment and decided it was a good idea.

"Yeah, just think you're like Michael Jackson or someone like that," Benny suggested. "But don't get carried away."

During rehearsal, Mr. Roybal, nervous about his debut as the school's talent coordinator, cursed under his breath when the lever that controlled the speed on the record player jammed.

"Darn," he growled, trying to force the lever. "What's wrong with you?"

"Is it broken?" Manuel asked, bending over for a closer look. It looked all right to him.

r. Roybal assured Manuel that he would have a good record player at the talent show, even if it meant bringing his own stereo from home.

Manuel sat in a folding chair, twirling his record on his thumb. He watched a skit about personal hygiene, a mother-and-daughter violin duo, five first-grade girls jumping rope, a karate kid breaking boards, three girls singing, and a skit about the pilgrims. If the record player hadn't been broken, he would have gone after the karate kid, an easy act to follow, he told himself.

As he twirled his forty-five record, Manuel thought they had a great talent show. The entire school would be amazed. His mother and father would be proud, and his brothers and sisters would be jealous and pout. It would be a night to remember.

Benny walked onto the stage, raised his trumpet to his mouth, and waited for his cue. Mr. Roybal raised his hand like a symphony conductor and let it fall dramatically. Benny inhaled and blew so loud that Manuel dropped his record, which rolled across the cafeteria floor until it hit a wall. Manuel raced after it, picked it up, and wiped it clean.

"Boy, I'm glad it didn't break," he said with a sigh.

That night Manuel had to do the dishes and a lot of homework, so he could only practice in the shower. In bed he prayed that he wouldn't mess up. He prayed that it wouldn't be like when he was a first-grader. For Science Week he had wired together a C battery and a bulb, and told everyone he had discovered how a flashlight worked. He was so pleased with himself that he practiced for hours pressing the wire to the battery, making the bulb wink a dim, orangish light. He showed it to so many kids in his neighborhood that when it was time to show his class how a flashlight worked, the battery was dead. He pressed the wire to the battery, but the bulb didn't respond. He pressed until his thumb hurt and some kids in the back started snickering.

But Manuel fell asleep confident that nothing would go wrong this time.

The next morning his father and mother beamed at him. They were proud that he was going to be in the talent show.

"I wish you would tell us what you're doing," his mother said. His father, a pharmacist who wore a blue smock with his name on a plastic rectangle, looked up from the newspaper and sided with his wife. "Yes, what are you doing in the talent show?"

"You'll see," Manuel said with his mouth full of Cheerios.

The day whizzed by, and so did his afternoon chores and dinner. Suddenly he was dressed in his best clothes and standing next to Benny backstage, listening to the commotion as the cafeteria filled with school kids and parents. The lights dimmed, and Mr. Roybal, sweaty in a tight suit and a necktie with a large knot, wet his lips and parted the stage curtains.

"Good evening, everyone," the kids behind the curtain heard him say. "Good evening to you," some of the smart-alecky kids said back to him.

"Tonight we bring you the best John Burroughs Elementary has to offer, and I'm sure that you'll be both pleased and amazed that our little school houses so much talent. And now, without further ado, let's get on with the show." He turned and, with a swish of his hand, commanded, "Part the curtain." The curtains parted in jerks. A girl dressed as a toothbrush and a boy dressed as a dirty gray tooth walked onto the stage and sang:

Brush, brush, brush
Floss, floss, floss
Gargle the germs away—hey! hey! hey!

After they finished singing, they turned to Mr. Roybal, who dropped his hand. The toothbrush dashed around the stage after the dirty tooth, which was laughing and having a great time until it slipped and nearly rolled off the stage.

Mr. Roybal jumped out and caught it just in time. "Are you OK?"

The dirty tooth answered, "Ask my dentist," which drew laughter and applause from the audience.

The violin duo played next, and except for one time when the girl got lost, they sounded fine. People applauded, and some even stood up. Then the first-grade girls maneuvered onto the stage while jumping rope. They were all smiles and bouncing ponytails as a hundred cameras flashed at once. Mothers "awhed" and fathers sat up proudly.

he karate kid was next. He did a few kicks, yells, and chops, and finally, when his father held up a board, punched it in two. The audience clapped and looked at each other, wide-eyed with respect. The boy bowed to the audience, and father and son ran off the stage.

Manuel remained behind the stage shivering with fear. He mouthed the words to "La Bamba" and swayed from left to right. Why did he raise his hand and volunteer? Why couldn't he have just sat there like the rest of the kids and not said anything? While the karate kid was on stage, Mr. Roybal, more sweaty than before, took Manuel's forty-five record and placed it on a new record player.

"You ready?" Mr. Roybal asked.

"Yeah . . ."

Mr. Roybal walked back on stage and announced that Manuel Gomez, a fifth-grader in Mrs. Knight's class, was going to pantomime Ritchie Valens's classic hit "La Bamba."

The cafeteria roared with applause. Manuel was nervous but loved the noisy crowd. He pictured his mother and father applauding loudly and his brothers and sisters also clapping, though not as energetically.

Manuel walked on stage and the song started immediately. Glassy-eyed from the shock of being in front of so many people, Manuel moved his lips and swayed in a made-up dance step. He couldn't see his parents, but he could see his brother Mario, who was a year younger, thumb-wrestling with a friend. Mario was wearing Manuel's favorite shirt; he would deal with Mario later. He saw some other kids get up and head for the drinking fountain, and a baby sitting in the middle of an aisle sucking her thumb and watching him intently.

hat am I doing here? thought Manuel. This is no fun at all. Everyone was just sitting there. Some people were moving to the beat, but most were just watching him, like they would a monkey at the zoo.

But when Manuel did a fancy dance step, there was a burst of applause and some girls screamed. Manuel tried another dance step. He heard more applause and screams and started getting into the groove as he shivered and snaked like Michael Jackson around the stage. But the record got stuck, and he had to sing

Para bailar la bamba
Para bailar la bamba
Para bailar la bamba
Para bailar la bamba

again and again.

Manuel couldn't believe his bad luck. The audience began to laugh and stand up in their chairs. Manuel remembered how the forty-five record had dropped from his hand and rolled across the cafeteria floor. It probably got scratched, he thought, and now it was stuck, and he was stuck dancing and moving his lips to the same words over and over. He had never been so embarrassed. He would have to ask his parents to move the family out of town.

After Mr. Roybal ripped the needle across the record, Manuel slowed his dance steps to a halt. He didn't know what to do except bow to the audience, which applauded wildly, and scoot off the stage, on the verge of tears. This was worse than the homemade flashlight. At least no one laughed then, they just snickered.

Manuel stood alone, trying hard to hold back the tears as Benny, center stage, played his trumpet. Manuel was jealous because he sounded great, then mad as he recalled that it was Benny's loud trumpet playing that made the forty-five record fly out of his hands. But when the entire cast lined up for a curtain call, Manuel received a burst of applause that was so loud it shook the walls of the cafeteria. Later, as he mingled with the kids and parents, everyone patted him on the shoulder and told him, "Way to go. You were really funny."

Funny? Manuel thought. Did he do something funny?

Funny. Crazy. Hilarious. These were the words people said to him. He was confused, but beyond caring. All he knew was that people were paying attention to him, and his brothers and sisters looked at him with a mixture of jealousy and awe. He was going to pull Mario aside and punch him in the arm for wearing his shirt, but he cooled it. He was enjoying the limelight. A teacher brought him cookies and punch, and the popular kids who had never before given him the time of day now clustered around him. Ricardo, the editor of the school bulletin, asked him how he made the needle stick.

"It just happened," Manuel said, crunching on a star-shaped cookie.

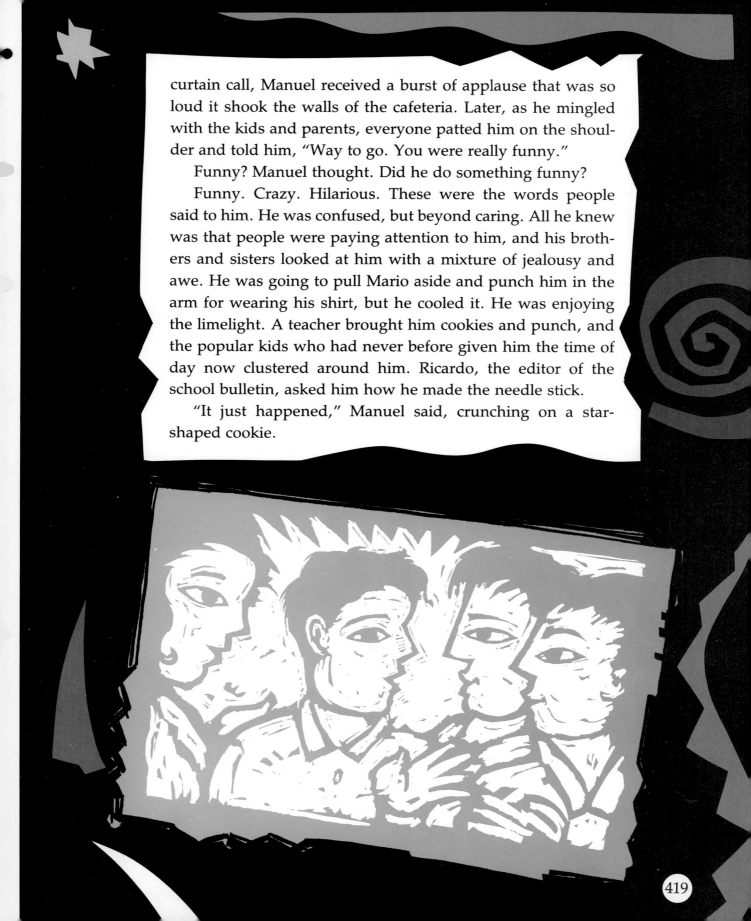

At home that night his father, eager to undo the buttons on his shirt and ease into his La-Z-Boy recliner, asked Manuel the same thing, how he managed to make the song stick on the words *"Para bailar la bamba."*

Manuel thought quickly and reached for scientific jargon he had read in magazines. "Easy, Dad. I used laser tracking with high optics and low functional decibels per channel." His proud but confused father told him to be quiet and go to bed.

"Ah, *que niños tan truchas,*[1]" he said as he walked to the kitchen for a glass of milk. "I don't know how you kids nowadays get so smart."

Manuel, feeling happy, went to his bedroom, undressed, and slipped into his pajamas. He looked in the mirror and began to pantomime "La Bamba," but stopped because he was tired of the song. He crawled into bed. The sheets were as cold as the moon that stood over the peach tree in their backyard.

He was relieved that the day was over. Next year, when they asked for volunteers for the talent show, he wouldn't raise his hand. Probably.

Should Manuel volunteer for the talent show next year? Explain why or why not.

Why is Manuel confused by the crowd's reaction to his performance?

What are some of the emotions that Manuel experiences? Describe the story event that causes each emotion.

WRITE Imagine that you performed in the talent show, too. Write a paragraph describing your act and the audience's reaction to it.

---

[1] what clever little rascals

Unforgettable Performances

In the selections, why is each public performance unforgettable for the person who gives it as well as for the audience?

WRITER'S WORKSHOP

Does the performance of Oliver Hyde or Manuel remind you of any performance you have witnessed or taken part in? Compare Oliver's or Manuel's performance to the one you're thinking about. Write a paragraph or two describing the similarities and the differences.

Writer's Choice
What do you think makes an experience unforgettable? Write what you think. Share your thoughts in some way.

CONNECTIONS

Multicultural Connection

Performing in Front of the Nation

Your family is watching the top-rated television news show in the nation. The team of newscasters on the show tell you not only what is happening but why it's happening.

Ed Bradley is a key member of that team. He's a special type of newscaster called a broadcast journalist. This means that he doesn't read stories written by other people but researches and writes his own. He flies all over the world to interview people and find out facts. He tells camera crews what he needs taped. After he creates a program from the facts and the tape, he goes on television to present the news.

Bradley's hard work, attention to detail, and fair presentations have won him the respect of his co-workers. He has won the Emmy, television's top award, three times.

Choose a broadcaster from a local or a national news program. Write a brief "TV Profile" describing that person's usual subject matter and style of reporting.

Social Studies Connection

The Week in Review

Collect the top newspaper stories about community events for one week. With a small group, use the facts from these to write a script for a news report that you and your classmates will perform. Have someone record your performance on videotape or on audiotape.

Science Connection

Performing Everywhere at Once

How is news broadcast across the world so fast? What part do satellites play? How are signals passed from place to place? Find out how our communication systems work. With a partner, create a diagram or a mural that shows the facts you learned.

UNIT FIVE 5

Lifelines

In time of silver rain
The earth
Puts forth new life again.
 — *Langston Hughes*

Nature can be kind, but it can also be challenging. A Papago Indian girl faces the challenge of a raging flood in the Sonoran Desert. Environmentalists such as Harrison Ngau [nou] urge people to meet the challenge of befriending the earth. As you read the selections in this unit, think about what you can do to treat the earth with kindness.

THEMES

BOOKSHELF

SUGARING TIME

by Kathryn Lasky
photographs by Christopher G. Knight
Wade out into the deep snow with the Lacey family as they harvest their own maple syrup during the season they call "sugaring time."
Newbery Honor
Harcourt Brace Library Book

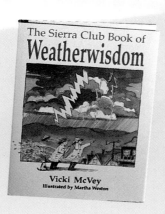

THE SIERRA CLUB BOOK OF WEATHERWISDOM

by Vicki McVey
Are you weatherwise? Can you spot the signs that foretell the weather in your area? Read about kids from all over the world who can, and learn how you can too.
Children's Choice,
Outstanding Science Trade Book for Children
Harcourt Brace Library Book

VOLCANO: THE ERUPTION AND HEALING OF MOUNT ST. HELENS

by Patricia Lauber

Fascinating photographs of the state of Washington in 1980 show the destructive power of a volcano and the slow return of life to the area.

Newbery Honor, ALA Notable Book, Outstanding Science Trade Book for Children

WALTER WARTHOG

by Betty Leslie-Melville

A two-hundred-pound warthog takes up residence in a family's yard in Kenya and refuses to leave. The author shares her family's true experience.

Award-Winning Author

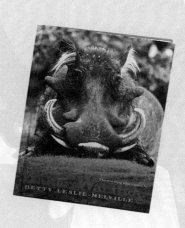

SALVEN MI SELVA/SAVE MY RAINFOREST

by Monica Zak

Omar Castillo and his father set out on foot on a desperate journey to save the last rainforest in Mexico.

Award-Winning Author

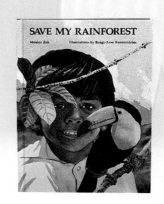

THEME

Life in the Desert

When you think of a desert, do you think of a hot, dry, lifeless place? Would you be surprised to read about the desert as a place overflowing with life and activity? To its many inhabitants, including humans, that's exactly what it is.

CONTENTS

One Day in the Desert

by Jean Craighead George

illustrated by Oleana Kassian

Award-Winning Author

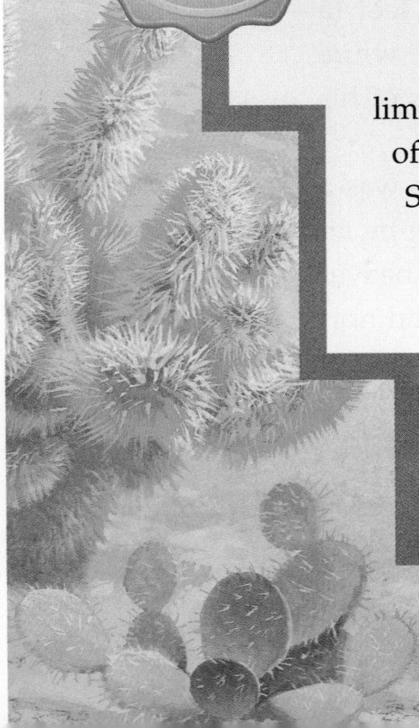

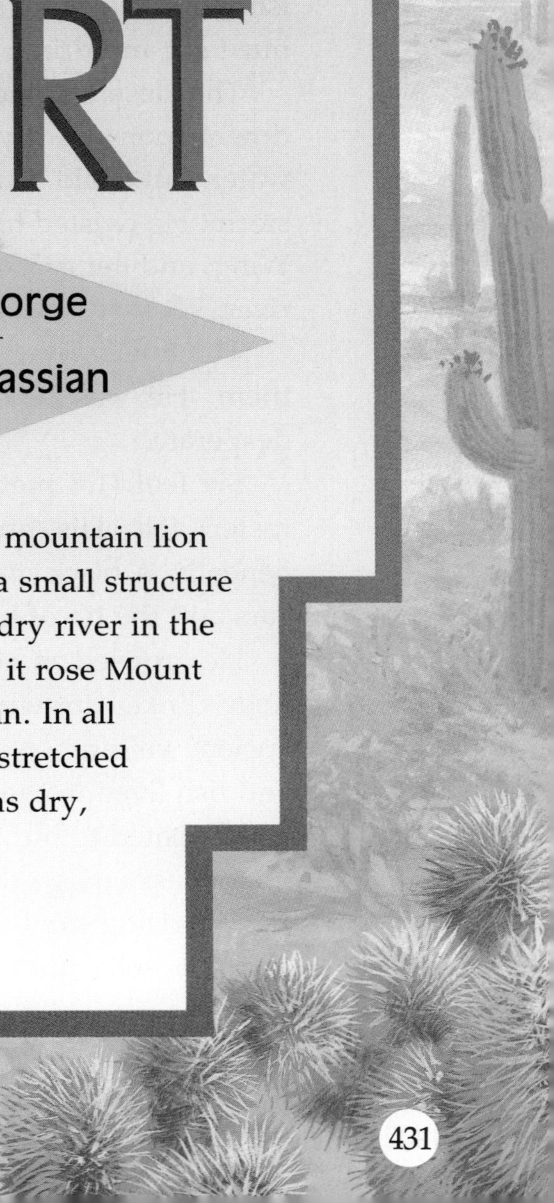

At daybreak on July 10th a mountain lion limped toward a Papago Indian hut, a small structure of grass and sticks on the bank of a dry river in the Sonoran Desert of Arizona. Behind it rose Mount Scorpion, a dark-red mountain. In all directions from the mountain stretched the gray-green desert. It was dry, hot and still.

The cactus wrens began to sing. The Gila woodpeckers squawked to each other across the hot air, arguing over their property lines. The kit foxes who had been hunting all night retreated into underground dens. The bats flew into caves on the mountain and hung upside down for the day.

The lion was hungry and desperately thirsty. A poacher's bullet had torn into the flesh of his paw, and for two weeks he had lain in his den halfway up the mountain nursing his feverish wound. As the sun arose this day, he got to his feet. He must eat and drink.

The desert stretched below him. He paused and looked down upon the dry river called an arroyo. It was empty of water, but could be a raging torrent in the rainy season after a storm. He twisted his ears forward. A Papago Indian girl, Bird Wing, and her mother were walking along the bank of the dry river. They entered the hut.

The lion smelled their scent on the air and limped toward them. He was afraid of people, but this morning he was desperate.

Six feet (1.8 meters) in length, he stood almost 3 feet (a meter) tall. His fur was reddish brown above and white beneath. A black mustache marked his face. The backs of his ears and the tip of his tail were also black.

He growled as he came down the mountain, which was a huge clinker thrown up from the basement of the earth by an ancient volcano. Near its summit were pools where beaver and fish lived in the desert and which the mountain lion normally visited to hunt and drink. But today he went down, for it took less energy than going up.

The rising sun burned down from space, heating the rocks and the soils until they were hot even through the well-

padded feet of the lion. He stood in the shade of a rock at 8 A.M. when the temperature reached 80° Fahrenheit (26.6° Celsius).

This day would be memorable. Bird Wing, her mother, the lion and many of the animals below Mount Scorpion would be affected by July 10th. Some would survive and some would not, for the desert is ruthless.

The Sonoran Desert is one of four deserts marked by distinctive plants that make up the great North American Desert, which extends from central Mexico to almost the Canadian border. The North American Desert covers more than 500,000 square miles (1,300,000 square kilometers).

All of the four deserts have one thing in common—little rain. Less than 10 inches (24 centimeters) a year fall on the greater parts of these deserts. The temperatures, however, vary from below freezing to the low 120s F. (about 50° C.).

Each one is slightly different. The Great Basin desert of Oregon, California, Idaho, Nevada, Utah and Wyoming—the most northern and the coldest—is largely covered with sagebrush, a plant that has adapted to the dry cold.

The Mojave Desert of California is the smallest and driest, with less than 4 inches (10 centimeters) of rain a year. The teddy-bear cactus called cholla (choy • ya), a cactus so spiny it seems to have fur, dominates this desert.

The third, the Chihuahuan (chee • wa • wan) Desert, lies largely in Mexico. Only 10 percent of it is in the United States, in New Mexico, Arizona and Texas. On this desert the yuccas and agaves, or century plants, have adapted and grow abundantly, lending a special look to the land.

The fourth and most magnificent is the Sonoran Desert of Mexico and Arizona. Unlike the other deserts, it has two rainy seasons—showers in March and deluges in July and August. The rains nourish magnificent plants that support a great variety of creatures. The outstanding plant in this desert is the giant saguaro cactus, a tall plant that resembles a telephone pole with upturned arms. All the cacti—the saguaro, barrel, teddy bear and prickly pear—are unique to North America. They have evolved nowhere else in the world.

The North American Desert is dry because it is robbed of rain by the Pacific coast mountains. The clouds coming in from the ocean strike the high cold peaks and dump most of their moisture on the western side of the mountains. Practically no rain reaches the eastern side, which is in what is called the "rain shadow" by scientists.

All deserts are lands of extremes: too hot, too dry, too wet. Yet they abound with living things that have adjusted to these excesses. To fight dryness, plants store water in their tissues or drop their leaves to prevent evaporation from their broad surfaces. They also grow spines, which do not use much water and which cast shadows on the plant to protect it from the blazing sun. They thicken stems and leaves to hold water.

The animals adapt by seeking out cool microclimates, small shelters out of the terrible heat. The microclimates are burrows in the ground where it is cool, crevices and caves in rocks, or the shade. Because of the dryness, the thin desert air does not hold heat. Shady spots can be 20° F. (11° C.) cooler than out in the sun.

A few animals adapt to the harsh conditions by manufacturing water from the starch in the seeds they eat. The perky kangaroo rat is one of these. Others move in the cool of the night.

The coyote hunts in the dark, as do the deer, ring-tailed "cat" (cacomistle), desert fox, raccoon and lion. The honeypot ant, on the other hand, has such a tough outer skeleton that it can walk in extremely hot sunshine.

On July 10th the wounded mountain lion was forced to hunt in the heat of the day. He could not wait for darkness. He made his way slowly down the trail toward the Papago Indian hut.

By 9 A.M. he was above the dwelling on a mountain ledge. The temperature climbed another degree. He sought the shade of a giant saguaro cactus and lay down to rest.

The scent of lion reached the nose of a coyote who was cooling off under the dark embankment of the dry river not far from the Papago Indian hut. He lifted his head, flicked his ears nervously and got to his feet. He ran swiftly into his burrow beneath the roots of the ancient saguaro cactus that grew beside the hut.

The huge cactus was over 100 years old, stood 75 feet (22.5 meters) tall and weighed more than 6 tons (5.5 metric tons). The last of its watermelon-red fruits were ripe and on the ground. Bird Wing and her mother were going to gather them and boil them in the water they had carried in buckets from the village. The fruit makes a sweet, nourishing syrup.

At 11 A.M. they stretched out on their mats in the hut. It was much too hot to work. The temperature had reached 112° F. (44.4° C.).

The old cactus was drying up in the heat. It drew on the last of the water in the reservoir inside its trunk and shrank ever so slightly, for it could expand and contract like an accordion.

The mountain lion's tongue was swollen from lack of moisture. He got to his feet again.

A roadrunner, a ground-dwelling bird with a spiny crest and a long neck and legs, saw the lion pass his shady spot in the grass. He sped down the mountain, over the riverbank and into the dry riverbed. He stopped under the embankment where the coyote had been. There he lifted his feathers to keep cool. Bird feathers are perhaps the best protection from both heat and cold, for they form dead air space, and dead air is one of the best insulations.

The roadrunner passed a family of seven peccaries, piglike animals with coarse coats, tusks and almost no tails. They stay alive in the dry desert by eating the water-storing prickly pear cactus, spines and all. They were now lying in the cool of the paloverde trees that grow in thickets. Like the pencil-straight ocotillo and almost all the desert leafy plants, the paloverdes drop their leaves when the desert is extremely hot and dry. On July 10th they began falling faster and faster.

The scent of the lion reached the old boar. He lifted his head and watched the great beast. The lion turned away from the peccary family and limped toward the Indian hut. All the pigs, big and little, watched him.

A warm moist wind that had been moving northwest across the Gulf of Mexico for a day and a night met a cold wind blowing east from the Pacific coast mountains. The hot and cold air collided not far from the Mexico-Arizona border and exploded into a chain of white clouds. The meeting formed a stiff wind. It picked up the desert dust and carried it toward Mount Scorpion.

As the lion limped across the embankment under which the roadrunner was hiding, the air around him began to fill with dust.

Near the coyote den dwelled a tarantula, a spider almost as big as a man's fist and covered with furlike hairs. She looked like a long-legged bear, and she was sitting near the top of her burrow, a shaft she had dug straight down into the ground. The hot desert air forced her to let go with all eight of her legs. She dropped to the bottom of her shaft, where the air was cooler. The spider survives the heat by digging underground and by hunting at night. The moist crickets and other insects she eats quench her thirst.

A headstand beetle felt the heat of the day and became uncomfortable. He stopped hunting in the grass and scurried into the entrance of the tarantula hole. He was not afraid of the spider, with her poison fangs that kill prey, but he was wary of her. Hearing the spider coming up her shaft to see who was there, the headstand beetle got ready to fend her off. He stood on his head, aimed his rear end and mixed chemicals in his abdomen. The tarantula rushed at him and lifted her fangs. The headstand beetle shot a blistering-hot stream of a quinonoid chemical at the spider. She writhed and dropped to the bottom of her den. The headstand beetle hid under the grass plant by the tarantula's door.

The temperature rose several more degrees.

At 12:30 P.M. a desert tortoise, who was protected from the heat by two unusually thick shells of bone, went on eating the fruit of a prickly pear cactus. He was never thirsty. The moisture from the plants he ate was stored in his enormous bladder, a reservoir of pure water that desert tortoises have devised over the ages to adapt themselves to the dry heat. The water cools the reptiles on the hottest days and refreshes them on the driest.

The temperature reached 117° F. (47.2° C.). At last the tortoise felt warm. He turned around and pushed up on his toes. On his short legs he walked to his burrow under the paloverde bushes where the peccaries hunched, their eyes focused on the lion.

Inside his burrow the tortoise came upon a cottontail rabbit who had taken refuge there out of the hot sun. The tortoise could not go on. The heat poured in, and to lower the temperature he plugged up the entrance with his back feet. On the ceiling above his head clung a spiny-tailed lizard and a Texas banded gecko, reptiles who usually like the heat. At 12:30 P.M. on July 10th they sought the protection of the tortoise's burrow.

The temperature rose one more degree. A cactus wren who had sung at dawn slipped into her nest in a teddy-bear cactus at the edge of the paloverde thicket. She opened her beak to release heat.

The peccaries heard soft sounds like rain falling. Hundreds of small lizards who usually hunted the leaves of the paloverde, even on the hottest days, could no longer endure the high temperature. They were dropping to the ground and seeking shelter under sticks and stones.

A kangaroo rat was in her labyrinth under the leafless, pencillike ocotillo plants. She awakened when the temperature reached 119° F. (47.3° C.). Her bedroom near the surface of the desert floor had become uncomfortably hot. Her body was drying out. She scurried along a tunnel, turned a corner and ran down a slope toward a room under the giant saguaro cactus. She paused at her pantry to eat seeds of the mesquite tree before retiring to the cool, deep chamber. While she slept, her internal system converted the starch of the seeds into water and revived her dry body.

The lion walked into the paloverde bushes. The peccaries squealed in fright and trotted out into the terrible sunshine. In a cloud of dust they sped into the dry riverbed and frightened the roadrunner. He ran out from under the overhang and flew into the saguaro forest on the far side of the dry river. The pigs hid under the embankment where the roadrunner had been.

The injured lion could not chase the peccaries. He lifted his head, smelled the sweet piglets and climbed up the Indian trail till he was at the hut. Bird Wing and her mother were sleeping. He stared at them and crouched. Slinking low, he moved to a bucket, drank long and gratefully, then lay down in the doorway of the hut.

The temperature climbed one more degree. The birds stopped singing. Even the cicadas, who love hot weather and drum louder and faster in the heat, could no longer endure the fiery temperature. They stopped making sounds with their feet and wings and sat still. The Gila woodpecker flew into his hole in the giant saguaro. Below him, in one of his old nests, sat the sparrow-sized elf owl. He opened his beak and lifted his feathers.

Bird Wing was awakened by thirst. She tipped one of the water buckets and drank deeply. The desert was so quiet she became alarmed.

Clouds were racing toward Mount Scorpion. They were black and purple. Constant flashes of lightning illuminated them from within. She crept to the back of the hut and lay down beside her mother. She closed her eyes.

At 1:20 P.M. the temperature reached 121° F. (49.4° C.).

This hour on July 10th was the hottest hour on record at the bottom of Mount Scorpion.

Even the well-insulated honeypot ants could not tolerate the temperature. They ran toward the entrance of their labyrinth near a pack rat nest by the hut. Some managed to get underground in the caverns where sister ants hung from the ceilings. Forager honeypot ants store the sweets from plants they have gathered in the bellies of hanging ants, some of which become as round as balloons and as big as marbles. The last two foraging ants ran across the hot soil to get home. They shriveled and died in seconds.

The peccaries under the embankment dug into the earth to find coolness.

The clouds covered the sun.

Instantly, the temperature dropped four degrees.

The tortoise shoveled more dirt into the mouth of his burrow.

The thunder boomed like Indian drums.

The kangaroo rat felt the earth tremble. She ran to her door, smelled rain on the air and scurried to a U-shaped tunnel. She went down it and up to a room at the top. There she tucked her nose into her groin to sleep.

The temperature dropped five more degrees. A rattlesnake came out of the pack rat's nest and slid back to his hunting spot at the rear of the hut. The cicadas sang again. The cactus wren looked out of the entrance of her ball nest in the teddy-bear cactus.

A thunderclap exploded sharply. Bird Wing awoke. She saw the lion stretched in the doorway. She took her mother's arm and shook her gently until she awoke. Signaling her to be quiet, she pointed to the mountain lion. Bird Wing's mother parted the grass at the rear of the hut and, after pushing Bird Wing out, backed out herself.

The rattlesnake buzzed a warning.

The sky darkened. Lightning danced from saguaro cactus to saguaro cactus. Bird Wing's mother looked at the clouds and the dry arroyo.

"We must get out of here," she said. "Follow me up the mountain." They scrambled over the rocks on hands and feet without looking back.

Huge raindrops splattered onto the dust. Bird Wing and her mother reached an overhanging rock on the mountain. Lightning flashed around them like white horsewhips.

The thunder cracked and boomed. Then water gushed out of the sky. The rain fell in such torrents that Bird Wing and her mother could not see the dry river, the hut or the old saguaro. They sat quietly, waiting and listening.

A flash of lightning shot out of a cloud and hit the old saguaro cactus. It smoked, split and fell to the ground. The elf owl flew into the downpour. His wings and body became so

wet, he soared down to the grass beneath the paloverde bushes. The woodpecker stayed where he was, bracing himself with his stiff tail.

The crash of the saguaro terrified the coyote. He darted out of his den under the tree and back to the dry riverbed. The peccaries dug deeper into the embankment. The roadrunner took to his feet and ran up the slope beyond the giant saguaro forest.

The rain became torrents, the torrents became waterfalls and the waterfalls cascaded out of the sky until all the moisture was wrung from the clouds. They drizzled and stopped giving rain. The storm clouds rumbled up the canyon above the dry riverbed.

The sun came out. Bird Wing and her mother did not move. They listened. The desert rocks dripped and the cacti crackled softly as they swelled with water. Cactus roots lie close to the surface, spreading out from the plants in all directions to absorb every possible drop of water. The roots send the water up into the trunks and barrels and pads to be stored.

A drumroll sounded up Scorpion Pass.

The peccaries heard it and darted out from under the embankment. They struggled up the bank and raced into the saguaro forest.

The lion got to his feet. He limped through the door.

The coyote rushed out of the dry riverbed. The wet elf owl hooked his beak around a twig of a paloverde and pulled himself upward toward higher limbs.

Water came bubbling and singing down the arroyo. It filled the riverbed from bank to bank, then rose like a great cement wall, a flash flood that filled the canyon. It swept over the embankment, over the hut, over the old saguaro cactus. It rose higher, thundered into the paloverdes and roared over the

rocks at the foot of the mountain. It boomed into the valley, spread out and disappeared into the dry earth.

The coyote was washed out from under the embankment. He tumbled head over heels, swam to the surface and climbed onto an uprooted mass of prickly pears. On this he sailed into the valley and was dropped safely onto the outwash plain when the water went into the ground. Stunned, he shook himself and looked around. Before him the half-drowned pack rat struggled. Recovering his wits, the coyote pounced upon him.

The lion was lifted up by the flood and thrown against a clump of ocotillo. He clung to it for a moment, then, too weak to struggle, slipped beneath the water.

The flash flood that had trickled, then roared, trickled and then was gone. The banks of the arroyo dripped. Bird Wing and her mother walked to the spot where their hut had been. There was no sign of house, pack rat nest, saguaro or lion.

"But for the lion, we would be dead," said Bird Wing. "We must thank him." She faced the mountain and closed her eyes for a moment. Her mother picked up an ocotillo stick and turned it over in her hand.

"We will rebuild our house up the mountain above the flood line," she said. Bird Wing nodded vigorously and gathered sticks, too.

The kangaroo rat sat in her room above the U trap that had stopped the water from reaching her. She waited until the floodwaters seeped into the ground. Then she began to repair her labyrinth.

The peccaries came out of the saguaro forest and rooted for insects among the billions of seeds that had been dumped on the land by the flood. The land was greening, the sky was blue. The roadrunner came back to the saguaro forest, ran down a young snake and ate it. The cactus wren and owl did not call. The rattlesnake did not rattle. They had not survived the wrath of the desert on this day, July 10th.

Bird Wing walked to the arroyo edge. The earth trembled at her feet. She looked down. Plugs of sand popped out of the wet bank like corks. In each hole sat a grinning spadefoot toad, creatures who must grow up in the water. Then what were they doing in the desert? Waiting for just this moment.

They hopped into the brilliant sunshine and leaped into the puddles in the arroyo. Quickly they mated, quickly they laid eggs and quickly they ate and dug backward into the sand with the spades on their feet. Far underground their skins secreted a sticky gelatin that would prevent them from drying up. In this manner they survived the hot waterless desert.

The warm sunlight of late afternoon heated the water in the puddles, speeding up the development of the toad eggs. They must hatch into pollywogs and change into toads before the blazing heat dried up the puddles.

At 7:33 P.M. soft blue and purple light swept over the beautiful desert. In the puddles pollywogs swam.

Would you like to live in this desert? Explain why or why not.

Describe the changes in weather in the Sonoran Desert on July 10th, from 8 A.M. to 7:33 P.M.

Do you think the author is correct when she says that the desert is ruthless? Explain your answer.

After the flood, why does Bird Wing say that she wants to thank the mountain lion?

WRITE   The author describes many different animals in this story. Choose one desert animal that interests you and write a name poem about it. Use each letter in the animal's name to start a line of the poem.

Jean Craighead George

Jean George doesn't mind getting up at 5:30 on Sunday morning if she can share the wonders of nature. That is what she does when she leads nature walks in the town where she lives. She has been in love with nature since she was a child.

"All through my childhood, my parents had taken the three of us (I have identical twin brothers) into the forests along the Potomac River outside of Washington, D.C., where I was born," she remembers.

Jean George spent summers on a farm in Pennsylvania, where she learned a lot about nature. She learned about trees, flowers, birds, and insects. She camped on the sandy islands and went canoeing and fishing. She felt close to nature even though she grew up in a big city, and she has kept this feeling all her life.

Jean George's family helped get her love for nature started. Her father was an entomologist. He studied insects. Her twin brothers grew up to be ecologists. They study the ways plants and animals live in nature. Ms. George and her family often took care of wild animals right in their home. When Jean George won the Newbery Medal for *Julie of the Wolves*, she especially thanked her parents. She said they gave her "a love of nature and a deep respect for the earth and its precious cargo of life."

AWARD-WINNING AUTHOR

JACKRABBIT

from *Desert Voices*

by Byrd Baylor

illustrated by Peter Parnall

ALA NOTABLE BOOK

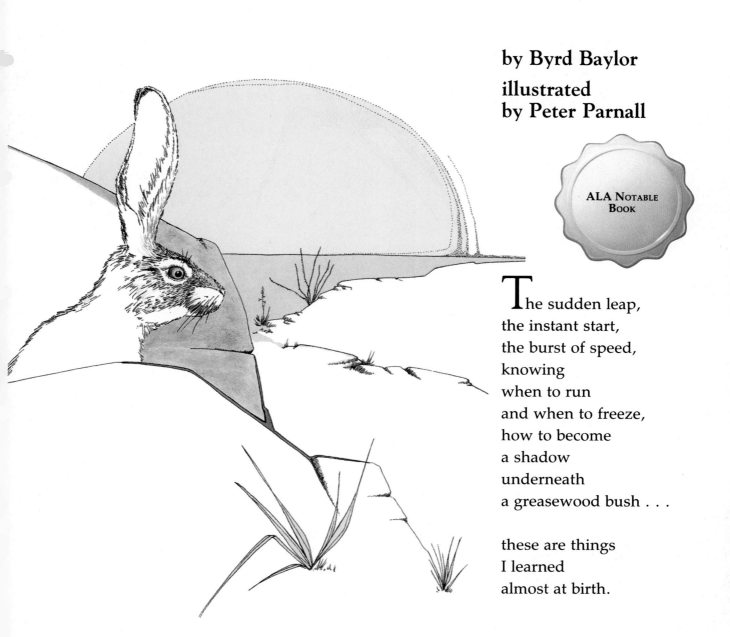

The sudden leap,
the instant start,
the burst of speed,
knowing
when to run
and when to freeze,
how to become
a shadow
underneath
a greasewood bush . . .

these are things
I learned
almost at birth.

Now
I lie
on the shadow-side
of a clump of grass.
My long ears bring me
every far-off footstep,
every twig that snaps,
every rustle in the weeds.

I watch
Coyote move
from bush to bush.

I wait.
He's almost here.

Now . . .

Now I go
like a zig-zag
lightning flash.
With my ears laid back,
I sail.

Jumping gullies
and bushes and rocks,
doubling back,
circling,
jumping high
to see where my enemy is,
warning rabbits
along the way,
I go.

I hardly touch
the ground.

And suddenly
I disappear.

Let Coyote stand there
sniffing
old jackrabbit trails.

Where I am now
is a
jackrabbit secret.

452

Life in the Desert

What difficulties and dangers do the desert animals in the selections face? What characteristics do they have in common that help them survive these dangers?

WRITER'S WORKSHOP

What makes a desert a desert? What are some deserts around the world? Choose a topic about deserts that interests you. Do research on your topic at a library. Take notes and use them to write a research report. You may want to include photographs, drawings, or charts in your report.

Writer's Choice

What do you think about life in the desert now that you have read "One Day in the Desert"? Write down your thoughts. Then share your ideas with others.

THEME

Seasons Within Seasons

There are some events that happen only at one certain place at one certain time of the year. Come along with a writer and a photographer as they experience these special events.

CONTENTS

455

MONARCHS

BY KATHRYN LASKY

Monarchs

KATHRYN LASKY

photographs by Christopher G. Knight

The Cubbyhole

In a bay off the coast of Maine there is an island with a cove on its northeast side. At the head of this cove is a deep notch between the rocks, like a cubbyhole, that is wind-safe and cozy. On one side of the notch a pine forest grows right down to the water's edge; on the other side the rocks give way to marsh grass growing thick and pale. Here the land dips to a swale sprigged with wildflowers and a tangle of sea roses, called rugosas. It then climbs steeply upward to a dirt road where a thick stand of milkweed grows.

A monarch butterfly has lighted on the leaf of a milkweed and has squeezed out a single egg, white and shiny, no bigger than the head of a pin. She flies off to another leaf, where she lays another egg. A single female can lay approximately four hundred eggs.

The little egg is very tough. A summer gale with pelting rain and scouring winds blows from the northeast and invades the usually wind-safe cove. Trees are ripped up and the marsh grass tosses wildly about, but the little egg stays on the leaf of the wind-bent milkweed plants.

Within a few days the egg hatches. The larva is so tiny— about one twenty-fifth of an inch long—it is barely visible to the naked eye. At one end of its grayish white body is a black dot perhaps one hundredth of an inch across. Amazingly, this is the head. And on this little head is a mouth one thousandth of an inch wide, and near this mouth is a pair of very short antennae that help the larva sense its way around a milkweed leaf. A pair of long black filaments near the front of the caterpillar and a shorter pair near the rear of its body are not antennae. They are used like small whips or clubs when the caterpillar twists its body about in defense against predators.

The tiny caterpillar also has eight pairs of legs. The front three pairs have small claws that help grab leaves for eating. The back five pairs, called prolegs, are stubbier and have hooks, or crotchets, which help the caterpillar cling and move along stems and leaves. When the caterpillar becomes a butterfly, the first three pairs of legs will become the butterfly's legs, while the prolegs will shrivel and disappear.

The larva's first meal is often its own egg case. Its next meal might be the hairlike filaments covering the surface of the milkweed leaf. Then it will begin on the leaf itself. All day and all night it munches, pausing only occasionally to rest. Milkweed is the only food that monarch caterpillars eat. For many other animals, especially birds, milkweed is poisonous. If they do not die from eating it, they get very sick. The poisons that accumulate in the bodies of the caterpillars, and later the butterflies, provide a natural defense against such predators as blue jays and other birds that might otherwise try to eat them.

After three days of almost nonstop eating, the little caterpillar has grown too big for its own skin. It stops and fastens itself to a leaf with a bit of silk produced from the spinneret just below its mouth. A shiver ripples through the caterpillar as it begins its first molt, or shedding of old skin. At this stage the old skin is as hard as a fingernail, and it splits down the middle of the caterpillar's back. The caterpillar will molt four or five times over the next few weeks, and with each molt it will grow bigger, adding more yellow and black stripes to its body.

After two weeks of eating, the caterpillar is now two inches long and is more than 2,700 times its original weight. If a six-pound human baby grew as fast as a caterpillar, it would weigh eight tons in twelve days. The caterpillar finally stops eating. For its next development stage it can travel to any twig or branch or stay on a milkweed plant. But wherever it goes, the caterpillar will climb straight up. Once it has decided on a spot, it produces more silk and weaves a button on the twig or branch it has chosen. Near the rear legs of the caterpillar is a tiny hook-shaped structure called a cremaster. The

caterpillar stabs the cremaster into the silk button and wriggles hard to see if it will hold. If it does, the caterpillar seems to relax and hangs from the silk button. Within minutes, the head curls up and the caterpillar looks like the letter J. For several hours it will stay this way, preparing for its final molt. Then the skin begins to split as the caterpillar twists and shivers, and as this last skin splits off, the bright bands of yellow and black dissolve into a milky green sheath called a chrysalis. Because the chrysalis seems to wrap itself around the form of the butterfly in the same way an infant is wrapped in swaddling clothes, this period of development is often called the pupal stage, from the Latin word *pupa* meaning "doll."

Within a short time the chrysalis hardens into a beautiful jade-green case studded with gold dots. It hangs like an exquisite magic lantern, inside which marvelous, seemingly magical changes are occurring. The body of the caterpillar melts away into a solution of transforming cells and tissues. Inside the chrysalis, the metamorphosis from caterpillar to butterfly takes approximately fifteen days.

New Wings Shimmer in the Sunlight

Clara Waterman is in a hurry to leave her store on North Haven Island in Penobscot Bay, Maine. But this morning the mail boat from the mainland has come and is turning right around for the return trip. All the supplies for the Waterman store have to be unloaded double-quick. At eighty-two Clara can beg off unloading thirty-pound crates of Georgia peaches and cases of soft drinks, but it means she has to stay on the cash register while the others unload the boat. Then everybody in town starts craving the big fat peaches as soon as they see them on the dock. Soon the line of customers at the Waterman store practically goes out the door.

Clara isn't going to be able to go home at noon as planned. She knew she should have brought the chrysalis down to the

store in the morning and set it right by the cash register. Now she'll probably miss it hatching out. She has seen hundreds of monarchs hatch out in her lifetime, and she never tires of it. For Clara there is only one thing better than seeing a butterfly emerge, and that is watching a child see it hatch. It's almost as

if two miracles are happening at the same time—the emerging butterfly and the wonder in the child's face.

The morning following the arrival of the peaches at the Waterman store, five children from another island come over to North Haven to talk to Clara about butterflies. She wants to take them to the cubbyhole where the milkweed grows so they can look for caterpillars. Maybe there will even be some chrysalises they can take home to watch hatch.

Monarch chrysalises hatch just about anyplace. All summer long Clara brings home bunches of milkweed that are crawling with caterpillars. She props the branches in jars filled with water to keep the plants fresh and builds little shoebox terrariums to put the jars in. When the chrysalises hatch, Clara releases the butterflies into her yard. Sometimes she just puts the jars of milkweed on a table or a bookshelf. And caterpillars can travel! She remembers a summer years ago when she was a young girl. She went up to her closet to get out her best dress for a party and found a chrysalis hanging from the sash. When the children come to Clara's house, they are amazed to see where the caterpillars have crept to form their chrysalises.

465

"That one just flew off before sunset last night," Clara says, pointing straight up at the door frame as they walk into her kitchen. An empty chrysalis, dry and transparent, quivers in the noon breeze. The children spot another chrysalis that has not yet hatched on the handle of a pail in the sink.

And out on the porch a small darkened lantern hangs from the leaf of a potted milkweed plant. Inside this chrysalis is an orange glimmer like the flame of a flickering candle: the wings of the monarch. The chrysalis shakes and begins to split. Within minutes a new monarch has hatched. Wet and crumpled, it seems completely exhausted. But soon the monarch begins pumping fluid from its swollen body into its wings.

"Maybe it will fly away while we're here." Clara's voice swells with excitement. The children press around her. She explains that before the butterfly flies off, its feeding tube, or proboscis, must be assembled. The proboscis is a hollow tube through which the butterfly sucks nectar and water. When the butterfly first hatches, the two parts forming the proboscis are not yet interlocked, and until they are, the butterfly cannot feed. When the butterfly is not drinking nectar, the proboscis coils up under its head like a watch spring.

Gradually, over an hour's time, the once wrinkled and wet wings begin to spread, becoming bright and velvety. The children look closely. The edges of the wings are bordered in black with a double row of white spots. The body of the butterfly also has white spots. A web of black veins spreads across the orange wings, making them as bright as stained-glass windows with the sun shining through. This monarch is a female. If it were a male, it would have a single black dot on each hind wing.

The colors and patterns of a butterfly's wings are made by tens of thousands of microscopically small flat scales that overlap like shingles on a roof. If the scales are rubbed off, which can happen, the wing underneath is bare and colorless. The butterfly can still fly, however, even missing a few scales. On either side of the butterfly's head is a compound eye, which is actually many little eyes pressed into one. These little individual eyes have six sides and are called facets. The two compound eyes of the monarch are made up of thousands of these facets. So instead of seeing one image, a butterfly sees thousands of little images. Compound eyes are very good at detecting movement as well as perceiving a wide range of colors, which helps the butterfly find nectar-rich flowers.

"It's getting ready!" Clara's voice trembles with anticipation. The butterfly's wings shimmer in the noon sun, there is a quiver, and then silently it lifts into gentle fluttering flight.

What did you like or not like about this selection?

Describe the stages a monarch goes through from egg to butterfly.

Would you like to be in Clara Waterman's house to watch a monarch emerge? Explain why or why not.

WRITE If you had the chance to study an animal or an insect closely, which one would you choose? Write a paragraph explaining your choice.

Words About the Author:
Kathryn Lasky

Writer Kathryn Lasky and her husband, photographer and filmmaker Christopher G. Knight, enjoy working as a team. They met when Lasky was running the sound equipment for one of Knight's films. After they married, the couple began combining their talents to create books for children.

Lasky and Knight have traveled near and far to capture, on film and in words, the images they turn into books. Both *Sugaring Time* (about tapping sugar maples) and *The Weaver's Gift* (about the weaving of sheep's fleece into soft blankets) take place in Vermont, not far from the couple's New England home. To write *Dinosaur Dig*, the author and photographer traveled to the Badlands of Montana.

People are an important element in Lasky's books. The many members of the Lacey family are the focus of *Sugaring Time*. Thinking about the Laceys' tradition of tapping sugar maples,

Lasky remarked, "It was a wonderful break for them, right near the end of winter; the sugaring time is like a little season unto itself." *Dinosaur Dig* depicts the excitement that six families share digging for dinosaur bones.

Lasky and Knight's research for *Monarchs* led them to more interesting places and people. They started out in Maine, where they watched the monarchs hatch from their chrysalises, and then followed the butterflies to California and to Mexico. Lasky got the idea for the book from an article in the *New York Times* about a town in California that decided to raise their own taxes so they could buy a grove where the monarchs rested during the winter. The people wanted to buy the grove because the owner of the property was planning to tear down the trees and build condominiums. "I was so impressed by this," Lasky said, "I decided I'd like to write a book about the monarchs. I'll never forget something the townspeople said—it has always stuck with me: 'You can't put a price on beauty, on how this beauty adds to our lives.'"

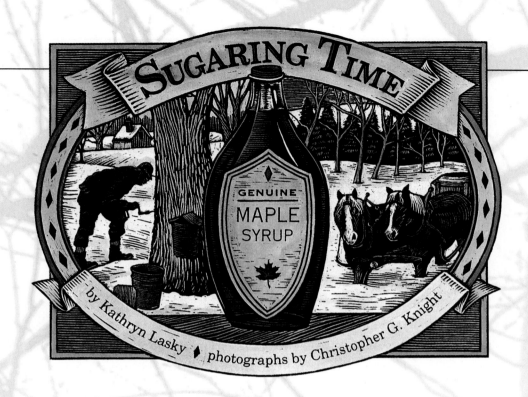

SUGARING TIME

by Kathryn Lasky ◆ photographs by Christopher G. Knight

A TIME OUT OF TIME

There is a time between the seasons. It comes in March when winter seems tired and spring is only a hoped-for thing. The crystalline whiteness of February has vanished and there is not yet even the pale green stain in the trees that promises spring. It is a time out of time, when night, in central Vermont, can bring a fitful late winter storm that eases, the very next day, into sunshine and a melting wind from the southeast.

NEWBERY HONOR
ALA NOTABLE BOOK
NOTABLE CHILDREN'S
TRADE BOOK FOR THE
LANGUAGE ARTS

◆✳◆ ✳◆✳ ◆✳◆ ✳◆✳ ◆✳◆ ✳◆✳ ◆✳◆

Many people complain about this time of year. Snow cannot be counted on for sledding or skiing; cars get stuck in muddy roads; clothes are mud-caked and hard to clean; and the old folks' arthritis kicks up. Everyone, young and old, gets cranky about staying indoors.

But for a few people, this time is a season in its own right. For them it is *sugaring time*, when the sap begins to flow in the maple grove or sugarbush, as it is called. It is a time that contradicts all farming calendars that say crops are planted in the spring, cared for in the summer, and harvested in the fall. This crop, maple sap, is harvested in March, and that is part of the specialness of sugaring time. It is special, too, because young people have a reason to go outside, snow or no snow, mud or no mud, and older people have a reason to believe in the coming spring.

Alice and Don Lacey and their three children live on a farm that has a small sugarbush. They have been waiting almost two weeks for the sap to start running. Last year they had started to hang buckets by town meeting time in early March. But this year's town meeting has come and gone by more than a week and the snow is still almost as high as the bellies of their Belgian workhorses, Jumping Jack and Tommy. It covers the meadow leading up to the sugarbush in a wind-packed, crusty blanket.

The Laceys wonder if the sap will get a jump on them this year. Before they can begin sugaring, they will have to spend a day or more using their horses to break out the trails to the sugarbush. And they cannot start breaking out until the days turn warm enough to loosen up the snow so the horses can get through it. The sap might be running for some time before

❖✳❖ ✳❖✳ ❖✳❖ ✳❖✳ ❖✳❖ ✳❖✳ ❖✳❖

they can get to the stand of maples covering the hillside at the
top of the meadow. But there is no other way to get there.

By the end of the second week in March, however, the
weather begins to change. The nights are still cold, below
freezing, but one midmorning the thermometer is above
freezing and still climbing. Icicles that have hung like scepters
since December suddenly begin dripping like popsicles in
August.

"It really feels like sugaring weather," Alice says.

"Tomorrow?" "Tomorrow?" "Tomorrow?" Jonathan, Angie,
and Jeremy all ask their mother at once.

"Maybe," she replies. "If this holds. If it's cold tonight and
warm again tomorrow, we'll be able to start breaking out, and
then by the next day hang some buckets."

❖✳❖ ✳❖✳ ❖✳❖ ✳❖✳ ❖✳❖ ✳❖✳ ❖✳❖

Tomorrow comes. It is warm but raining. Fog swirls through the valley and up into the meadow, covering the hills and mountaintops beyond. Everything is milky white. Snow-covered earth and sky melt together. Pines appear rootless, like ghost trees, their pointy tops wrapped in mist. It is a groundless world without edges or distances, a world that floats, private and cozy and detached, through the fog and clouds. There will be no breaking out today.

BREAKING OUT

Finally the day does come. A northwest wind blows the clouds and rain away, then quickly dies, and the sun shines until the mountaintops break through to a clear day. Snow is loosening up and the Laceys can almost hear the sap dripping in the sugarbush. Even a baby down in town was ready to get born and go! Don Lacey, who is a doctor, was up before the sun to deliver it.

Back home, Don harnesses up Tommy and Jumping Jack and walks behind them, urging them through the three-foot-deep snow. They are reluctant, even though there is no sled to pull on this first circuit. The snow is heavy, and their muscles are stiff.

Breaking out is the hardest part of sugaring. After three months of easy barn living with no loads to pull and not even a fly to swish away, the horses are winter lazy and stubborn. But the trails have to be broken if the trees are to be tapped and the sap gathered.

Don guides the horses toward the sugarhouse. Jonathan, who is eight, and Angie, six, follow on skis. The hoofprints that the horses leave are nearly a foot across and one and a

❖✤❖   ✤❖✤   ❖✤❖   ✤❖✤   ❖✤❖   ✤❖✤   ❖✤❖

half times as deep. With a sound like muffled thunder, their hoofs crush the snow.

This snow of early spring is called corn snow because the crystals are big and granular, like kernels of corn. But it is really more sugary in its texture, and when Jonathan skis it sounds as if he is skimming across the thick frosting of a wedding cake. He and Angie, on their skis, move faster than the horses across the snow, but at last the first loop to the sugarhouse and across the low ridge behind it is complete. Don turns the horses and circles back to the lower meadow. There, he and Alice hook the harnesses to a sturdy sled. They are going to cut out some runner marks on the trail.

◆✳◆　✳◆✳　◆✳◆　✳◆✳　◆✳◆　✳◆✳　◆✳◆

Max, a young neighbor, has his first sled ride on Alice's lap as she skillfully guides the horses through the ups and downs and twists and turns of the half-broken trail that leads through the sugar maze. The horses are even more obstinate, now that they are pulling the sled. They balk at a muddy trickle of a creek, they stop on the incline of a curve. They are like two stubborn babies—each weighing nearly a ton. But Alice is firm. She scolds and cajoles them through the heavy snow and gradually coaxes the winter laziness out of their bones. Two hours later the first trail is completely broken out. Tomorrow, they will go for the higher ones.

The next day is warmer still. The meadow is scored with dozens of small rivulets of melting snow, and the road and

◆❋◆ ❋◆❋ ◆❋◆ ❋◆❋ ◆❋◆ ❋◆❋ ◆❋◆

lower paths are muddy. Streams that have lain as still as black ribbons in the snow now rush, muddy and raucous, down the hills. The world slips and slides in the thick mud. Early this morning, a car slid into a ditch down the road, and another one followed while trying to get the first one out. Then a neighbor's dog got into the Laceys' sheep yard, barked, chased around, raised havoc, and scared the wits out of a pregnant ewe, who in her panic skidded headfirst into the creek. Alice came out when she heard the commotion and rescued the ewe. It is late morning by the time the horses are hitched up. But breaking out is easier this time and goes much faster.

TAPPING TIME

The big trails have been broken out. Another cold spell comes, giving the Laceys just enough time to get the tapholes drilled into the maple trees and the buckets hung before the sap starts rising again.

They load up the sled with buckets and lids, called hats, and spouts. In all, nearly two hundred holes will be drilled, two hundred spouts hammered into the holes, and two hundred buckets hung. Alice fetches the drill and bit. When the sled is stacked with buckets, spouts, and hats, there is room only for Alice and two small children, not medium-sized, but really small children, who would get stuck in the deep drifts of snow if they were not snug in the sled. So Jeremy and Max are packed aboard with the sugaring tools, while Don, Jonathan, and Angie strap on their skis.

The runners glide over the freshly broken trails. It is a cold, windless day. The sky is clear, and in the deep silence of the woods one bird can be heard singing. The trees stand

◆✱◆　✱◆✱　◆✱◆　✱◆✱　◆✱◆　✱◆✱　◆✱◆

waiting, ready to give up some of the clear sap that circulates just beneath the bark. Alice and Don will drill carefully. Often, more than one hole is drilled in a tree, especially if it is a good running tree. But they will not go too deep or drill too many holes at a time in one tree. They mean to take only a little of each tree's sap, for that is its source of vitality, its nourishment, its life.

The sugar sap is made in the tree primarily for its own use, not for people's use. It helps the tree to live and grow. Sunlight and warmth start the sugar-making activity beneath the surface of the tree.

Some people, especially a long time ago, gashed maple trees with an ax or chopped big notches into their trunks. Like gaping wounds, these cuts would pour forth the sap, but they would never heal and within a few years the sugar maples would die.

❖✿❖ ✿❖✿ ❖✿❖ ✿❖✿ ❖✿❖ ✿❖✿ ❖✿❖

❖✳❖　✳✳✳　❖✳❖　✳✳✳　❖✳❖　✳✳✳　❖✳❖

Alice and Don begin to drill. The bit, or pointed part of the drill, is just under one-half inch in diameter and the holes are no more than one and one-half inches deep. The holes are slanted upward into the tree to catch the sap, for although the saying is "Sap's rising!," the movement of the sap within the tree is downward as well as upward, around about, and every which way. Last year, Jonathan hammered in the spouts; this year he will do that again and help with the drilling, too.

Angie is now tall enough to reach up and put the hats on the buckets to keep out the rain and snow. Jeremy, three, and Max, four, still too small to walk a long way in the big drifts, will hand her the hats from the sled.

❖✳❖ ✳❖✳ ❖✳❖ ✳❖✳ ❖✳❖ ✳❖✳ ❖✳❖

◆✳◆   ✳✳✳   ◆✳◆   ✳✳✳   ◆✳◆   ✳✳✳   ◆✳◆

Seventy-five buckets have been hung by the end of this first day. Alice has steered the huge Belgians and her sledful of spouts and buckets and children through the twists and turns and dips and rises of the sugar maze without spilling a child or a hat.

"SAP'S RISING!"

The buckets have hung for over three days but the weather has not been the kind that makes for a real flow of sap. It

has been below freezing, day and night, with thick cloud cover. No sun, no warmth, no flow. Standing in the sugarbush, you can hear the creaking of maples as the cold wind blows in from Canada.

Finally, after a freezing cold night, the next morning is sunny. It is not the pale, thin, low-angle sunlight of November, but the direct, strengthening light of

a sun that has passed the year's equator, the vernal equinox. It is the sun of longer days that feels warm on the cheeks, makes birds sing, and helps all things loosen up and stretch.

❖❀❖ ❀❖❀ ❖❀❖ ❀❖❀ ❖❀❖ ❀❖❀ ❖❀❖

The frost designs on Jonathan's bedroom window have melted before he has dressed this morning. Bright lances of sunlight do a crazy crisscross dance on Angie's covers if she wiggles her knees. Little Jeremy climbs up on a stool by his window and takes a quiet look at the sunlit world outside.

"Sap's rising!" Alice calls up. "It's going to flow today!"

And it will flow, because sunlight is the energy for the tree's sugar-making process. Last year, sunlight from the sky, carbon dioxide from the air, and chlorophyll in the green leaves worked together to make the sugar that nourishes the tree. All winter, the sugar has been stored in the bark and wood of roots and stems. Long before the first leaf is seen, watery sap carrying the sugar begins to stir under the bark, reviving the tree for a new cycle of growth.

❖✷❖ ✷❖✷ ❖✷❖ ✷❖✷ ❖✷❖ ✷❖✷ ❖✷❖

The sap flows all day, not in little drips or plinks, but in what Jonathan calls long "drrriiips." It is the sweet maple song of spring to Jonathan's and Angie's ears as they stand in the sugarbush. By tomorrow, they tell each other, the buckets will be full enough to gather. Angie and Jonathan lift the hats and peek into the buckets. The sparkling sap, clear and bright, runs like streams of Christmas tinsel. They each take a lick and wonder how so much crystal sweetness can come from a gnarled tree older than all their grandparents put together.

Would you like to visit and help the Laceys at sugaring time? Why or why not?

What is the right time in March to go sugaring?

Everyone works together at sugaring time. Explain the jobs each Lacey family member has.

In what ways do the Laceys protect their sugar maples when they tap them?

WRITE Sugaring time is an important season to the Laceys. What important seasonal thing happens in your area at about the same time every year? Write a short travel report to tell visitors what happens and where to go to see this special seasonal occurrence.

❖✻❖ ✻❖✻ ❖✻❖ ✻❖✻ ❖✻❖ ✻❖✻ ❖✻❖

Seasons Within Seasons

What are the seasons within seasons in "Monarchs" and "Sugaring Time"? Why is it important to recognize these seasons?

WRITER'S WORKSHOP

You learned how Clara Waterman collects monarch chrysalises and how the Laceys collect maple syrup. Find out how something else involving nature is done. Then write a how-to paragraph, giving the steps.

Writer's Choice

You have read that there are other types of seasons within the regular seasons of winter, spring, summer, and autumn. What do you think about this idea? Write your response. Then plan a way to share your writing.

THEME

Trees of Life

Some people think of trees as mere decorations. Some think of them as raw material for paper and lumber, or as bearers of fruit. The following selections show a few of the many ways in which people and trees depend upon each other.

CONTENTS

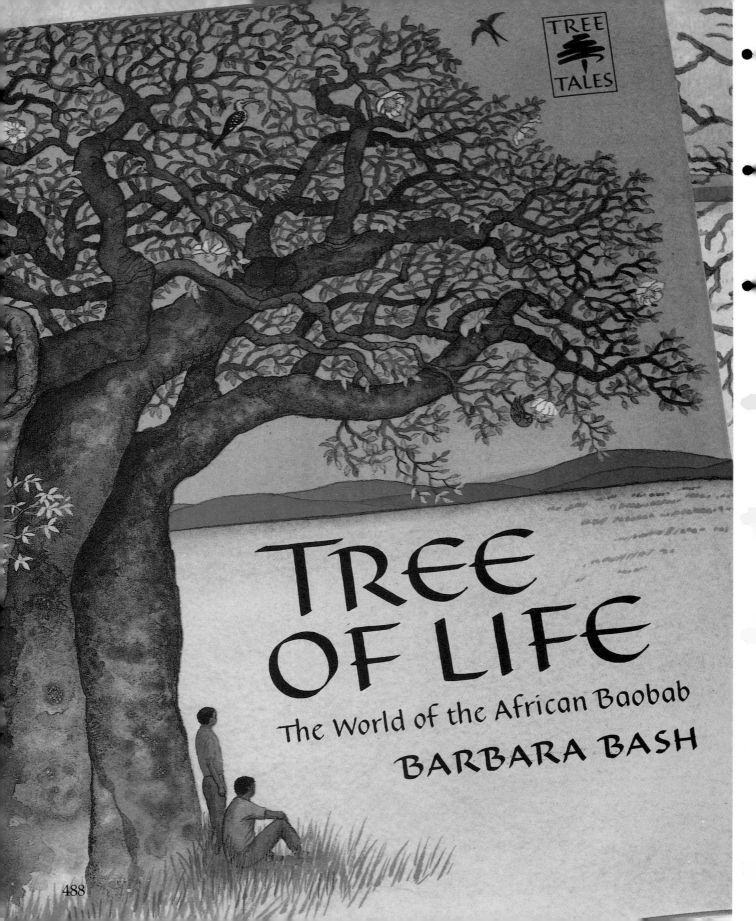

TREE
TALES

TREE
OF LIFE

The World of the African Baobab

BARBARA BASH

In the oldest times, as the !Kung Bushmen of Africa tell the story, the Great Spirit gave each animal a tree to plant. Hyena arrived late and was given the very last tree, the baobab. Being a careless creature, he planted it upside down—and that is why its branches look like gnarled roots.

The baobab grows on the dry savannahs of Africa. Reaching crookedly into the air, it stands silent and ancient. Many people believe there are no young baobabs—that they spring into being full grown. Perhaps this is because the young, slender trees look so different from the older ones. They begin to thicken and twist after forty years of growth and can eventually measure up to forty feet across and sixty feet high. With a life span of more than one thousand years, baobabs outlive nearly everything on earth.

For most of the year the baobab stands leafless and bare, but twice a year the rains come, and for a brief period the tree leafs out and blooms. Sometimes even before the rains begin, the baobab senses the coming moisture and sends out its soft new leaves and flower buds.

AWARD-WINNING AUTHOR/ ILLUSTRATOR

489

Soon birds arrive to make their nests in the baobab's hollows. The yellow-collared lovebird and the mosque swallow perch in the high branches. The old tree starts to hum with life.

At twilight, the large white flowers begin to open. Small furry creatures called bushbabies emerge from their hollows in the tree and smell the sweet nectar. They dart from branch to branch like little elves, pushing their faces into the flowers, lapping up the nectar, and carrying the sticky yellow pollen on to the next bloom. The soft leaves rustle as the bushbabies chirp and scurry about.

In the morning, the flowers that opened the night before have fallen to the ground, and a pair of eland comes to lap up the soft petals. A trio of impalas also munches the petals quietly, keeping a watchful eye on the horizon for signs of danger. No one seems to notice the tiny dik-dik that hides in the lush grass nearby. In the distance, a lone giraffe reaches for the baobab's tender leaves.

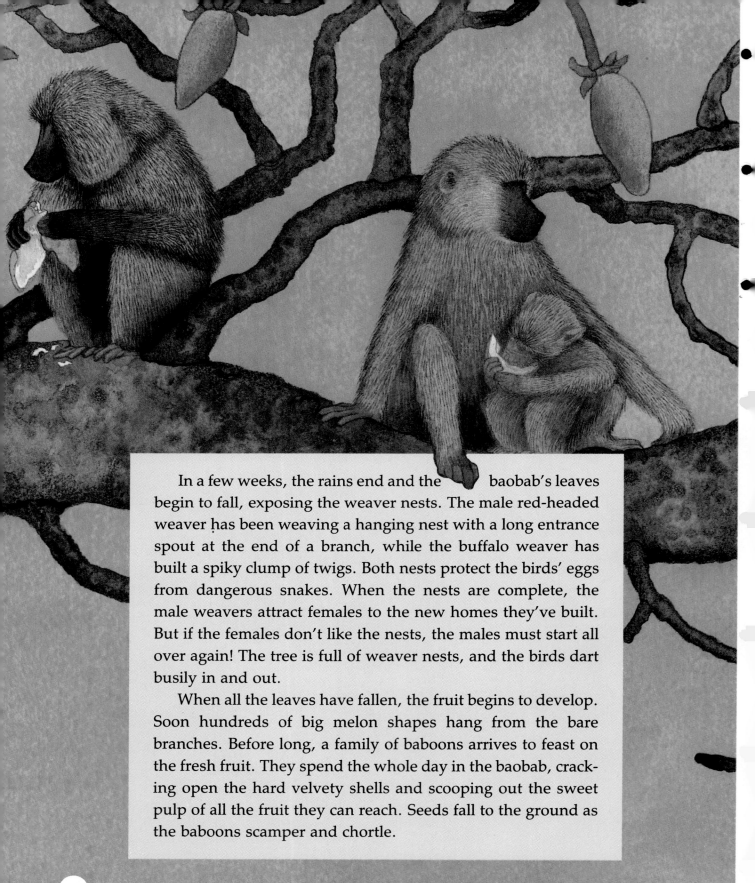

In a few weeks, the rains end and the   baobab's leaves begin to fall, exposing the weaver nests. The male red-headed weaver has been weaving a hanging nest with a long entrance spout at the end of a branch, while the buffalo weaver has built a spiky clump of twigs. Both nests protect the birds' eggs from dangerous snakes. When the nests are complete, the male weavers attract females to the new homes they've built. But if the females don't like the nests, the males must start all over again! The tree is full of weaver nests, and the birds dart busily in and out.

When all the leaves have fallen, the fruit begins to develop. Soon hundreds of big melon shapes hang from the bare branches. Before long, a family of baboons arrives to feast on the fresh fruit. They spend the whole day in the baobab, cracking open the hard velvety shells and scooping out the sweet pulp of all the fruit they can reach. Seeds fall to the ground as the baboons scamper and chortle.

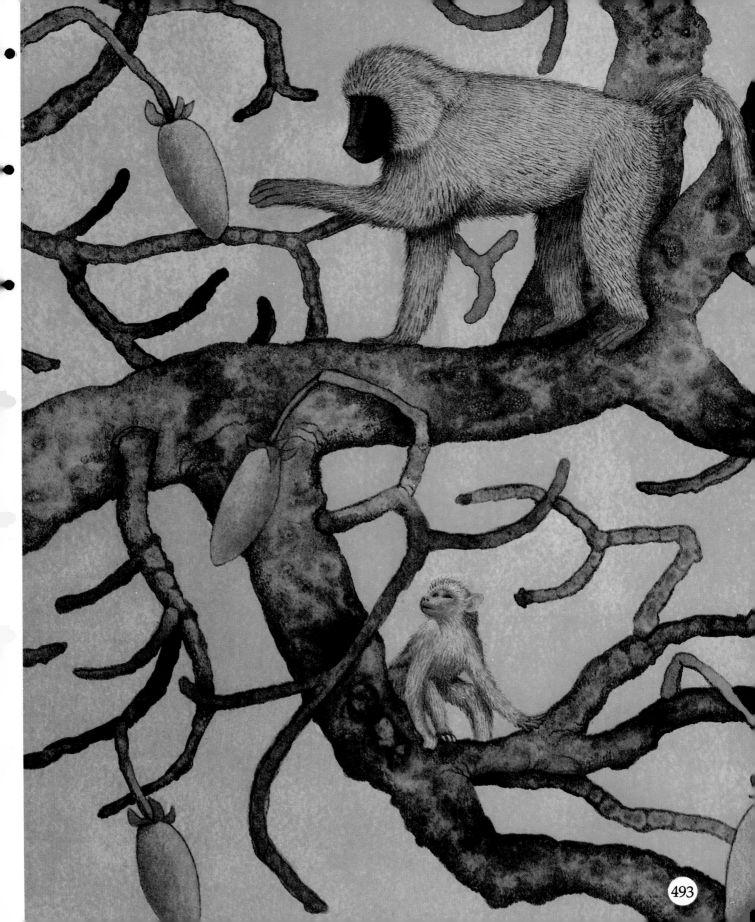

After the fruit is gone, the baobab is very still. A boomslang snake drapes its long body over a gnarled branch and waits. A praying mantis turns its head, its large eyes ever-watchful. A stick insect hides from the snake in plain sight, looking very much like a twig. A flap-eared chameleon is also camouflaged in the branches; it turns the color of its surroundings and does not move.

Sometimes the stillness is broken by the call of the honey guide bird—*aje-je-je-je*—and the voices of tribesmen who follow close behind. The bird dips and swoops, flashing its white tail feathers, until it gets close to a hive in the baobab. Then the honey guide perches quietly nearby and waits for the hunters to find the hive. The men climb the baobab, smoke out the bees, and scoop out the honey. But they always leave some beeswax behind, as thanks to the honey guide bird.

To the African people, the baobab is more than a source of honey. Its bark is stripped for baskets and rope; its fruit is made into candy and sweet drinks; and its roots and leaves are used as medicine. On the hot, dry savannah, the hollow trunks of ancient baobabs can also become water containers and even shelters.

At the end of the long, dry season, the thirsty elephants arrive and begin to eat the baobab bark, extracting juices from the soft fiber. With their enormous strength, the elephants strip away all the bark and pull down large chunks of wood, leaving gaping holes in the trunk. But the baobab heals its wounds, produces new bark, and keeps growing.

Finally, after many, many years, the old baobab dies. Perhaps too many elephants have chewed the wood and weakened its structure, or insects have broken down its inner core.

One day it collapses in on itself, a melted heap of ruins. Over time, only a soft mound of powdery fragments is left. The wind will blow these away until nothing of the baobab remains.

In the sky, the clouds begin to build for the coming rains. Near the dust of the dead tree, a baobab seed has sprouted. It is all alone on the wide savannah. Now the story of the baobab begins all over again.

Do you agree that the African baobab should be called the "tree of life"? Why or why not?

Why does the !Kung legend explain that the hyena planted the first baobab tree upside down?

Which animals help the baobab tree? How do they help?

Name some of the animals and people that depend on the baobab tree.

WRITE Imagine that you lived for one season in a tree house in your neighborhood. Write about that season in a brief journal entry describing events such as those in "Tree of Life."

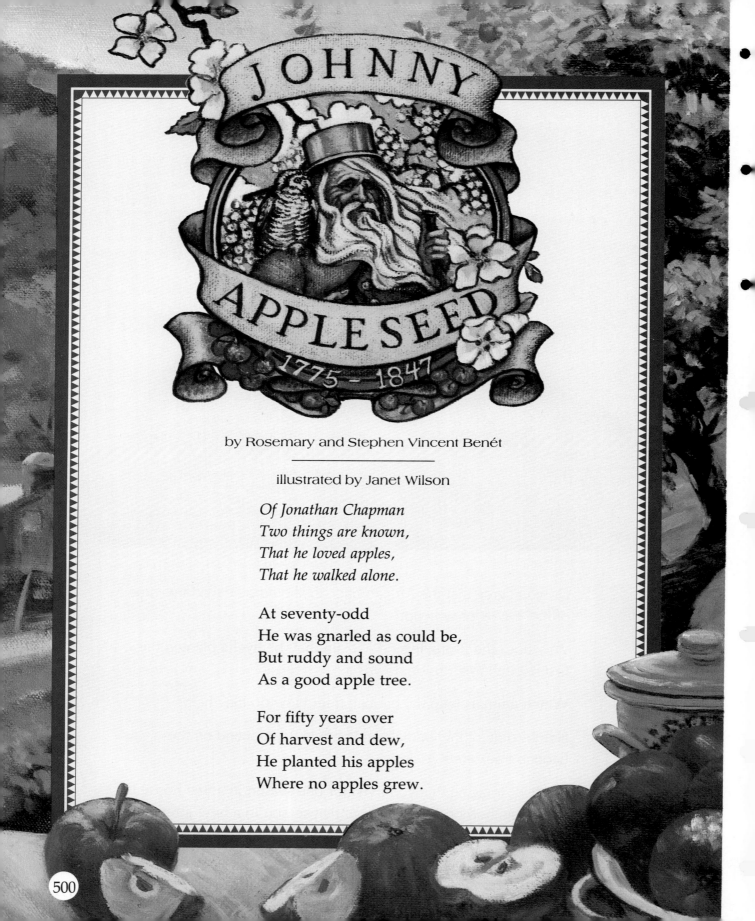

JOHNNY APPLESEED
1775 - 1847

by Rosemary and Stephen Vincent Benét

illustrated by Janet Wilson

Of Jonathan Chapman
Two things are known,
That he loved apples,
That he walked alone.

At seventy-odd
He was gnarled as could be,
But ruddy and sound
As a good apple tree.

For fifty years over
Of harvest and dew,
He planted his apples
Where no apples grew.

The winds of the prairie
Might blow through his rags,
But he carried his seeds
In the best deerskin bags.

From old Ashtabula
To frontier Fort Wayne,
He planted and pruned
And he planted again.

He had not a hat
To encumber his head.
He wore a tin pan
On his white hair instead.

He nested with owl,
And with bear-cub and possum,
And knew all his orchards
Root, tendril and blossom.

A fine old man,
As ripe as a pippin,
His heart still light,
And his step still skipping.

Why did he do it?
We do not know.
He wished that apples
Might root and grow.

He has no statue.
He has no tomb.
He has his apple trees
Still in bloom.

Consider, consider,
Think well upon
The marvelous story
Of Appleseed John.

The Growin' of PAUL BUNYAN

by William J. Brooke   illustrated by Alex Murawski

CHILDREN'S CHOICE

ALA NOTABLE BOOK

502

THIS IS A STORY about how Paul Bunyan met up with Johnny Appleseed an' what come about because o' that meetin'. But it all got started because o' the problems Paul had with his boots one mornin'.

The hardest thing for ole Paul about gettin' started in the mornin' was puttin' on his boots. It wasn't so much the lacin' up that got him down (although when your bootlaces are exactly 8,621 feet an' four an' three quarters inches long, an' each one has to be special ordered from the Suwanee Steamship Cable Company in New York City, an' if because you're strong as ole Paul you tend to snap about two laces a week as a rule, then just tyin' your boots can be a bit of an irritation, too).

No, the hardest part o' puttin' on his boots was makin' sure he was the only one in 'em. Because, you see, they was so big an' warm that all the critters liked to homestead in 'em. So he'd have to shake 'em for nine or ten minutes just to get out the ordinary rattlesnakes an' polecats. Then he'd reach in an' feel around real careful for mountain lions an' wolf packs an' the occasional caribou migration. Fin'ly he'd wave his hand around real good to see if any hawks or eagles was huntin' game down around the instep. Then he could start the chore o' lacin'.

But ever' now an' then, no matter how careful he was, he'd miss a critter or two an' then he'd just have to put up with it. 'Cause once he had those laces all done up, it just wasn't worth the trouble to untie 'em all again.

So on this partic'lar day ole Paul is out o' sorts because of a moose that's got stuck down betwixt his toes. Paul's appetite is so spoiled he can't get down more than three hunnert pancakes an' about two an' a half hogs worth o' bacon afore he grabs up his ax an' takes off to soothe his ragged nerves in his usual way by shavin' a forest or two.

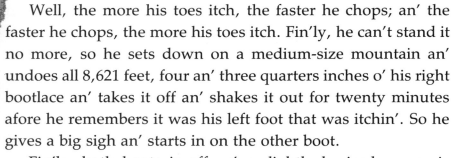

Well, the more his toes itch, the faster he chops; an' the faster he chops, the more his toes itch. Fin'ly, he can't stand it no more, so he sets down on a medium-size mountain an' undoes all 8,621 feet, four an' three quarters inches o' his right bootlace an' takes it off an' shakes it out for twenty minutes afore he remembers it was his left foot that was itchin'. So he gives a big sigh an' starts in on the other boot.

Fin'ly, both boots is off an' a slightly bruised moose is shakin' his head an' blinkin' his eyes an' staggerin' off betwixt the stumps. An' Paul has his first chance to take a deep breath an' have a look round. An' he's surprised, 'cause he can't see any trees anywheres, only stumps. So he gets up on a stump an' looks around an' he still can't see any standin' timber. He'd been so wrought up, he'd cleared all the way to the southern edge o' the big woods without noticin'.

Now this annoys Paul, 'cause he's too far from camp to get back for lunch, an' nothin' upsets him like missin' grub. An' when he's upset, the only thing to soothe him is choppin' trees, an' all the trees is down so that annoys him even worse.

There he sits, feelin' worse by the minute, with his stomach growlin' like a thunderstorm brewin' in the distance. An' then he notices somethin' way off at the horizon, out in the middle o' them dusty brown plains. All of a sudden there's somethin' green. As he watches, that green starts to spread in a line right across the middle of all that brown.

Now the only thing I ever heard tell of that was bigger than ole Paul hisself was ole Paul's curiosity. It was even bigger than his appetite. So quick as he can get his boots on, he's off to see what's happenin'. What he sees makes him stop dead in his tracks. 'Cause it's trees, apple trees growin' where nothin' but dirt ever growed before. A whole line of apple trees stretchin' in both directions as far as you can see.

It makes him feel so good he just has to take up his ax an' start choppin'. An' the more he chops, the better he feels. An' as he marches westward through all the flyin' splinters an' leaves an' applesauce, he sees that the trees is gettin' shorter until they're just saplin's, then green shoots, then just bare earth.

Paul stops short then an' leans on his ax handle to study the funny little man who turns around an' looks up at him. He's barefoot an' wears a gunnysack for clothes with a metal pot on his head for a hat. He looks up at Paul for a second, then he reaches in a big bulgy bag hangin' at his side an' takes out somethin' teeny-tiny, which he sticks in the ground. He gathers the dusty brown dirt around it an' pats it down. He stands up, an' out of a canvas waterbag he pours a little bit o' water on the spot. Then he just stands an' watches.

For a few seconds nothin' happens, then the tiniest littlest point o' green pokes out o' the dust an' sort o' twists around like it's lookin' for somethin'. All at once, it just stretches itself toward the sky an' pulls a saplin' up after it. An' it begins to branch an' to fill out an' its smooth green skin turns rough an' dark an' oozes sap. The branches creak an' groan an' stretch like a sleeper just wakin' up. Buds leaf out an' turn their damp green faces to the sun. An' the apples change from green to red an' swell like balloons full to bustin' with sweet cider.

The funny little man looks up an' smiles an' says, "My name's John Chapman, but folks call me Johnny Appleseed."

"Pleased to meet you," says Paul.

The little man points at his tree. "Mighty pretty sight, don't you think?"

"Sure is," says Paul, an' with a quick-as-a-wink flick o' his ax, he lays the tree out full length on the ground. "My name's Paul Bunyan."

The little man lifts his tin pot an' wipes his bald head while he stares at the tree lyin' there in the dirt. Then he squints up at Paul an' kneels down an' puts another seed in the ground. Paul smiles down at him while the tree grows up, then he lays it out by the first. The little man pops three seeds into the ground fast as can be. Paul lets 'em come up, then he lops all three with one easy stroke, backhand.

"You sure make 'em come up fast," says Paul, admirin'-like.

"It's a sort o' gift I was born with," says Johnny Appleseed. He looks at the five trees lyin' together. "You sure make 'em come down fast."

"It's a talent," says Paul, real humble. "I have to practice a lot."

They stand quiet awhile with Paul leanin' easy on his ax an' Johnny lookin' back along the line o' fallen trees to the horizon. He lifts his tin pot again an' rubs even harder at his head. Then he looks up at Paul an' says, "It seems like we got somethin' of a philosophical difference here."

Paul considers that. "We both like trees," he says real friendly.

"Yep," Johnny nods, "but I like 'em vertical an' you like 'em horizontal."

Paul agrees, but says he don't mind a man who holds a dif- ferin' opinion from his own, 'cause that's what makes America great. Johnny says, "Course you don't mind, 'cause when my opinion has finished differin' an' the dust settles, the trees is in the position you prefer. Anybody likes a fight that he always wins."

Paul allows he's sorry that Johnny's upset. "But loggin's what I do, an' a man's gotta do what he does. Besides, without my choppin' lumber, you couldn't build houses or stoke fires or pick your teeth."

"I don't live in a house an' I don't build fires an' when I want to clean my teeth I just eat an apple. Tell me, when all the trees are gone, what'll you cut down then?"

Paul laughs. "Why, there'll always be trees. Are you crazy or somethin'?"

"Yep," says Johnny, "crazy to be wastin' time an' lung power on you. I got to be off. I'm headin' for the Pacific Ocean an' I got a lot o' work to do on the way. So why don't you head north an' I'll head west an' our paths won't cross till they meet somewheres in China."

Paul feels a little hurt at this, but he starts off north, then stops to watch as Johnny takes off at a run, tossin' the seed out in front o' him, pressin' it down into the ground with his bare toes an' tricklin' a little water behind, all without breakin' stride. In a minute he's vanished at the head o' his long line of apple trees.

Now Paul has figured that Johnny hadn't really meant to offend him, but it was more in the nature of a challenge. An' Paul loves any kind of a challenge. So he sets down an' waits three days, figurin' he should give a fair head start to Johnny, who's a couple hunnert feet shorter'n he is. Then at dawn on the fourth day, he stands up an' stretches an' holds his ax out level a foot above the ground. When he starts to run, the trees drop down in a row as neat as the cross ties on a railroad line. In fact, when it came time to build the transcontinental rail-road, they just laid the iron rails down on that long line o' apple trees an' saved theirselves many thousands o' dollars.

Anyways, Paul runs for two days an' two nights, an' when the sun's settin' on the third day, he sees water up ahead. There's Johnny Appleseed plantin' a last tree, then sittin' on a high bare bluff lookin' out over the Pacific Ocean. Paul finishes the last o' the trees an' swings the ax over his head with a whoop an' brings it down on the dirt, buryin' its head in the soil an' accident'ly creatin' the San Andreas Fault. He mops his brow an' sits down beside Johnny with his feet danglin' way down into the ocean.

Starin' out at the orange sun, Johnny asks, "Are they all gone?" Paul looks back over his shoulder an' allows as how they are. Paul waits for Johnny to say somethin' else, but he just keeps starin', so Paul says, "It took you six days to plant 'em and it took me only three days to chop 'em down. Pretty good, huh?"

Johnny looks up an' smiles sadly. "It's always easier to chop somethin' down than to make it grow." Then he goes back to starin'.

Now that rankles Paul. When he beats somebody fair an' square, he expects that someone to admit it like a man. "What's so hard about growin' a tree anyway?" he grumps. "You just stick it in the ground an' the seed does all the work."

Johnny reaches way down in the bottom o' his bag an' holds out a seed. "It's the last one," he says. "All the rest o' my dreams is so much kindlin' wood, so why don't you take this an' see if it's so easy to make it grow."

Paul hems an' haws, but he sees as how he has to make good on his word. So he takes the little bitty seed an' pushes it down in the ground with the tip o' one fingernail. He pats the soil around it real nice, like he seen Johnny do. Then he sits down to wait as the sun sets.

"I'm not as fast as you at this," Paul says, "but you've had more practice. An' I'm sure my tree will be just as good as any o' yours."

"Not if it dies o' thirst," says Johnny's voice out o' the dark.

Paul hasn't thought about that. So when the moon comes up, he heads back to a stream he passed about two hunnert miles back. But he don't have nothin' to carry water in, so he scoops up a double handful an' runs as fast as he can with the water slippin' betwixt his fingers. When he gets back, he's got about two drops left.

"Guess I'll have to get more water," he says, a mite winded.

"Don't matter," says Johnny's voice, "if the rabbits get the seed."

An' there in the moonlight, Paul sees all the little cotton-tails hoppin' around an' scratchin' at the ground. Not wishin' to hurt any of 'em, he picks 'em up, one at a time, an' moves 'em away, but they keep hoppin' back. So, seein' as how he still needs water, he grabs 'em all up an' runs back to the stream, sets the rabbits down, grabs up the water, runs back, flicks two more drops on the spot, pushes away the new batch o' rabbits movin' in, an' tries to catch his breath.

"Just a little more water an' a few less rabbits an' it'll be fine," Paul says between gasps.

Out o' the dark comes Johnny's voice. "Don't matter, if the frost gets it."

Paul feels the cold ground an' he feels the moisture freezin' on his hands. So he gets down on his knees an' he folds his hands around that little spot o' dirt an', gentle as he can, breathes his warm breath onto that tiny little seed. Time passes and the rabbits gather round to enjoy the warmth an' scratch their soft little backs up against those big callused hands. As the night wears on, Paul falls into a sleep, but his hands never stop cuppin' that little bit o' life.

Sometime long after moonset, the voice o' Johnny Apple-seed comes driftin' soft out o' the dark an' says, "Nothin's enough if you don't care enough."

Paul wakes up with the sun. He sets up an' stretches an' for a minute he can't remember where he is. Then he looks down an' he gives a whoop. 'Cause he sees a little tiny bit o' green pokin' up through the grains o' dirt. "Hey, Johnny," he yells, "look at this!" But Johnny Appleseed is gone, slipped away in the night. Paul is upset for a minute, then he realizes he don't need to brag to anybody, that that little slip o' green is all the happiness he needs right now.

As the sun rises, he fetches more water an' shoos away the crows an' shields that shoot from the heat o' the sun. It grows taller an' straighter an' puts out buds an' unfurls its leaves. Paul carries in all the animals from the surroundin' countryside, coyotes an' sidewinders an' Gila monsters, an' sets 'em down in a circle to admire his tree growin' tall an' sturdy an' green.

Then Paul notices somethin'. He gets down on his hands an' knees an' looks close. It's a brown leaf. "That's not too serious," he thinks an' he shades it from the sun. Then he sees another brown leaf an' he runs back to get more water. When he gets back, the little saplin' is droopin' an' shrivelin'. He gets down an' breathes on it, but as he watches, the leaves drop off an' the twigs snap. "Help me, somebody," he cries out, "help me!" But there's no answer 'cept the rustlin' o' the critters as they slink away from him. An' while he looks down at the only thing he ever give birth to, it curls up an' dies.

For a second he just stands there, then he pounds his fists on the ground an' yells, "Johnny! Johnny! Why didn't you tell me how much it could hurt?"

He sets down an' he stares till the sun begins settin'. Then he jumps up an' says, "Only one thing's gonna make me feel better. I'm gonna cut me some timber! Maybe a whole forest if I can find one!" He reaches for his ax.

An' that's when he sees it. It stretches right up to the sky, with great green boughs covered with sweet-smellin' needles an' eagles nestin' in its heights. Johnny must have worked some o' his magic afore he left, 'cause when Paul struck it into the ground it wasn't nothin' but an ax. But now, in the light o' the settin' sun, it shines like a crimson column crowned in evergreen.

"I'll call it a redwood," says Paul, who knew now he'd never want an ax again as long as there was such a tree.

So he waited for the cones with the seeds to form an' drop, an' he planted them all over the great Northwest an' nurtured them an' watched a great woodland spring up in their shelter. An' he never felled a tree again as long as he lived.

For years he worked, an' there are those who say you can still catch a glimpse o' him behind the highest mountains in the deepest woods. An' they say he's always smilin' when you see him.

'Cause Paul learned hisself somethin': A little man who chops somethin' down is still just a little man; but there's nobody bigger than a man who learns to grow.

Is it fair that Johnny Appleseed doesn't tell Paul Bunyan how much a tree's death hurts? Give reasons for your answer.

In what way does Paul Bunyan grow in this story?

How does the author let you know that this is a legend and not a true story?

Paul Bunyan and Johnny Appleseed have very different opinions about trees. In what other ways are they different?

Why does Johnny Appleseed give his very last seed to Paul Bunyan?

WRITE   Which character in this story do you like better? Write an opinion paragraph explaining why you like that character. Use events in the story to support your opinion.

Trees of Life

For what reasons might the trees described in the selections be called "trees of life"?

WRITER'S WORKSHOP

What other important message about protecting nature could a folktale deliver? With your classmates, brainstorm a list of living things that might be in danger. For example, a baobab might be threatened by an African woodcutter, or a wild bear might be in danger from Davy Crockett. Choose the one you would most like to save. Brainstorm ways in which a wise character might save it. Use your ideas to write a folktale.

WRITER'S CHOICE   Do you feel any differently about trees after reading the selections in the theme Trees of Life? Think of a way to express your feelings, and share your work with your classmates.

CONNECTIONS

MULTICULTURAL CONNECTION

Prizing Our World

Harrison Ngau [nou] grew up in the rain forests of Sarawak, a state in northern Borneo. He watched these forests being slowly destroyed by timber companies that sold the lumber worldwide. He knew that all rain forests are important to the health of our planet. He also knew that the rain forests of Borneo were home to the Irak and other native peoples.

To save the Irak culture as well as the forests, Ngau organized people to halt the logging in every way they could. For his efforts, Harrison Ngau was awarded the Goldman Environmental Prize in 1990. He quickly put his $60,000 prize money to work and financed a successful bid for a seat in his nation's parliament.

Ngau has shown that one person can do a lot to help our environment. Write a character sketch about someone you know who is making a difference in our world.

516

SOCIAL STUDIES CONNECTION

Saving the World Begins at Home

People all over the world are working to save the environment. What are your community's environmental problems? What groups are already trying to solve these problems? Create posters that tell how people can make a difference in your community.

MATH CONNECTION

Harrison Ngau won the Goldman Environmental Prize in 1990.

Calculating the Future

What percentage of the earth's surface is covered by rain forests? How fast are the forests being destroyed? Collect these and other statistics that show how our environment is changing. Use the information to compute the changes that may take place on our planet in the next ten years. Report your conclusions.

UNIT SIX

Flights

We have always been fascinated by the skies above us. This fascination goes back over 3,000 years, to the ancient astronomers of China, Babylonia, and Egypt. And our fascination has led us beyond mere looking. We actually travel into space for close-up views. Think about what fascinates you about the skies as you read the selections in this unit.

THEMES

BOOKSHELF

TO SPACE & BACK

by Sally Ride with Susan Okie

Spectacular photos and the words and thoughts of astronaut Sally Ride allow you to take a ride on the space shuttle *Challenger*.

ALA Notable Book, Outstanding Science Trade Book for Children

Harcourt Brace Library Book

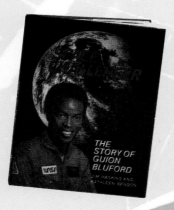

SPACE CHALLENGER: THE STORY OF GUION BLUFORD

by Jim Haskins and Kathleen Benson

Aerospace engineer and astronaut Guy Bluford pursued his childhood love of flying machines to the limit, riding into space aboard the *Challenger*.

Outstanding Science Trade Book for Children

Harcourt Brace Library Book

SELF-PORTRAIT WITH WINGS

by Susan Green

Be careful what you wish for. Jennifer wishes that she could grow wings—never believing that her wish could come true!

BEFORE THE WRIGHT BROTHERS

by Don Berliner

Who were the people who planned, built, and used the flying machines of the nineteenth century? Find out in this collection of short biographies.

THE SECRET GROVE

by Barbara Cohen

Two boys grow up in a city divided by religious and ethnic hatreds. What will happen when they meet accidentally in the grove?

Award-Winning Author

T H E M E

Through Space and Time

Is time always ticking away at the same pace, second by second? Or can time be condensed? Or expanded? Or even wrinkled?

C O N T E N T S

523

New Provid

A CHANGING CITYSCAPE

1910

New Providence is thriving. Cobblestone streets bustle with activity—Model T Fords, streetcars, and horse-drawn carts carrying meat, milk, and ice. There is no concert in the bandstand today, but a crowd has gathered in the square in front of the Town Hall and the Tenebo County Courthouse. A fountain has been built in commemoration of Chief Tenebo, a Native American from a local tribe. The statue is about to be unveiled. Around the base of the fountain is an inscription: GOOD CITIZENS ARE THE RICHES OF A CITY.

ence

CONCEIVED BY
RENATA VON TSCHARNER AND RONALD LEE FLEMING,
THE TOWNSCAPE INSTITUTE
ILLUSTRATIONS BY DENIS ORLOFF

NOTABLE
CHILDREN'S TRADE
BOOK IN SOCIAL
STUDIES

NEW PROVIDENCE
A CHANGING CITYSCAPE

*Put the city up; tear the city down;
put it up again; let us find a city. . . .*

CARL SANDBURG

New Providence's good citizens—women in long skirts and men
in hats—buy fruit at the sidewalk stand in front of the grocery and
most of their clothing and household items at Getz & McClure's, the
largest store in town. They shop for shoes and jewelry and office
supplies and have supper at Gilman's or at the Butler House Cafe.

The rural hillsides surrounding the city are lush, with
comfortable Victorian homes dotting the landscape and the Bloom
mill and worker housing in the distance. The large red brick
schoolhouse is attended by all school-age children in the region. A
flock of birds flies peacefully overhead.

1935

As a mist rolls into New Providence, effects of the Great Depression are visible; the city has fallen on hard times. Gone is the bandstand from the courthouse square, where homeless men now huddle over trash can fires for warmth. A WPA sign publicizes the Works Progress Administration, a jobs program funded by the government. A line of jobless men waits for free bread outside the post office, and hoboes are taking a free ride out of the city on trains. Many buildings are in need of repair.

But even in times such as these, life goes on. A Charlie Chaplin movie is playing at the Strand Theater. A huge Coca-Cola advertisement goes up on the side of a building. A streetlight now controls automobile traffic. The Bloom mill—expanded before the stock market crash—is still in operation, the grocery has become a shoe store, and the dry goods store, a jeweler's. The Colonel Fleming House now accommodates three small businesses. Art Deco chrome and glass streamline some of the storefronts, contrasting with the older styles of the upper stories. A modern yellow apartment building squats on the hillside, while a biplane and a blimp cruise the skies.

1955

Apostwar prosperity settles over New Providence, although there are signs that downtown is deteriorating.

The night sky glows with neon, Christmas lights, and lighted billboards advertising bread, used cars, and cigarettes. Part of the courthouse square is now paved with asphalt to make room for more and larger cars. Buses have replaced streetcars. Franchises like Rexall's and Woolworth's have moved into town, and the Alpine Motel attracts traveling businessmen. Walt Disney's *Lady and the Tramp* is playing at the Strand.

The elegant Butler House is now a liquor store and a boarding house for transients. Next to it, a Victorian cast-iron building is being covered with prefabricated siding. Getz & McClure's has already been sheathed with stark metal grillwork and a currently popular style of lettering. Two of the small businesses in the Colonel Fleming House are boarded up. Behind it, a bland new building has been erected to house Monarch Insurance. The old slate roof of the Town Hall has been replaced by asphalt shingles. A fire is raging at the train station, while the citizens of New Providence go about their holiday shopping.

1970

By 1970, downtown New Providence is an uninspired jumble of old and new. To attract people from thriving suburbia, part of Main Street has been converted into a pedestrian mall, dominated by a harsh concrete fountain. But there is less traffic than ever in the city center, and fewer people actually live there.

A number of people in town today are gathered outside the courthouse, taking part in a protest march against the Vietnam War. Across the newly sunken and cemented square, a mugging is in progress. Graffiti mars the area, as do more and more billboards—

advertising beer, cigarettes, whiskey, and an Army/Navy surplus
store. The post office and several other buildings have been
demolished and turned into parking lots, the Bloom mill is for rent,
and the train station tower remains burnt out.

The Alpine Motel is now a Holiday Inn, a Fotomat has opened,
and the Beatles' *Let It Be* is playing at the Strand. A day school has
opened, complete with colorful murals and giant toadstools. The
Colonel Fleming House seems about to be rescued by a preservation
group. Victorian homes in the hills are disappearing to make room
for highways, look-alike suburban housing, and another addition to
the school. In the afternoon sky, a jet flies over the increasing
number of powerlines strung across the horizon.

1980

Ten years later, there are signs that downtown New Providence is sadly in need of recovery—and also signs that help is on the way.

Chief Tenebo's statue has been vandalized; debris blows around its dry base and across the square. Graffiti is everywhere, street lamps are smashed, and a police box has appeared. The Colonel Fleming House has been moved across the street, but its placement does not look permanent. In its old location are a Cor-Ten steel sculpture and Monarch Insurance's new highrise, which bears no architectural relationship to the buildings around it.

But the streets seem more populated, and people are again living—even barbecuing—downtown in the new red brick infill structure next to McDonald's. The only billboard in town advertises health food and a cultural event. The old Strand Theater is being expanded into a Cultural Center. And although the Butler House has been all but abandoned, a sign shows that rehabilitation is being planned. A superhighway now cuts through the hillside, making downtown more accessible to summer holiday travelers. A large parking structure has been built, and well-tended plantings soften the mall.

1987

In the sunny afternoon sky a flock of birds heads back to its winter home. Below, people have returned to the city—living, shopping, working, playing. New Providence has never looked better. Sidewalk vendors sell their produce once more, and traffic again flows through handsomely paved streets. Buses are made to look like old-fashioned trolleys. Chief Tenebo has been restored, and the bandstand is back, a concert in full swing. Gone are graffiti, billboards, and harsh sculptures. Plants and fall flowers are everywhere—even the parking structure has been elegantly camouflaged.

It is wisdom to think the people are the city . . . .

CARL SANDBURG

All of the old building facades have been renovated, and the condition of most buildings is strikingly similar to what it was in 1910. The Town Hall's slate roof has been restored, and the air-raid siren is gone. Street furniture is comfortable and compatible with the architecture. The circular clock is back in front of the Butler House, now beautifully refurbished. An arcaded building where people live and work occupies the site of the controversial tower, serving as an entry into the restored train station, and an atrium full of plants softens the Monarch Insurance skyscraper. A Fitness Center has replaced the Feminist Health Center, and a film festival is in progress at the Strand Cultural Center.

The good citizens of New Providence have worked hard to make the city livable again—and true to its heritage.

New Providence, a small American city, will not be found on any map. It is the creation of a team of architectural historians and designers, and yet its fictional cityscape is truly authentic. The buildings, the signs, even the street furniture can be found somewhere in urban America. Almost every detail was discovered in old photographs and assembled by the design team at The Townscape Institute.

Baltimore, Maryland (McDonald's building and H_2O fountain); Binghamton, New York (courthouse lights); Boston, Massachusetts (church in center and 1970 concrete plaza); Brookline, Massachusetts (church); Cambridge, Massachusetts (signs); Chelsea, Massachusetts (storefront); Chicago, Illinois (metal awning on the Butler House); Cincinnati, Ohio (1987 City Identity System booth); Denver, Colorado (building across the street from courthouse in 1910); Eugene, Oregon (1970 modern concrete fountain); Flint, Michigan (1910 shoe sign and street awnings); Fresno, California (1970–80 sculptural clock tower); Garland, Utah (Bloom mill); Grand Rapids, Michigan (City Hall); Heber City, Utah (water tower); Junction City, Kansas (corner bank); Knoxville, Tennessee (billboard); Los Angeles, California (Getz & McClure building); Milwaukee, Wisconsin (suburban villas); Montclair, New Jersey (Colonel Fleming House); Montgomery, Alabama (Victorian cast-iron building); New York, New York (Butler House and train station); Portland, Oregon (fountain base); Richmond, Virginia (signs on Reiter's shoe store); Salem, Ohio (cornice on Main Street); San Diego, California (circular clock); Scottsdale, Arizona (parking structure with plantings); Staunton, Virginia (stained glass in McDonald's building); Syracuse, New York (layout of courthouse square); Topeka, Kansas (Alpine Motel sign); Townsend, Massachusetts (bandstand); Traverse City, Michigan (mansard roof on Butler House); Upper Sandusky, Ohio (horse fountain and pavilion); Waltham, Massachusetts (bench); Washington, D.C. (Masonic building); Westerville, Ohio (gas station); Wilkes-Barre, Pennsylvania (park outline); Wilmington, Delaware (1970 metal Main Street shelters); Winooski, Vermont (Main Street building).

Would you like to live in New Providence? Explain why or why not.

In what ways did New Providence change with the times?

How do you think the authors feel about the changes made in New Providence? Explain your answer.

Which would you say was a better year for New Providence—1910 or 1987? Explain why you think as you do.

WRITE Would you like to be involved in city planning? List some reasons why you would or wouldn't want to be a city planner.

A Wrinkle

Meg Murry's father disappeared several years ago while working on a top secret project. Did he somehow slip through a wrinkle in time? Meg, her friend Calvin, and her brother Charles Wallace are determined to find out. Aided by a trio of superhuman helpers named Mrs. Who, Mrs. Which, and Mrs. Whatsit, they investigate a series of strange places, including the capital city of Camazotz.

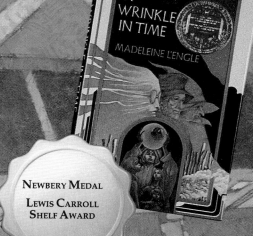

NEWBERY MEDAL

LEWIS CARROLL SHELF AWARD

IN TIME

by Madeleine L'Engle

Illustrations by Kate Muellar

Below them the town was laid out in harsh angular patterns. The houses in the outskirts were all exactly alike, small square boxes painted gray. Each had a small, rectangular plot of lawn in front, with a straight line of dull-looking flowers edging the path to the door. Meg had a feeling that if she could count the flowers there would be exactly the same number for each house. In front of all the houses children were playing. Some were skipping rope, some were bouncing balls. Meg felt vaguely that something was wrong with their play. It seemed exactly like children playing around any housing development at home, and yet there was something different about it. She looked at Calvin, and saw that he, too, was puzzled.

"Look!" Charles Wallace said suddenly. "They're skipping and bouncing in rhythm! Everyone's doing it at exactly the same moment."

This was so. As the skipping rope hit the pavement, so did the ball. As the rope curved over the head of the jumping child, the child with the ball caught the ball. Down came the ropes. Down came the balls. Over and over again. Up. Down. All in rhythm. All identical. Like the houses. Like the paths. Like the flowers.

Then the doors of all the houses opened simultaneously, and out came women like a row of paper dolls. The print of their dresses was different, but they all gave the appearance of being the same. Each woman stood on the steps of her house. Each clapped. Each child with the ball caught the ball. Each child with the skipping rope folded the rope. Each child turned and walked into the house. The doors clicked shut behind them.

"How can they do it?" Meg asked wonderingly. "We couldn't do it that way if we tried. What does it mean?"

"Let's go back." Calvin's voice was urgent.

"Back?" Charles Wallace asked. "Where?"

"I don't know. Anywhere. Back to the hill. Back to Mrs. Whatsit and Mrs. Who and Mrs. Which. I don't like this."

"But they aren't there. Do you think they'd come to us if we turned back now?"

"I don't like it," Calvin said again.

"Come *on*." Impatience made Meg squeak. "You *know* we can't go back. Mrs. Whatsit *said* to go into the town." She started on down the street, and the two boys followed her. The houses, all identical, continued, as far as the eye could reach.

Then, all at once, they saw the same thing, and stopped to watch. In front of one of the houses stood a little boy with a ball, and he was bouncing it. But he bounced it rather badly and with no particular rhythm, sometimes dropping it and running after it with awkward, furtive leaps, sometimes throwing it up into the air and trying to catch it. The door of his house opened and out ran one of the mother figures. She looked wildly up and down the street, saw the children and put her hand to her mouth as though to stifle a scream, grabbed the little boy and rushed indoors with him. The ball dropped from his fingers and rolled out into the street.

Charles Wallace ran after it and picked it up, holding it out for Meg and Calvin to see. It seemed like a perfectly ordinary, brown rubber ball.

"Let's take it in to him and see what happens," Charles Wallace suggested.

Meg pulled at him. "Mrs. Whatsit said for us to go on into the town."

"Well, we *are* in the town, aren't we? The outskirts anyhow. I want to know more about this. I have a hunch it may help us later. You go on if you don't want to come with me."

"No," Calvin said firmly. "We're going to stay together. Mrs. Whatsit said we weren't to let them separate us. But I'm with you on this. Let's knock and see what happens."

They went up the path to the house, Meg reluctant, eager to get on into the town. "Let's hurry," she begged, "*please!* Don't you want to find Father?"

"Yes," Charles Wallace said, "but not blindly. How can we help him if we don't know what we're up against? And it's obvious we've been brought here to help him, not just to find

him." He walked briskly up the steps and knocked at the door.
They waited. Nothing happened. Then Charles Wallace saw a bell,
and this he rang. They could hear the bell buzzing in the house,
and the sound of it echoed down the street. After a moment the
mother figure opened the door. All up and down the street other
doors opened, but only a crack, and eyes peered toward the three
children and the woman looking fearfully out the door at them.

"What do you want?" she asked. "It isn't paper time yet;
we've had milk time; we've had this month's Puller Prush
Person; and I've given my Decency Donations regularly. All my
papers are in order."

"I think your little boy dropped his ball," Charles Wallace
said, holding it out.

The woman pushed the ball away. "Oh, no! The children in
our section *never* drop balls! They're all perfectly trained. We
haven't had an Aberration for three years."

All up and down the block, heads nodded in agreement.

Charles Wallace moved closer to the woman and looked past her into the house. Behind her in the shadows he could see the little boy, who must have been about his own age.

"You can't come in," the woman said. "You haven't shown me any papers. I don't have to let you in if you haven't any papers."

Charles Wallace held the ball out beyond the woman so that the little boy could see it. Quick as a flash the boy leaped forward and grabbed the ball from Charles Wallace's hand, then darted back into the shadows. The woman went very white, opened her mouth as though to say something, then slammed the door in their faces instead. All up and down the street doors slammed.

"What are they afraid of?" Charles Wallace asked. "What's the matter with them?"

"Don't *you* know?" Meg asked him. "Don't you know what all this is about, Charles?"

"Not yet," Charles Wallace said. "Not even an inkling. And I'm trying. But I didn't get through anywhere. Not even a chink. Let's go." He stumped down the steps.

After several blocks the houses gave way to apartment buildings; at least Meg felt sure that that was what they must be. They were fairly tall, rectangular buildings, absolutely plain, each window, each entrance exactly like every other. Then, coming toward them down the street, was a boy about Calvin's age riding a machine that was something like a combination of a bicycle and a motorcycle. It had the slimness and lightness of a bicycle, and yet as the foot pedals turned they seemed to generate an unseen source of power, so that the boy could pedal very slowly and yet move along the street quite swiftly. As he reached each entrance he thrust one hand into a bag he wore slung over his shoulder, pulled out a roll of papers, and tossed it into the entrance. It might have been Dennys or Sandy or any

one of hundreds of boys with a newspaper route in any one of hundreds of towns back home, and yet, as with the children playing ball and jumping rope, there was something wrong about it. The rhythm of the gesture never varied. The paper flew in identically the same arc at each doorway, landed in identically the same spot. It was impossible for anybody to throw with such consistent perfection.

Calvin whistled. "I wonder if they play baseball here?"

As the boy saw them he slowed down on his machine and stopped, his hand arrested as it was about to plunge into the paper bag. "What are you kids doing out on the street?" he demanded. "Only route boys are allowed out now, you know that."

"No, we don't know it," Charles Wallace said. "We're strangers here. How about telling us something about this place?"

"You mean you've had your entrance papers processed and everything?" the boy asked. "You must have if you're here," he answered himself. "And what are you doing here if you don't know about us?"

"You tell me," Charles Wallace said.

"Are you examiners?" the boy asked a little anxiously. "Everybody knows our city has the best Central Intelligence Center on the planet. Our production levels are the highest. Our factories never close; our machines never stop rolling. Added to this we have five poets, one musician, three artists, and six sculptors, all perfectly channeled."

"What are you quoting from?" Charles Wallace asked.

"The Manual, of course," the boy said. "We are the most oriented city on the planet. There has been no trouble of any kind for centuries. All Camazotz knows our record. That is why we are the capital city of Camazotz. That is why CENTRAL Central Intelligence is located here. That is why IT makes ITs home here." There was something about the way he said "IT" that made a shiver run up and down Meg's spine.

But Charles Wallace asked briskly, "Where is this Central Intelligence Center of yours?"

"CENTRAL Central," the boy corrected. "Just keep going and you can't miss it. You *are* strangers, aren't you! What are you doing here?"

"Are you supposed to ask questions?" Charles Wallace demanded severely.

The boy went white, just as the woman had. "I humbly beg your pardon. I must continue my route now or I will have to talk my timing into the explainer." And he shot off down the street on his machine.

Charles Wallace stared after him. "What is it?" he asked Meg and Calvin. "There was something funny about the way he talked, as though—well, as though he weren't really doing the talking. Know what I mean?"

Calvin nodded, thoughtfully. "Funny is right. Funny peculiar. Not only the way he talked, either. The whole thing smells."

"Come *on*." Meg pulled at them. How many times was it she had urged them on? "Let's go find Father. He'll be able to explain it all to us."

547

They walked on. After several more blocks they began to see other people, grown-up people, not children, walking up and down and across the streets. These people ignored the children entirely, seeming to be completely intent on their own business. Some of them went into the apartment buildings. Most of them were heading in the same direction as the children. As these people came to the main street from the side streets they would swing around the corners with an odd, automatic stride, as though they were so deep in their own problems and the route was so familiar that they didn't have to pay any attention to where they were going.

After a while the apartment buildings gave way to what must have been office buildings, great stern structures with enormous entrances. Men and women with brief cases poured in and out.

Charles Wallace went up to one of the women, saying politely, "Excuse me, but could you please tell me—" But she hardly glanced at him as she continued on her way.

"Look." Meg pointed. Ahead of them, across a square, was the largest building they had ever seen, higher than the Empire State Building, and almost as long as it was high.

"This must be it," Charles Wallace said, "their CENTRAL Central Intelligence or whatever it is. Let's go on."

"But if Father's in some kind of trouble with this planet," Meg objected, "isn't that exactly where we *shouldn't* go?"

"Well, how do you propose finding him?" Charles Wallace demanded.

"I certainly wouldn't ask *there!*"

"I didn't say anything about asking. But we aren't going to have the faintest idea where or how to begin to look for him

until we find out something more about this place, and I have a
hunch that that's the place to start. If you have a better idea, Meg,
why of course just say so."

"Oh, get down off your high horse," Meg said crossly.
"Let's go to your old CENTRAL Central Intelligence and get
it over with."

"I think we ought to have passports or something," Calvin
suggested. "This is much more than leaving America to go to
Europe. And that boy and the woman both seemed to care so
much about having things in proper order. We certainly haven't
got any papers in proper order."

"If we needed passports or papers Mrs. Whatsit would have
told us so," Charles Wallace said.

Calvin put his hands on his hips and looked down at Charles
Wallace. "Now look here, old sport. I love those three old girls
just as much as you do, but I'm not sure they know *everything*."

"They know a lot more than we do."

"Granted. But you know Mrs. Whatsit talked about having
been a star. I wouldn't think that being a star would give her much
practice in knowing about people. When she tried to be a person
she came pretty close to goofing it up. There was never anybody
on land or sea like Mrs. Whatsit the way she got herself up."

"She was just having fun," Charles said. "If she'd wanted to
look like you or Meg I'm sure she could have."

Calvin shook his head. "I'm not so sure. And these people
seem to be *people*, if you know what I mean. They aren't like us, I
grant you that, there's something very off-beat about them. But
they're lots more like ordinary people than the ones on Uriel."

"Do you suppose they're robots?" Meg suggested.

Charles Wallace shook his head. "No. That boy who dropped
the ball wasn't any robot. And I don't think the rest of them are,
either. Let me listen for a minute."

They stood very still, side by side, in the shadow of one of the big office buildings. Six large doors kept swinging open, shut, open, shut, as people went in and out, in and out, looking straight ahead, straight ahead, paying no attention to the children whatsoever, whatsoever. Charles wore his listening, probing look. "They're not robots," he said suddenly and definitely. "I'm not sure *what* they are, but they're not robots. I can feel minds there. I can't get at them at all, but I can feel them sort of pulsing. Let me try a minute more."

The three of them stood there very quietly. The doors kept opening and shutting, opening and shutting, and the stiff people hurried in and out, in and out, walking jerkily like figures in an old silent movie. Then, abruptly, the stream of movement thinned. There were only a few people and these moved more rapidly, as if the film had been speeded up. One white-faced man in a dark suit looked directly at the children, said, "Oh, dear, I shall be late," and flickered into the building.

"He's like the white rabbit," Meg giggled nervously.

"I'm scared," Charles said. "I can't reach them at all. I'm completely shut out."

"We have to find Father—" Meg started again.

"Meg—" Charles Wallace's eyes were wide and frightened. "I'm not sure I'll even know Father. It's been so long, and I was only a baby—"

Meg's reassurance came quickly. "You'll know him! Of course you'll know him! The way you'd know me even without looking because I'm always there for you, you can always reach in—"

"Yes." Charles punched one small fist into an open palm with a gesture of great decision. "Let's go to CENTRAL Central Intelligence."

How did you feel as you read about the characters walking through the capital city of Camazotz?

How are the homes and the people of Camazotz similar to places and people anywhere else? How are they different?

What might be an Aberration in Camazotz?

Do you believe the children are in danger? What in the story makes you believe that?

WRITE Do you think you would like to live in a place where people do everything exactly the same? Write a paragraph or two to explain your opinion.

WORDS ABOUT THE AUTHOR:

Madeleine L'Engle

Madeleine L'Engle can't remember a time in her life in which she wasn't writing. As an only child, she enjoyed spending many hours alone, reading books and writing her own stories.

According to L'Engle, the main characters in her stories, male and female, are based on herself. The settings for her books are usually places she has visited. An exception is *A Wrinkle in Time*, in which three children traveling through space and time visit fantastic places beyond our world. *A Wrinkle in Time* was at first rejected by several editors who considered it to be too unusual for the general reading public. When the book was published, it was awarded the Newbery Medal "for the most distinguished contribution to American literature for children" in 1963.

L'Engle once said, "There are forces working in the world . . . for standardization, for the regimentation of us all, or what I like to call making muffins of us, muffins like every other muffin in the muffin tin." She believes that reading for pleasure can help children avoid such standardization and lead them to creativity.

L'Engle enjoys experimenting with all forms of writing—science fiction, suspense, young adult novels, poetry, playwriting, and nonfiction. But she is best known as a children's writer and has written her most difficult works for children because she believes "that children's minds are open to the excitement of new ideas and that they are able to understand what their parents have rejected or forgotten."

Through Space and Time

Do you think the city of New Providence could ever become like the capital city of Camazotz? Why or why not?

WRITER'S WORKSHOP

Two cities are described in the selections you read. The authors give details about the buildings, the landscapes, and the people who live there. The authors use specific language to express how they feel about the towns. Write a descriptive paragraph about the town you live in or one you have visited. Give details about the town you choose, and use specific, vivid words to let your audience know how you feel about it.

Writer's Choice

What do you think of the theme Through Space and Time now that you have read "New Providence: A Changing Cityscape" and "A Wrinkle in Time"? Plan a way to respond. Then carry out your plan.

555

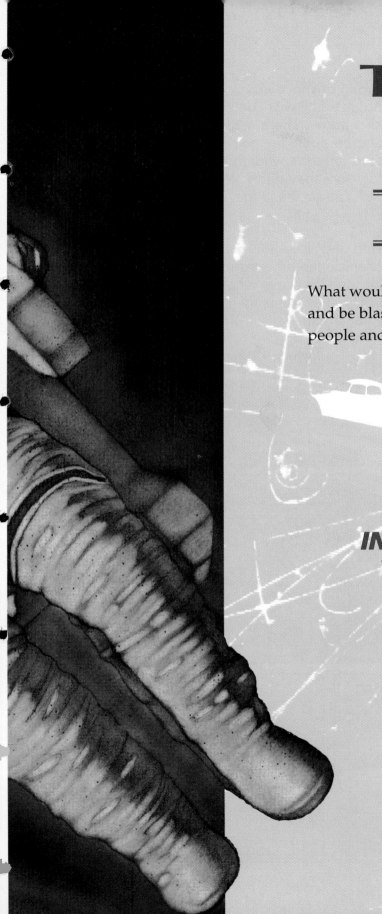

T H E M E

Space Flights

What would it be like to report to work in the morning and be blasted into space? Read about some fictional people and some real people who do just that.

C O N T E N T S

BUCK ROGERS IN THE 25TH CENTURY
by Phil Nowlan and Dick Calkins

TO SPACE & BACK
by Sally Ride with Susan Okie

BUCK ROGERS

The idea of space travel was once so fantastic that it was confined to the comics pages. There, writers and illustrators could let their imaginations soar to describe what the future might hold. Were they right? Were they even close? You be the judge.

IN THE 25TH CENTURY

In 1929, writer Phil Nowlan and illustrator Dick Calkins began to chronicle the adventures of Buck Rogers, a man trapped in a cave who woke up 500 years into the future. Running until 1967, this comic strip entertained Americans well into the real space age.

IN THE TEST FLIGHT OF OUR INTERPLANETARY SHIP, WE HAD LANDED ON THE MOON. WHILE THERE A MARTIAN SHIP SUDDENLY LOOMED THREATENINGLY ABOVE US.

DAZED FROM THE JAR OF OUR TERRIFIC TAKE-OFF, WE ROCKETED FULL BLAST AT THE SPHERICAL CRAFT.

WHEN WE RECOVERED, I STAGGERED TO THE EMERGENCY CUT-OFF.

THERE! I'LL EASE OFF OUR SPEED A BIT.

WH-WHAT HAPPENED? DID WE HIT THE MARTIAN SHIP?

HAVE KNOCKED IT TO FLINDERS.

WE MUST. OUR NOSE PLATES ARE DENTED BUT SAFE.

ONLY A FEW HOURS LATER WE PLUNGED DOWN THROUGH THE ATMOSPHERE OF EARTH.

WHY THAT LOOKS LIKE ITALY. WE'RE ON THE WRONG SIDE OF THE EARTH!

AND WE CAN'T SPEED HOME. AIR FRICTION WOULD BURN US UP. WHAT SHALL WE DO?

TO BE CONTINUED

WE HAD COME DOWN OVER ITALY. OUR PROBLEM WAS HOW TO GET BACK TO NIAGARA AT FULL SPEED WITHOUT SUFFERING FROM AIR FRICTION.

I ROCKETED **UPWARD** AND WESTWARD.

COPYRIGHT JOHN F. DILLE CO. REG. U. S. PAT. OFF.

558

ABOVE THE STRATOSPHERE THERE WAS NO AIR. I COULD MAKE SPEED.

THEN I REVERSED THE SHIP AND DROPPED DOWN OVER NIAGARA.

ROARING CROWDS WELCOMED US.

QUICK STODDARD! RUSH REPAIRS! LOAD SUPPLIES!

I'LL REPORT TO THE PRESIDENT RIGHT AWAY

WHILE SUPPLIES WERE RUSHED ABOARD—

WE MUSTERED OUR CREW FOR THE FIRST MARTIAN EXPEDITION EVER TO LEAVE EARTH—

I, MYSELF WAS CAPTAIN

I WAS FIRST MATE

I WAS SECOND MATE

I WAS CHIEF ENGINEER AND CHEMIST

I CAME ALONG AS ASTRONOMICAL NAVIGATOR AND GRAVITATIONIST

I WAS ELECTRONIST

I WAS CHIEF ROCKET GUNNER

BUCK ROGERS   WILMA DEERING   LIEUTENANT BURKE   PROFESSOR STODDARD   BOB BYRON   JOE MARTIN   JUD HANCOCK

WHAT'S THE DELAY?

THE PRESIDENT IS COMING! WE HAVE TO CHRISTEN THE SHIP PUBLICLY. WHAT SHALL WE CALL IT?

WE WERE ABOUT TO LAUNCH THE MOST DARING EXPEDITION EVER ATTEMPTED BY MAN — A TRIP TO MARS —TO RESCUE SALLY, WILMA'S LITTLE SISTER, AND ILLANA THE GOLDEN PRINCESS, FROM THE HANDS OF THE SINISTER TIGER MEN WHO DOMINATED THAT PLANET.

FIRST, WILMA NAMED OUR ROCKET SHIP—

I CHRISTEN THEE SATELLITE!

WE RECEIVED A SPECIAL COMMISSION FROM THE PRESIDENT HIMSELF.

--AND WHATEVER BEFALLS, MAY YOU UNFALTERINGLY UPHOLD THE HONOR OF EARTH!

THEN WE SHOT SKYWARD, ON OUR FORTY SEVEN MILLION MILE JOURNEY THROUGH SPACE, TOWARD MARS AND WE KNEW NOT WHAT!

382

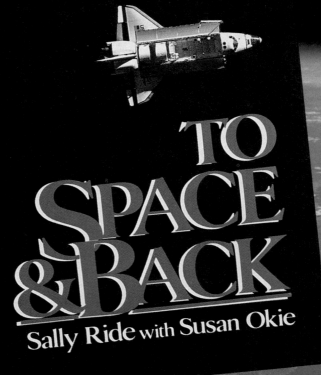

U.S. Astronaut Sally Ride
shares the adventure of outer space

ALA
NOTABLE BOOK
SLJ BEST BOOKS
OF THE YEAR

TO
SPACE
&BACK

Sally Ride with Susan Okie

My first space flight was in June 1983, with four other astronauts: Bob Crippen, Rick Hauck, John Fabian, and Norm Thagard. We went up in the space shuttle, the world's first spaceplane, which carries all of today's astronauts into space. We blasted off from a launch pad in Florida; then we circled the Earth for seven days. As we went around and around the planet, we launched two satellites, studied the Earth, and learned about weightlessness. After a week in orbit we returned to Earth. Our adventure ended as the space shuttle glided back through the atmosphere to a smooth landing in California.

Crip, Rick, John, Norm, and I have each had a chance to visit space again. We have found time on every trip to relax, enjoy weightlessness, and admire the view of the Earth and the stars. And, like all astronauts, we have found time to take pictures. The pictures help us to capture the excitement of our trip into space and share the adventure with our friends when we get back.

Most of the photographs in this book were taken by astronauts on board the space shuttle. Some were taken on my flights, some on other space shuttle flights. They will show you what it's like to eat from a spoon floating in midair, to put on a spacesuit for a walk in space, and to gaze at the Earth's oceans far below.

When I was growing up, I was always fascinated by the planets, stars, and galaxies, but I never thought about becoming an astronaut. I studied math and science in high school, and then I spent my years in college learning physics—the study of the laws of nature and the universe. Just as I was finishing my education, NASA, the United States space agency, began looking for scientists who wanted to become astronauts. Suddenly I knew that I wanted a chance to see the Earth and the stars from outer space. I sent my application to NASA, and after a series of tests and interviews, I was chosen to be an astronaut.

On January 28, 1986, this book was almost ready to go to the printer, when the unthinkable happened. The space shuttle *Challenger* exploded one minute after lift-off. After the accident I thought a lot about the book, and whether or not I wanted to change any part of it. I decided that nothing except the dedication and the words I write here should be changed.

I wrote this book because I wanted to answer some of the questions that young people ask of astronauts. Many of the questions are about feelings, and one that now may have added meaning is, "Is it scary?"

All adventures—especially into new territory—are scary, and there has always been an element of danger in space flight. I wanted to be an astronaut because I thought it would be a challenging opportunity. It was; it was also an experience that I shall never forget.
                                                                —*Sally Ride*

LAUNCH MORNING.

6 . . . 5 . . . 4 . . .

The alarm clock counts down.

3 . . . 2 . . . 1 . . .

Rrring! 3:15 A.M. *Launch minus four hours.* Time to get up.

It's pitch black outside. In four hours a space shuttle launch will light up the sky.

Nine miles from the launch pad, in the astronaut crew quarters, we put on our flight suits, get some last-minute information, and eat a light breakfast.

Launch minus three hours. It's still dark. We leave the crew quarters, climb into the astronaut van, and head for the launch pad.

The space shuttle stands with its nose pointed toward the sky, attached to the big orange fuel tank and two white rockets that will lift it—and us—into space.

The spotlights shining on the space shuttle light the last part of our route. Although we're alone, we know that thousands of people are watching us now, during the final part of the countdown.

When we step out onto the pad, we're dwarfed by the thirty-story-high space shuttle. Our spaceplane looked peaceful from the road, but now we can hear it hissing and gurgling as though it's alive.

The long elevator ride up the launch tower takes us to a level near the nose of the space shuttle, 195 feet above the ground. Trying hard not to look down at the pad far below, we walk out onto an access arm and into the "white room." The white room, a small white chamber at the end of the movable walkway, fits right next to the space shuttle's hatch. The only other people on the launch pad—in fact, the only other people for miles—are the six technicians waiting for us in the white room. They help us put on our escape harnesses and launch helmets and help us climb through the hatch. Then they strap us into our seats.

Because the space shuttle is standing on its tail, we are lying on our backs as we face the nose. It's awkward to twist around to look out the windows. The commander has a good view of the launch tower, and the pilot has a good view of the Atlantic Ocean, but no one else can see much outside.

Launch minus one hour. We check to make sure that we are strapped in properly, that oxygen will flow into our helmets, that our radio communication with Mission Control is working, and that our pencils and our books—the procedure manuals and checklists we'll need during lift-off—are attached to something to keep them from shaking loose. Then we wait.

The technicians close the hatch and then head for safety three miles away. We're all alone on the launch pad.

Launch minus seven minutes. The walkway with the white room at the end slowly pulls away. Far below us the power units start whirring, sending a shudder through the shuttle. We close the visors on our helmets and begin to breathe from the oxygen supply. Then the space shuttle quivers again as its launch engines slowly move into position for blast-off.

Launch minus 10 seconds . . . 9 . . . 8 . . . 7 . . . The three launch engines light. The shuttle shakes and strains at the bolts holding it to the launch pad. The computers check the engines. It isn't up to us anymore—the computers will decide whether we launch.

3 . . . 2 . . . 1 . . . The rockets light! The shuttle leaps off the launch pad in a cloud of steam and a trail of fire. Inside, the ride is rough and loud. Our heads are rattling around inside our helmets. We can barely hear the voices from Mission Control in our headsets above the thunder of the rockets and engines. For an instant I wonder if everything is working right. But there's no more time to wonder, and no time to be scared.

In only a few seconds we zoom past the clouds. Two minutes later the rockets burn out, and with a brilliant whitish-orange flash, they fall away from the shuttle as it streaks on toward space. Suddenly the ride becomes very, very smooth and quiet. The shuttle is still attached to the big tank, and the launch engines are pushing us out of Earth's atmosphere. The sky is black. All we can see of the trail of fire behind us is a faint, pulsating glow through the top window.

Launch plus six minutes. The force pushing us against the backs of our seats steadily increases. We can barely move because we're being held in place by a force of 3 g's—three times the force of gravity we feel on Earth. At first we don't mind it—we've all felt much more than that when we've done acrobatics in our jet training airplanes. But that lasted only a few seconds, and this seems to go on forever. After a couple of minutes of 3 g's, we're uncomfortable, straining to hold our books on our laps and craning our necks against the force to read the instruments. I find myself wishing we'd hurry up and get into orbit.

Launch plus eight and one-half minutes. The launch engines cut off. Suddenly the force is gone, and we lurch forward in our seats. During the next few minutes the empty fuel tank drops away and falls to Earth, and we are very busy getting the shuttle ready to enter orbit. But we're not too busy to notice that our books and pencils are floating in midair. We're in space!

The atmosphere thins gradually as we travel farther from Earth. At fifty miles up, we're above most of the air, and we're officially "in space." We aren't in orbit yet, though, and without additional push the shuttle would come crashing back to Earth.

We use the shuttle's smaller space engines to get us into our final, safe orbit about two hundred miles above Earth. In that orbit we are much higher than airplanes, which fly about six miles up, but much lower than weather satellites, which circle Earth more than twenty-two thousand miles up.

Once we are in orbit, our ride is very peaceful. The engines have shut down, and the only noise we hear is the hum of the fans that circulate our air. We are traveling at five miles a second, going around the Earth once every ninety minutes, but we don't feel the motion. We can't even tell we're moving unless we look out the window at Earth.

We stay much closer to home than the astronauts who flew space capsules to the moon in 1969. When those astronauts stood on the moon, they described the distant Earth as a big blue-and-white marble suspended in space. We are a long way from the moon, and we never get far enough from Earth to see the whole planet at once.

We still have a magnificent view. The sparkling blue oceans and bright orange deserts are glorious against the blackness of space. Even if we can't see the whole planet, we can see quite a distance. When we are over Los Angeles we can see as far as Oregon; when we are over Florida we can see New York.

We see mountain ranges reaching up to us and canyons falling away. We see huge dust storms blowing over deserts in Africa and smoke spewing from the craters of active volcanoes in Hawaii. We see enormous chunks of ice floating in the Antarctic Ocean and electrical storms raging over the Atlantic.

Sunrises and sunsets are spectacular from orbit. Since we see one sunrise and one sunset each time we go around the Earth, we can watch sixteen sunrises and sixteen sunsets every twenty-four hours. Our sightseeing doesn't stop while we are over the dark

side of the planet. We can see twinkling city lights, the reflection of the moon in the sea, and flashes of lightning from thunderstorms.

These natural features are not the only things we can see. We can also spot cities, airport runways, bridges, and other signs of civilization. When our orbit takes us over Florida, we are even able to see the launch pad at Cape Canaveral, where we crawled into the space shuttle just hours earlier.

Astronauts are sent into space to launch new satellites into orbit, to return orbiting satellites to Earth, to fix broken satellites, and to perform many different types of scientific experiments.

The space shuttle carries satellites into orbit in its cargo bay. Satellites may be as small as a basketball or as large as a bus. Most are designed to be released from the spaceplane; a few are retrieved before the shuttle returns to Earth, but generally they are left in orbit to do their jobs. Some relay television signals across the country, some point telescopes at distant stars, and some aim weather cameras back at Earth.

It is not an easy job to launch a satellite. Before a flight, astronauts practice every step over and over so that they will be able to release the satellite at exactly the right time, at exactly the right spot over the Earth, and with the shuttle pointing in exactly the right direction. During the countdown to the satellite launch, the crew works as a team—a very well trained team working very closely together. Each astronaut "plays a position" on the flight deck: two are seated (wearing seatbelts to avoid floating away from the computers at a critical moment), one is near the windows, and one is floating behind the seats near the satellite switches.

What kind of scientific experiments do we conduct in space? We observe the stars and the Earth from our position two hundred miles up. On some flights we carry telescopes outside in the cargo bay. Because our orbit is above the atmosphere, these telescopes get a clearer view of the sun, stars, planets, and galaxies than any telescope on Earth. On some flights we carry sensitive cameras to take pictures of the land, sea, and weather back on Earth. Information gathered at shuttle height can help scientists study storms, air pollution, and volcanic eruptions and learn more about the planet we live on.

Inside the space shuttle, astronauts perform experiments exploring ways to make new substances—medicines, metals, or crystals—in weightlessness. We also record data about our own bodies to help scientists understand the effects of weightlessness. Before astronauts can set out on a two-year trip to Mars, scientists must be able to predict what will happen to people who stay in space that long.

THE DAY BEFORE THE SHUTTLE RETURNS TO EARTH, astronauts have to put away all loose equipment. Cameras, food trays, and books will stay attached to the ceiling or walls with Velcro as long as they are weightless, but they would come crashing to the floor if we left them out during re-entry. We drift around collecting things and stowing them in drawers. An amazing number of lost pencils and books turn up floating behind wall and ceiling panels.

Immediately after launch we folded and put away all but two of our seats to give us more room inside. Now we have to reattach them to the floor so we can sit in them during re-entry. We must also find the suits, boots, helmets, and life vests that we haven't worn since launch and put them on again for landing. It is often hard to remember where we stored everything. Once I almost had to come back to Earth barefoot because I had forgotten where I had put my boots!

Four or five hours before landing, we begin to drink liquid—four or more big glasses each—and take salt pills to keep the liquid in our bodies. We have to do this because our bodies have gotten rid of some water during the flight to adjust to weightlessness. Now we are about to feel Earth's gravity again, and if we do not replace the lost fluid ahead of time, we will feel very thirsty and lightheaded—and maybe even pass out—as gravity pulls the fluid in our bodies toward our legs.

We also put on "g-suits," pants that can be inflated to keep the blood from pooling in our legs. If we begin to feel lightheaded as we re-enter the atmosphere, a sign that not enough blood is reaching the brain, we can inflate our g-suits.

Finally we strap ourselves into our seats, connect our helmets to the oxygen supply, and fire the shuttle's small space engines. This "de-orbit burn" slows the shuttle down and brings us back into Earth's atmosphere. Once the engines are fired to start re-entry, there is no turning back.

The space shuttle re-enters the atmosphere about thirty minutes later. It is moving very fast, and as it collides with molecules of gas in the air it becomes very hot—in places, over twenty-five hundred degrees Fahrenheit. Only the special heat tiles glued on the outside of the spaceplane keep it from melting. The tiles protect the shuttle so well that inside we do not even feel the heat. But we can tell that it is very hot outside, because all we can see through the windows is a bright, flickering orange glow from the hot air around us.

After we have traveled a short distance down into the atmosphere, we begin to hear the rushing of wind as we shoot through the thin air. We feel a little vibration, like what passengers might feel on a slightly bumpy airplane ride. Gravity slowly begins pulling us into our seats, and we start to feel heavier and heavier. Since we are used to weightless books, pencils, arms, and heads, all these things now seem very heavy to us. It's an effort even to lift a hand.

As the shuttle falls farther down into the atmosphere, it flies less and less like a spacecraft and more and more like an airplane. It gradually stops using its small space jets to maneuver and starts using the control surfaces on its tail and wings instead. These surfaces were useless in the vacuum of space, but they become more effective as the air thickens. When the shuttle is about as low as most airplanes fly, it is only a few miles from the runway and is traveling below the speed of sound. At this point it is flying like a glider—an airplane with no engines.

Until this stage of re-entry the computers have been flying the spaceplane, but now the commander takes control. We approach the runway much more steeply than we would in an ordinary airplane, and we feel almost as if we're flying straight down. We slide forward in our seats, held back only by our shoulder harnesses, as the shuttle dives toward the ground. The pilot lowers the landing gear when the spaceplane is only a few hundred feet above the ground. The landing gear slows us down, but we still land at about two hundred miles per hour—quite a bit faster than most airplanes. The rear wheels touch the runway first, so gently that inside we can't even be sure we've landed. Then the nose wheel comes down with a hard thump, and we know we're back on Earth.

The space shuttle rolls to a stop. As I unstrap myself from my seat and try to stand up, I am amazed at how heavy my whole body feels. My arms, my head, my neck—each part of me seems to be made of lead. It is hard to stand straight, it is hard to lift my legs to walk, and it is hard to carry my helmet and books. I start down the ladder from the flight deck to the mid-deck—the same ladder that was unnecessary just an hour ago—and I have to concentrate just to place my feet on the rungs. My muscles are nearly as strong as they were before the one-week space flight, but my brain expects everything to be light and easy to lift.

My heart, too, has gotten used to weightlessness. For several days, it has not had to pump blood up from my legs against gravity. Now it is working harder again, and for several minutes after we land it beats much faster than normal.

My sense of balance also needs to adjust to gravity. For a few minutes I feel dizzy every time I move my head. I have trouble keeping my balance or walking in a straight line for about fifteen minutes after landing.

We stay inside the spaceplane for a little while to give ourselves a chance to get over these strange sensations. We do knee bends and practice walking while the ground crew moves a boarding platform over to the shuttle and opens the hatch. Then a doctor comes on board to make sure everyone is in shape to get off. We are all still a little wobbly, but about thirty minutes after landing we are ready to climb out of the space shuttle and walk down the stairs to the runway.

Once my feet are on the ground, I look back and admire the space shuttle. I take a few moments to get used to being back on Earth and to say goodbye to the plane that took us to space and back.

What did you learn about a space shuttle launch and flight that you didn't know before?

When, do you think, are the most dangerous times for astronauts during shuttle flights?

Describe the changes that the astronauts' bodies go through upon their return to Earth.

How does Sally Ride feel about space flight? What in her story makes you believe that?

WRITE Would you want to blast off in the space shuttle? Write a paragraph explaining why you would or would not want to be part of a shuttle crew.

Space Flights

Think about how the selections provide contrast to one another. How does what we really know about space and space travel differ from what we enjoy imagining about them?

WRITER'S WORKSHOP

Many writers have been inspired to write about space or space exploration. Some write stories; some write poems. Think of a topic about space or space travel that is fascinating to you. Then write a poem that expresses your feelings about your topic.

Writer's Choice
You have read how space flights can be dangerous as well as thrilling. What do you think of space flights? Respond in some way to the theme. Share your writing with your classmates.

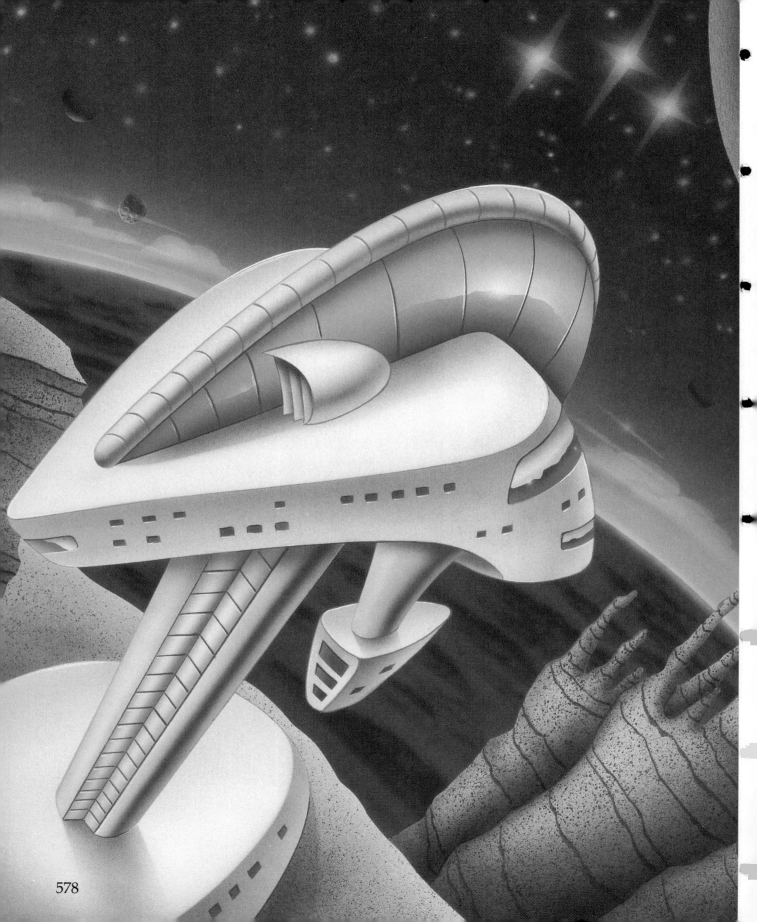

THEME

Beyond the Solar System

Many authors have written about people going on spaceships to colonize other planets. But what if a disaster destroyed our own planet? Would we have enough spaceships to take us away from here? Would we have any other place to go?

CONTENTS

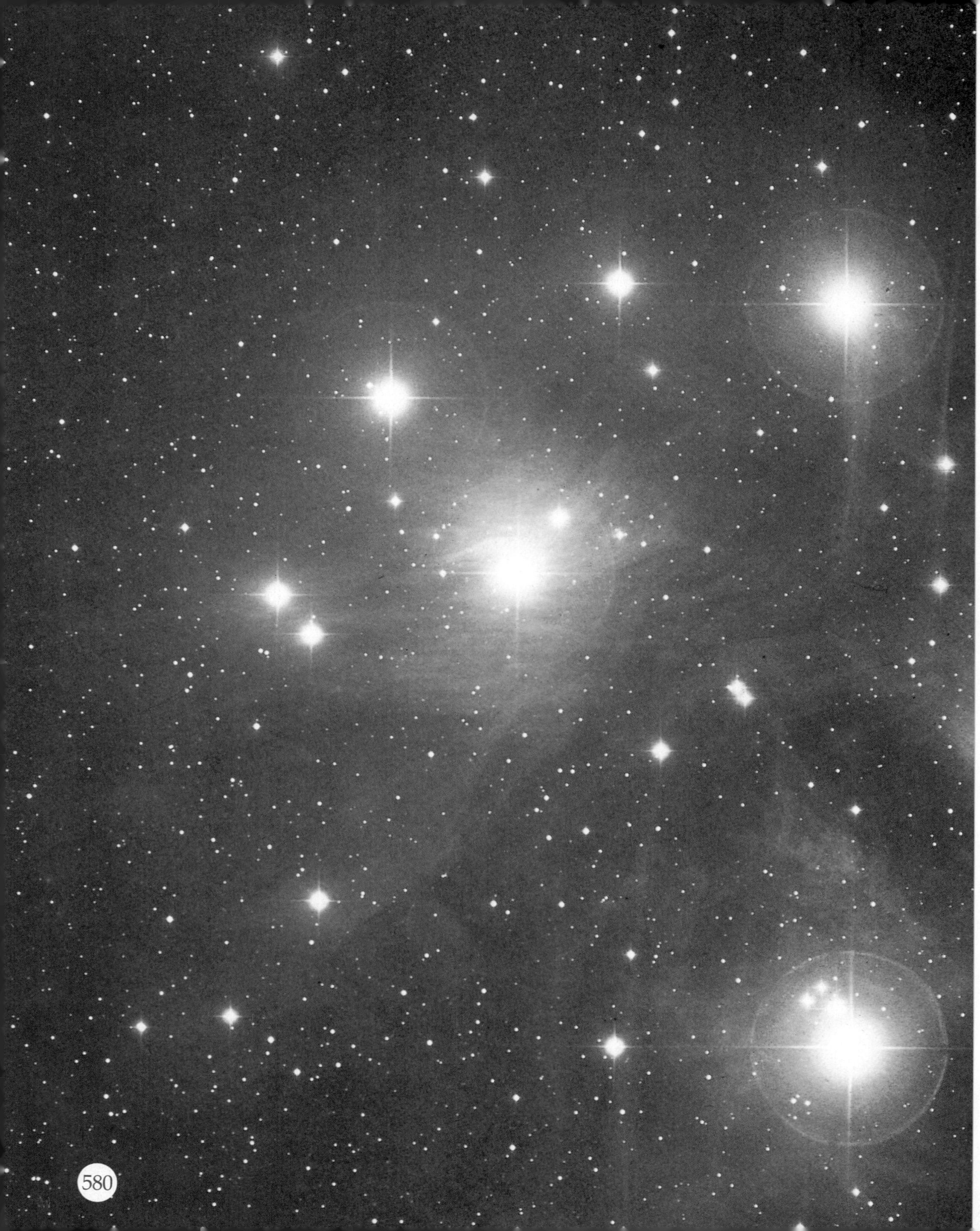

SECRETS

from
Space Songs
by Myra Cohn Livingston

AWARD-WINNING
AUTHOR

Space keeps its secrets
hidden.

It does not tell.

Are black holes time machines?
Where do lost comets go?

Is Pluto moon or planet?

How many, how vast
unknown galaxies beyond us?

Do other creatures
dwell   on distant spheres?

Will we ever know?

Space is silent.

It seldom answers.

But we ask.

THE
GREEN BOOK

JILL PATON WALSH

SLJ BEST BOOKS
OF THE YEAR

Will Pattie and her family survive on the planet Shine?

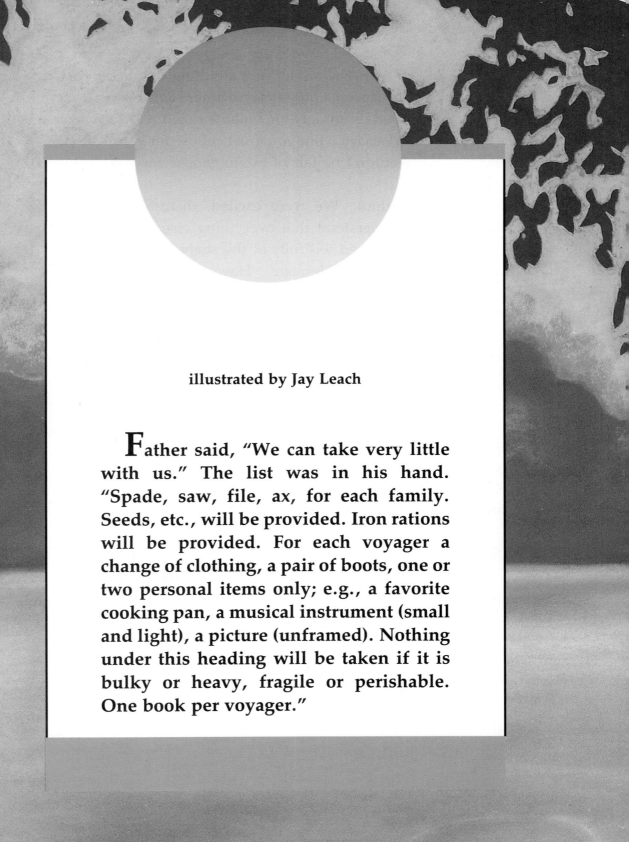

illustrated by Jay Leach

Father said, "We can take very little with us." The list was in his hand. "Spade, saw, file, ax, for each family. Seeds, etc., will be provided. Iron rations will be provided. For each voyager a change of clothing, a pair of boots, one or two personal items only; e.g., a favorite cooking pan, a musical instrument (small and light), a picture (unframed). Nothing under this heading will be taken if it is bulky or heavy, fragile or perishable. One book per voyager."

It was easy to pack. We were allowed so little, and we didn't have to bother about leaving anything tidy behind us. Only the books caused a little delay. Father said, "I must take this." He showed us an ugly big volume called *A Dictionary of Intermediate Technology*. "But you must choose for yourselves," he said. "It wouldn't be fair of me to choose for you. Think carefully."

We didn't think. We were excited, disturbed, and we hadn't really understood that everything else would be left behind. Father looked wistfully at the shelves. He picked up *The Oxford Complete Shakespeare.* "Have you all chosen your books?" he asked. "Yes," we told him. He put the Shakespeare back.

We had time to waste at the end. We ate everything we could find.

"I don't want to eat iron," Pattie said, but nobody knew what she meant.

Then Father got out the slide projector, and showed us pictures of holidays we had once had. We didn't think much of them.

"Have they all gone brownish with age, Dad?" said Joe, our brother, the eldest of us.

"No," said Father. "The pictures are all right. It's the light that has changed. It's been getting colder and bluer now for years . . . but when I was young it was this lovely golden color, just like this—look."

But what he showed us—a beach, with a blue sea, and the mother we couldn't remember lying on a towel, reading a book—looked a funny hue, as though someone had brushed it over with a layer of treacle.

Pattie was glad that Father wasn't going to be able to take the slide projector. It made him sad.

And the next day we all went away, Father and Joe, and Sarah, and Pattie, and lots of other families, and left the Earth far behind.

When this happened, we were all quite young, and Pattie was so young that later she couldn't remember being on the Earth at all, except those few last hours, and even the journey was mostly forgotten. She could remember the beginning of the journey, because it was so exciting. When we could undo our seat belts, and look out of the windows, the world looked like a Chinese paper lantern, with painted lands upon it, and all the people on the ship looked at it, and some of the grownups cried. Father didn't cry; he didn't look, either.

Joe went and talked to Father by and by, but Sarah and Pattie stood at a porthole all day long, and saw the world shrink and shrink and diminish down till it looked like a round cloudy glass marble that you could have rolled on the palm of your hand. Pattie was looking forward to going past the moon, but that was no fun at all, for the ship passed by the dark side and we saw nothing of it. And then we were flying in a wide black starry sky, where none of the stars had names.

At first there were voices from the world below, but not for long. The Disaster from which we were escaping happened much sooner than they had thought it would, and after two days the ship was flying in radio silence, alone, and navigating with a calculator program on the computer, and a map of magnetic fields.

The journey was very boring. It was so long. The spaceship was big enough to frighten us when we thought of it flying through the void. Joe kept telling Pattie not to worry. "Heavy things *don't* fall down in space," he told her. "There's nowhere for them to fall; no gravity."

"When I knock things over, they fall down, just like at home," Pattie said, doubtfully.

"That's just the ship's gravity machine, making it happen inside the ship," said Joe. "To make us feel normal."

But the ship was *small* enough to frighten us too, when we thought of spending years inside it. "We will still be here when I'm fourteen!" said Joe, as though he found that as hard to believe as Pattie found the lack of gravity.

"Better get used to it, then," said Sarah. We had pills to make us sleep a lot of the time, but the rules said everyone had to be awake some of each forty-eight hours. When people were awake, they played games, which were all on the ship's computer and could be played with the video screens. And one of the grownups had even brought along as his special luxury a funny hand set for playing chess which let you play it with another person instead of with the computer. When we weren't playing games, we could read the books we had brought. Joe asked Father why there were no books to read on the computer screens.

Father told us that all the new, well-equipped spaceships belonged to big wealthy countries. They had flown off to find distant, promising-looking planets. "We were the bottom of the barrel," he said, "the last few to go from an old and poorer country, and only an old ship available, and no time to outfit it properly. Our computer was intended for exploration journeys, not for colonization. It has no spare memory; it can barely manage our minimum needs. And there was so little fuel we couldn't get lift-off with anything extra on board—no useful livestock, like sheep or cows; just ourselves, and what the organizers thought we needed for survival. But we are lucky to be away at all, remember, and they allocated us a much nearer destination so that our old ship could get us somewhere."

There were some chickens in cages on the ship, with two very noisy cocks who had lost their sense of timing in the flight through darkness and crowed at all the wrong times when we were trying to sleep. And there were rabbits too; we could let them out and play with them. Rabbits are fun when you are very small and like furry things, but they aren't much fun, really. You can't teach them tricks. All they ever think about is munching. And when we got bored with rabbits, all we had was that one book each to go back to. Of course, we tried to read slowly. "Read each sentence at least twice, before you read another," the rule books said, under "Helpful Suggestions." But Sarah couldn't read that slowly. At home she read four or five books every week. She finished her book quickly and then wanted to borrow Pattie's.

Pattie wouldn't let her. So she swapped with Joe, and read his. He had brought *Robinson Crusoe.* Sarah didn't much like *Robinson Crusoe.*

"You'd better think about him, old girl," Joe said to her. "That island is just like where we're going, and we have to scratch a living on it, just like Crusoe."

Joe didn't like Sarah's book any better than she liked his. Hers was called *The Pony Club Rides Again.* Joe didn't like horses, and he couldn't resist telling Sarah that, after all, she would never see a horse again as long as she lived.

So then they both wanted to borrow Pattie's book. Pattie wouldn't lend it. "I haven't finished it myself yet," she kept saying. "It's not fair. You finished yours before you had to lend it."

In the end, Father made her give it to them. It was thin and neat, with dark green silky boards covered with gold tooling. The edges of the pages were gilded and shiny. It had a creamy silk ribbon to mark the place, and pretty brown and white flowered endpapers. And it was quite empty.

"There's nothing in it!" cried Sarah, staring.

"It's a commonplace book," said Joe.

"What's that?" asked Sarah.

"A sort of jotter, notebook thing, for thoughts you want to keep."

"And she's been pretending to read it for months!" said Sarah, beginning to giggle. They both laughed and laughed. Other people came by and asked what the joke was. Everyone laughed.

"Oh, Pattie, dear child," said Father when he heard about it. He didn't laugh, he looked a mixture between sad and cross.

"It was my choose," said Pattie very fiercely, taking her book back and holding it tight.

Father said, "She was too young. I should have chosen for her. But no use crying over spilt milk."

We did get used to being on the ship, in the end. A funny thing happened to the way people felt about it. At first, everyone had hated it, grumbled all the time about tiny cubicles, about no exercise, about nothing to do. They had quarreled a lot. Grownup quarreling isn't very nice. We were luckier than most families; we didn't seem to quarrel, though we got very cross and scratchy about things, just like other people. But time went by, and people settled down to playing games, and sleeping, and talking a little, and got used to it, and so when at last everyone had had four birthdays on the ship, and the journey had been going on for what seemed like forever and ever, and the Guide told us all there were only months to go now, people were worried instead of glad.

"We shall be lucky if we can walk more than three steps, we're so flabby," said Father, and people began to do pushups in their cabins, and line up for a turn on the cycle machine for exercising legs.

589

Joe began to ask a lot of questions. He didn't like the answers he got and he talked to Pattie and Sarah about it after lights-out in sleeping times. "They just don't know what this place is going to be like," he told them. "They *think* it should support life; they know there is plant growth on it, and they suppose that means we could grow wheat. But there may be wild animals, or any kind of monster people on it already, they don't know."

"Couldn't there possibly be wild ponies, Joe?" said Sarah.

"No, sis, I don't think so," said Joe, very kindly. "And if this place isn't any good, we can't go anywhere else. The fuel won't last."

* * * * *

A time came when we reached the light of a new sun. Bright golden light filled the spaceship from the starboard portholes. The cocks woke up and crowed as if for all the missing mornings on the whole long trip. The sun warmed the ship, and made it hard to sleep at sleeping time. And then the new planet loomed up on the starboard side. It looked unlike the Earth, said the grownups, who could remember what the Earth had looked like. It was redder and shinier; it had no cloud drifts around it. When it got near, it looked like maps in bright colors. It didn't look green. People spent all day looking anxiously through the portholes at it, trying to guess the meaning of what they could see. Just before touchdown, we could all see a land with mountains, craggy and rocky, and large lakes lying on the land surface everywhere; but as the ship came in to land, nightfall was racing us across the ground—a big black shadow, engulfing everything, moving faster than we were ourselves, its crescent edge going at a dizzy speed, and leaving us behind, so that we landed in total darkness. It was an auto-control landing anyway. It happened smoothly. The ship landed at a steep angle, but immediately straightened up by leveling its podlike legs. Then it switched off its own gravity and hummed quietly into run-down cycles.

When the gravity machine switched off, everyone felt lightheaded, and, indeed, light. The planet's own gravity was less than the ship had got us used to. Pattie found she could jump up and touch her cabin roof, and land without thudding enough to make anyone cross. Everyone felt full of energy, and eagerness to get out. But the Guide said the ship must be kept locked till daylight. So little was known, it would be dangerous to go out.

Arthur, the head of one of the families, said he would go and have a look, at his own risk, and then the Guide spoke to us very sternly.

"It's natural to feel excited," he said. "But this is not a holiday. We are a handpicked group; we are the minimum number that can possibly survive and multiply. Between us we have the skills we require. But the loss of a single member of our party will endanger the survival of us all. There is no such thing, Arthur, as 'your own risk.' Not any more. And may we all remember that."

We sat around, fidgeting, restless, talking together in lowered voices, waiting for dawn. None of the games interested us now. Pattie couldn't sleep, though Father made her lie down on her bunk. The feeling of suspense, the unfamiliar rhythm of the machines running themselves toward shutdown, the altered pitch of the voices around her kept her awake so late, so long, that when dawn broke at last she was fast asleep and did not see it.

But Sarah told her it had come like a dark curtain being swept aside in a single rapid movement; for a few minutes there was a deep indigo light, and after that, brilliance.

The Guide walked around the ship, looking out of each porthole in turn. All that he could see was rocks, white and gray, rather glittery crags, all very near the ship, blocking any distant view. They gave Arthur a breathing mask and put him through the inner door to the ship's main hatch, closing it behind him before he opened the outer door. He came back very quickly. "Come out," he said. "The air is good."

592

So we trooped down the ramp and found ourselves in the shadow of the ship, in a narrow gully between one rock face and another. It seemed to be a sort of hanging valley in a hill. A tiny runnel of flowing clear liquid threaded between rocks in the bottom of the dip, over a bed of silver-white sand and pebbles. Malcolm, the party's chemist, took a sample of the stream in a little specimen bottle, to test it.

Pattie was so sleepy after the night before that she could hardly walk, and Father picked her up and carried her, nodding with drowsiness, rather than leave her alone in the ship. She went in his arms, up the slope toward a gentle saddle between one side of the valley and the other, where all the others were walking. It was easy to walk, even up the slope; Pattie felt light and easy to carry. So up we all went to the rim of the hollow, and looked over.

Before us lay a wide and gentle plain sloping to the shores of a round wide lake some miles across. Beyond the lake, a very high mountain with perfectly symmetrical slopes rose into the sky, topped with snow. A mirror image of the lovely mountain hung inverted in the lake, quite still, for the surface was like glass, perfectly unruffled by even the slightest impulse of the air. The surface of the plain was gray and silver, shining like marcasite in places, in others with a pewter sheen. To the left and right of the plain, on gentle hills, were wide sweeps of woodland, with quite recognizable and normal trees, except that the leaves upon them were not green but shades of red, and shining, like the blaze of an amazing autumn. It was very beautiful, and perfectly silent, and perfectly still.

The children ran forward onto the open expanse of land before them, shouting. And at once we were limping, crying, and hopping back. We were still wearing the soft ship slippers we had been given to keep down the noise in the corridors of the spacecraft, and the pretty gray grass and flowers had cut through the thin leather at once, and cut our feet. The Guide ordered the crate of boots to be brought from the store and unpacked. Someone fetched ointment and bandages. Meanwhile, we stooped and picked the sharp plants, which broke easily in our fingers when gathered; they seemed to be made of glass, sharp and shining like jewels. But as soon as we all had boots on, we could walk over them safely, for the growth was crushed beneath the soles, as fragile and as crunchy to walk on as the frost-stiffened grass of winter on Earth.

We all walked over the crisp and sparkling frost plain, down toward the shores of the lake. It took an hour to reach it. The lake shore was a wide silver beach, made of soft bright sand, like grains of worn-down glass. And all the time we walked toward the lake, it did not move, or ruffle, even enough to shake the curtains of reflected mountain and reflected sky that hung in it. And though the air smelled good and sweet to breathe, it was windless, and as still as the air in a deep cave underground. Only the little rivulet that followed us across to the lake from the crag valley where the ship had lodged moved; it chuckled gently from stone to stone, and sparkled as brightly as the glass leaves and grass. When we got to the beach, Pattie went to look where it joined the lake, to see if it would make some splash or ripples for just a little way, but it seemed to slide beneath the surface at once and made only the faintest ripple ring, quickly dying in the brilliant mirror of the lake.

"I think we may be lucky," said the Guide. "I think this place is good."

People laughed, and some of the grownups kissed each other. The children ran to the edge of the lake and made it splash. Jason's mother ran along the beach, calling to the wading children not to drink from the lake until Malcolm had made sure it was water. Everyone was thirsty from walking, and the lake looked clear and good, but we all obediently drank from the flagons of recycled water from the ship.

"Right," said the Guide. "We shall begin the settlement program. And first we need to name the place we are about to build. The instructions suggest that the youngest person present should give the name. That can't include the real babies, obviously; Pattie or Jason—which is the youngest?"

Jason's mother and Pattie's father spoke together.

"It is Pattie, by a few days," said Father. "Well, Pattie, where are we?"

"We are at Shine, on the first day," said Pattie, solemnly.

"Good girl," said the Guide. "This place, then, is Shine. And now we must all work, and fast, for we do not know how long the days are here, or what dangers there may be." And he began to hand out jobs to each one in turn.

So people went back to the ship to unload the land truck, fill it with tents and food and sleeping bags, and bring them to the shore. Malcolm went to complete his tests for water. A work party was formed to unload the land hopper and put it together. The land hopper would glide or fly just above the ground, and let us explore quickly, and then it would run out of fuel and be of no more use. And the Guide had two men standing with guns ready, one each side of the camping ground, in case of wild beasts, or enemies.

"In science fiction, bullets go right through things and they come right on anyway, roaring, *urrrrrr*!" said Jason. "And we're in science fiction now, aren't we, so what good are guns?"

"We are in Shine," said Pattie. "And no monsters will come." Jason hadn't talked to her much on the flight; he was much shorter than she, and he thought she was older. But now he had found that, although she was taller, she was younger, and he got friendlier.

There was no job for either, so they watched Joe setting up a tally stick. It was a huge plastic post with rows and rows of holes in it, and black pegs to move in the holes.

"What's it for, Joe?" they asked.

"It's a calendar," said Joe. "We have to count the days here, or we'll lose track. All the things on the ship will run down and stop working—clocks, calculators, everything. So this thing just keeps a count—you move one hole for each day. You move the peg, and you remember when you are."

"A tree of days," said Pattie.

The grownups brought a stove from the ship, and a can of fuel, and set it up to cook supper on the beach, for the sand was soft and easy to sit and walk on, unlike the gray glass grass. A ring of tents went up around the stove. Malcolm decided that the little stream and the huge lake were both good water, fit to drink—and after the stale recycled water we had been drinking for so long, how fresh and clean and cool the lake water tasted! Everyone laughed again, and passed the cups from hand to hand, exclaiming.

The Guide said they must set a guard over the camp all night. "Any kind of living thing, harmless or savage, may be here," he said. The wilderness seemed so beautiful and so still it was hard to believe that, but they chose five of the men to take turns on watch.

And only just in time, for soon after the watch was chosen, the night came upon us. A curtain of deep lilac light swept across the lake, obscuring the sight of the mountain, and sinking almost at once to a deepening purple, then inky darkness. It got dark much quicker that it would have done on Earth—in less than half an hour. The darkness was complete for a moment or two; and then as our eyes got used to it, it was

596

pierced by hundreds of bright and unknown stars—nameless constellations shining overhead. People began to spread their bedding in the tents, and to settle to sleep, and as they did so, a gust of air shook the tent walls, and there was a sighing sound of wind in the woods, and a lapping of water on the shore close by, unseen in the dark. And then the air was quite still again, and it began to rain, heavily and steadily, though the stars were still bright and clear above. When Pattie fell asleep she could hear Father and Malcolm talking together in low voices at the other end of the tent.

"There must be no dust at all in this atmosphere," said Malcolm. "That would scatter light and delay the dark. No wonder it feels so invigorating to breathe."

Father took his turn on watch, but nothing stirred all night, he said. The rain stopped in an hour or so, and not so much as a gust of air moved anywhere around. At the sudden return of daylight, all was well.

Would you want to set out on a four-year voyage to an unknown planet? Explain your answer.

Who are the people on the spaceship? Why are they making this journey to another planet?

Will people be allowed to do things their own way on the planet Shine? Why or why not?

What are the most important tasks facing the travelers once they land on their new planet?

WRITE   The children are allowed to take only one book apiece on the journey. Write a paragraph explaining what book you would take and why.

Words About the AUTHOR:
Jill Paton Walsh

AWARD-WINNING
AUTHOR

Jill Paton Walsh grew up in London, England, during World War II. It was a time of danger, upset, and change for the whole world—especially for children.

Ms. Walsh was born with Erb's palsy, which causes her right hand to be weak. When she was little, people thought she could not do many things and that she would have trouble learning easily in school. But young Jill found out she could do most things if she tried. In fact, when people thought she couldn't do something, it made her want to do that thing even more. Over the years, Ms. Walsh has learned there are only a few things she cannot do. She cannot lift heavy things from high shelves or be a

bell-ringer or put curlers in her hair. But these things are not important to her. What are important are all the things she is able to do despite her weak hand.

Ms. Walsh graduated from Great Britain's famous Oxford University. Then she got married and became a teacher. She quit teaching when her first baby was born, but soon she was bored. She got an old typewriter and began to write children's books. Why children's books? She says, "It never occurred to me to write any other kind." Even when she was a busy mother of three, she continued to write them because "you always have the time for what you really want to do."

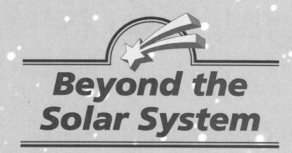

Beyond the Solar System

How did you picture outer space as described by Jill Paton Walsh in "The Green Book"? Compare your mental picture to the artist's illustration of outer space for "Secrets."

WRITER'S WORKSHOP

Many stories, movies, and television shows have outer space as their setting. They have unique characters and plots to go along with this setting. Think of your own unusual characters and plot for an outer-space setting. Then write a play in which your characters solve an exciting problem that they might encounter in space.

Writer's Choice
You have read about an imaginary trip to an imaginary planet beyond our solar system. Think about the new frontier beyond our solar system. Write down your thoughts, and come up with a way to share your response with your classmates.

CONNECTIONS

Multicultural Connection

Ancient Astronomers

Humans studied the heavens long before they believed it possible to explore them. Among the earliest and cleverest astronomers were those of ancient Egypt, in North Africa.

The Egyptians made maps of the night sky, identifying the paths of the moving stars. Their observations led them to create the most accurate of the early calendars. It had twelve months, each with thirty days, along with five extra days in each year. They also divided day and night into twelve equal parts of time and invented a very exact water clock.

Besides astronomy, these Egyptians excelled in engineering, medicine, agriculture, and many arts. They developed one of the greatest civilizations of the ancient world.

With your classmates, create a bulletin board display that shows the knowledge and the methods of early astronomers. Research such groups as the Anasazi, Aztec, Maya, Olmec, Pawnee, Tairona, Arabs, Babylonians, Chinese, Greeks, Romans, (east) Indians, and Khmer.

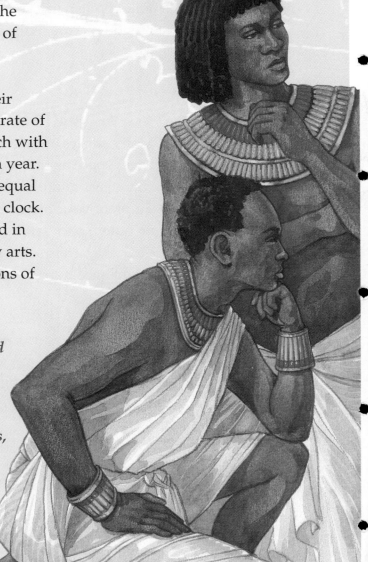

Social Studies Connection

Space Explorers

Since people first studied the sky long ago, we have gradually learned more about it. Research an astronomer, a pilot, an inventor, or an astronaut who helped add to our knowledge of the heavens. Share what you learn by writing a news story about this person.

Science Connection

Your Own Sky Chart

The winter nighttime sky is different from the summer nighttime sky. Find out how and why star positions change over a year. Look for interesting and unusual facts. In an oral report to your classmates, share what you have learned.

Astronaut
Guy Bluford

Aviator
Amelia Earhart

GLOSSARY

The **pronunciation** of each word in this glossary is shown by a phonetic respelling in brackets—for example, [ak′rə·bat′iks]. An accent mark (′) follows the syllable with the most stress: [pes′kē]. A secondary, or lighter, accent mark (′) follows a syllable with less stress: [i·vap′ə·rā′shən]. The key to other pronunciation symbols is below. You will find a shortened version of this key on alternate pages of the glossary.

Pronunciation Key*

a	add, map	m	move, seem	u	up, done
ā	ace, rate	n	nice, tin	û(r)	burn, term
â(r)	care, air	ng	ring, song	yōo	fuse, few
ä	palm, father	o	odd, hot	v	vain, eve
b	bat, rub	ō	open, so	w	win, away
ch	check, catch	ô	order, jaw	y	yet, yearn
d	dog, rod	oi	oil, boy	z	zest, muse
e	end, pet	ou	pout, now	zh	vision, pleasure
ē	equal, tree	o͝o	took, full	ə	the schwa, an
f	fit, half	o͞o	pool, food		unstressed vowel
g	go, log	p	pit, stop		representing the
h	hope, hate	r	run, poor		sound spelled
i	it, give	s	see, pass		a in *above*
ī	ice, write	sh	sure, rush		e in *sicken*
j	joy, ledge	t	talk, sit		i in *possible*
k	cool, take	th	thin, both		o in *melon*
l	look, rule	t̶h̶	this, bathe		u in *circus*

*The Pronunciation Key, adapted entries, and the Short Key that appear on the following pages are reprinted from *HBJ School Dictionary*. Copyright © 1990 by Harcourt Brace & Company. Reprinted by permission of Harcourt Brace & Company.

A

a·bate [ə·bāt′] *v.* **a·bat·ed, a·bat·ing** To gradually become less.

ab·er·ra·tion [ab′ə·rā′shən] *n.* A departure from what is right, correct, or natural: **A four-leaf clover is an** *aberration* **of nature.**

a·brupt·ly [ə·brupt′lē] *adv.* Suddenly: **Felix** *abruptly* **stopped singing when he forgot the words.**

a·bun·dant [ə·bun′dənt] *adj.* Very plentiful: **Tomatoes from the garden were so** *abundant* **this year that we couldn't eat them all.** *syn.* ample

ac·ro·bat·ics [ak′rə·bat′iks] *n.* Showy, skillful, and difficult movements: **The monkeys were swinging from branch to branch and doing** *acrobatics* **in the treetops.** *syn.* gymnastics

a·dapt [ə·dapt′] *v.* **a·dapt·ed, a·dapt·ing** To change to fit certain conditions. *syns.* adjust, conform

ad·just [ə·just′] *v.* **ad·just·ed, ad·just·ing** To reposition or reset something. *syns.* re-arrange, regulate

al·le·giance [ə·lē′jəns] *n.* A strong support of something: **On some national holidays, we sing patriotic songs to show our pride in and our** *allegiance* **to our country.** *syns.* devotion, loyalty

al·lo·cate [al′ə·kāt′] *v.* **al·lo·cat·ed, al·lo·cat·ing** To set something apart for a spe-cial use: **Mr. Flores** *allocated* **a part of his garden for beans and a part for peppers and tomatoes.**

am·a·teur [am′ə·choͦor *or* am′ə·t(y)oͦor] *adj.* For enjoy-ment rather than money; not professional: **Joyce plays in an** *amateur* **soccer league on weekends.**

am·ble [am′bəl] *v.* **am·bled, am·bling** To walk very slowly: **The young puppy scurried rapidly across the room, but its mother merely** *ambled.* *syn.* stroll

a·nat·o·my [ə·nat′ə·mē] *n.* The structure of a person, a plant, or an animal: **Doctors must understand human** *anatomy* **thoroughly.**

anx·ious·ly [angk′shəs·lē] *adv.* In a worried way: **We waited** *anxiously* **during my sister's surgery.** *syn.* uneasily

ap·pro·pri·ate [ə·prō′prē·it] *adj.* Right or proper; right to do at a certain time: **It is** *appropriate* **to send flowers when some-one is sick.** *syn.* suitable

ar·ti·fi·cial [är′tə·fish′əl] *adj.* Not made from nature: **Mr. Fernandez bought an** *artifi-cial* **Christmas tree for his family last year.**

as·bes·tos [as·bes′təs] *n.* A min-eral that will not burn or let heat pass through it: **Before it was found to be harmful to our lungs,** *asbestos* **was used to keep heat from escaping from homes.**

amateur Athletes who are paid for playing are called *professionals.* Those who take part in sports for the sheer love of it, with-out payment, are known as *amateurs.* Indeed, this word means "lover." It came into English by way of French from the Latin word *amare,* meaning "to love."

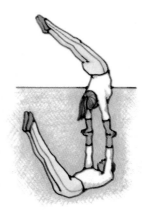

acrobatics

a	add	oͦo	took
ā	ace	oͦo	pool
â	care	u	up
ä	palm	û	burn
e	end	yoͦo	fuse
ē	equal	oi	oil
i	it	ou	pout
ī	ice	ng	ring
o	odd	th	thin
ō	open	th	this
ô	order	zh	vision

ə = { a in *above*   e in *sicken*
i in *possible*
o in *melon*   u in *circus* }

camouflage

cartwheel

chortle Sometimes writers like to coin, or invent, words. Once in a while, these words catch on with readers and become an everyday part of the language. In 1872, Lewis Carroll, the author of *Alice's Adventures in Wonderland*, coined the word *chortle*. Actually he took two words, *chuckle* and *snort*, and, as linguists say, "blended" them.

as·sure [ə·shŏŏr′] *v.* **as·sured, as·sur·ing** To make someone feel certain or convinced. *syn.* guarantee

a·stray [ə·strā′] *adv.* Off the correct path; away from the mark.

at·mos·phere [at′məs·fir] *n.* The air around the earth.

au·thor·ize [ô′thə·rīz′] *v.* **au·thor·ized, au·thor·iz·ing** To give the right or permission to do something: **Mr. Wilson** *authorized* **Carmello to take attendance before every meeting.**

au·to·mat·i·cal·ly [ô′tə·mat′ik·lē] *adv.* Like a machine; without trying or thinking first: **Lindell** *automatically* **washes his face every morning before getting dressed.**

B

beam [bēm] *v.* **beamed, beam·ing** To smile happily: **When the teacher praised his poem, Cesar** *beamed* **with pride.** *syn.* grin

beck·on [bek′ən] *v.* **beck·oned, beck·on·ing** To call by motioning silently or by sending a signal.

brack·ish [brak′ish] *adj.* Somewhat salty: **Thomas tasted the** *brackish* **water on his lips.**

C

ca·jole [kə·jōl′] *v.* **ca·joled, ca·jol·ing** To coax, plead, or persuade: **I hope Alex** *cajoles* **Mark into joining us.**

cam·ou·flage [kam′ə·fläzh′] *v.* **cam·ou·flaged, cam·ou·flag·ing** To hide by changing one's looks to blend in with the surroundings: **The soldier** *camouflaged* **herself in the woods by putting green, leafy tree branches on her helmet.**

car·a·van [kar′ə·van′] *n.* A group of people traveling together.

car·bo·hy·drate [kär′bō·hī′drāt′] *n.* An important class of foods, supplying energy to the body: **People all over the world eat bread, which provides them with** *carbohydrates.*

ca·reen [kə·rēn′] *v.* **ca·reened, ca·reen·ing** To sway or lean over to one side: **The speeding car hit a curb and then** *careened* **on two wheels, throwing the passenger across the seat.**

cart·wheel [kärt′(h)wēl′] *n.* A sideways flip that is done by springing the body onto one hand and then the other, followed by the feet: **The gymnast turned three** *cartwheels* **and landed perfectly on his feet.**

cha·grined [shə·grind′] *adj.* Upset because of disappointment or failure: **After she dropped the ball, Maria looked** *chagrined.*

chauf·feur [shō′fər] *n.* A person employed as a driver: **The contest winner will be picked up by a** *chauffeur* **in a limousine.**

chor·tle [chôr′təl] *v.* To make a chuckling or snorting noise. *syn.* chuckle

cir·cu·late [sûr′kyə·lāt′] *v.* To move about or around: **I opened the window to let the air** *circulate.*

cit·i·zen [sit′ə·zən] *n.* A person whose legal home is in a certain place: **Elena and Ramon became U.S.** *citizens* **six years after they moved from Mexico.**

civ·il de·fense [siv′əl di·fens′] *n.* Program for protecting the public from attack or disaster, such as a flood or tornado.

col·lide [kə·līd′] *v.* **col·lid·ed, col·lid·ing** To come together with great force: **The car raced through a red stoplight and** *collided* **with a truck.** *syns.* crash, smash

col·o·ni·za·tion [kol′ə·nə·zā′shən] *n.* The act of setting up homes in a new place with the purpose of living there a long time: **Some people believe we should consider** *colonization* **of the moon.**

com·mo·tion [kə·mō′shən] *n.* Noisy confusion: **The** *commotion* **was caused by raccoons trying to get into the garbage cans.** *syns.* disturbance, uproar, agitation

com·pli·ment [kom′plə·mənt] *n.* Praise; nice words said about someone: **Lucia gave her brother a** *compliment* **for the careful way he had planned the party.** *syn.* flattery

com·pound [kom·pound′] *v.* **com·pound·ed, com·pound·ing** To make by mixing together.

com·pute [kəm·pyoot′] *v.* **com·put·ed, com·put·ing** To figure mathematically. *syns.* calculate, reckon

con·ceal [kən·sēl′] *v.* To hide something.

con·jure [kon′jər *or* kun′jər] *v.* **con·jured, con·jur·ing** To seem to create by magic.

con·sis·tent [kən·sis′tənt] *adj.* Sticking to the same principles or ways of acting: **Julia's leadership with her playmates is** *consistent* **with her leadership with her classmates.**

con·tra·dict [kon′trə·dikt′] *v.* **con·tra·dict·ed, con·tra·dict·ing** To state the opposite of: **The defendant admits his guilt after an eyewitness** *contradicts* **his testimony.**

con·trap·tion [kən·trap′shən] *n. informal* An invention, such as a machine, that is odd and unusual: **Miguel built a** *contraption* **for watering his lawn from some wood, a hose, and a power lawn mower.**

cor·ri·dor [kôr′ə·dər] *n.* A long hallway or passageway with rooms opening onto it: **We walked down three** *corridors* **before we found our hotel room.**

cre·a·tiv·i·ty [krē′ā·tiv′ə·tē] *n.* The ability to make or invent things: *Creativity* **is a quality shared not only by artists and scientists but by anyone who is good at solving problems.** *syns.* originality, inventiveness

crim·i·nal [krim′ə·nəl] *adj.* Having to do with crime or those involved in crime.

crit·i·cal [krit′i·kəl] *adj.* Very important: **Completing every assignment is** *critical* **to your success.** *syns.* crucial, decisive

conceal

contraption If you created a device from assorted parts of different objects, you might refer to your invention as a *contraption*. Indeed, the word *contraption* is itself a kind of contraption: It is believed by some word experts to be a humorous blend of the words *contrive, trap,* and *invention.*

a	add	oo	took
ā	ace	ōō	pool
â	care	u	up
ä	palm	û	burn
e	end	yōō	fuse
ē	equal	oi	oil
i	it	ou	pout
ī	ice	ng	ring
o	odd	th	thin
ō	open	th	this
ô	order	zh	vision

ə = { a in *above*   e in *sicken*
i in *possible*
o in *melon*   u in *circus* }

605

debut When a rookie baseball player steps up to the plate for the first time in the major leagues, we say that he is making his *debut*. This is an especially appropriate use of *debut* because the word first appeared in the world of sports. It came from an Old French word, *desbuter*, meaning "to play first" in a game or sports match.

dedication

cul·prit [kul′prit] *n.* A person guilty of a crime or misdeed: **Based on the evidence, the police arrested him as the** *culprit.* *syn.* offender

cu·ri·os·i·ty [kyŏŏr′ē·os′ə·tē] *n.* The feeling of wanting to know about something: **Emiko's great** *curiosity* **about our school led her to ask many questions about our courses and teachers.**

cur·ric·u·lum [kə·rik′yə·ləm] *n.* The classes that a school requires or offers: **Math, reading, and science are part of the fifth-grade** *curriculum* **in our school.**

D

de·but [dā·byōō′ *or* dā′byōō′] *n.* A first appearance or performance before an audience.

de·cline [di·klīn′] *v.* **de·clined, de·clin·ing** To steadily become less: **Attendance at the football games has** *declined* **in the past year because the admission prices have risen.** *syn.* shrink

ded·i·ca·tion [ded′ə·kā′shən] *n.* **1** Devotion to something: **The doctor received an award for her** *dedication* **to her patients. 2** A personal note in a book in which the author thanks or remembers someone: **The author's** *dedication* **to her father was on the third page of her new book.**

de·fi·ant [di·fī′ənt] *adj.* Opposing or resisting power or authority: **The angry criminal stood before the judge with a** *defiant* **look on his face.**

des·per·ate [des′pər·it] *adj.* With great need; very anxious: **Marie was** *desperate* **to get home because she was afraid she had left the iron plugged in.** *syn.* frantic

de·te·ri·o·rate [di·tir′ē·ə·rāt′] *v.* **de·te·ri·o·rat·ed, de·te·ri·o·rat·ing** To become worse or less valuable: **The new owners were alarmed to discover that the old house was** *deteriorating* **at a rapid pace.**

de·ter·mined [di·tûr′mind] *adj.* Feeling very strongly about making sure that something is done: **Allison was** *determined* **to finish building the model, even if it meant she had to work all night.** *syns.* committed, resolute

dig·ni·ty [dig′nə·tē] *n.* The quality of being respected and respecting oneself: **The winners of the trophies received the applause with pride and** *dignity.* *syns.* worth, pride

di·lem·ma [di·lem′ə] *n.* A situation in which a person must make a difficult choice: **The boys' difficult** *dilemma* **was whether to tell what they saw and risk punishment or to keep quiet and let a crime go unpunished.**

di·min·ish [di·min′ish] *v.* To become smaller or look smaller: **We watched the kite** *diminish* **as it went higher.**

dis·charge [dis′chärj *or* dis·chärj′] *n.* Something that is released or sent out from its source.

dis·cour·aged [dis·kûr′ijd] *adj.* Having lost courage or confidence: **Angela looked** *discouraged* **because her experiment would not work.**

dis·grun·tled [dis·grun′təld] *adj.* Resentful, discontented: **The** *disgruntled* **fans started to leave before the game was over.** *syn.* dissatisfied

dis·mayed [dis·mād′] *adj.* Feeling alarm and confusion: **The audience was** *dismayed* **when a stage light caught fire.** *syn.* uneasy

dra·mat·i·cal·ly [drə·mat′ik·lē] *adv.* In a sudden or alarming way: **The principal's voice boomed** *dramatically* **from the public address system.**

drape [drāp] *v.* draped, drap·ing To cover with a piece of cloth: **The statue was** *draped* **so that no one would see it before the party.**

drear·y [drir′ē] *adj.* Causing sadness: **The house with its sagging roof and broken porch was a** *dreary* **sight in the rain.** *syn.* gloomy

dumb·found [dum′found′] *v.* dumb·found·ed, dumb·found·ing To make silent from surprise; to shock.

dwarf [dwôrf] *v.* dwarfed, dwarf·ing To make something look small by comparison: **My baby sister is** *dwarfed* **by the trees she is playing under.**

E

e·lab·o·rate [i·lab′ər·it] *adj.* Complicated; carefully planned out; detailed: **The suspect told an** *elaborate* **story about where he was and what he was doing at the time of the crime.** *syn.* complex

e·lec·tri·cal [i·lek′tri·kəl] *adj.* Having to do with electricity, a form of energy used for light and heat. *syn.* electric

em·bank·ment [im·bangk′mənt] *n.* A wall used to hold back water: **Mr. Payo walked down the steep** *embankment* **toward the river.**

em·brace [im·brās′] *v.* em·braced, em·brac·ing To hug; to accept something completely: **Carlos** *embraced* **his stepfather's way of doing things because it was usually better.**

en·er·get·ic [en′ər·jet′ik] *adj.* Lively; not easily tired: **The most** *energetic* **dancer was Stephanie, who didn't stop once.**

en·gulf [in·gulf′] *v.* en·gulfed, en·gulf·ing To cover completely; to close over.

en·light·en·ing [in·līt′(ə)n·ing] *adj.* Educating, informative: **After Ms. Estrella's** *enlightening* **talk, we felt we had learned a great deal about whales.** *syn.* instructive

en·to·mol·o·gist [en′tə·mol′ə·jist] *n.* A scientist who studies insects: **The** *entomologist* **identified the insect as an earwig.**

drape

entomologist You may already know that the word ending *-logist* means "a person who studies." You probably don't know that the ancient Greek word for "insect" was *entomon*. If you put the parts together, you now know that an *entomologist* is someone who studies insects.

a	add	o͝o	took
ā	ace	o͞o	pool
â	care	u	up
ä	palm	û	burn
e	end	yo͞o	fuse
ē	equal	oi	oil
i	it	ou	pout
ī	ice	ng	ring
o	odd	th	thin
ō	open	t͟h	this
ô	order	zh	vision

ə = { a in *above*   e in *sicken*
      i in *possible*
      o in *melon*   u in *circus* }

607

e·rect [i·rekt'] *v.* **e·rect·ed, e·rect·ing** To build or construct: **The students** *erected* **a pyramid made from cardboard boxes.**

et·i·quette [et'ə·kət] *n.* Rules that one should follow for polite behavior: *Etiquette* **requires that you write a thank-you note to someone who sends you a gift.** *syn.* manners

e·vap·o·ra·tion [i·vap'ə·rā'shən] *n.* The loss of water into the air: **In science class we compared the rate of** *evaporation* **from pans of water during humid and dry days.**

e·ven·tu·al·ly [i·ven'choō·əl·ē] *adv.* After the passing of some time: **The drive home from Grandmother's was very long, but we knew that we would** *eventually* **get there.** *syn.* ultimately

ev·i·dence [ev'ə·dəns] *n.* One or more facts or items that can be used as proof.

e·volve [i·volv'] *v.* **e·volved, e·volv·ing** To come into being: **Over the years, the quiet little town** *evolved* **into a big, busy city.** *syn.* develop

ex·hib·it [ig·zib'it] *n.* An item on display: **The museum has** *exhibits* **of Civil War uniforms.**

ex·pan·sion [ik·span'shən] *n.* The increase in the size of something: **The** *expansion* **of his business meant that he had to hire more employees.**

ex·pose [ik·spōz'] *v.* **ex·posed, ex·pos·ing** To make something easy to see: **The boy lifted up the heavy rock,** *exposing* **an active colony of ants underneath.** *syns.* reveal, uncover

ex·tinct [ik·stingkt'] *adj.* No longer existing or living: **If dinosaurs were not** *extinct,* **we would be able to study them in the wild and perhaps keep some in zoos.**

ex·trav·a·gant [ik·strav'ə·gənt] *adj.* Beyond reason or proper limits: **They spent an** *extravagant* **amount of money on a merry-go-round and performing clowns for the child's birthday party.**

F

fa·nat·ic [fə·nat'ik] *n.* A person whose interest in something is greater than normal: **Bonita loved baseball so much that she was not just a fan, but a** *fanatic.*

fas·ci·nate [fas'ə·nāt'] *v.* **fas·ci·nat·ed, fas·ci·nat·ing** To attract and hold interest: **She was so** *fascinated* **by the bird building its nest that she couldn't stop watching it.**

fa·tigue [fə·tēg'] *n.* A tired condition resulting from hard work, effort, or strain: **After two miles of walking,** *fatigue* **overtook me and I had to stop to rest.** *syn.* weariness

etiquette Knowing proper *etiquette* could be the ticket for a "commoner" to mix with "polite society"—and with good reason! In French, the literal meaning of *etiquette* is "ticket."

exhibits

feist·y [fī′stē] *adj. informal* Very active or spirited.

flail [flāl] *v.* **flailed, flail·ing** To move wildly as if beating something: **Charles was** *flailing* **around in the water so violently that the people on the beach thought he was drowning.** *syn.* thrash

flax [flaks] *n.* A slender plant with blue flowers, used to make linen cloth: **Whenever we visit the farm, we see** *flax* **growing in the meadow.**

flick·er [flik′ər] *v.* **flick·ered, flick·er·ing** To change unsteadily from bright to dim light: **The light was** *flickering* **during the thunderstorm.**

for·lorn [fôr·lôrn′] *adj.* Sad or pitiful because alone or neglected: **The tall weeds made the house look old and** *forlorn.*

fran·tic·al·ly [fran′tik·lē′] *adv.* In a manner wild with fear, worry, pain, or rage: **The boy searched** *frantically* **for a way out of the tunnel.**

free·style [frē′stīl′] *n.* A contest in which any style of swimming may be used: **Gus's parents were proud because he won a medal for the** *freestyle* **race at the swimming meet.**

fret·ful [fret′fəl] *adj.* Restless and unhappy or seeming to be: **The music sounded** *fretful,* **like screeching birds.** *syn.* irritable

fruit·less [frōōt′lis] *adj.* Without any success; useless: **Teresa knew it would be** *fruitless* **to try pushing the fallen tree, so she took a different path.**

frus·tra·tion [frus·trā′shən] *n.* A feeling of anger or disappointment at not being able or allowed to do something: **Antonia's** *frustration* **increased when she could not finish the test.**

fun·nel [fun′əl] *n.* An open cone, wide at the top with a smaller end: **Mrs. Francisco used a** *funnel* **to pour cereal into a jar.**

fur·tive [fûr′tiv] *adj.* Done in secret: **The child took a** *furtive* **peek through the curtains.** *syn.* stealthy

funnel

G

gap·ing [gāp′ing] *adj.* Wide open: **The explosion left a** *gaping* **hole in the wall.**

gasp [gasp] *v.* **gasped, gasp·ing** To pant breathlessly. *syns.* puff, wheeze

gin·ger·ly [jin′jər·lē] *adv.* In a careful or reluctant manner: **I** *gingerly* **lifted the priceless vase.** *syn.* cautiously

gnarled [närld] *adj.* Twisted or knotted. *syn.* tangled

goad [gōd] *v.* **goad·ed, goad·ing** To use some object to make an animal move: **Luz was** *goading* **the horse with a small stick so that it would run faster.**

graf·fi·ti [grə·fē′tē] *n. pl.* Words illegally written or painted in public places: **The** *graffiti* **on the buildings and fences made the city look very ugly.**

gnarled

a	add	ŏŏ	took
ā	ace	ōō	pool
â	care	u	up
ä	palm	û	burn
e	end	yōō	fuse
ē	equal	oi	oil
i	it	ou	pout
ī	ice	ng	ring
o	odd	th	thin
ō	open	th	this
ô	order	zh	vision

ə = { a in *above* e in *sicken*
      i in *possible*
      o in *melon* u in *circus* }

grap·ple [grap'əl] *v.* **grap·pled,
grap·pling** To grab and struggle. *syns.* wrestle, contend

grove [grōv] *n.* A group of trees.

guile [gīl] *n.* Cleverness; the
ability to trick others: **The spy
used** *guile* **to win the trust of
the official and trick her into
giving him the plans.** *syn.*
slyness

gun·ny·sack [gun'ē·sak'] *n.* A
sack made out of heavy cloth.

gunnysack When you
say *gunnysack,* you are
repeating yourself. *Goni* is
the word for "sack" in
Hindi, a language of
northern India. So a
gunnysack is really a "sack
sack."

H

hail·stone [hāl'stōn'] *n.* A small,
round pellet of frozen rain.

hav·oc [hav'ək] *n.* Widespread
destruction of life and property:
**The hurricane roared across
three states, leaving** *havoc* **in
its wake.** *syns.* ruin, devastation

hoarse [hôrs] *adj.* Sounding
husky or rough.

home·ly [hōm'lē] *adj.* Plain
looking: **His** *homely* **face suddenly looked beautiful as he
rocked the child to sleep.**

home·stead [hōm'sted'] *v.* To
make a place one's home:
**Pioneers of the West had to
homestead land to earn the
right to own it.** *syn.* occupy

hor·i·zon·tal [hôr'ə·zon'təl] *adj.*
Level from side to side, the
way the horizon looks: **Book
shelves are** *horizontal.*

HORIZONTAL

VERTICAL

horizontal

hy·giene [hī'jēn'] *n.* Practices
that keep people clean and
healthy: **Good dental** *hygiene,*
**like toothbrushing, helps pre-
vent cavities.**

I

i·den·ti·cal [ī·den'ti·kəl] *adj.*
The very same: **The twin sisters wore clothes that were
identical in every way.**

ig·no·rant [ig'nər·ənt] *adj.*
Not knowing something: **The
students were** *ignorant* **of the
history of their state until
they studied it in school.**
syn. unaware

il·lu·mi·nate [i·lōō'mə·nāt'] *v.*
**il·lu·mi·nat·ed,
il·lu·mi·nat·ing** To fill with
light: **We lit several candles, which** *illuminated*
the room.

im·pro·vise [im'prə·vīz'] *v.*
im·pro·vised, im·pro·vis·ing
To make up at the time of
performance; to make from
whatever material is available: **The campers used
large, flat rocks to** *improvise*
a table.

in·crim·i·nat·ing
[in·krim'ə·nāt'ing] *adj.* Showing proof of guilt: **The bur-
glary tools found in the trunk
of his car were considered
incriminating evidence by
the jury.**

in·di·cate [in'də·kāt'] *v.* To
show or describe: **The directions** *indicate* **which way we
should turn.**

in·dig·nant [in·dig'nənt] *adj.*
Angry because of some-
thing that is not right, just,
or fair: **Ricardo became** *indignant* **when his older brother
wouldn't let him play the
game.**

in·flu·en·tial [in'flŏŏ·en'shəl] *adj.* Important; able to change people's thoughts on something: **Albert Einstein was an *influential* scientist because his work changed the way people think about the universe.**

in·her·it [in·her'it] *v.* To receive something, usually from a parent or relative, after that person dies: **When his aunt dies, Sergio will *inherit* her house.**

in·i·ti·a·tive [in·ish'(ē·)ə·tiv] *n.* The ability to start something or take the first step: **Mr. Díaz has the *initiative* necessary to become a good salesman.**

in·suf·fi·cient [in'sə·fish'ənt] *adj.* Not enough: **We could not make tacos because we had *insufficient* amounts of tomatoes and cheese.** *syn.* inadequate

in·tel·lec·tu·al·ly [in'tə·lek'chŏŏ·əl·ē] *adv.* In a way that uses or shows the reasoning powers of the mind: **Computer programming can be *intellectually* satisfying work.**

in·tim·i·date [in·tim'ə·dāt'] *v.* To make someone afraid: **Lorenzo looks tough, but he is too nice to *intimidate* anyone.**

in·ven·tive·ness [in·ven'tiv·nis] *n.* Skill at creating things: **Luisa's *inventiveness* helped her win first prize in her class's Build-a-Better-Mousetrap contest.** *syns.* creativity, originality

ir·re·sis·ti·bly [ir'i·zis'tə·blē] *adv.* In a way that cannot be overcome or opposed: **Although I was unsure of what might be in the room, my curiosity drew me *irresistibly* toward the door.** *syn.* magnetically

ir·ri·ta·tion [ir'ə·tā'shən] *n.* Something that makes a person mildly angry: **At the picnic, the bee buzzing around our food was an *irritation*.** *syn.* annoyance

J

jave·lin [jav'(ə·)lin] *n.* A spear that is thrown for distance as an athletic event: **My father won an athletic scholarship for throwing the *javelin*.**

K

keen·ing [kēn'ing] *adj.* Sharp; mournful: **The *keening* howl of the coyote made shivers run down my spine.**

L

lab·y·rinth [lab'ə·rinth] *n.* A place that has a complicated layout, like a maze: **The princess in the fairy tale could not find her way out of the forest because it was a *labyrinth* of many paths.**

labyrinth When *Labyrinth* is spelled with a capital "L," it refers to the maze in Greek mythology where the Minotaur, a mythical monster, was imprisoned.

javelin

a	add	ŏŏ	took
ā	ace	ōō	pool
â	care	u	up
ä	palm	û	burn
e	end	yōō	fuse
ē	equal	oi	oil
i	it	ou	pout
ī	ice	ng	ring
o	odd	th	thin
ō	open	th	this
ô	order	zh	vision

ə = { a in *above* e in *sicken* i in *possible* o in *melon* u in *circus* }

limelight The chemical calcium oxide was discovered in 1808. This material, often called lime, shone with a bright white light when heated. This quality made it useful for lighting plays and shows in dark theaters. Even in the age of electrical lighting, people who are the center of public attention are "in the limelight."

lopsided

mandolin

laugh·ing·stock [laf′ing·stok′] *n.* A person or thing that is the object of ridicule: **Lorraine had turned in her homework late so many times that she was afraid she would be the** *laughingstock* **of her class.**

lime·light [līm′līt′] *n.* The attention or notice of other people. *syn.* spotlight

lop·sid·ed [lop′sī′did] *adj.* Hanging over to one side; uneven: **The cake was lower on one side, so it looked** *lopsided.*

lux·u·ry [luk′shər·ē] *n.* An item that adds to pleasure and comfort but is not necessary: **The Dillman family decided to cut back on buying** *luxuries,* **so they decided not to get a video camera.**

M

ma·chet·e [mə·shet′ē *or* mə·shet′] *n.* A long, curved knife used for cutting tall vegetation.

man·do·lin [man′də·lin *or* man′də·lin′] *n.* A musical instrument with eight to ten strings.

ma·neu·ver [mə·n(y)ōō′vər] *v.* **ma·neu·vered, ma·neu·ver·ing** To move in a skillful way: **Elbowing her way through the crowd, the photographer** *maneuvered* **herself to a position near the stage.**

mar·vel [mär′vəl] *n.* Something that is remarkable or exciting: **The white tiger was a** *marvel* **to the patrons of the circus.** *syns.* sensation, wonder

mas·sive·ly [mas′iv·lē] *adv.* Hugely; with much size and weight: **The house,** *massively* **enlarged by the two new wings, now seemed to sprawl across the whole hilltop.**

me·chan·i·cal [mə·kan′i·kəl] *adj.* Having to do with machines.

meg·a·phone [meg′ə·fōn′] *n.* A cone or electric device that makes the voice sound louder when it is spoken into.

met·a·mor·pho·sis [met′ə·môr′fə·sis] *n.* A change from one form, shape, or substance into another: **In science class, we watched the** *metamorphosis* **of a tadpole into a frog.**

me·te·or·ol·o·gist [mē′tē·ə·rol′ə·jist] *n.* A person who studies the weather.

mim·ic [mim′ik] *v.* **mim·icked, mim·ick·ing** To imitate: **The parrot** *mimicked* **every word I said.**

min·gle [ming′gəl] *v.* **min·gled, min·gling** To join or mix together: **At the party Oscar** *mingled* **with the other guests, but he still felt out of place.** *syn.* associate

mis·er·a·ble [miz′ər·ə·bəl] *adj.* **1** Causing unhappiness. **2** Shameful: **The** *miserable* **conditions at the jail caused problems among the prisoners.**

mis·giv·ing [mis·giv′ing] *n.* A feeling of worry: **Michael had** *misgivings* **about the picnic because dark storm clouds were gathering.** *syn.* qualm

mo·bile [mō′bēl] *n.* A sculpture with objects attached that moves lightly as air passes it: **Rosa made a *mobile* out of wood and paper and hung it over her sister's crib.**

mol·e·cule [mol′ə·kyool′] *n.* A tiny particle: **Scientists tell us that *molecules* and atoms are the basic building blocks of everything in the world.**

mor·sel [môr′səl] *n.* A little piece of food: **Kay loved the cake, and she ate every tiny *morsel* on her plate.** *syn.* bit

mourn·ful·ly [môrn′fəl·ē] *adv.* In a sad manner. *syn.* sorrowfully

muf·fled [muf′əld] *adj.* Having a deadened sound: **Even though the twins laughed into their pillows, Mother could hear their *muffled* giggles through the door.**

mus·ket [mus′kit] *n.* An old type of gun with a long barrel, similar to a rifle: **Each soldier in the volunteer army brought his own *musket*.**

mys·ti·fied [mis′tə·fīd] *adj.* Puzzled or not able to figure something out: **Rick was *mystified* by the strange sound and decided to find out exactly where it was coming from.**

N

nau·seous [nô′shəs *or* nô′zē·əs] *adj.* Sick to the stomach.

nav·i·gate [nav′ə·gāt′] *v.* **nav·i·gat·ed, nav·i·gat·ing** To control or decide in which direction something will go: **Bernardo was *navigating* the boat, and I was rowing.**

near·sight·ed [nir′sī′tid] *adj.* Able to see only things close by: **Nearsighted people often need glasses so they can see what is written on signs.** *syn.* myopic

nes·tle [nes′əl] *v.* **nes·tled, nes·tling** To sit very close to someone else: **All five children *nestled* together on the small couch.** *syns.* cuddle, snuggle

neu·tral [n(y)oo′trəl] *n.* Someone who is not on either side during a war: **During the American Revolution the *neutrals* refused to take the side of either the colonists or the British.**

non·cha·lant [non′shə·länt′] *adj.* Showing a jaunty coolness: **Paulo seemed *nonchalant* about winning the tennis match, but we knew he was excited.** *syns.* unexcited, unconcerned

O

ob·sti·nate [ob′stə·nit] *adj.* Stubbornly holding to one's opinions or purposes: **The *obstinate* child refused to eat his carrots.** *syn.* unyielding

ob·vi·ous [ob′vē·əs] *adj.* Easily noticed or understood: **The rainstorm makes it *obvious* that we can't play outside today.**

musket

nauseous Have you ever been seasick? The ancient Greeks associated this feeling with sea voyages and named it *nausia* from *naus,* their word for "ship." Some dictionaries state that *nauseous* strictly means "causing sickness," not "being sick." However, other dictionaries do accept the latter meaning as standard.

a	add	oo	took
ā	ace	ōō	pool
â	care	u	up
ä	palm	û	burn
e	end	yoo	fuse
ē	equal	oi	oil
i	it	ou	pout
ī	ice	ng	ring
o	odd	th	thin
ō	open	th	this
ô	order	zh	vision

ə = { a in *above*   e in *sicken*
{ i in *possible*
{ o in *melon*   u in *circus*

pendulum

parlor The room in your house called the *living room* was once known as the *parlor*. This word is related to the French word *parler*, meaning "to speak." A *parlor*, then, was a room in which people gathered to talk with each other.

off·hand·ed [ôf′han′did] *adj.* Without a lot of care or planning: **Because Tom told us about the play in an *offhanded* way, we didn't think he cared if we came.** *syn.* casual

op·po·nent [ə·pō′nənt] *n.* A person or group that takes the opposite position, as in sports. *syn.* rival

or·i·gin [ôr′ə·jin] *n.* The first use or the beginning: **Our class learned about the *origin* of the use of silver by Native American artists.**

or·nate·ly [or·nāt′lē] *adv.* In a way that involves much decoration: **Renaldo gave Lydia a package *ornately* wrapped with gold paper and silver ribbons.**

out·skirts [out′skûrts′] *n. pl.* The outer edges or areas far from the center of a city: **We drove to the *outskirts* of town to picnic by a quiet lake.**

P

pan·to·mime [pan′tə·mīm′] *n.* A play in which actors use only gestures with no speech. *v.* To express in gestures alone.

parch·ment [pärch′mənt] *n.* A scraped and dried piece of animal skin used to write or paint upon.

par·lor [pär′lər] *n.* A room that is usually used for talking or entertaining.

par·tic·i·pa·tion [pär·tis′ə·pā′shən] *n.* The act of getting involved with others: *Participation* in team sports can be fun.

pe·cul·iar [pi·kyool′yər] *adj.* Oddly different from the usual: **My dog has a *peculiar* habit of eating cat food.**

pe·des·tri·an [pə·des′trē·ən] *n.* A person who walks: **A *pedestrian* must obey traffic signals too!**

pel·ting [pel′ting] *adj.* Striking over and over: **Seeking cover from the *pelting* rain, the kitten ran under the porch.**

pen·du·lum [pen′joo·ləm *or* pen′də·ləm] *n.* A weight that hangs down and swings evenly from side to side: **A large clock with a *pendulum* is usually called a grandfather clock.**

per·ish·a·ble [per′ish·ə·bəl] *adj.* Likely to spoil.

per·ma·nent [pûr′mən·ənt] *adj.* Meant to last without changing: **This time, Robert's cure was *permanent*, and the illness did not come back.** *syn.* enduring

per·mis·sion [pər·mish′ən] *n.* An act by one person that allows someone else to do something: **Ashley asked for her mother's *permission* to go to the dance.** *syns.* approval, consent

per·sist [pər·sist′] *v.* **per·sist·ed, per·sist·ing** To keep doing something; insist: **Lome *persisted* in bouncing the ball on the floor, even after I asked him not to.** *syn.* continue

pes·ky [pes′kē] *adj. informal* Annoying; being like a pest.

phy·si·cian [fi·zish′ən] *n.* A medical doctor: **Our family *physician* prescribed penicillin when I had a sore throat and a fever.**

plum·met [plum′it] *v.*
plum·met·ed, plum·met·ing
To fall quickly: **The heavy
rock** *plummeted* **to the bottom
of the pond.**

pounce [pouns] *v.* **pounced,
pounc·ing** To jump onto something: **The cat** *pounced* **happily
on the ball of yarn.** *syn.* leap

pred·a·tor [pred′ə·tər] *n.* A person or animal that lives by
preying on others: **A porcupine uses its quills as a
defense against** *predators.*

pre·fer [pri·fûr′] *v.* **pre·ferred,
pre·fer·ring** To like one thing
better than another: **Mrs.
McCormick** *preferred* **working
in her vegetable garden to
seeing a movie.**

pre·his·tor·ic [prē′his·tôr′ik]
adj. From the time before historical records were kept:
**Since they left no written
records, the only way to learn
about** *prehistoric* **humans is to
study their drawings and the
things they made.** *syn.* ancient

pre·miere [pri·mir′] *n.* The first
showing or display: **We're
going to the** *premiere* **of
Ellen's new play.**

pres·er·va·tion
[prez′ər·vā′shən] *n.* The act of
keeping from danger or harm:
**Juan helped raise money for
the** *preservation* **of the city's
oldest schoolhouse.**

prick·le [prik′əl] *v.* **prick·led,
prick·ling** To tingle or sting.
syn. tingle

priv·i·lege [priv′ə·lij] *n.* A special benefit, favor, or advantage:
**News reporters often enjoy the
privileges of meeting interesting people and traveling to far-
away places.**

pro·ce·dure [prə·sē′jər] *n.* The
specific way in which something is done: **To learn how to
work this machine, you have
to follow the** *procedure*
described in the manual.

prom·i·nent [prom′ə·nənt] *adj.*
Important; well-known: **The
mayor is the most** *prominent*
woman in our town.

pros·per·i·ty [pros·per′ə·tē] *n.*
A condition that includes
material wealth and success:
**The new mayor promised to
help the townspeople open
businesses that would bring
prosperity to their city.**

pros·per·ous [pros′pər·əs] *adj.*
Doing well: **The Joneses are a
happy,** *prosperous* **family
with good jobs, healthy children, and a big garden full of
vegetables.** *syn.* successful

pro·tein [prō′tēn′ *or* prō′tē·ən]
n. One of several substances
that are a necessary part of our
diet: **Meat, fish, dairy products, nuts, and beans can
supply needed** *protein* **in
our diet.**

R

ran·kle [rang′kəl] *v.* To make
someone annoyed and mad:
**Losing the game by forfeit
still** *rankles* **Yoshio and
makes him feel angry whenever he thinks about it.**

rau·cous [rô′kəs] *adj.* Rough
in sound: **The** *raucous* **sounds
of football practice broke
through the half-open classroom windows.** *syns.* hoarse,
harsh

premiere

rankle When someone's
insulting remark *rankles*
inside you, you might
imagine that a little
dragon is gnawing at you.
The Latin word for
"dragon" was *draco.* A
"little dragon" was called
dracunculus.

a	add	o͝o	took
ā	ace	o͞o	pool
â	care	u	up
ä	palm	û	burn
e	end	yo͞o	fuse
ē	equal	oi	oil
i	it	ou	pout
ī	ice	ng	ring
o	odd	th	thin
ō	open	th	this
ô	order	zh	vision

ə = { a in *above*   e in *sicken*
       i in *possible*
       o in *melon*   u in *circus* }

savannah It was Arawak people, speaking Taino, who greeted Christopher Columbus when he landed in the West Indies. The Arawak are no more, but their language gave us the word *zabana*, which has survived as *savannah*.

reservoir

re·as·sur·ance [rē′ə·shŏŏr′əns] *n.* Freedom from doubt or fear: **Sonya was nervous about giving her speech, and she looked to her teacher for** *reassurance*. *syn.* confidence

re·con·struct [rē′kən·strukt′] *v.* To put something together or make it again: **After the barn blew down in the storm, we worked to** *reconstruct* **it.** *syn.* rebuild

re·en·act [rē′in·akt′] *v.* To act out again; to perform as if for the first time: **Mr. Jackson's seventh-grade class will** *reenact* **several scenes from American history for the school assembly.**

ref·uge [ref′yōōj] *n.* A place to hide: **When the bears came into the camp, the family ran to the car because it was a safe** *refuge*.

re·lieve [ri·lēv′] *v.* **re·lieved, re·liev·ing** To free from worry, pain, or unhappiness. *syn.* ease

re·luc·tant [ri·luk′tənt] *adj.* Unwilling: **Phillip was so warm and comfortable by the fire that he was** *reluctant* **to go outside into the cold.**

ren·o·vate [ren′ə·vāt] *v.* **ren·o·vat·ed, ren·o·vat·ing** To make as good as new: **These buildings looked old and shabby before they were** *renovated*. *syn.* repair

rep·re·sent [rep′ri·zent′] *v.* To act or speak for someone or something; to stand for something.

res·er·voir [rez′ər·vwär′ *or* rez′ər·vwôr′] *n.* A place where water is stored.

rest·less [rest′lis] *adj.* Not relaxed; eager to do something else: **Anna felt bored and** *rest-less* **having to sit still during the long movie.**

re·sume [ri·zōōm′] *v.* To start again after stopping: **My father's cooking class** *resumes* **after two weeks of vacation.**

re·treat [ri·trēt′] *v.* To turn around and go back to where one came from. *syn.* withdraw

rit·u·al [rich′ōō·əl] *n.* A set action or series of actions: **Andy went through a** *ritual* **of pulling up his socks and tugging on his shirt every time he shot a free throw.**

rook·ie [rŏŏk′ē] *n.* A first-year player in sports; a beginner.

S

sar·cas·tic·al·ly [sär·kas′tik·lē] *adv.* In a mocking or taunting way: **Tracy is so clumsy that her family has** *sarcastically* **nicknamed her "Miss Graceful."**

sa·van·nah [sə·van′ə] *n.* A grassy plain that has very few trees.

scoot [skōōt] *v. informal* **scoot·ed, scoot·ing 1** To move quickly. **2** To slide something, especially while seated.

scur·ry [skûr′ē] *v.* To move about quickly. *syn.* scamper

sem·i·cir·cu·lar [sem′ē·sûr′kyə·lər] *adj.* Shaped like a half-circle: **Tiffany draws** *semicircular* **lines that look like smiles.**

set·tle·ment [set′(ə)l·mənt] *n.* A new place for people to live: **When the pioneers first reached the valley, they built a** *settlement.*

shin·dig [shin′dig′] *n. slang* A party with noise and dancing.

shrewd·ly [shrōōd′lē] *adv.* In a practical way: **Edward** *shrewdly* **talked his sister, who was dieting, into trading her large piece of pie for his smaller one.** *syn.* slyly

shriv·el [shriv′əl] *v.* **shriv·eled, shriv·el·ing** To contract into wrinkles; shrink and dry up: **I forgot to water the plant, so its leaves have begun to** *shrivel* **and fall off.**

shud·der [shud′ər] *n.* A quick, light shaking motion; shiver: **The cold air made a** *shudder* **run through my body.**

si·mul·ta·ne·ous·ly [sī′məl·tā′nē·əs·lē] *adv.* Happening, done, or existing at the same time: **Everyone in the audience jumped** *simultaneously* **when the villain burst onstage.**

slan·der [slan′dər] *n.* A cruel, false, and sometimes illegal spoken public statement made about a person: **Anyone who publicly says something untrue about another person is guilty of** *slander.*

sleigh [slā] *n.* A carriage with runners instead of wheels that is pulled by a horse over ice or snow: **After the last snowfall, Mr. Cowley let us hitch up the horses and ride in both** *sleighs.*

smoth·er [smuth′ər] *v.* **smoth·ered, smoth·er·ing** To hide or suppress: **She** *smothered* **a laugh with her handkerchief.**

so·ber·ing [sō′bər·ing] *adj.* Serious; causing to be suddenly aware and able to think clearly.

sol·emn·ly [sol′əm·lē] *adv.* Quietly and seriously: **Mr. Jenkins** *solemnly* **read the names of the people who had been injured.**

star·board [stär′bərd] *adj.* The right-hand side of a ship as one faces the bow: **We looked for sharks and whales over the** *starboard* **railing.**

stat·ic [stat′ik] *n.* A rough sound that comes from a radio or television set that is not receiving properly.

stow [stō] *v.* **stowed, stow·ing** To store; put away.

stu·pen·dous [st(y)ōō·pen′dəs] *adj.* Wonderful. *syn.* fabulous

sub·mit [səb·mit′] *v.* To say or to put something forward for someone else's reaction; to suggest in a formal way.

sue [sōō] *v.* To ask a court to solve a problem legally.

suf·fra·gist [suf′rə·jist] *n.* A person who thinks that the right to vote should be extended to others.

sum·mit [sum′it] *n.* The top of a mountain. *syn.* peak

sup·port [sə·pôrt′] *v.* To provide food and clothing and other necessities: **Mrs. Swoboda will** *support* **the family while her husband looks for a new job.**

shindig The only thing word experts agree on is that *shindig* comes from Ireland. The word may have come from a game called *shindy,* a wild kind of hockey played on a field with balls and curved sticks. Or *shindig* may go back to the Irish word *sinteag,* which means "a skip" or "a jump."

sleigh

a	add	o͝o	took
ā	ace	o͞o	pool
â	care	u	up
ä	palm	û	burn
e	end	yo͞o	fuse
ē	equal	oi	oil
i	it	ou	pout
ī	ice	ng	ring
o	odd	th	thin
ō	open	th	this
ô	order	zh	vision

ə = a in *above*   e in *sicken*
i in *possible*
o in *melon*   u in *circus*

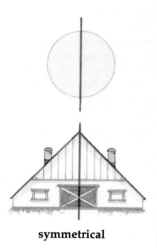

symmetrical

unanimously If you and your classmates voted *unanimously* on an issue, you would all be in agreement, or of one mind. *Unanimous* comes from the Latin words *unus,* meaning "one," and *animus,* meaning "soul or mind."

tumble

sur·feit [sûr′fit] *n.* Too much of something. *syn.* overabundance

swag·ger [swag′ər] *v.* **swag·gered, swag·ger·ing** To walk in a boastful and proud way. *syn.* strut

sym·met·ri·cal [si·met′ri·kəl] *adj.* Alike on both sides.

T

ta·per [tā′pər] *v.* To fade; to decrease in amount or size.

tech·nol·o·gy [tek·nol′ə·jē] *n.* A way to use science to produce useful things: **Computers and cars both make use of modern *technology.***

temp·ta·tion [tem·tā′shən] *n.* An instant urge or desire: **The *temptation* to eat the cookies may be too much to resist.**

ter·rain [tə·rān′] *n.* The features of an area of land: **The race was run on rough *terrain* of steep hills and rocky valleys.**

ter·rar·i·um [tə·râr′ē·əm] *n.* A transparent container in which small land animals or plants are kept: **Our group built a *terrarium* for hermit crabs.**

tes·ti·mo·ny [tes′tə·mō′nē] *n.* The answers that must be given truthfully to a lawyer's questions in court.

tour·na·ment [toŏr′nə·mənt *or* tûr′nə·mənt] *n.* A set number of contests that includes many teams or players and produces one winner overall.

trai·tor [trā′tər] *n.* A person who goes against his or her family, friends, or country to join the opposite side during a war. *syn.* betrayer

trans·form [trans·fôrm′] *v.* **trans·formed, trans·form·ing** To change the form or appearance of: **The caterpillar is now *transforming* itself into a butterfly.**

trans·mis·sion [trans·mish′ən] *n.* The sending of pictures or sounds through the air, as by radio or television.

trans·par·ent [trans·pâr′ənt] *adj.* Easily seen through: **The wings on this butterfly look as if they are *transparent. syn.* clear**

tum·ble [tum′bəl] *v.* **tum·bled, tum·bling** To turn over and over: **The puppies were rolling and *tumbling* on the carpet.**

tur·bu·lence [tûr′byə·ləns] *n.* Wind currents that move very quickly.

U

ul·ti·mate·ly [ul′tə·mit·lē] *adv.* Finally; at the end: **We will *ultimately* arrive in California after we stop in Arizona for a rest.**

u·nan·i·mous·ly [yoŏ·nan′ə·məs·lē] *adv.* With all voters voting the same way: **Sasheen was *unanimously* elected class president when all the students voted for her.**

un·in·spired [un′in·spīrd′] *adj.* Showing no originality: **The committee rejected the building plans as boring and** *uninspired.* *syn.* unimaginative

un·veil [un·vāl′] *v.* **un·veiled, un·veil·ing** To remove the covering from: **The new statue will be** *unveiled* **today.** *syn.* reveal

V

vague [vāg] *adj.* Not clearly understood.

ve·ran·da [və·ran′də] *n.* A long, open, outdoor porch along the outside of a building: **The addition of a** *veranda* **made the small house more comfortable.**

ver·ti·cal [vûr′ti·kəl] *adj.* Straight up and down.

vig·or·ous·ly [vig′ər·əs·lē] *adv.* Very fast or with great energy: **The chief** *vigorously* **waved his arms to get our attention.** *syns.* energetically, rapidly

vi·o·lent·ly [vī′ə·lənt·lē] *adv.* Harshly; with destructive force.

vis·u·al·ize [vizh′o͞o·əl·īz′] *v.* To imagine; to see something in the mind.

volt [vōlt] *n.* A measure of electricity.

W

wal·low [wol′ō] *v.* To tumble or roll with slow and lazy movements: **My cat likes to** *wallow* **in the warm sand.**

war·i·ly [wâr′ə·lē′] *adv.* In a watchful and suspicious way: **Kevin watched** *warily* **as the magician put his watch into the hat.** *syns.* carefully, cautiously

weight·less·ness [wāt′lis·nəs] *n.* Having little or no weight: **A helium-filled balloon's** *weightlessness* **will allow it to float away if you do not hold it.**

wind·break [wind′brāk′] *n.* Anything that blocks the force of the wind, such as a wall or a line of trees.

wist·ful·ly [wist′fəl·ē] *adv.* Wishing for something.

wretch·ed [rech′id] *adj.* Very unhappy: **My ankle ached so badly that I had a** *wretched* **day at school.** *syns.* miserable, poor

vague If the details of that story you just read are *vague*, maybe your mind was wandering as you turned the pages. *Vague*, in fact, is closely connected to the Latin word *vagari*, meaning "to wander." We call people who wander around aimlessly *vagabonds* and *vagrants*.

windbreak

a	add	o͝o	took
ā	ace	o͞o	pool
â	care	u	up
ä	palm	û	burn
e	end	yo͞o	fuse
ē	equal	oi	oil
i	it	ou	pout
ī	ice	ng	ring
o	odd	th	thin
ō	open	t͟h	this
ô	order	zh	vision

ə = { a in *above*   e in *sicken*
      i in *possible*
      o in *melon*   u in *circus* }

INDEX OF
TITLES AND AUTHORS

Page numbers in light print refer to biographical information.

Acknowledgments continued

HarperCollins Publishers: "The Growin' of Paul Bunyan" from *A Telling of the Tales* by William J. Brooke. Text copyright © 1990 by William J. Brooke. "Fireflies" from *Joyful Noise* by Paul Fleischman, illustrated by Eric Beddows. Text copyright © 1988 by Paul Fleischman; illustrations copyright © 1988 by Eric Beddows. *One Day in the Desert* by Jean Craighead George. Text copyright © 1983 by Jean Craighead George. Text and cover illustration from *In the Year of the Boar and Jackie Robinson* by Bette Bao Lord, cover illustration by Marc Simont. Text copyright © 1984 by Bette Bao Lord; cover illustration copyright © 1984 by Marc Simont. *Sarah, Plain and Tall* by Patricia MacLachlan. Text and cover illustration copyright © 1985 by Patricia MacLachlan. Cover illustration by Ruth Sanderson from *The Facts and Fictions of Minna Pratt* by Patricia MacLachlan. Illustration © 1988 by Ruth Sanderson. From *Flower Moon Snow: A Book of Haiku* by Kazue Mizumura. Copyright © 1977 by Kazue Mizumura. Text and cover illustration from *Night of the Twisters* by Ivy Ruckman, cover illustration by Jim Spence. Text copyright © 1984 by Ivy Ruckman; cover illustration © 1984 by Jim Spence.

Holiday House: "My Horse, Fly Like a Bird" and illustrations from *Dancing Teepees: Poems of American Indian Youth*, selected by Virginia Driving Hawk Sneve, illustrated by Stephen Gammell. Text copyright © 1989 by Virginia Driving Hawk Sneve; illustrations copyright © 1989 by Stephen Gammell. Cover illustration from *Ferret In the Bedroom, Lizards In the Fridge* by Bill Wallace. Copyright © 1986 by Bill Wallace.

Houghton Mifflin Company: From *The Sign of the Beaver* by Elizabeth George Speare, cover illustration by Robert Andrew Parker. Text copyright © 1983 by Elizabeth George Speare; cover illustration copyright © by Robert Andrew Parker.

Richard Kennedy: "Oliver Hyde's Dishcloth Concert" from *Richard Kennedy: Collected Stories* by Richard Kennedy. Text copyright © 1987 by Richard Kennedy.

Alfred A. Knopf, Inc.: Like Jake and Me by Mavis Jukes, illustrated by Lloyd Bloom. Text copyright © 1984 by Mavis Jukes; illustrations copyright © 1984 by Lloyd Bloom. From *Flying Machine* by Andrew Nahum. Copyright © 1990 by Dorling Kindersley Limited, London. From pp. 61–72 in *The Kid in the Red Jacket* by Barbara Park, cover illustration by Rob Sauber. Text copyright © 1987 by Barbara Park; cover illustration copyright © 1987 by Rob Sauber.

Lerner Publications Company: Cover illustration from *Before the Wright Brothers* by Don Berliner. Copyright © 1990 by Lerner Publications Company.

Little, Brown and Company: Cover illustration by Ted Lewin from *Self-Portrait with Wings* by Susan Green. Copyright © 1989 by Susan Green.

Little, Brown and Company, in conjunction with Sierra Club Books: From *Tree of Life: The World of the African Baobab* by Barbara Bash. Copyright © 1989 by Barbara Bash. Cover illustration by Martha Weston from *The Sierra Club Book of Weatherwisdom* by Vicki McVey. Illustration copyright © 1991 by Martha Weston.

Lothrop, Lee & Shepard Books, a division of William Morrow & Company, Inc.: From *To Space & Back* by Sally Ride and Susan Okie. Text and cover photograph copyright © 1986 by Sally Ride and Susan Okie.

Macmillan Publishing Company: From *Sugaring Time* by Kathryn Lasky, photographs by Christopher G. Knight. Text copyright © 1983 by Kathryn Lasky; photographs copyright © 1983 by Christopher G. Knight. From *The House of Dies Drear* by Virginia Hamilton, cover illustration by Eros Keith. Text copyright © 1968 by Virginia Hamilton; illustration copyright © 1968 by Eros Keith.

McIntosh and Otis, Inc. and Union of American Hebrew Congregation: Cover illustration by Michael J. Deraney from *The Secret Grove* by Barbara Cohen. Illustration copyright © 1985 by Michael J. Deraney. Published by Union of American Hebrew Congregation.

Joseph T. Mendola Ltd., on behalf of Steve Brennan: Cover illustration by Steve Brennan from *A Gathering of Days* by Joan W. Blos. Illustration copyright © 1990 by Steve Brennan.

The Metropolitan Museum of Art: The trademark of The Metropolitan Museum of Art. The Renaissance M is a registered trademark of The Metropolitan Museum of Art.

Morrow Junior Books, a division of William Morrow & Company, Inc.: From *Storms* by Seymour Simon. Text copyright © 1989 by Seymour Simon. Cover photograph courtesy of the National Center for Atmospheric Research. Cover illustration by Paul O. Zelinsky from *Dear Mr. Henshaw* by Beverly Cleary. Copyright © 1983 by Beverly Cleary.

Philomel Books, a division of The Putnam & Grosset Group: Cover illustration by Mitsumasa Anno from *Anno's Hat Tricks* by Akihiro Nozaki. Illustration copyright © 1984 by Kuso-Kubo and Akihiro Nozaki.

Jerry Pinkney: Cover illustration by Jerry Pinkney from *Pride of Puerto Rico: The Life of Roberto Clemente* by Paul Robert Walker.

Poetry: "Kansas Boy" by Ruth Lechlitner. Text copyright 1931 by The Modern Poetry Association. Originally published in *Poetry*.

Marian Reiner: "Elizabeth Blackwell" from *Independent Voices* by Eve Merriam. Text copyright © 1968 by Eve Merriam.

Marian Reiner, on behalf of Myra Cohn Livingston: "Secrets" from *Space Songs* by Myra Cohn Livingston. Text copyright © 1988 by Myra Cohn Livingston.

Melodye Rosales: Cover illustration by Melodye Rosales from *Beetles, Lightly Toasted* by Phyllis Reynolds Naylor. Illustration copyright © 1987 by Melodye Rosales.

Scholastic Inc.: From *You Be the Jury* by Marvin Miller. Text copyright © 1987 by Marvin Miller.

Charles Scribner's Sons, an imprint of Macmillan Publishing Company: "Jackrabbit" from *Desert Voices* by Byrd Baylor, illustrated by Peter Parnall. Text copyright © 1981 by Byrd Baylor; illustrations copyright © 1981 by Peter Parnall.

Smithsonian Institution Press: "Sun, Moon, Stars" from *Twenty-seventh Annual Report of the Bureau of American Ethnology 1905–06*, Smithsonian Institution, 1911.

Rosemary A. Thurber: Many Moons by James Thurber. Text copyright 1943 by James Thurber; text copyright renewed 1970 by Rosemary Thurber.

Viking Penguin, a division of Penguin Books USA Inc.: From *A Long Way to Go* by Zibby Oneal. Text copyright © 1990 by Zibby Oneal.

Volcano Press, Inc.: Cover illustration by Bengt-Arne Runnerström from *Save My Rainforest* by Monica Zak, English version by Nancy Schimmel. Originally published in Sweden under the title *Rädda Min Djungel* by Bokförlaget Opal, 1989.

Neil Waldman: Cover illustration by Neil Waldman from *Hatchet* by Gary Paulsen. Illustration copyright © 1987 by Bradbury Press.

Walker Books Limited: Cover illustration by Iain McCaig from *Boat Girl* by Bernard Ashley. Illustration © 1990 by Iain McCaig.

Photograph Credits
KEY: (t) top, (b) bottom, (l) left, (r) right, (c) center.

UNIT 1
130–131, HBJ/Dan Peha

UNIT 3
338, Harry Landgon Photography/Office of March Fong Eu; 339, State Bar of Arizona; 339, used by permission, *Mel Bay's American History Songbook*, © 1992, Mel Bay Publications, Inc., Pacific, Missouri, all rights reserved

UNIT 4
422 (b), CBS; 422–423(t), TRW, Inc.; 423(c), HBJ Photo; 423(b), HBJ/Erik Arnesen

UNIT 5
424–425, 426–427, 429, 453, 455, 485, 487, 515, 516–517 (bkgrds.) Earth Scenes/© Francis Lepine; 516, The Goldman Environmental Foundation; 517, © Luiz C. Marigo/Peter Arnold, Inc.

UNIT 6
518–519, 520–521, 557, 577 (bkgrds.) *Atomic Particle Tracks in Bubble Chamber*/Fermilab Visual Media Services, Fermi National Accelerator Laboratory, Batavia, IL; 579, 599 (bkgrds.), 601(t), NASA; 601(b), Historical Pictures Service

Illustration Credits
KEY: (t) top, (b) bottom, (l) left, (r) right, (c) center.

Theme Opening Art
Janice Castiglione, 396–397; Vince Chiaramonte, 302–303, 556–557; Renee Daily, 240–241; Chris Ellison, 280–281, 486–487; Deborah Haeffele, 370–371; Jennifer Hewitson, 428–429; Gay Holland, 88–89; John Kane, 170–171, 578–579; Kristin Kest, 344–345; Ruben Ramos, 136–137; Roni Shepherd, 196–197; Andrea Tachiera, 454–455; Russell Thurston, 522–523; Cristina Ventoso, 56–57; Darryl L. Warfield, 20–21

Connections Art
Rondi Collette, 601(t); Renee Daily, 600–601(b); Mouli Marur, 422–423, 516–517(b); Steve Shock, 234–235, 338–339; Dean Williams, 130–131

Unit Opener and Bookshelf Border Art (4/c)
Tony Caldwell, 4–5, 16–17; Pat and Robin DeWitt, 426–427, 516–517(t); Mary Jones, 10–11, 340–341, 342–343

Selection Art
Barbara Bash, 488–499; Eric Beddows, 346–347; Lloyd Bloom, 348–359; Dick Calkins, 558–559; Harvey Chan, 74–86, 186–194; Lambert Davis, 324–336; David Diaz, 410–420; Katy Farmer, 360–368; Michael Garland, 22–37; Sheldon Greenberg, 288–300; Amy Hill, 38–51; Ronald Himmler, 164–168; Irmeli Holmberg, 90–125; Thomas Hudson, 58–73; Oleana Kassian, 430–447; Jay Leach, 582–597; Gary Lippencott, 260–278; Davy Liu, 128; Jack Malloy, 306–323; Kazue Mizumura, 372–373; Kate Mueller, 538–553; Alex Murowski, 502–514; Michelle Nidenoff, 260–261; Peter Parnall, 449–452; Jerry Pinkney, 138–140; Mark Reidy, 202–231; Marcia Sewall, 398–409; Marc Simont, 374–393; Jeffery Terreson, 150–163; Rick Tom, 242–256; Janet Wilson, 500–501